INSIDERS' GUIDE® TO CIVIL WAR SITES
IN THE SOUTHERN STATES

D0166720

HELP US KEEP THIS GUIDE UP TO DATE

Every effort has been made by the author and editors to make this guide as accurate and useful as possible. However, many things can change after a guide is published—phone numbers change, facilities come under new management, etc.

We would love to hear from you concerning your experiences with this guide and how you feel it could be improved and be kept up to date. While we may not be able to respond to all comments and suggestions, we'll take them to heart and we'll also make certain to share them with the author. Please send your comments and suggestions to the following address:

> The Globe Pequot Press
> Reader Response/Editorial Department
> P.O. Box 480
> Guilford, CT 06437

Or you may e-mail us at:

> editorial@GlobePequot.com

Thanks for your input, and happy travels!

INSIDERS' GUIDE®

INSIDERS' GUIDE® SERIES

INSIDERS' GUIDE® TO
CIVIL WAR SITES
IN THE SOUTHERN STATES

THIRD EDITION

JOHN McKAY

SEQUOYAH REGIONAL LIBRARY SYSTEM
CANTON, GA

INSIDERS' GUIDE®

GUILFORD, CONNECTICUT
AN IMPRINT OF THE GLOBE PEQUOT PRESS

The prices and rates in this guidebook were confirmed at press time. We recommend, however, that you call establishments before traveling to obtain current information.

To buy books in quantity for corporate use or incentives, call **(800) 962–0973, ext. 4551,** or e-mail **premiums@GlobePequot.com.**

INSIDERS' GUIDE ®

Text design by LeAnna Weller Smith
Maps by Trailhead Graphics © The Globe Pequot Press

ISSN 1544-2640
ISBN 0-7627-3407-8

Manufactured in the United States of America
Third Edition/First Printing

CONTENTS

CONTENTS

Directory of Maps

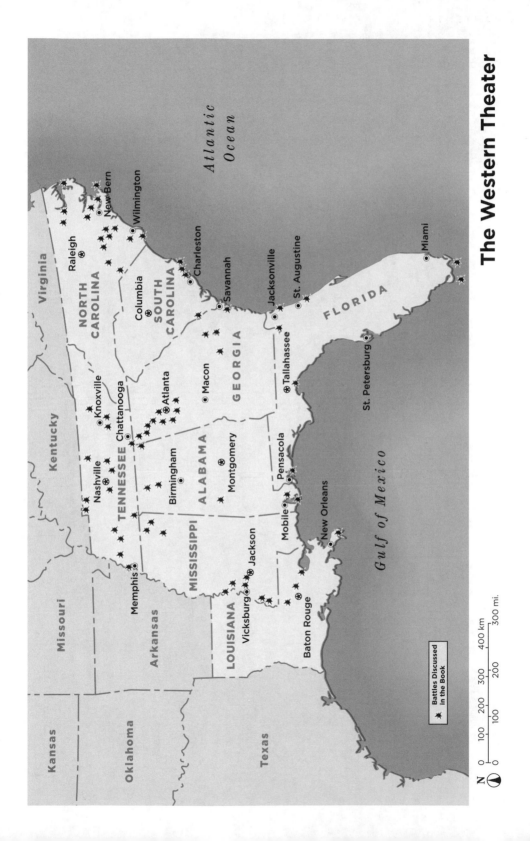

The Western Theater

Battles Discussed
in the Book

N

0   100   200   300   400 km
0   100   200   300 mi.

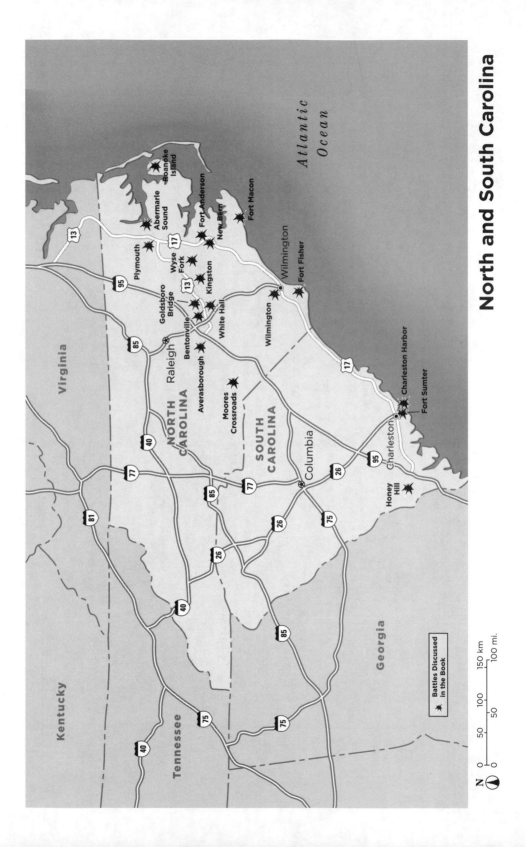

North and South Carolina

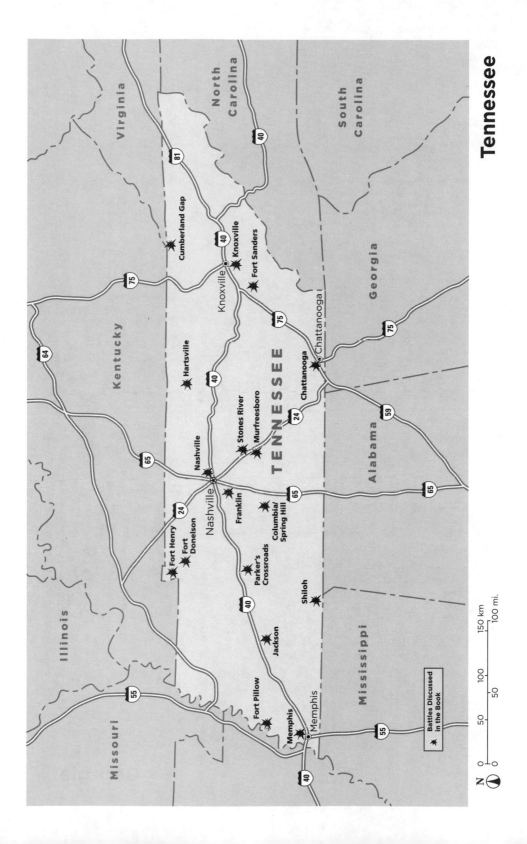

Tennessee

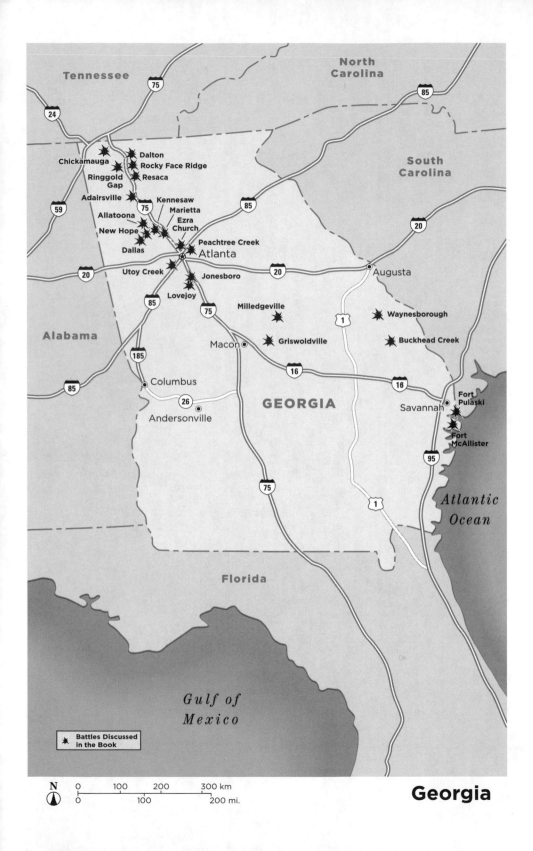

Tennessee

North Carolina

South Carolina

Chickamauga
Dalton
Rocky Face Ridge
Ringgold Gap
Resaca
Adairsville
Kennesaw
Allatoona
Marietta
New Hope
Ezra Church
Dallas
Peachtree Creek
Atlanta
Utoy Creek
Jonesboro
Lovejoy
Milledgeville
Waynesborough
Macon
Griswoldville
Buckhead Creek
Columbus
Andersonville
GEORGIA
Savannah
Fort Pulaski
Fort McAllister

Alabama

Augusta

Atlantic Ocean

Gulf of Mexico

Florida

Battles Discussed in the Book

N

0   100   200   300 km
0   100   200 mi.

Georgia

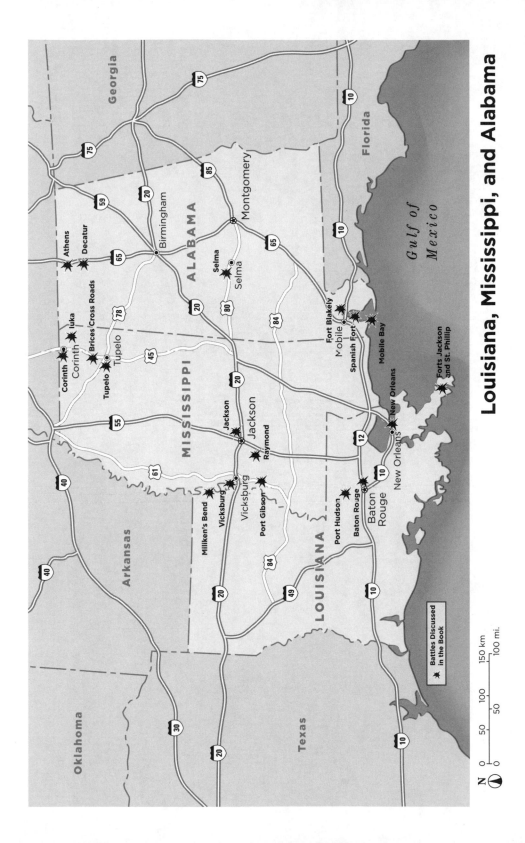

Louisiana, Mississippi, and Alabama

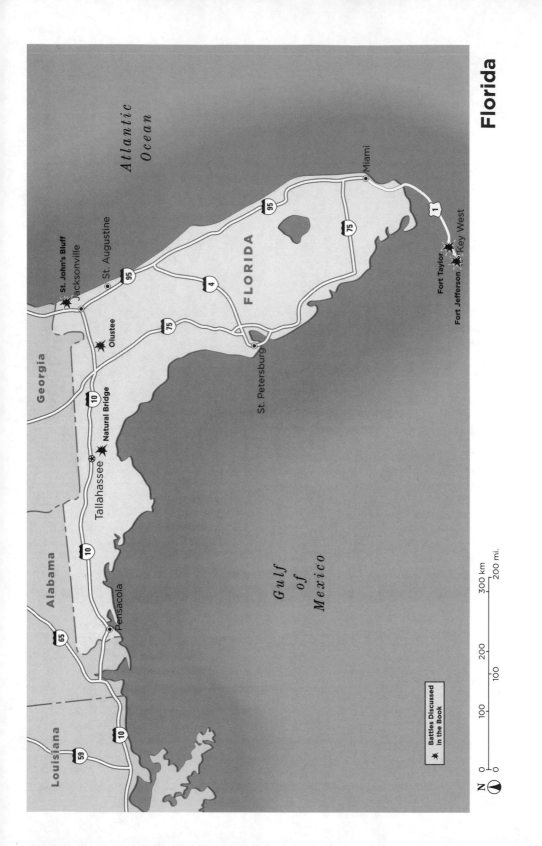

Florida

ACKNOWLEDGMENTS

As I mentioned in past editions of this work, there is no such thing as an author producing a book of this sort in a vacuum, and I have many dedicated curators, researchers, historians, and other professionals to thank as a result. Although a revision of a work of this type requires much less in the way of peer support than the original does, there are still quite a number of debts I owe for kindness rendered. By no means is this an inclusive list of all those who lent support in this revision, but any inadvertent exclusions between this and the previous edition are entirely the fault of this author's faulty memories.

As always, I owe my greatest debts of gratitude to Bill Kinsland of the Hometown Bookstore in Dahlonega, Georgia, my dear friend and a most enthusiastic research associate for this and other Civil War–related projects; I am deeply grateful for all he has done to assist in this and innumerable other projects. Gordon Jones and Beth Woodward of the Atlanta History Center have been both good friends and gracious hosts to me on many occasions in their exquisite facility, and I was deeply grateful and honored for the opportunity to speak there in 2001. Myers Brown, late of the Atlanta History Center and newly of the Wheeler Plantation Historic Site, Ranger Joe Brehn of the Castello de San Marcos in St. Augustine, Florida, and Ranger Stephanie Gray of the Antietam National Battlefield have been (and hopefully will remain!) wonderful historians with whom to passionately debate theories and ideas long after the day's work (should have) ended.

Finally, my most heartfelt thanks and gratitude must go, as always, to Bonnie Kathleen McKay, my beloved wife and best friend, who is both my greatest motivator and sharpest critic and too often has had to endure solitary pursuits while I delved into completely obscure issues of one stripe or another. Her endless support of my work, a field in which she does not always share my passionate enthusiasm, has been among the greatest of gifts she has bestowed upon me throughout our marriage, and for this and many other things I thank God every day for slamming us together enough times so it took.

HOW TO USE THIS BOOK

As a high school history teacher, I have frequently experienced "that look" from students in my classroom, the "please-God-let-the-bell-ring" expression that telegraphs all too well that the subject at hand is somewhat boring. Not coincidentally, I notice these looks most frequently when the subject bores me as well. (Yes, teachers sometimes have to cover material they personally think is as exciting as watching grass grow.) Although trained as an academic historian, and therefore in theory disdainful of "popular" history, with all the cute little stories and anecdotes, I have found that the books I take on vacation and to read at lunch are almost invariably of this genre. As sort of an experiment, I started modifying my approach in the classroom to one that was more inclusive of the "cute anecdotes," mixed in among all the names and dates and battles and generals. At a parent-teacher conference later, one parent told me in delight how much her daughter now enjoyed the history class and related a long story about how we had discussed one of the paintings in the textbook and some of the background about the different elements of it.

I thought long and hard about all this when I started writing *Insiders' Guide to Civil War Sites in the Southern States*. I very much wanted to produce the sort of guidebook I was always looking around for: one that talked about the battles and campaigns in some, but not obsessive, detail; that gave enough driving details to let me find the place without delving into tenths-of-mile directions and specific mile marker locations; and that was the sort of book I would enjoy sitting down and reading in the comfort of my home, instead of being just another tote-along accessory to the maps. At the same time, although I personally find great delight (and have spent much of my professional life) in studying the minute-by-minute movements of regiments and officers, I know that the guides I have read that do this tend not to be very accessible except to the obsessed. And finally, I do enjoy the anecdotal stories about what people saw and experienced that bring a human face to the mask of war. In this book I very much hope to have done all of this, just as I so enjoy seeing the look of quiet fascination on my students' faces when we are talking about some dusty, previously unnoticed corner of history.

Although there have been somewhere between 75,000 and 100,000 books published about the Civil War since 1865 (depending on which source you consult), the overwhelming majority have been on the Eastern Theater (Virginia, Pennsylvania, Maryland) and the grand campaigns and huge battles fought there that have become part of the American lexicon. However, the battles and campaigns that really brought the Confederacy to a close happened elsewhere, at Vicksburg in Mississippi, at Shiloh in Tennessee, at New Orleans and Port Hudson in Louisiana, at Wilmington and Durham Station in North Carolina, at Charleston in South Carolina, and, most important, at Atlanta and Savannah in Georgia. While Gettysburg, a name known literally around the world, has long been known as "the battle" of the war, it really was just a meeting engagement followed by a three-day battle of assault and maneuver, where the Union Army hung on by its fingernails most of the battle and only a grievous error (some might argue a series of errors) of judgment by Lee handed the victory to the North. In comparison, the same day that Lee's final charge up Cemetery Ridge broke the back of his own army, Pemberton in Vicksburg surrendered to Grant after a long, painful campaign that featured brilliant maneuvering on Grant's part, superb gunnery by the Confederate cannoneers guarding the Mississippi River approaches to the city, heroic though unsuccessful assaults on the ramparts of the surrounding forts by Sherman's men, six weeks of unbroken siege and heavy bombardment that resulted in the starving civilians of the city moving into caves and basements for cover, and, finally, an honorable surrender of an infantry garrison that had not been defeated in any direct assault on the city.

Similarly, although various Union armies maneuvered and fought all around the northern and eastern approaches to Richmond (their target from the very beginning) most of the four-year-long war, the city was finally taken only after Lee's decimated Army of Northern Virginia was no longer able to resist the overwhelming Union armies opposing it. On the other hand, Atlanta was an even more important target from a military standpoint than Richmond itself, having manufacturing facilities to make the weapons and uniforms impossible to import through the Union naval blockade, warehouses to store all the supplies, and three major rail lines crossing in the middle of town able to take all those needed supplies to any point of the Confederacy. Richmond's major exports were ill-advised orders and advice from the politicians and hangers-on that plagued the city like so many vermin-infested mice. Atlanta fell after less than four months of a brilliant, determined, and well-led campaign by Sherman, and his subsequent sightseeing trip down to Savannah really and finally cut the Confederacy in half. The loss of both supplies and transport doomed the Confederacy, itself toppling less than six months afterwards.

With all this in mind, we decided to limit the scope of this book to the combat actions in the Deep South, covering eight states in 15 individual chapters. As the actions described in this book did not all occur within a given state, geographic area, time frame, or campaign, or even have anything at all to do with one another in some cases, we decided to follow a standard but admittedly artificial format in each chapter and in the layout of the book as well. We have tried to stick to an east-to-west and north-to-south format overall, with North Carolina as the first chapter and Florida the last. Within each chapter, whenever possible, we tried to stick to a chronological order, as in the Atlanta Campaign chapter, which starts with Dalton and ends with Jonesboro. Six of the chapters cover specific battles or limited campaigns, while four others discuss protracted and widespread campaigns. Three chapters cover entire states, while one covers two states, and the remaining chapter is centered around one tiny rail stop in rural southwestern Georgia. Whenever possible, we have used the discussion of a given battle or location as a springboard from which to discuss larger issues—the Andersonville chapter, for example, discusses the prisoner-of-war issue and how it affected the war as a whole, while the New Orleans chapter is used to discuss riverine warfare.

The first part of every chapter discusses the history and chronology of the area, with as many anecdotal stories packed in as our editors would allow, and is followed by a section entitled The Tour where basic travel information is provided. This section is by no measure comprehensive—we really saw no need to tell you about the 16 fast-food establishments parked at the entrance gate of a national battlefield, for example, nor did we feel the need to review the amenities of standardized chain motels that clog the exit ramps of freeways these days like so many sutlers rows. We have attempted to let you know how to find these places in the rare instances it was not absolutely obvious upon arrival at a historic site. Some lodging and dining establishments were so overwhelmingly superior, however,

Increased Security

Please be aware that many of the sites, museums, and historic areas mentioned in this book are either on the grounds of current military bases or are managed by state and national government agencies. Due to the response to the September 11, 2001, terrorist attacks, these places may either be closed to the public or have limited operating hours. Other areas may require a search of your vehicle or person before allowing you entry, and in literally every facility we visited after the attacks, there was a much higher awareness and attention paid to general security measures.

As always, it pays to make a quick phone call to the facilities at your destination, before you start out on a lengthy road trip, to confirm hours of operation and other new developments. It also pays to be aware that you will likely be subject to a search before being allowed entry to any current military facility, so it would be advisable to leave weapons or anything that might be viewed with suspicion at home. Ask at the gate if photography or videotaping is allowed at your destination, as we can tell from personal experience how discomforting it is to gain the attention of military police in this manner!

that we felt as if we just had to bring them to your attention. We must point out that many of the areas we discuss are covered in thorough detail in some of our sister publications, such as *Insiders' Guide to Atlanta*, *Insiders' Guide to Savannah*, and *Insiders' Guide to North Carolina's Outer Banks*. Those with Internet access can find the latest list of available guides at www.InsidersGuide.com.

The last portion of many chapters, entitled Day Trips, includes mostly Civil War–oriented attractions that were not really a part of whatever we were discussing in the chapter, along with some unrelated features and attractions that the average history buff should enjoy. Your mileage may vary, but as an aviation buff as well as a Civil War historian, I saw no conflict or disparity whatsoever in visiting Ft. Barrancas at Pensacola and then immediately going around the corner to the Museum of Naval Aviation (both of which are discussed in the Florida chapter).

The Civil War and the military have a specialized language that may trip up the uninitiated. The next chapter is a glossary that can help you understand terms and expressions that have no plain-language equivalent.

It is often remarked that the Civil War took place in 10,000 places (a number that is absolutely impossible to argue either for or against successfully, by the way), but we do not discuss all of the 8,000 or so that took place in the areas we covered in this book. Although we have tried to be as reasonably comprehensive as possible, our rule of thumb was that, aside from the obvious major battles and campaigns, we would look at the strategically important smaller battles and campaigns (like Corinth, Mississippi), any significant sites reasonably near the major ones already on our list (Roswell, Georgia, for example), and those we felt played a role that surpassed the station usually assigned them by general histories of the war (Griswoldville, Georgia, and St. Augustine, Florida, spring to mind here). There were a few somewhat significant sites that we left out, partly for brevity, but primarily because of either their remoteness or the fact that they have little or nothing left from the war to see. Key West and Tampa, Florida, and Murphy, North Carolina, are examples of this. Inevitably, someone will be just amazed that we did not discuss this battle, that campaign, or those campgrounds somewhere in the rural South, but as it was, this book took over two years of dedicated research, nearly 30,000 miles of driving, and every spare minute of our lives to produce. We do plan on producing additional updated versions of this guide in the years to come and continue to collect suggestions from other historians, park rangers, reenactors, and Civil War buffs on places to add, so your favorite battlefield may well be discussed in a future edition.

One last caveat: This work is the product of some very opinionated and somewhat biased historians (as if there were any other kinds!). You may feel that Braxton Bragg represented the be all, end all of the modern major general, but we do not. Similarly, many of his own men loved and respected William Starke Rosecrans, but we feel that he was the Dan Quayle of Union generals. As professional historians, we have tried to lay aside these biases and opinions in order to take fresh looks at the events that unfolded here, but as interpreting history is an entirely subjective exercise, one cannot work in the vacuum of sober objectivity. The opinions presented here are our own and do not necessarily represent The Globe Pequot Press, Insiders' Guides, the National Park Service, the Sons of Confederate Veterans, or any other interested parties.

PRICE CODES
Accommodations

Based on information available at the time of publication, we offer the following price code (average one-night charge for double occupancy rates in peak season) as a general guide. Please note that fluctuations in price and availability occur frequently. Extra charges may apply for special weekends, additional people in the room, efficiency apartments, or pets. These prices do not include local or state taxes. Unless otherwise indicated, accommodations accept major credit cards.

$	$35 to $69
$$	$70 to $99
$$$	$100 to $130
$$$$	$131 and up

Restaurants

The price code below is for a dinner entree (or lunch if dinner is not served) for one person. Appetizers, desserts, alcohol, and gratuity are additional.

$	$10 and under
$$	$11 to $20
$$$	$21 to $30
$$$$	$31 and up

GLOSSARY

The Civil War, and the military in general, produced such a set of specialized terminology and phrases that it almost constitutes a separate language. While we attempted to write this book in as clear and ordinary a style as possible, on many occasions there was simply no way to avoid the use of specialized terms. Here is a selection of terms used in the book.

Abatis or abattis: a defensive "wall" made of cut trees, usually arrayed in a thick, interconnected tangle, which would not completely stop a charging enemy attack but would slow one, giving the defenders additional time to bring heavy fire to bear on the points affected.

Amphibious: an attack launched from transports at sea or on a river; implies a coordinated army-navy attack, although this was not always the case.

Assault: a concentrated attack on a specific target or area; implies the maximum use of force that will fit into a given quadrant of the battlefield. It also implies an all-out attack that does not stop until the objective is taken or the attacking force is destroyed, but the term is used frequently as a synonym for any attack.

Battle flag: the flag used by each regiment on both sides for unit identification and signaling. Most battles during this period tended to break down into mass chaos and confusion unless the commander kept a firm control of his men, and the battlefield was far too noisy to hear a spoken order or even a bugle call. Soldiers were trained to recognize their regimental flag and to always follow it wherever it went. The flag bearer was given both a high honor and a great responsibility; he had to stay right by his commander at all times, he was usually not armed, and he could not break and run no matter how bad the situation was, as his whole regiment would then follow him to the rear. The casualty rate among flag bearers was appalling.

Bayonet: a long spike or thick knife blade with mountings to attach to the muzzle end of a rifle, enabling the soldier to stab his enemy at more than an arm's length away. Both the Enfield and Springfield bayonets were 18 inches long and triangular in section, which would cause a ghastly wound that usually would not heal properly and frequently caused a fatal infection in those who lived through the initial event. The "spirit of the bayonet" is a hallowed tradition for even modern infantrymen, although its use in battle has been greatly exaggerated. Most "hand to hand" combat actually involved the use of the butt end of the rifle, swung like a club, or even just fists, rocks, and heavy sticks. The bayonet-equipped rifle is a lethal and intimidating-looking weapon, but it took great skill and discipline to effectively employ it in the heat of combat. Soldiers usually used their issued bayonets for other purposes, as skewers to cook their meat or rammed into trees or walls to serve as coat hooks. Quite often they were heated and bent into hook shapes to drag the dead bodies of their comrades off the battlefield.

Blockade: to cut off and isolate a position or area from any resupply or reinforcement. During the Civil War this almost always referred to the Union Navy's blockade of the entire Southern Atlantic and Gulf coastlines, preventing most supplies from England and France from coming into the Confederacy.

Blockade runners: Civil War–era privateers, almost always civilians, who earned huge profits through great risk in sneaking their ships loaded with cargo through the Union Navy's coastal blockade. Although usually from the ranks of the lower classes and ordinary seamen before the war, they were the toast of Southern society as well as a major source of critical supplies for the embattled Southern armies. Northern newspapers universally decried them as the utter scourge of mankind.

Bomb-proof: a heavily reinforced, usually underground structure designed and built to protect the occupants, either civilians in an area under siege or troops in a combat area, from nearby artillery fire. Rarely would these structures protect from a direct hit by a large-caliber weapon.

Break contact: to pull back from a combat engagement, either to retreat or to shift the direction of a given assault. This is sometimes used as a polite way of saying that the men involved simply ran away.

Breastworks: a defensive barricade wall made of whatever materials were immediately available, usually logs, rocks, or fence rails. When placed in front of trenchlines, they usually were covered with the excavated earth itself, piled up, and formed into steep-faced walls. By the second year of the war, "spades is trumps" as Private Sam Watkins said, and nearly every time troops on either side stopped for more than a few minutes, their officers would put them to work constructing defensive works. On most battlefields today, these works are the only remaining evidence of the war.

Casements: refers to the lower areas in a masonry fort where the main artillery is mounted. These are usually some of the strongest parts of the fort's walls, built-up areas of stone or brick surrounding a narrow port or slit through which the cannon would fire.

Casualties: the losses for a unit, including deaths, injuries, capture or "missing" (usually from desertion), as well as losses from sickness or disease, by far the biggest killer of all during the war. On occasion the reports include losses resulting from discharge.

Chevaux-de-frise: somewhat like an early version of barbed wire, these barricades were in effect and construction very similar to abatis, with the exception of being somewhat portable. These were constructed by taking a log or (more rarely) a piece of iron post 9 to 15 feet long, drilling holes through it every 6 to 12 inches and through both angles, and inserting sharpened stakes about 4 to 6 feet long through the post. From an end view they looked like a crude cross, while from a frontal view they vaguely resembled a large version of an aerator used today on lawns. Many of these would be constructed and placed in front of other static defenses, sometimes fastened together, and always in the direct line of fire from the defenders. Although they could be moved by a squad or less of men, they slowed down infantry attacks long enough to provide an effective "kill zone" where they were placed.

Color bearer: the man assigned to carry the colors of the regiment. As the flag was usually large and unwieldy, he would most usually be unarmed, and as the rest of the regiment followed his actions to the letter (at least in theory), he must be a very brave and trustworthy man, unlikely to bolt and run from the battlefield. He would always be found standing very close to the regimental commander. Casualties were very high among color bearers; at Shiloh six color bearers from three Wisconsin regiments were all shot and killed in the first few hours of battle on the first day.

Colors: the distinctive flag unique to each regiment. As most of the soldiers of this time were illiterate, and the smoke and noise of battle precluded effective use of shouted orders, the men were taught to recognize their own colors (in a formal ceremony, still done in today's army, called "parading the colors") and to follow them wherever they went on the battlefield.

Column: a road march formation of troops, usually in company or regimental order and as long as 3 to 9 miles. When these columns were ambushed or otherwise surprised by an enemy force, it took quite some time to get the force arrayed into a combat formation, allowing plenty of time for "hit and run" attacks to succeed in delaying the column and inflicting casualties with relatively little risk to the attacker.

Counterattack: to aggressively assault an attacking force, to try to turn the momentum from the offensive to the defensive side.

Deploy: to move into either an offensive assault formation or to man defensive positions. Occasionally used to indicate simply being sent somewhere.

Doctrine: the established way of doing a particular mission or task; doing it "by the book." Most of both the Confederate and Union general officer staffs had trained at West Point, and early in the war it was clear who had done their homework better, as tactics and strategies used were nearly identical. Later in the war the doctrine of the Confederate armies was to maintain their forces intact even at the cost of positions and territory, while Union doctrine was to bring the heaviest mass possible of men and supplies into every given situation.

Earthwork/sandwork: a fort with outer defense walls made from earth or sand rather than some sort of masonry. Ironically, although these forts were made of local materials due to supply or cost problems, they turned out to be much better

at handling incoming artillery fire than the massive, expensive masonry forts.

En barbette: guns or cannon mounted on a low platform on the top floor of a fort, able then to fire over the top of the parapet without any firing slit or cutout needed. This was a very exposed and dangerous position for the artillerymen.

Enfilade: attacking an enemy force from a sharp angle, the side, or the rear. This usually implies the direction of fire, rather than an assault or such action.

Envelopment: to attack the sides and/or rear at the same time, usually requiring a high level of command coordination. Many well-planned attacks of this nature turned into disasters when the attack went in piecemeal, allowing the defenders to concentrate their forces as needed rather than spread them out to face multiple attacks.

Flanks: the sides or rear of a formation or position, usually one of the weakest points for an attacker to hit given the "line of battle" tactics of the day. The emphasis throughout most of the war was for an attacking force to maneuver into a position where they could hit the enemy's flanks; Grant and Lee in Virginia and Sherman and Johnston in Georgia provided classic examples of this.

Fleet: a group of warships and/or transports under a single commander, usually detailed for a general mission or task. A "flotilla" is generally a smaller grouping of the same sort, used for a single specific action or task.

Garrison: the body of troops assigned to a single fixed position, usually for a prolonged length of time and normally used only for guard duty or action from that one position. Just as the war began, many U.S. forts along the Atlantic and Gulf coasts in the South had a garrison of just one man (an ordnance sergeant), while by the fall of 1864 Atlanta had a Union Army garrison consisting of a full corps.

Gundeck: on a ship, the main deck where cannon or guns are mounted; in a fixed fortification, any of the positions where artillery is mounted.

Ironclads: special warships armored with iron plating, usually enough to deflect both rifle and smaller cannon fire. Early in the war these were just standard wooden naval vessels hastily outfitted with crude armor, but by the second year of the war, ships were being designed from the hull up to be steam-powered armored warships. The USS *Monitor* is the most familiar example of this genre, a low-freeboard hull mounting a single movable turret housing two large guns.

Lunette: a special type of earthwork fort consisting of an angled, L-shaped wall, with the rear completely exposed. These were used primarily as outlying artillery positions.

Militia: prewar local defense groups organized originally in colonial days for protection from Indian attacks. Later used as the core of the Continental Army and organized extensively in the South after the Revolutionary War to guard against slave insurrections. As the United States had only a tiny "professional" standing army well into the 20th century, the militias were relied upon to provide a trained cadre of fighting men that could be called up quickly in times of war (this is the "well-regulated militia" spoken of in the Second Amendment to the Constitution). By the 1840s the militias had become a sort of social culture, with many units dressing in all sorts of outlandish uniforms and drilling primarily for show in parades and such. These militias were quickly absorbed into the regular Union and Confederate Armies after the start of the war and their stylish uniforms soon packed away.

OR: a shorthand reference to the massive reference work *War of Rebellion: Official Records of the Union and Confederate Armies.* This 128-volume set began as an 1864 project to preserve all the correspondence of Union officers and other government papers pertaining to the war. Soon after the Confederate surrender, its papers were collected and work began on indexing them. The last volume was not compiled and published until 1901, with a "second series" of assorted and miscellaneous papers begun in the 1980s. These two sets, an associated (and exquisite) atlas, and a 31-volume sister compilation of naval records are the holy grail so far as Civil War research is concerned. Every significant fact in this book was checked against entries in the *OR*—helped in no small part by an excellent CD-ROM version produced by Guild Press of Indiana (available in most museum and battlefield bookstores for around $70). This is the most significant advance in Civil War research in quite some time, because, while the *OR* did have a three-volume index, it was not inclusive by any stretch of the imagination, and the "keyword search" function of electronic documents is a far more efficient and effective way of looking up references. It is also the most cost-efficient way of having your own copy of the *OR*, which costs around $3,500 for a new set (available from Broadfoot Publishing Company; www.broadfootpublishing.com) and takes up an incredible amount of shelf space.

Palisade: the steep outer walls of an earthwork or masonry fort.

Parapets: a low wall or fence along the top of a fort's ramparts, to provide some protection for the gunners manning en barbette positions. It now serves in existing forts to help keep the tourists from falling off the upper gundecks and ramparts.

Picket: a guard or sentry for either a fixed position or mobile force, these were usually placed well outside friendly lines or the head of the column, where they could best look for or hear any enemy movement. They were almost always the first to fight in any engagement and suffered appallingly high casualties. This duty would usually rotate from company to company in a regiment. During times of battle, they would work in conjunction with skirmishers and vedettes.

Quick-time: to walk in step at 120 steps per minute—the standard pace for infantry on the march. "Double quick time" is 180 steps per minute, which means you are moving at a sort of jog, but still in step with the men around you in a formation. "Charge" means to run flat-out at whatever lies ahead; obviously, calling for a faster pace or to run should only be done when nearly in contact with the enemy, as otherwise you have a bunch of worn-out infantrymen able to do little but gasp for breath.

Rampart: the top of a position's palisade, usually flattened so that artillery may be mounted and men may move about for guard and combat duties. To "take the ramparts" means the position has been breached by an enemy force that now holds the high ground and thus the tactical advantage.

Redoubt: another term for a reinforced protective shelter, usually made of logs covered with earthwork, but implies that this is a fighting position as well, as opposed to the bomb-proof, which implies simply a hideout or isolated shelter. This term is also used frequently as a reference to any defensive trenchwork or earthwork.

Refuse: a line of battle or wall of fortifications that is angled sharply back from the main enemy advance or attack. This helps prevent the enemy force from attacking the flank of a formation or position.

Reinforcements: troops brought into the battle either from an already established reserve force or from other commands moved into the area.

Reserve: troops kept back away from the main battle area to use to exploit any breach in the opponent's line, to replace casualties in the main battle force, or to use as the last line of defense. The rule of thumb is 2:1, keeping two parts of your command on the line of battle and one back as a reserve. There were some Civil War commanders who prided themselves on never using their reserves, no matter the situation, and others who would plug them in at the slightest sign of trouble.

Salient: a part of a defensive line or fortification that juts out from the rest of the line toward the enemy. Before the war this was taught to be something desirable, as it would naturally break up any enemy line of attack (and in theory allow the defender to fire straight into the flanks of an attacker on either side), but during the war most attacks focused on this feature to the distress of the defender. The "Dead Angle" at Cheatham's Hill (Kennesaw Mountain campaign in Georgia, 1864) is an excellent example of what can go wrong with a feature in the line of this sort.

Sapper or Sappier: a specially assigned soldier, charged with the construction of mines and associated structures, usually aimed at the destruction of an enemy's works.

"See the elephant": an expression used to refer to engaging in combat. A soldier who has just lived through his first battle has "seen the elephant." While it is debatable (and fiercely argued over in some circles) where this expression came from, the most plausible explanation is that it refers to the circus. During a time when the vast majority of the population were cloistered on farms, rarely going more than 20 miles from home in their entire lifetime, seeing the exotic animals in a circus was one of the highlights of their lives.

Shrapnel: listed under Artillery section.

Siege: to surround and cut off an enemy position from resupply or reinforcement and then "starve them out." The earliest known military histories (Homer's *The Iliad,* for one) mention this kind of warfare, which is brutally effective if one is facing an enemy position without hope of a strong relief effort and if one is very patient. During the Civil War a siege was usually accompanied by bombardment from heavy artillery manufactured and brought in for this specific situation. Vicksburg, Atlanta, and Petersburg are the three most often cited examples of this during the war.

Skirmishers: troops, usually of company strength or less, assigned to protect the head and flanks of a main battle formation. These infantrymen fought very much as modern infantrymen do, using cover, concealment, and individual maneuvers to "pick away" as much as possible from the main enemy force before withdrawing into their own lines. During times of battle, they would work in conjunction with pickets.

Squadron: a naval formation, usually consisting mostly of gunboats and other armed vessels and usually assigned to a given geographic area. Sometimes used as an alternative term for fleets or flotillas.

Staging bases: main bases usually well removed from the battle areas where men and supplies are funneled out to the necessary commands. This is where the main supply depots would be located, as well as training camps for the men.

Strategy: the overall plan for conducting the war or even just a single battle. A good example is the "Anaconda Plan," the grand overall plan for conducting the war against the Confederacy. Army commands and above would deal with plans on this level, leaving the specifics of exactly how to carry out these objectives to the lower commands.

Tactics: the specifics of how a particular strategy will be carried out on the battlefield. For example, Sherman's strategy was to drive southeast from Chattanooga and take Atlanta, but his tactical plans included details on which specific commands would move where and when. There are some sources in military science and theory circles that claim a distinction between strategy and tactics is ridiculous, as both talk about more or less the same thing, but we believe it is a useful distinction to mean you are talking about the grand strategies of politicians and top generals versus the battle tactics of field commanders and soldiers.

Theater: the general area of combat or a large area covered by a single command. For example, "theater armies" means all the combatant forces in a given major geographic area. The "theater armies" referred to at Resaca (during the Atlanta campaign) meant all four armies commanded by Sherman as well as the three corps commanded by Johnston—all the troops they had immediately available to them. A "theater" can also mean something such as the "Western Theater," which included everything in the South from the Carolinas to the Mississippi. This book concentrates on this theater of the war.

Transports: unarmed ships attached to fleets or flotillas, carrying army troops to use in assaults or amphibious invasions.

Trench work: a line of dug-out ditches, providing both cover and concealment for infantrymen who fought from inside them. Depending on how long the troops had been in their position before being attacked, these could be as crude as a shallow, scratched-out series of "foxholes" or a deep and elaborate series of interconnected ditches, bomb-proofs, and redoubts.

Vanguard: the forwardmost elements of a command or column. In modern military parlance, this is the "point element," the troops most vulnerable to a sudden ambush or attack.

Vedette or vidette: a mounted guard or sentry, who otherwise did the same duty as a picket. During times of battle, vedettes would work in conjunction with pickets and skirmishers.

Volley fire: a line of infantry all firing at the same time on command. A central element of the Napoleonic tactics used throughout the war, massed infantry firing volleys was the only way that smoothbore muskets of limited range could gain a real advantage on a fluid battlefield; the infantrymen would form three lines slightly offset one behind another, and each would fire in turn on the order of their officer. By the time the third line fired the first would be reloaded, so a near continuous volume of outgoing fire could be maintained so long as the ammunition held out. As Civil War–era rifles had ranges 3 to 10 times longer than Revolutionary War–era muskets, could be reloaded a bit faster, and had a much more lethal ammunition load, the same close-in volley fire tactics resulted in appalling casualties.

ARTILLERY

Artillery had its own specialized language; the following list is a sampling of the most commonly used terms.

Barrage: to use multiple guns firing on a single target or to saturate an area with as heavy a rate of fire as possible.

Battery: the basic organization of artillery units, which contained four, five, or six guns of single or multiple type, which usually worked together in a combat action. Occasionally batteries were broken up into two-gun sections for use in special circumstances.

Bombardment: the use of artillery to reduce either a military or civilian target to rubble. Atlanta withstood nearly six weeks of a high rate of fire from some of the heaviest guns the Union possessed;

Most soldiers fired fewer than 10 shots during training before going into combat. Most weapons training consisted of a rapid reloading drill and bayonet drill.

some sources claim that it is the "heaviest bombarded" city in North America. Other sources claim the same for Vicksburg, Port Hudson, Charleston, Petersburg, etc.

Caisson: the ammunition wagon and container for an artillery piece. Usually the piece and the caisson were hauled together by a single team of horses, called the caisson team. As these wagons were very sturdily built and had flat tops, they were often used as ambulances and even as hearses. The U.S. Army still uses caissons in formal military funerals; the 3rd Infantry, the "Old Guard" at Arlington National Cemetery, is often seen using caissons to haul the coffins of the honored dead to their final rest.

Canister/grapeshot: a tin can similar to a coffee can filled with either 27 or 48 iron balls, designed to burst open right after it left the muzzle and spray the area in front of the piece like a giant shotgun. Grapeshot is a slight variation that uses nine larger iron balls either sewn together in a cloth sleeve or held together in a light iron frame. The size of these balls varied with the caliber of the gun they were used in. This round was useful out to about 300 yards but was more usually employed at much closer range, including at literally point-blank range. When things were really bleak for the artillery crews, they would load up with "double canister," knocking the powder bag off the rear of the second round and ramming it in on top of the first. This cut the range roughly in half, but doubled the effectiveness up close. This was a deadly weapon to use against closely packed infantry charges and would result in the lines being literally blown apart, creating huge gaps.

i

At the usual combat range, 300 yards, bullets from the .58 caliber rifled muskets used by both sides could penetrate up to 11 inches of seasoned white-pine boards.

Cannon: a generic term for a piece of artillery, not specific as to the type or size.

Columbiad: a very heavy-barreled, smoothbore weapon originally introduced in 1811, which could fire either shot or shell from either flat or high trajectories, giving it the combined characteristics of guns, howitzers, and mortars. For many years these were the backbone weapon of coastline defense, and nearly every coastal fort featured them at the outbreak of war. Early Columbiads could fire a 50-pound solid round shot about 1,800 feet. A variation of this gun, known as a Rodman, was manufactured in a way that created an exceptionally strong barrel, giving the improved guns the ability to fire shells that weighed up to 320 pounds out to nearly 3 miles away.

Counter-battery: to use artillery fire against an enemy artillery position to try to knock their guns out of the fight.

Dahlgren: a very heavy-barreled weapon, very similar in look to a Columbiad. These were used primarily on board naval vessels (the USS *Monitor* mounted two 11-inch Dahlgrens in its turret) and came in both smoothbore and rifled varieties. They were built in sizes ranging from 12-pounders to 150-pounders, as well as 9-inch to 20-inch calibers, with the 15-inch smoothbores being the most popular.

Friction primer: the "match" that was used to set off a cannon. It consisted of two short pieces of copper tubing soldered together at right angles, with one tube filled with mercury fulminate and the other, slightly longer tube filled with gunpowder. After the charge had been loaded and the gunpowder-filled charge bag torn open by a vent prick, the friction primer was inserted into the vent hole, directly over the now-opened charge bag, and attached to a lanyard. The mercury-filled tube had a short, twisted wire inserted that, when pulled out rapidly, created a friction spark with the mercury fulminate. This caused the gunpowder in the other tube to flash and, in turn, caused the pricked charge bag inside the tube to deflammate, expelling the round from the tube.

Fuse: a length of flammable cording inside a plug that burned at a known rate and that was used to cause an explosive shell to go off at a given time after firing. A gun crewman cut the fuse to the length (time) desired and then inserted the fuse and plug assembly into a shell before handing it off to be loaded into the piece. The firing of the piece ignited the fuse, and artillery officers were well trained in the mathematics of figuring out exactly when a shell would arrive over a given target at a given range. The advantage of this was the ability to do "air bursts," which spread the lethal shrapnel over a much wider arc than if the shell had hit the ground before bursting.

Gun: a generic term for any artillery piece, although, to be precise, it really refers only to rifled cannon.

Hot-shot: solid shot heated to red-hot in special ovens and then quickly loaded and fired at flammable targets: ships and their rigging, wagons and caissons, wooden palisades, abatis, etc.

Lanyard: a 12-foot-long rope with a wooden handle on one end and a hook on the other that was attached to a small loop in the wire of a friction primer. Used to fire the artillery piece.

Mortar: a short, very heavy-barreled artillery piece that used exceptionally heavy powder charges in order to loft solid shot or shell nearly vertically. These were extremely useful in lobbing charges over a walled enemy position or trench-work that was resistant to direct fire.

Parrott rifle: a rifled, muzzle-loading cannon, ranging in size from a 3-inch (or 10-pounder) to a 10-inch (300-pounder). These are some of the easiest cannons to identify, having a thick band attached around the rear of the barrel, used to help withstand the tremendous pressures rifled cannons build up during firing. These rifled guns fired oblong "bolts," cucumber-shaped solid shot and explosive shells, that had brass rings attached to the base that "grabbed" the rifling during firing. Many accounts of soldiers on the wrong end of Parrott rifles firing talk about the particular "whiffling" shrill noise these bolts made when flying overhead. A deadly accurate weapon found in both armies in every theater of the war.

Piece: another generic term for a cannon, although usually used to indicate a specific or singular gun.

Shell: a hollow round filled with gunpowder, which would burst either from striking a target or by the action of a timed fuse.

Shot: solid round balls or oblong "bolts," usually used against masonry structures or other such heavy, solid objects. However, cannoneers had absolutely no qualms about using solid shot against infantry formations; one of the author's great-grandfathers lost a leg to just such a round at South Mountain, Maryland.

Shrapnel: red-hot, jagged bits of metal flying about at high rates of speed, produced by the exploding casing of a bursting shell. A shell bursting in the air above an infantry formation could produce many times the casualties of a solid shot blasting through the line.

Spike: to render a cannon unable to fire, usually by driving a soft iron nail through the vent hole and cutting off the protruding end. This would be done, if possible, when an enemy force was about to overrun an artillery position and the guns could not be withdrawn. There were frequent occasions, especially late in the war, when Union gunners simply shot all their caisson horses when on the verge of being overrun and left the guns intact, knowing that the Confederates would lack the horses needed to take the guns when they retreated. Then the Union gunners could simply move back in and resume their firing with little fuss.

Trails: the rear "legs" of the gun carriage, which had a short pole (called a trail handspike) attached for ease of aiming by moving the gun left and right. This is also where the cannon was attached to the rear of the caisson, being hauled tube pointed backward.

Tube: sometimes used as a generic term for cannon, it is the heavy iron or bronze casting that is the barrel of the gun. It is attached to the gun carriage by means of two trunnions cast on either side, near the barrel's center of gravity, and raised up and down by means of various attachments to the knob and neck cast on the rear of the barrel.

BACKGROUND
TO THE WAR

The Civil War is perhaps both the most significant single event in our nation's history and probably the most divisive—even 140 years after it ended. Although the last of the combat soldiers died more than 70 years ago (1933) and the last of the people known to be present on those battlegrounds died more than 50 years ago (1951), there are still a few living links to the past that bring this period alive. As late as fall 2002, two widows of Civil War veterans were alive and still collecting their late husbands' veterans' benefits. One former Confederate state still maintains part of the "battle flag" as part of its official state flag design, while another only very recently quit flying the "Naval Jack" alongside the state and national flags over its capitol. Civil War reenacting has become one of the fastest growing hobbies in the nation, leading some to remark that it has become a distinct and readily apparent subculture all its own. Most small (and a few large) Southern towns have one or two well-preserved antebellum homes that suffered minor damage during the local skirmish or battle and that are now proudly displayed as cherished artifacts. In some parts of the South, it is still an ordinary and everyday sort of question to be asked, "Are you a legacy?" meaning, "Did you have any relations who fought in The War?"

The very name for this period of conflict is in itself a still-festering point of contention. Merely calling it the "Civil War," although dryly accurate from a historian's point of view, is seen in some circles as a Northern political statement. Frequently, especially in the rural parts of the Deep South, you will hear it referred to with equal political overtones as the "War of Northern Aggression," "The War Between the States," and even (our favorite) "The Late Unpleasantness."

The Civil War did not just spring up overnight, nor were the issues involved simple. The seeds were sown much earlier in our nation's history, with some elements of what grew into the bitter and often violent sectional crisis apparent in some of the earliest attempts at colonization. The very first attempts at colonizing North America were done purely for means of profit, making the United States the only country in the world that was created for financial purposes and whose national anthem mentions rockets and bombs! The New England colonies soon turned into conservative, religious, small-plot farming, trading, and manufacturing states, while the Southern colonies established their status as major agricultural producers of products requiring large numbers of workers. To turn a profit, these large plantations required the use of slave labor or, at a bare minimum, very poorly paid workers or sharecroppers.

The period between 1830 and 1860 was a time of rapid growth throughout the United States that emphasized the basic sectional differences. It also was a time of erratic and ever-changing political leadership and allegiances. It was a time in which America was attempting to define its identity and trying to overcome or ignore the fact that very real and very extreme differences in the character of the major regions made a single "identity" impractical. The nation's population during these three decades increased from 12.8 million to nearly 31.5 million—an amazing 140 percent increase. The number of states grew from 24 to 34, reflecting the country's intense interest in settling beyond the Ohio and Mississippi River valleys. New states emerged in every region: Arkansas, Florida, and Texas in the South; Iowa and Kansas in the nation's heartland; Michigan, Wisconsin, and Minnesota in the "Old Northwest"; Oregon and California on the Pacific coast. Despite the nation's growth, however, people habitually referred to the nation as "these" United States, a subtle reference to the ongoing struggle between the power of the individual states and overriding federal control.

There were 10 presidents during these 30 years. Andrew Jackson, the first "modern" Democrat, was inaugurated as the nation's 7th president in 1829. Abraham Lincoln, the first "modern" Republican, was sworn in as the 16th chief executive in 1860. In between, there was not a single two-term president. The struggle for partisan leadership in the White House resembled a game of political badminton. Jackson and his fellow Democrats controlled presidential politics through the 1830s. A third party, the Whigs, was reorganized in the mid-1830s in an attempt to unite various coalitions opposed to what they considered Jackson's executive tyranny. They were remarkably successful during most of the 1840s, but party leaders never developed a strong, identifiable party program. Democrats reclaimed control of the White House in the 1850s. Republican Lincoln was elected in 1860 without even appearing on the ballot in most Southern states, an act that "proved" to secessionists that the North would not allow the South to hold or maintain any political power in Washington.

SLAVERY

Slavery was a practice begun in the Virginia colony in 1609. It was particularly Southern, where economics centered primarily on large-scale, manpower-intensive agriculture. In the North, an area with more advanced manufacturing and industrialization, the sentiment—based on moral or religious objections—usually was against slavery.

The United States never declared war against the Confederacy. The official position was that the states of the Confederacy had not in fact seceded and formed a new nation; they were simply being held hostage by hostile, rogue governments. This makes the "conditions" the U.S. Congress forced for their "readmission" to the Union a rather interesting issue.

Slavery existed in every single Northern state until the time of the American Revolution, although it was usually restricted to a relatively small group per owner, working on family farms or in factories and mines. It was ironic that most abolitionists turned a blind eye to the condition of newly arrived immigrant workers in Northern factories who replaced these slaves, many of whom were also the victims of exploitation and wage slavery.

As new states were admitted to the union, pro- and antislavery proponents became more and more vocal. The 1820 Missouri Compromise allowed the admission of Missouri as a slave state, while Maine was cut from Massachusetts and admitted as a free state to balance Congress with an equal number of representatives from slave and free states. This compromise outlawed slavery in the remainder of the Louisiana Territory north of Missouri's southern boundary. "We have a wolf by the ears," Thomas Jefferson said of the problem of slavery, "and we can neither safely hold him, nor safely let him go."

POLITICAL DEBATES

As the debate over slavery raged in the 1820s and 1830s, two particular positions arose as a Southern answer to the seeming pro-Northern stance taken by Washington politics: "states' rights" and "nullification." "States' rights" was a term usually associated with South Carolina and its prominent political leader John C.

CLOSE-UP

John Brown's Raid

John Brown's Raid was an 1859 violent attack against the federal arsenal at Harpers Ferry, in the mountains of what was then western Virginia (now West Virginia). Brown, the Kansas abolitionist, plotted for months before raiding the town because it was what he described as "the safest natural entrance to the Great Black Way." According to Brown, "Here, amid the mighty protection of overwhelming numbers, lay a path from slavery to freedom." Brown, a self-described "instrument of God sent to liberate all slaves," captured the federal arsenal and refused to surrender. He was captured two days later when U.S. Marines, led by Colonel Robert E. Lee of the U.S. Army, stormed the arsenal. Brown was tried for and convicted of treason in nearby Charles Town and was hanged on December 2, 1859. To many blacks and non-slave-owning whites, he was a hero and a

John Brown, circa 1856. COURTESY OF THE NATIONAL ARCHIVES

martyr. Ironically, the first man killed in the raid was a freed slave.

Calhoun. This political position suggests a strict interpretation of the U.S. Constitution as it relates to federal powers and state autonomy. A "strict" interpretation means that only what is literally written into the document itself has any legal power, while a "loose" interpretation holds that the Constitution is a relatively simple framework that cannot possibly address every given circumstance but that should be used as a basic reference to infer how it holds in specific cases. By the time Calhoun became President Andrew Jackson's vice president, states' rights were a source of heated debate in Washington and elsewhere in the country.

"Nullification" was another term commonly attributed to Calhoun. He, along with fellow South Carolinians and other Southerners, said individual states existed prior to the formation of the United States. Therefore the states themselves could interpret the U.S. Constitution and "nullify" any action by the Federal government they considered unauthorized or unconstitutional. South Carolina put its nullification philosophy into action in 1832, after Congress passed legislation that put protective duties, also know as tariffs, on imported manufactured goods. Congressmen from the North and West supported the bill; Southerners, who had few manufacturing concerns, disliked it. To be forced to pay tariffs that were decided on in Washington and heavily influenced by Northern business interests was just another point on which Southerners came to believe that their interests and needs were being ignored. South Carolina enacted an ordinance of nullification, which declared the national law as not applicable within the state's boundaries.

South Carolina considered its right to nullify a federal law an issue important enough to merit seceding from the union. To secede (pronounced c-seed or sa-seed, depending on one's own regional accent) means to withdraw from membership in an association. After South Carolina enacted its ordinance of nullification, President Jackson charged Calhoun with treason and threatened to have him hanged. To the nullifiers, the president said, "Secession, like any other revolutionary act, may be morally justified by the extremity of oppression; but to call it a constitutional right is confounding." Jackson added, "The laws of the United States must be executed. I have no discretionary power on the subject."

PREWAR PRESIDENTS AND POLITICS

In 1833, as Jackson began his second term in the White House, his trusted friend, Martin Van Buren, was the new vice president. Calhoun had broken with Jackson over the tariff issue and had resigned in protest to return to a South Carolina leadership position. That same year, Senator Henry Clay of Kentucky helped the nation avoid a serious crisis over the tariff issue. Clay, a native Virginian and former secretary of state, had been an unsuccessful presidential candidate against Jackson the previous year. Clay devised a new tariff law designed to lower duties over a period of years. His plan gave South Carolina enough political elbow room to repeal its nullification ordinance, and in

time Clay became known as the Great Compromiser.

In 1840 the nation's population topped 17 million. Jackson's handpicked successor, Van Buren, faced a military hero, Whig William Henry Harrison, in his bid for reelection. Earlier in the year, Clay had challenged Harrison for the Whig nomination and lost. Clay, a presidential candidate in 1824, 1832, and later in 1844, commented, "I am the most unfortunate man in the history of parties; always run by my friends when sure to be defeated, and now betrayed when I, or anyone, would be sure of an election." An antislavery group called the Liberty Party also ran a candidate. Harrison won and was inaugurated the following March, but he became ill and lived just one more month.

Vice President John Tyler, a man of more obscure political leanings, succeeded Harrison, and Calhoun became Tyler's secretary of state. In 1844 Clay ran for president again and lost to Democrat James Polk. Four years later, Whig Zachary Taylor, another war hero, became a presidential candidate. Taylor won the election. He, too, died in office and was succeeded by Vice President Millard Fillmore.

Senator Daniel Webster of Massachusetts was a member of President Fillmore's cabinet. Webster gained national fame in 1830, when he spoke out against South Carolina's nullification principles. He served as secretary of state for both Presidents Harrison and Tyler, and he was an unsuccessful Whig candidate for president in 1836. Webster was appointed secretary of state in July 1850, just four months after delivering his stirring speech in the U.S. Senate in support of the Compromise of 1850. This compromise was designed to prevent a national split over the issue of territorial slavery. In his famous speech, Webster said, "I wish to speak today, not as a Massachusetts man, nor as a Northern man, but as an American." He urged his fellow Northerners to accept a stronger fugitive slave law and Southerners to give up all thought of secession.

There were a total of 432,650 slaves in the "free" and border states at the outbreak of war.

"Peaceable secession!" Webster exclaimed, "Heaven forbid."

Senator Stephen Douglas of Illinois, at 5-foot-4 and 90 pounds known as the Little Giant, efficiently maneuvered the Clay-inspired Compromise of 1850 through Congress. The bill authorized the acquisition of the Southwest Territory after the Mexican War and again raised the issue of territorial slavery. California was admitted as a free state; the rest of the Southwest was divided into two sections, one with slavery and one without. While adopting the 1850 compromise legislation, Congress passed another act to abolish slave trading in the District of Columbia and help slave owners recover runaways. Known as the Fugitive Slave Act, it inflamed ill feelings between sectionalist leaders as well as proponents of both slavery and abolitionism. *Uncle Tom's Cabin* was written in 1852 by Harriet Beecher Stowe and heralded by abolitionists. It avoided self-righteous accusations and described slaves as victims of an evil, Southern system. The book had a major impact on Northern sympathizers. In England, Queen Victoria was said to have cried when she read it. An undocumented anecdote holds that when President Lincoln met Stowe in the White House during the war, he remarked, "So, this is the little woman who started this great big war."

Senator Clay died in Washington in 1852; funeral services were held in the U.S. Senate chambers. Four months later, Secretary of State Webster died in Marshfield, Massachusetts. Senator Douglas, meanwhile, was an unsuccessful candidate for the Democratic presidential nomination. The nod went instead to Franklin Pierce, who defeated Winfield Scott, a hero of the Mexican-American War. Pierce was inaugurated in Washington in March 1853.

Among Pierce's cabinet members was Secretary of War Jefferson Davis.

Senator Douglas returned to national prominence in 1854, when he introduced the Kansas-Nebraska Bill to establish a territorial government west of Missouri, divide the region into slave and free sections, and repeal the law that banned slavery north of Missouri's southern border. The Kansas-Nebraska Act, the result of Senator Douglas's bill, prompted thousands of both pro- and antislavery supporters to pour into Kansas to try and overthrow the established government. There was considerable death and destruction (thus the term "Bleeding Kansas"), including a raid at Pottawatomie led by abolitionist John Brown. Northerners, including Douglas's own supporters, were outraged by the Kansas act. The legislation destroyed the senator's presidential aspirations and led the nation farther down the road toward an inevitable national conflict.

"Free Soil, Free Speech, Frémont" was the slogan of the new Republican Party in the 1856 presidential campaign. The slogan was used by advocates who wanted to ban territorial slavery, end abolitionist literature, and elect John C. Frémont as president. The Republicans skipped over Douglas to run Frémont against a Pennsylvania bachelor, James Buchanan, the ultimate victor. Buchanan did little to stop the widening split between the North and South. In the Panic of 1857, a number of banks collapsed after American grain producers dropped grain prices in response to increased Russian grain exports. The South survived the 1857 panic, in large part, because of Europe's continued demand for cotton. Southerners, aware of the power of the cotton trade and convinced the North would avoid interfering with their states' rights philosophy, proclaimed "Cotton is King" as a term of assumed triumph over Northern trade policies.

In its famous Dred Scott Decision, the U.S. Supreme Court ruled in 1857 that the

Missouri Compromise was unconstitutional because it deprived slave owners the right to take their "property" where they wanted. In this case, Scott, a slave, was taken into the Wisconsin Territory, where slavery was banned.

A one-term Illinois congressman named Abraham Lincoln rose to prominence in 1858, challenging incumbent Senator Douglas. Lincoln, in his famous "House Divided" speech at the senatorial nominating convention, predicted "This government cannot endure permanently half slave and half free." Many, including conservative Northerners, took his speech as a call for abolishing slavery. Throughout the campaign, particularly in a notable joint appearance in Freeport, Illinois, Lincoln pressed Douglas on two issues: the senator's Kansas-Nebraska Bill and the Supreme Court's Scott decision. Of Douglas, it can be said he won the battle but lost the war: He defeated Lincoln in the Illinois senate race, but he lost to Lincoln in the presidential election two years later.

The Constitutional Union Party was a third-party faction that adopted a platform in 1860 in support of the Union and the U.S. Constitution, without regard to sectional issues. While Lincoln and Douglas were the prime contenders for the presidency in 1860, the Constitutional Union Party ran Tennessean John Bell, a former U.S. senator and secretary of war. Bell said Americans had a patriotic duty to "recognize no political principle other than the Constitution, the Union of the States, and the enforcement of the laws." He carried his home state plus Kentucky and Virginia, where sharply divided voters clearly realized that any possible bloodshed likely would erupt in their region.

Lincoln was elected president in 1860, and South Carolina seceded a month later. Then, in quick succession prior to the 1861 inaugural, the Union lost six more states: Mississippi, Florida, Alabama, Georgia, Louisiana, and Texas. Within a few months, four more states joined the new Confederate States of America: Virginia, Arkansas, Tennessee, and North Carolina. Lincoln was inaugurated in March 1861. Douglas, the new president's old nemesis, held Lincoln's hat during the inaugural ceremony. Three months later, Senator Douglas died in Chicago, barely a month after the outbreak of the Civil War.

Kansas was admitted to the Union just five weeks before Lincoln's inaugural. This new state aligned with 18 other Northern, non-slave states in the Northeast, north of the Ohio River, and just beyond the Mississippi River. The North included the states of California, Connecticut, Illinois, Indiana, Iowa, Kansas, Maine, Massachusetts, Michigan, Minnesota, New Hampshire, New Jersey, New York, Ohio, Oregon, Pennsylvania, Rhode Island, Vermont, and Wisconsin and the territories of Colorado, Dakota, Nebraska, Nevada, and Washington. Separating the North and South were so-called border states—Delaware, Maryland, Kentucky, and Missouri, as well as the District of Columbia and the New Mexico Territory, all of which contained a significant population of slaves. In addition, many parts of the South were heavily pro-Union, including eastern Tennessee, western North Carolina, and northern Georgia and Alabama, but most notably western Virginia, which was admitted to the Union as a separate state in 1863.

INTRODUCTION TO THE WESTERN THEATER OF THE WAR

The Civil War is frequently said to have occurred "in 10,000 places," but the overwhelming majority of books and writings on the subject would lead one to believe that the war might have started in South Carolina, but then it moved quickly to Virginia and stayed there, with a few isolated skirmishes here and there elsewhere. Actually, the war in the Eastern Theater, which included Virginia, Maryland, and Pennsylvania, included roughly one-third of the men and material and featured a long series of battles geographically relatively close to Richmond, Virginia. In contrast, the other theaters of the war ranged from as far east as North Carolina's Outer Banks all the way west to New Mexico and from as far north as Canada and Vermont south to the Florida Keys, and even south into Brazil (where Confederate expatriates set up communities after the war), and featured some of the largest campaigns, biggest armies, most horrifying sieges, and bloodiest battles of the entire war.

The word "theater" in a military sense means a large geographic area under one commander, that commander being subordinate only to the army's commander in chief. For example, in World War II, General Dwight D. Eisenhower was SHAEF commander (Supreme Headquarters, Allied Expeditionary Forces) and commander of the European theater of the war. He reported directly to the Army chief of staff, General George C. Marshall, just as did his counterpart in the Asian/Pacific Theater, General Douglas C. MacArthur.

During the Civil War, the term "theater" was not widely used; it's a modern historian's shorthand way of keeping track of the area being studied. Instead, the term "department" was used, which did not have a standard size of composition but which was used to designate the largest area to have a single field commander. Early in the war, Confederate authorities created two departments centered around the Mississippi River. "Department No. 1" consisted of most of Louisiana and all of Alabama and Mississippi south of the 31st parallel, including Mobile Bay. "Department No. 2" consisted of northern Mississippi and Alabama, western Tennessee, and parts of Arkansas. These department organizations, which changed constantly during the war, recognized the fact that control of the rivers and ports, and especially the Mississippi River, was going to be central to the preservation of the Confederacy. Other departments covered other, irregular portions of the remaining Southern states. Within a year, these designations started giving way to statewide department organizations—by the time of Shiloh in early April 1862, General Albert Sidney Johnston commanded Department No. 2, which evolved shortly afterward into the Department of the West, inclusive of a reduced Department No. 2 and a newly created Department of Mississippi and East Louisiana. A year later the No. 2 disappeared completely when a new Department of Tennessee was created.

All this very confusing organization was typical across the lower South, done in both the Confederate and Union armies. In the massive reference work *War of Rebellion: Official Records of the Union and Confederate Armies, OR* for short, a vast and bewildering array of departments, military divisions, territorial divisions, and field armies appear at different times of the war. Similar to today's constantly shifting business organizations, these redesignations were usually in response to the shifting focus of military actions, both real and imagined. A sampling of the departments that appear in the OR gives an idea of the complexity of this issue:

Confederate Department of Alabama, Mississippi, and East Louisiana
Confederate Department of Alabama and West Florida
Confederate Department of West Florida
Confederate Department of Middle and Eastern Florida
Confederate Department of Georgia
Confederate Department of the Gulf
Confederate District of the Gulf
Confederate Department of Louisiana
Confederate Department of East Tennessee
Confederate Department of Tennessee and Georgia
Confederate Department of the West

Union Department of Alabama
Union Department of Florida
Union Department of Georgia
Union Department of the Gulf
Union Military Division of the Gulf
Union Department of Key West, Florida
Union Department of Louisiana and Texas
Union Department of Mississippi (two different ones)
Union Department of the Mississippi
Union Military Division of the Mississippi
Union Military Division of West Mississippi

In this book, for the sake of both brevity and sanity, we refer to the area we cover as the "Western Theater." This covers the area from North Carolina to the Mississippi River and from Tennessee south to Florida. This, of course, shows our Southern bias, as the Union Army preferred to call most of this area the "Southern The-

Julia Dent Grant, wife of Union Lieutenant General Ulysses S. Grant, owned four slaves. She brought them with her into Union army camps when she visited Grant during the war and kept them under bondage until the 13th Amendment to the U.S. Constitution was passed after the hostilities ended.

ater." Areas in Virginia, Maryland, Pennsylvania, and Washington, D.C., are habitually referred to as the "Eastern Theater," while areas west of the Mississippi River are usually referred to as the "Trans-Mississippi Theater." Although fighting did occur in Kentucky and other points not included in these three broad definitions, they are either ignored (usually) or simply referenced by the individual campaigns or battles without theater labels being attached.

The war, or at least the combat actions of the war, started in this theater, whether you hold to the standard story of the "first shots" being fired at Fort Sumter in Charleston, adhere to the *Star of the West* incident, or even the small firefight at Fort Barrancas in Pensacola as the first true shots. Although the earliest major battles did shift to the Eastern Theater (Bull Run/Manassas), some of the largest and most significant battles were fought there (Antietam/Sharpsburg, Fredericksburg, Petersburg), and the largest battle ever fought in North America occurred there (Gettysburg), the most important battles and campaigns from a strategic sense occurred in the Western Theater.

The Union's overall plan for the war consisted of three major parts: first, to control shipments of arms from overseas to the South by building a naval blockade of the Atlantic and Gulf coastlines and ports; second, to take control of the Mississippi and split the Confederacy in half; and third, to seize the Confederate capital at Richmond. General Robert E. Lee was extremely successful in avoiding the latter with his Army of Northern Virginia until

CLOSE-UP

A President for the Confederacy

Jefferson Davis, a Kentucky native and longtime Mississippi resident, was a West Point graduate. His first wife, the daughter of President Zachary Taylor, died of malaria only a few months after they were married. Davis served in the Mexican-American War and as a U.S. senator and was President Franklin Pierce's secretary of war. He was elected president of the Confederate States of America (CSA) at a meeting of 37 delegates from five seceded states who met in assembly in February 1861 in Montgomery, Alabama.

Davis was rail-thin, chronically ill with what were more than likely stress-related problems, ill-tempered, and highly opinionated, and he did not suffer being questioned or debated—all poor qualifications for the post he held. The very nature of the Confederate cause was centered on "states' rights," another try on the old Articles of Confederation style of government that had failed so completely 70 years before. Davis was tasked with both recognizing the rights of complete sovereignty of each state in the Confederacy, while simultaneously trying to lead them all in a coalition to fight the overwhelmingly superior Union armies.

Complicating his task were the actions of Governor Joseph Brown of Georgia and Governor John West Ellis of North Carolina, both of whom were ardent supporters of "states' rights," to the point of helping to defeat their own cause. Brown was consumed throughout the war with attempts to form his own "state army," completely separate from the Confederate high command and answerable only to him, while Ellis refused

the last few days of the war, while keeping the eastern Union armies bottled up in a long and costly series of battles around the capital city. In the West, the blockade was successfully positioned within the first year of the war but was unable to completely cut off blockade-runners with their precious cargoes. That job was only accomplished with the fall of the port cities of Wilmington, Savannah, Mobile, and New Orleans later in the war. The campaign for control of the Mississippi River started off well for the Union, with the quick and relatively painless fall of Forts Henry and Donalson to the north and New Orleans to the south. However, it took two years and many thousands of lives to wrest control of the river via the long siege campaigns at Vicksburg and Port Hudson. One may reasonably claim that July 3, 1863, was the brightest day of the entire war for the Union, as it featured the near simultaneous victories at Gettysburg, the "high tide of the Confederacy," and Vicksburg, opening up the "Father of the Waters" to the Union Navy's unimpeded passage.

Even with two-thirds of the Union master plan accomplished by that day, the Confederacy showed no signs of imminent collapse. Lee's army, though battered and needing resupply and reorganization, successfully retreated back into Virginia more or less intact, while the railroads across the South successfully took over the task of shipping men and supplies

to supply uniforms and equipment to other states' troops, even while his own warehouses were nearly bursting at the seams with unissued uniforms.

Davis had one last fault that doomed his own army—a near-fanatic devotion to his friends and fellow combat veterans. Braxton Bragg had fought with Davis in Mexico, forming a lifelong friendship that resulted in Davis placing Bragg in high command positions to which he was clearly unsuited. Davis reacted angrily to criticisms of Bragg, not only leaving his old friend in command but transferring out or even firing the very able officers who dared to complain about him. The result was that Bragg and later John Bell Hood, another old friend, made mistake after mistake in the Western Theater that destroyed their own armies and handed victory after victory to the Union commanders.

Jefferson Davis, a prewar photo. COURTESY OF THE NATIONAL ARCHIVES

from the Union-controlled river ways. Factories sprang up all across the South to manufacture the military supplies no longer available in quantity from England and the rest of Europe (although the "homemade" variety were almost always crude imitations, they were still useful in killing quantities of Yankees), railroads were expanded and improved in order to move these supplies around more efficiently, while Atlanta, a town that hadn't even existed 20 years beforehand, became a critically important transportation and logistics center (a role it still plays today). It would take two more years and a massive campaign through Georgia and the Carolinas to finally bring the Confederacy to its knees.

Some of the final chapters in the Confederacy occurred in the Western Theater as well: first, with the surrender of the pitiful remnants of General Joseph Eggleston Johnston's Army of Tennessee near Durham, North Carolina, on April 26, just over two weeks after Lee's own surrender in Virginia. On May 4 Lieutenant General Richard Taylor surrendered his small army outside Mobile, Alabama, and then President Jefferson Finis Davis was captured by Union cavalrymen near Irwinville, Georgia, on May 10.

The last surrenders, ironically, took place in the nearly forgotten Trans-Mississippi Theater, first with Lieutenant General Simon B. Buckner surrendering all the Trans-Mississippi commands (not all of which he actually commanded) at New Orleans on May 27. The actual commander of this theater, Lieutenant General E. Kirby Smith, refused to surrender and soon led more than 2,000 of his men south into Mexico rather than submit to federal authority. He eventually returned quietly to the United States in November 1865. The final holdout was the chief of the Cherokee Nation, Stand Watie, a Confederate brigadier commander leading a battalion of Native Americans, who finally led his command into Doaksville, Indian Territory (now Oklahoma), and surrendered on June 23. The last combat action of the war occurred in this theater as well, at Palmito Ranch, Texas, on May 12 and 13, interestingly enough a Confederate victory.

MAJOR PERSONALITIES

Throughout the text of this guide, for the sake of brevity, most soldiers are listed only by their last name, preceded by their rank and full name the first time mentioned in each chapter. While it would take a massive chapter to list every name mentioned, here, for easy reference, we list the full names and ranks of the most prominent figures mentioned more than once in the text.

CONFEDERATE

Adams, Brigadier General Daniel West
Anderson, Brigadier General Joseph Reid
Anderson, General Robert Heron
Avery, Colonel Clark
Baker, Brigadier General Alpheus
Barron, Commodore Samuel
Bate, Major General William B.
Baucum, Colonel George
Beauregard, General Pierre Gustave
    Toutant (P. G. T.)
Benning, Brigadier General Henry L.
Bragg, General Braxton
Branch, Brigadier General Lawrence O'Bryan
Brantley, Colonel William F.
Brown, Brigadier General John C.
Campbell, Colonel R. P.
Cheatham, Major General Benjamin
    Franklin "Frank"
Clark, Colonel H. J. B.
Clayton, Brigadier General Henry D.
Cleburne, Major General Patrick R.
Colquitt, Colonel Peyton H.
Deas, Brigadier General Zach C.
Ewell, Lieutenant General Richard S.
Forrest, Brigadier General Nathan Bedford
Fulton, Brigadier General John S.
Galt, Colonel Edward M.
Gatlin, Brigadier General Richard Caswell
Gilmer, Major John A.
Gist, Brigadier General States Rights
Govan, Brigadier General Daniel C.

Granbury, Brigadier General Hiram M.
Gwynn, Brigadier General Walter
Hardee, Lieutenant General William Joseph
Helm, Brigadier General Benjamin H.
Hill, Major General Daniel Harvey
Hindman, Major General Thomas C.
Hoke, Major General Robert Frederick
Holmes, Major General Theophilus Hunter
Hood, Lieutenant General John Bell
Hume, Brigadier General William
Jackson, Brigadier General William H.
Jenkin, Brigadier General Micah
Johnson, Brigadier General Bushrod R.
Johnston, General Albert Sidney
Johnston, General Joseph Eggleston
Kelly, Brigadier General John
Kershaw, Brigadier General Joseph B.
Lamb, Colonel William
Lee, Colonel Charles C.
Lee, General Robert Edward
Lee, Lieutenant General Stephen D.
Liddell, Brigadier General St. John R.
Longstreet, Lieutenant General James
    "Old Pete"
Loring, Major General William W.
Lowe, Lieutenant Colonel Thomas L.
Lowrey, Brigadier General Mark P.
Maney, Brigadier General George East
Manigault, Brigadier General Arthur M.
Martin, Colonel William F.
Martin, Colonel William H.
McCowan, Major General John
McLaw, Major General Lafayette
McNair, Brigadier General Evander
Mercer, Brigadier General Hugh W.
Mosby, Colonel John Singleton
Pelham, Major John
Pemberton, Lieutenant General John
    Clifford
Pickett, Major General George Edward
Polk, Major General Leonidas K.
Preston, Brigadier General William
Roberton, Brigadier General Jerome B.
Ross, Brigadier General Lawrence S.
Scott, Brigadier General Thomas M.

Shaw, Colonel H. M.
Sinclair, Colonel James
Smith, Major General Gustavus W.
Stevenson, Major General Carter L.
Stewart, Major General Alexander P.
Stovall, Brigadier General Marcellus A.
Vance, Colonel Zebulon B.
Walker, Major General William Henry Talbot
Walthall, Major General Edward C.
Watkins, Corporal Sam
Wheeler, Major General Joseph
White, Colonel Moses J.
Whiting, Major General William Henry Chase
Winder, Brigadier General John H.
Winder, Captain William Sidney
Wirz, Captain Henry
Wise, Brigadier General Henry Alexander

UNION

Ames, Brigadier General Adelbert
Baird, Brigadier General Absalom
Banks, General Nathaniel Prentiss
  "Commissary"
Beatty, Brigadier General Samuel
Blair, Major General Frank P.
Boyd, Colonel Robert K.
Brannon, Brigadier General John M.
Burnside, Major General Ambrose Everett
Butler, General Benjamin Franklin "Spoons"
Butterfield, Major General Daniel
Cameron, Colonel Daniel
Carlin, Brigadier General William Passmore
Connell, Colonel John M.
Cox, Major General Jacob Dolson
Crittenden, Major General Thomas L.
Curtis, Colonel Newton Martin
Davis, Brigadier General Jefferson C.
DeGress, Captain Francis
Derveer, Colonel Ferdinand Van
Dodge, Major General Grenville M.
Elliott, Brigadier General Washington
Farragut, Rear Admiral David Glasgow
Foster, Brigadier General John Gray
Frémont, General John Charles
French, Major General Samuel G.
Garfield, Brigadier General James A.
Garrard, Brigadier General Kenner

Geary, Brigadier General John West
Gibson, Colonel William H.
Goldsborough, Rear Admiral L. M.
Granger, Major General Gordon
Grant, Lieutenant General Ulysses S.
Harker, Brigadier General Charles G.
Hawkins, Colonel Rush Christopher
Hazen, Brigadier General William B.
Hoffman, Colonel William H.
Hooker, Major General Joseph
Howard, Major General Oliver Otis
Johnson, Brigadier General Richard W.
Jones, Colonel Patrick H.
Judah, Brigadier General Henry M.
Kilpatrick, Brigadier General Judson
Kimball, Brigadier General Nathan
King, Brigadier General John H.
Knefler, Colonel Frederick
Leggett, Brigadier General Mortimer D.
Lightburn, Brigadier General Joseph
Logan, Major General John A.
McClellan, General George Brinton
McCook, Major General Alexander McDowell
McCook, Colonel Daniel
McCook, Brigadier General Edward M.
McLean, Brigadier General Nathaniel
McPherson, General James Birdseye
Minty, Colonel Robert
Mitchell, Colonel John G.
Morgan, Brigadier General James Dada
Mower, Major General Joseph Anthony
Newton, Brigadier General John
Paine, Brigadier General Charles Jackson
Palmer, Major General John M.
Parke, Brigadier General John Grubb
Pennypacker, Colonel Galusha
Porter, Rear Admiral David Dixon
Ransom, Private John
Reno, Brigadier General Jesse Lee
Reynold, Major General Joseph J.
Rosecrans, Major General William Starke
Rousseau, Colonel Laurence H.
Schofield, Major General John McAllister
Scott, General in Chief Winfield "Fuss and
  Feathers"
Shaw, Colonel Robert Gould
Sheridan, Major General Philip H.
Sherman, Major General William Tecumseh
Slocum, Major General Henry Warner

Smith, Brigadier General Giles A.
Smith, Brigadier General Morgan L.
Stanley, Major General David S.
Stoneman, Major General George
Stringham, Commodore Silas Horton
Sweeney, Brigadier General Thomas W.
Terry, Major General Alfred Howe
Thomas, Major General George Henry

Wagner, Brigadier General George D.
Weber, Colonel Max
Whitaker, Brigadier General Walter C.
Wilder, Colonel John T.
William, Brigadier General Alpheus S.
Willich, Brigadier General August
Wood, Brigadier General Thomas J.

ORGANIZATION OF THE ARMIES

Both Union and Confederate armies were organized along the same lines as a result of practices in the prewar U.S. Army. The following lists the smallest usual organization of troops up to the largest field command, but remember that these are just the "way it was supposed to be" numbers and that very few field units came anywhere close to these strengths. Confederate forces toward the end of the war were especially decimated—with no replacements available, desertion widespread, and each battle taking a heavier and heavier toll; many regiments or brigades were represented by a mere handful of men when they surrendered.

Corporal Sam Watkins of the Confederacy talked about this in his book, *Co. Aytch,* when he mentioned that his regiment, the 1st Tennessee Infantry, left for the war in 1861 with 1,250 officers and men. Even after consolidating with the 27th Tennessee Infantry Regiment and another independent infantry battalion and adding another 350 replacements over the next four years to a grand total of 3,200 men in the combined regiments, only 65 were still standing next to their colors at the end. Some other regiments combined with three, four, or even five others toward the end, yet had fewer to surrender than Watkins's regiment.

Ranks of officers who commanded at each level were as irregular as the number of men they commanded. Listed below are the "book" numbers, those that at least on paper were the authorized commander's rank and number of men, but these also tended to vary wildly, especially toward the beginning and end of the war. Battlefield casualties among the upper ranks were very high when compared with other conflicts; this was a war where by and large the officers took seriously their charge to lead their men into battle. The Battle of Franklin is an excellent example of the danger in this; nearly half of all the Confederate regimental commanders were killed or wounded. Of the 12 general officers on the field that day, 6 were killed, 1 was captured, and 3 of the other 5 were wounded so badly that they never were able to command again. See the chapter on Nashville and Franklin for the complete story.

COMPANY

A company was the basic unit to which a soldier belonged and was usually raised in a single county, often having a great percentage of its men related by birth or marriage. It was supposed to have 100 (sometimes 101) men and officers and was usually commanded by a captain. In the postwar South, it became habitual to refer to a distinguished veteran as "Captain John Smith"; some sources suggest this was a title given to the last survivor of a company, and thus the de facto company "commander," but this seems highly speculative. Depending heavily on which theater and which army, companies also had one to three lieutenants, one to six sergeants, and assorted numbers of corporals. A first sergeant usually ran the nuts and bolts of the company and stood behind them in battle to help keep the lines properly formed and to make sure no one ran away.

BATTALION

More usual in today's army than during the Civil War, a battalion consisted of three to five companies, usually commanded by a major. Most independent battalions were assimilated into regiments by the second year of the war, but a few stayed on as organizations of sappers, snipers, engineers, or other such special-duty troops.

REGIMENT

The central and often most important element of both sides' armies, a regiment consisted of 10 companies with 1,000 men, commanded by a lieutenant colonel or sometimes a full colonel. Regiments usually had a strength of 200 to 500 on the battlefield. Almost always raised from the same geographic area, the men identified with their regiment both on and off the battlefield and always looked to the "colors," the unique regimental battle flag, for where they should stand, fight, and advance during battle.

Most regiments, particularly Union regiments, had a small command staff consisting of a major as adjunct (doing the same duties today's executive officer does); a surgeon and one or more of his assistants to treat the wounded and sick; a quartermaster, who looked after their supplies; a commissary, who controlled the kitchens and food supplies; and one or more senior sergeants.

BRIGADE

Brigades were composed of two to seven (or even more on occasion) regiments and usually commanded by a brigadier general. Some brigades had artillery or cavalry commands attached to them, particularly early in the war, and would almost always have a brigade staff very similar in size and positions to the regimental staffs. Brigades at full strength would, at least in theory, have somewhere between 3,000 and 6,000 men, but most often had in the neighborhood of 1,500 to 2,000 effective troops.

DIVISION

A division was composed of two to six brigades and was almost always commanded by a major general, accompanied

The best way to get information about a specific Union regiment is to consult F. H. Dyer's A Compendium of the War of Rebellion, *a two-volume set present in most large and research libraries.*

by a larger staff than on the brigade level, but again performing almost the same tasks. Divisions were the usual maneuver organization, meaning that when the highest headquarters involved in a battle planned an attack, divisional level organizations were usually sent in to perform a specific task. In theory a division commanded some 6,000 to 15,000 troops but only rarely had more than 10,000 available at any given time.

CORPS

A corps was the largest usual maneuver organization on either side, commanded by Union major generals or Confederate lieutenant generals and composed of two to six divisions. Again, in theory, they could field about 20,000 to 60,000 troops but most often had in the neighborhood of 35,000 men. A very large staff was the norm for corps, with a large and ungainly staff encampment that was difficult to move swiftly. This resulted in several almost comical incidents during the war, when a fast-moving attack swept through an enemy's corps headquarters, as happened at Shiloh and Chickamauga.

ARMY

Armies were generally associated with an entire theater of action in the Confederacy, while the Union generally used them as their largest maneuver organizations, as at Shiloh and on the march to Savannah. An army might consist of only one corps, such as the XIV Corps during Sherman's Atlanta and Georgia campaigns of 1864, while other examples had as many as four corps. Union major generals and Confederate (full) generals commanded this organizational force that included

The best sources for information on Confederate regiments are Stewart Sifakis's Compendium of the Confederate Armies *and Joseph Crute's* Units of the Confederate States Army, *available in most research libraries.*

widely varying numbers of men—from as few as 30,000 to as many as 120,000.

Cavalry and artillery units were organized under the same basic structure, with a few levels known by different terms.

CAVALRY

The basic unit was the troop, which was otherwise the same as an infantry company. Some Union cavalry formations were called squadrons, which consisted of two or three troops. Both sides removed their cavalry from troops supporting infantry formations and collected them together in all-cavalry battalions, divisions, and corps.

ARTILLERY

The basic formation of artillery was a battery, which almost always had four or six guns, usually of the same or just two different types (this made ammunition supply easier). Initially these batteries were deployed as semi-independent units loosely attached to an infantry brigade or division, but later in the war they tended to be grouped under one specified division or corps level artillery commander, usually a major or lieutenant colonel.

CAVALRY, ARTILLERY, AND INFANTRY

Early in the war the Confederacy organized several legions, which were combined infantry, artillery, and cavalry formations of between 1,000 and 2,000 men. Few, if any, actually saw any combat; most were broken up when they were assigned to an army and reorganized into their respective

branches. Other "special" formations were marines, heavy artillery, engineers, sappers, sharpshooters, prison garrisons, and dedicated skirmishers, all of which tended to be organized similarly to infantry companies.

Cavalry

The simplest definition of "cavalry" is the use of armed soldiers mounted on horseback. Starting at about the time of Darius I of Persia's invasion of western Asia and the Greek city-states (circa 500 B.C.E.), mounted soldiers began developing into the preeminent force on the battlefield. While infantry was certainly still used and was an important element of military tactical deployment, the cavalry became the fighting element that all military planning revolved around. This situation continued into the early medieval period in Europe, finally fading out in favor of concentration on infantry combat around the period bookmarked by the battles of Stirling Bridge, Scotland (1198 C.E.), and Agincourt, France (1415 C.E.), both of which demonstrated the complete failure of heavy cavalry formations to break up an infantry position.

By the time of the American Civil War, cavalry had been relegated to the tasks of scouting and forward patrolling, guarding railroads, and providing keen-looking escorts to politicians and generals. During combat actions, they were primarily used as "first strike" attackers, charging at full tilt toward the enemy line, firing pistols and screaming as loudly as possible, the tactic designed to try to either scare off the enemy or at least blow a hole in his lines that follow-up infantry attacks could exploit. At the beginning of the war, cavalrymen bore the brunt of sometimes mean-spirited ridicule from the infantry, who regarded them as dandies at best and shirking cowards at worst. A frequent jibe, admittedly hard to translate into today's culture, was an infantryman's cry when he saw a line of cavalry approaching: "Mister! Here's your mule!" That was a real knee-slapper back in 1862.

By 1863 things had started to change across the board in military thought, including the role and use of cavalry in combat. Still maintaining their primary role as advance scouts and vedettes (mounted sentries), the cavalry on both sides began being used for dedicated attacks on enemy flanks and marching columns, even when unsupported by infantry. That same year, cavalry-on-cavalry battles became more common, peaking with the cavalry-only battle at Brandy Station, Virginia, which was the opening fight of the Gettysburg campaign. This rapidly escalated into the use of regular army cavalry in roles—raids into enemy camps, supply depots, and even cities—that had been reserved for the disdained "guerrilla" and "partisan ranger" units (thought to be roughly on the same level as murderous mercenaries). The end result of all this expansion in the use of cavalry was that garrison units had to be expanded and changed from those staffed by the sick, lame, and lazy into combat-ready units that had to be able to respond to a lightning-fast attack by a raiding cavalry unit.

The relatively small cavalry units, especially the Confederate regiments led by Lieutenant General Nathan Bedford Forrest and Major General Joseph Wheeler, had an impact on grand campaigns far beyond what their size would suggest. During the 1863 approach to Vicksburg, Major General Ulysses S. Grant of the Union Army was forced to abandon his initial overland movement across Mississippi after Forrest's raids on his supply lines in southern and western Tennessee threatened to leave his men cut off without ammunition and food deep inside the Confederacy. Later that same year, Wheeler led a raid through central Tennessee that cut off the besieged Union garrison at Chattanooga from desperately needed supplies, routed Union supply columns, caused havoc with the central Union command structure in the area, and could have resulted in a collapse of the entire Union control of the area if

General Braxton Bragg, the local area commander, could have bothered to follow up on the advantages Wheeler had handed him.

War means fightin', and fightin' means killin'.

> Lieutenant General Nathan Bedford Forrest, Confederacy, 1864

The last act of the war in the Western Theater was a cavalry raid, led by Brigadier General James Harrison Wilson of the North. After routing what was left of General John Bell Hood's decimated Army of Tennessee after the battle of Nashville, in 1864 Wilson rebuilt his force into a 13,500-man command, all mounted, based out of Gravelly Springs in northern Alabama. In late March 1865 he led his command south to Selma, taking and destroying the essential Confederate arsenal there, routing most of Forrest's command in the process, and then turned toward Georgia. For the next three weeks, his command ranged all through central Alabama and central and southern Georgia, destroying warehouses and manufacturing facilities and capturing scores of local militias and independent commands, almost without opposition. Finally, on May 10, near Irwinville, Georgia, an element of his command captured the fleeing Confederate president himself, Jefferson Davis.

Despite the enmity of the infantry, the life of a cavalryman was far from glamorous or safe. As the fastest moving military force in the field at the time, a cavalryman could be in the midst of battle literally at a moment's notice, and the swift movement of combat meant that near-instantaneous decisions and lightning-quick reflexes were an absolute necessity in order to live to tell about it. The individual weapons that the cavalrymen used changed as rapidly as their tactics, with the early-war drawn-saber charges changing into the near-abandonment of edged weapons in favor of pistols and eventually rapid-fire, breechloading carbines.

One similarity to the infantry, however, was the grossly overloaded manner in which they left home. One Texas cavalryman with the W. P. Lane Rangers, described by eminent historian Bell Irvin Wiley in his monumental work *The Life of Johnny Reb*, carried a typical load with him when he first marched off:

. . . saddle, bridle, saddle-blanket, curry comb, horse brush, coffee pot, tin cup, 20 lbs. ham, 200 biscuit, 5 lbs. ground coffee, 5 lbs. sugar, one large pound cake presented to me by Mrs. C. E. Talley, 6 shirts, 6 prs. socks, 3 prs. drawers, 2 prs. pants, 2 jackets, 1 pr. heavy mud boots, one Colt's revolver, one small dirk, four blankets, sixty feet of rope with a twelve inch iron pin attached . . . and divers and sundry little momentoes from friends.

Again, similar to their infantry counterparts, carried equipment rapidly downgraded until the typical load consisted of a light steel saber (rarely used after 1863 and abandoned completely in Forrest's and other Southern commands), one or two .36 or .44 caliber six-shot pistols, a short-barreled carbine, a saddle and other horse-related necessities, a shelter half, blanket, poncho, sometimes a change of clothes and socks, and a saddle bag holding coffee, food, and other absolute necessities.

One element of the cavalry that never completely died out during the war was their dash and elan, perceived or real as it was. Largely promoted by the dashing personality of Major General James Ewell Brown Stuart of Lee's Army of Northern Virginia, the image of the cavalryman developed into one of the gallant cavalier, forever prancing about the battlefield in a rather hyperactive sort of way or swooping down into an unprotected Northern town, where the women would be romanced, the men respectably placed out of the line of danger, and some random supplies would be gathered up to take back to the unglamorous, starving infantry. Dressed in a rather fancy yellow-trimmed uniform (the color associated with the cavalry), tall polished boots, a gleaming saber buckled over a yellow silk sash, topped with a slouch hat trimmed with a large ostrich feather, and his own personal band in tow (literally), the rather weak-chinned and somewhat homely Stuart somehow proved irresistible to Southern (and some Northern) women, particularly after he hid his shortcomings behind a thick and usually immaculately groomed beard. The popular perception of his cavalry, promoted in newspapers both North and South, was that his war was a sort of grand adventure, fought in a gentlemanly manner and treated by friend and foe alike as some sort of great lark, in which both sides could not wipe their grins off their faces from the pure joy of it all. This was helped in no small part by a popular song of the day, said to be Stuart's favorite:

JINE THE CAVALRY
(by Sam Sweeney, one of Stuart's musicians)

CHORUS:
If you want to have a good time, jine the cavalry!
Jine the cavalry! Jine the cavalry!
If you want to catch the Devil, if you want to have fun,
If you want to smell Hell, jine the cavalry!

We're the boys who went around McClellian,
Went around McClellian, went around around McClellian!
We're the boys who went around McClellian,
Bully boys, hey! Bully boys, ho! (Chorus)

We're the boys who crossed the Potomicum,

*Crossed the Potomicum, crossed the
Potomicum!
We're the boys who crossed the
Potomicum,
Bully boys, hey! Bully boys, ho! (Chorus)*

*Then we went into Pennsylvania,
Into Pennsylvania, into Pennsylvania!
Then we went into Pennsylvania,
Bully boys, hey! Bully boys, ho! (Chorus)*

*The big fat Dutch gals hand around the
breadium,
Hand around the breadium, hand around
the breadium!
The big fat Dutch gals hand around the
breadium,
Bully boys, hey! Bully boys, ho! (Chorus)*

*Ol' Joe Hooker, won't you come out of The
Wilderness?
Come out of The Wilderness, come out of
The Wilderness?
Ol' Joe Hooker, won't you come out of The
Wilderness?
Bully boys, hey! Bully boys, ho! (Chorus)*

The truth, of course, is not anywhere close to this romantic fantasy, but as in so many other situations, image won out over substance. The sight of a dirty, nasty cavalry trooper mounted on top of an unbathed, rather fragrant horse could set the heart of a Southern belle all aflutter, while the sight of an equally dirty, unkempt infantryman would usually make her wonder if she had adequately hidden all the silverware. The media of the day, and many latter days, kept up this romantic hogwash, with images of saber-drawn cavalry at the gallop toward lines of faceless enemy remaining popular well into the 20th century. On a related note, the last-known charge by horse cavalry into the face of the enemy was during the 1939 German invasion of Poland—the attack by saber- and lance-equipped Polish cavalry against the armored tank formations was not successful.

Artillery

The subject of Civil War artillery could encompass (and has done so) whole books in and of itself. From an ancient tradition of a branch of military service used primarily for harassment and minor support of the more dashing infantry and cavalry branches, the science of artillery underwent a renaissance in the post-Napoleonic antebellum years. Along with the field of military engineering, artillery became the branch of choice for some of the brightest minds emerging from West Point in the 1830s and 1840s (including Confederate general Pierre Gustave Toutant Beauregard and his old friend, West Point instructor and opponent at Fort Sumter, Major Robert Anderson of the Union Army) and had evolved into a central part of planning for both defense and offense. During the war, the use of artillery further evolved in the disparate directions of "flying" batteries (horse-drawn, relatively light, and very mobile), used to support rapidly moving cavalry operations, and in the deployment of heavy siege guns, used as the primary offensive weapon in a static situation, as at Petersburg, Vicksburg, and Atlanta.

Basically put, artillery was the use of heavy cannons designed to toss a solid or explosive round for distances varying from point-blank to more than 10,000 yards (just under 6 miles). Artillery weapons came in three basic types: rifled guns, long-barreled heavy cannons designed to fire heavy solid shot great distances at very high velocities and with very flat trajectories in order to hit distant targets or batter down masonry structures; smoothbore guns, relatively short-barreled howitzers originally designed to shoot explosive shells with less of a powder charge needed and used for more rapid and direct fire, which also had the advantage of having a shorter and lighter tube than the rifled guns, making them easier to transport and set up; and mortars, very short, very thick, and heavy barreled weapons used to shoot large explosive shells at very high trajectories, able to drop their charges in almost vertically.

Each of these three basic types came in several varieties and a wide range of sizes, measured by their "caliber," the internal diameter of the tube, or the weight of the ammunition itself. However, to make this subject as confusing as humanly possible, there never was a universally agreed upon standard of how to name cannons. In antebellum days, it was more or less standard to designate cannons based on the weight of the solid shot ammunition, e.g., a cannon that fired a solid round shot that weighed six pounds would have an inside barrel diameter (or "caliber") of a bit over 3.5 inches (3.67 inches, to be precise) and would be designated a "six-pounder." The advent of rifled cannons caused this system to collapse, as they fired oblong rather than round shot and therefore had no standard weight: The longer the round, the heavier it could be, depending on whether it was solid shot or explosive shell. One of the most common (and notorious) artillery pieces, the 10-pounder Parrott rifle, fired a range of ammunition that weighed between the 9-pound shell to an 11.5-pound case shot, and the tube itself had a caliber of 2.9 inches (1861 model) to 3.0 inches (1863 model). Larger models of the Parrott rifle, the so-called 200-pounder and 300-pounder, actually fired shells weighing 175 and 250 pounds apiece, respectively. Confused? Don't feel lonely, even experts in the field of Civil War–era artillery sometimes have a hard time keeping up with the whole mess.

Just like their infantry counterparts, artillery weapons were almost all muzzle-loaders, requiring a team of six to eight men to set up, load, aim, and fire the weapon. A well-drilled team could fire two shots per minute "by the book," but in the heat of combat shortcuts were sometimes undertaken that increased this rate to an average of three or even four shots a minute. A battery could keep up a sustained fire of one shot every 5 to 10 seconds, and larger assemblies of cannon could put out amazing rates of fire. At Shiloh, Brigadier General Daniel Ruggles of the South gathered up as many artillery batteries and individual gun crews as he and his staff could locate, ending up with 53 guns parked axle to axle on the west border of the Duncan field, 400 to 500 yards directly across open ground from the Union position in the Hornet's Nest. For nearly one-half hour the assembled artillery kept up a fire that averaged *three shots per second* going into the Union position.

Union batteries usually had four or six guns, almost always of the same type and size. Confederate batteries were almost invariably four guns and very frequently had two or sometimes even three different types and sizes of weapons within them, making supply and logistics a nightmare. As per the usual in artillery, even this basic setup was not universally standard—during the Atlanta campaign, the Union armies had 1 five-gun, 29 four-gun, and 22 six-gun batteries, while their Confederate counterparts had 44 four-gun batteries, all organized into 3 twelve-gun battalions (while maintaining their four-gun battery designations and internal command system within this structure), and two independently assigned four-gun batteries. A battery was usually commanded by a captain, called the "battery commander." Early in the war batteries were usually assigned to infantry brigades, and the captain would answer directly to the general commanding the brigade. Later in the war both sides gradually moved away from this system into one where the artillery was organized into independent artillery battalions (Confederates) or brigades (Union), headed by divisional "chiefs of artillery," usually of the rank of colonel, and having three to five individual batteries.

Obviously, with all this variation in command structure, it is impossible to set a precise figure on how many men each battery contained, but on average, a four-gun battery would have about 70 men and 45 horses, while the largest batteries might have more than 170 men and 100 horses. Organization structure within the battery itself was remarkably similar on both sides; a lieutenant "section chief" would command two guns, each individual gun was commanded by a sergeant "chief of the piece," two corporals were the "gunner," in charge of the firing operation, and the "chief of caisson," in charge of supply and reloading operations. Six privates rounded out the individual gun crew, all with very specialized and specific tasks to perform during a firing operation. Other assigned personnel were the first sergeant (sometimes known as the orderly sergeant), who assisted the captain in administrative matters and served as a second-in-command of the battery; a quartermaster sergeant, responsible for the logistics and supply of the battery; drivers, teamsters, and wagoneers of the horse teams, usually privates; an artificer (blacksmith) and farrier (who kept the horses and mules shod); musicians, usually just one or two buglers; a guidon, who carried the battery's colors and was usually the most trusted and reliable man. In the smoke and noise of battle, verbal orders were impossible to properly relay, so the guidon stayed with the commander or at a place of his choosing. The men were trained to always keep an eye on the colors and to go where they went. If they suddenly went flying toward the rear, the prudent thing to do was to follow them, as chances were the commander had called for a sudden retreat. Obviously, if you had a skittish or untrustworthy man carrying the colors, his option to run away could take an entire unit off the field with him.

Because hauling the heavy cannons across rough roads and open fields wore out horses at an alarming rate, the cannoneers usually walked alongside their rig, riding on the horses or caisson only when very rapid movement was necessary. The "flying batteries" attached to the cavalry doubled the number of horses assigned to the battery and tended to use the lighter howitzers so that everyone could habitually ride and keep up with the fast pace.

Infantry

The very heart, soul, and backbone of any army, at least since early medieval times, is the infantry. These are the so-called foot soldiers who carry the battle literally on their shoulders into the face of the enemy. In all periods of history, these men have been unappreciated by the unlearned; suffering under the burden of whatever wacky uniforms their generals had decided were in fashion at the moment; carrying food, shelter, and other comforts in packs or slings as they trudged down one dusty road after another; forever in movement but always at the snail's pace of the route march; sometimes walking down one endless road after another, sometimes even back and forth along the same road for days on end. At other times the lowly infantryman might sit in camp for weeks or even months at a time, only to be hastily summoned by the bugle's insistent call to pack up and move out, sometimes into battle, other times only to sit in yet another camp for days, weeks, or even months.

Whenever you see something blue, shoot at it, and do all you can to keep up the scare.

> Lieutenant General Nathan Bedford Forrest,
> Confederacy, 1864

Most histories of the Civil War ignore these men—and almost all were men, even though there are at least 200 documented cases of women posing as men in order to fight (and at least 400 documented cases of men posing as women so they wouldn't have to)—reserving the prose for those whose names ring with the brassy tone of importance: Lee, Johnston, Grant, Sherman, and so on. However, as essential as the direction of these great generals might have been (and as disastrous as it was in certain other cases—Bragg and Rosecrans spring to mind here), it was the lowly infantryman who did the actual fighting and dying. Sam Watkins, the self-described "high private" from Columbia, Tennessee, wrote after the war about his personal experiences, stating that "the histories are all correct" when they speak only of the high and mighty, but that infantrymen had a different view of the war and that their story needed telling as well.

> In the following pages I propose to tell of the fellows who did the shooting and killing, the fortifying and ditching, the sweeping of the streets, the drilling, the standing guard, picket and videt, and who drew (or were to draw) eleven dollars per month and rations, and also drew the ramrod and tore the cartridge.
>
> from Co. Aytch, or
> A Sideshow of the Big Show

The average infantryman of the war was between 19 and 21 years old (although there are both much younger and much, much older examples), single, and a farmer by trade and had never been as much as 20 miles from his home in his entire life. He was more than likely illiterate or nearly so and deeply religious, yet given to drink and playing cards when the opportunity arose—most would get rid of their cards and "dirty pictures" before battle so that if they were killed, it would not pain their mothers to see such things if and when their personal effects made it back home. The Confederate infantryman was, for the most part, reasonably comfortable living in the field and acceptably accurate with firearms and almost always a volunteer. His Union counterparts tended toward these same desirable traits but had much more of a sprinkling of city boys, foreigners, and draftees among their ranks, along with a higher literacy rate. Despite all the eloquent speeches and patriotic rhetoric, both most likely joined for the adventure and stayed because they could not desert their friends.

The commonly heard nicknames of the two opponents, Johnny Reb and Billy Yank, seem to have arisen from the common appellations that pickets would holler across the lines to one another, usually in a friendly way in order to set up a trade of some sort. Coffee, the universal infantryman's fuel, was almost completely absent in the South by the third year of the war, as was good Virginia tobacco, that other grunt's vice, in the North, so both sides were eager to trade whenever possible, including during battle.

When the two armies left their home bases in 1861, both were burdened heavily by three things—inexperienced officers; gaudy, impracticable uniforms; and far too much baggage. While many officers on both sides had trained at West Point, the majority had either no military training whatsoever or just a smattering that they had picked up while drilling with their local militias. This did not necessarily mean they were bad officers or poor combat leaders—one prime example is the well-known commander of the 20th Maine Infantry, Colonel Joshua Lawrence Chamberlain. Although completely unschooled in military sciences (he was a professor of "real and found religion" in civilian life), he turned into one of the most outstanding tactical leaders in the Union Army, primarily by reading every book on tactics he could lay his hands on. The real weakness in the officer corps was that, by prewar militia tradition, most field officers (company and regimental commanders) were elected into office by the men they were to lead. While the thought was nice, that men would more likely follow those they trusted well enough to vote for, this, like all other political processes, soon turned into a beauty contest. Some turned into capable leaders, some destroyed their own commands though sheer incompetence, and others muddled along until the forge of combat produced the real leaders.

Uniforms were another early-war burden on the infantrymen, whose commanders were mightily impressed with the European, and specifically French, methods of making their armies look just divine. One telling example was the adoption by both sides of so-called Zouave units, inspired by a troop of the French Algerian soldiers who had traveled the prewar United States giving displays of their precision marching to standing-room-only crowds. The Zouave uniform consisted of white leggings or gaiters, usually bright red or brilliant blue pantaloons (very baggy, knicker-length pants), white shirts under red or blue Arab-style velvet or wool vests, darker colored shell jackets, usually decorated with brass or gold trim and buttons, sometimes a short blue or red cape, and the whole affair topped off with a fez or turban. These units were noted for their esprit de corps and their drilling abilities, but the gaudy uniforms made them minié-ball magnets on the battlefield (when faced with an indistinct mass of infantry, the tendency is to pick a target out of whatever stands out—a different sounding weapon, a poorly camouflaged position, or a brilliantly dressed Arab in the woods of Tennessee). Most of these units soon abandoned these outfits in favor of more standard uniforms, but a handful wore them throughout the war, most notably Wheat's Tigers out of New Orleans.

In the collection of the Atlanta History Center is a splendid display of the junk sold to soldiers by equally unenlightened (or uncaring) sutlers, including Spanish conquistador–style "armor" breastplates (which could not stop or deflect rifled musket fire), backpacks containing a sort of sling chair that might fit the smallest of all imaginable infantrymen, early sorts of tin helmets, heavy iron pots, and all sorts of smaller ephemera—daguerreotypes of loved ones, fancy stationery sets, elaborate grooming and mustache-trimming sets, and even folding tables and chairs. By the end of the first year of the war, these excesses had, for the most part, been ejected by the side of some dusty road or another or sent home for safekeeping.

The standard infantry uniform in both armies (after all the prewar glamour had faded) was a wool shell or sack coat worn over a three-button white or natural-colored cotton shirt, with wool trousers held up by cotton or leather suspenders, usually with the pants stuffed into the top of tall wool socks, and topped off by either a cowboy-style "slouch" hat or short-brimmed kepi. Shoes were usually pegged-soled "Jefferson" bootees—high-topped brogans made on a straight last, meaning that there was not a distinct right or left shoe. A waist belt fastened with a lead-filled buckle held a cap box on the right front and a bayonet scabbard on the left hip. A cartridge box filled with a standard load of 60 rounds was slung over the left shoulder, resting on the right hip. A canteen and a canvas haversack (sometimes tarred for waterproofing—it contained rations and small personal items) were slung over the right shoulder (resting on the left hip).

The difference in the two armies was reflected in two things—the color of their uniforms and equipment and the way they carried their bedrolls and personal supplies. The Union Army almost universally wore dark blue coats and jackets over sky-blue pants, usually trimmed with brass buttons bearing letters designating their branch of service—"I" for infantry, "A" for artillery, and so on. Their belts and other leather gear were usually black, and most infantrymen carried black-colored canvas or leather knapsacks, with their bedroll tied on top. Their Confederate counterparts wore uniforms that were by regulation "Richmond gray" but that ranged in hue from a gray so dark it was almost black all the way to barely dyed examples that soon turned white in the sun. The late-war usual Confederate (especially in the west) color, "butternut," came from the use of plant dyes that could not truly replicate the designated gray colors and soon turned into shades of light to medium brown. As an unintended consequence, this provided a sort of camouflage for outlying pickets and vedettes. Buttons ranged from brightly polished, state-seal decorated brass, to stolen Union buttons, down to ones made of wood or bone.

Confederate leather gear was by regulation brown in color, although equipment shortages followed by the use of captured

Union equipment meant that many men had mixtures of black and brown leather gear. Unlike their Union counterparts, Confederate cartridge boxes rarely had lead-filled plates attached (used both for decoration and to help keep the unfastened flap down while running), almost never had polished brass cartridge breast strap plates attached (again, used mostly for decoration), and the fancy lead-filled, brass waist-belt buckles were replaced in the Western Theater by "Georgia frame" buckles—very similar to today's minimalist belt buckles. Toward the end of the war, shortages in obtaining leather led to the use of painted canvas for belts and straps. Confederate-issue canteens tended toward the thick, round, heavier wooden type, but the Union tin "bullseye" pattern canteens were very popular and were scavenged from the dead on battlefields whenever possible.

Rather than use uncomfortable knapsacks, most Confederate infantrymen placed what little they carried—an extra pair of socks, a "wiper" to clean their weapon, a "housewife" containing sewing supplies, tobacco tin, occasionally a wallet, maybe a small Bible, and a photograph of their loved ones or a letter—inside their single blanket, rolled it up, fastened the ends together with a thick rubber band or piece of rope, and slung it cross-chest over their right shoulder.

Once again, after the noise and fuss of the early war wackiness had settled, weapons on both sides became more-or-less standardized and remarkably similar. The Union adopted the 1861 Springfield rifled musket, .58 caliber, weighing a bit over 9 pounds, with a 39-inch-long barrel, about 56 inches in length overall, and capable of hitting targets well over 500 yards distant. The Confederacy used a wide variety of weapons and calibers throughout the war, but the most prevalent was the imported British 1853 model Enfield 3-band rifled musket, .577 caliber, weighing about 9½ pounds, 55 inches long with a 38-inch barrel, and even more accurate than the Springfield in the right

hands. The paper cartridge ammunition used in both weapons was interchangeable, making resupply from captured enemy ammo chests easier. Both weapons used an "angular" bayonet that was triangular in cross-section and 18 inches long—a fearsome-appearing weapon indeed. However, it took a high degree of expertise and discipline to properly use a bayonet in combat. Imagine trying to hold a poorly balanced, 11-pound, 6-foot-long stick with an off-center pointed end (the bayonet attached to the muzzle end of the weapon and was offset from the center of mass about 2 inches so that the weapon could be fired with it attached) and trying to stick it in a moving, similarly equipped, and very highly motivated (to move out of the way) target, while your hands are slick with sweat and shaking with fear and adrenaline. For these reasons, the bayonet was either "lost" by the roadside, along with the equally useless-in-combat huge Bowie and other such knives also carried along on the early fights, or put to use as candleholders, rammed into trees as coathooks, used as spits to roast the evening meal, or heated and bent into hook shapes to drag the dead bodies of their compatriots off the battlefield.

Much has been made of the incredibly high casualty rate during the war—more were killed in the single-day battle of Antietam than in all previous American wars combined (26,134 dead, wounded, and missing, total). Not only had the majority of senior officers on both sides trained together at West Point but they had learned a set of battlefield tactics that were based on the use of smoothbore, relatively inaccurate, and slow-to-reload weapons. In the 1850s a new class of weapon emerged, the rifled-barrel muzzleloader. A series of lands and grooves cut in a spiral fashion down the inside of the barrel "grabbed" the bullet as it was fired and gave it a spinning motion that helped stabilize its flight, much like a football quarterback giving a spin to the ball as he releases it. This simple change not only helped stabilize the round, increasing its accuracy, but also dramatically increased its effective range (again using the football analogy, imagine throwing a football by grabbing one end and pushing it forward—which will most likely result in the ball tumbling wildly and not going very far—just like a ball leaving a smoothbore weapon). On top of this new rifle technology, a new bullet was designed in the 1840s by a French army captain, Claude Minié, that was elongated, with a hollow base, and slightly smaller than the rifle's bore diameter. Thus the bullet could be rammed down the barrel much faster, and the gases from discharge would expand the base, engaging the rifling and giving the bullet a very stable flight. The soft lead bullet (called a minié "ball," in the parlance of the day), weighing 500 grains (about the same as 11 modern copper pennies), tended to "mushroom" when it struck anything solid, depleting the entire kinetic energy of the shot onto the target. For example, this meant that if an infantryman was struck in the shoulder, his arm would most likely be ripped off, or a hit in the leg would shatter the bone into so many irreparable fragments that amputation was the only option.

Through the first months and years of the war, nicely dressed massed lines of battle drawn up 50 to 75 yards from the enemy were the desired formations, as the earlier smoothbore weapons only had an effective range of about 100 yards maximum, and massed firepower was the only reliable way to break up an enemy's line. Using this formation with the modern weapons, with their effective range of six times that of smoothbores, the ability to fire about three times as fast (up to three shots a minute), and the incredible damage the minié ball would do to the human body resulted in an incredibly high casualty count, including large numbers of combat-ineffective wounded. It took far too many casualties from good infantry before the powers that be woke up to the realization that a new day in combat technology had arisen. Most grunt infantrymen realized this about the time the first shots were fired in the first battle, but officers throughout history have always been about three steps behind the ones they theoretically lead. It was not long before "spades is trumps" was the order of the day, meaning the men dug out trenches and created well-protected firing positions whenever they stopped marching for more than a few minutes.

With all of these tactical changes, battlefield casualties were impressive, even at extreme ranges. Common infantrymen were able to pick off individual targets at ranges of 500 to 600 yards, using just their ordinary issued weapons. Special "sniper" rifles were acquired in both armies and issued either to special riflemen units, mostly in the Union Army, or to one or two of the best shots in a regiment, as was the fashion in the Confederate Army. The most common of these special weapons, the British-made Whitworth, had a heavy barrel and a full-length scope, weighed about 35 pounds, and, in the hands of a trained sharpshooter, could pick off even moving targets at ranges over 1,000 yards. One of the better-known examples of long-range sniping occurred at Spotsylvania, in Virginia, on May 9, 1864. Major General John Sedgewick was walking the ramparts of his redoubts, fully exposed, looking over at the Confederate lines a good 800 yards away, nearly one-half mile. When his men pleaded for their beloved "Uncle John" to get under cover after Confederate sharpshooters had sent several rounds their way, he merely laughed at them, "What? Men dodging this way for single bullets? What will you do when they open fire along the whole line? I am ashamed of you. They couldn't hit an elephant at this distance." About two minutes later came the crack of a Whitworth rifle fired by Sergeant Grace of the 4th Georgia from the distant Confederate trenchline. Sedgewick stiffened and then fell dead, a neat hole about one-half inch under his left eye.

NORTH CAROLINA: OUTER BANKS TO THE LAST GREAT BATTLE

At the beginning of the "secessionist crisis" after the election of Lincoln in 1860, North Carolina was not overwhelmingly in favor of leaving the Union, as opposed to the position held by its namesake to the south. Although a primarily agricultural state, there were relatively few slaves in the state, which was marked more by disparate, isolated elements mostly either neutral or outright hostile to both slavery and secession. Several meetings across the state in late 1860 only produced more evidence that if secession was inevitable, it would be done without widespread support.

As the talks raged, South Carolina declared itself free and independent on December 20, the first state to openly declare secession from the Union. In North Carolina the only large public celebration was a mass gun firing in Wilmington, a city noted for its strong support of secession. This act touched off even more heated debate across the state, the majority of citizens tending to support staying within the Union but radically opposed to any force being used to keep any state within it. In the middle of this continued crisis, the state legislature disbanded for the Christmas holidays.

With most of the politicians safely out of the way, staunch secessionists in Wilmington went into action. On December 31 the citizens of that coastal city wired Governor John Willis Ellis of North Carolina, asking permission to seize nearby Forts Caswell and Johnston, as they constituted a "threat" to access to the city via the Cape Fear River. Ellis refused, but the citizens went ahead and seized the forts based on an erroneous rumor that U.S.

troops were on the way to garrison them. Ellis then immediately demanded that the Carolinians evacuate the posts and, when they had removed themselves, sent a letter of apology to President James Buchanan (Lincoln had been elected but not yet sworn in at the time).

All through the winter and early spring of 1861, Ellis continued to act in an equally conservative manner, backed up by a February 28 popular vote against a secession convention. Even the secession of six fellow Southern states and the bombardment of Fort Sumter at Charleston on April 12 and 13, 1861, did not sway Ellis from his Unionist stance. The deciding factor, however, was an April 15 letter from Lincoln asking Ellis to provide two regiments of militia to "suppress the Southern insurrection." Ellis regarded such a request as a violation of the 10th Amendment to the Constitution, which addresses the rights of the individual states, and "a gross usurpation of power" on Lincoln's part.

Ellis immediately ordered the seizure and occupation of "Federal" (or Union) installations and forts throughout the state and called for a secession convention. On May 20 the convention met and, by the day's end, had both adopted an ordinance of secession and ratified the Confederate constitution. North Carolina was officially separated from and at war against the United States government.

THE WAR IN NORTH CAROLINA BEGINS

Although General in Chief Winfield "Old Fuss and Feathers" Scott had warned at the very beginning that the war with the South would be long and bloody, most military personnel and civilians alike, North and South, scoffed at the 75-year-old general's words. The initial rush of volunteers was fueled partially by the desire to see combat "before it's all over," and 90-day enlistments of both individuals and militia companies were common on both sides.

Several small battles won by the Confederacy in the summer of 1861 seemed to indicate that the South was en route to an early victory, and both armies readied for what each thought would be a single, gigantic, and ultimately decisive battle. On July 21 these armies—28,452 Union troops facing 32,232 Confederates—met at Bull Run Creek, Virginia, in a daylong clash that ended with the whipped Union Army running in sheer panic from the field back to Washington. The First Manassas, as Southerners referred to the battle, was both a resounding major victory for the Confederacy and a signal that this was to be a long, bloody war, just as Scott, who was active only in the earliest stages of the war, had predicted.

After getting over the shock of initial Confederate victories and the threat against Washington itself, Union Army planners settled down and devised a multiphase strategy to use against the Confederacy, ironically based on Scott's original ideas. One of the first offensive operations would be against North Carolina's eastern coast to seize the vital ports and cut the north-south supply lines from Virginia. To start carrying out these plans, Major General Benjamin Franklin Butler and Commodore Silas Horton Stringham were given the task of attacking and capturing the most important Outer Banks access to mainland ports, Hatteras Inlet.

HATTERAS ISLAND

When the war began, one of the Union strategies was to blockade the entire Southern coastline to prevent supplies from coming in and amphibious forces from going out. To counter the threat on the Outer Banks, Confederate authorities had given their blessing to a quasi-military fleet of small sailing vessels, dubbed the "mosquito fleet" by the Southerners and "privateers" or outright "pirates" by the Union, that ran supplies through the blockade, helped defend the coastline, and raided Union ships when the opportunity arose. To back up these small ships, five strong forts and associated batteries were constructed all along the narrow coastal islands and placed under the overall command of Brigadier General Walter Gwynn and Brigadier (later Major) General Theophilus Hunter Holmes.

Battle of Hatteras Inlet

To defend the vital access to the mainland ports, North Carolina had constructed two forts on either side of the small village on the north bank of Hatteras Inlet: Fort Hatteras, mounting twelve 32-pounder guns, was on the west side and closer to the channel itself, while Fort Clark, mounting five 32-pounders, was a smaller post closer to the ocean. Commanding the Hatteras Island Garrison was Colonel William F. Martin, with about 400 men and 35 artillery pieces. With news of the approach of Union naval forces, Martin requested and received somewhere between 200 and 400 reinforcements (accounts vary significantly on this point).

Sailing down from Fort Monroe, Virginia, was a Union naval force of seven ships under the direct command of Stringham mounting 143 cannon, accompanied by transports carrying the Colonel Rush Christopher Hawkins 9th (Hawkins's Zouaves) and Colonel Max Weber's 20th (United Turner Rifles) New York Infantry Regiments and the 2nd U.S. Artillery Battery, under overall command of Butler. Arriving off the Outer Banks on the afternoon of August 27, Stringham spent the rest of the night getting his ships into position to begin a bombardment of the Confederate posts the next morning.

On the morning of August 28, Stringham opened a heavy bombardment of Fort Clark and landed roughly half of Weber's regiment under its cover. Weber's men easily overran the Confederate defenses after Fort Clark's defenders ran out of ammunition and retreated to Fort Hatteras. Watching the Confederates running over the sand dunes toward the westernmost fort, Stringham initially thought both posts had been abandoned. The USS *Monticello* was ordered into the inlet to give chase, only to be pounded by heavy fire from the still-ready-and-able defenders at Fort Hatteras. Ironically, the only Union casualty of the day's action was an infantryman killed by one of Stringham's guns. As the seas were rough, Stringham was forced to pull offshore, leaving Weber's small command to hold Fort Clark.

During the night, as Martin was preparing to attack and retake Fort Clark, Commodore Samuel Barron, chief of Confederate Coastal Defenses, landed with about 200 reinforcements and took over command of the operation. His first action was to cancel any offensive plans, and he spent the rest of the night repairing and building up the sandwork fort.

The next morning, August 29, Stringham sailed back into the inlet over calm seas and began a heavy bombardment of Fort Hatteras. Unusual for the time, he kept his ships moving while firing and stayed just out of range of the Confederate guns. After just three hours of intense fire, Barron was forced to surrender his post and troops.

After Hatteras

After the fall of Forts Clark and Hatteras, Confederate authorities saw that defense of the narrow Outer Banks was going to require major manpower and resources, neither of which was in abundance. Fort Morgan at Ocracoke Inlet and Fort Oregon at Oregon Inlet were quickly evacuated and just as quickly taken over by Butler's forces, leaving just Fort Fisher at the Cape Fear River inlet to guard the outer coast.

The only other action on this part of the Outer Banks was a bizarre set of pursuits between Hatteras and Chicamacomico (now called Rodanthe). On October 5, 1861, Hawkins had advanced toward the tiny north Hatteras Island town, aiming to capture and garrison it against the threat of a Confederate overland attack. As they closed in, six Confederate gunboats suddenly appeared, as well as part of a small Georgia infantry regiment (the 3rd Georgia Volunteers). A chase ensued, with the Union force running the 20 miles back to the safety of Fort Hatteras. The next morning, the chase began again, but this time Hawkins's men pursued the Confederates all the way back to Chicamacomico. Both sides' navies joined in on the fun, running on either side of the narrow banks in support of their troops. Besides a relative handful of casualties, absolutely nothing came out of what the locals referred to as the "Chicamacomico Races."

BURNSIDE'S 1862 NORTH CAROLINA EXPEDITION

With the quick fall of all Confederate defenses on the Outer Banks, two things became glaringly obvious: First, there would be a major effort by Union forces to capture the mainland ports, and second, the only thing standing in their way was the small garrison on Roanoke Island. As the defense of the entire area was now under Confederate control, Governor Clark, who had replaced Governor Ellis after his death, had little control over the buildup of a strong defense network, which the civilian population was demanding from him. Richmond responded to his appeals by simply stating that all available trained men were urgently needed in Virginia (not coincidentally, where the officials stating this were also located) and that only newly recruited units were available.

Brigadier General Richard Caswell Gatlin was placed in command of the newly formed Confederate Department of North Carolina. Brigadier (later Major) General Daniel Harvey Hill was initially given the responsibility of defending Albemarle and Pamlico Sounds (the body of water between the Outer Banks and the North Carolina mainland), and Brigadier General Joseph Reid Anderson took command of the District of Cape Fear, based out of Wilmington. Hill was apparently less than happy with his new command and soon resigned in order to return to General Robert E. Lee's Army of Northern Virginia. To replace him, Gatlin placed Brigadier General Henry Alexander Wise in charge of the area north of Roanoke Island and Brigadier General Lawrence O'Bryan Branch in charge of the stretch from Roanoke Island to New Bern.

Exact numbers are very hard to pin down, but Wise and Branch had somewhere around 8,000 men between their commands, most with Branch in New Bern. Roanoke Island itself was guarded by a few earthwork forts; on the east (seaward) side of the island was a tiny, unnamed two-gun redoubt at Ballast Point, and in the center was Fort Russell, a three-gun redoubt having a clear field of fire over the only road. On the northwest (landward) side of the island were three small sandwork forts, Forts Huger, Blanchard, and Bartow, mounting a total of 25 guns. No posts were established on the southern side of the island, possibly because the land was marshy and difficult to build on.

The most unusual defensive position was Fort Forrest, a partially sunken ship on the mainland side of the sound that had been reinforced and mounted with eight guns. The entire Confederate garrison numbered a mere 1,434 North Carolinians and Virginians, soon placed under direct command of Colonel H. M. Shaw, after Wise became too ill to lead the defense. Shaw was intensely disliked by his own men; one source quotes a soldier remarking that he was "not worth the powder and ball it would take to kill him."

Sailing rapidly toward this unhappy situation was the largest amphibious force the United States had ever mounted to that time; 67 gunboats and troop transports under command of Commodore (later Rear Admiral) L. M. Goldsborough, carrying more than 13,000 soldiers under command of Brigadier (later Major) General Ambrose Everett Burnside, an undistinguished commander better known for his namesake whiskers than his military prowess. In his postwar memoirs, General in Chief Ulysses S. Grant said that Burnside was "an officer who was generally liked and respected. He was not, however, fitted to command an army." By February 4, 1862, the fleet had crossed Hatteras Inlet safely and prepared to sail north into combat against Confederate forces.

THE ASSAULT OF ROANOKE ISLAND

Burnside's fleet moved north through Pamlico Sound and arrived just off Roanoke Island on February 7, opening fire on Fort Barrow between 10:30 and 11:00 A.M. Out of range, none of the Confederate batteries was able to return in kind the pounding artillery barrage. The Union Navy kept up their fire all day long, and as darkness approached, Burnside began landing his infantry at Ashby's Harbor, about 3 miles south of the southernmost Confederate fortification. A scouting force of about 200 Confederates was nearby when the first Union troops came ashore, but the Southerners elected to retreat to Fort Russell without firing a shot. By midnight, more than 10,000 Union soldiers were ashore, along with several artillery batteries, and making preparations to move north at first light.

At dawn, three Massachusetts infantry regiments (the 23rd, 25th, and 27th) attacked Fort Russell, strung in a line formation across the road and into the swamps on both sides. The 400 Confederate defenders opened a heavy fire down the road, blocking the 25th Massachusetts advance, but they were soon forced to pull out when the other Union infantry appeared out of the swamps on both flanks. As the Massachusetts men entered the redoubt to take the abandoned guns, Hawkins's Zouaves (the 9th New York Infantry Regiment) burst out of the woods and ran screaming over the redoubt's walls. Hawkins claimed ever after that his men had bravely charged and taken the "heavily defended" post.

As the rest of the Union infantry regiments rapidly advanced north on the small island toward the remaining three forts, Shaw decided that any further action was futile and surrendered without firing another shot. In all, 23 Confederate soldiers, including Wise's own son, were killed in the brief action, 58 were wounded, 62 missing, and about 2,500 captured, including nearly a thousand newly landed reinforcements from Nags Head. Burnside reported his losses at 37 killed, 214 wounded, and 13 missing, including 6 sailors killed and 17 wounded by return fire from Fort Bartow.

ACTIONS IN EASTERN NORTH CAROLINA

With the Outer Banks and Roanoke Island secured and available as staging bases, Burnside turned his attention to the mainland. His overall strategy from this point on seems a little less clear-cut than the assault on the Outer Banks; his postwar writings in Battles and Leaders only state that he had presented a rather vague plan to General of the Army George B. McClellan, to outfit an amphibious force "with a view to establishing lodgements on the Southern coast, landing troops, and penetrating into the interior . . ."

With the Confederate "mosquito fleet" fleeing with hardly a shot fired before the powerful Union naval task force, elements of Commandant Goldsborough's fleet set off after their base at Elizabeth City, across Albemarle Sound from the newly captured island, taking it with little resistance on February 10. Part of Burnside's infantry command joined the navy for "assaults" on other, nondefended towns off the sound; Edenton was ransacked on February 11, and Winton was burned to the ground on the 20th. Burnside and Goldsborough then turned their attention to the south, across Pamlico Sound toward New Bern and Morehead City.

To defend against the oncoming Union force, Branch had about 4,000 ill-trained and untested troops, stretched in a line from an old earthwork named Fort Thompson near the Neuse River, across the Atlantic and North Carolina Railroad track to Morehead City, and on nearly 2½ miles to the bank of the Trent River. Later Civil War doctrine called for a line this size to be held by at least 10 times this number of men. Six smaller earthwork redoubts surrounded the city, and an incomplete line of trenchworks and redoubts ran around the outside of Fort Thompson, all unmanned due to the manpower shortage. Branch's only real defensive advantage was the 13 guns inside Fort Thompson and the 12 scattered down the line of battle. The other forts were mounted with cannon, but none was positioned to resist a land-based attack.

On March 12 the Union fleet arrived in the Neuse River about 14 miles south of New Bern, and that night Burnside gave his orders for the attack. The men were to land the next morning, march north along the Morehead City Road, and attack the Confederate line at the earliest opportunity.

The Battle of New Bern

Branch had arranged his men in an interesting fashion, possibly due to his total lack of experience or training as a military officer (he was a lawyer turned politician turned politically appointed general).

From the fort to the railroad track, he placed four regiments, Major John A. Gilmer's 27th, Lieutenant Colonel Thomas L. Lowe's 28th, Colonel James Sinclair's 35th, and Colonel Charles C. Lee's 37th North Carolina Infantry, with Colonel Clark Avery's 33rd North Carolina Infantry Regiment just behind them in reserve. To the right (west) of the railroad, he placed Colonel Zebulon B. Vance's 26th and Colonel R. P. Campbell's 7th North Carolina Infantry Regiments. In the middle, at the critical point in his line pierced by the railroad, he placed the least able of his men, the newly recruited, still un-uniformed and mostly shotgun-equipped Special Battalion, North Carolina Militia, led by Colonel H. J. B. Clark.

On the morning of March 13, Burnside's troops waded ashore unopposed, the entire force able to join on land by 1:00 P.M. It had begun raining, and by the time the Union troops started moving north, the roads had become a quagmire of mud. Burnside said later it was "one of the most disagreeable and difficult marches that I witnessed during the war." It took until dark to move north to the Confederate picket line, where it was decided to bivouac for the night and attack the next morning. Without tents or shelters of any kind, the night must have been a most difficult one for the rain-soaked infantrymen.

As dawn approached on the 14th, Burnside split his command into three brigades: Brigadier General John Gray Foster's 1st Brigade was to attack on the right, Brigadier General John Grubb Parke's 3rd Brigade the center, and Brigadier General Jesse Lee Reno's 2nd Brigade was to roll up the extreme left. As dawn broke, the three Union brigades moved out.

Burnside had camped for the night much closer to the Confederate line than he had thought, and the lead brigade, Foster's 1st, was in action almost immediately. Branch ordered the landward-facing guns of Fort Thompson to open up, which was answered by return fire from Union gunboats sailing in support up the Neuse

River. Foster's men were caught in the crossfire, suffering heavy casualties, and were soon forced to withdraw. Seeing the attack was bogging down on his right and spotting the break in the Confederate line at the railroad track, Reno led the four regiments under his command into the breach, the 21st Massachusetts Infantry in the front.

With the Union infantry storming down the road toward their position, the militiamen broke and ran, most without firing a single shot. With the line to their right caving in, the 35th North Carolina soon followed suit. The only reserve regiment, the 33rd North Carolina, quickly moved up to plug the hole in the line and, between their volley fire and that of the 26th North Carolina to the right, soon broke up the Union attack and hurled it back. Reno moved further to his left and prepared to attack once again.

By this time, the third Union brigade, Parke's, had moved into position, and all three brigades launched a renewed attack on the Confederate line at nearly the same time. This time the attack was successful, with Union infantry pouring through gaps in the line and raising their battle flags on the ramparts of the Confederate defenses. Branch, seeing his entire command caving in, ordered everyone to disengage and move back into New Bern. Once there, apparently believing Burnside was hot on his heels when in fact the Union assault had stopped for a rest within the breastworks, Branch ordered New Bern to be immediately evacuated and his headquarters moved to Kinston, 40 miles farther east.

When Burnside's men moved into town on the afternoon of the 14th, all Confederate troops had fled, and the town was taken without further incident. Rather than trashing and burning the place, as was the Union custom, Burnside decided to garrison the town and use it as a supply and headquarters station for raids into the rest of North Carolina. Union troops held the town for the rest of the war. The short campaign had cost Burnside 90 killed and 380 wounded and another 4 sailors wounded, while Branch lost 64 killed, 101 wounded, and 413 captured or missing.

Beaufort and Morehead City

With New Bern newly secured, Burnside had only one task left to bring the entire central and eastern coasts under Union control—the seizure of Fort Macon on Bogue Banks, just across Bogue Sound from Beaufort just 33 miles to the southwest, guarding the only inlet left in Confederate control along the Outer Banks. With this post under Union control, the port of Morehead City would be open to Union troop and supply shipments to use in the planned invasion of central and southern North Carolina.

Fort Macon was named for Nathaniel Macon, who was Speaker of the House of Representatives and a U.S. senator from North Carolina. The five-sided structure was built of brick and stone with outer walls 4.5 feet thick with more than 9.3 million locally produced bricks, and it mounted 54 artillery pieces of various calibers. At the beginning of the war it was seized, in a scene repeated all over the coastal South, by local militia who demanded the post from the single ordnance sergeant who manned it.

At the time of Burnside's expedition, Fort Macon was commanded by Lieutenant Colonel (later Colonel) Moses J. White of Vicksburg, Mississippi, with a garrison of about 450 (some accounts say 480 to 500) infantry and artillerymen.

THE BATTLE FOR FORT MACON

With the Union Navy already under way to lay siege to the fort, Burnside ordered Parke to take his 3rd Brigade, with about 1,500 men fit for duty, south along the road through Morehead City and to lay siege to the Confederate outpost by land. Parke left New Bern on March 18 and

walked into Morehead City without resistance five days later. After taking Beaufort the next day, also without resistance, Parke immediately and politely requested Fort Macon's surrender; White, also politely, turned down his request. White knew that, without reinforcement or resupply, his post was doomed, but he was determined to fight it out as long as possible.

Over the next month the Union Navy landed men and supplies on Bogue Banks west of the fort and constructed a series of artillery redoubts and firing pits that gradually extended closer and closer to the fort. White's men could only stand and watch and fire at the occasional ship or redoubt that came too close. By April 22 Parke had managed to emplace heavy cannon and siege mortars within 1,200 to 1,400 yards of the fort's walls. Parke once again asked for a surrender and was once again turned down.

The Union land batteries opened fire at dawn on April 25, and the Navy joined in a little after 8:00 A.M. White's were high-velocity, flat trajectory guns unable to hit the well-entrenched redoubts, but they raked the Union ships with a murderous fire, causing them to break off and retreat in less than one hour. Parke kept up an accurate and heavy fire for nearly 11 hours, helped in no small part by a Union signal officer in nearby Beaufort who watched the impact of each round and signaled corrections to the artillerymen. With his help, about 560 of the 1,100 rounds fired landed inside the fort, an amazingly high statistic for the time.

By 4:00 P.M. White had suffered enough and signaled that he was ready to ask Parke for a truce. The firing stopped immediately. The next morning, White went aboard the schooner USS *Alice Price* and surrendered his post and his command. By noon the 5th Rhode Island Infantry Regiment marched inside the fort's walls and raised the Stars and Stripes once again. Losses on both sides were quite light for such a heavy bombardment; 7 Confederates were killed and another 18 wounded, while Parke suffered the loss of 1 dead and 3 wounded.

AFTER THE BATTLE

Beaufort served as a supply station for the Union Army and Navy for the rest of the war, despite several rather weak attempts to recapture it. With all eastern water accesses of the state now under Union control, Confederate authorities prudently pulled their overmatched forces back into the interior and north to support Lee's army in Virginia. By springtime Union troops had marched in and taken Plymouth and Washington, North Carolina, without opposition.

With the exception of a continuous series of Union and Confederate raids that produced nothing for either side, no major offensive was launched in North Carolina for nearly three more years. The major battles had shifted away from the supply and farming region of eastern North Carolina to the heart of the Confederacy in Tennessee, Mississippi, and Georgia and to the seemingly endless struggle around Richmond, Virginia.

Wilmington, 1864–65

After Burnside's successful 1861–62 campaign in the eastern portion of the state had cut off Confederate supply and transport routes into Virginia, Wilmington inherited a vital role as the most important safe port for blockade runners. The supplies they managed to sneak past the Union fleet were then transferred to trains on the Wilmington & Weldon Railroad and sent north to Lee's army. Lee remarked on several occasions that he would not have been able to fight on so long without this steady flow of supplies. Two other railroads carried some supplies to the western portion of the state and then on to Tennessee and Georgia, and down to Charleston and Columbia in South Carolina.

Wilmington had a very favorable and easily defended location 26 miles inland on the wide and deep Cape Fear River, whose twin entrances from the Atlantic Ocean were well fortified. Also to the Union Navy's grief, it was very nearly impossible to sail into the river inlet without the use of local, firmly Confederate guides to show the way through the treacherous Frying Pan Shoals.

To guard against even the remote possibility of a Union attempt to assault the city by water, there were no less than six forts. The two channels into the Cape Fear River are separated by Smith's Island (now called Bald Head Island), the location of Fort Holmes. On the west bank of the river above the island were Forts Johnston (later renamed Pender) and Anderson, while the lesser used Old Inlet was guarded by Fort Caswell and Battery Campbell. To guard the much more heavily used New Inlet, a massive sandwork fortification called Fort Fisher was constructed on Federal Point starting in the summer of 1861. Fisher was not a fort in the classic sense, as it did not have encompassing walls. Instead, it was L-shaped, with the longest side facing the expected avenue of attack, the Atlantic Ocean. Several earthwork redoubts and batteries surrounded each fort, adding to an already impressive amount of available firepower.

The Union blockade fleet had initially considered Wilmington an insignificant port, ignoring it at first and then placing only a single ship, the USS *Daylight,* off the coast in July 1861. By late 1864 its importance was clear even to Union planners in Washington; by that time more than 50 blockade ships lay just offshore. Even with this tight noose around the supply lanes, blockade runners managed to slip through up until the time of the battle itself.

THE BATTLES FOR WILMINGTON

While Grant was tied up in the months-long battle around Petersburg, he realized that in order to bring the stalemated fight to a successful conclusion, he was going to have to cut Lee's supply lines. Until the only remaining port supplying the Army of Northern Virginia, Wilmington, could be cut off or taken over, this was not going to be possible. Grant ordered General Benjamin Franklin Butler and Rear Admiral David Dixon Porter to take their forces south to capture the city. Butler had two divisions of infantry—Brigadier General Adelbert Ames's 2nd of the XXIV Corps and Brigadier General Charles Jackson Paine's 3rd of the XXV Corps—as well as two batteries of artillery, with a grand total of nearly 8,000 men. Porter commanded the largest force of ships ever assembled at that time in the United States under one command, nearly 60 ships mounting a total of 627 guns.

As attack on the port city was likely at some point, Confederate president Davis sent General Braxton Bragg to take over command of the defenses in December 1864. The previous area commander, Major General William Henry Chase Whiting, was a competent officer well liked by both his troops and the local citizens, and Davis's choice of the notoriously inept Bragg to replace him (he was actually placed over Whiting, who stayed on to directly command the garrison) was loudly protested. The size of the command then around Wilmington is highly debatable, but it can be safely assumed that Bragg initially commanded somewhere around 3,000 men.

Lee was fully aware of the critical and vulnerable nature of the port city and warned Davis that, if the city fell, he would be forced to pull back and abandon Richmond itself. When the Virginia general learned of Butler and Porter's advance down the coast, he sent Major General Robert Frederick Hoke's division to help defend the vital port, adding another 6,000 men to the line.

The First Battle for Fort Fisher

Butler, considered by many on both sides to be Bragg's equal in ineptness, was determined to open the Cape Fear River by reducing its strongest defense, Fort Fisher. On December 20, 1864, the Union fleet began arriving off the Wilmington coast in the midst of a severe storm, taking nearly three days to get organized. Finally, on the night of December 23, with nearly all his command present and ready to assault, Butler sprang his "secret weapon" on the unsuspecting Confederates.

Butler had decided that a ship loaded to the gills with gunpowder, floated to the outer defenses of Fort Fisher and then exploded, would reduce at least one wall of the sandwork post to dust and allow his troops to pour in through the opening. Amazingly, he managed to sell Porter on the idea and got Grant's grudging approval to go ahead (Butler and Grant were mortal enemies, and the supreme Union commander had simply wanted to fire Butler rather than allow him another chance to screw up but could not due to Butler's political connections).

At 1:45 A.M. on December 24, an unnamed "powder ship" loaded with 215 tons of gunpowder was sailed to within 200 yards of the fort and then exploded. The resulting massive blast failed to even superficially damage the well-constructed fort, and the sleepy defenders peered out wondering if one of the Union ships had just suffered a boiler explosion or something of a similarly innocuous nature. Despite the failure of his secret weapon, Butler ordered the planned attack to proceed.

As dawn crept over the horizon, Porter's gunboats began a heavy bombardment of the fort, while Butler ordered his troops ashore to the peninsula just north of the Confederate stronghold. Capturing two small batteries and pushing back Confederate skirmishers, the Union troops had made it to within 75 yards of the fort by the morning of Christmas Day. Butler learned that General Hoke's division was then only 5 miles away and moving in fast. Panicking, Butler ordered his troops to break off and return to the troop transports, which he in turn ordered to hoist anchor and sail away so fast that more than 600 infantrymen were left stranded on the beach. Porter, who had no idea what Butler was up to, was forced to send his own ships and sailors to the beachhead under fire from the defenders of Fort Fisher to rescue the stranded troops. Butler reported a loss of 15 wounded and 1 killed in action (by drowning), while the Confederates suffered about 300 killed, wounded, and captured, as well as the loss of four precious artillery pieces.

A furious Grant immediately fired Butler, damning the political consequences, and hurriedly assembled another, stronger assault force under Major General Alfred Howe Terry. He sent Porter a message: "Hold on, if you please, a few days longer, and I'll send you more troops, with a different general." Porter pulled about 25 miles offshore, to the general line of the Union blockade fleet, to await Terry's arrival.

The Second Battle for Fort Fisher

Porter did not have long to wait. Terry left Bermuda Landing, Virginia, on January 4, 1865, with a total of 8,000 soldiers. Joining Porter's squadron just off Beaufort, the force sailed once again for the Cape Fear River, again through a strong storm, arriving late on the afternoon of January 12.

Whiting had received word that the Union force was en route to try again and, fearing that this attempt would be much stronger, personally led 600 North Carolina troops from the garrison at Wilmington to reinforce Colonel William Lamb's garrison of 1,200. Hoke's newly arrived command deployed on the peninsula north of the fort, in case the second assault followed Butler's attempted route.

A few hours after the Union fleet arrived, Porter ordered all guns to open fire on the Confederate fort while the infantry landed north of Hoke's line. Terry spent the next two days carefully bringing his total force ashore and deploying them in a semicircle around the fort. One Union

brigade under Colonel Newton Martin Curtis was sent to the western end of the peninsula, capturing a small redoubt and digging in close to the fort.

At dawn on January 15, Porter's ships once again opened up a massive bombardment, lasting more than five hours, until Terry signaled his men to advance. Riflemen from the 13th Indiana Infantry Regiment led the assault, dashing forward under fire to dig in less than 200 yards from the fort and then rake the parapets with a deadly accurate fire.

While this rifle fire kept the Confederate defenders' heads down, Terry ordered forward Curtis's brigade, now reinforced with Colonel Galusha Pennypacker's brigade, against the western face of the fort. As the Union troops cut through the wooden palisades and dashed up the sand walls, Lamb's men rose out of their shelters and met the Union soldiers with fixed bayonets and drawn swords.

As the western wall defenses broke down into a massive hand-to-hand melee, 2,200 sailors and marines from Porter's command sprang forward to assault the northeastern corner of the fort. There, the Confederate defenders were able to return a disciplined fire, killing or wounding more than 300 of the naval command and forcing them to quickly retreat.

The Union's Terry left the rest of his command before Hoke's Confederate line, and Hoke never sent any of his men to help relieve the fort's defenders at Bragg's direct order. About 10:00 P.M., after hours of unrelenting and vicious hand-to-hand combat and the commitment of the last Union reserves, the seriously wounded Lamb finally surrendered his post. The exact numbers of dead and wounded Confederates are difficult to assess, as records of this fight are spotty and highly debatable as to accuracy, but somewhere between 500 and 700 were killed or wounded and another approximately 2,000 captured. The South's Whiting himself was mortally wounded during the assault, dying less than two months later. Terry reported Union losses of 184 killed,

749 captured, and 22 missing, including the seriously wounded Curtis, who was shot three times while leading the way over the ramparts, while Porter reported the loss of 386 in addition to the casualties in his marine assault force.

As a morbid postscript to the hard-fought battle, on the morning of January 16 two drunk sailors (sometimes identified as U.S. Marines) were walking around looking for something worth stealing when they came to a heavy bunker door. Opening it, they lit a torch and stuck it in the dark opening. The resulting explosion of about 13,000 pounds of gunpowder killed 25 more Union soldiers, wounded another 66, and killed an unknown number of wounded Confederate prisoners in the next bunker.

The Fall of Wilmington

With the main defense post now in Union hands, Bragg wasted little time mounting any sort of renewed defense. The next day Fort Caswell's garrison was withdrawn and the walls blown up, followed in quick order by most of the rest of the forts, batteries, and redoubts. Fort Anderson was left manned to cover Bragg's withdrawal. This post stayed until February 20, when Major General Jacob Dolson Cox's XXIII Corps moved upriver and forced them out without much of a fight. The next day Hoke's troops were finally withdrawn and escaped north with the last remnants of Bragg's force to Goldsboro. On February 22, Mayor John Dawson of Wilmington rode out to surrender his city to the Union invaders.

THE LAST OF THE ARMY OF TENNESSEE

As the campaign to take Wilmington wound to a close in February 1865, Confederate operations in the Deep South were rapidly coming together near the eastern North Carolina town of Goldsboro. Bragg's

defeated force was withdrawing there to regroup (and for its commander to figure out whom to blame for his latest disaster); Sherman was pounding through South Carolina, driving what was left of the Confederate Army of Tennessee and various attached militias before him toward Goldsboro; and the newly appointed U.S. Department of North Carolina commander, Major General John McAllister Schofield, had been directed to move in from New Bern and take Goldsboro under Union control.

Desperately seeking some way out of the disastrous conclusion now looming before him, Davis finally came to a long-overdue decision and appointed Robert E. Lee as General in Chief of all of the combined Confederate armies. One of Lee's first acts was to place General Joseph Eggleston Johnston once again as commander of the Army of Tennessee and almost incidentally as commander of the CSA Department of the Carolinas, with an aggregate total of about 45,000 men of widely varying skill and training levels. Bragg was reduced to command of a division under Johnston, a move that no doubt humiliated him but delighted his many political enemies.

Johnston promptly ordered most of his command to concentrate with him in the central portion of the state, to make a stand against Sherman's oncoming force. From reports filtering up from South Carolina, where Sherman was advancing without any real resistance, he knew that the Union commander was arrayed in a column four corps abreast in a nearly 60-mile-wide front. Johnston planned to concentrate his forces so as to hit Sherman from one flank and then attack each corps' flank and defeat each in turn.

THE BATTLE OF WYSE FORK

As Wilmington had been effectively, if hastily, abandoned by Bragg's troops, Schofield found no wagons or trains there available to move his Union troops rapidly inland. Undeterred, he ordered his forces under Cox in the longer-held base at New Bern to also move inland, and by late February two great Union columns were heading west. Bragg had pulled some of his troops safely out of Wilmington and now had about 8,500 men under Hoke near Kinston to protect his headquarters at Goldsboro. Johnston had sent a few green troops under Hill to reinforce Hoke's line, including a unit known as the "North Carolina Junior Reserves," consisting mostly of completely untrained teenage boys.

On the morning of March 8, as Cox rather blandly moved up the Kinston Road toward Southwest Creek, Hoke and Hill moved out of the trenchline in a well-timed attack and assaulted the Union column on both flanks. Several thousand surprised and horrified Union soldiers either ran or surrendered on the spot, while Cox hastily ordered the remainder to dig in and fight back. Sporadic fighting lasted the rest of the day and into the next, while some Union reinforcements came up to replace the scattered force. By nightfall on March 9, Cox had about 12,000 men in his trenchline.

At dawn on March 10, Hoke swung around and hit the Union left flank while Hill struck the right flank, forcing a few troops to pull back or run, but both Confederate commands were forced to withdraw after a relatively short fight.

Seriously weakened by the three-day battle, Hoke and Hill were forced to withdraw back into Kinston and then almost immediately pull out as Cox's stronger force approached. Cox entered the city on March 14, as Bragg pulled what was left of his forces back into Goldsboro.

SHERMAN'S ADVANCE

Sherman had stormed through South Carolina without any real resistance and by the first of March was approaching Cherhaw, near the North Carolina border. After evacuating Charleston, also without a fight, Beauregard had directed Lieutenant General William Joseph Hardee to take his corps (with two divisions and 8,000 men) to Cherhaw and delay Sherman's advance while everyone else got into some kind of order. Johnston determined that he should concentrate his forces near Fayetteville in order to best strike at Sherman's flank, no matter if he went south toward Goldsboro or north toward Raleigh.

Schofield and Sherman agreed that they should link up their respective commands at Goldsboro before moving on Raleigh to cut the main Confederate supply line there; Johnston determined to strike hard at Sherman's column and was maneuvering his forces to hit before that linkup could be accomplished.

Hardee wisely pulled his infantry steadily back from Sherman's advance, leaving most of the fighting up to Major General Joseph Wheeler's Cavalry Corps, who kept up a running battle with Sherman's cavalry chief, Brigadier General Judson Kilpatrick, most of the way to Fayetteville. Sherman's infantry moved steadily forward, reaching Fayetteville on March 12. There he rested his troops for three days before starting out again.

The Battle of Averasborough

As he had in Georgia and South Carolina, Sherman had arranged his force of four corps into two great columns covering a 60-mile front; on the left were the XIV and the XX Corps, collectively referred to as the Army of Georgia, under Major General Henry Warner Slocum. On the right were the XVII and XV Corps under one-armed Major General Oliver Otis Howard, collectively referred to as the Army of the Tennessee. On March 15 the great Union army marched out of Fayetteville northeast toward Goldsboro and an expected linkup with Schofield's army.

Hardee had pulled back to a strong defensive position near the tiny settlement of Averasborough, on the Raleigh

Road, atop a ridgeline between a swamp and the Cape Fear River. On the afternoon of March 15, not long after leaving Fayetteville, Kilpatrick's Cavalry Corps, attached to Slocum's Corps, ran into the line of Confederate defenses and immediately tried to ram their way through them. Hardee's men held fast, forcing Kilpatrick to withdraw and request infantry support. Slocum deployed his men during the night and at dawn on March 16 assaulted Hardee's line.

Hardee's only task was to delay the Union force, and he did an outstanding job here. Alternately pulling back and counterattacking, Hardee's fewer than 6,000 men forced Slocum to deploy his entire XX Corps and then order up the XIV Corps for reinforcements late in the afternoon. By nightfall, well over 25,000 Union soldiers were engaged or deployed for battle, while Sherman's lines were starting to become unstrung, just as Johnston had hoped. Rather than turn and support Slocum's fight, for some unknown reason, Howard's right wing kept moving forward, separating the two armies by more than a day's march by the morning of March 17.

As darkness fell, Hardee broke contact and moved his small force rapidly back toward Johnston's line outside Goldsboro, no doubt pleased that his actions had delayed the Union left wing by at least two days. About 600 Union soldiers were killed or wounded, while Hardee reported a loss of about 450.

The Battle of Bentonville, Day One, March 19, 1865

Unknown to both Sherman and Slocum, Johnston was massing his available forces just 20 miles north, outside the tiny village of Bentonville and hidden in the woods on the north side of the Goldsboro Road. Howard's right wing was advancing down the New Goldsboro Road about 4 miles to the southeast and was well down the road by the time Slocum got his troops reorgan-

ized and on the road again. Sherman was convinced that Johnston, the defensive genius, was entrenching around Raleigh at that very moment. With Hardee's corps still advancing up the road from Averasborough, the Confederate commander could muster about 21,000 men, as opposed to the 30,000 in Slocum's command alone.

As Brigadier General William Passmore Carlin's 1st Division, the lead elements of Slocum's XIV Corps, moved up the Goldsboro Road early on the morning of March 19, his skirmishers started engaging what they thought were local militia. Instead, they were running straight into Hoke's newly reinforced command arrayed across the road, fresh up from the battles around Wilmington. Slocum ordered an envelopment movement to his left, which instead had his men running straight into the middle of Johnston's main line of battle.

As the battle started unfolding, Major General Lafayette McLaw's division, the vanguard of Hardee's command, finally arrived. Johnston, responding to panicked requests for reinforcements from Bragg, sent the road-march-weary soldiers over to the far left of his lines to join Hoke, arriving only to see the Union troops retreating in disarray. Johnston's tactical plan had been to stop and break up the Union column and then spring a strong attack into their flank from his wooded position as soon as possible. Thanks to Bragg's continued ineptness as a battlefield commander, the chance to do this with McLaw's troops was lost.

While the rest of Hardee's command moved into position and Johnston prepared to attack, Slocum had his men hastily dig in and sent word for his XX Corps to move up as soon as possible. The Union commander also sent word to Sherman that he had found Johnston's army and requested Howard's army be moved north into the rapidly growing battle.

Just before 3:00 P.M., with all his forces now in place and ready, Johnston gave the order to start what became the last major Confederate offensive of the war. Led by Hardee, Johnston's combined force swept out of the woods and thundered down on Carlin's seriously outnumbered division. In minutes the Union line fell apart, and Johnston's screaming men ran down the road toward the next Union division coming into the line, Brigadier General James Dada Morgan's 2nd Division.

Morgan had ordered his men to quickly construct a log breastwork soon after encountering Hoke's men, and this hastily built barricade broke up the Confederate assault. Under heavy fire, Hardee's men hit the ground and returned fire, while Hoke was ordered out of his trenchline into the assault. Soon, every reserve Johnston could muster was thrown into the fight, while Slocum's XX Corps made it into the line in time to withstand the assault. As darkness fell, Johnston ordered his men to break contact and pull back to a strong defensive position near Mill Creek, while Sherman ordered Howard's entire Army of the Tennessee north into battle.

The Battle of Bentonville, Days Two and Three, March 20–21, 1865

Very little fighting occurred during the day of March 20, with Johnston strengthening his position around Mill Creek and Howard's two corps moving into the line of battle. As day dawned on March 21, both armies stood static in their defensive lines, with Johnston trying to keep his force intact and Sherman simply wondering when his Confederate opponent would withdraw and allow him to proceed to his rendezvous with Terry and Cox at Goldsboro.

By the middle of the afternoon, hot-headed Major General Joseph Anthony Mower grew impatient and ordered his division to advance, totally without orders from either Slocum or Sherman. Moving west along a narrow path along Mill Creek, Mower's men blew past pickets set up in the rear of Johnston's line and soon advanced to within 600 feet of Johnston's

headquarters. Commanding a hastily assembled counterattack, Hardee personally led a Texas cavalry unit into Mower's left flank, followed in short order by cavalry and infantry attacks on every flank of the Union command. Mower was soon forced out of the Confederate lines with heavy losses, but his division managed to inflict the ultimate blow on Hardee. Private Willie Hardee, his son, was a member of the very Texas cavalry brigade the general led into battle and was mortally wounded in the heavy exchange of fire.

Johnston had had enough. During the night of March 21, he pulled the remnants of his command out of the line and headed back toward Raleigh. The ill-conceived stance had cost him 2,606 men killed, wounded, captured, or missing, while Sherman's forces suffered a loss of 1,646. The only objective Johnston managed was the delay of Sherman's march for a few days, while nearly destroying his own army in the attempt. With hindsight, it is clear that, even if Johnston had managed the unlikely result of totally destroying Slocum's Army of Georgia, he would have still faced the 30,000-plus-strong Army of the Tennessee shortly thereafter.

POSTSCRIPT

Johnston had once commanded a powerful, relatively well-equipped, and extremely well-trained Army of Tennessee, 42,000 strong, before Sherman's grinding "total war" tactics had reduced it to a pitiful shell of its former glory. "High" Private Sam Watkins, of the Maury Grays, 1st Tennessee Infantry Regiment, had marched for the South as part of this great army since the very beginning. In his postwar memoirs he remarked that his regiment had once numbered 1,250 men, had received about 350 replacements, and had joined with other regiments throughout the war bringing it to a grand total of about 3,200 men, but after the battle of Bentonville, it was reduced to just 65 officers and men.

Sherman rather halfheartedly moved on to Goldsboro on March 23, where he met up with Terry's and Cox's commands newly arrived from the coast, then moved north to take the abandoned city of Raleigh. There he received word on April 16 that Johnston wanted to discuss surrender terms. The two generals met at Bennett Place between Durham and Hillsborough, where very generous terms were offered to the courtly Confederate general after two days of talks. Both generals had just learned of Lincoln's assassination on April 14, which no doubt added some haste to their efforts to end the fighting.

Grant traveled south to tell his old friend Sherman that these terms were not acceptable to the new administration in Washington and that he would have to insist the Confederates accept the same terms offered to and accepted by Lee on April 9. Jefferson Davis, newly arrived in Goldsboro in flight from the Union armies, rudely ordered Johnston, his political enemy, to break away from Sherman's armies and join him in flight to the south. Johnston quietly ignored him and, as Davis continued his escape attempt southward, met again with Sherman to discuss the surrender. After agreeing to the new, harsher terms, Johnston surrendered his once-great army on April 26, 1865.

THE TOUR

Reasoning with Hurricane Season

Since our first research trips into this area, no fewer than seven major hurricanes have either hit this area or passed close by. The resulting floods and damage to roads, buildings, and beaches meant that many businesses had to shut down to undergo repairs. Most reopened, but next year will undoubtedly play host to another major hurricane season. Weather experts say that hurricane seasons peak and ebb in relative strengths and numbers of major hurricanes and that the East and Gulf Coasts can expect high levels of both for the next eight years or so. It is strongly suggested that you call ahead just before your trip to make sure that the roads are passable and your hotel is open, and it pays to monitor weather conditions during the hurricane season (roughly June through November, peaking in late August and September).

Getting There: Hatteras Island

Hatteras Island is a long, narrow, sandy barrier island well off the mainland coast, accessible either by highway or ferry. U.S. Highway 64 accesses the central portion of the Outer Banks and the northern end of Hatteras Island; it can be accessed from Interstate 95 (exit 138) or off U.S. Business Route 40, which runs around Raleigh. The entrance to the Outer Banks is roughly 60 miles east of the nearest larger town, Plymouth, so make sure to fill your tank and get any necessary supplies before leaving there. As in any other resort/vacation area, prices tend to be much higher east of Plymouth. Once you cross the bridge onto Roanoke Island, stay on US 64 through Manteo and across the Washington Baum Bridge to Nags Head/Bodie Island. Turn right onto North Carolina Highway 12, which goes straight south to Hatteras Island, just across the Oregon Inlet.

The lower end of Hatteras Island and Hatteras Village can be accessed via toll ferries from Swan Quarter on the mainland (just off U.S. Highway 264, east of Greenville) or from Cedar Island, east of Morehead City on U.S. Highway 70. The latter ferry is recommended because you'll be farther down the coastline, where most of the actions between 1861 and 1864 took place. Both ferries land at Ocracoke Village, where a drive north on NC 12 and another short (but free) ferry takes you to Hatteras Village.

Hatteras-Ocracoke Ferry
End of NC 12, Hatteras Village to
beginning of NC 12 on Ocracoke Island
(252) 986-2353, (800) BY FERRY
The only link between Hatteras and Ocra-coke Islands, this free state-run ferry car-ries passengers and vehicles across Hatteras Inlet daily, year-round, with trips at least every hour from 5:00 A.M. to mid-night. A fleet of 10 ferry boats, some 150 feet long, carry up to 30 cars and trucks each on the 40-minute ride.

MODERN TIMES AT FORTS HATTERAS AND CLARK

Due to wind, tide, and time, nothing re-mains of either post, save a marker near the ferry station indicating where the two forts were, now a spot in the Atlantic Ocean. A small museum at the base of the Cape Hatteras Lighthouse houses a dis-play about the Civil War activities here.

Despite the dearth of actual Civil War sites in this area, we recommend a visit as part of a tour of eastern North Carolina; while the Outer Banks have radically changed shape and size in the past 140-plus years, you can get a good idea of the terrain and weather that both sides had to endure in this campaign.

POINTS OF INTEREST

Outer Banks Visitors Bureau
704 US 64/264, Manteo
(252) 473-2138, (800) 446-6262
The Outer Banks Visitors Bureau relocated in the summer of 2002 to a 10,000-square-foot facility near the eastern termi-nus of the Croatan Sound Bridge. The bureau houses both the Outer Banks Wel-come Center and administrative offices, and it offers a sizable collection of brochures, maps, and promotional materi-als about area attractions. Staffers can also supply information on local demographics and business opportunities. The center features a rest area, toilets, and an RV dump station. Hours are 8:00 A.M. to 6:00 P.M. Monday through Friday and noon to 4:00 P.M. Saturday and Sunday, year-round.

Nags Head Visitor Center
Whalebone Junction (US 64 and NC 12)
(252) 441-6644
Operated by the Dare County Tourist Bureau, this wooden visitor center sits just south of the Whalebone Junction inter-section on NC 12. It's open daily from Memorial Day to October 1 from 9:00 A.M. until 5:00 P.M. and on weekends in April, May, and November. The staff can answer all kinds of questions about southern des-tinations along the Outer Banks. The pub-lic restrooms are some of the few you'll find on this remote stretch of NC 12.

Bodie Island Lighthouse
and Keeper's Quarters
West of NC 12, 6 miles south of
Whalebone Junction
(252) 441-5711
This black-and-white beacon with hori-zontal bands is one of four lighthouses still standing along the Outer Banks. It sits more than a half mile from the sea, in a field of green grass. The site is a perfect place to picnic.

In 1870 the federal government bought 15 acres of land for $150 on which to build the lighthouse and keeper's quar-ters. When the project was finished two years later, Bodie Island Lighthouse was very close to the inlet, stood 150 feet tall, and was the only lighthouse between Cape Henry, Virginia, and Cape Hatteras. But the inlet is migrating away from the beacon, and the current lighthouse is the third one to stand near Oregon Inlet since the inlet opened during an 1846 hurricane. The first light developed cracks and had to be removed. Confederate soldiers destroyed the second tower to frustrate Union shipping efforts.

Wanchese resident John Gaskill served as the last civilian lightkeeper of Bodie Island Lighthouse. As late as 1940, he said, the tower was the only structure between Oregon Inlet and Jockey's Ridge. Gaskill helped his father strain kerosene before pouring it into the light. The kerosene pre-vented particles from clogging the vapor-izer that kept the beacon burning.

Today the lighthouse grounds and keeper's quarters offer a welcome respite during long drives to Hatteras Island. Wide expanses of marshland behind the tower offer enjoyable walks through cattails, yaupon, and wax myrtle. You can stick to the short path and overlooks if you prefer to keep your shoes dry.

The National Park Service added new exhibits to the Bodie Island keeper's quarters in 1995. The visitor center there is open daily from Memorial Day through Labor Day from 9:00 A.M. to 6:00 P.M. and from 9:00 A.M. to 5:00 P.M. in the off-season. The lighthouse itself is not open, but you can look up the tall tower from below when National Park Service employees are present to open the structure. Even a quick drive around the grounds to see the exterior is worth it.

Pea Island National Wildlife Refuge
North end of Hatteras Island,
both sides of NC 12
(252) 987-2394
Pea Island National Wildlife Refuge begins at the southern base of the Herbert C. Bonner Bridge and is the first place you'll come to if you enter Hatteras Island from the north. The beach along this undeveloped stretch of sand is popular with surfers, sunbathers, and shell seekers. On the right side of the road, heading south, salt marshes surround Pamlico Sound and birds seem to flutter from every grove of cattails.

With 5,915 acres that attract more than 250 observed species of birds, Pea Island is an outdoor aviary well worth venturing off the road, and into the wilderness, to visit. Few tourists visited this refuge when Hatteras Island was cut off from the rest of the Outer Banks and people arrived at the southern beaches by ferry. But after the Oregon Inlet bridge opened in 1964, motorists began driving through this once isolated outpost.

Four miles south of the Bonner Bridge's southern base, at the entrance to the new portion of NC 12, the Pea Island Visitor Cen-

ter offers free parking and easy access to the beach. If you walk directly across the highway to the top of the dunes, you'll see the remains of the more than 100-year-old federal transport Oriental. Her steel boiler is the black mass, all that remains since the ship sank in May 1862.

The *Monitor*
Off Cape Hatteras, in the Atlantic Ocean
Launched January 30, 1862, the *Monitor* is one of the nation's most famous military ships. Its watery grave is the first National Underwater Marine Sanctuary. Divers sanctioned by the National Oceanic and Atmospheric Administration have spent four years trying to retrieve the four-pronged propeller from the ironclad boat, which rests upside down in 230 feet of water about 17 miles off Cape Hatteras.

The *Monitor* was owned by Union forces and was their counterpart to the Confederate ship *Virginia* during the Civil War. The *Virginia* was the world's first ironclad warship, built from the hull of the Union frigate *Merrimac,* which Southern forces captured and refitted. On March 8, 1862, the pup tent–shaped steamer *Virginia* cruised out of Norfolk to challenge a blockade of six wooden ships. By day's end, the *Virginia* had sunk two of those Union ships and damaged another.

Built by Swedish-American engineer John Ericsson and appropriately dubbed the "Cheesebox on a Raft" because of its unusual design, the *Monitor* was a low-slung ironclad that included a revolving turret to carry its main battery. This strange-looking ship arrived in Norfolk on March 9 and soon battled the *Virginia* to a draw. Retreating Confederates eventually destroyed the *Virginia.* The *Monitor* was ordered to proceed farther south.

The New Year's Eve storm of 1862 caught the Union ironclad off Cape Hatteras, far out in the Atlantic. The *Monitor* sank completely, taking its crew with it. Its whereabouts were unknown until university researchers discovered the *Monitor* in 1973.

Although they haven't been able to retrieve the heavy propeller, federally permitted scuba divers have brought a few small artifacts off the *Monitor*'s waterlogged decks, including bottles, silverware, and china pieces. In 1983 they even brought up the ship's distinctive four-blade anchor. During the summer of 2002, the U.S. Navy successfully recovered the distinctive turret, which now is undergoing preservation at Virginia's Mariners' Museum.

Cape Hatteras Lighthouse
Cape Point, Buxton
(252) 995-4474

The nation's tallest brick lighthouse, this black-and-white-striped beacon is open for free tours from early spring through the fall and is well worth the climb. It contains 268 spiraling stairs and an 800,000-candlepower electric light that rotates every 7.5 seconds. Its bright beacon can be seen more than 20 miles out to sea.

The original Cape Hatteras Lighthouse was built in 1803 to guard the area known as the "Graveyard of the Atlantic," but it was poorly designed with an underpowered light. One sea captain dubbed it the "worst light in the world." Standing 90 feet tall and sitting about 300 yards south of its current site, the first lighthouse at Cape Hatteras was fueled with whale oil, which didn't burn bright enough to illuminate the dark shoals surrounding it. This was an invitation to disaster, as just off this eastern edge of the Outer Banks, the warm Gulf Stream meets the cold Labrador Current, creating dangerous undercurrents around the ever-shifting offshore shoals. Erosion weakened the structure over the years. Finally, in 1861 retreating Confederate soldiers took the light's lens with them, denying the Union Navy the light's harboring safety but also leaving Hatteras Island in the dark.

The lighthouse that's still standing was erected in 1870 on a floating foundation and cost $150,000 to build. More than 1.25 million Philadelphia baked bricks are included in the 180-foot-tall tower. A special Fresnel lens that refracts the light increases its visibility.

During the summer of 1999, the National Park Service moved the lighthouse 1,500 feet inland, at a cost to the federal government of $12 million. This move was literally in the nick of time, as multiple hurricanes shortly thereafter seriously eroded the coastline near the old location.

Staffed entirely by volunteers, the Cape Hatteras Lighthouse is open all the way to the outdoor tower at the top. The breathtaking view is like looking off the roof of a 20-story building. And the free adventure is well worth the effort. The climb is strenuous, so don't attempt to carry children in your arms or in kid carriers. Climbing is permitted from 9:00 A.M. to 5:00 P.M. from Good Friday through Columbus Day. Hours are subject to change, so call first. Nearby structures originally housing the lightkeepers and their families now house a fascinating museum of the history of both the lighthouse and Cape Hatteras itself.

Frisco Native American Museum
NC 12, Frisco
(252) 995-4440

This fascinating museum on the sound side of NC 12 in Frisco is stocked with unusual collections of Native American artifacts gathered over the past 65 years plus numerous other fascinating collections unrelated to native peoples. Opened by Carl and Joyce Bornfriend, the museum boasts of one of the most significant collections of artifacts from the Chiricahua people and has displays of the work of other Native American tribes from across the country, ranging from the days of early man to modern time. Hopi drums, pottery, kachinas, weapons, and jewelry abound in homemade display cases with hand-lettered placards.

Many visitors are astonished at the variety, amount, and eclectic appeal of the displays in the museum. A souvenir gift shop offers everything including antiques, books, Civil War uniforms, and an amazing Wedgwood china collection. Native craft items made by about 40 artisans from across the country are also available for sale. Other unusual collectibles for sale include prints of Lincoln and an old blanket that belonged to Lincoln, a basket from General George Washington, and political memorabilia. A small military section in the museum displays Revolutionary and Civil War items, such as uniforms, medals, and trench art made from copper shell cases.

The book section and natural history center have recently been expanded. With advance notice, the Bornfriends will give guided tours of their museum and lectures for school and youth groups. Call for prices. The museum property also includes outdoor nature trails through three acres of woods, with a screened-in pavilion, a large pond, and three bridges on the land. Hours are 11:00 A.M. to 5:00 P.M. Tuesday through Sunday, year-round. Admission is $2.00 per person, $5.00 per family, or $1.50 for seniors.

ACCOMMODATIONS

Rates vary dramatically from one area of the Outer Banks to another, from oceanfront rooms to those across the highway, between in- and off-season times, and especially depending on the amenities offered with each unit. In general, however, fall, winter, and early spring prices are at least one-third lower than midsummer rates—often as little as $25 per night. The most expensive season, of course, is between mid-June and mid-August, when rates in general range from $50 a night for two people with two double beds to more than $150 per night in some of the fancier establishments.

As this is a major resort and vacation area for the entire mid-Atlantic coastal region, finding hotels and motels is absolutely no problem. Nearly every major national and regional chain has at least some presence here, located conveniently on NC 12, which runs the length of the Outer Banks.

Many hotels and motels honor AARP and other discounts. And children stay free with paying adults in many of these accommodations.

Cape Hatteras Motel $$$
NC 12, Buxton
(252) 995-5611, (800) 995-0711
When you arrive in Buxton, you'll see the Cape Hatteras Motel situated on both sides of the road. Owners Carol and Dave Dawson maintain this motel, parts of which have been here for more than 34 years. The 11 motel rooms and 23 units with kitchens are popular with anglers, surfers, and folk who just plain enjoy Hatteras Island's beaches. Windsurfers especially like this facility because it is near some of the best windsurfing conditions on the East Coast at nearby Canadian Hole.

Most of the units with kitchens sleep up to six comfortably and offer double as well as queen- and king-size beds. The newer, more modern town houses are located on the ocean. The motel has an outdoor swimming pool and spa. The motel's position at the north end of Buxton is not only convenient to pristine uncrowded beaches but also is near restaurants and services, making this a very popular place in the busy summer season.

Most of the units rent weekly during the season, but nightly rentals also may be available, depending on supply. Book reservations early. Cape Hatteras Motel is open year-round.

Falcon Motel $$
NC 12, Buxton
(252) 995-5968, (800) 635-6911
The Falcon offers some of the best prices for accommodations on the Outer Banks. The traditional Outer Banks–style rooms here appeal to family-oriented guests who appreciate moderate prices, accommodations with character, and the peaceful environment of Hatteras Island. The Falcon, owned by Chris and Tracy Latta, is known for its attention to detail, which is apparent in the clean, well-maintained rooms and grounds.

This motel includes 35 units with 30 rooms and 5 fully equipped apartments, all at ground level. Nonsmoking rooms are available. The spacious rooms have a light, airy feel and include cable TV with HBO. Many rooms have refrigerators and microwaves. Some have wooden deck chairs on a wide, covered porch. Park right outside your door.

Guests have use of the swimming pool and boat ramp as well, and you'll find a shaded picnic area with barbecue grills amid mature oak trees, away from the road. The landscaping includes martin and bluebird houses and planted shrubs and flowers that attract the local bird population. Don't miss seeing the osprey platform on the sound-side area beyond the trees.

The Falcon Motel is located in the heart of Buxton within easy walking distance of several shops and restaurants. The beach is a short walk away.

The apartments generally rent on a weekly basis. The motel is open from March through mid-December.

RESTAURANTS

Just as with the hotel situation, finding a meal on the Outer Banks is not difficult at all. Although the area is seriously crowded during the school vacation months of summer, and many of these establishments close up completely during winter, there is still quite a variety to choose from at any time of year. It is also comforting to note that the fast-food and midlevel chains have made little headway on the Outer Banks, where the independent and mom-and-pop establishments still rule. Here are a few places we recommend.

Down Under Restaurant & Lounge $$–$$$
Waves, off NC 12
(252) 987–2277

Water views are spectacular at this Australian-style restaurant. You can sit at the bar in this warm and friendly eatery and watch the sun set over the sound. Or you can enjoy your meal in the dining room and see the pelicans glide over Atlantic waves or the moon rise over the dark sea. Decorated with authentic Australian art and memorabilia, Down Under is one of a kind on the Outer Banks. Lunch specialties include the Great Australian bite, similar to an Aussie burger, made with hamburger, a fried egg, grilled onions, cheese, and bacon. Spicy fish burgers, Vegemite sandwiches, and marinated chicken sandwiches are good authentic options too. Kangaroo, a delicious meat and very popular at Down Under, is imported from Australia for 'roo stew, 'roo burgers, and kangaroo curry.

Dinner selections include Down Under shrimp stuffed with jalapeño peppers and cream cheese and wrapped in bacon. We also enjoy a side order of the foot-high onion rings and a Foster's lager. Happy hour is from 3:00 to 6:00 P.M. daily. Steamed, spiced shrimp are 15 cents each. Parents will appreciate the children's menu, and kids will appreciate the extraordinary decor. Everyone will enjoy the view. Down Under is open seven days a week for lunch and dinner from Memorial Day through Labor Day and Wednesday through Sunday in the off-season.

The Channel Bass $$–$$$
NC 12, Hatteras Village
(252) 986–2250

Well known for its fishing heritage, this canalside restaurant has been a Hatteras Village institution for more than 30 years. The Channel Bass has one of the largest menus on the beach, loaded with seafood platters, no-filler crab cakes, veal, and charbroiled steaks that the chefs slice in-house. An old family recipe is used for the hush puppies, and all the salad dressings are homemade. Make sure you try the homemade coconut, Key lime, and chocolate cream pies. A private dining room is available, and large groups are welcome. A nice selection of beer and wine is served; brown bagging is allowed. A children's menu is available. Dinner is served six nights a week from mid-March through November. The Channel Bass is closed on Sunday.

Sonny's Restaurant $$-$$$
NC 12, Hatteras Village
(252) 986-2922

This casual, family-run eatery serves breakfast and dinner seven days a week year-round. Breakfast begins at 6:00 A.M. for fishermen and includes hash browns, grits, Western omelets, ham and cheese omelets, and hot cakes—just a few of Sonny's specialties. There's a dinner buffet each evening, with an 18-item salad bar, breads, crabmeat bisque, soft-shell crabs in season, sea scallops, popcorn and regular shrimp, prime rib, clams, oysters, macaroni and cheese, fettuccine Alfredo, and desserts such as carrot and chocolate cakes, rice pudding, and a soft-serve ice-cream bar. Salad bar, soup, and dessert are all included in the price.

Regular menu items range from steaks to seafood to pasta. Alcoholic beverages aren't served here, but you're welcome to bring your own. Sonny even will provide frosty beer mugs and wineglasses for you. Senior citizen's and children's menus are offered. Reservations are accepted for large parties.

Getting There: Roanoke Island

Roanoke Island is just off the coast of mainland North Carolina, between the shoreline and Nags Head in the Outer Banks. The only road access is via US 64 east from I-95, through Rocky Mount, Williamston, and Plymouth, about 120 miles in total. East of Plymouth the road is primarily two-lane through very scenic and rural stretches, with very few amenities along the way. Deep canals line one or both sides of the road in places, so be extremely careful if you have to pull over for any reason.

MODERN TIMES

Roanoke Island today is a bustling community centered around the small town of Manteo and heavily oriented toward the tourists that flock in during the spring and summer heading for the Outer Banks beaches. Although wind, time, and tide have erased all original signs of the forts and redoubts, there are some signs indicating where they stood.

As soon as you cross the US 64/264 bridge onto the island from the mainland, look immediately to your right. A side road leads to a small park, where a small plot of raised land indicates the west wall of Fort Huger. The rest of the fort lies as far out as 300 feet into the sound, although at the time it was on dry land a good piece from the water. A narrow walkway south leads to the location of Fort Blanchard, although the walls have long ago washed away. Just down the street from this park is a small rest area, with signs indicating exactly where each fort on the island stood, along with a good description of the short battle.

The location of Fort Bartow is just off US 64, about 3 miles east of the rest stop. Turn right onto Burnside Road (just past the library), and take the right fork of the road about a quarter mile down. About another mile down the road you will pass Payne Road; the area from this point on was very heavily shelled, and live ordnance is still occasionally found. We strongly urge you not to go "relic hunting" here, for two reasons: First, it is all private property, and second, disturbing a potentially unstable artillery round can let you have a "Civil War experience" the hard way! Yes, a Parrott shell can still explode after 140-plus years, as too many have learned to their grief. Turn right onto Burnside Drive into the Burnside Forest subdivision, the site of Fort Bartow; again, no signs remain of the post.

Back out on US 64, travel southeast to the intersection with North Carolina Highway 345. A small park on NC 345 just south of the intersection contains the site of Fort Russell, and a historic marker next to a white picket fence gives the precise location. About a mile south of the intersection on NC 345, turn right onto Skyco Road and drive to the end. The beach in front of you is where Burnside's infantry landed the night of February 7, 1862.

POINTS OF INTEREST

Weirs Point and Fort Huger
North end of Roanoke Island, off US 64/264
At the Roanoke Island base of the bridge to Manns Harbor, Weirs Point is an attractive, easily accessible public beach on Croatan Sound. Free parking is available at the turnoff on Roanoke Island just before the end of the bridge. The brackish water is warm and shallow here. Sandy beaches are wide enough to picnic, sunbathe, or throw a Frisbee across.

About 300 yards north of Weirs Point, in 6 feet of water, lie the remains of Fort Huger. This was the largest Confederate fort on the island when Union troops advanced across the Outer Banks during the Civil War battles of 1862. The island has migrated quite a bit in the past 130 years. The fort used to sit securely on the north end on solid land.

Picnic benches, a Dare County information kiosk, and restrooms are provided at Weirs Point. Watch for stumps and broken stakes in the water. The tide also creeps up quickly, so beware of needing to move beach blankets away from its encroaching flow.

Outer Banks History Center
Roanoke Island Festival Park
(252) 473-2655
Next to the *Elizabeth II*, across from the Manteo Waterfront on Ice Plant Island, the Outer Banks History Center is the most remarkable repository of northeastern North Carolina chronicles collected in any place. More than 25,000 books, 4,500 official documents of the U.S. Coast Guard and the U.S. Life Saving Service, 25,000 photographs, 1,000 periodicals, 700 maps, and hundreds of audio and video recordings are housed in this state-supported

cultural site. Special collections include the David Stick Papers, the Frank Stick Collection, the Cape Hatteras National Seashore Library, the Cape Lookout National Seashore Oral History Collection, and the Aycock Brown Tourist Bureau Collection of 17,000 photographs. There are maps of the area more than 400 years old here.

Opened in 1988 on the right-hand side of the *Elizabeth II* visitor center building, the Outer Banks History Center includes a comfortable reading room with long tables for research and a gallery with rotating exhibits that are free to the public. North Carolina natives will enjoy exploring their own history here. Visitors will find the Outer Banks legacy equally enchanting.

Most of the collections included in this library belonged to Outer Banks historian David Stick, who still serves as an adviser to the history center and lives in Kitty Hawk. The author of many books on the Outer Banks, Stick gathered much of the information during his years of research and writing. Stick's father, also David Stick, helped found the Cape Hatteras National Seashore as part of the National Park Service.

Staffers at the history center are knowledgeable and happy to help anyone access the facility's vast resources. Journalists, history buffs, students, archaeologists, writers, and even interested tourists will find the stop well worth their time. The reading room is open year-round from 9:00 A.M. until 5:00 P.M. Monday through Friday. Gallery hours are 10:00 A.M. to 5:00 P.M. Monday through Friday, year-round. Call for weekend hours.

ACCOMMODATIONS

The Elizabethan Inn $$-$$$
US 64, Manteo
(252) 473-2101, (800) 346-2466
The Elizabethan Inn is a year-round resort facility with spacious shaded grounds, country manor charm and Tudor architecture that reflects the area's heritage. Only 7 miles from the beach, the hotel consists of three buildings providing 78 rooms,

efficiencies, and apartments, plus conference facilities, a health club, a gift shop, and a restaurant. Nonsmoking and wheelchair-accessible rooms are available. All rooms have cable TV with HBO, refrigerators, and direct-dial phones. Rooms are available with a king-size bed or two queen-size or standard double beds, and two rooms have whirlpool baths. All rooms are comfortable and well suited for a quiet, Roanoke Island–style vacation.

The Virginia Dare Restaurant, on the premises, offers a full menu year-round and a popular breakfast buffet daily during summer. The lobby is filled with interesting antiques, and a friendly staff makes you feel welcome. A small shop offers a selection of fine gifts plus local books, souvenirs, and personal items.

The inn's Nautics Hall Health and Fitness Center, the largest and most complete health club in the area, is available for guests of the inn. Guests may also use the small outdoor pool and a heated, competition-size indoor pool. Another nice touch: Guests have free use of bicycles to tour the nearby village or travel the paved bike path.

Inquire about special rate packages. The inn is open year-round.

RESTAURANTS

Weeping Radish Brew Pub $$–$$$
US 64, Manteo
(252) 473-1157

Located next to the Christmas Shop on the main highway in Manteo, this large Bavarian restaurant includes an outdoor beer garden, separate pub, children's playground, and two-story dining room. A European flavor prevails throughout. Traditional German meals include veal, sauerbraten, and a variety of sausages. Homemade noodles, also called spaetzle, and cooked red cabbage are flavorful side dishes offering unusual tastes you won't find elsewhere on the Outer Banks. Continental cuisine also is available.

The restaurant's name comes from the radish served in Bavaria as an accompaniment to beer. Cut in a spiral, it's sprinkled with salt and packed back together. The salt draws out the moisture and gives the radish the appearance of weeping. Beer isn't served with radishes here except by special request, but the brews are certainly the best part about this place. A microbrewery opened at the Weeping Radish in 1986 offering pure, fresh-malt German brews without chemical additives or preservatives. You can watch this "nectar of the gods" being brewed on-site. Or take home a pint or small keg to enjoy later. The Weeping Radish is open seven days a week for lunch and dinner in summer. Lunch is served daily in the off-season. Call for dinner hours.

Big Al's Soda Fountain & Grill $$–$$$
US 64, Manteo
(252) 473-5570

You can't miss Big Al's, across from the Christmas shop in downtown Manteo. Owners Vanessa and Allan Foreman were originally planning to open a little ice-cream parlor, but the concept expanded into a full-blown soda fountain and family restaurant. It's definitely a place to take the kids. With '50s decor and memorabilia, Big Al's is a great place to kick back and enjoy some good ol' American food and fountain treats.

Children's meals are available, and kids can check out the game room, with a pinball machine, video games, and a juke box. Big Al's serves lunch and dinner daily.

Waterfront Trellis $$$–$$$$
Waterfront, Manteo
(252) 473-1727

Overlooking Shallowbag Bay and the state ship, *Elizabeth II*, this is one of our favorite Manteo eateries where diners can watch boats on the water and see birds diving for fish. At this casual, relaxing restaurant with good service and equally admirable food, the lunch menu has delicious sandwiches and salads, hot soups, and an ever-changing specials board. We order the black beans and rice most frequently. All the dinners are excellent, especially the mixed grill of shrimp and scallop kabobs, filet mignon, and tuna. Caesar salads are a cool alternative on warm summer evenings. And the steam bar showcases local seafood of all sorts.

Historic photos lining the walls will remind you of what Manteo's waterfront looked like in the early days. And since this restaurant is less than a 10-minute drive from The Lost Colony amphitheater, it's a good place to take in an early meal before the outdoor drama begins. Beer, wine, and champagne are available, and brown bagging (carrying in your own alcohol) is allowed. A children's menu is provided. Waterfront Trellis is closed in January but serves lunch and dinner daily the rest of the year and also offers a Sunday brunch.

**The Green Dolphin
Restaurant & Pub**   **$$-$$$**
**Sir Walter Raleigh Street, Manteo
(252) 473-5911**
This downtown Manteo eatery has been a popular pub for more than two decades. It's casual and dark inside, with wooden booths and tables fashioned from the hatch covers taken off old ships. Other nautical memorabilia lines the walls, and a long bar stretches along the back of the restaurant. Food here is simple, cheap, and satisfying. Hamburgers, she-crab soup, crab cakes, lasagna, manicotti, Italian sausage, and french fries are just a few of the offerings served for lunch and dinner. Appetizers and desserts also are available, and the pub serves pizzas and small-fry portions for the kids. The Green Dolphin is open year-round Tuesday through Saturday.

Getting There: New Bern

New Bern is located in south-central North Carolina and easily accessed via US 70, which intersects I-95 (exit 97) about 70 miles northwest of the city. US 70 continues on through Morehead City and ends at the intersection with NC 12 in the small town of Atlantic. NC 12 then continues north and east through the Outer Banks, with two ferry rides along the way. From the south, U.S. Highway 17 comes in from Wilmington and Jacksonville.

MODERN TIMES

New Bern today is a pleasant, small riverside city, with a decidedly southern European look about it. Originally founded by Swiss and German immigrants in 1710, it is the second oldest city in North Carolina. Downtown is undergoing an urban revival, and the major local industry is related to tourism and water sports. Literally everywhere are historic markers and signs attesting to its long history, and a slew of historic houses and museums dot the area, besides the Civil War–related venues we've listed below.

We cannot emphasize enough what a nice place this is: The town is beautiful, the people are quite friendly and helpful to the lost and clueless (we know this firsthand, unfortunately), and the only complaints we consistently heard were about the badly timed stoplights (which really are atrocious) and the lack of "big city" clubs and bars.

POINTS OF INTEREST

**Dixon-Stevenson House
609 Pollock Street, New Bern
(252) 514–4900, (800) 767–1560**
Erected in 1828 on a lot that was originally a part of Tryon Palace's garden, the Dixon-Stevenson House epitomizes New Bern's lifestyle in the first half of the 19th century, when the town was a prosperous port and one of the state's largest cities.

The house, built for a New Bern mayor, is a fine example of neoclassic architecture. Its furnishings, reflecting the Federal period, reveal the changing tastes of early America. At the rear of the house is a garden with seasonal flowers, all in white. When Union troops occupied New Bern during the Civil War, the house was converted to a regimental hospital.

First Presbyterian Church
418 New Street, New Bern
(252) 637-3270

The oldest continually used church building in New Bern, First Presbyterian was built in 1819–22 by local architect and builder Uriah Sandy. The congregation was established in 1817. The Federal-style church is similar to many built around the same time in New England but is unusual in North Carolina. Like that of nearby Christ Episcopal Church, the steeple on First Presbyterian is a point of reference on the skyline. The church was used as a Union hospital and lookout post during the Civil War, and the initials of soldiers on duty in the belfry can still be seen carved in the walls. Visitors are welcome to tour the church between 9:00 A.M. and 2:00 P.M. weekdays.

Bellair Plantation and Restoration
1100 Washington Post Road, New Bern
(252) 637-3913

The last and largest brick plantation country house of the 18th century in North Carolina, the Bellair Plantation (circa 1734) is a majestic three-story brick building approached from North Carolina Highway 43 North by two long driveways, one lined by lavish old cedars. Georgian handcrafted woodwork greets visitors at the imposing eight-paneled door and continues through the main rooms. Original family furnishings are still in the house, probably because Bellair was specifically guarded from harm during the Civil War by order of Major General Ambrose Burnside of the North. The written order, dated March 20, 1862, still hangs on the wall at Bellair. The basement holds the cooking fireplaces with tools and ironworks of the period.

Cedar Grove Cemetery
Queen and George Streets, New Bern

If you're one of those people who loves wandering through old graveyards, you'll not want to miss this one. Statuary and monuments beneath Spanish moss–draped trees mark burial traditions from the earliest days of our nation. One smallish obelisk lists the names of nine children in one family who all died within a two-year time span. The city's monument to its Confederate dead and the graves of 70 soldiers are also here. The cemetery's main gate features a shell motif, with an accompanying legend that says if water drips on you as you enter, you will be the next to arrive by hearse.

ACCOMMODATIONS

All hotels and bed-and-breakfasts accept most major credit cards.

Palace Motel $
1901 Martin Luther King Boulevard
New Bern
(252) 638-1151

A basic, no-real frills establishment, the low-cost Palace Motel sits a bit off from the "main drag." There are 66 rooms here, all of which have the usual amenities, and a small but clean pool.

Sheraton Grand New Bern $$$$
1 Bicentennial Park, New Bern
(252) 638-3585, (800) 326-3745

With a total of 153 rooms and 19 suites, the five-story-tall Sheraton is not only New Bern's largest hotel but also one of its nicest. Modeled in the style of the old Southern grand hotels, the grounds are immaculately gardened, an adjacent marina provides a scenic view of the Trent River waterfront, and an in-house restaurant offers both fine dining and a decent wine list. All the expected amenities of a truly grand hotel are present, updated to include such niceties as an exercise room and a jogging/nature trail through the extensive landscaped grounds.

RESTAURANTS

Clementine's $$-$$$
104 Marina Drive, Fairfield Harbour
(252) 637-2244

This is a great place to end a day. Overlooking the Northwest Creek Marina at

Fairfield Harbour, this hospitable establishment offers sunsets, refreshing beverages, and casual dining on deck or inside. The menu offers a nice range of fare from light supper options such as burgers, salads, soups, or a terrific Reuben to Cajun-style shrimp Creole, New York strip steak, or Texas ribs. Board specials are announced nightly. A variety of sandwiches, soups, and salads are also available for lunch. Reservations are not accepted. Dinner is served daily; lunch is offered Monday through Friday, with a brunch on Sunday.

The Chelsea $$$
335 Middle Street, New Bern
(252) 637-5469
The Chelsea is exactly the kind of restaurant we are always looking for—in a building with an interesting architecture or history (in this case it's a circa 1912 brick building that housed the drugstore where Pepsi-Cola was invented) with a well-trained head chef who likes to experiment with eclectic cuisine. "Eclectic" is the operative term here, showing influences of French, German, Cajun, and Asian traditions, fused with traditional American fare. A very interesting seafood gratin is our suggested appetizer, a baked blend of seafood, herbs, minced vegetables, and cheeses on toast. Fresh pecan-crusted catfish topped with Cajun meunière sauce is one example of the unusual entrees here, and an in-house pastry chef provides a changing selection of desserts daily. The wine list runs a bit too much toward the lighter (weight and quality) Californias, but any place that keeps Guinness, Bass, and Newcastle Brown on tap can't be all bad! We do heartily recommend the Chelsea, to the point that it would be worth driving out of your way to enjoy.

*Should my demand be refused,
I cannot be responsible for the fate
of your command.*

Lieutenant General Nathan
Bedford Forrest of the Confederacy, at Fort Pillow

Getting There: Beaufort and Morehead City

Fort Macon is on the narrow Bogue Banks, also called Atlantic Beach, across Bogue Sound from Morehead City. From New Bern, US 70 is a fast, four-lane highway straight to Morehead City. Just past the central portion of the city, turn right (south) onto 23rd Street and go over the bridge to Atlantic Beach. Turn left (east) onto North Carolina Highway 58 and go about 3 miles. Here, on the right side of the road, is a historic marker indicating where some of the Union artillery redoubts were located. Just ahead about a mile is the well-marked entrance to Fort Macon.

POINTS OF INTEREST

Fort Macon State Park
MP 0, East Fort Macon Road (NC 58)
Atlantic Beach
(252) 726-3775
Fort Macon State Park, at Milepost 0 on the east end of Bogue Banks, is North Carolina's most visited state park, and with around 1.4 million visitors each year, it is the Crystal Coast's most visited attraction. Initially the fort served to protect the channel and Beaufort Harbor against attacks from the sea. Today the danger of naval attack is remote, but during the 18th and 19th centuries this region was very vulnerable. The need for defense was clearly illustrated in 1747, when Spanish raiders captured Beaufort, and again in 1782, when the British took over the port town.

Construction of Fort Dobbs, named for Governor Arthur Dobbs, began here in 1756 but was never completed. In 1808-09 Fort Hampton, a small masonry fort, was built to guard the inlet. The fort was abandoned shortly after the War of 1812 and by 1825 had been swept into the inlet.

The fort was deactivated after 1877 and then regarrisoned by state troops in 1898 for the Spanish-American War. It was abandoned again in 1903, was not used in World War I, and was offered for sale in

1923. An Act of Congress in 1924 gave the fort and the surrounding land to the state of North Carolina to be used as a public park. The park, which is more than 400 acres, opened in 1936 and was North Carolina's first functioning state park.

At the outbreak of World War II, the army leased the park from the state and, once again, manned the fort to protect a number of important nearby facilities. In 1944 the fort was returned to the state, and the park reopened the following year.

Today Fort Macon State Park offers the best of two worlds: beautiful, easily accessible beaches for recreation and a historic fort for exploration. Visitors enjoy the sandy beaches, a seaside bathhouse and restrooms, a refreshment stand, designated fishing and swimming areas, and picnic facilities with outdoor grills. A short nature trail winds through dense shrubs and over low sand dunes. The park is abundant with wildlife, including herons, egrets, warblers, sparrows, and other animals.

The fort itself is a wonderful place to explore with a self-guided tour map or with a tour guide. A museum and bookstore offer exhibits to acquaint you with the fort and its history. The fort and museum are open daily year-round. Fort tours are guided through late fall. Reenactments of fort activities are scheduled periodically from spring to fall. Talks on the Civil War and natural history and a variety of nature walks are conducted year-round. The fort is open daily from 9:00 A.M. to 5:30 P.M. The fort office is open Monday through Friday from 8:00 A.M. to 5:00 P.M.

Carteret County Historical Society/ The History Place
1008 Arendell Street, Morehead City
(252) 247–7533

In 1985 the Carteret County Historical Society was given the old Camp Glenn School building, circa 1907, which had served the community first as a school and later as a church, a flea market, and a print shop. The society moved the building from its earlier location to Wallace Drive, facing the parking lots of Carteret Community College and the Crystal Coast Civic Center, just off Arendell Street in Morehead City. The members renovated the building and created a museum to show visitors and residents how life used to be in Carteret County.

There are rotating exhibits with emphasis on the area's Native American heritage, schools, businesses, and homes. The museum houses the society's research library, including an impressive Civil War collection, that is available to those interested in genealogy and history. The museum conducts occasional genealogy workshops. Monthly exhibits feature area artists, and there is a gift shop. The museum is open Tuesday through Saturday from 10:00 A.M. until 4:00 P.M. There is no admission charge.

"When you were near enough for our rifles to do good work we commenced pumping lead. [When the Federal troopers closed in] we dropped our carbines (which were strung by a strap across the shoulder), drew our navy sixes, one in each hand—we had discharged sabres as fighting weapons—then we fed you on lead so fast and furious you whirled your backs to us."

Unidentified Confederate cavalry trooper, on Lieutenant General Nathan Bedford Forrest's defensive fighting technique, to his Union captor

ACCOMMODATIONS

Although Fort Macon directly guarded and is just across the sound from Beaufort, the closest amenities accessible by land are in Morehead City. There is a choice of several chain motels, all offering the usual amenities, on Arendell Street, the "main drag" of the business district there.

RESTAURANTS

Like the motel situation, nearly all the usual fast-food and midlevel dining establishments are clustered together in Morehead City on Arendell Street. Besides these, we can recommend one locally owned establishment.

Bistro by the Sea
Restaurant & Banquet Room $$$
4031 Arendell Street, Morehead City
(252) 247-2777
Bistro by the Sea, a favorite of locals for both food and hospitality, opened in its current location (next to the Hampton Inn) in 1997. The Bistro celebrates its space, like moving into a dream house, after five cramped years in the restaurant's old 1,000-square-foot area. Chef-owner Tim Coyne serves reliably wonderful dinner entrees using very fresh vegetables, seafood, and tasty cuts of beef. Seafood entrees vary nightly according to freshness and availability. Other than seafood specialties, we also recommend the chargrilled filet mignon or rib eye, liver in orange liqueur, or stir-fried chicken with rice and wontons. We also like the pasta creations, such as seafood-and-cheese-filled pasta shells, eggplant Parmesan, and capellini with pesto, vegetables, and scallops. Sandwiches are available along with a tempting selection of desserts. Bistro by the Sea has all alcohol permits, a piano and martini bar, and a cigar patio.

Getting There: Wilmington

Wilmington is at the southeast corner of North Carolina, at the end of Interstate 40 and only 40 miles east of the South Carolina border. I-40 intersects I-95 near Benson, about 75 miles north of Wilmington. An alternate route is US 17 paralleling the coast from Myrtle Beach to the west (72 miles) or Jacksonville (50 miles) to the east.

All the military action took place south of the city itself, near where the Cape Fear River meets the Atlantic Ocean. U.S. Highway 421 south out of downtown will take you straight to Carolina Beach (Fort Fisher), while the bare remains of other fortifications can be found on Oak Island, in Southport, at Caswell Beach Road (Fort Caswell), and at the corner of Davis and Bay Streets (Fort Johnson). A ferry from Carolina Beach will take you straight into Southport, or it can be accessed via North Carolina Highway 133 south from US 17, west of the river.

MODERN TIMES

Wilmington today is a fair-size city of about 95,000, almost all working in some facet of support for the tourism industry, the leading employer of the area. A surprising number of movies and television shows have been filmed here, prompting local wags to dub the place "Wilmywood."

As in most other places around the South, not many period structures remain from the war, but a few have been preserved and can be toured.

POINTS OF INTEREST

Fort Fisher State Historic Site
US 421, south of Kure Beach
(910) 458-5538
Fort Fisher was the last Confederate stronghold to fall to Union forces during the War between the States. It was the linchpin of the Confederate Army's Cape Fear Defense System, which included Forts Caswell, Anderson, and Johnson and a series of batteries. Largely due to the tenacity of its defenders, the port of Wilmington was never entirely sealed by the Union blockade until January 1865. The Union bombardment of Fort Fisher was the heaviest naval demonstration in history up to that time.

Today all that remains are the earthworks, the largest in the South. The rest of the fort has been claimed by the ocean. However, a fine museum, uniformed demonstrations, and reenactments make Fort Fisher well worth a visit. Don't miss the underwater archaeology exhibit, Hidden beneath the Waves, housed in a small outbuilding beside the parking lot. Thirty-minute guided tours allow you to walk the earthworks, and slide programs take place every half hour. The Cove, a tree-shaded picnic area across the road, overlooks the ocean and makes an excellent place to relax or walk. However, swimming here is discouraged due to dangerous currents and underwater hazards.

Since Fort Fisher is an archaeological site, metal detectors are prohibited. Museum hours are 9:00 A.M. to 5:00 P.M. Monday through Saturday and 1:00 to 5:00 P.M. Sunday with shorter winter, off-season hours. It is open year-round, and admission is free (donations are requested). The site, about 19 miles south of Wilmington, was once commonly known as Federal Point. The ferry from Southport is an excellent and time-saving way to get there from Brunswick County.

Fort Caswell
Caswell Beach Road, Caswell Beach
(910) 278-9501

Considered one of the strongest forts of its time, Fort Caswell originally encompassed some 2,800 acres at the east end of Oak Island. Completed in 1838, the compound consisted of earthen ramparts enclosing a roughly pentagonal brick-and-masonry fort and the citadel. Caswell proved to be so effective a deterrent during the Civil War that it saw little action. Supply lines were cut after Fort Fisher fell to Union forces in January 1865, so before abandoning the fort, the Caswell garrison detonated the powder magazine, heavily damaging the citadel and surrounding earthworks. What remains of the citadel is essentially unaltered and is maintained by the Baptist Assembly of North Carolina, which owns the property. A more expansive system of batteries and a seawall were constructed during the war-wary years from 1885 to 1902. Fort Caswell is open for self-guided visits Monday through Friday 8:00 A.M. to 5:00 P.M. and Saturday 8:00 A.M. to 4:00 P.M. Admission is $3.00. The fort is closed to tours from Memorial Day to Labor Day.

Fort Johnson
Davis and Bay Streets, Southport
(910) 457-7927

The first working military installation in the state and reputedly the world's smallest, Fort Johnson was commissioned in 1754 to command the mouth of the Cape Fear River. A bevy of tradespeople, fishermen, and river pilots soon followed, and so the town of Smithville was born (renamed Southport in 1887). During the Civil War, Confederate forces added Fort Johnson to their Cape Fear Defense System, which included Forts Caswell, Anderson, and Fisher. Fort Johnson's fortifications no longer stand, but the site is redolent with memories of those times. The remaining original structures house personnel assigned to the Sunny Point Military Ocean Terminal, an ordnance depot a few miles north.

Cape Fear Museum
814 Market Street, Wilmington
(910) 341-4350

For an overview of the cultural and natural histories of the Cape Fear region from prehistory to the present, the Cape Fear Museum, established in 1898, stands unsurpassed. A miniature re-creation of the second battle of Fort Fisher and a remarkable scale model of the Wilmington waterfront, circa 1863, are of special interest. The Michael Jordan Discovery Gallery, including a popular display case housing many of the basketball star's personal items, is an interactive natural history exhibit for the entire family. The Discovery Gallery includes a crawl-through beaver lodge, Pleistocene-era fossils, and an entertaining Venus flytrap model you can feed with stuffed "bugs." Children's activities, videos, special events, and acclaimed touring exhibits contribute to making the Cape Fear Museum not only one of the primary repositories of local history but also a place where learning is fun.

The museum is open Tuesday through Saturday 9:00 A.M. to 5:00 P.M. and Sunday 1:00 to 5:00 P.M. and is wheelchair-accessible. Admission is $5.00 for adults 18 to 65, $1.00 for children 3 to 17, and $4.00 for college students with valid ID and seniors older than 65. Children younger than 3 and Museum Associates are admitted free. Admission is free to all on the first and third Sundays of each month.

First Baptist Church
411 Market Street, Wilmington
(910) 763-2471

This is Wilmington's tallest church. The congregation dates to 1808, and construction of the redbrick building began in 1859. The church was not completed until 1870 because of the Civil War, when Confederate and Union forces in turn used the higher steeple as a lookout. Its architecture is Early English Gothic Revival with hints of Richardson Romanesque in its varicolored materials and its horizontal mass relieved by the verticality of the spires, with their narrow, gabled vents. Inside, the pews, galleries, and ceiling vents are of native heart pine. Being the first Baptist church in the region, this is the mother church of many other Baptist churches in Wilmington. The church offices occupy an equally interesting building next door, the Conoley House (1859), which exhibits such classic Italianate elements as frieze vents and brackets and fluted wooden columns.

Poplar Grove Plantation
10200 US 17, Scotts Hill
(910) 686-9518

The 1850 Greek Revival house was the focus of this 628-acre plantation that was supported by as many as 64 slaves prior to the Civil War. Today costumed guides lead visitors and recount its history. Skills important to daily 19th-century life, such as weaving, smithery, and basketry, are frequently demonstrated. A restaurant and country store add to Poplar Grove's attraction, as do the many events held here throughout the year, including Halloween hayrides and the Down Home Antique Fair in May. Listed on the National

Register of Historic Places, Poplar Grove Plantation is 8 miles outside Wilmington on US 17 at the Pender County line. It is open to the public Monday through Saturday 9:00 A.M. to 5:00 P.M. and Sunday noon to 5:00 P.M. Fees are $7.00 for adults, $6.00 for senior citizens and military personnel with active IDs, and $3.00 for students ages 6 to 15.

Wrightsville Beach Museum of History
303 West Salisbury Street
Wrightsville Beach
(910) 256-2569

A recent attraction on Wrightsville Beach, this museum is housed in the Myers cottage, one of the oldest cottages on the beach (built in 1907). The museum presents beach history and lifeways through permanent exhibits featuring a scale model of the oldest built-up section of the beach, photos, furniture, artifacts, a slide show, and recorded oral histories, plus rotating exhibits on loggerhead turtles, surfing, the Civil War, shipwrecks, hurricanes, and beach nightlife at such bygone attractions as the Lumina Pavilion. The museum is open Tuesday through Friday 10:00 A.M. to 4:00 P.M., Saturday noon to 5:00 P.M., and Sunday 1:00 to 5:00 P.M. Admission is $3.00 for adults, children under 12 are free. Upon crossing the drawbridge, bear left at the WELCOME TO WRIGHTSVILLE BEACH sign; the museum is on the right near the volleyball courts beyond the fire station.

Old Brunswick Town State Historic Site
Off NC 133, Southport
(910) 371-6613

At this site stood the first successful permanent European settlement between Charleston and New Bern. It was founded in 1726 by Roger and Maurice Moore (who recognized an unprecedented real estate opportunity in the wake of the Tuscarora War, 1711–13), and the site served as a port and political center. Russelborough, home of two royal governors, once stood nearby. In 1748 the settlement was attacked by Spanish privateers, who were soundly

Confederate General
Pierre Gustave Toutant Beauregard

Two generations of Southern men are saddled with the middle name "Beauregard" in tribute to this immortal man; perhaps no other single Confederate officer so completely epitomized the aristocratic "gentleman officer." Beauregard was born in St. Bernard Parish, Louisiana, on May 28, 1818, a true Creole who could speak French before English. He graduated second in his class at West Point in 1838, going on to help build the system of fortifications along the Gulf Coast and various command positions in and around New Orleans. During the Mexican-American War he served with a conspicuous flair,

winning two promotions for gallantry as well as suffering two slight wounds. Immediately before the outbreak of hostilities, he was appointed superintendent of West Point but lost the post a few days later when he made it clear that he was not about to turn his back on a seceding Louisiana.

Upon resigning his U.S. Army commission in February 1861, he was almost immediately given a Confederate brigadier general's commission and shortly placed in command of the Charleston defenses. There, on April 12, 1861, he directed the "opening shots" of

---

defeated in a surprise counterattack by the Brunswick settlers. A painting of Christ presented to the People (*Ecce Homo*), reputedly 400 years old, was among the Spanish ship's plunder and now hangs in St. James Episcopal Church in Wilmington. At Brunswick Town in 1765, one of the first instances of armed resistance to the British Crown occurred in response to the Stamp Act. In time, the upstart upriver port of Wilmington superseded Brunswick. In 1776 the British burned Brunswick, and in 1862 Fort Anderson was built there to help defend Port Wilmington. Until recently, occasional church services were still held in the ruins of St. Philip's Church. The other low-lying ruins and Fort Anderson's earthworks may not be visually impressive, but the stories told about them by volunteers dressed in period garb are interesting, as is the museum.

Admission to the historic site is free. Hours are 10:00 A.M. to 4:00 P.M. Tuesday through Saturday. From Wilmington, take NC 133 about 18 miles to Plantation Road. Signs will direct you to the site (exit left), which lies close to Orton Plantation Gardens.

Orton Plantation Gardens
Off NC 133, Southport
(910) 371-6851

This property represents one of the region's oldest historically significant residences in continuous use. The family names associated with it make up the very root and fiber of Cape Fear's history. Built in 1725 by the imperious "King" Roger Moore, founder of Brunswick Town, the main residence at Orton Plantation underwent several expansions to become the archetype of Old Southern elegance. It

the war against Fort Sumter, commanded then by Major Robert Anderson of the U.S. Army, Beauregard's close friend and artillery instructor at West Point. His next command was over the Confederate forces in northern Virginia near Manassas Junction, where he commanded the main battle line in a great victory over superior Union forces on June 1. One of five brigadier generals subsequently promoted to full general (the others being Samuel Cooper, Albert Sydney Johnston, Robert E. Lee, and Joseph Eggleston Johnston), he was soon sent west after feuding with both President Jefferson Davis and his War Department.

At Shiloh, Beauregard served as second-in-command to A. S. Johnston, assuming command of the Confederate Army of the Mississippi upon Johnston's death. A few months later, too ill to command, he turned over his command to General Braxton Bragg while he recovered, but Davis personally blocked his return to command later. He spent most of the rest of the war in command of the Carolinas and Georgia coastal defenses, briefly serving alongside Lee at Petersburg, and ended up serving under J. E. Johnston in his last stand in the Carolinas.

So great was Beauregard's reputation here and abroad that he was offered command of both the Romanian and Egyptian armies, both of which he refused. He lived out the rest of his life in Louisiana, working in several administrative posts, and died in New Orleans on February 20, 1893.

survived the ravages of the Civil War despite being used as a Union hospital after the fall of Fort Fisher. Thereafter it stood abandoned for 19 years until it was purchased and refurbished by Colonel Kenneth McKenzie Murchison of the Confederacy. In 1904 the property passed to the Sprunt family, related to the Murchisons by marriage, and the plantation gardens began taking shape. In 1915 the family built Luola's Chapel, a Doric structure of modest grandeur available today for meetings and private weddings.

ACCOMMODATIONS

Best Western Coast Line Inn $$-$$$$
503 Nutt Street, Wilmington
(910) 763-2800, (800) 617-7732
An unusually pleasant establishment, the Coast Line Inn has 53 rooms, each with a view of the waterfront. The usual amenities are enhanced by wireless Internet connections and coffeemakers in each room, and a nice touch is the continental breakfast placed outside your room in a basket each morning. Any establishment that makes it possible to eat breakfast and drink coffee without dressing any more so than I would at home gets extra points for quality! There are several decent restaurants within a short walking distance, and a waterfront bar and lounge offers a pleasant way to end the day.

Cabana De Mar Motel $$-$$$$
31 Carolina Avenue North
Carolina Beach
(910) 458-4456, (800) 333-8499
Decidedly more upscale than the usual "beach" motel, the Cabana De Mar is really built more along the lines of attractive

condominiums, with one- or two-bedroom suites available, all with kitchen facilities. The usual amenities are present, some rooms have unobstructed ocean views and private balconies, and decent restaurants and shopping are a short walk away.

Ocean Crest Motel $$-$$$$
1417 East Beach Drive, Oak Island
(910) 278-3333
Another very nice, clean, and decent ocean-side motel, with one- and two-bedroom suites with kitchen facilities and private balconies facing the ocean. All the usual amenities are present, and a fishing pier is right next door.

RESTAURANTS

Elijah's Restaurant $$-$$$
2 Ann Street, Wilmington
(910) 343-1448
In a beautiful location on the Cape Fear River waterfront, Elijah's offers genuine Low Country fare as well as Cajun-style seafood and steaks. There are really two restaurants in this one location: the outside oyster bar, which features alfresco deck seating, and the more formal inside dining room. Seafood, poultry, pasta, and beef dishes are all available, although we recommend simply selecting whatever is offered as the special of the day. Lunch, supper, and Sunday brunch are all offered, and the oyster bar remains open until 11:00 P.M. on weekends.

Front Street Brewery $$
9 North Front Street, Wilmington
(910) 251-1935
As you may note in this guide, we have a weakness for microbreweries, and Front Street turned out to be one of our favorites. A distinctly German-flavored establishment, the food ranges from light bar-food, such as sandwiches and salads, to very well-prepared steaks and seafood. As with any microbrewery, the beer is the main attraction, and the quality of the products here is excellent. Although there is a changing variety of

seasonal and fest beers, the house brews include a Wurzburg-style unfiltered Hefe Weissbier, a hoppy and slightly bitter Dusseldorf Alt, and a wonderful Irish-style malt stout.

The Brewery is open for lunch and supper seven days a week, closing at 10:00 P.M. Sunday, midnight Monday through Thursday, and a little later Friday and Saturday.

Big Daddy's Seafood Restaurant $$
202 K Avenue, Kure Beach
(910) 458-8622
A huge building (it can seat about 500) houses this local institution, which offers primarily seafood prepared in a variety of ways. A decidedly casual establishment, Big Daddy's tends to attract large numbers of local families with children, drawn by the all-you-can-eat, Low Country, family-style dining; an inexpensive all-you-can-eat salad bar; and the 1950s style Surf and Turf Supreme (beef tenderloin with split Alaskan king crab legs). Although this is an independent establishment, the entrance to the restaurant is through a Cracker Barrel Restaurant–style gift shop offering novelties and candy. Big Daddy's is almost impossible to miss, located at the only stoplight in Kure Beach.

Getting There: Averasborough

The Battle of Averasborough was fought a few miles northeast of Fayetteville, just off I-95 between Fayetteville and the intersection with I-40 near Benson. Very little of the battlefield remains untouched, but the initial point of contact is well marked. Take exit 65 off I-95 onto North Carolina Highway 82, and go north toward Godwin. About 1.2 miles past the U.S. Highway 301 intersection is a large historic marker on the left in a curve on the road. This marks Hardee's initial position, and the battle moved more or less northwest from this point about 2 miles.

About another half mile north on NC 82 is Lebanon, one of a handful of period structures in the area, which was used as a Confederate hospital during the brief battle.

Getting There: Bentonville

As a village, Bentonville has all but disappeared. The original area of battle covered about 6,000 acres; now all that remains is a small field, a museum, and a few historic markers scattered about the country roads.

Bentonville battlefield is located just off I-40 about 14 miles southeast of the intersection with I-95. Take exit 341 onto U.S. Highway 13 and go about a mile east into Newton Grove. Go around the courthouse square and take U.S. Highway 701 North, and drive about 2½ miles north to State Route 1008 (Goldsboro Road). Turn right, and the battlefield is about 2½ miles down the road.

POINT OF INTEREST

**Bentonville Battleground
State Historic Site
5466 Harper House Road, Four Oaks
(910) 594-0789**
A small museum houses a few artifacts collected from the battlefield, and across the road is a set of reconstructed trenches. The museum has a set of maps that depict fairly well how the battle unfolded, and a short film presentation gives a good account of the fight here. A special high-tech battlefield map uses 3,500 small lights to illustrate the movement of soldiers in coordination with a recorded battle description. This museum reopened in August 1999, after its first renovation since 1965. This site hosts a yearly, popular reenactment of the battle on the weekend in April closest to the battle date (April 19–21).

Next door to the museum is the Harper House, used as a Confederate hospital and partly restored to its wartime condition. It is kept locked, but the site manager will open it up for a tour on request. For those into the occult, we should mention that we have heard quite a few ghost stories about this house from the reenactor community; quite frankly, the image we have of what this place must have looked like as a wartime hospital, filled with amputees and other seriously wounded soldiers, is eerie enough.

In the woods behind the trenchline is a portion of surviving earthworks constructed by Slocum's men; a small path leads back to them. The museum has both a free driving-tour map and a book for sale about the battle; either (or both) are recommended in order to travel down the country roads east of the museum to find the actual battle-site markers (this site is on the extreme western edge of the actual battlefield). Be aware that most of the battlefield is now private property and not open for walking. In fact, this battlefield has been named as one of the most endangered from development in the nation.

The battlefield site is open 10:00 A.M. to 4:00 P.M. Tuesday through Saturday and 1:00 to 4:00 P.M. on Sunday. Admission is free, but donations are accepted (and encouraged).

ACCOMMODATIONS

As there are few, if any, amenities in Bentonville or the surrounding immediate area, we suggest you look for food and lodging in Raleigh, 35 miles northwest, which gives you the added benefit of being in the area of Bennett Place (see the Day Trip at the end of this chapter).

**Best Western Raleigh North $-$$
2715 Capital Boulevard (junction of U.S. Highway 1 bypass, US 64, and US 401 at the Beltline), Raleigh
(919) 872-5000**
This hotel maintains clean and efficient service. Popular with traveling business-people because of its reasonable rates, it is close to a number of restaurants, including the authentic Mexican El

Dorado, and is close to the Highwoods business park. It has a pool and 139 rooms, complimentary breakfast, and an open bar Tuesday and Wednesday evenings. It sits across the highway from the Parker Lincoln office building.

Crabtree Summit Hotel $-$$
3908 Arrow Drive, Raleigh
(919) 782-6868

Formerly the Comfort Suites at Crabtree, the Crabtree Summit offers 83 rooms, all with refrigerators, coffeemakers, and other amenities to make your stay a comfortable one. Some rooms are equipped with whirlpool baths. A weekday stay in any room gets you a full breakfast buffet and free van service to and from the airport. An outdoor pool provides a means for exercise and relaxation while away from home.

Sheraton Capital Center $$$$
421 South Salisbury Street, Raleigh
(919) 834-9900

The interior of this 17-story downtown hotel is one of the most elegant of any in the city, and its 350 rooms make it among the largest. It is located next to and is connected through the underground parking lot with the city's Civic Center and the BB&T York-Hannover skyscraper. It is a block from Memorial Auditorium and the City Market. The indoor pool features a whirlpool, and the Raleigh Plaza has business meeting facilities for groups ranging from 15 to 700.

RESTAURANTS

Big Ed's City Market $
City Market, Raleigh
(919) 836-9909

Fresh vegetables from the farmers' market make this restaurant's country cooking truly down-home. Leftovers are donated to the Raleigh Relief Rescue Mission daily. Breakfast is served Monday through Saturday, and lunch is served Monday through Friday.

Five Eighteen West $$-$$$
518 West Jones Street, Raleigh
(919) 829-2518

This culinary addition to downtown Raleigh opened with the established reputation of its sister restaurant, 411 West in Chapel Hill, preceding it. The former warehouse has been beautifully renovated to resemble a Roman piazza with terrazzo floors, wrought iron balconies, and a tromp l'oeil–sky ceiling. The menu offers Italian contemporary cuisine with fresh seasonal pastas, seafood, vegetarian dishes, and pizzettes, individual wood-fired pizzas. Try the grilled shrimp polenta or the vegetarian steak. Desserts are made daily in-house, and weekly specials are available. Reservations are not accepted, so enjoy a drink and the atmosphere at the handcrafted cherry bar. Before you know it, you'll be enjoying the food, too.

Captain Stanley's Calabash Seafood $$
3333 South Wilmington Street, Raleigh
(919) 779-7878

If you're willing to wait in line, sometimes a very long line, this is the place for inexpensive seafood. Calabash seafood, named for a North Carolina coastal town, is dipped in batter and then deep fried.

Day Trips

Bennett Place
4409 Bennett Memorial Road, Durham
(919) 383-4345

You don't have to be a Civil War buff to appreciate the significance of what occurred on the farm of James and Nancy Bennett in April 1865. It was in the Bennetts' home that two battle-fatigued adversaries—Joseph E. Johnston and William T. Sherman—met to work out a peaceful settlement. Their original agreement was nixed in the wake of hostilities surrounding Abraham Lincoln's assassination, but their talks continued

and eventually resulted in Johnston's surrender. It was the largest troop surrender
of the Civil War, ending the fighting in the
Carolinas, Georgia, and Florida.

The Bennett grandchildren lived on
the farm until 1890. A fire destroyed the
farmhouse and kitchen in 1921. The present buildings were reconstructed in the
1960s from Civil War sketches and early
photos. To get to Bennett Place, take the
Hillsborough Road exit off U.S. Highway
15/501 Bypass or Interstate 85, and follow
the signs. It's open from 10:00 A.M. to 4:00
P.M. Tuesday through Saturday. Call about
extended summer hours. Admission is
free, and you can picnic on the grounds.

North Carolina Museum of History
**5 East Edenton Street, Raleigh
(919) 715-0200**

This elegant building opened in 1994
across the street from the capitol. It contains four grand display areas for North
Carolina historical collections. You can
visit the state's Sports Hall of Fame, a collection on North Carolina women, another
on folk life, and a fourth that is a chronological history of the state. The museum
also has a gift shop filled with items from
North Carolina, most of them made in the
state. The museum's open, spacious
rooms make popular spots for government receptions. The collections include
more than 350,000 artifacts, photographs, and videos and the museum
offers hands-on activities for children.
Admission is free, and the museum is
open Tuesday through Saturday 9:00 A.M.
to 5:00 P.M. and Sunday noon to 5:00 P.M.

SOUTH CAROLINA: FIRST TO FIGHT

For many people, the Civil War in South Carolina means one thing: Charleston. And in one sense they are quite correct. While South Carolina was the first to secede and one of the last to be brought under the Union Army's control, only two relatively small battles were fought in the state outside the immediate Charleston area. In all, most of the combat in the state primarily revolved around the struggle for control of Charleston and the relatively weak resistance to Sherman's 1864 march through the middle part of the state. Ironically, less fighting occurred in this most politically radical of the Confederate states than did in Florida, an oft-forgotten "backwater" theater of the war.

BACKGROUND TO THE WAR IN SOUTH CAROLINA

It can be (and is) endlessly debated whether the Civil War was fought over the issue of slavery, primarily or otherwise, but the fact is that this divisive issue was at least a motivation for the earliest efforts at secession. John Caldwell Calhoun of South Carolina, while a U.S. senator from 1832 to 1843 and again from 1845 to 1850, agitated constantly for "nullification," the right of individual states to declare null and void and subsequently ignore any Federal law, rule, or regulation that conflicted with their original agreement to join the Union. This was a widely popular stance in the South, whose slave-holding major landowners felt constantly threatened by abolitionist movements in the northern, "free" states.

The argument that "the Civil War was about freeing the slaves" doesn't adequately explain what was going on politi-

cally in the United States before 1860. A thorough discussion of this would fill many volumes; for a well-researched and reasonable presentation, we suggest reading *Battle Cry of Freedom* by James McPherson. The first 300 pages give a good overview of this very complex time and introduce the major issues and personalities.

In oversimplified terms, the South as a whole was obsessed with the idea that the 10th Amendment to the Constitution (among other documents) gives the individual states ultimate control over most acts of the federal government, and this control includes the right to declare itself separate from the Union if its citizens so desire. The North as a whole was equally obsessed with the idea that the federal government reigns supreme over acts of the individual states and that the Union as an entity was inviolate; once entered, it could not be exited without, at a minimum, the express consent of the federal government. This line of argument had been going on in one form or another since shortly after the United States became a sovereign nation, reaching an early peak in the federalist versus antifederalist arguments of Alexander Hamilton and Patrick Henry.

Whatever the base cause, tensions were running so high by 1860 that the election of Abraham Lincoln was reason enough for South Carolina politicians to start calling for secession, literally within hours of the vote. A secession convention was called for in short order, meeting on December 18 and unanimously passing an Ordinance of Secession on December 20. The two-day delay in passing this measure was not due to any real opposition to the document but was necessary so that each of the 169 delegates could stand up in turn and bombastically grandstand about the "Yankee outrages."

"THE UNION IS DISSOLVED"

Minutes after the signing, the *Charleston Mercury* newspaper published a special edition proclaiming the new independence of South Carolina and expressing the hope that its Southern brethren would soon follow. The same thought occupied the Northern politicians, and Union military officials moved quickly to protect forts and installations around the Southern coastline.

Garrison commanders in Florida and South Carolina reacted swiftly to the War Department order (to protect their posts as best as possible, preferably without igniting a shooting war), gathering up their men in the strongest and easiest-to-defend of their forts and preparing for what could be a long siege. In Charleston, Major (later Major General) Robert Anderson abandoned the low-walled Fort Moultrie on Sullivan Island and moved his small Northern command to still-unfinished Fort Sumter, in the middle of the cold night of December 26. Before leaving, he "spiked" the guns of Fort Moultrie, making them unable to fire and useless, and burned most of the remaining supplies and equipment. As a final act of defiance, he ordered the post flagpole to be chopped down so that any of the assorted flags of secession would not fly from it.

Once inside Fort Sumter, Anderson was faced with a serious tactical situation; only 48 guns had been mounted in the 140 gun positions, and 27 of these guns were mounted en barbette atop the upper ramparts, where their crews would be exposed to hostile fire. In addition, he only had 84 officers and men to run the post and was responsible for housing and feeding another 43 civilian workers still attempting to complete construction of the fort. On the positive side, he had enough rations and supplies to last more than four months, even if he could not be resupplied.

The night after Anderson made his move, a group from the 1st Regiment of Rifles, one of the Charleston militias under Colonel (later Brigadier General) James Johnson Pettigrew, rowed out into Charleston Harbor and seized Castle Pinckney, one of the batteries that guarded Charleston Harbor. The only Union soldier present, Lieutenant Richard K. Meade, protested the invasion verbally and then got in his own rowboat and went off to Fort Sumter in a dark cloud over his "treatment" by Pettigrew. This was the first seizure of U.S. property by a seceded state and coldly indicated that this was not to be a happy separation. Meade tendered his resignation from the U.S. Army soon thereafter and joined the Confederate Army as an engineer. Pettigrew went on to greater glory in the Confederate Army of Northern Virginia, leading a brigade under Major General Henry Heth and then taking over this division in charging Cemetery Ridge on the third day at Gettysburg (the so-called Pickett's Charge). He was wounded in this disaster and again wounded 10 days later at the Battle of Falling Waters, that time mortally.

THE LULL BEFORE THE STORM

Through the rest of the winter of 1860–61, things were relatively quiet in Charleston. Confederates and Union alike worked to build up their defenses, the South Carolinians constructing, reinforcing, or rearming some 60 forts, batteries, and redoubts all around the harbor. Anderson worked on completing his post as best as possible with what workers and materials he had on hand—the U.S. government had entered into an uneasy agreement not to reinforce or resupply any of its besieged garrisoned forts in the South if they were in turn left unmolested.

Fort Sumter was a five-sided fort, 300 feet wide by 350 feet long, with walls about 40 feet high made of locally procured brick; it was built on an artificial island in the middle of Charleston Harbor. Construction began about 1828 on the main post to guard this major harbor. No natural land was sufficient upon which to build a strong fort upon in the harbor itself, so more than 70,000 tons of rock were dumped on a low sandbar to form a firm foundation. Construction progressed at a glacial pace; the post was still unfinished and most of the guns still unmounted when Anderson was forced to withdraw within its walls in December 1860.

THE OPENING SHOTS OF THE WAR

As the first months of 1861 faded away, Anderson and his men worked to mount what guns they could and waited for their masters in Washington to figure out how to get them all out of this mess. While talks were going on, the USS *Star of the West* tried to slip into the harbor and resupply the garrison. As the Union supply ship sailed past the Confederate batteries on Morris Island on January 9, batteries manned by cadets from the nearby Citadel college opened fire. Moments later, two shots slammed into the ship's wooden hull, prompting the captain to do an immediate about-face and head for safety. Some historians regard this as the true opening act of the military phase of the war.

Little happened for the next three months, until early April. Anderson's garrison was running dangerously low on rations, the U.S. government seemed befuddled by the continued declarations of secession by the Southern states, seven in all by this time (in chronological order: South Carolina, Mississippi, Florida, Alabama, Georgia, Louisiana, and Texas). Newly appointed commander of Confederate forces in Charleston, Brigadier General (later full General) Pierre Gustave Toutant Beauregard, knew that Anderson's situation was growing critical and, with the full blessing of the new Confederate government, decided to take advantage of it. He also knew that a heavily armed

U.S. Navy squadron was en route with supplies for the fort, prepared to blast its way in if necessary, and he would have to act quickly.

On April 11, 1861, Beauregard sent Anderson, his friend and old artillery instructor at West Point, a formal request for surrender of his post. Anderson replied politely, asking if he could wait until April 15 to surrender. Beauregard knew that the Navy ships were due to arrive on the 14th and in turn refused. He further sent word to Anderson that he would fire on the fort if not surrendered by midnight. At 3:30 A.M. on Friday, April 12, Beauregard sent one last message to Anderson, stating that he intended to open fire in exactly one hour. Anderson then ordered his men down into the deepest and best-protected casements.

At 4:30 A.M., Captain George S. James yanked the lanyard of a 10-inch mortar mounted in Fort Johnson on James Island, sending an 88-pound shell arcing high over the dark harbor for 20 long seconds, which finally exploded with a bright flash and dull roar in the middle of the fort's parade ground, a perfect shot. This was the signal for which every Confederate artilleryman around the harbor had been waiting for weeks. Within minutes, 30 guns and 17 heavy mortars opened fire as well, aiming at the darkened target only 1,800 to 2,100 yards away.

Anderson kept his men in the casements until dawn and then allowed them to man their guns under strict orders not to man those on the upper, exposed parapets. Captain Abner Doubleday took the honor of yanking the lanyard to fire the first return shot. As each gun facing toward the Confederate-held fortifications came on line and began a disciplined return fire, Sergeant John Carmody snuck upstairs under heavy incoming fire and loaded up and fired a few of the barbette guns. As the fort had not been given a full load-out of ammunition before the secession crisis hit and had not been resupplied since, Anderson's guns soon burned up what was left in the magazines. By late afternoon, only six smaller-caliber guns were able to keep up a steady fire.

Beauregard kept up a pounding fire for 34 straight hours, seriously damaging the fort's three-story outer wall and raking the upper gundeck with hot shot and shrapnel. Noting that some of his hot-shot guns had set a few interior buildings ablaze, Beauregard ordered more guns to start firing the heated shells, quickly turning the fires into a massive blaze that threatened the otherwise protected gun crews. Finally, after more than 4,000 well-aimed rounds had slammed into his post, Anderson signaled his surrender, at 1:30 P.M. on April 13.

It is almost beyond belief that not a single man on either side had been seriously wounded or killed in the day-and-a-half exchange of heavy and very accurate artillery fire; even more incredibly, the subsequent single Union casualty occurred as Anderson's gun crews were firing a last salute before leaving their post. Private Daniel Hough of Battery E, 1st U.S. Artillery, was killed when his ammunition pile exploded while firing the 50th round of a planned 100-gun salute, becoming the first known casualty of the war. Two others in his crew were wounded, one later dying of his injuries. Anderson stopped the salute rounds and quietly embarked his command on a steamship bound for New York. Fort Sumter now belonged to the state of South Carolina.

THE CONFEDERATE OCCUPATION OF FORT SUMTER

Fort Sumter quickly became a symbol of the rebellion, both in the North and South, and both sides were equally determined to possess it. Literally the moment Anderson left, South Carolina troops moved in and started repairing some of the damage from the intense bombardment. The Confederates held Fort Sumter for the next 27 months, nearly to the end of the war, although there were no fewer than 2

The Confederate armies suffered 175,000 casualties in the first 27 months of the war—more soldiers than were in the entire army during the summer of 1861.

direct assaults and 11 major bombardments against its garrison. Over the course of almost two years, as many as 46,000 shells (approximately 3,500 tons of metal) were fired at the island fort.

The First Attack

On April 7, 1863, the Union Navy mounted the first attempt to take back their fort. A squadron of eight ironclad monitors and the capital ironclad battleship USS *New Ironsides,* a 3,500-ton, 20-gun frigate under Rear Admiral Samuel Francis Du Pont, attempted to blast past the defenses of Fort Sumter and force open an entrance to the harbor. In what was supposed to be a coordinated and mutually supporting attack, Major General David Hunter had his troops loaded on transports just offshore, preparing to land on Folly, Cole's, and North Edisto Islands.

The "battle," as it was, did not take long. Du Pont's small fleet sailed into the harbor, guns blazing on Confederate batteries at Fort Sumter and Sullivan Island, to no real effect. Beauregard's batteries returned a galling fire, pounding the ironclads with well-aimed shot and shell from at least nine separate gun emplacements. The USS *Keokuk* would sink the next day, struck by more than 90 shots and her armored hull breached. Other ships in his squadron had suffered a total of 351 hits from the cannoneers of Fort Sumter, while only returning a grand total of 55 ineffective hits on the masonry fort. Du Pont was unable to push past Fort Sumter and soon turned back to sea, at the cost of 22 of his sailors killed or wounded. Hunter never even attempted to land his troops.

CLOSE-UP

The First Shot

There is an ongoing controversy over who fired the "first shot" of the war. Most general histories rather blandly state that widely admired Virginia secessionist Edmund Ruffin fired this shot, usually accompanied by a really great photo of the irritable agitator sitting with his rifle, staring a hole in the camera. Ruffin was a member (probably honorary, as he was 67 years old at the time) of the Palmetto Guards and was supposedly present at Stevens Battery on Charleston Harbor that night (even this point is open to debate).

The "official" invitee to pull the lanyard for the first shot was supposed to be Congressman (later Brigadier General,

even later Private when he resigned his commission and joined Lee's army as a scout) Roger Atkinson Pryor, the former U.S. congressman from Virginia, who had endlessly preached not only for secession but for bombardment of Fort Sumter as well. "Strike a blow!" was his endless call to war, at least before he was actually given the chance. Pryor declined the invitation to fire the signal round, simply stating quietly, "I could not fire the first gun of the war." Captain George S. James stepped forward as commander of the battery and without ceremony yanked the lanyard.

At least one source, possibly hoping to preserve the old legend, suggests that

Beauregard suffered the loss of 14 killed and wounded in the brief attack.

A Second Attempt

By early September 1863, with the situation improving for Union forces besieging the islands surrounding Charleston Harbor, Admiral John Adolph Dahlgren, commanding the Union blockade fleet at Charleston, somehow got the idea that Beauregard was pulling out of Fort Sumter and relayed this bit of "intelligence" to area commander Major General Quincy Adams Gillmore, who advised Dahlgren to send a force in to retake the fort.

Once again, the attack didn't last long. The fort had not been abandoned but was instead fully manned and commanded by

Major (later Brigadier General) Stephen Elliott, whose home in nearby Beaufort was being used as a Union headquarters at the time. About 1:00 A.M. on September 9, 1863, a force of about 400 U.S. sailors and Marines rowed up to the fort's landing, only to be greeted by heavy and accurate rifle fire from the parapets. Some Confederate defenders even tossed down small cannon shells mounted with lit fuses, an early and crude version of hand grenades.

The Union sailors and Marines were totally overwhelmed, having been told not to expect any resistance at all. Within a few minutes 21 were killed or wounded, another 100 or so captured, and the rest were rowing like mad for the safety of Union-held islands. Elliott reported that he had not suffered a single casualty in the assault.

Ruffin fired the first "actual" shot from Stevens Battery after James fired the "signal" for him to do so. In opposition to all this, Shelby Foote, famed novelist-historian of the Civil War, repeats the Ruffin story in his mostly reliable and superbly written *The Civil War: A Narrative.*

This whole argument is simply a subset of the line of arguments that consume and delight historians. Where were the true "first shots" fired: at Fort Sumter, at Fort Barrancas in Pensacola Bay a few hours beforehand, at the *Star of the West,* elsewhere? Then, of course, there is an even bigger argument over where the first battle was fought. As you can see, historians tend to consume themselves at times over what are in all reality rather trivial points!

Edmund Ruffin in the uniform of the Palmetto Guards. COURTESY OF THE NATIONAL ARCHIVES

A Last Union Attempt

Realizing that direct assault on the well-protected post was rather unhealthy and that it was absolutely impossible to simply sail by its defenses, Gillmore determined the best course of action was to simply reduce both Fort Sumter and the city of Charleston to rubble by a heavy and prolonged artillery fire. With Morris Island now under Union control (see Battery Wagner later in this chapter), Gillmore ordered batteries to be set up and to begin firing as soon as possible. The first shots rang out on the morning of August 17, 1863, continuing unabated night and day until August 23. Other batteries gradually came into line, bombarding both the fort and the city more or less continually until both were evacuated in early 1865.

One famous siege gun was the "Swamp Angel," an 8-inch Parrott rifled gun weighing more than eight tons and mounted on a special carriage able to "float" on the swampy soil of Morris Island. It fired a 175-pound shell with deadly accuracy, but typical of this class of artillery piece, its barrel burst on the 36th round.

Although the heavy bombardment gradually leveled the fort's three-story walls down to a single story of casements, Confederate engineers simply used the rubble to reinforce this lowest tier, making it even more resistant to artillery fire. The fort never surrendered its garrison; with the approach of Sherman's grand army in February 1865, both it and the city were evacuated.

SECESSIONVILLE

During the buildup of defenses around Charleston Harbor early in 1861, a small mud redoubt was constructed on James Island near a small settlement called Secessionville. This redoubt, later dubbed Battery Lamar, was soon manned by a 500-soldier garrison, who thought that they were left out on the fringe of any action at their remote location.

General Hunter had placed two Union divisions under Brigadier General Henry Washington Benham on the southeastern portion of James Island early in June 1862, planning to use them to assault Charleston by land along the Stono River, having just learned that Beauregard had abandoned some of his outer defenses. Hunter gave strict and very specific orders to Benham not to take his force and try to assault either the city or nearby Fort Johnson until more infantry could be brought up.

Major General John Clifford Pemberton, newly appointed commander of the Confederate Department of South Carolina, Florida, and Georgia, noted the increased Union movements south of Charleston and ordered defenses there to be bolstered. Brigadier General Nathan George Evans was given command of the James Island defenses and directed to build additional earthworks and redoubts to meet the expected attack.

Battery Lamar was given a new commander, Colonel T. G. Lamar, and 350 additional artillerymen and infantry for its defense, and an additional three regiments of infantry were placed in a central location less than two hours march from any of the new defenses. Battery Lamar now mounted an 8-inch Columbiad, a 24-pounder rifled gun, another 24-pounder smoothbore cannon, and an 18-pounder smoothbore. Two 24-pounder smoothbores were placed in another redoubt on the north side of the small fort for flank protection and to serve as a reserve.

During the night of June 15, Benham decided to ignore his orders and directed his divisional commanders to ready for an immediate assault on Battery Lamar. At 5:00 A.M. on the 16th, four regiments moving at the double-quick abreast burst out of the muddy cotton fields and quickly overran the Confederate pickets. Lamar had worked his men through most of the night trying to improve their post, and they were caught asleep when the attack began. By the time the gun crew stumbled out of their quarters and manned their guns, the Union line was less than 200 yards away.

Lamar ordered all guns to immediately open fire. The Columbiad, loaded with a cannister charge, was the first to cut loose, tearing a gaping hole in the blue ranks. Soon the other guns were firing, joined by infantry coming into line on the ramparts. On the fort's left face, three Union regiments made it to the top of the ramparts before Confederate infantry racing into position forced them back with a staggering volley fire. On the fort's right face, the 79th New York Infantry, famous for their early-war Scottish Highlander kilt uniforms, actually made it over the ramparts and attacked the gun crews. A fierce hand-to-hand combat was broken up when Union artillery batteries zeroed in on that section of the fort, killing some of their own men and forcing the rest to withdraw.

Two more assaults proved no more successful, and Benham finally withdrew his troops a little after 9:00 A.M. Benham was forced to report to a furious Hunter that he had lost 685 killed, wounded, or missing. He was subsequently brought up on charges for disobeying orders and reduced in rank, which was restored later on the personal order of Lincoln. Lamar reported 204 killed, wounded, or missing in the brief action.

MORRIS ISLAND

By the summer of 1863, capture and control of the low-slung sandbar called Morris Island was viewed as the only way Union forces were ever going to be able to batter down the defenses of Charleston. As the city was well situated at the north end of a harbor and surrounded by mile after mile of swampy lowlands, the Union Army had been unable to penetrate close enough overland to establish siege gun emplacements within range, and the Union Navy had been severely beaten back when it tried to ram its way through the waterborne defenses.

On July 10, a well-coordinated attack on Morris Island began, with Dahlgren's ironclad squadron successfully landing Brigadier General George Crockett Strong's 1st Brigade (1st Division, X Corps) with about 3,000 troops on the southern tip of the island, supported by artillery batteries stationed on nearby Folly Island. Advancing under heavy fire from the island's main fortification, Battery Wagner, Strong's men advanced to within rifle range of the sandwork fort during the night. At dawn on July 11, he personally led an assault on the fort, with his 7th Connecticut Infantry managing to gain the ramparts, but they were soon forced back with the loss of 339 men. The 1,200 Confederate defenders of the 27th South Carolina Infantry, 51st North Carolina Infantry, and 1st South Carolina Artillery under Brigadier General William Booth Taliaferro lost only 12 men in the failed assault.

Gillmore ordered more troops landed later that same day and set up siege artillery to try to reduce the fort before another assault. Twenty-six heavy artillery pieces and 10 large mortars were manhandled into place and began firing on the fort by the afternoon of July 12, supported by heavy fire from Dahlgren's ironclads.

THE 54TH REGIMENT

In what was considered a radical experiment at the time, an all-black regiment led by white officers had been formed in Boston soon after Lincoln issued his Emancipation Proclamation—the 54th Massachusetts Infantry Regiment. Its commander,

When Major Robert Anderson of the Union Army was forced to surrender his post at Fort Sumter in 1861, he kept the flag he hauled down from the post flagpole. Four years to the day later, the fort retaken, he personally hauled the same flag back up.

Colonel Robert Gould Shaw, was the son of a prominent and wealthy abolitionist, and two of Frederick Douglass's sons marched in the ranks. After a rather prolonged period of training and fitting out, obstructed in no small part by widespread racism within the Union Army command structure, the 54th moved out to join Gillmore's command in South Carolina.

Shaw's regiment received their baptism of fire on Sol Legare Island on July 16, 1863. Confederate forces under Brigadier General Johnson Hagood swept down James Island, determined to attack the Union forces gathering on Folly Island on their flanks and drive them away from Morris Island. The 54th was standing a picket line that morning on the northernmost end of the Union line, when Brigadier General Alfred Holt Colquitt's brigade charged across the causeway. Shaw ordered the rest of his men up, and a vicious hand-to-hand brawl erupted while Brigadier General Alfred Howe Terry struggled to get the rest of his division up to support them.

The Union forces were gradually pushed completely off James Island, with the 54th remaining engaged and acting as a rear guard the whole way. By nightfall all the Union troops were on Folly Island and preparing to move over to Morris Island.

Battery Wagner

By July 18, Gillmore decided that the massive artillery barrage had reduced the fort's defenses down to the point where a strong assault would be successful.

Brigadier General Truman Seymour's 2nd Division was brought up in whole to take the fort, with the brigades of Strong and Brigadier General H. S. Putnam to lead the assault. The 54th was selected by Strong to be the spearhead regiment, to be followed closely by two other infantry regiments, with Putnam's brigade of three regiments close behind them.

The reason for the single-regiment frontal assault was simple. The only access to the fort, which spread nearly completely across Morris Island, was down a narrow strip of sand between the ocean and a swamp and then across a water- and abatis-filled moat before the men could even approach the walls.

Just before dusk on July 18, the 54th formed up in ranks and moved off down the beach toward the fort. The weeklong artillery barrage had failed to significantly damage the Confederate fort, however, and as the Union infantry approached, Taliaferro's men swarmed out of their bombproofs and manned their guns.

The assault was an unqualified disaster. Although a few of Shaw's men managed to fight their way through the outer defenses and gain the ramparts, they soon were shot down and the rest of his regiment hurled back. Shaw was killed in the assault, as well as nearly half his men. The rest of Strong's brigade fared no better; no other regiment managed to gain the ramparts, and five of the six regiment commanders were killed or wounded. Seymour himself was seriously wounded, and Putnam was killed in the attempt. In all, the Union forces suffered a total of 1,515 casualties out of the 5,300-man assault force. Taliaferro, reporting the loss of 174 killed and wounded in the attack, still held the fort.

Taliaferro and his men stayed in the sandwork fort, trading artillery fire with the Union Army and Navy, until September 1863, when Union reinforcements landing nearby made it clear the fort was about to be taken at any cost. Taliaferro then abandoned his post and moved his men back into Charleston. The battered remnants of the 54th were eventually refitted and reinforced, and the regiment stayed in service through the rest of the war, fighting primarily in Florida. The question as to whether African-American men could fight had been decisively answered, though at a terrible cost.

THE END FOR CHARLESTON

After the fall of Savannah in December 1864, Sherman wasted little time in turning his attention northward. Entering South Carolina with 63,000 men arranged in four great columns in late January 1865, almost no Confederate force was available to stand up against him. A single division under Major General Lafayette McLaws did their best at the Salkehatchie River Bridge east of Allendale, but all they managed to do was hold up one Union corps for a single day, at the cost of 170 men killed or wounded.

As Sherman's "bummers" ravaged through the middle of the state, Lieutenant General William Joseph Hardee, now in command of Confederate forces around Charleston, determined that he would have to immediately evacuate his troops or risk having them cut off and trapped between Sherman and the Union Navy. On the night of February 17, 1865, with the bulk of Union forces still several days away, burning Columbia, Hardee ordered Fort Sumter abandoned and marched out of the city heading for Cherhaw to support General Joseph Eggleston Johnston's Army of Tennessee, now in North Carolina and preparing for last-ditch defenses.

Sherman never moved toward Charleston, instead moving his grand army slowly northeast toward North Carolina, meeting almost no resistance along the way. Charleston's mayor surrendered the city a few days later to a handful of Union officers who had ridden up from Beaufort. The "grand affair," which had started out with so much grand talk and excitement less than four years before, came to a quiet end.

THE TOUR

Getting There: Charleston

Charleston is located at the southeastern end of South Carolina, directly on the Atlantic Ocean coast, about 80 miles northeast of Savannah, Georgia, and 114 miles southeast of the state capital of Columbia. Interstate 26 runs between Columbia and Charleston and intersects Interstate 95 about 50 miles northwest of Charleston, near Santee. U.S. Highway 17 connects Charleston with Savannah or Myrtle Beach and Wilmington, North Carolina, but is a decidedly low-speed two-lane road in parts.

POINTS OF INTEREST

Fort Sumter National Monument
Charleston Harbor
(843) 883–3123
Today Fort Sumter is a national monument administered by the National Park Service of the U.S. Department of the Interior. It is still accessible only by boat, and the only public tour of this tiny man-made island and world-famous fort is offered through Fort Sumter Tours. You can board the Fort Sumter tour boat at either Liberty Square in downtown Charleston or Patriots Point Maritime Museum in Mt. Pleasant (across the Cooper River). The trip out to Fort Sumter takes about an hour and 15 minutes. It affords delightful views of Charleston's waterfront and the tip of the peninsula from an ocean voyager's perspective. (There's a separate, two-hour tour that does not stop at the fort and includes a cruise under the Cooper River bridges on up to the vast facility that until recently was the U.S. Naval Base in North Charleston.) The specially built sightseeing boats are clean and safe and have onboard restrooms.

Once you're at Fort Sumter itself, you can walk freely about the ruins. There's a museum on-site with fascinating exhibits of the fort's history. National Park Service rangers are there to answer any questions you may have.

You'll need to check in for your tour at least 15 minutes early for ticketing and boarding. Departure times vary according to the season and the weather, so call for departure information (843–881–7337 or 800–789–3678). During the busy summer season, there are usually three tours a day from each location. Prices are $12.00 for adults and teens and $6.00 for children younger than 12. Children younger than 6 are free, but a boarding pass is required for them. Wheelchair access is available only at the Liberty Square departure location. Group rates are available, but advance reservations for groups are encouraged.

Fort Johnson
Wildlife and Marine Resources Center
James Island
(843) 762–5000
Fort Johnson is another Charleston-area fortress steeped in history and adaptively reused for modern needs. Since the early 1970s, the waterfront James Island site has been the home of the South Carolina Wildlife and Marine Resources Department, which researches and promotes the state's marine industries. But military buffs know Fort Johnson in another role. Like Fort Moultrie, this site has military significance that dates back several hundred years.

No trace now exists of the original Fort Johnson that was constructed on the site in about 1708. It was named for Sir Nathaniel Johnson, proprietary governor of the Carolinas at the time. A second fort was constructed in 1759, and small portions of that structure remain as "tabby" ruins there today. (Tabby is an early building material made from crushed lime and oyster shell.)

Records show the fort was occupied in 1775 by three companies of South Carolina militia under the leadership of

Lieutenant Colonel Motte. During the American Revolution, the fort remained in colonial hands until 1780, when the British forces advancing on Charleston reported finding it abandoned. A third fort was built in 1793, but a hurricane destroyed it in the 1800s. Some work on Fort Johnson was done during the War of 1812, but the following year another storm destroyed that progress. Shortly afterward, Fort Johnson was dropped from official reports of U.S. fortifications.

During early 1861, South Carolina state troops erected mortar batteries and an earthwork of three guns on the old fortress site. The signal shot that opened the bombardment of Fort Sumter and marked the beginning of the Civil War was fired from the east mortar battery of Fort Johnson on April 12, 1861.

All throughout the Civil War, building activity increased until Fort Johnson became an entrenched camp mounting 26 guns and mortars. However, apart from routine artillery firing from the site, the only major action at the fort occurred on July 3, 1864, when its Confederate defenders repulsed two Union regiments totaling about 1,000 men. The Union forces sustained 26 casualties and lost 140 men as captives. The Confederate loss was 1 killed and 3 wounded. On the night of February 17, 1865, Fort Johnson was evacuated during the general Confederate withdrawal from Charleston Harbor.

After the Civil War, Fort Johnson became a quarantine station operated by the state and the city of Charleston. It continued to be used in that capacity until the 1950s. Today's inhabitants at the site (the Marine Resources folks) do not prohibit exploration, so you might find this history-drenched spot worth a visit.

Fort Moultrie
(West) Middle Street, Sullivan's Island
(843) 883-3123

From the earliest days of European settlement along the eastern seaboard, coastal fortifications were set up to guard the newly found, potentially vulnerable harbors. In this unique restoration, operated today by the National Park Service, visitors to Fort Moultrie can see two centuries of coastal defenses as they evolved.

In its 171-year history (1776 to 1947), Fort Moultrie defended Charleston Harbor twice. The first time was during the Revolutionary War, when 30 cannon from the original fort drove off a British fleet mounting 200 guns in a ferocious, nine-hour battle. This time, Charleston was saved from British occupation, and the fort was justifiably named in honor of its commander, William Moultrie. The second time was during the long Union siege of Charleston.

Today the fort has been restored to portray the major periods of its history. Five different sections of the fort and two outlying areas each feature typical weapons representing a different historical period. Visitors move steadily back in time from the World War II Harbor Entrance Control Post to the original, palmetto log fort of 1776.

Fort Moultrie is open from 9:00 A.M. to 5:00 P.M. daily. It is closed on Thanksgiving, Christmas, and New Year's Day. Groups should make reservations for guided tours. Pets are not allowed. Admission is free.

From Charleston, take US 17 North (Business) through Mt. Pleasant to Sullivan's Island and turn right on Middle Street. The fort is about 1½ miles from the intersection.

Secessionville
Fort Lamar, James Island

While the small settlement has disappeared without a trace (the area is now a subdivision called Secessionville Acres), the earthwork fort is now a South Carolina Heritage Preserve and is undergoing preservation and restoration efforts by volunteers. A reenactment of the Battle of Secessionville is held annually.

To get to the site, drive south out of Charleston on US 17, and turn left onto Folly Road (South Carolina Highway 171) just past the Ashley River Bridge. Turn left onto Grimball Road, right onto Old Military Road, and almost immediately left again onto Fort Lamar Road. The preservation site is about 1¼ miles down the road on the left.

Battery Wagner
Morris Island

Of all the forts and battlegrounds that dot the Low Country landscape and pay quiet tribute to the area's military history, perhaps the most muted one is Battery Wagner. The story is a brief one in the long struggle of the Civil War, but it is a significant one that is especially poignant today. In 1989 the story of Battery Wagner was portrayed in the acclaimed film *Glory,* which starred Matthew Broderick, Denzel Washington, and Morgan Freeman.

Time and tides have long since removed all traces of Battery Wagner. Today Morris Island is vacant and uninhabited. It was annexed by the city of Charleston and is expected to one day be developed to become a vital part of the ever-growing metropolitan area surrounding the city. Although a monument at Battery Wagner is planned, the site remains remarkably overlooked by the public at large. But whatever its future may hold, the story of Morris Island will always include the story of Battery Wagner and the 54th Massachusetts Regiment.

The Battery

One can argue that Charleston's White Point Gardens, which most people know as The Battery, shouldn't officially be called an "attraction," like a museum or a fort. On the other hand, it's a darn good bet that no first-time visitor to the city ever left here without making it a point to walk there or at least drive by.

In a city where almost every other building or street holds some historical significance, few sites afford a better view of Charleston's 300-year-long parade of history than The Battery.

That seaside corner of land at the end of East Bay Street, where it turns and becomes Murray Boulevard, is now a pleasant park with statues and monu-

Some Civil War sites are inside unrelated state parks—Fort McAllister near Savannah, Georgia, for example. These parks are great places to let uninterested spouses and children play while you "go exploring," but be sure to note if you need to pay only once per site or if there are separate charges for admission to the historic sites and parks. At Fort McAllister, there are separate charges.

ments, long-silent cannon, and spreading live oak trees. There's even a Victorian bandstand that looks as if it could sport a uniformed Sousa band any Sunday afternoon. But the atmosphere on The Battery hasn't always been so serene.

The Battery has been a prominent feature in Charleston since the earliest days of the English settlement. Then it was known as Oyster Point because it was little more than a marshy beach covered in oyster shells—bleached white in the Carolina sun.

At first, it was mostly a navigational aid for the sailing vessels going into and out of the harbor. The peninsula was still unsettled, and the first colonial effort was farther upstream on the banks of the Ashley River at what is now called Charles Towne Landing. Later, when the settlement was moved to the much more defensible peninsula site, the point was a popular fishing area, too low and too easily flooded to be much of anything else. Charts used during the years 1708 to 1711 show only a "watch tower" on the site and just a few residences built nearby.

Remember, Charles Towne was still a walled city at that time, the southernmost wall being several blocks north, near what is now the Carolina Yacht Club on East Bay Street. The point was definitely a "suburban" location. The area took a decidedly higher public profile about a decade later, when pirate Stede Bonnet and some 40 or 50 scalawags like him were hanged there from makeshift gallows. The local authorities must have gotten the right ones, as they were apparently quite effective in bringing an end to the pirate activity that had plagued the Carolina coast.

The first of several real forts built on the site came along as early as 1737. This and subsequent fortifications were crudely built, however, and none lasted long against the tyranny of the sea. By the time of the American Revolution, White Point was virtually at the city's door and no longer considered a strategic site for defense.

Hurricanes in 1800 and again in 1804 reduced whatever fortification remained there to rubble. Another fort, this version constructed for the War of 1812, apparently gave White Point a popular new name: The Battery. At least, the new name appears on maps beginning about 1833.

The seawall constructed along East Battery (the "high" one) was built after a storm in 1885. Storms and repairs have traded blows at the seawall for many years: in 1893, 1911, 1959, and, of course, with Hugo in 1989.

The area's use as a park dates back to 1837, when the city rearranged certain streets to establish White Point Gardens. It was from this vantage point that Charlestonians watched the battle between Confederate fortifications across the river and the small band of Union troops holed up in Fort Sumter on April 12, 1861. Once the war had started, this peaceful little garden was torn up and convulsed into two massive earthwork batteries, part of Charleston's inner line of defense. And while one of these battery sites housed a Blakely rifle (a 3.50 caliber rifled cannon that fired a variety of specially flanged shot and shell in the 12-pound range), neither battery ever fired a shot in anger. (Some incoming artillery rounds landed here during the extended bombardment of the city from late 1863 until Charleston fell in February 1865.)

The end of the Civil War was the end of The Battery's role in Charleston's military defense, although several subsequent wars have left poignant souvenirs behind for remembrance. Today no fewer than 26 cannon and monuments dot The Battery's landscape, each of which is described on a nearby plaque or informational marker.

General Cheatham, all the time, was calling on the men to go forward, saying, "Come on, boys, and follow me"... as he was passing me I said, "Well, General, if you are determined to die, I'll die with you."

Private Sam Watkins of the Confederate Army, at Stones River

Powder Magazine
79 Cumberland Street, Charleston

Only a couple of blocks from the bustling market area is, quite simply, the oldest public building in the Carolinas. And yet, as Charleston attractions go, the Powder Magazine is relatively unknown to tourists and to some locals as well.

Perhaps the site is overlooked because it's dramatically upstaged by Charleston's sumptuous house museums and romantic streetscapes. And in truth, the utilitarian Powder Magazine actually predates Charleston's legendary aesthetics. It was built for a time when the still-new English settlement was predominantly interested in self-defense and basic survival.

In the early years of the 18th century, Charles Towne was still threatened by Spanish forces, hostile Indians, rowdy packs of buccaneers, and an occasional French attack. It was still a walled city, fortified against surprise attack.

In August 1702 a survey of the armament in Charles Towne reported "2,306 lbs. of gunpowder, 496 shot of all kind, 28 great guns, 47 Grenada guns, 360 cartridges, and 500 lbs. of pewter shot." In his formal request for additional cannon, the royal governor requested "a suitable store of shot and powder . . . (to) make Carolina impregnable." And so in 1703 the Crown approved and funded such a building, which was completed in 1713 on what is now Cumberland Street.

The Powder Magazine was the domain of the powder receiver, a newly appointed city official entitled to accept a gunpowder tax levied on all merchant ships entering Charleston Harbor during this period.

The building served its originally intended purpose for many decades. But eventually, in an early colonial version of today's base closings, it was deemed unnecessary (or too small) and sold into private hands.

This multigabled, tile-roofed architectural oddity was almost forgotten by historians until the early 1900s. In 1902 it was purchased by the National Society of Colonial Dames of America in the State of South Carolina. It was maintained and operated as a small museum until 1991, when water damage, roof deterioration, and time had finally taken too high a toll. What the Powder Magazine needed to survive at all was a major stabilization and restoration—something beyond the resources of the owners.

In an agreement whereby Historic Charleston Foundation did the needed work under a 99-year lease, the Powder Magazine underwent a $400,000 preservation effort, its first ever. This included a temporary roof over the entire structure, allowing the massive walls to dry out before necessary repairs could even begin. Much-needed archaeological and archival research was also done on the site.

The Powder Magazine opened to the public in the summer of 1997. Inside, an interactive exhibit interprets Charleston's first 50 years, a time when it was still a relatively crude colonial outpost of the British Empire.

The Charleston Museum
360 Meeting Street, Charleston
(843) 722-2996

Directly across Meeting Street from the Visitor Reception and Transportation Center is one of Charleston's finest jewels: the Charleston Museum. Because it is the first and oldest museum in America, having been founded in 1773, the museum's collection predates all modern thinking about what should be kept or discarded in preserving the artifacts of a culture.

Instead, the Charleston Museum is heir to the collected memorabilia of real American patriots, early Charlestonian families, and early colonial thinkers, explorers, scientists, and planters. It is their opinion of what mattered then . . . and what they thought should matter to us today. Although the collection is housed in modern buildings and has the benefit of modern conservation methods and enlightened interpretation, the collection is uniquely eloquent. It speaks of a city that already knew it was great and sought early on to record itself for posterity. That difference alone makes the Charleston Museum a must-see.

The museum's scope is the social and natural history of Charleston and the South Carolina coastal region. Objects from natural science, cultural history, historical archaeology, ornithology, and ethnology are presented to illustrate the importance each had in the history of this area. The Charleston Silver Exhibit contains internationally recognized work by local silversmiths in a beautifully mounted display. Pieces date from colonial times through the late 19th century.

Visitors will see what the museum's many archaeological excavations have revealed about some of the city's best and worst times. Some artifacts date from the early colonial period, while others are from the Civil War years. Some exhibits focus on early Native Americans who lived in this region. Others trace changes in trade and commerce, the expansive rice and cotton plantation systems, and the important contributions made by African Americans.

Children will be intrigued by the Discover Me room with amazing things to touch, see, and do. They'll see toys from the past, games children played, the clothes they wore, furniture they used, and more. The photographs, ceramics, pewter, and tools reveal a very personal portrait of Charlestonians from the past.

The Charleston Museum is open Monday through Saturday from 9:00 A.M. to

5:00 P.M. and 1:00 to 5:00 P.M. on Sunday. Admission is $9.00 for adults and teens and $4.00 for children ages 3 through 12.

> *The result (of the fall of Atlanta) had a large effect on the whole country for solid and political reasons. But I had not accomplished all, for Hood's army, the chief objective, had escaped. Then began the real trouble.*
>
> Major General William T. Sherman of the Union Army, from his 1888 memoirs

Magnolia Cemetery
70 Cunnington Street, Charleston
(843) 722–8638

One of the most telling places in all Charleston has to be the remarkably distinctive 19th-century cemetery at the north end of the peninsula, not far off East Bay Street/Morrison Drive.

Not on any contemporary beaten path and clearly not a tourist destination, Magnolia Cemetery is the quiet, final resting place of many important Charlestonians and other players in the city's long-running and colorful drama. It is also an intriguing collection of Southern funerary art in an almost unbearably romantic setting, yet another eloquent expression of Charlestonian pride and prejudice.

The site was originally on the grounds of Magnolia Umbria Plantation, which dates back to 1790 and where rice was the principal crop in the first half of the 19th century. By 1850, however, a 181-acre section of that land had been surveyed for a peaceful cemetery, dedicated on November 19, 1850, on the edge of the marsh. From that time on (even to the present), many of Charleston's most prominent families chose Magnolia as the place to bury and commemorate their loved ones.

Many of the city's leaders, politicians, judges, and other pioneers in many fields of endeavor are interred beneath the ancient, spreading live oaks of Magnolia.

Among them are five Confederate brigadier generals. There is a vast Confederate section, with more than 1,700 graves of the known and unknown. Eighty-four South Carolinians who fell at the Battle of Gettysburg are included.

There are literally hundreds of ornate private family plots, many of which bear famous names. You will find the monument of Robert Barnwell Rhett—"Father of Secession," U.S. senator, attorney general of South Carolina, and author. There's also the grave of George Alfred Trenholm, wealthy cotton broker who served as treasurer of the Confederacy and organized many a blockade run for the cause. Trenholm is thought by many to be the man on whom Margaret Mitchell's Rhett Butler was based for *Gone with the Wind*. Among the famous artists and writers buried in Magnolia are Charleston's Alice Ravenel Huger Smith and John Bennett.

To find Magnolia, drive north on East Bay/Morrison Drive and turn right at the traffic light onto Meeting Street/South Carolina Highway 52. Turn right at the first opportunity onto Cunnington Street; Magnolia's gates (open daily from 8:00 A.M. to 6:00 P.M.) are at the end of the street.

Patriots Point Naval and Maritime Museum
40 Patriots Point Road, Mt. Pleasant
(843) 884–2727

While this large indoor/outdoor museum has absolutely nothing to do with the Civil War, other than being one of the embarking sites for the Fort Sumter tour, it is so proximate to historic sites and is so overwhelmingly enjoyable that we just couldn't resist including it. Patriots Point is the name given to a huge maritime museum complex that consists mainly of four in situ ships (permanently situated): a submarine, a destroyer, a Coast Guard cutter, and an aircraft carrier with 25 vintage aircraft. For this you'll need comfortable shoes and plenty of time.

Considering all there is to see, Patriots Point Naval and Maritime Museum is a real bargain. Admission is $13.00 for adults and teens, $6.00 for children ages 6 through 11, and free for children younger than 6. There's a $2.00 discount for senior citizens and anyone with a military ID. Plan on spending the better part of your day at Patriots Point; it's open from 9:00 A.M. to 7:30 P.M. Here's a detailed rundown of the ships on display:

USS *Yorktown* (aircraft carrier). No one comes or goes through Charleston via US 17 across the Cooper River bridges without noticing the giant aircraft carrier moored off Mt. Pleasant. It dominates—no, commands—a vast stretch of the Cooper's Mt. Pleasant shore at the very gates into Charleston Harbor. She is none other than the *Yorktown* (CV-10), the famous "Fighting Lady" of World War II and the proud flagship of Patriots Point, the world's largest naval and maritime museum. Of the four vessels permanently anchored and open to the public, the *Yorktown* is the most impressive. She was commissioned April 15, 1943, in the darkest days of the war, and served valiantly in some of the worst engagements ever witnessed at sea. Her planes inflicted heavy losses against the Japanese at Truk and the Marianas, and she supported the American ground troops in the Philippines, at bloody Iwo Jima, and at Okinawa.

Shortly after the *Yorktown* was commissioned and sent into battle, 20th Century Fox put a film crew on board to record—on Technicolor film—the continuing war story of a typical U.S. Navy carrier in action. The spectacular footage shot at unnamed, secret locations during then-unnamed battles became the Academy Award–winning documentary film feature of 1944. The film was called *The Fighting Lady,* and it is shown daily at the *Yorktown*'s onboard theater at regularly scheduled intervals. Don't miss it. Nothing brings the World War II drama of the *Yorktown* to life like this amazing celluloid time capsule. The terrible explosions and blistering fires, the fierce fighting, and all the brave young faces who served on her are there to be seen and appreciated by generations then unborn.

But the *Yorktown* story doesn't end there. She patrolled the western Pacific during the Cold War and even fought in Vietnam. In fact, the *Yorktown* received the crew of Apollo 8, the first manned space flight around the moon, in 1968.

The flight deck, hangar deck, and many of the *Yorktown* crew's living and working quarters are open to visitors today. You'll find actual carrier aircraft and Vietnam-era antisub planes on display, 25 aircraft in all. And there are other fascinating exhibits on everything from mines to shipbuilding.

One of the newer exhibits is the true-to-scale Vietnam Naval Support Base, showing the living conditions and work areas of a typical support base during the Vietnam War. You'll also find the Congressional Medal of Honor Museum, featuring displays representing the eight different eras of our military history in which the Medal of Honor was awarded. You'll see actual Medals of Honor and some of the artifacts related to their original recipients.

Mercifully, you'll find a snack bar on board the *Yorktown* and another in the riverside gift shop, so excited youngsters and foot-weary veterans can stop for lunch and a rest.

USS *Laffey* (destroyer). The heroic destroyer *Laffey* (DD-724) was commissioned on February 8, 1944, and participated in the giant D-Day landings of Allied troops at Normandy four months later. Transferred to the Pacific, she was struck by five Japanese kamikaze suicide planes and hit by three bombs off Okinawa during one hour on April 16, 1945. Her gallant crew not only kept her afloat but also managed to shoot down 11 planes during the attack. After World War II, the *Laffey* served during the Korean War and then in the Atlantic Fleet until she was decommissioned in 1975. A tour route on the *Laffey* lets you see her bridge, battle stations, living quarters, and various displays of destroyer activities.

USS *Clamagore* (submarine). The World War II submarine *Clamagore* (SS-343) was commissioned on June 28, 1945.

CLOSE-UP

The Rebel Yell

Of the myriad symbols and images of the old Confederacy, the rebel yell is perhaps the one most widely known yet most misunderstood. This particular battle cry was first heard at the First Manassas (First Bull Run), shortly after the war had begun. The originator of this cry was none other than the revered Brigadier (later Lieutenant) General Thomas Jonathan "Stonewall" Jackson (who earned his nickname in this very same battle). As Union infantry approached his Virginians, he rode calmly down the line of battle and gave his order: "Hold your fire until they're on you. Then fire and give them the bayonet. And when you charge, yell like furies!" Minutes later, the "weird halloo of the rebel yell" (as Shelby Foote put it) was heard for the first time, as 20,000 Confederate soldiers swept the Union Army from the field.

A Union survivor of that battle later recalled, "There is nothing like it on this side of the infernal region. The peculiar corkscrew sensation that it sends down your backbone under these circumstances can never be told. You have to feel it."

There are no known recordings of an actual full-volume rebel yell, the nearest approximation being a snippet of high-pitched "yipping" recorded on a 1920s-era movie about Civil War veterans. These men were in their 70s and 80s and obviously not in the prime of life or health anymore, so the sound was more reminiscent of a soft call to one's dog rather than a fear-inducing battle cry. One aged veteran, noting the rather weak attempt at the sound, leans toward the camera and, with a wink in his eye, explains, "That's the famous rebel yell!"

From scattered descriptions, it is apparent that the familiar "yee-haw!" heard from the stands at college football games is not the actual cry; many veterans compared it to a lusty and truly frightening version of a fox-hunter's yelp. One

She operated in the Atlantic and Mediterranean throughout her entire career and patrolled tense Cuban waters during 1962. Twice modified, she survived as one of the U.S. Navy's last diesel-powered subs until she was decommissioned in 1975.

The *Clamagore* tour route covers her control room, berth and mess areas, engine rooms, maneuvering room, and displays of submarine warfare. Note: Spaces are very cramped onboard. Visitors with health problems or claustrophobia are strongly cautioned against going inside.

USCGC *Ingham* (Coast Guard cutter). The *Ingham* was the most decorated vessel in the U.S. service, with a total of 18 ribbons earned during her career of more than 50 years. Commissioned in 1936, the *Ingham* took part in 31 World War II convoys, 6 Pacific patrols, and 3 Vietnam tours. In 1942 she sank the German U-boat 626 with one depth charge, called *Ingham's* Hole-in-One. In recent years the cutter tracked illegal immigrants and drug runners. She was decommissioned in 1988 and is now open for tours.

of the better descriptions comes from notes taken at an 1891 veterans convention in Memphis, when the widow of Admiral Raphael Semmes asked Captain Kellar Anderson (of the famed Kentucky Orphan Brigade) to let her hear a rebel yell. Anderson gave a rather lengthy reply, starting with a description of the hellish action around Snodgrass Hill at the battle of Chickamauga. Then he went on:

> There they go, all at breakneck speed, the bayonet at charge. The firing appears to suddenly cease for about five seconds. Then arose that do-or-die expression, that maniacal maelstrom of sound; that penetrating, rasping, shrieking, blood-curdling noise, that could be heard for miles on earth, and whose volumes reached the heavens; such an expression as never yet came from the throats of sane men, but from men whom the seething blast of an imaginary hell would not check while the sound lasted.

> The battle of Chickamauga is won.

> Dear Southern mother, that was the Rebel yell, and only such scenes ever did or ever will produce it.

> Even when engaged, that expression from the Confederate soldier always made my hair stand on end. The young men and youths who composed this unearthly music were lusty, jolly, clear-voiced, hardened soldiers, full of courage and proud to march in rags, barefoot, dirty and hungry, with head erect to meet the plethoric ranks of the best equipped and best fed army of modern times. Alas! Now many of them are decrepit from ailment and age, and although we will never grow old enough to cease being proud of the record of the Confederate soldier, and the dear old mothers who bore them, we can never again, even at your bidding, dear, dear mother, produce the Rebel yell. Never again; never, never, never.

ACCOMMODATIONS

As nearly all the significant Civil War sites are in and around Charleston, we have limited our suggestions for hotels/motels and restaurants to this city.

A friendly word of advice: Charleston attracts droves of visitors year-round, and we strongly recommend that you make reservations well in advance. For major events like Spoleto and holiday weekends, it's advisable to think up to six months in advance. See *Insiders' Guide to Charleston* for more information.

Charleston Place Orient Express $$$$
205 Meeting Street, Charleston
(843) 722-4900, (800) 611-5545

In terms of size, the former Omni is the granddaddy of Charleston hotels, with 444 units sprawling across a massive complex in the shopping district. The hotel, with its impressive lobby and reception area, opens into the walkway of a minimall that includes such famous stores as Laura Ashley, Talbot's, and Gucci. The luxury fitness center has an on-staff masseur and masseuse as well as an indoor-outdoor swimming pool among the quality amenities. Under the auspices of Orient Express, the rooms at Charleston Place are taking on the aura of Europe in the 1930s. Expect to find marble bathtubs and gold fixtures in the roomy baths. And notice the little touches in the rooms like Art Deco lighting and the subdued use of color. It adds just that much more romance to your lodging experience.

Several superb dining options are available right under the Charleston Place roof. Foremost among them is the Charleston Grill, tucked away among the shops and boutiques.

Doubletree Guest Suites at Charleston–Historic District $$$$
181 Church Street, Charleston
(843) 577–2644, (800) 254–0637

Located in The Market area, Doubletree Guest Suites is a comfortable courtyard hotel consisting of oversize suites. Units have "the Charleston look" and include complete kitchens, separate bedrooms, and living rooms. Life is made easy with a complimentary breakfast buffet, and you can unwind with on-the-house refreshments at the afternoon reception. For those who enjoy burning the calories they consume, there's a fitness center and a heated whirlpool spa in the courtyard that seats at least 12 comfortably (great for relaxing while gazing at the stars). When energy levels diminish, the hotel's VCR tape library is available to complement your cable television service. Noteworthy is the fact that 12 suites have complete access and amenities for handicapped guests.

RESTAURANTS

Hyman's Seafood Company $$
215 Meeting Street, Charleston
(843) 723–6000

A casual seafood dining experience for lunch or dinner, Hyman's offers a large selection of fresh-caught fish and a wide variety of shellfish. A raw bar and lounge are upstairs. Hyman's fries in olive oil, or you can order your fish broiled or blackened. Try the okra soup, even if you have always shied away from the vegetable. The she-crab soup is award-winning. Open every day, the restaurant serves meals all day long. We suggest parking in the Charleston Place garage.

Tommy Condon's Irish Pub and Seafood Restaurant $-$$
160 Church Street, Charleston
(843) 577–3818

The most authentic Irish pub in Charleston, Tommy Condon's has live Irish entertainment Wednesday through Sunday and serves a wide variety of imported beers and ales such as Bass and Newcastle Brown. The menu is a mixture of Irish and Low Country items including shrimp and grits, seafood jambalaya, and fresh fish of the day. There is a covered deck for outside dining, and patrons are welcome for lunch or dinner any day of the week. The kitchen closes at 10:00 P.M., but the bar stays open until midnight.

Union Hall $$-$$$
16 North Market Street, Charleston
(843) 377–1090

What was until fairly recently a trade union office and general hangout for Charleston's stevedores and dockworkers is now part of the city's cutting-edge restaurant scene. Union Hall is an upscale restaurant featuring some of the best-presented dinner entrees in town. The fare is essentially Northern Italian, on the lighter side, with a full range of classic Italian seafood specialties (from paella to lobster linguine) and some enticing meat choices (roasted suckling pig or young duckling) turned out on a European-style rotisserie. The decor is deliberately understated and just right for a quiet luncheon tête-à-tête or special evening. The extensive wine list will help with the latter. You'll find something really different here, and Charleston's evolving waterfront is the better for it. Union Hall is open for dinner only, Monday through Saturday.

NASHVILLE AND FRANKLIN: DESTRUCTION OF THE CONFEDERATE ARMIES IN TENNESSEE

On a short list of all the bone-headed maneuvers during the Civil War, General John Bell Hood's invasion of Tennessee for the Confederacy in late 1864 without a doubt ranks at or near the very top. Possibly influenced by his reported use of large doses of laudanum as a pain reliever for his serious injuries from Gettysburg and Chickamauga, Hood concocted this plan after being thoroughly trounced by Major General William T. Sherman's three grand armies around Atlanta in the late summer of 1864.

Maintaining to his death that the only way to defeat Sherman was to draw him into battle on terrain of his own choosing (possibly true), Hood decided to take what was left of his Army of Tennessee and march north out of the Atlanta area, "forcing" Sherman to follow and then defeating him by parts as the Union armies marched after him.

BACKGROUND TO THE BATTLE

In May 1864 three grand armies with a total of 110,123 men and 254 cannon under Sherman marched south out of their winter quarters at Chattanooga, Tennessee, aiming for the heart of the Southern Confederacy, Atlanta. Standing in their way was General Joseph Eggleston Johnston with a single army of 54,500 men and 144 artillery pieces. Within four months, Sherman tore a path through northwest

Georgia, resoundingly defeated the Confederate Army in nearly every battle, besieged Atlanta, and finally took the city when the last defenders slipped out during the night of September 1.

Johnston was a defensive genius, probably delaying the inevitable far longer than any other Southern general could have. His primary handicaps, ironically, had nothing to do with his overt enemy, Sherman, but lay in the enmity of President Jefferson Davis's military adviser, General Braxton Bragg, and one of his own corps commanders, Hood. Both conspired against Johnston behind his back to Davis, making outrageous charges that he was "reluctant to fight" and that his tactics would lead to ruin. Davis was all too willing to listen; although Bragg had proved a disaster as an army commander and even General Robert E. Lee warned that Hood was out of his league above a corps command (and others warned he wasn't particularly good at that position, although a capable and outstanding divisional commander), Davis held a grudge against Johnston. The exact reason for this enmity is open to debate, but most likely it resulted from political infighting at the very beginning of the Confederate government.

When Johnston was finally forced south of the Chattahoochee River just north of Atlanta, Davis mocked outrage at this act of "incompetence" and promptly fired him. Placed in his stead was Hood, who promised to go on the offensive, and whose appointment dashed the morale of the men he was to lead. Johnston had been their hero, a man they trusted and who trusted in them as well, who had placed their lives above holding property, and who had been forced to withdraw nearly a hundred miles but had done it without leaving behind any command or even a single artillery piece.

Hood, on the other hand, was well known for his "battlefield heroism," actions that played well in the press but tended to get a lot of his own men killed for no real gain. His charges at Devil's Den at Gettysburg in July of 1863 had lost him the use of an arm, and his charge on the second day at Chickamauga a little more than two months later cost him his right leg. He carried this same flair for dashing off into the face of the enemy into his leadership of the Army of Tennessee, which he ordered on the offensive the same day he assumed command, July 17, 1864.

Hood at Atlanta

On July 20, 1864, Hood ordered an assault at the Battle of Peachtree Creek, just north of Atlanta. Two days later he tried another assault at the Battle of Atlanta, actually a few miles east of the city, and on July 28 he tried yet another at the Battle of Ezra Church, west of Atlanta. The only result in three actions was to reduce his fighting force to fewer than 37,000, with a few thousand Georgia militiamen thrown in for good measure. A final series of battles at Jonesboro shattered his own army, and Hood promptly abandoned Atlanta. Sherman's armies walked in unmolested on September 2.

Davis "encouraged" Hood to attack Sherman and recapture the city, but that overwhelming task daunted even the "attack at all costs" Texan. Instead, he proposed to march north of the city to strike and cut Sherman's supply line from Chattanooga, which, hopefully, would force the Union Army out of the city and north in pursuit. Although neither Hood nor John-

ston had yet decisively defeated Sherman in a major pitched battle the entire campaign, with the Southern army intact, he now convinced the Confederate president that by choosing his defensive terrain carefully, he could defeat a well-armed, well-equipped, and relatively fresh force four times his size. Amazingly, Davis bought the idea and approved the plan.

Hood Moves North

With three corps in his command, led by Major General Benjamin Franklin "Frank" Cheatham, Lieutenant General Stephen Dill Lee, and Major General Alexander Peter Stewart, a cavalry corps commanded by Major General Joseph "Fighting Joe" Wheeler, and a separate cavalry division commanded by Brigadier General William Hicks "Red" Jackson, Hood moved out of his last Atlanta base of Lovejoy on September 18, swinging wide around the western flank of the Atlanta defenses, and headed north. Sherman had anticipated the maneuver and had already sent Brigadier General George Henry Thomas (the "Rock of Chickamauga") with three infantry divisions back to Chattanooga to prepare.

Hood moved relatively slowly, crossing the Chattahoochee River near Campbellton on October 1. He continued north for two days, finally encamping near Hiram. Stewart was ordered to move east and attack and cut the Western & Atlantic Railroad line at Big Shanty (now Kennesaw), Acworth, and Allatoona.

The Attack at Allatoona Pass

Stewart's men surprised and captured about 170 Union troops at Big Shanty on October 4 and then quickly moved north and captured a larger garrison at Acworth. Flushed with these easy successes, Hood personally ordered Major General Samuel G. French to take his division on up the tracks to capture and destroy the bridge and railroad cut at Allatoona Pass in Georgia. Hood was under the impression that the pass was only lightly held, as the two previous rail stops had been. However, Sherman had made the tiny settlement on the south side of the deep railway cut into a central base of logistical operations, had it heavily fortified, and had ordered another division under Brigadier General John M. Corse forward to garrison it. On both peaks over the 90-foot-deep railroad cut, heavily reinforced emplacements had been built. The westernmost set of peak defenses was dubbed the Star Fort, because of the arrangement of railroad ties surrounding it.

French divided his force and approached Allatoona from the north, west, and south. Once all were in position, he rather arrogantly sent Corse a terse message:

> Sir: I have the forces under my command in such positions that you are now surrounded, and, to avoid a needless effusion of blood, I call upon you to surrender your forces at once, and unconditionally. Five minutes will be allowed for you to decide. Should you accede to this, you will be treated in the most honorable manner as prisoners of war.

Corse was somewhat less than impressed, and 15 minutes later he replied, "Your communication demanding surrender of my command, I acknowledge receipt of, and respectfully reply, that we are prepared for the 'needless effusion of blood' whenever it is agreeable with you."

French wasted no time in sending Brigadier General Francis M. Cockrell's Missouri Brigade and Brigadier General William H. Young's (Ector's) Brigade to assault from the west. Both pushed through the first line of defense, then the second, and then through a third line of defense, all the while fighting hand-to-hand with clubbed rifles and bayonets. Advancing to within a few feet of the Star Fort, the fighting rapidly intensified, with the Confederate advance finally being stopped before it could overrun the fort. With warnings coming from outposts that a Union force had been spotted moving rapidly toward the battle area, French disengaged and marched his depleted force west to rejoin Hood.

All through the daylong battle, a Union signal post at Kennesaw Mountain sent a message to Corse: "General Sherman says hold fast; we are coming." This message, which popularized the expression "hold the fort," was nothing more than a morale booster, for Sherman did not order any additional infantry to the area until the next day, and none arrived until two days later. The forces spotted by the Confederate side were apparently just cavalry on a scouting mission.

Casualties in this little-remembered battle were exceptionally high, with Corse reporting 706 dead and wounded, and French also reporting 706 (including 70 officers), about 30 percent of either side's total force. Young himself was wounded just outside the fort and captured shortly afterward. Corse reported in a message to Sherman that he, too, had been wounded: "I am short a cheek bone and an ear but am able to lick all hell yet!" When Sherman came up later, he was unimpressed with the severity of his wounds and said, "Corse, they came damn near missing you, didn't they?"

The Armies Advance in Opposite Directions

Following the decisive loss at Allatoona Pass, Hood elected to continue north, moving west around Rome through Cedartown, Cave Springs, and Coosaville, while Sherman moved north after him with a force of 40,000 men (55,000 in some accounts), a partial vindication of

Hood's audacious plan. Wheeler's cavalry joined the campaign at this point, screening his movement from Sherman's force, while Jackson's cavalry stayed below Rome near the Coosa River. Attacks at Resaca on October 12 and 13 were failures, but Lee's and Cheatham's corps were able to capture the railroad north of Resaca the next day. In one of the only real successes in north Georgia, the 2,000-man Union garrison at Dalton was forced to surrender, but with Sherman hot on his heels, Hood was unable to hold the city.

Hood moved west again toward northwestern Georgia near the Alabama state line, setting up a line of battle near La Fayette on October 15. Hood's strategy here is uncertain, as he was moving away from the mountainous terrain he had claimed would be to his advantage. There are mountains here, and rugged ones in places, but this was the same area in which Sherman had already demonstrated an ability to operate. The northeastern mountains were not specified in Hood's plans but were his most likely original destination. If his plan was to keep Sherman bottled up in northern Georgia, it both succeeded and failed.

When Hood slipped away after the Union troops deployed for battle at La Fayette on October 17, Sherman remarked that Hood's tactics were "inexplicable by any common-sense theory . . . I could not guess his movements as I could those of Johnston." After a total of three weeks of chasing the now fast-moving Confederate Army of Tennessee, Sherman ordered his forces to return to Atlanta and prepare for a march to the south.

Warned by Grant that Hood was taking his army north into Tennessee to threaten his supply lines, Sherman remarked, "No single force can catch Hood, and I am convinced that the best results will follow from our defeating Jeff Davis's cherished plan of making me leave Georgia by maneuvering."

At the same time, Davis was begging Hood "not to abandon Georgia to Sher-

man but defeat him in detail before marching into Tennessee." Hood replied that it was his intent to "draw out Sherman where he can be dealt with north of Atlanta." In his postwar memoirs, Hood clung to this unrealistic stance and hopes of defeating both Sherman and Thomas's powerful force in Tennessee:

I conceived the plan of marching into Tennessee . . . to move upon Thomas and Schofield and capture their army before it could reach Nashville and afterward march northeast, past the Cumberland River in that position I could threaten Cincinnati from Kentucky and Tennessee . . . if blessed with a victory (over Sherman coming north after him), to send reinforcements to Lee, in Virginia, or to march through gaps in the Cumberland Mountains and attack Grant in the rear.

It was whispered by not a few members of the Army of Tennessee that Hood was half-mad from his injuries—a shot in the arm at Gettysburg and a leg shot off at Chickamauga shortly thereafter. Widely viewed as a gallant fighter, his leadership did not impress those under him in the sense that his tactics killed a lot of his men. Private Sam Watkins said, "As a soldier, he was brave, good, noble and gallant, and fought with the ferociousness of the wounded tiger, and with the everlasting grit of the bull-dog; but as a general he was a failure in every particular."

Hood continued his march north, and Sherman, upon hearing the news, couldn't have been happier, saying, "If he will go to the Ohio River, I will give him rations." He sent Major General John M. Schofield's Army of the Ohio, consisting of Major General David F. Stanley's IV and Brigadier General Jacob B. Cox's XXIII Corps, to Thomas to defend Tennessee and then turned his attention to his March to the Sea.

Hood in Alabama

The Confederate Army of Tennessee reached Decatur, Alabama, on October 26, where Hood met General Pierre Gustave Toutant Beauregard, commander of the Division of the West. Beauregard approved Hood's plan to invade Tennessee but made him give up Wheeler's cavalry, which was sorely needed in the coming campaign against Sherman in south Georgia. In exchange, Major General Nathan Bedford Forrest's Cavalry Corps was moving down from eastern Tennessee to provide coverage.

While waiting for Forrest to arrive, Hood moved his force west, retaking and fortifying Florence, Alabama, and Corinth, Mississippi, and repairing the railroad line between the cities to shuttle his supplies as needed. Forrest took nearly three weeks to arrive, finally appearing on November 17.

To counter Hood's move west, Thomas sent Stanley's corps, reinforced with one division from Cox's corps, to Pulaski, Tennessee, directly astride the Nashville & Decatur Railroad that he expected Hood to advance on. On November 14 Schofield arrived in Pulaski to establish his headquarters and detail the defense against Hood's army. At that time Schofield commanded an army of 25,000 infantrymen and 5,000 cavalry, while Thomas had another 40,000 troops scattered between Nashville and north Georgia, nearly all relatively fresh and well supplied. With Forrest's arrival, Hood had about 33,000 infantrymen and 6,000 cavalrymen, all tired, battle-weary, and poorly supplied.

Hood Marches North

On November 19 Hood at long last moved out on his great campaign, led by Forrest's cavalry and Lee's corps. Rather than following the railroad as Schofield expected, Hood moved along three parallel roads to the west of the small town of Pulaski, heading toward Columbia, 31 miles to the north. The weather was wretched—a cold rain mixed with snow and sleet turning the muddy roads to ice, which cut and burned the bare feet of most of the tattered infantrymen.

Recognizing the danger of his flank being turned, Schofield hustled all but one brigade of his army to Columbia, arriving and fortifying the bridges over the Duck River by November 24. Hood's army closed in on the town on the morning of November 26. That night he outlined yet another strategy to his three corps commanders. He told them that Nashville was an "open city" and a ripe prize to be easily taken. To do so, they had to move fast toward the capital city, bypassing what Union forces they could and overwhelming those they could not.

Once again, it is difficult to see just what Hood's overall intent was. Originally moving north to draw Sherman out of Atlanta, he succeeded but then ran into Alabama rather than finding suitable terrain to fight from. Once in Alabama, he ignored Davis's pleas not to abandon Georgia completely and convinced Beauregard that he could defeat Thomas's forces in Tennessee piecemeal, recover the state for the Confederacy, then either help reinforce Robert E. Lee's army in Virginia or invade Ohio. To do either he had to eliminate any Union threat from his own base of support by defeating Thomas, or at the very least by forcing him to retire from Tennessee. Yet, when literally given the opportunity to challenge parts of the Union Army with a superior force, at Pulaski and now at Columbia, he chose to outflank them and continue north.

HOME

One company of Hood's army had arrived back home after nearly four years of combat—Captain A. M. Looney's Company H of the 1st Tennessee Infantry Regiment, the "Maury County Grays." One surviving original member, Private Sam Watkins, was overcome with emotion at what had happened to his friends and comrades:

The Maury Grays . . . left Columbia, four years ago, with 120 men. How many of these 120 original members are with the company today? Just twelve. Company H has twenty listed. But we twelve will stick to our colors till she goes down forever, and until five more of this number fall dead and bleeding on the battlefield.

Spring Hill

Realizing early on that Hood had no intent of forming a direct assault at Columbia, and possibly was going to try to envelop him to the north, Schofield sent Stanley's corps reinforced with additional infantrymen and artillery to the smaller city. The Union corps arrived at Spring Hill about 2:00 P.M.

Hood had sent Forrest to the north to bypass the Union defenses north of Columbia, and they arrived at Spring Hill at nearly the same time Stanley did. Both sides skirmished to no real gain on either side until just before dark. Lee's corps had stayed outside Columbia to "make a racket" while Hood moved Cheatham's and Stewart's corps around to the east to Davis Ford on the Duck River, crossing through pastures, woods, and creeks before remerging on the Rally Hill (Franklin) Turnpike toward Spring Hill just at dark on November 29, neatly flanking Schofield in the maneuver.

Arriving just at dark, part of Cheatham's corps came up and helped push the Union force back into town. Stanley managed to hold the town and keep the road to Columbia open. Hood's army was exhausted by the rough marching and combat action, however, and nearly immediately lay down in the mud on either side of the road to catch some badly needed sleep.

As the Confederate infantry slept, Schofield slipped out of Columbia and passed through a mere 200-yard-wide gap between the two Southern corps without being detected, making it to Spring Hill without incident. When Hood found out, a huge fight between him and Cheatham erupted in which he blamed Cheatham for the escape and requested that Richmond send a replacement, while Cheatham complained he had not been specifically ordered to take and cut the road. While the rest of the Southern generals joined in the fun and argued through the night, Schofield and the rest of his corps moved out of Spring Hill and on toward Franklin, reaching the outer defenses by dawn on November 30. Once there, Schofield discovered he was not going to be able to move his men and heavy supply trains into the city until his engineers rebuilt the bridges and fords destroyed by Forrest's raids. He ordered his men to hastily throw up earthwork defenses on the south edge of town in case Hood was following too closely. He planned on withdrawing back across the river after dark and then to move on up to Nashville during the night.

FRANKLIN

Hood was indeed following closely. After withdrawing his request for Cheatham's replacement and making a few last rude comments, he got his army moving north again, chasing after Schofield. The vanguard of the Southern force arrived atop a low range of hills just south of Franklin just before 3:00 P.M., and Hood immediately gave orders to attack the Union lines they could clearly see being constructed. The three corps commanders were incredulous. Dusk was only a bit over two hours away, the army was still in a column formation with parts of it still hours away, and the Union troops clearly had a superior and fortified position well protected by artillery batteries.

This is when Hood threw another one of his fits. He had habitually considered anyone who disagreed with him an enemy and was loath to change any plan he had created, even in the face of overwhelming evidence that it was a poor one. In addition, he had often remarked since taking command that the men and officers loyal to former Army of Tennessee commander Johnston were "soft" and too prone to retreating in the face of the enemy. He insisted that they were to march right down there and take those works, even at the cost of their own lives, almost as a punishment for daring to disagree with him.

The Battle of Franklin

After 3:00 P.M., the two Confederate corps present started forming in line of battle, Cheatham's corps on the left, Stewart's corps on the right. At the same time, the bridge and ford work had been completed, and Schofield was getting ready to pull his forces back north across the river. At 3:30 P.M. the signal trumpets blew, and a mass of butternut-clad infantry charged across the open ground toward the Union emplacements. Major General John Calvin Brown's and Major General Patrick Ronayne Cleburne's Confederate divisions briefly overran Brigadier General George B. Wagner's division, which was left out on the road south of the main defense belt in an ill-thought-out move.

Mounting a strong counterattack, Colonel Emerson Opdyke's 1st Brigade (Wagner's Division), which had been the rear guard all day and was taking a well-deserved rest at the river, leapt back over the defense wall and charged Cleburne's men. A furious fight erupted with point-blank shots and hand-to-hand combat all along the line. One of his officers, Major Arthur MacArthur, father of the World War II hero Douglas MacArthur, managed to slash one Confederate regiment's color bearer with his sword and take the prize, even though he was shot three times in the process.

All along the rest of the line, individual regiments and brigades reached the second Union line of defense, but none was able to pierce it. The field behind them now raked by constant canister and shot from the Union batteries, there was no place left to retreat either. Both sides stood just yards apart for hours, pouring musket and artillery fire into each other's ranks, without either side giving way.

The slaughter finally stopped about 9:00 P.M., well after dark, when gun by gun, the firing slowly petered out. Surviving Confederate regiments literally crawled back across the dead-strewn field to the safety of their original positions. Schofield promptly abandoned the field, leaving his dead and wounded behind, and immediately marched back to Nashville, arriving about noon on December 1.

Hood's casualties were almost unfathomable. Of the 26,000 he had sent into battle, 5,550 were dead or wounded, with another 702 missing. Thirty-two regimental and brigade battle flags had been taken. No less than 54 regimental commanders were killed, wounded, or missing. The worst loss was that of six generals: Cleburne, Brigadier General John Adams, Brigadier General Otho French Strahl, Brigadier General States Rights Gist, Brigadier General John Carpenter Carter, and Brigadier General Hiram Bronson Granbury. Of the other six generals on the battlefield, one had been captured and only two were left unwounded and fit for service.

Schofield's casualties, although heavy, were still lighter than Hood's. Of the 28,000 men Schofield had on the line that afternoon, 1,222 were killed or wounded, while 1,104 were captured or missing.

THE MARCH TO NASHVILLE

Hood's army was in no shape to fight after the beating at Franklin, but nothing would deter Hood from his determination to take the Tennessee capital back. Schofield's forces had quit the field at Franklin immediately after the battle, and

i

At Franklin, only 2 of the 12 Confederate generals walked away unwounded.

Hood followed suit. Ordering his men up and at 'em, the depleted Confederate Army of Tennessee stood outside the defenses of Nashville by December 2.

Once again, we face the question of what Hood was planning to do. He admitted himself after the war that he knew his army was too depleted to assault the Nashville emplacements and that Schofield was well placed and well supplied and had reinforcements on the way. By no stretch of the imagination could one follow or endorse his plan (as outlined in his postwar memoirs, *Advance and Retreat*): wait outside for Thomas's combined army to come out and attack his own fortifications and hope that promised reinforcements (which probably did not even exist) of his own could manage to travel from Texas in time to help him.

Thomas, on the other hand, was quite comfortable and in no mood to hurry into a fight. Major General Andrew Jackson Smith arrived with his three divisions of XVI Corps by the time Schofield came in from Franklin, and Major General James Blair Steedman brought up a division of 5,200 men detached from Sherman's command the next day. By December 4, Thomas had a total of 49,773 men under his command, some of whom were well rested and had not seen combat recently, while Hood could muster (on paper) only 23,207 tired, cold, and demoralized troops. This figure did not take into consideration the large number of desertions of battle-hardened veterans the South's Army of Tennessee was beginning to experience.

The Battle of Nashville

Under growing pressure from Grant to go into action, Thomas made preparations to decisively defeat the weaker Confederate

Army and gain "such a splendid and decisive victory as to hush censure for all time." Finally, at 6:00 A.M. on the foggy morning of December 15, his army moved out. Thomas planned to hit both of Hood's flanks with a coordinating attack that would destroy his lines of battle in a matter of minutes. Thomas had no desire to simply push Hood away from Nashville; he was determined to destroy that Confederate army once and for all.

Steedman started the attack at 8:00 A.M. on Hood's right, the coordinated plan falling apart immediately due to the poor weather and bad roads. Two hours later Smith's corps hit Hood's left flank, followed by Wood and Schofield over the next few hours. Hood was steadily pushed back, but his lines held fast and pulled together to form a tight, straight line of battle. By nightfall, Hood had been pushed back about a mile, where he formed a new line of battle that stretched between Shy's Hill and Overton Hill.

At dawn on December 17, Thomas's forces started probing the new Confederate line for weakness. At 3:00 P.M. a strong attack was made against the defense atop Overton Hill, followed a half hour later by initial actions against Shy's Hill. By 4:00 P.M. the attack on Hood's right had been repulsed with heavy losses, but the attack on Shy's Hill succeeded in routing the Confederate defenders and effectively bringing the battle to an end.

The Confederate Army of Tennessee was at long last broken. All semblance of order broke down as many soldiers either ran for the rear or allowed themselves to be taken prisoner. Many more simply dropped their rifles and returned home, too defeated to fight any more. Hood pulled what was left south out of Nashville and marched through a brutal winter landscape all the way back down to Tupelo, Mississippi. Once there, Hood quietly asked to be relieved of command on Friday, January 13, 1865.

Hood insisted that his losses were "very small," but he was not the sort to admit defeat or desertion of his own men.

Various sources give wildly disparate figures, but a rough guess is that Hood lost about 1,500 killed and wounded in the battle, with another 4,500 captured. He lost a grand total of nearly 20,000 men in the whole failed campaign. Thomas reported losses of 387 killed, 2,562 wounded, and 112 missing in the battle.

Even after this shattering defeat, the end of this great army was not yet at hand. Reorganizing yet again, the Army of Tennessee was reunited with its beloved commander, General Joseph Eggleston Johnston and moved back east to confront Sherman once again, this time in his march through the Carolinas.

THE TOUR

Getting There: Allatoona Pass

The battlefield is accessible from Interstate 75 north from Atlanta. Take exit 283 (Emerson-Allatoona Road), turn right (east), and go about 2 miles to the pass area. On the way you will cross over a set of railway tracks, which are the modern relocation of the tracks the soldiers were fighting over.

MODERN TIMES

Nearly all the area covered by the battle is today heavily overgrown or equally heavily developed, and the east side of the battlefield is under the murky waters of Lake Allatoona. The dug railroad gap is heavily overgrown, and it is difficult to get a clear picture of the tactical situation, but at least one period structure remains. The Mooney House, the yellow-and-white tin-roofed structure in the sharp curve in the road at the pass entrance, was used as a field hospital during the battle and can be seen in a famous photograph of the area by George M. Barnard taken just after the battle.

There is a small parking area with two historic markers across the street from the Mooney House, which indicate quite well

the 1864 layout and tactical situation. One contains a fair reproduction of the Barnard photo, which pictures landmarks still visible today. The Star Fort is still present, although overgrown and in deteriorating condition on top of the left peak of the railway cut. A warning: Both the fort and the Mooney House are private property and not open to the public. Please be respectful and observe them from the parking lot. The eastern redoubt, on top of the right peak, is on U.S. Army Corps of Engineers property and can be accessed by a steep, partially overgrown path just inside the entrance to the pass walking north.

Getting There: Franklin

Franklin is about 20 miles south of Nashville on U.S. Highway 431 and easily accessible off Interstate 65. Take exit 65, then drive west 3 miles on Tennessee Highway 96. The battle was fought on the south part of town, but the only remaining undisturbed portion of it is on the state-owned Carter House property. Take U.S. Highway 31 about a mile south off the main square, turning left onto the well-marked property.

MODERN TIMES

Franklin today is both a thriving small town on its own and a rapidly growing bedroom community for nearby Nashville. Time and development have erased nearly every sign of the battle.

POINTS OF INTEREST

Carter House
1140 Columbia Avenue, Franklin
(615) 791–1861
This 1830 brick house was the center of fighting in the Battle of Franklin in 1864, one of the bloodiest battles of the Civil War. The house, built by Fountain Branch Carter, was used as a Federal command post while the Carter family, friends, and neighbors hid in the cellar during the bat-

CLOSE-UP

Braxton Bragg

Perhaps one of the most hated and vilified men in the entire Confederate Army, Braxton Bragg's greatest advantage as a military commander was his close friendship with President Jefferson Davis. Born on March 22, 1817, in North Carolina, Bragg graduated high in his class at West Point in 1837 and served with Davis in the Mexican War before resigning from the army to start a plantation in Louisiana.

When the war began, Bragg served first as a high-ranking officer in the Louisiana militia before being tapped for duty as a Confederate general officer in charge of part of the Gulf Coast defenses. Soon promoted to major general, he was transferred to A. S. Johnston's command at Corinth and commanded a corps at Shiloh. Thanks to his close friendship with

Davis, Bragg was soon promoted to full general and given command of the Army of Tennessee. Despite his earlier heroics (mostly in the Seminole and Mexican-American Wars) and his relative competence as a corps commander, Bragg was a near unmitigated disaster as an army commander. Serious defeats followed his invasion of Kentucky, the fights at Perryville and Stones River, and his actions during the Tullahoma Campaign. A resounding victory at Chickamauga can be traced not strictly to his battlefield strategy, but more to the timely arrival of Major General James Longstreet's corps and a simultaneous Union defensive blunder.

Just after the battle at Chickamauga, Bragg returned to his usual form, refusing

tle. Among the dead in the battle was Captain Tod Carter, the youngest son of the Carter family, who fought for the South and died at the home 48 hours after being wounded.

The Carter House is a registered National Historic Landmark. A video presentation, access to the visitor center museum featuring Confederate artifacts and photos of soldiers, and a guided tour of the house and grounds are included with admission to the attraction. Admission is $8.00 for adults and teens, $3.00 for children ages 7 through 13, and $6.00 per person for seniors and for groups of 25 or more. From April through October, hours are 9:00 A.M. to 5:00 P.M. Monday through Saturday, 1:00 to 5:00 P.M. Sunday. November through March, hours are 9:00

A.M. to 4:00 P.M. Monday through Saturday, 1:00 to 4:00 P.M. Sunday.

Carnton Plantation
1345 Carnton Lane, Franklin
(615) 794-0903

This 1826 antebellum plantation was built by Randal McGavock, who was Nashville's mayor in 1824 and 1825. The late-neoclassical plantation house is considered architecturally and historically one of the most important buildings in the area. In its early years, the mansion was a social and political center. Among the prominent visitors attending the many social events there were Andrew Jackson, Sam Houston, and James K. Polk.

On November 30, 1864, after the bloody Battle of Franklin, the home was

against strong protest to pursue the crushed Union Army (he was deathly afraid of running headlong into a possible Union ambush) and allowing it time to regroup. A subsequent and complete defeat at Chattanooga finally resulted in his loss of command for good; his actions there were so incompetent that Davis could no longer overlook them. His removal from command brought great celebration in the ranks, reinforced when the beloved J. E. Johnston was placed in his stead. Davis placed Bragg as his chief of staff, where he continued to plague the Confederate armies with a series of interfering moves, unnecessary commands and directives, and political retaliations. At the very end of the war, he returned to combat duty and served as a divisional commander under J. E. Johnston at the Battle of Bentonville.

Bragg's postwar life was no more successful than his wartime life. He served briefly as the chief engineer for the state of Alabama before moving on to Galveston, Texas. He died there on September 27, 1876, suddenly struck by a stroke while walking down the street. Few postwar memoirs have the slightest positive comments about him—other than proclaiming his devotion to the Confederate cause; perhaps the kindest comments are that he was an able and effective organizer and staff officer. His defenders admit to a person that his battlefield accomplishments were few and far between but point out that he suffered from chronic migraine headaches and was often ill, sometimes quite seriously, from other causes during his campaigns.

used as a hospital. Wounded and dead soldiers filled the house and yard. The Confederates lost 10 generals during the battle to death, injury, or capture. The bodies of five of the generals were laid out on the mansion's back porch. At that time, Carnton was the home of McGavock's son, Colonel John McGavock, and his wife, Carrie Winder McGavock. In 1866 the McGavock family donated two acres adjacent to their family cemetery for the burial of some 1,500 Southern soldiers. The McGavock Confederate Cemetery is the country's largest private Confederate cemetery.

A guided tour of the house costs $8.00 for adults and teens, $7.00 for seniors, and $3.00 for children ages 5 through 11. Group rates are available.

Admission to the grounds and cemetery is free. From April through October hours are 9:00 A.M. to 5:00 P.M. Monday through Saturday and 1:00 to 5:00 P.M. Sunday. November through March hours are 9:00 A.M. to 4:00 P.M. Monday through Saturday and 1:00 to 4:00 P.M. Sunday.

Getting There: Nashville

Nashville is in upper-middle Tennessee, easily accessed via Interstate 24 from Chattanooga and Paducah, Kentucky; Interstate 40 from Knoxville and Memphis; I-65 from Louisville, Kentucky, or Birmingham, Alabama; or the delightfully scenic Natchez Trace Parkway from Tupelo, Mississippi. The major areas of battle were on the south side of the city, accessible from I–65 South.

MODERN TIMES

Nashville is a major metropolitan city and, like Atlanta, has become a city "too busy to preserve its past." With the exception of a fair number of historic markers, few signs of the battle remain. The major action took place along what is today Granny White Pike, 21st Avenue, 12th Avenue, US 31, and Tennessee Highways 106 and 6 in the south part of the city. Some earthworks remain inside the campus of Vanderbilt University near its entrance on 21st Avenue.

About the most significant spot remaining more or less intact is Shy's Hill, part of Hood's line of battle on December 17. Take Battery Lane off US 31 (it extends east to Harding Road at I–65) and travel west about 2 miles to Benton Smith Drive. Drive a very short distance down this road until you see the historic marker; beside it is a set of steps leading to the top of the low hill.

POINTS OF INTEREST

Belle Meade Plantation
5025 Harding Road, Nashville
(615) 356–0501
Relive a bit of the Old South at Belle Meade Plantation, the 1853 mansion known as the "Queen of the Tennessee Plantations." The Greek Revival mansion was once the centerpiece of a 5,400-acre plantation known the world over in the 19th century as a Thoroughbred farm and nursery. In 1807 John Harding purchased a log cabin and 250 acres of land adjacent to the Natchez Trace from the family of Daniel Dunham. Harding and his wife, Susannah, enlarged the cabin as their family grew. In the 1820s they began construction of the present-day Belle Meade (a French term meaning "beautiful meadow") mansion, originally a two-story, Federal-style farmhouse.

Harding, who built a successful business boarding and breeding horses, con-

tinued to add to his estate. In 1836 his son, William Giles Harding, established the Belle Meade Thoroughbred Stud. William Giles Harding made additions to the mansion in the 1840s and in 1853. The Hardings also maintained a wild deer park on the property and sold ponies, Alderney cattle, Cotswald sheep, and cashmere goats. During the Civil War, the Federal government took the horses for the army's use and removed the plantation's stone fences. Loyal slaves are said to have hidden the most prized Thoroughbreds. The mansion was riddled with bullets during the Battle of Nashville.

After the war, William Giles Harding and his son-in-law, William H. Jackson, expanded the farm. It enjoyed international prominence until 1904, when the land and horses were auctioned. The financial crisis of 1893, an excessive lifestyle, and the mishandling of family funds led to the downfall of Belle Meade, which in the early 1900s was the oldest and largest Thoroughbred farm in America. The stables housed many great horses, including Iroquois, winner of the English Derby in 1881. The mansion and 24 remaining acres were opened to the public in 1953 under the management of the Nashville Chapter of the Association for the Preservation of Tennessee Antiquities. For more information on Belle Meade, read *Belle Meade: Mansion, Plantation and Stud* by Ridley Wills III (1991: Vanderbilt University Press, Nashville). Wills is the great-great-grandson of William Giles Harding and the great-grandson of Judge Howell E. Jackson.

The beautifully restored mansion is listed in the National Register of Historic Places. It is elegantly furnished with 19th-century antiques and art of the period. The site also includes the 1890 carriage house and stable filled with antique carriages; the 1790 log cabin (one of the oldest log structures in the state); and six other original outbuildings, such as the garden house, smokehouse, and mausoleum. Guides in period dress lead tours of the property, offering a look back at the lifestyles of early Nashville's rich and famous. The shaded lawn is a popular site for festivals. Admission is $10.00 for adults, $8.50 for seniors, and $4.00 for children 6 through 12; group rates are available. Belle Meade Plantation is open year-round except Thanksgiving, Christmas, and New Year's Day. Hours are 9:00 A.M. to 5:00 P.M. Monday through Saturday and 11:00 A.M. to 5:00 P.M. Sunday.

Tennessee State Capitol
Charlotte Avenue between Sixth and Seventh Avenues, Nashville
(615) 741-2692

The Greek Revival–style building was begun in 1859. Its architect, William Strickland of Philadelphia, began his career as an apprentice to Benjamin Latrobe, architect of the U.S. Capitol in Washington, D.C. Strickland died before the Tennessee State Capitol was completed and, per his wishes, was buried in the northeast wall of the building, near the north entrance. Strickland's son, Francis Strickland, supervised construction until 1857, when Englishman Harvey Akeroyd designed the state library, the final portion of the building.

The capitol stands 170 feet above the highest hill in downtown Nashville. On the eastern slope of the grounds is the tomb of President and Mrs. James K. Polk and a bronze equestrian statue of President Andrew Jackson. During the Civil War the capitol was used as a Union fortress. In the 1930s the murals in the governor's office were added. Various restoration projects have taken place over the years. In 1996 a bronze statue of Andrew Johnson was erected so that all three U.S. presidents from Tennessee are commemorated on the capitol grounds.

The building is open Monday through Friday from 9:00 A.M. to 4:00 P.M.; guided tours are conducted from 9:00 A.M. to 3:00 P.M. A brochure is available for self-guided tours. Admission is free. The building is closed on weekends and state holidays.

Oaklands Historic House Museum
900 North Maney Avenue, Murfreesboro
(615) 893-0022

One of the most elegant antebellum homes in Middle Tennessee, this house began around 1815 as a one-story brick home built by the Maney family. The family enlarged the house with a Federal-style addition in the early 1820s and made more changes in the 1830s. The last addition was the ornate Italianate facade, completed in the 1850s.

Oaklands was the center of a 1,500-acre plantation. Union and Confederate armies alternately occupied the house during the Civil War. On July 13, 1862, Confederate Brigadier General Nathan Bedford Forrest led a raid here, surprising the Union commander at Oaklands. The surrender was negotiated here. In December 1862 President Jefferson Davis of the Confederacy boarded at Oaklands while visiting nearby troops. There is a gift shop on the property. Admission is $7.00 for adults and $5.00 for children 6 through 17. Groups of 10 or more receive a $1.00 discount per person. Hours are 10:00 A.M. to 4:00 P.M. Tuesday through Saturday and 1:00 to 4:00 P.M. Sunday.

Sam Davis Home Historic Site
1399 Sam Davis Road, Smyrna
(615) 459-2341

This Greek Revival home, built around 1820 and enlarged around 1850, sits on 169 acres of the original 1,000-acre farm that was the home of Sam Davis. Davis, called the "Boy Hero of the Confederacy," enlisted in the Confederate Army at the age of 19. He served as a courier, and while transporting secret papers to General Braxton Bragg in Chattanooga, he was captured by Union forces, tried as a spy, and sentenced to hang. The trial officer was so impressed with Davis's honesty and sense of honor that he offered him freedom if he would reveal the source of military information he was caught carrying. Davis is reported to have responded, "If I had a thousand lives I would give them all gladly rather than betray a friend." He was hanged in Pulaski, Tennessee, on November 27, 1863. The home is a typical upper-middle-class farmhouse of the period. A tour of the property also includes outbuildings. Several annual events take place here. Admission is $8.50 for adults and teens, $6.50 for seniors 65 and older, and $3.00 for children 6 through 12. Group discounts are available. From June through August, hours are 9:00 A.M. to 5:00 P.M. Monday through Saturday and 1:00 to 5:00 P.M. Sunday. September through May, hours are 10:00 A.M. to 4:00 P.M. Monday through Saturday and 1:00 to 4:00 P.M. Sunday.

Stones River National Battlefield
3501 Old Nashville Highway
Murfreesboro
(615) 893-9501

One of the bloodier Civil War battles took place at this site between December 31, 1862, and January 2, 1863. More than 83,000 men fought in the battle; nearly 28,000 were killed or wounded. Both the Union army, led by Major General William S. Rosecrans, and the Confederate army, led by General Braxton Bragg, claimed victory. However, on January 3, 1863, Bragg retreated 40 miles to Tullahoma, Tennessee, and Rosecrans took control of Murfreesboro.

The Union constructed a huge supply base within Fortress Rosecrans, the largest enclosed earthen fortification built during the war. The battlefield today appears much as it did during the Battle of Stones River. Most of the points of interest can be reached on the self-guided auto tour. Numbered markers identify the stops, and short trails and exhibits explain the events at each site. Plan to spend at least two hours to get the most out of your visit, and stop first at the visitor center. An audiovisual program and museum will introduce you to the battle. A captioned slide show is available, too. Pick up a brochure guide or recorded guide to use on the self-guided auto tour.

During summer, artillery and infantry demonstrations and talks about the battle are scheduled. The park is administered by the National Park Service. Stones River National Battlefield is open daily except Christmas. Hours are 8:00 A.M. to 5:00 P.M. Admission is free. (See the Other Tennessee Battlefields chapter for a complete description of this battle.)

ACCOMMODATIONS

As a major metropolitan area and convention destination, Nashville is literally filled with chain motels and hotels, mostly clustered near the airport and around the interstate highway exits.

Steeplechase Inn $$$-$$$$
5581 Franklin Pike Circle, Brentwood
(615) 373-8585

One of the Nashville area's rare privately owned and operated hotels, the Steeplechase Inn promises luxury at an affordable rate. It's popular with business travelers, who account for about 70 percent of bookings. The hotel also welcomes a lot of guests in town for weddings and family reunions.

Steeplechase Inn opened in 1986 and features 47 rooms, including 23 suites. The large rooms have 9-foot ceilings, which add to their spacious feel. The decor includes floor-to-ceiling draperies and cherry-wood furniture. The 650-square-foot suites have fully furnished kitchens. Daily deluxe breakfast is included in the room rate. Other perks include free access to Brentwood's YMCA (about a mile away), cable TV, and free parking.

The inn is off I-65 on the east side of Old Hickory Boulevard. There are plenty of affordable restaurants and good shops across the interstate in Brentwood, and the Cool Springs area, about 6 miles south on I-65, has a great mall and lots of good restaurants. Downtown Nashville is about 7 miles north on I-65.

RESTAURANTS

F. Scott's $$–$$$
2210 Crestmoore Road, Nashville
(615) 269–5861

Casually elegant, warm, and inviting, F. Scott's is considered by many to be one of the best restaurants in Nashville. This is a place where the sophisticated feel comfortable, but it's not necessary to dress up to the hilt; you'll fit in, whether you're in jeans or coat and tie. F. Scott's serves American bistro-style food. The menu changes seasonally, but there is always plenty of pasta, chicken, duck, lamb, pork, and fresh fish. Grilled tuna on spinach with shallots and pommes frites, roasted butternut squash soup, grilled salmon with purple sticky rice, and center-cut pork chop in orange cumin butter are just a few tempting examples of the contemporary dishes you might find here. F. Scott's has three dining rooms and a jazz bar with live entertainment each night. In addition to a wonderful dining experience, this is a very pleasant place to stop for a drink. F. Scott's is open only for dinner, and reservations are recommended.

Sunset Grille $$–$$$
2001-A Belcourt Avenue, Nashville
(615) 386–3663

Sunset Grille is one of Nashville's favorite restaurants. Since it opened in fall 1990, this Hillsboro Village hot spot has developed a reputation as a good place to see and be seen. It's a music-business hangout and draws lots of other business people and sports personalities, too. On weekdays when the weather is nice, diners don their dark sunglasses and power-lunch on the patio. In winter the patio is enclosed for those who prefer a more casual setting than the main dining room. Sunset Grille serves new American cuisine in a casually elegant atmosphere. Any night of the week you're apt to see customers in jeans dining next to a group in tuxedos.

The Voodoo Pasta is a menu staple. It has grilled chicken, baby shrimp, andouille sausage, and roasted red-pepper marinara sauce dusted with Black Magic seasonings and tossed with Cajun fettucine. The Vegetarian Voodoo Pasta has zucchini, eggplant, mushrooms, and onions. Other menu favorites include blackberry duck and lamb dijonnaise. There is a good selection of vegetarian dishes, such as Veggies Lee Ann—steamed seasonal veggies over garlic-herb orzo pasta with black beans. The desserts are beautiful. Try the chocolate bombe, a brownie crust with double-thick chocolate mousse filling, drenched in chocolate glaze. You can also order a large dessert trio or half-portions. If you want to go all out, order the dessert mirror, 10 full portions of various desserts served on a mirrored tray.

Sunset Grille has an excellent wine selection—one of the best in town—with more than 200 wines, 60 available by the glass. The Tuesday afternoon wine tasting classes have become quite popular; seating is limited for these, so make a reservation if you don't want to miss out. Sunset Grille is one of the few places in town that has a late-night menu. You can order till 1:30 A.M. Monday through Saturday and until 11:00 P.M. Sunday.

Hog Heaven $
115 27th Avenue North, Nashville
(615) 329–1234

This is a good time to apply the "don't judge-a-book-by-its-cover" rule. Hog Heaven doesn't look like much—it's a tiny white cinder-block building tucked in a corner of Centennial Park behind McDonald's—but once you taste their barbecue, you'll know why they attached the word "heaven" to the name. This is some good eatin'. Hog Heaven's hand-pulled pork, chicken, beef, and turkey barbecue is actually pretty famous among Nashville's barbecue connoisseurs.

The menu is posted on a board beside the walk-up window. After you get your order, you might want to hop on over to Centennial Park and dig in, since the only seating at the restaurant is two picnic tables on a slab of concrete right in front of the window. You can order barbecue sandwiches, barbecue plates that come with two side orders, and barbecue by the pound. The white barbecue sauce is just right on top of the chicken, and the regular sauce comes in mild, hot, or extra hot. Quarter-chicken and half-chicken orders are available, and Hog Heaven has spareribs, too. Barbecue beans, potato salad, coleslaw, turnip greens, white beans, green beans, black-eyed peas, and corn on the cob are among the side dishes. The homemade cobbler is a heavenly way to end a memorable Hog Heaven meal. Hog Heaven delivers to areas nearby and is open Monday through Saturday for lunch and dinner.

CHATTANOOGA: THE BATTLE ABOVE THE CLOUDS

BACKGROUND TO THE BATTLE

In the late afternoon of September 20, 1863, following the disaster at Chickamauga (see chapter on Chickamauga), Union troops streamed back in a near panic to their stronghold at Chattanooga. Many abandoned both arms and equipment in their haste to escape the Confederate force they thought would surely pounce at any moment. Amid them (and in front of a great number of them) rode their dispirited commander, Major General William Starke Rosecrans, no doubt wondering how to tell his bosses that earlier dispatches predicting victory in the north Georgia battle were premature at best.

Although his able lieutenant, Major General George Henry Thomas, the "Rock of Chickamauga," still held his ground at the northern end of the battleground, Rosecrans was in near hysterics on hearing (untrue) rumors that 20,000 or more Confederate troops under Lieutenant General Richard S. Ewell were on their way from Virginia. In quick succession, Rosecrans telegraphed Washington begging for "all reinforcements you can send hurried up," and he sent other telegrams stating he could stand and fight and others that claimed he would soon have to withdraw north. To complete his rushed and distracted set of actions, he ordered Thomas to retreat and join him in Chattanooga and that small outposts atop Lookout Mountain be abandoned as "undefensible."

Chattanooga had first fallen into Union hands in early September 1863, the Confederate force under General Braxton Bragg pulling out without a shot being fired when Rosecrans's three columns including 60,000 men moving south threatened to cut the rail line to Atlanta. At the same time, Major General Ambrose Burnside's Union Army of the Ohio, divided into four columns including 24,000 men, swept down on the smaller Confederate garrison at Knoxville, also forcing it to abandon the city without a fight. The two Confederate forces combined under Bragg in northwest Georgia, just below the Tennessee line. For all practical purposes, Tennessee was then under complete Union control.

Problems in the Armies

Strangely enough, at this time both forces were closely matched in both troop strength (56,359 Union to 65,165 Confederate) and the controversial nature of their sometimes simply incompetent commanders. Bragg was intensely despised by both officers and ordinary soldiers and kept his rank and position primarily by way of his personal friendship with President Jefferson Davis. Private Sam Watkins of the Maury Grays, 1st Tennessee Infantry, said, "None of General Bragg's soldiers ever loved him. They had no faith in his ability as a general. He was looked upon as a merciless tyrant."

Bragg also was noted for his personal vendettas against his "enemies," those fellow Confederate officers who disagreed with him on one point or another. In the midst of renewed Union offenses in the summer of 1863, Bragg chose instead to pay more attention to his conspiracies against outstanding generals such as Major Generals Benjamin Frank Cheatham and John McCowan and Lieutenant General William J. Hardee.

Rosecrans, on the other hand, was considered a dangerous tactician by his Confederate foes, but while loved by his men and admired for his generalship in most battles, his own peers thought him unstable and prone to panic under stress. Lincoln later remarked that Rosecrans had acted "confused and stunned like a duck hit on the head." In the midst of Rosecrans's rushed preparations for the retreat to Chattanooga, one glaring problem escaped his notice—his own supply lines. Confederate forces had cut his northern rail access, steep and nearly impassable mountains surrounded him on three sides and were soon to be manned with Confederate artillery and infantry emplacements, and a low-water situation combined with adjacent Confederate outposts on the Tennessee River flowing past his command prevented resupply by riverboat. To add to his woes, most of a more than 800-hundred-wagon supply train coming in on the one inadequate road was captured on October 2 by Major General Joseph Wheeler's cavalry raiders. Rations at this point were estimated at a mere 10 days' worth, and ammunition existed for only about two days of fully involved combat. Instead of a fortified redoubt, Rosecrans's muddled planning had placed them in an isolated prison.

Tell old Bragg for God's sake not to let the Yanks whip him as he usually does when this army gains a victory . . . If the armies of the West were worth a goober we could soon have piece [sic] on our own terms.

Private W. C. McClellan of Lee's Army of Northern Virginia, in a letter to his father in northern Alabama, as quoted in Bell Irvin Wiley's *Life of Johnny Reb*

On the Confederate side, things were hardly better. At Chickamauga, to the outrage of his senior commanders, Bragg refused to allow them to press on after the rapidly retreating routed majority of Union forces, ordering instead a concentration of effort on Thomas's sparse force holding fast to Horseshoe Ridge. Even after Thomas's men slipped away after nightfall on September 20, Bragg refused to allow a pursuit, believing the noises the retreating Union forces were making indicated they were preparing for an assault the next morning. Not until two full days later did Bragg move forward to Missionary Ridge, only to see the Union forces already well entrenched within Chattanooga below.

After some patrol and light skirmishing action on September 22 showed the extent of the Union army's fortifications, Bragg settled down to try to starve out the besieged city garrison. Within a few days, Union rations were reduced by half, then to one-quarter. Even with some supplies coming in through a torturous 65-mile mountain route constantly under attack by Wheeler's cavalry, it became nearly impossible to maintain even this inadequate ration. Guards were posted to prevent soldiers from stealing the feed of the most essential horses; another 15,000 horses and mules simply died of starvation.

After heavy rains washed out the only bridge on their own supply line, Confederate men were reduced to the same meager rations as their Union foe. With the infantry obviously dissatisfied with Bragg's tactics and personal vendettas, as well as the bleak supply situation, President Davis decided to make a mid-October visit to the battlefield to shore up morale. It didn't work as planned, as Sam Watkins describes:

And in the very acme of our privations and hunger, when the army was most dissatisfied and unhappy, we were ordered into line of battle to be reviewed by Honorable Jefferson Davis. When he passed by us, with his great retinue of staff officers and play-outs at full gallop, cheers greeted them, with the words, "Send us something to eat, Massa Jeff. Give us something to eat, Massa Jeff. I'm hungry! I'm hungry!"

Sherman to the Rescue

Unknown to either side at Chattanooga, at least at first, once word of the situation reached Washington, four divisions of General William T. Sherman's Army of the Tennessee set out from Vicksburg and two corps under Major General Joseph Hooker set out from Virginia. On October 30 the forward elements of Hooker's corps reached Bridgeport, Tennessee, and Rosecrans made plans to assault and seize the closest ferry point, Brown's Ferry, just west of Lookout Mountain itself. Before all could be made ready, Rosecrans was relieved of command and replaced by Thomas. Major General U. S. Grant himself arrived with reinforcements from Vicksburg on October 23, and both commanders agreed to continue with Rosecrans's plans.

Led by Lieutenant Colonel James C. Foy of the 23rd Kentucky Infantry, hastily gathered pontoons and other flatboats floated quietly downriver on the night of October 27 and captured Brown's Ferry with hardly a shot being fired by the small Confederate outpost. While engineers and pioneers hastily assembled a pontoon bridge to bring reinforcements across, Foy had his men entrench for the attack that was sure to come.

The only Confederate troops nearby did soon mount an attack, but only about one-half of a regiment under Colonel William C. Oates could be summoned for the assault. In a 20-minute fight, Oates's men were routed by both Foy's men and other Union units hastily brought across

the still-unfinished bridge. The key to Bragg's entire strategy—Brown's Ferry—had been guarded by a tiny, unsupported percentage of the men under his command.

On October 28, with Bragg and Lieutenant General James Longstreet personally observing from atop Lookout Mountain, Brigadier General John West Geary's 2nd Division of Hooker's 12th Corps crossed the newly finished pontoon bridge and entered Lookout Valley, stopping at the Wauhatchie rail junction. At midnight that same night, Brigadier General Micah Jenkin's Division of Longstreet's corps attacked Geary, now reinforced by two other brigades. The three-hour fight resulted in both Jenkin's being thrown back and a complete Confederate withdrawal out of the valley and up onto the slopes of Lookout Mountain, leaving all the good supply lines into the city in Union hands. The Confederates still held all the high ground surrounding the city, and Bragg remained confident that this was the only advantage he would really need.

THE FIGHT BEGINS: ORCHARD KNOB

With the Union situation improving by the day with fresh men and supplies coming in, and the Confederate supply problems mounting, Bragg amazingly decided to concentrate on his own personal vendettas once again. Blaming Longstreet for the Union successes at Brown's Ferry and Wauhatchie, Bragg ordered him and two other generals to prepare for an all-out assault on the strong Union positions in Lookout Valley. Longstreet duly reported for the three of them that such an attack would be "impracticable."

Viewing this sensible report as a personal affront, Bragg decided Longstreet's attitude was unacceptable. In a letter to Jefferson Davis, Bragg complained that Longstreet was "disrespectful and insubordinate" and reported that he planned to send him off with his corps to the renewed campaign around Knoxville. On November 4, Longstreet left by rail with nearly a third of Bragg's entire force.

Sherman's forces finally began arriving on November 21, and with this encouraging news, Grant ordered attacks to begin as soon as possible. His first target was a small, steep hill in front of Missionary Ridge called Orchard Knob. On the morning of November 23, three Union brigades led by Brigadier Generals William B. Hazen, August Willich, and Samuel Beatty stormed the lightly held outpost, capturing the knob in about five minutes of heavy fighting. The surviving Confederates fled back to the entrenchments at the base of Missionary Ridge, and almost before they knew it, the Union held one of the best strategic observation posts for the coming battle. The cost was very high, though, with Hazen alone losing 167 men.

LOOKOUT MOUNTAIN: CRAVENS HOUSE FIGHT

Early the next morning, with Sherman's forces fully across the river (but mistakenly out of position to strike at Missionary Ridge), Hooker was ordered to make a "demonstration" against Lookout Mountain, to draw attention away from the main assault on Missionary Ridge. With a low fog enveloping the mountain and obscuring the view of Confederate artillery and infantry outposts atop the mountain at Point Lookout, Geary's division supported by Brigadier General Walter C. Whitaker's brigade moved quietly up the flank of the rough, boulder-encrusted mountainside, aiming not to take the upper crest (which Hooker thought was completely immune to direct assault) but to capture the middle and lower reaches of the mountainside. When they at last encountered a line of Confederate entrenchments and emplacements manned by Brigadier General Edward C. Walthall's brigade, they found to their joy that the Confederate force was positioned to repulse a direct assault up the slope, not from across the steep mountainside. In less than 15 minutes of furious fighting, the Confederate force was driven out and sent fleeing back to its main line of defense at the Cravens House.

Storming around the mountain after the fleeing Confederates, the Union forces, led now by the 60th and 137th New York Regiments, advanced through a furious cannonade toward the white farmhouse, close behind Walthall's retreating Confederates. They closed in so tight that a two-gun battery at the Cravens House itself was unable to fire upon them, for fear of hitting its own troops, and the house was soon overrun and captured. More Confederate forces arrive to shore up the trenchlines of the tiny battleground, but they were soon routed and sent fleeing down the mountain by Whitaker's reserve brigades coming onto the field.

POINT LOOKOUT

Geary sent word to Hooker of their achievement and asked for resupply so that they could advance farther. Amazed and almost upset that this "demonstration" had gone so far, Hooker ordered Geary and Whitaker to entrench and stay put. With the Confederate forces above and around them in the woods keeping up a steady fire and even rolling large boulders down the mountainside at them, the Union forces manned their enemies' previous breastworks and waited.

Bragg, alerted to his plight on Lookout Mountain by the sound of heavy Union artillery being placed atop it, made a fatal decision. Convinced that this action constituted a major assault on his commanding position, he ordered the withdrawal of all units from atop and on Lookout Mountain, and the valley below as well, to concentrate his forces on Missionary Ridge. By sunrise on November 25, Hooker had complete command of the entire mountain, at least by default. As a final act, men of the North's 8th Kentucky and 96th Illinois Infantry Regiments climbed the nearly sheer rocky cliffs to plant their flags on the abandoned emplacements.

The oft-remarked "battle above the clouds" in fact never really occurred; at best, it could be accurately called the "battle within the fog." Grant himself grumbled over the brief fight's wide exposure and exaltation in the press, stating that it had hardly even constituted a skirmish. In his postwar memoirs he remarked, "The Battle of Lookout Mountain is one of the romances of the war. There was no such battle and no action even worthy to be called a battle on Lookout Mountain. It is all poetry."

Missionary Ridge

With reinforcements from the withdrawn positions around Chattanooga coming in line, Bragg had a strong position on Missionary Ridge. Aside from the natural defense of the steep mountain terrain, he had positioned his men in two main defensive bands. The first line of defense was a set of interlocking rifle pits at the mountain's base and the second was a set of strongly reinforced breastworks nearly atop the ridgeline, reinforced by artillery emplacements.

Turning attention immediately toward his main objective, Grant ordered Sherman to attack the far right of the Confederate line on Missionary Ridge early on the morning of November 25. Moving forward on the afternoon of the 24th, Sherman discovered too late that the hill his men were already assaulting, Billy Goat Hill, was not continuous with the ridgeline but separated by a steep and wooded ravine. With his typical bullheadedness, Sherman attempted to push through the ravine and hit the far right of the Confederate line anyhow, only to be halted by Major General Patrick R. Cleburne's still entrenching troops. Even with a near seven-to-one advantage, the Union forces could not push through the strong Confederate

At Franklin, Tennessee, 23 of the 88 Confederate regiments engaged in the battle each suffered over 40 percent casualties, while 40 percent of their commanders were killed or wounded.

position. Even worse, a counterattacking downhill bayonet charge by Cleburne's men at a part of the ridge called Tunnel Hill pushed the Union line back to the base of the hill and captured nearly a whole Union brigade's worth of men after an incredibly fierce hand-to-hand fight.

With Sherman stuck on the Union left, Grant ordered Hooker to cross the valley and strike on the low ridges on the right, with Thomas's men to make a "demonstration" from Orchard Knob toward the middle of the Confederate line. As planned, this center attack would force the Confederates to shift their men away from the flanks, giving Sherman and Hooker the edge they needed to take the flanks.

The Infantry Assault on Missionary Ridge

Once more, the "demonstration" became the battle centerpiece. About 3:30 P.M., Thomas's men moved forward with orders to engage the first set of rifle pits and halt. Charging across the nearly half mile of open ground, under inaccurate and ineffective Confederate artillery fire all the while, the Union troops quickly took over the Confederate rifle pits, earlier ordered to be abandoned when attacked in a serious tactical blunder by Lieutenant General William J. Hardee. Under heavy and accurate fire from above, Thomas's men realized that to stay in this exposed position was sheer suicide. Ignoring his orders, Lieutenant Colonel William P. Chandler of the 35th Illinois Infantry leapt to the top of the breastwork and, with a cry of "Forward!," led his men up the steep hillside.

CLOSE-UP

Sam Watkins

Sam Watkins was born near Columbia, Tennessee, in 1839, and was attending college there when the war broke out. He immediately quit school and joined Company H, 1st Tennessee Infantry Regiment of the Confederate Army, afraid that the war would soon end and he would not see any action. Self-described "High-Private" Watkins served until the end of the war and amazingly survived in the midst of some of the fiercest fighting in the Western Theater. His unit, soon joined by the 27th Tennessee Infantry Regiment and another independent battalion, fought from just after the First Manassas (First Bull Run) until the surrender of General Joseph Eggleston Johnston's Army of Tennessee at Greensboro, North Carolina, in April 1865. Although his combined regiments counted some 3,200 men in their ranks throughout the war (by his own estimation), Watkins was one of only 65 original members still standing after four years of fighting, and one of only seven survivors of the original 120 men of Company H.

Although Watkins was in the first line of battle in most of his unit's engagements, he managed to survive nearly unscathed—seriously wounded only once. He lived to tell about his experiences in one of the greatest memoirs of the Civil War, *Co. Aytch*, or *A Sideshow of the Big Show*, published in 1882. Originally written in serial form for the Columbia *Herald*, the book is an emotional and quite philosophical journey through the heart and mind of a combat infantryman separated from all he knows and loves and forced into brutal savagery simply to survive. Watkins took an ironic and somewhat humorous view of "what I saw as a humble private in the rear rank of an infantry regiment," and his memoir is distinctly different from the legions of other, more self-aggrandizing memoirs and diaries published after the war.

Watkins's view of the war was from the trenches, and throughout the book he commented that he was not aware of and did not care about the grander strategies;

This was all the motivation that the rest of Thomas's command needed, and company by company, roaring at the top of their lungs, soon all were in full assault uphill. Atop Orchard Knob, Grant was horrified at the sight. With the memory of Sherman's men in full flight down Tunnel Hill still very fresh, he had a terrible vision of Thomas's men being chewed to pieces and routed. Turning in anger, he demanded of his corps commanders who had ordered that charge. Thomas and Major General Gordon Granger both calmly answered, truthfully, that they had not. Grant turned back to watch the scene unfolding, muttering that if that attack failed, someone would pay dearly. One does get the impression that he was not referring to the infantrymen.

Sweeping like a wildfire up the mountainside, the uncoordinated attacks all along the center of the Confederate lines could not be stopped. About 5:00 P.M., the 32nd Indiana and 6th Ohio Infantry Regi-

he just marched where he was led and fired when he was told. However, his observations of those mostly vain and self-serving men who led his regiment and army stand out as piercingly accurate. He saw General Braxton Bragg as a "merciless tyrant" that no one in the ranks "ever loved or respected." About the best thing Watkins could say about Bragg was a simple postwar observation, "But he is dead now." Watkins thought General John Bell Hood a "failure in every particular" as a general and leader, but "brave, good, noble and gallant," although he stated that Hood was both mentally and physically incompetent for command.

Johnston was held in much higher regard by Watkins and most of his men and is also well thought of by most modern historians. Watkins said, "He was loved, respected, admired; yea, almost worshipped by his troops. . . . The veriest coward that was ever born became a brave man and a hero under his manipulation." While Johnston did not have the support of the higher Confederate command and authorities, his men loved him because he "made us love ourselves," and Watkins mentioned time and again how they would have followed the little general literally anywhere. Watkins's own regimental commander, Colonel Hume R. Field, was equally admired; Watkins said that he was the "bravest man, I think, I ever knew" and that the War Department should have placed him in charge of whole armies instead of a mere regiment. Watkins's view of officers in general, however, was more practical: "I always looked upon officers as harmless personages," and on the battlefield, "I always shot at privates."

Watkins went on after the war to marry his beloved Jennie, who was mentioned throughout his memoir, and to raise eight children. He died in Columbia in 1901.

ments reached the crest at Sharp's Spur, right in the center of Colonel William F. Tucker's Mississippi Brigade. Quickly capturing one 12-pounder Napoleon of Captain James Garrity's Alabama Battery, the Ohio men forced the Confederate gunners at bayonet point to fire on their own retreating men.

Other Union regiments soon reached the crest and fanned out to both sides, with Confederates making only token resistance before pulling back. With strong attacks now coming from three points atop the ridge, Bragg gave hasty orders to retreat. Mostly in ragged groups and as individual soldiers, some in quickly organized defensive postures, the Confederates streamed back toward Georgia. Hooker was ordered to give chase. Cleburne was ordered to save what was left of the army and to protect their retreat at the north Georgia town of Ringgold.

i *There are pieces of original hardtack—a crackerlike ration—in several museums. The soldiers were not kidding when they said it was too hard to eat!*

THE FIGHT AT RINGGOLD

Receiving these orders just before the Union advance elements arrived, Cleburne elected to set up his defensive position just south of the small town atop two small hills on either side of the rail line. With only a little more than 4,000 men and two small artillery pieces, he knew that he could not withstand a direct assault by Hooker's 12,000 troops.

Hooker's men passed through the small town nearly uncontested on the morning of November 27 and immediately set out along the south rail line, led by the 13th Illinois Infantry. Waiting until the Union men were less than 150 yards away, Cleburne ordered both cannon to open fire with both solid shot and cannister. The resulting carnage was extreme, with the 13th Illinois being shot to pieces within minutes, and the flanking regiments on either side of the gap suffering equally immense casualties.

Cleburne kept up his defensive position until shortly after noon, when Union artillery finally arrived on scene. Less than an hour later, he had his men and both artillery pieces safely off the hilltops and heading back toward Dalton. At a cost of 110 casualties, he had both stopped the Union advance and bloodied Hooker to the tune of at least 500 casualties. Many of Hooker's own men grumbled that this official figure was far too low.

Grant arrived in town later that same day and ordered Hooker to stop the pursuit. Intending to sit out the winter in relative comfort in Chattanooga, he ordered Hooker to stay put for a few days, and then withdraw to the north. Hooker finally left on November 30, burning the small Georgia town in his wake. The bitter fight for control of the gateway city to the Deep South finally came to an end, ironically with a Confederate tactical victory.

THE TOUR

Getting There: Chattanooga

Chattanooga is a rapidly growing major city (only one Georgia county along the 100-plus-mile Interstate 75 corridor is not within either metropolitan Chattanooga or Atlanta), and its Civil War heritage stands front and center in its images and advertisements. Curiously, there is relatively little remaining untouched of the most fought-over battleground, Missionary Ridge, and it and some of the other major landmarks are very poorly marked and somewhat hard to find. Due to the city's growth alongside the meandering Tennessee River, streets are laid out in a confusing array, and it is a bit difficult to find your way around town at first.

Looming over the city like a great granite guardian angel is Lookout Mountain, the focal point for most Civil War–related activities. However, even this obvious landmark suffers from having its only real battleground (the Cravens House) barely marked and easily overlooked. On the positive side, the original Confederate artillery emplacements at the mountain's crest are still in place, encompassed by a small but tidy park run by the National Park Service. Although no skirmish transpired here, one can get a magnificent view of the city and on clear days see all the major battle landmarks in the area.

Three major interstate highways meet in Chattanooga (Interstates 24, 59, and 75), giving easy access to the area from all directions. The suggested route, if convenient, is I-75 north from Atlanta, turning onto I-24 northbound and exiting at exit 178 (Broad Street/Lookout Mountain). An abundance of signs at the end of the ramp will guide you to whichever site or area you wish to visit first.

Take the Battlefield Parkway exit off I-75 (Georgia Highway 2, exit 141) and travel west about 5 miles, then head south on U.S. Highway 27 about 1 mile to the park. The visitor center is just inside the north entrance and is very well marked.

To follow closely the track that Rosecrans's retreating army took from Chickamauga to Chattanooga, from Chickamauga stay on US 27 North about 3 miles to a large ridgeline bisecting the state line. This is the left flank of the Confederate Missionary Ridge line. A right turn onto Crest Road will take you across what was once the second and highest set of emplacements, nearly on top of the highest point of the mountain ridge, all the way to the far right flank where Crest Road meets Campbell Street. Please note that nearly all of this avenue is private property, even where historic markers and cannon monuments abound. Also note that this road is narrow and twisting, and parking is difficult to find in most places. A good choice if you are physically able is to park at the Sherman, DeLong, or Iowa Reservations (very few parking slots are at each) and walk along the route.

MODERN TIMES

Today most of the area of operations of this short campaign has been altered or covered up by the rapidly growing city of Chattanooga. The most significant battlegrounds are now federal property, with the National Park Service preserving and operating several separate areas around the city. The largest continuous preserved area consists of Point Park and Lookout Mountain and includes the Cravens House, Point Lookout, and much of the northwest face of the large ridgeline. A very small, 1-city-block-square park encompasses the highest elevation of Orchard Knob, and several small "reservations" dot the top of Missionary Ridge.

We strongly suggest you visit at least the visitor center of Chickamauga Battlefield (see our chapter on Chickamauga for a complete description), which the National Park Service operates as the centerpiece of the two-state Chickamauga and Chattanooga National Military Park.

SHILOH: THE BLOODIEST DAYS OF 1862

THE CONFEDERATE SITUATION

In early 1862, after decisive Confederate losses in Kentucky and upper Tennessee, General Albert Sidney Johnston pulled his forces together in northern Mississippi and, along with General Pierre Gustave Toutant Beauregard, began plans for a Confederate campaign to retake the lost territory. Part of the Union strategy was to divide the Confederacy in half by taking middle Tennessee and then Atlanta; the Confederate overall strategy was much more daunting than the Union's: Stop the Union forces when the opportunity arose, grind them up when possible, and simply survive until the North grew tired of the fight.

Johnston's newly organized Army of Mississippi, based in the important rail center of Corinth, Mississippi, steadily built up strength through March 1862. Major General Leonidas Polk, Brigadier General (and former U.S. vice president) John C. Breckinridge, and Major General William J. Hardee brought the remnants of their corps down from Kentucky; Major General Braxton Bragg brought most of his corps north from Pensacola, Florida; and Brigadier General Daniel Ruggles's division marched east from New Orleans. Other commands scattered around the Deep South detached individual regiments and brigades, which arrived in the northern Mississippi town all through the last two weeks of March. By April 1, Johnston had a roughly organized, ill-trained, and mostly inexperienced force of about 45,000 officers and men under his command.

THE UNION SITUATION

After taking Fort Henry in the north-central region of Tennessee, Flag Officer Andrew Hull Foote sailed his small gunboat fleet down the Tennessee River nearly unmolested all the way to Florence, Alabama, decisively demonstrating just how vulnerable the South was to invasion via the river systems. One of the very few attempts at a Confederate resistance to his mission was on March 1, when Gibson's Battery of the 1st Louisiana Artillery Regiment, mounted on a bluff just downstream from Savannah, Tennessee, lobbed a few shells at the fleet as they passed. Colonel Alfred Mouton's infantry from the adjacent 18th Louisiana Infantry joined in, ineffectively shooting up the side of the armored gunboats. Foote returned fire, and the shelling soon stopped.

Two weeks later, Union forces started moving south under the overall command of Major General Henry Wager Halleck with two missions: Take control of and repair roads through middle Tennessee, and clear the area of any Confederate forces they encountered. Once all of his forces were concentrated at Savannah, Halleck intended to move farther south, into Mississippi, and destroy the rail junctions in Corinth, Jackson, Humbolt, and Iuka. To accomplish this mission, Halleck had two grand armies: Major General Ulysses S. Grant's Army of the Tennessee and Major General Don Carlos Buell's Army of the Ohio, with a combined total of just under 63,000 men on the march south.

A heavy reconnaissance force under Brigadier General Charles Ferguson Smith (promoted one week later to Major General) arrived in Savannah on March 13, charged by Halleck to seize and hold or at least cut the Memphis & Charleston Railroad at Corinth without engaging the Confederate forces rumored to be gathering in the area. Brigadier General William Tecumseh Sherman arrived from Kentucky the next day, and Smith promptly sent him off toward Eastport, Mississippi, to see if he could cut the railroad there. As he sailed south on the Tennessee River aboard Lieutenant William Gwin's gunboat, Tyler, Gwin pointed out the location of their earlier skirmish with the Confederate artillery battery. Alarmed at the close presence of the enemy to his intended target, Sherman sent word back to Smith that this location should be occupied in force as soon as possible. Smith agreed and immediately dispatched Brigadier General Stephen Hurlbut's 4th Division to occupy the small bluff, Pittsburg Landing, about 3 miles northeast of a tiny settlement called Shiloh Church.

THE BUILDUP

Sherman soon returned from his reconnaissance, after finding Confederates were present in force at his intended target, and joined Hurlbut at Pittsburg Landing. Scouting the area, he reported back to Smith that the area was "important" and easily defended by a relatively small force, although the ground provided a good encampment space for several thousand troops. The few settlers at the landing had fled with the arrival of Union gunboats, and the only "locals" remaining were small-plot farmers scattered about the county. The small Methodist meetinghouse, Shiloh Church, was described by one source as a "rude one-room log cabin, which would make a good corncrib for an Illinois farmer." Sherman urged Smith to relocate the majority of forces to this small landing,

the northernmost road link to their intended target of Corinth, Mississippi.

General Grant arrived in Savannah on March 17 to take over direct command of the Tennessee River operation from Smith, setting up his headquarters in the Cherry Mansion on Main Street. He soon ordered his (roughly) 35,000-man force to deploy on the west side of the river, save a small garrison in Savannah, with five divisions to join with Sherman at Pittsburg Landing, and Brigadier General Lewis "Lew" Wallace's 2nd Division to occupy Crump's Landing, 6 miles north of Sherman's position.

Another major Union army, Major General Buell's Army of the Ohio, was on the way south from Nashville with another 30,000 men (both this figure and Grant's total command size are wildly disparate in differing accounts). Grant planned to rest his men and wait for Buell's arrival before starting his operation against Corinth. Although he was aware that the Confederates were present in force just 20 miles away, he believed that they would simply entrench around Corinth and have to be forced out. An attack on Pittsburg Landing was, quite literally, the last thing he expected the Confederates to do.

The Deployment

It took well over a week to transport all the Union forces south to the new position, and the divisions moved inland and encamped in a loose semicircle south of the landing and across the Corinth Road as they arrived. Sherman's own 5th Division headquarters was just to the west of the Corinth Road. Colonel John A. McDowell's 1st, Colonel Ralph P. Buckland's 4th, and Colonel Jesse Hildebrand's 3rd Brigades deployed from Owl Creek left (east) to just south of Shiloh Church. Colonel David Stuart's 2nd Brigade of Sherman's division encamped separately about 2 miles farther east, at the far left and southernmost of the combined Union line, just above Locust Grove Branch at the Hamburg-Savannah Road. Hurlbut's 4th Division encamped to the left (due east) of Sherman's main line, with Colonel Nelson G. Williams's 1st, Colonel James C. Veatch's 2nd, and Colonel Jacob G. Lauman's 3rd Brigades arrayed across the intersection of the Corinth and Hamburg-Savannah Roads.

Major General John A. McClernand's 1st Division deployed behind (north of) Sherman's. Colonel Abraham M. Hare's 1st, Colonel C. Carroll Marsh's 2nd, and Colonel Julius Raith's 3rd Brigades encamped along the Corinth Road as it ran due west to the Hamburg-Purdy Road intersection. Smith's division stayed close to Pittsburg Landing itself, Colonel James M. Tuttle's 1st, Colonel Thomas West Sweeny's 3rd, and Brigadier General John McArthur's Brigades encamped just north of the end of the Corinth Road and west to Snake Creek. Brigadier General Benjamin M. Prentiss's newly organized 6th Division landed and moved the south to the right (west) of Stuart's Brigade. Colonel Madison Miller's 2nd and Colonel Everett Peabody's 1st Brigades made camp to Sherman's southeast, in the woods across and to the west of the Eastern Corinth Road.

By March 19, all six divisions were in place and comfortably making camp. Smith had been injured while jumping from one boat to another during the landing and was soon forced to hand over command of his 2nd Division to Brigadier General William Harvey Lamb Wallace. Smith died on April 25 of an infection in his foot from the wound.

The Confederate Advance

Johnston was well aware of Grant's presence to the north of his headquarters and received a message on April 2 that Buell's force was nearby as well. Still waiting in

Corinth for the last of his assigned forces to arrive, Johnston decided that he would go ahead and attack the gathering Union force before Buell's addition could make it stronger. The orders he issued were simple: March north and engage the enemy between his encampments and the river, turning their left flank and forcing them away from their line of retreat until they were forced to surrender.

Beauregard planned out the tactical details of the coming attack and issued orders to move out on the morning of April 3. Confederate units scattered across upper Mississippi and lower Tennessee were to converge by April 4 at Mickey's farmhouse, 8 miles south of Pittsburg Landing, where final preparations for the attack would begin. Hardee's and Bragg's corps would march north from Corinth, along with one division of Polk's corps, along the parallel Bark and Pittsburg Landing Roads. Breckinridge's corps moved north from Burnsville and Polk's other division (Major General Benjamin Franklin Cheatham's) would move southeast from Purdy, Tennessee, to join at the rendezvous farm.

The march took much longer than Beauregard had planned due to poor preparation and a steady rain that turned the dirt roads into mud quagmires. It was late in the evening of April 5 before everyone was in position at the junction of Corinth and Bark Roads, with Hardee's corps arrayed in the front only a half mile from the Union picket line. Union cavalry patrols had engaged with forward elements of each column on both April 4 and 5, leading Beauregard to ask Johnston to call off the attack. He stated that his carefully scheduled attack plan was now "disrupted" and that with the cavalry attacks, surely all aspects of surprise were long gone. Johnston was adamant about continuing the attack, telling Beauregard, Polk, and Bragg, "Gentlemen, we shall attack at daylight tomorrow." Moments later, he remarked to one of his staff officers, "I would fight them if they were a million. They can present no greater front between these two creeks than we can, and the more men they crowd in there, the worse we can make it for them."

The Night of April 5

All through the dark, damp night, Confederate soldiers lay in the woods, listening to Union bands playing patriotic tunes just yards away. Union soldiers had listened to them advancing into position all evening and had sent a slew of frantic messages up the chain of command warning of their presence. Amazingly, all these warnings were ignored by Grant's staff, who believed they amounted to nothing more than reconnaissance patrols. Grant was still firmly convinced that Johnston's men were continuing to entrench heavily at Corinth and was only concerned with how difficult it was going to be to "root them out."

To top off the Union army's lack of combat preparedness, Halleck had ordered Grant not to be pulled into a fight that would distract him from his goal of taking Corinth, and Grant followed suit by ordering no patrolling of his own forces, for fear they might engage the enemy "patrols" and create a general battle. His brigade commanders farthest south were growing increasingly nervous, passing on report after report to headquarters that their men were spotting more and more Confederate cavalry, infantry, and even artillery. Their frantic requests for reinforcement, or even for permission to mount their own scouting missions, were denied; their division commanders only reiterated Grant's orders.

Finally, as darkness fell on April 5, Peabody decided it would be better to beg forgiveness if he was wrong than to ask permission again and gave orders for a combat patrol to go out as early as possible the next morning. At 3:00 A.M. on April 6, Major James Powell led his 25th Missouri and the 12th Michigan Infantry Regiments, with a total of 250 men, out into the predawn blackness, heading south toward the Corinth Road. They marched southwesterly down a narrow farm lane only about a quarter mile before running into Confederate cavalry vedettes. Both sides exchanged fire briefly before the Confederate cavalrymen suddenly broke contact and withdrew. Just before 5:00 A.M. Powell deployed his men into a line-abreast skirmish line and continued southeast, toward Fraley's cotton field.

THE FIRST DAY, APRIL 6, 1862: THE BATTLE BEGINS

Powell's men moved into the cotton field and soon came under fire. Major Aaron B. Hardcastle's 3rd Mississippi Battalion had observed the Union troops entering the field and waited until they closed within 90 yards before opening fire. The Union soldiers hit the ground and returned a heavy volume of fire. The exchange lasted until 6:30 A.M., both sides suffering moderate casualties, until Powell observed Hardcastle's men suddenly disengaging and moving back into the woods. Believing they were retreating, Powell ordered his men up and was preparing to move out again when, to his horror, a mile-wide mass of Confederate soldiers suddenly appeared at the woodline before him—9,000 men of Hardee's corps on their way north.

The Confederate force was fully up and moving, their surprise attack only slightly tripped up by Powell's tiny force. Behind Hardee was Bragg's corps, also in a near mile-wide line of battle, followed by Polk's corps in route-march formation (columns of brigades) on the Corinth Road. In the rear, and also in columns of brigades, was Breckinridge's reserve corps. The whole formation was T-shaped, almost a mile wide, and more than 2 miles long, all moving forward at a quick-time march toward the Union encampments.

Before he was killed and his small patrol force scattered, Powell managed to get word back to Peabody about the general attack. Peabody immediately moved his brigade south to try to aid Powell.

Hardee was having a tough time moving his large force north—the Union patrol and skirmishers delayed his general movement, and the terrain was not conducive to moving such a heavy mass of troops and equipment very quickly. As the two forces moved toward each other, Prentiss rode up to Peabody and began berating him for sending out the patrol and "bringing this battle on." After a few minutes of argument, Peabody set his men up in a line of battle near his original encampment, while Prentiss set his force up on the left, making ready to engage the oncoming Confederates.

The time was 7:00 A.M., and the sun was dawning on what looked like a beautiful, cloudless day.

Hardee's Assault

Hardee's corps had broken up into the individual brigades, which spread out to engage the Union encampments in an almost 2-mile front. At Spain field on the Eastern Corinth Road, Brigadier General Adley H. Gladden's brigade burst out of the woodline directly across from Prentiss's line, the field itself swept with heavy artillery fire from both sides. A galling fire came from the Union line that staggered the Confederates. Able to stand for only a few minutes, the brigade retreated to the woodline, dragging with them the mortally wounded Gladden, who died later that same day.

Over on the left, at about the same time, Brigadier General Sterling A. M. Wood's brigade hit Peabody's right flank, pushing the Union infantry out of their line and back. Johnston, no longer able to stand being out of the line of fire, turned over operations in the rear to Beauregard and rushed forward to lead the battle from the front. Arriving just in time to see Wood's success and Gladden's repulse, he ordered all four brigades now up on the line to fix bayonets and assault the Union line at the double-quick, and 9,800 men ran screaming forward into the Union lines.

As his command withered under the assault, Peabody rode forward to rally his men and was hit four times in a matter of minutes by rifle fire as he moved down the line. Finally, in front of his own tent, watching the butternut-clad ranks closing in on him from two sides, Peabody was shot from his saddle, dying instantly. His command completely crumbled, followed shortly by Prentiss's own men. Even as William Wallace's and Hurlbut's brigades moved south to reinforce them, most of the Union infantry had had enough of this fight and retreated toward Pittsburg Landing.

Bragg's Assault

As the Union men broke and ran, the victorious Confederate infantry raced into their just-abandoned encampment and fell over the piles of fresh food and good equipment. Exhortations from their officers to return to the fight did no good, as the brigades and regiments dissolved into a rabble, pillaging the camps. Beauregard and Johnston had to take several precious minutes getting the men back under control and reorganizing them to renew their attack, while the Union line stopped its headlong retreat and fell into new positions for defense.

Johnston ordered Bragg's corps into the growing battle, splitting his five brigades between the left and right of Hardee's men and ordering Bragg to take command of the assault on the right flank. On the right, Brigadier General John K. Jackson's and Brigadier General James R. Chalmer's brigades briefly joined the rout of Prentiss, while on the left Colonel Preston Pond's and Brigadier General Patton Anderson's brigades joined Brigadier General Patrick Ronayne Cleburne's brigade, which was steadily advancing on Sherman's position at Shiloh Church. Colonel Randall L. Gibson's brigade continued straight northeast, in between the two ongoing major assaults, to try to break the Union center and turn Sherman's left flank. In an attempt to bring the strongest force on his right flank and force the Ohio general's division away from the river, Johnston brought up Polk's corps and sent his four brigades into the line alongside Bragg. Hardee was instructed to take direct command of the left flank and to hammer hard on Sherman's position.

The Second Union Line

By 9:00 A.M., 13 Confederate brigades were fully engaged along a nearly 3-mile front, steadily pushing back Union forces. Sherman was soon reinforced by McClernand's division, while the newly arriving commands of Hurlbut, William Wallace, and McArthur joined in a hastily organized line along with what was left of Prentiss's brigade to Sherman's left over to the Hamburg-Savannah Road. Wallace was particularly well positioned along a narrow wagon trace, hardly even a road, that was concealed in an oak forest atop a low ridgeline with a good field of fire before him across the open Duncan field. This position in the center of Grant's defense line was later referred to as the Sunken Road.

Sherman, wounded in the hand during his stand around the church, was forced to retreat at 10:00 A.M. when a heavy attack by five Confederate brigades broke through to his left and threatened to envelop his position. Alongside Sherman, McClernand's division had already set up a defensive perimeter within the confines of their own camp, extending the line east to the southern border of Duncan field, directly across from William Wallace's position.

Grant had heard the cannon fire from Savannah, nearly 10 miles to the north, and had hastily traveled south via his headquarters steamship, the *Tigress*. Before leaving, he ordered Lew Wallace to march south to the growing battle and newly arrived Brigadier General William "Bull" Nelson's 4th Division of Buell's Army of the Ohio to travel down the east bank of the

The only time the issue of secession came before the U.S. Supreme Court, for an official ruling on its constitutionality, was in the 1869 case Texas v. White *(74 U.S. 700). The Court decided that Texas had never actually seceded, as an act of that sort was not permitted under any interpretation of the Constitution, and thus, the various "secession" legislations were "absolutely null."*

Tennessee River to where they could be transported across to Pittsburg Landing. Arriving about 9:00 A.M. only to find the landing choked with fleeing Union soldiers, Grant painfully saddled his horse (he had been injured in a fall several days earlier and could walk only with the aid of crutches) and rode south to assess the situation. Sherman met him in the woods just north of his new position, just north of the Hamburg-Purdy Road, and assured him that he could hold this new line. Satisfied, Grant returned to the landing after riding down his left flank (closest to the river).

The Union lines were seriously disrupted and unstable, but the Confederates were having their own problems. The massive, 3-mile-long front had broken down into a series of uncoordinated attacks due to the thickly wooded and hilly terrain, and Johnston was no longer able to control the entire line. The three corps commanders and Johnston decided to break up overall command into a series of sector commands; Johnston controlled the right side of the battlefield (east and closest to the river) from Prentiss's camp, Bragg took the right-center at the Eastern Corinth Road, Polk took the left-center at the Corinth Road and Shiloh Church, while Hardee moved west to Owl Creek to take control of the left flank.

A little after 10:30 A.M., just after Grant finished his visit with Sherman, Polk initiated a gigantic attack on Sherman's and McClernand's positions with 10 reinforced brigades, more than two-thirds of the entire Confederate force on the field. The Union lines reeled under the massive attack and soon broke, falling back almost three-quarters of a mile to Jones field before regrouping. Ironically, this attack produced the exact opposite of what Johnston wanted: It drove the Union line back, but the Union right flank rather than the left, and moved it *toward* Pittsburg Landing.

The Hornet's Nest

At the same time, a smaller attack on the Union left flank by Chalmer's and Jackson's brigades slammed into McArthur's and Stuart's brigades, wounding both Union commanders and forcing them to retreat. By 11:00 A.M. a strong Union line was forming, centered on William Wallace's and Prentiss's position, hidden along the Sunken Road. Several Confederate attacks on this position were thrown back with heavy losses before Bragg realized what a strong force was concentrated there. As Gibson's brigade attacked through a dense thicket just east of Duncan field toward the Sunken Road, Union artillery canister fire and infantry rifle fire raked through the brush. The bullets and canister balls ripping the leaves apart reminded the Confederate infantrymen of a swarm of angry hornets, and they named the place the Hornet's Nest.

To the left (west) of the Hornet's Nest, Bragg once again displayed his irritated impatience and ordered attack after attack around or across Duncan field on the well-positioned Union line, each one being broken and thrown back in turn. (There is some controversy about the exact nature of this series of attacks; traditionally, the story holds that these attacks went straight across the wide-open field itself, while some more recent research seems to indicate that the attacks actually went down the relatively concealed roads on either side of the field.) To add to Bragg's problems, Sherman and McClernand managed to regroup

their scattered forces and counterattack Hardee's and Polk's forces, briefly regaining their own original camps. To reestablish his gains, Beauregard threw his last reserves in the lines, which stopped the Union counterattack. A fierce battle raged between the two armies in Woolf field, near the Water Oaks Pond just north of the Corinth Road, for just under two hours before the Union troops were once again thrown back to Jones field.

The Peach Orchard

On the right of the Hornet's Nest, multiple attacks against Hurlbut and McArthur had been repulsed with heavy losses, until at last some of the Confederate soldiers refused to mount another assault. Riding forward at about 2:00 P.M., Johnston announced that he would get them going and told the battered force that he would personally lead the next attack. Riding down the line of infantry, he tapped on their bayonets and said, "These must do the work. Men, they are stubborn, we're going to have to use the bayonet." He then turned, and with a shouted command for them to follow him, he headed toward the Union left flank. The line of infantry rose with a scream, and four brigades followed Johnston into battle.

At this same time, Stuart's brigade, which was directly in front of where Johnston was headed, had nearly completely run out of ammunition, and Stuart ordered a retreat. With Johnston's men sweeping forward, both Hurlbut's and McArthur's flanks were exposed and caved in. Both Union brigades retreated north to the upper end of Bell's field, near a small peach orchard. Returning a heavy volume of fire on the advancing Confederate force, newly opened peach blossoms fell like snow on the ground as bullets and shot sprayed through the trees.

As Johnston watched the battle unfolding a little after 2:30 P.M. from across the Hamburg-Savannah Road at the southeast corner of Bell's field, a bullet ripped through his right leg just below the knee. It probably was fired by one of his own men (the ball came in from the rear); the wound, amazingly, went almost unnoticed by Johnston. Years earlier, Johnston had been struck in the same leg during a duel, which damaged the nerves and possibly numbed the leg to the point that he couldn't feel a gunshot wound. Minutes later he nearly tumbled from his horse but was caught by his aide, Governor Isham Green Harris of Tennessee, and placed on the ground in a nearby ravine. No medical help was immediately available, as Johnston had sent his personal surgeon out a few minutes earlier to check on some wounded Union prisoners. Harris frantically tore open Johnston's uniform looking for a significant wound, but dismissed the leg wound as minor. Unfortunately, the leg wound had opened up a major artery, dumping blood into the general's knee-high boot, and Johnston bled to death within minutes. A tourniquet was later found in the general's pocket, the quick application of which would have saved his life.

Beauregard Assumes Command

At about 3:00 P.M. Beauregard was informed that Johnston was dead and took over command of all the Confederate forces in the field. Responding to the growing sounds of battle around the Hornet's Nest, he ordered most of his left flank to shift over to the right (east) to reinforce the attack there. By doing so he committed two major mistakes. First, his assault that threw back Sherman's counterattack had been highly successful, pushing the Union right flank far back across the north end of Jones field and on across the Tilghman Branch, seriously decimating the Union ranks. A follow-up attack could well have split the Union line of battle, sending Sherman and McClernand north and west away from Pittsburg

Landing, precisely as Beauregard had originally planned.

Second, the growing battle on his right flank was due to a continued hammering at a relatively small Union force well positioned at the Sunken Road forest area, but which was isolated from retreat, resupply, or reinforcement. Bypassing this position would have undoubtedly resulted in a surrender of the entire command by nightfall and could possibly have led to a successful capture of the steamboat landing itself. Instead, not only did Beauregard order a continued hammering at the isolated Union position, but the shift of units from other isolated fights on the battlefield relieved pressure on other Union units, which were then able to withdraw and reestablish a line along the Hamburg-Savannah and Corinth-Pittsburg Roads, protecting Pittsburg Landing as a landing place for Buell's rapidly approaching command.

The lack of control Beauregard, or any other high commander, had over the spread-out Confederate forces became painfully obvious in the fight around the Hornet's Nest; even if Beauregard had not ordered a concentration of forces there, it most likely would have occurred anyway. Individual regiments and brigades that were not already engaged elsewhere and that had rookie or undisciplined commanders started following what Shiloh park ranger Stacy D. Allen called the "make yourself useful policy," drifting over toward the sound of battle without specific orders to do (or even not to do) so.

Bloody Pond

With news of the death of Johnston, Bragg shifted over and took direct control of the Confederate right. Hurlbut had established a new line on the north end of the Peach Orchard (which was what Johnston was observing when shot), and despite having an unsupported left flank, he was making things hot for the assaulting Confederates. Just behind his position was a small, shallow pond that had the only fresh water

i

The last-known, documented Confederate survivor of the war, Pleasant Crump of the 10th Alabama Infantry, died in 1951.

available on this part of the battlefield. Wounded and parched infantrymen and horses alike crawled over to its shores to get a cool drink; many men were too badly wounded to raise their heads once in the pond and drowned in the foot-deep water. Dozens of blue-clad infantry were piled up in heaps of the dead and dying all around the water, their wounds dripping into the damp ground, staining the pond a deep crimson. When Confederates advanced past the ghastly scene, someone remarked what a "bloody pond" it was; the name stuck.

About 4:00 P.M., Hurlbut's line finally caved in under the intense Confederate fire, and he retreated up the Hamburg-Savannah Road. Jackson's and Chalmers's brigades, now supported by Clanton's Alabama Cavalry Regiment, rushed through the hole left by Stuart's and McArthur's collapse and began advancing north to the east flank of the Hornet's Nest. About the same time, the seventh direct assault against the Hornet's Nest was hurled back; bleeding and battered troops of Florida, Louisiana, and Texas pulled back to try to reestablish their ranks.

The Surrender of the Hornet's Nest

Brigadier General Ruggles had seen enough. Gathering up as many artillery batteries and individual gun crews as he and his staff could locate, by 4:30 P.M. he had 53 guns parked axle to axle on the west border of Duncan field, 400 to 500 yards directly across open ground from Wallace's and Prentiss's position in the Hornet's Nest. This was the largest assembly of artillery arrayed against a single target ever seen in the Western Hemisphere

at that time. Given the order to fire, the entire line of artillery opened up with a thunderous roar. Ruggles had ordered a mixed load of shot, shell, and canister fired as rapidly as possible. For nearly a half hour the artillery kept up a fire that averaged three shots *per second* going into the Union position.

When at last the murderous fire lifted, another Confederate assault charged the Union lines led by Wood, this time sweeping all around both flanks and meeting at the junction of the Hamburg-Savannah and Corinth Roads north of the Hornet's Nest. As the assault came down upon them, both Wallace and Prentiss ordered a retreat, trying to break out of their position before being surrounded. While leading an Iowa brigade north to the Corinth Road, Wallace was struck on the head; he lived a few more days and died in his wife's arms in nearby Savannah. With the death of Wallace and the impossibility of his situation painfully obvious, Prentiss finally surrendered what was left of the two brigades—himself and 2,250 men—a little after 5:30 P.M., the largest surrender to date in the war.

Grant's Last Line of Defense

While the remainder of his forces were slowly dissolving away to the west and south, Grant hurriedly brought up as much artillery and as many men as he could scrape together to guard the critically important landing. By the time the last survivors of the Hornet's Nest surrendered, Grant had about 70 cannon and 20,000 infantrymen in line for defense. His 1¼-mile-long last-ditch defense line started at Dill Branch on the left flank (east), where it entered the Tennessee River just south of the landing, ran due west to the Hamburg-Savannah Road, then turned north along the road to just north of Perry's field. The majority of artillery was placed just below the crest of the low, rolling hills above the landing, obviously intended to be used for point defense should an evacuation prove necessary.

As the last artillery batteries pulled into position, the vanguard of Buell's Army of the Ohio finally appeared across the river from the landing. Hastily transported across the river, Nelson's division had to force their way through several thousand Union soldiers desperately trying to flee the battlefield. As they fell into place, one last Confederate charge came up the hill at them.

The Last Charge of April 6

About 6:00 P.M., Jackson's and Chalmer's brigades moved through the Dill Branch ravine, aiming straight at the hill above Pittsburg Landing. The mass of Union artillery opened fire on them, joined by the Union gunboats *Lexington* and *Tyler* with their 8-inch guns. As these two brigades struggled through the flooded branch and rugged ravine, the remnants of Anderson's, Stephens's, and Wood's brigades joined in the attack without overall coordination, a mere 8,000 Confederates attacking uphill and across rugged terrain without artillery support into a strongly fortified Union position manned by at least 10,000 infantry, studded with nearly 40 artillery pieces, and with reinforcements hustling down the road to join in.

Within minutes the Confederate assault petered out, the butternut-clad infantry slipping away in squads and companies to find shelter as the early spring sun set on the horizon. Only Chalmer's and Jackson's infantrymen managed to briefly get within rifle range of the Union line; most of them were out of ammunition by that point, intent on closing and using the bayonet.

Beauregard sent word to all his commanders to suspend the attack for the night and pull back to the captured Union encampments. One by one, guns fell silent as the Confederates moved out of range. Units were in serious disarray on both sides, and the long night would be needed just to restore some semblance of order. Some Confederate units had not slept more than naps in two days, and most had not eaten since the day before. Although warned that Buell was nearby, Beauregard disregarded the threat and decided along with Bragg, Polk, and Hardee that the best plan was to rest and wait until daylight to get the army back into proper organization and to renew the assault. All felt that the only task remaining was to sweep up Grant's line and force him to retire north, a task that should not take more than a few hours.

Losses on both sides were very high in the daylong battle, with both sides suffering near identical casualties—almost 8,500 dead, wounded, and missing. The critical factor in these losses, however, was that Grant had reinforcements on the way, while Beauregard was on his own, without hope of relief.

THE NIGHT OF APRIL 6–7, 1862

Just as fighting was ending for the day, Lew Wallace's division finally arrived on the battlefield. It was only 6 miles away when sent for at 11:00 A.M.; a march that should have taken about two hours had taken more than seven. Grant was livid, but mistakes in navigation had simply tied up the men all day and left them wandering around muddy country roads north of the battlefield while Wallace tried to find the right one to lead him to Sherman's support. Grant used Wallace's tardiness later as an excuse to blame away some of the Union Army's disaster of April 6, but if he had shown up on time where he was headed, his division would have entered the brunt of the fighting around Shiloh Church and most likely would have been routed as Sherman and McClernand had been. Wallace, the postwar author of *Ben*

William Tecumseh Sherman

Just the mention of this Union general's name is enough to raise the blood pressure of many a loyal Southerner. In 1998 a land transaction in South Carolina was completed under a number of rather unusual conditions, including that no one named Sherman or whose name could be unscrambled to spell out Sherman could ever be permitted to purchase that property.

Born in Lancaster, Ohio, in 1820, Sherman was sent from his home to live with the family of Senator Thomas Ewing after his own father died in 1829. Nicknamed "Cump" by his boyhood friends, Sherman was appointed to West Point by his foster father, graduating in 1840 ranked 6th out of 42. His first assignment as a brevet 2nd lieutenant was to the 3rd Artillery, and through the 1840s and early 1850s he was assigned to posts in Florida, South Carolina, Georgia, and California. During the Mexican War he saw very little action, assigned as an aide to Captain Philip Kearny and Colonel Richard B. Mason. Assigned to a post in California after the war, he resigned his commission as a captain and went to work in the banking industry there. In 1857 he moved to Fort Leavenworth, Kansas, and opened a law and real estate practice, moving on to become superintendent of the Louisiana State Seminary of Learning and Military Academy in 1859. He remained in that capacity until Louisiana seceded in 1861.

With the outbreak of war, Sherman was quickly recommissioned, this time at the rank of colonel, and placed in command of the 13th Infantry Regiment.

Rapid promotions being the norm in the early, confused months of the war, he was soon promoted to command of a brigade in Brigadier General Irvin McDowell's army, defeated in battle shortly thereafter at the First Manassas. Sherman was soon promoted to brigadier general and sent to Kentucky as second in command to Brigadier General Robert Anderson. When Anderson became too ill to lead a short time later, Sherman assumed command. Sherman was never what one would describe as a temperate or thoughtful man, and when the press questioned him endlessly about his plans (similar to today's braying mob at press conferences), his irritated, snappish responses caused the newspapers to start rumors that he was "off in the head," a charge that would haunt him throughout the war. Various sources report that Sherman suffered a mild mental breakdown during this period.

The Union high command, affected by the news stories and showing a lack of leadership common throughout the war, reassigned Sherman, who was doubtlessly relieved to be out of such a bad situation. He was sent to command the 5th Infantry Division of Major General Henry West Halleck's army in Missouri, which was building up to invade western Tennessee and northern Mississippi. In April 1862, as part of Major General Ulysses S. Grant's corps, Sherman's division was encamped near Shiloh Church, 23 miles north of their target of Corinth, Mississippi, when they were suddenly attacked by 25,000 men of General Albert Sydney Johnston's combined

Confederate Army of the West. Although wounded in the early phases of the battle, Sherman stayed in the field and helped organize a successful counterattack.

When Grant replaced Halleck in command of all the western armies, Sherman, now promoted to major general, stayed with him, commanding a corps. Sherman successfully fought guerrillas at Memphis and in the grand land-water campaign at Vicksburg, before being sent to relieve the besieged forces at Chattanooga. In March 1864 Grant was recalled east to take over as commander in chief of all Union armies, leaving his friend Sherman in command of the western armies. Building up his Army of the Tennessee in Chattanooga over the winter and spring of 1863–64, Sherman unleashed the 100,000-man force on northern Georgia in May. Slowly pushing his Confederate opponent (and friend), General Joseph Eggleston Johnston, back toward the defenses of Atlanta, Sherman did not receive a real break until Johnston was replaced by Lieutenant General John Bell Hood at the end of July. Five weeks later, the campaign came to a close, with Sherman firmly in control of Atlanta and northern Georgia. With this, the war in the Western Theater was for all practical purposes over.

Sherman's reputation today largely stems from his March to the Sea, the Georgia campaign where he brought 60,000 men from Atlanta to Savannah, but truthfully, this wasn't much of a military campaign. Resistance was almost nonexistent, consisting of one small battle and a handful of skirmishes. Sherman's biggest problem on the march was feeding his vast army off the depleted

Major General William T. Sherman of the Union Army. COURTESY OF THE LIBRARY OF CONGRESS

countryside. However, the behavior of his "bummers" through this march and the subsequent one through the Carolinas, encouraged by the "total war" thinking commander, gave him his reputation as a thief and firebug. He ordered that anything of military value be taken or burned, and his men applied this order very liberally. Leaving only 10 percent of the buildings standing in their wake in Atlanta, his army burned and looted their way across a 40- to 60-mile-wide swath through central and south Georgia and an equally wide, depleted path in South and North Carolina. The destruction was so complete that certain buildings in those areas today are celebrated for their *survival*.

After accepting Johnston's surrender of the Western Theater armies in April 1865, Sherman turned to fighting and rounding up Indians in the far west. When his old friend Grant was elected presi-

dent, he appointed Sherman a full general and placed him as commander in chief of the army. He finally retired from the service in 1886 and died in New York in 1891. One of the pallbearers at his funeral was none other than his friend and ancient nemesis, Joseph Johnston.

Hur, lived with this series of mistakes the rest of his life, dying with the thought on his mind that his errors may have killed Union soldiers.

As the two battered armies settled down for a fitful rest, clouds gathered and a heavy, cold rain started to fall shortly after 10:00 P.M. Grant wandered around his headquarters, reluctant to go inside, as the building had been converted to a hospital, and the shrieking wounded and charnel-house atmosphere were simply unendurable. Sherman, wounded again in the shoulder during the afternoon, finally found him under a large oak tree, holding a lantern and smoking one of his ever-present cigars. "Well, Grant, we've had the devil's own day, haven't we?" remarked the fiery Ohioan. Grant, far from demoralized, replied simply, "Yes. Lick 'em tomorrow, though."

Grant ordered the gunboats stationed in the Tennessee River to keep up a steady bombardment all night, but their shells mainly burst among the Union wounded still left out in the killing fields. The Confederates had pulled back to the former Union encampments and were comfortably housed in their enemies' tents while they feasted on the abundant supplies. Cleburne, sitting in a tent and watching the shells burst around the bodies of the Union dead and wounded, remarked, "History records few instances of more reckless inhumanity than this."

As the night wore on, Buell's Army of the Ohio traveled south from Savannah

and crossed over into Grant's line; by 8:00 A.M. on April 7 more than 13,000 fresh, well-equipped troops stood ready to renew the fight. Beauregard had no reinforcements to bring up but remained optimistic. Upon hearing a false report that Buell's force was actually moving on Decatur, Alabama, he fired off a report to Richmond that he had "won a complete victory" that day and would finish off Grant's force in the morning.

As morning approached, Grant had about 45,000 men ready for an assault on the Confederate positions, most of them well rested and spoiling for a fight, while Beauregard could field only about 28,000 (some accounts say 20,000) tired men not yet re-formed into their brigades or even completely resupplied.

THE SECOND DAY, APRIL 7, 1862

Just before dawn on Monday morning, April 7, 1862, Grant ordered his combined armies to move out. Buell's fresh troops moved nearly due south, toward Hardee's and Breckinridge's lines, while Grant's resupplied and reinforced army moved southwest in two lines of battle toward Bragg's and Polk's lines. Led by heavy artillery fire from the massed Union guns, the sudden dawn attack caught their Confederate opponents completely by surprise, turning the tables from the day before.

No organization existed, the Confederate infantry had simply dropped in place the night before at whatever camp was handy, and few had bothered to resupply their depleted cartridge boxes from the piles of captured Union ammunition boxes scattered literally everywhere. Most likely believed that, if Grant were smart, he would leave the field during the night rather than suffer another "lickin'."

To top off Beauregard's problems, Polk had withdrawn his corps nearly 4 miles to the south, to the site of his previous night's encampment, and it took nearly two hours after the Union's initial attack to locate him and get his corps moving. Once in the line, none of the four corps commanders actually commanded his entire corps as the units intermingled and were confusingly arrayed in the haste to mount a defense.

The Confederate Defense

With great effort, the four Confederate corps commanders managed to form a meandering defense line in the face of the Union attack, roughly running northwest to southeast from the Jones field across Duncan field south of the Hornet's Nest to just about the place of Johnston's death the day before, on the Hamburg-Savannah Road. They managed to hold this line under great pressure until about 11:00 A.M., when a general pullback in order was called. The line moved back intact about a half mile on the left and extended another half mile on the right to counter increased pressure from Buell's forces on its right flank.

By noon the Confederate line had again pulled back under pressure to a line centered on Shiloh Church. Union units all along the line kept up a steady artillery and infantry fire; Grant's plan was to simply roll south using his fresh troops to grind up the tired Confederate infantry. The plan worked quite well; several counterattacks by Hardee, Breckinridge, and Bragg were absorbed and thrown back with heavy casualties.

The Confederate Retreat

By 1:00 P.M. it was obvious to Beauregard that not only were they not going to be able to win this battle, he was also in danger of being swept in pieces from the field. He hesitated for nearly an hour, however, before finally passing orders down the line for his commands to break contact and retreat to Corinth. Several artillery batteries repositioned at Shiloh Church, along with Colonel Winfield S. Statham's and Colonel Robert P. Trabue's brigades of Breckinridge's corps, to act as a heavy rear guard.

Cavalrymen were ordered to hastily destroy all the Union equipment and supplies that the retreating infantry weren't able to carry off with them. As the piles of broken tents and wagons blazed into the stormy afternoon, Breckinridge broke off contact and withdrew in good order at the rear of the long Confederate column. As the Confederate line moved south about 5:00 P.M., Grant's exhausted infantry was simply too tired to follow. Breckinridge stopped for the night and redeployed at the intersection of Bark and Corinth Roads. No Union force challenged their rest, and at dawn he moved south into Corinth.

Grant had won a magnificent victory, but at a heavy price. Of his 65,000-man combined army (with Buell's), 1,754 were killed, 8,408 wounded, and 2,885 captured or missing in action—a fifth of his whole command. The tattered remnants of his proud regiments were too shot up and exhausted after two solid days of combat to pursue the retreating Confederates, who made it back into Mississippi without resistance.

Beauregard suffered worse; in addition to losing the beloved army commander Albert Sidney Johnston, he had to report losses of 1,728 killed, 8,012 wounded, and 959 missing or captured. This loss of

10,699 soldiers constituted nearly a fourth of all the men he had helped bring into the campaign. Once back in Corinth, he ordered the town prepared for defense against an attack by Grant and set about turning nearly the entire small community into one vast hospital for his thousands of wounded.

THE TOUR

Getting There: Shiloh

Shiloh is in a relatively remote part of Tennessee, very close to the common border of Tennessee, Alabama, and Mississippi. The nearest city with access to an interstate highway is Jackson (Interstate 40 between Memphis and Nashville), 52 miles to the northwest via U.S. Highways 64 and 45. The nearest large cities are Memphis, 113 miles west on US 64, and Chattanooga, 204 miles east via US 64 and Interstate 24.

As we came in to Shiloh from the east, we took I–24 north out of Chattanooga to exit 134 (Monteagle), turning west on U.S. Highway 41 Alternate through Sewanee and turning west/south on US 64 just outside Winchester. US 64 is a pleasant but long journey through southern Tennessee about 140 miles to Savannah. This small town lies just 10 miles northeast of the national military park. Continue on US 64 until you cross the Tennessee River into Crump, and then take the first major road intersection to the left, Tennessee Highway 22, which runs straight through the park.

MODERN TIMES

Shiloh today is a quiet, wooded, and serene place little changed overall from 1862. The surrounding towns are larger, and instead of steamboats on the adjoining Tennessee River, there are pontoon boats and fishermen. It is just as remote, though, and one can easily imagine the reaction of Grant's inexperienced troops placed in such a "crude and hostile environment," as one Ohio private wrote. The majority of the original battlefield has been preserved as a national military park and is operated by the National Park Service.

The original little wooden Shiloh Church is long gone, but the congregation is still present and meets every Sunday in a brick-and-stone sanctuary built on the same spot in 1949. A replica of the original church has recently been constructed near this site. The surrounding graveyard has some gravestones that were present when Sherman made his stand here, and most of the roads both armies walked down are still in existence, albeit now paved and improved.

Be aware that the weather in this area tends to be extremely hot during summer; snow and ice are not unknown during the winter, and violent weather (including tornadoes) is often a feature of springtime. Visits to some of the battlefield areas involve quite a bit of walking, so make sure to dress appropriately and carry sufficient water with you during hot weather.

POINT OF INTEREST

Shiloh National Military Park
TN 22, Route 1, Box 9, Shiloh
(731) 689–5696

This 3,960-acre park covers all but a small fraction of the original battlefield and contains all the significant sites. A very nicely appointed visitor center graces the hill just above Grant's last line of defense, containing a small but well-presented set of artifacts, a friendly and quite knowledgeable staff, and a 25-minute film, *Shiloh—Portrait of a Battle,* shown every 90 minutes. We recommend it for its good description of both the battle and events that led up to it.

Just across the parking lot is the bookstore, run by a private concessionaire, Eastern National, which has made a great effort to provide a well-stocked and well-selected choice of books, maps, and some nice souvenirs. An unusual item we noticed was small ceramic replicas of some of the state monuments scattered around the park. Eastern National has earned our gratitude for resisting promotion of the "anything with a rebel flag on it" school of souvenir shop. Behind the bookstore is a selection of soft drink and snack machines, restrooms, and a pay phone.

Make sure you pick up a copy of the driving tour brochure in the visitor center, and we recommend arming yourself with a copy of Trailhead Graphics' "Shiloh National Military Park" battlefield map, available in the bookstore. The driving tour will get you around the major sites in a reasonable amount of time, while Trailhead's map lists the exact location of every one of the 151 monuments, 600 or so unit position markers, and 200 artillery pieces. A very nice adjunct to these maps is the *Guide to the Battle of Shiloh* by Jay Luvass, Stephen Bowman, and Leonard Fullenkamp, part of the excellent U.S. Army War College "Guides to Civil War Battles" series. This battle was a very large, confusing, and widespread campaign, and this book was our constant companion when trying to understand certain movements and actions—although as it is meant for professional historians and military officers, it, too, tends to be confusing and hard to understand in places! It is available in the park's bookstore.

Directly adjacent to the bookstore is the Shiloh National Cemetery, the final resting place of 1,227 known and 2,416 unknown Union dead from this battle and others nearby. A unit of the national cemetery system, it also contains remains of veterans from later wars. Grant's headquarters was located in the middle of this field and is marked by a vertical cannon barrel.

All across the battlefield are mass graves of the Confederate dead, hastily buried and mostly unmarked by the Union troops, who stayed on the field for another six weeks. Five of the mass graves have been located and marked; one is on the driving tour. Admission to the park (actually more like a parking fee) is $3.00 for adults, $5.00 for families. Pay the fee and get the dashboard card for your car at the visitor center.

ACCOMMODATIONS

The closest cities with a selection of services are Savannah, about 10 miles north of the park via TN 22 and US 64, and Corinth, Mississippi, about 23 miles south via TN 22 and US 45.

The small settlement of Shiloh, just outside the south park boundary at the intersection of TN 22 and TN 142 has exactly one service station/convenience store, one restaurant, and one souvenir shop.

There are very few accommodations in the immediate area of the battlefield park, but the usual array of chain establishments are in Savannah to the northeast and Corinth to the south; of the two, Corinth is farther away but has a larger selection.

RESTAURANTS

There is nothing available in the park besides soft drink and candy machines, so you will have to drive either north or south on TN 22 for anything more substantial. As with the accommodation situation, the usual array of fast-food and lower-end sit-down chains are available either way, but a wider array of offerings is in Corinth.

Ed Shaw's Restaurant $
TN 22, Shiloh
(731) 689–0322
A typical small-town, country, meat-and-three restaurant with a really great location, Ed Shaw's leans heavily toward seafood—offering shrimp, crab, fish, and oysters, as well as chicken, steaks, hamburgers, and salads. Frog legs are also available for the more adventurous. Ed Shaw's is located just south of the National Battlefield itself, in the small crossroads hamlet of Shiloh.

Sonic Drive-In $
1706 Wayne Road (US 64), Savannah
(731) 925–5552
We don't usually recommend fast-food chains but must admit that we have a serious weakness for the hard-to-find

Sonic. This is a '50s-style drive-in where you give your order into individual parking-place menu speakers; carhops still occasionally wear roller skates to deliver your food, which hangs in those archaic trays that clip onto the driver's window. The food can best be described as unabashedly anti–Martha Stewart: chiliburgers and footlong hot dogs; high-cholesterol-count greasy onion rings and french fries; some of the world's best milk shakes; and even, be still my (still) beating heart, cherry Cokes.

SUTLERS

Shiloh Civil War Relics and Museum
4730 TN Highway 22, Shiloh
(731) 689–4114
With a rather unusual combination of well-selected museum artifacts and stuff for sale, this small building just outside the northern park boundary is well worth a stop after visiting the battlefield. We really couldn't decide if this was a museum with a really big gift shop that had higher-caliber souvenirs than the norm or if the artifacts were there to help whet the appetite for more sales. Complete uniforms, buttons, belt buckles, artillery shells, and even a complete artillery piece are on display; some of the authentic items are for sale, as are some more reasonably priced replicas, books, and videos. Open Monday and Wednesday through Saturday 9:30 A.M. to 5:00 P.M., and Sunday 1:00 to 5:00 P.M.; closed Tuesday.

Ed Shaw's Gift Shop
TN 22 and 142, Shiloh
(731) 689–5080
Everything and anything you could possibly want with a "rebel flag" printed or stitched on it, and then some. With some reservations we recommend that you stop by for a visit, even if just to marvel at the sheer vastness of the offerings of T-shirts, bumper stickers, mugs, beer coolers, pocket knives, pens, pencils, hats, and much, much more—all prominently displaying the Southern Cross. The sticker

selection is a particular favorite of the "forgit hell!" crowd; a typical offering: "If I had known they felt that way about it, I'd have picked my own damn cotton!" Be forewarned: Judging by the stickers on local vehicles, this apparently is the general consensus of the area, just on the southern boundary of the park.

Day Trips

Corinth, Mississippi, 23 miles south, was the site of Confederate actions before and after the battle; for a complete list of places to visit there, please see our chapter on Other Alabama and Mississippi Battlefields. In Savannah, 10 miles north, there are two sites worth visiting.

Tennessee River Museum
507 Main Street, Savannah
(731) 925–2364, (800) 552–FUNN (3866)
Housed in the chamber of commerce building next to the county courthouse, this small museum has set a daunting task for itself, which has partially been fulfilled: to chronicle the life and times of the Tennessee River Valley from prehistoric times to today. Still obviously under development, several exhibits tell the story of the Native American mound builders, the Trail of Tears, the Golden Age of Steamboats, and the river gunboats used during the battle here.

The museum is open Monday through Saturday 9:00 A.M. to 5:00 P.M. and Sunday 1:00 to 5:00 P.M. Admission is $2.00 for adults; children and students are admitted for free.

Cherry Mansion
101 Main Street, Savannah
(731) 925–2364 (Hardin County Tourism)
This 1830 two-story house was used by Grant as his headquarters immediately before and after the battle but is unfortunately not open for tours. The grounds are open for strolling, and a nearby monument commemorates Grant's stay here.

OTHER TENNESSEE BATTLEFIELDS

The 16th state to be admitted to the Union (1796), Tennessee was the last to secede and join the new Confederacy and did so, ironically, partly as a reaction to a request by President Lincoln for troops to put down the "insurrection" in other states. Parts of the state were heavily pro-Union, most notably the far-eastern, mountainous sections that were part of the one-time separate state of Franklin. Some of the largest battles in the Western Theater were fought here, although the Union controlled most of the state for most of the war. As a final irony, even Lincoln's September 1862 Emancipation Proclamation did not apply to Tennessee; by that time it was fully under Union control and no longer "presently in rebellion."

It is tempting to note that Tennessee was also the first state to be brought back under Union control, as is so often claimed, but the rather "fuzzy" situations in Maryland and Kentucky raise some doubts here. Kentucky was proclaimed by its legislature to be officially neutral, and several of Maryland's most influential legislators were arrested by Federal authorities to prevent a vote of secession, but both were slaveholding states with very strong ties to the Confederacy. Both supplied combat troops and supplies to the South, even though both were ruled by what has been referred to as a "hostile foreign government," i.e., the United States.

Battles, skirmishes, and raids occurred across the entire length and breadth of Tennessee, although the largest occurred in the central and southern portions of the state. Outside the major battles that are discussed in other chapters, these actions can be divided into three broad categories: the campaigns for Knoxville, the Battle of Stones River, and the struggle for control of the northwestern rivers. Smaller actions ranged all through the state largely as a result of Major General Nathan B. Forrest's and Colonel John Hunt Morgan's cavalry raids for the South.

THE CAMPAIGN FOR KNOXVILLE

Today the third largest city in Tennessee, during the Civil War Knoxville was a strong Confederate outpost in an otherwise remote area that was heavily pro-Union. It also was the key communication and transportation point between the Confederate armies in Tennessee and Virginia.

President Abraham Lincoln had a personal interest in the Unionists in Knoxville; like him, they were small-plot farmers strongly opposed to slavery and secession and strong advocates of the Republican stance. For this, their pro-Confederacy neighbors persecuted them, sometimes to the point of torture and murder. Early in 1863 Lincoln directed his western armies to take Knoxville as soon as possible to "relieve" the Unionists in the area.

Background to the Campaign

The combined Union armies in the west had had their fill of fighting since shortly after the war began and for nearly two years had been unable to mount an offensive in force into the eastern reaches of the Confederate heartland. Major General Ulysses S. Grant, on siege outside Vicksburg in May and June of 1863, had been urging his fellow Union army generals to launch an offensive in central Tennessee in order to cut off General Joseph Eggleston Johnston's attempts to relieve the embattled Confederate garrison there. Major General William Stake "Rosy" Rosecrans, comfortably encamped with his Union Army of the Cumberland in Murfreesboro, Tennessee, finally and reluctantly agreed to mount an offensive. On June 23 his army moved out and slogged southward through a cold rain toward the Confederate force at Tullahoma.

General Braxton Bragg had sent a good portion of his Confederate Army of Tennessee to Mississippi and was at that time in no shape to stand up to Rosecrans. During the nine days it took the Union force to arrive, Bragg withdrew all of his remaining men and most of his supplies south to Chattanooga, where he heavily entrenched. Rosecrans took Tullahoma without a shot being fired and then he did nothing for the next eight weeks while Bragg reinforced both his army and his fortifications at Chattanooga.

With increasing pressure from Lincoln, Rosecrans finally moved out eastward to retake the strongly pro-Union east Tennessee from Confederate control. Rosecrans was to take the vital rail and manufacturing center at Chattanooga, while Major General Ambrose Everett Burnside's Army of the Ohio was to march from their base in Cincinnati to take Knoxville.

The Capture of Knoxville

The Confederate Department of East Tennessee was commanded at the time by Major General Simon Bolivar Buckner, newly sent up from Mobile to prepare for Burnside's threat to the region. In Knoxville was a single infantry brigade and two cavalry brigades—all told, only 2,500 men. The northern approach to the city, Cumberland Gap at the Kentucky state line, was guarded by only a single

brigade under the command of Brigadier General John W. Frazer, with 2,000 men and 14 pieces of artillery in total.

Before Burnside could even get a good start southward, Rosecrans was threatening Chattanooga, and Buckner was ordered to withdraw from Knoxville to help defend the river and rail center to the west. Leaving Frazer in place at Cumberland Gap and one infantry brigade just east of Knoxville, Buckner left town with all the rest of his infantry and cavalry on August 16.

Cumberland Gap had been taken and lost three previous times by Union forces, and Burnside knew better than to directly confront Frazer's strong defensive position there. His Army of the Ohio then consisted of Brigadier General Robert Brown Potter's IX and Major General George Lucas Hartsuff's XXIII Corps, with about 24,000 men total. Sending one division of the advance brigade of the IX Corps to "demonstrate" against Frazer's command, Burnside moved the rest of his force several miles to the west, crossing the Cumberland Mountains at Winter's Gap and Big Creek Gap.

Burnside's command entered Knoxville unopposed on September 3, welcomed by a large crowd of local Unionists. The single Confederate infantry brigade still present prudently declined to engage the overwhelmingly superior Union force and quietly slipped out of the area to join Buckner in Chattanooga. Burnside detached two brigades to confront Frazer's entrenched Cumberland Gap position from the south; faced with strong Union forces on either side of the gap, Frazer surrendered his command without a fight on September 9.

The Occupation of Knoxville

Burnside, the Union general better known for his namesake facial hair than his military prowess, set up his headquarters in newly captured Knoxville with the intent of using it as a base to raid western Virginia. So intent was he on this task that he ignored a number of requests for help from Rosecrans, first as the fight at Chickamauga was going badly and again when Chattanooga was besieged.

As Bragg made his plans to break back into Union-held Chattanooga in late 1863, he committed a grievous tactical error and ordered Lieutenant General James "Old Pete" Longstreet to take his corps (nearly a third of Bragg's entire army) to the east and retake Knoxville. Bragg, a personal friend of President Jefferson Davis but an erratic commander and occasionally poor judge on the battlefield, had a personal feud with the South Carolinian and sent him east mainly just to be rid of him.

Longstreet's 10,000-man force consisted of Major General Lafayette McLaw's and Brigadier General Micah Jenkin's division (of Lieutenant General John Bell Hood's corps) and Colonel Robert Porter Alexander's and Major A. Leyden's Artillery Battalions (35 guns total), along with Major General Joseph "Fighting Joe" Wheeler's Cavalry Corps with 5,000 men. The Confederate task force moved out of the Chattanooga line on November 5, riding on trains so old and tracks so worn out that nearly everyone had to get off and walk up each hill. It took eight days to cover the first 60 miles and another three to finally reach the Tennessee River 30 miles west of Knoxville. Wheeler's cavalry had been sent ahead to probe around the city and find an undefended high spot to set up artillery.

The Defense of Union-Held Knoxville

Burnside had not been idle in the intervening months, setting up a ring of strong earthwork forts and redoubts around the hilly city. Wheeler was soon forced to report back to Longstreet that there was no undefended high ground from which to

launch an attack. While Longstreet made ready to cross the Tennessee River and pondered just how to launch his attack, Burnside decided to take the offensive.

Burnside was well known in the Union Army as being a poor battlefield commander, which he would be the first to admit, and the decision to leave the strong defenses of Knoxville and personally lead a 5,000-man force west to directly confront the oncoming Confederate troops was a poor one, indeed. The lead elements of both forces first encountered each other at the Tennessee River between Louden and Lenoir City. All the bridges and ferries there had been burned in an effort to further slow down Longstreet's advance.

Longstreet was delighted. With Burnside out of the city, all he needed to do was find a quick ford and race around him, cutting the Union force off from its home base. Wheeler reported in short order that a suitable crossing was only one-half mile to the south, at Huff's Ferry. Longstreet quickly rerouted his army there and crossed a still-under-construction pontoon bridge just after noon. Burnside was still unaware that Longstreet had drawn so close and was caught completely by surprise when the first elements of the Confederate force engaged his pickets in Lenoir City just at dusk.

Rapidly backpedaling, Burnside managed to hold off the ineffective assaults and withdrew his forces intact through Concord heading for Campbell's Station (today known as Farragut). The Union forces left Lenoir City at dawn on November 16, "temporarily abandoning the valley of the Tennessee south of Louden," according to Brigadier General Orlando M. Poe of the North, and making all speed back to the fortifications under construction in Knoxville. Longstreet realized that if he could reach the crossroads at Campbell's Station first, he could cut off Burnside's force from the main body in Knoxville and defeat both in turn. Almost a footrace ensued, with both armies racing up parallel roads toward the small crossroads settlement.

Campbell's Station

Burnside's troops, led by Colonel John F. Hartranft's 2nd Division, won the race but just barely. Hartranft deployed his men facing west on the Kingston Road just before noon to cover the baggage train that continued east toward Knoxville without stopping. The rest of Burnside's combat troops formed a second line about one-half mile behind Hartranft's. About 15 minutes later, the vanguard of Longstreet's force, McLaw's division, arrived and immediately assaulted the Union line still forming up.

McLaw's attack was at first successful, driving the left of the Union line back and forcing it to reform to the rear. Jenkin had been ordered to simultaneously strike the Union right, but his maneuver was ineffective and the line held. With two more Union divisions now in place and ready just behind him, Hartranft broke contact just after noon and withdrew to the new Union line of battle.

Longstreet's men stayed in close contact, assaulting the Union line on the right and center just as Hartranft fell into position, again without any gain. As the attacks continued, Burnside ordered his force to fall back under pressure to a ridgeline about three-fourths of a mile to their rear. The Union withdrawal was brilliantly executed; the troops keeping up a steady fire while slowly moving back to the higher ground. McLaw and Jenkin kept the pressure on, one attacking head-on while the other attempted maneuvers to turn the Union flank, all to no avail. As darkness fell, the Union line held and the Confederates ceased their assaults. Burnside ordered his troops to march through the night farther east, into the defenses of

Knoxville, arriving there by dawn on November 17.

The running battle produced a surprisingly small number of casualties for so many hours of contact—approximately 400 Union and 570 Confederate.

The Second Defense of Knoxville

While Burnside had gone west to confront Longstreet, his remaining force had not been idle. Ten hilltop fortifications and miles of trenchlines now ringed three-fourths of the city, the fourth side protected by the Holston River (now called the Tennessee River). The most prominent fortification was Fort Sanders, on the northwest corner of the defense belt and manned by about 440 troops with 12 artillery pieces. This strong fortification was surrounded by a dry ditch 12 feet wide and 8 feet deep, and the walls rose almost vertically 15 feet above the ditch. Although the designer, Poe, was worried that the hilltop post stuck too far forward of the main defensive belt and thus presented an inviting target to the oncoming Confederates, he relocated his cannon to be able to fire straight down the ditch and added a new type of defense feature.

Poe had his engineers string telegraph wire about 1 foot off the ground between stumps and stakes just outside the ditch, weaving a densely knotted pattern several feet wide that would slow down and break up the line of any attacking force. This "trip foot" is now a common military defense feature, and Knoxville is the first place it is known to have been used in battle.

Longstreet brought his forces up close to the Knoxville defenses and then halted. Although the weather was turning bitterly cold and some of his barefoot soldiers were literally freezing, he decided to wait until reinforcements arrived to make his move. Scouting the Union defense line while he waited, Longstreet determined that the only spot he had a real chance of taking

---

i *Future President Grover Cleveland had been drafted for service during the war but paid $150 for another man to serve in his place. This practice, known as substitution, was legal at the time but not considered entirely honorable.*

was Fort Sanders, sited atop a low hill but just 200 yards away from a thick tree line that would cover and conceal his troops.

Brigadier General Bushrod R. Johnson arrived with 2,600 men in Colonel John S. Fulton's and Brigadier General Archibald Gracie's brigades on the night of November 25, along with Brigadier General Danville Ledbetter, Bragg's chief engineer for the Army of Tennessee, who scouted the Union emplacements along with Longstreet. Based primarily on Ledbetter's assessment of the situation, Longstreet modified his plans and ordered the assault to begin just before dawn on Sunday, November 29. With his newly arrived reinforcements, the Confederate commander had nearly 20,000 troops at his disposal to counter the estimated 12,000 of Burnside's force.

> Today, April 14, 1882, I say, and honestly say, that I sincerely believe the combined forces of the whole Yankee nation could never have broken General Joseph E. Johnston's line of battle, beginning at Rocky Face Ridge, and ending on the banks of the Chatta-hoochee.
>
> Corporal Sam Watkins of the Confederacy, in Co. Aytch

The Battle for Fort Sanders

The night of November 28 was freezing cold, with a misty rain turning to ice and sleet as the hours wore on. Longstreet assigned three brigades to make up the assault force: Brigadier General Benjamin G. Humphreys's Mississippi, Brigadier General Goode Bryan's Georgia, and Colonel S. Z. Ruff's (Wofford's) Georgia, all of McLaw's division. Brigadier General G. T. Anderson's Georgia Brigade of Jenkin's division was ordered to "demonstrate" at their left flank against the northernmost wall of the fort.

About 11:00 P.M. skirmishers were ordered forward to capture the Union rifle pits before the fort; this action also alerted the Union defenders that action was imminent. For the rest of the night, small firefights broke out between pickets and skirmishers of both sides, joined in occasionally by canister rounds from the fort. Longstreet's assault troops lay on the frozen ground atop their guns, trying to keep them dry and catch a little sleep. Fires had been forbidden, as they were too close to the Union line, and the freezing drizzle undoubtedly made everyone miserably cold.

At the first sign of light on the eastern horizon, three signal guns of Alexander's artillery fired arcing red flares that exploded over the fort. With this the mass of Confederate infantry sprang to their feet and charged the ramparts of the earthwork redoubt. Twelve guns of Alexander's artillery fired as rapidly as possible for a few minutes and then ceased firing so as not to strike the onrushing infantry.

Poe's tripwire broke up the mass charge, but in quick order the assault troops gathered themselves and rushed onward, firing as they went. In the confused darkness, under rifle and artillery canister fire from the fort and stumbling through the outer defenses, all three brigades accidentally merged into one mass, meeting at the northwest bastion of the earthwork fort. Their massed fire at that point caused the Union guns to go silent, leading Longstreet and Alexander alike to believe the fort's defenses had already been reduced. Casualties to this point had been extremely light, and a massive wave of butternut-clad troops pushed into the ditchwork defenses.

No scaling ladders had been constructed, as the walls were not thought to be unusually steep, but both the reality of the construction and the ice-covered ground brought the assault to a sudden halt. As Union defenders stayed down, occasionally raising an unaimed rifle over the rampart to fire at the massed infantry, men formed human ladders to gain the heights, standing on each other's shoulders and passing their fellow soldiers on up. As dawn slowly brought light to the fort, officers and color bearers began planting the Georgia and Mississippi battle flags on the parapet.

As the first Confederates gained the top of the walls, the Union troops inside opened fire with every gun available. Nearly as soon as a color bearer planted a flag, he was shot down, and officers lifting their swords to urge on their troops were equally swiftly gunned down. One after another the fallen bloodred "damned flags of the rebellion" were lifted up by an infantrymen and then fell as he, too, was gunned down by the determined Union infantry and artillery gunners. As the Confederate troops came too close to the Union line to fire their cannon, Lieutenant Samuel N. Benjamin, commander of Company E, 2nd U.S. Artillery within the fort, had his men light the fuses of cannon shells and throw them over the walls like hand grenades, exploding more than 50 of the lethal devices in the very faces of the Confederates in the ditch.

As the full light of dawn revealed the hopelessness of taking even one bastion of the fort, Longstreet reluctantly recalled his troops. As the first wave was withdrawing, Anderson ordered his men forward, unaware that his attack had also been canceled. The scene repeated itself, with the Georgians thrown back with heavy losses after a 40-minute pitched fight atop the ramparts.

Aftermath

As Jenkin was preparing for yet a third assault, word came to Longstreet that Bragg had been decisively defeated at Chattanooga and his help was urgently needed in Dalton. The attempt to regain Knoxville came to a sudden end as Longstreet immediately pulled out of the battle and marched south.

Longstreet quickly learned that Rosecrans had sent Sherman with two full corps to break his siege of Knoxville and now stood between him and Bragg. Reluctantly he abandoned his plans to march into Georgia and turned up toward northeastern Tennessee, hoping that Sherman would pursue him there and relieve the pressure on Bragg's Army of Tennessee. Sherman probably saw right through that idea and shortly returned to Chattanooga, leaving two divisions behind to reinforce Burnside should Longstreet backtrack and try again. Longstreet spent a miserable winter with the remains of his command in Greenville, Tennessee, and returned to General Robert E. Lee's Army of Northern Virginia in the spring.

Left behind, atop, and around Fort Sanders were the bodies of 129 killed and many of the 458 wounded from Longstreet's ill-conceived assault. Ruff, Colonel H. P. Thomas, and Colonel Kennon McElroy all lay dead on the parapet next to a number of their color bearers. Confederate losses for this entire campaign were 198 dead, 850 wounded, and 248 missing, with Burnside losing 92 dead, 393 wounded, and 207 missing.

STONES RIVER

With the full knowledge that in order to hold on to their commands and perhaps even their commissions, they must win the coming day's battle, both General Rosecrans, Union Army of the Cumberland commander, and General Braxton Bragg, Confederate Army of Tennessee commander, sat on either side of a line of battle just west of Murfreesboro, Tennessee, on the night of December 30, 1862. Studying their maps and consulting with their cavalry scouts, both commanders came up with identical plans: Strike the enemy's right flank at daylight.

Bragg hoped to rout the Union force, cut it off from a retreat route back to Nashville, and then batter it to pieces against the riverbanks. Rosecrans equally hoped to rout the Confederate force, cut it off from a retreat through Murfreesboro, and then defeat the scattered force in detail.

As the two great armies lay just yards apart in the cold darkness, knowing that the morning might bring their own "great gettin' up day," regimental bands began playing patriotic tunes in the hopes of bucking up the morale. Confederate bands played "Dixie," which would be defiantly replied to by Union bands playing "The Battle Hymn of the Republic." Finally, after much catcalling across the lines and general amusement, both sides' bands joined together to play the heart-wrenching "Home Sweet Home." Blue-coated and butternut-clad troops joined in singing together, a chorus of tens of thousands plaintively wishing for home and hearth in the windy, rainy night. As the last notes faded away, both sides grew silent, waiting in the dark for the morning's scheduled carnage.

Background to the Battle

Following his disastrous loss at Perryville during his aborted invasion of Kentucky in the fall of 1862, General Braxton Bragg retreated completely out of the state, falling back to Morristown in eastern Tennessee to try to resurrect his rebel army. Protecting the retreat was Brigadier General Joseph "Fighting Joe" Wheeler's Cavalry Corps, who fought a running battle with the closely pursuing Union forces all the way to London, fighting no fewer than 26 engagements along the way. Bragg's army moved into Knoxville on October 23, after a 200-plus-mile unbroken retreat march.

Bragg's subordinates were outraged at his conduct during the campaign and considered him not only a poor commander but also a danger to the Confederate Army itself. One after another, Lieutenant General William Hardee, Lieu-

tenant General Leonidas Polk, and Major General Edmund Kirby Smith all traveled to Richmond, Virginia, to demand Bragg's removal, echoed by a host of politicians and influential civilians. After a short visit to the Confederate capital to prop up his status once again with his old friend, President Jefferson Davis, Bragg not only held on to his command but also received permission to move back into middle Tennessee and threaten Nashville.

Concentrating his forces near the small town of Murfreesboro, about 30 miles south of Union-held Nashville, Bragg allowed his great cavalry commanders, Morgan and Forest, to roam throughout northern Tennessee and Kentucky. This disrupted Union commanders more than any concentration of infantry ever could hope to, with the Confederate cavaliers cutting supply lines, disrupting lines of communication, and destroying miles of rail lines and vital supply depots.

Morgan's Attack on Hartsville

One such cavalry raid netted more than the usual: Morgan's raid on Hartsville. In early December 1862, Colonel Absalom B. Moore's 39th Brigade (Union Army of the Cumberland) was guarding the isolated river crossing at Hartsville, 40 miles northeast of Nashville. Under orders from Bragg to disrupt Rosecrans's lines of supply and communication north of Nashville in the late fall of 1862, Morgan soon learned how isolated the small Union outpost was from any support and resolved to take it at once. Morgan's force consisted of four regiments and one battalion of cavalry, two regiments of infantry, and one battery of artillery all told, with about 5,000 men. Moore's force consisted of a single infantry brigade with about 2,000 men.

On the night of December 6–7, 1862, Morgan's men crossed the Cumberland River near the Union encampments. Moore claimed in his report that they were wearing captured Union uniforms to fool the outer pickets. The inner line of picket guards sounded the alarm, and by 6:45 A.M. the fight was on. The outnumbered Union troops hastily formed a line of battle and briefly held their ground, while Morgan's men surrounded the beleaguered command. Without hope of timely relief from other, much larger Union encampments only 9 miles away, Moore surrendered at 8:30 A.M.

Morgan immediately retreated south toward Bragg's lines, taking with him some captured supplies, wagons, horses, mules, and about 1,800 prisoners. Union losses in the brief fight were 58 killed and 204 wounded, besides those taken prisoner. Morgan lost a total of 139 dead, wounded, and missing.

Davis Steps In

In response to the disaster in Kentucky, partly to quiet Bragg's critics and partly to ease his own growing distrust of Bragg's command strategies, Davis had ordered the reorganization of Bragg's Army of Mississippi. His force was combined with Lieutenant General Edmund Kirby Smith's Army of Kentucky and Lieutenant General John C. Pemberton's Army of Mississippi (at Vicksburg), and Bragg was placed in charge of the new Army of Tennessee. Given overall command of the Department of the West was General Joseph Eggleston Johnston, technically then Bragg's superior officer, but a man intensely despised by Davis and constantly overruled by him.

Johnston's first act as the new theater commander was to recommend the abandonment of Vicksburg and the concentration of forces in Tennessee to overwhelm Rosecrans and cut off the flow of supplies to Grant's army outside Vicksburg, which could be dealt with in a weakened condition later. The idea was to handle each Union army in turn with a united Confederate force, instead of trying to fight a

two-, three-, or four-front war. Davis not only refused, he traveled to Bragg's headquarters in Murfreesboro and personally ordered him to detach the 7,500 troops of Major General Carter Littlepage Stevenson's division to reinforce Pemberton in Vicksburg. This cut nearly one-sixth of the fighting force out of Bragg's command at a time and a place where action was imminent.

General Hood was in command of the Army of the Tennessee at this time and if anything was ever out of all sorts it was the Army of the Tennessee. Old Joseph E. Johnston looked after his men and did not run them into any unnecessary engagements. Hood would fight at the drop of the hat and drop it himself, so he thought he would show Sherman a few things out of the ordinary.

Private Robert C. Carden, of the South's Company B, 16th Tennessee Infantry, about Lieutenant General John Bell Hood

The Advance to Murfreesboro

Upon hearing of the action at Hartsville and other Confederate cavalry operations in west Tennessee and Kentucky, Rosecrans assumed that Bragg was now without scouts and therefore blind to any Union troop movements. From his own cavalry scouts, he had learned that the Confederates were at Murfreesboro preparing to go into camp for the winter, and he immediately issued orders for his army to march out and confront them. The North's Army of the Cumberland moved southeast from Nashville on December 26 with roughly half the available troops, organized into three wings with a total of just over 44,000 men. Major General Thomas Leonidas Crittenden's left wing moved straight down the Nashville & Chattanooga Railroad tracks, while Major General Alexander McDowell McCook's right and Major General George Henry Thomas's center wings marched to his right down the McLensville Turnpike and part of the Franklin Turnpike.

Bragg had plenty of warning from both his scouts and Wheeler's cavalry, still operating between his command and Nashville. He spread his forces out into a 32-mile-wide front from Triune through Murfreesboro itself to Readyville, covering any possible approach from the north. The ill-tempered Confederate commander had two corps at his disposal: Lieutenant General William J. Hardee's corps on the left and Lieutenant General Leonidas Polk's corps on the right. Wheeler's cavalry both slowed down the Union advance and protected the army's flanks; all told, about 32,000 men were available for combat.

Bragg's scouts soon reported the exact approach route and composition of the Union force, and he pulled his troops into a tight semicircle just north and west of Murfreesboro, astride the West Fork of the Stones River. Ironically, Rosecrans himself was blind to the Confederate movements and strength, having sent his own cavalry north and west chasing off after Forrest and Morgan. About 3:00 P.M. on December 29, without any warning, Crittenden's corps made contact with the Confederate forces of Major General John Cabell Breckinridge's 2nd Division (of Hardee's corps) along the Stones River bank, northwest of Murfreesboro. A small skirmish erupted, ending shortly when both forces moved back a bit to await orders on how to proceed.

While Rosecrans hastily brought up the rest of his force to concentrate on what he believed, for some unknown reason, to be a Confederate force in full retreat, Wheeler sprang into action. Riding in a giant arc through the Union rear, he captured about 1,000 prisoners, burned more than a million dollars' worth of ammunition and medical supplies, and

caused a general panic that nearly turned into a rout back to Nashville.

Both Sides Prepare for Battle

Unprepared to immediately launch into battle against the strong Confederate position before him, Rosecrans hesitated through most of the day of December 30, finally meeting with his top lieutenants to hammer out a plan of action in the afternoon. Together they agreed that the Confederates' weakest point was on the right of their line, where Breckinridge stood to the far north of the line of battle. While units were shifted north to prepare for an assault the next morning, McCook's men were directed to light a large number of campfires on the far right of the Union line to fool their adversaries into thinking that units were being shifted for an attack coming from that angle, instead.

McCook's wing was arrayed, from right to left, by Brigadier General Richard W. Johnson's 2nd, Brigadier General Jefferson C. Davis's 1st, and Brigadier General Philip H. Sheridan's 3rd Divisions. In the center of the line was Brigadier General James S. Negley's 2nd Division of Thomas's wing, and on the left was Brigadier General John M. Palmer's 2nd and Brigadier General Thomas J. Wood's 1st Divisions of Crittenden's wing, which extended the Union line all the way to the river. Two other divisions were in an assembly area behind the lines, readying for an assault scheduled for 7:00 A.M. on December 31. Rosecrans had passed orders down that his men were to finish their breakfast before the attack began.

All through the day of December 30, Bragg expected a Union assault on his lines and shifted his troops to better meet the Union formation. Late in the afternoon, noting the Union troop movements and fooled by the fake campfires, he was convinced that the main attack would come

Corps Confusion

The Army of the Cumberland under Rosecrans was officially designated the XIV Corps (formerly Buell's Army of the Ohio) on its creation on October 24, 1862. Although the army as a whole was far larger than the traditional corps, the true corps-level organizations under its command were designated "wings" instead. This confusing mess was finally rectified on January 9, 1863, when the wings were redesignated the XXI, XIV, and XX Corps.

from that direction, onto his left flank. He ordered his troops to be shifted to meet the perceived threat and readied for his own attack on what he thought was the mass of enemy, on the Union right. The attack was to begin at first light, a little after 6:00 on the morning of December 31.

Breckinridge stayed in position on the right, while the other two divisions of Hardee's corps swung around to Polk's left. The left of the Confederate line consisted of Major General John Porter McCown's and Major General Patrick Ronayne Cleburne's divisions of Hardee's corps. The center consisted of Major General Jones Mitchell Wither's division of Polk's corps, with Major General Benjamin Franklin "Frank" Cheatham's division just to the rear as a reserve. Brigadier General John A. Wharton's Cavalry Brigade took up the far left flank of the Confederate line.

The Confederate Assault Begins

At 6:22 A.M. 4,400 butternut-clad and battle-hardened troops of McCown's division stormed out of the gray, misty predawn twilight into the right of the Union line, catching totally by surprise the Northern soldiers leisurely eating breakfast, shaving, and getting dressed. Most of McCook's regiments still had their weapons at stack arms and unloaded as they were routed or shot to pieces where they stood.

Cleburne's division, advancing behind and in support of McCown's, found itself alongside their fellow division in the front line, as the Union army hastily retreated to the north and west, dragging the Confederate assault behind them. As their assault slowed, mainly from the rough terrain and exhaustion, Cheatham's division entered the attack and helped push the Union line farther north. Davis's and Sheridan's divisions managed to hastily assemble a sufficiently strong line of battle and put up a strong resistance that slowed the Confederate advance. About 9:30 A.M. Sheridan even managed to mount a limited counterattack, which pushed back Cheatham long enough to allow a more orderly retreat. By 10:00 A.M. the Union line was compacting into a strong position just west of and running parallel to the Nashville Pike.

Although the morning had gone very well for Bragg, casualties were appalling; Hardee and Polk had both lost about one-third of their men and were begging for reinforcements. Bragg had none to send.

Rosecrans Responds

The Union line had formed, "bending back their line, as one half-shuts a knife-blade," according to Colonel David Urquhart of Bragg's staff, with the sharp angle forming a salient in a four-acre patch of woods called the Round Forest, which the troops soon renamed "Hell's Half-Acre." Rose-crans ordered his remaining uncommitted units, originally tasked to assault the Con-federate right, into this salient for a last-ditch defense. Brigadier General Horatio Philips Van Cleve's 2nd and Brigadier General Thomas John Wood's 1st Division got into position in the woods just in the nick of time.

Bragg ordered what he thought would be a final assault into the Union position in the small patch of woods, led by Brigadier General James Ronald Chalmer's 2nd Mis-sissippi Brigade. These men were some of the freshest available, having just spent the previous 48 hours lying in shallow trenches on the far right of the line, await-ing an attack that never came. One regi-ment, the 44th Mississippi, went into the assault with most of the men unarmed; their rifles had been collected up a few days earlier to distribute to units thought more in danger of attack, and just before going into the line of battle, they were reissued what the brigade ordnance offi-cer declared as "refuse guns." Most either could not be fired at all or had to be reassembled after each shot.

Chalmer's brigade "moved forward in splendid style," according to one of their opponents, Colonel Thomas Sedgewick of the 2nd (U.S.) Kentucky, but almost imme-diately began receiving murderous fire from the well-positioned 2nd Kentucky and 31st Indiana Regiments. The Confederates with-ered under the intense fire, but then recov-ered and closed to within 150 feet of the Union troops, where they exchanged fire for nearly 30 minutes before retreating with heavy losses. Chalmer himself was seriously wounded, and some regiments lost as many as eight color bearers in the brief assault.

As the last of Chalmer's men retreated, at about 9:30 A.M., a brief lull fell over the fighting. Fresh Union regiments were brought into the salient, while another Confederate attack was organ-ized. Brigadier General Daniel Smith Donelson led his Tennessee Brigade into the same sector about 10:00 A.M., this time

successfully breaching the Union line to the right (west) of the Round Forest, tak-ing prisoners and capturing some artillery pieces. As the Confederate attack suc-cessfully progressed, more and more units were fed into the line by commanders of both sides, both determined to take and hold this critical position.

The fierce battle for possession of the wooded salient raged on for more than two hours before the Confederates were forced to withdraw. "Appalling casualties" is hardly an apt description of what the Tennesseans endured; Colonel W. L. Moore's 8th Tennessee Infantry Regiment, which had advanced far beyond any other unit, coming close to the turnpike itself, finally retreated leaving behind 301 dead and wounded of the 440 troops it had advanced with, including Moore himself. This loss, 68 percent casualties, was the worst suffered by a Confederate regiment in any single battle of the entire war.

The Afternoon Battle of December 31

With the failure of the morning assaults, the battlefield grew quiet for another few hours. About 4:00 P.M. the last four Con-federate brigades that had not yet seen action assaulted the Round Forest posi-tion once again. Brigadier General Daniel Weisiger Adam's 1st and Brigadier General John K. Jackson's brigades were repulsed with heavy losses. Colonel Joseph Ben-jamin Palmer's and Brigadier General William Preston's brigades were sent in for the same results.

With the attacks over for the day with the approaching darkness, the Confeder-ates held most of the field, now covered with dead and wounded soldiers of both sides. Rosecrans considered withdrawing back to Nashville but decided to stay and attack again, that is, if his opponent Bragg did not. Bragg returned to his headquar-ters in Murfreesboro and, somehow con-vinced that his army had been totally successful in the assault, telegraphed Richmond that "God has granted us a happy New Year."

Neither side attacked the next day, January 1, 1863, Rosecrans ordering his men to heavily entrench. Bragg took the quiet along the line, for some unknown reason, to indicate that the Union soldiers were on retreat back to Nashville. Wheeler's and Wharton's cavalry spent the day harassing the Union supply lines, with some moderate success. Bragg decided to assault the high ground to the left of the main Union line, hoping to find a place he could mount artillery and pour enfilading fire down on the rest of the Union line. Breckinridge was given the task of taking this position the next afternoon.

January 2, 1863

Breckinridge was horrified by his orders. Acting on his own, he had ordered a reconnaissance of the very area Bragg was proposing to attack. On his return from the dangerous scouting mission, Captain W. P. Bramblett of H Company, 4th Kentucky, the Orphan Brigade (so called because Kentucky was occupied by Union forces and the men could not go home until the war was over), had remarked that not only was this position already strongly held but that more Union regiments were moving in, and it looked like "Rosecrans is . . . setting a trap" for Bragg to fall into.

Traveling to Bragg's headquarters, the Kentuckian presented his findings and requested the attack be canceled or moved. Bragg, ever intractable when told his ideas were faulty, insisted that the attack go ahead as scheduled and set the hour of assault for 4:00 P.M., one hour before the winter sun set. Breckinridge angrily returned to his command, proclaiming to some of Bragg's staff officers that he was carrying out the attack under protest and fully expected it to fail.

As Breckinridge's men moved slowly into position, word was passed to drop their packs (which infantrymen were loath to do, rightfully worried that a rapid retreat would mean the loss of their personal possessions) and prepare for a rapid assault. Hanson rode down his regiments forming up, stopping before each and ordering the regimental commander, "Colonel, the order is to load, fix bayonets and march through this brushwood. Then charge at double-quick to within a hundred yards of the enemy, deliver fire, and go at him with the bayonet." As the men aligned themselves, a cold, wet sleet started coming down hard, numbing bare hands and feet and soaking what threadbare clothes they had left.

At exactly 4:00 P.M., a signal round went off from an artillery battery, and the assault force fixed bayonets and moved forward at the double-quick. Leading on the left was Brigadier General Roger Weightman Hanson's 4th Brigade with Brigadier General Gideon Johnson Pillow's 2nd Brigade to his left, followed about 150 yards to the rear by Colonel Randall Lee Gibson's 1st and Preston's 3rd Brigades—all told, about 4,500 men.

The first 900 yards of the assault went well. Although almost immediately coming under fire from Union positions on the hilltop, Hanson's and Pillow's brigades advanced without seriously disturbing their formation, brushing aside the Union skirmishers in front of the main line of battle with hardly a casualty. Colonel Samuel Beatty Price's 3rd Brigade of Van Cleve's division, atop and just in front of the targeted hill, held their fire until the Confederates were nearly upon them.

With the onrushing Kentuckians only 60 yards away, Price ordered his command on their feet to fire a volley into the butternut-clad ranks. The men of the Orphan Brigade never slowed down. Returning their own volley, the men let out their weirdly high-pitched battle yell and charged the Union line, bayonets glistening in the late-afternoon rain and sleet. The Union troops fired one last ragged volley and then bugged out, leaving the hill to the assaulting Confederates. As

Hanson's men jumped over the abandoned Union breastworks, a Union artillery shell hit the general in his leg. Breckinridge, riding up to assess the success of his assaulting units, jumped off his horse and frantically tried to stop the bleeding, but to no avail. Although an ambulance soon arrived and Hanson was soon in the care of a surgeon, he died minutes later.

Storming over the hill and into the valley below, the Confederate assault continued unbroken to the east banks of Stones River itself. No doubt recalling how artillery had broken the Union ranks at Shiloh's Hornet's Nest a few months previous, Major John Mendenhall of the Union, Crittenden's artillery officer, had hastily assembled every available artillery battery and positioned them on a rise overlooking the west bank of the river. Fifty-eight guns commanded the river approach with unobstructed fields of fire onto both banks. As the Confederates boiled out of the woodline and ran to the river, running over a small rise next to the riverbank, Mendenhall ordered his batteries to open fire.

The explosion of artillery shattered the Confederate assault. More than 100 shots per minute rained down on the assault force, blowing apart whole regiments in a matter of minutes. The attack almost instantly turned into a matter of holding what they had gained; within minutes it turned into just getting out alive. No order given, the Southern soldiers simply retreated as best they could, dragging behind them a counterattack that ended up regaining all the Union losses of the afternoon. Confederate losses amounted to more than 1,700 of the best men on the field, nearly half of what had started out.

His attacks muted, his offense stalled, and his ranks shattered, Bragg stayed on the field one more day without contact with the Union forces, and then quietly withdrew during the night of January 3 south of Murfreesboro to Shelbyville. Rosecrans's force was too spent to pursue, staying in the area another five months before resuming any offensive operations.

Neither side could really claim victory, both being mauled to the point where their armies were rendered nearly useless for many months, but Rosecrans's army held the field at the end, and Bragg failed in his attempt to retake Nashville. Rosecrans lost a total of 12,906 dead, wounded, and missing; Bragg, a total of 11,740.

RIVERS CAMPAIGN

Background to the Campaign

After Lincoln's election and the parade of Southern states seceding from the Union, it was not at first thought that any grand scheme or strategy for defeating the strong Confederate armies would have to be devised. General Winfield Scott, aged commander in chief of all Union armies, suggested early on a plan that would cut off trade and supply to the South, effectively starving it into submission. This so-called Anaconda Plan was initially rejected by Northern politicians, who in the manner of politicians everywhere and throughout history, demanded a "quick 'n' easy" solution to a complex and deadly problem. Their idea, which was unfortunately happily carried out by the army, was to simply march out and "show the grand old flag," and the Southerners would run screaming from the field.

Southerners proved a bit more intractable than the Northern politicians had predicted. With the Union disaster at the First Manassas (First Bull Run to the Yankees), realization set in that this was not going to be any sort of "90-day war" and that a real, workable strategy would have to be adopted. Based on Scott's plan, a three-part strategy was approved and adopted: first, a tight naval blockade of the entire Southern Atlantic and Gulf Coasts to cut off supplies and trade with foreign nations; second, an invasion of Virginia as soon as possible with the goal of capturing the Confederate capital of Richmond; and

Joseph Eggleston Johnston

One of the most beloved of all Civil War generals, second only to Lee in this regard, Joseph Eggleston Johnston was born in Farmville, Virginia, in 1807 and was appointed to West Point in 1825. He graduated 13th in his class of 46 in 1829 and was initially assigned to the 4th Artillery, seeing service during the Black-hawk War, on the western frontier, and during the Seminole War in Florida. He resigned his commission in 1837 to work as a civil engineer in Florida, only to run into further combat situations with hostile Indians while working with John Wesley Powell's expedition. Although seriously wounded in the head, Johnston rallied a defense and successfully moved the party to a safer area.

In 1838, partly in recognition of his exploits with Powell, Johnston was recommissioned in the engineering corps of the army and promoted to captain. He served under General Winfield Scott during the Mexican War, was wounded five times in combat, and led the final charge at Chapultepec.

Johnston resigned his U.S. Army commission on April 22, 1861, and was almost immediately commissioned as a major general of Virginia and brigadier general of the Confederacy (mixed commissions like this were common in the Confederacy). He commanded the combined Confederate forces at the opening major battle at Manassas and was subsequently one of four promoted to the highest rank of full general (along with Robert E. Lee, Albert Sydney Johnston, and Samuel

Cooper). Johnston did have a personal fault of occasionally complaining about things of little consequence, and his comment that he should have been given seniority over Lee in this set of four, based on his rank and position in the prewar U.S. Army, served only to irritate President Jefferson Davis of the Confederacy, turning him into a lifelong enemy. Davis had several personal faults as well, and his thin skin and inability to stand criticism were his worst. Soon afterward, Johnston was seriously injured at the battle of Seven Pines and was relieved from duty. When he returned to service in November 1862, he was placed in charge of the newly formed Department of the West, theoretically in command over General Braxton Bragg's Army of Tennessee and Lieutenant General John Clifford Pemberton's Department of Mississippi, Tennessee, and East Louisiana, although he was given no support by Davis in having his orders and directives obeyed.

After Pemberton had lost Vicksburg and Bragg lost Tennessee, partly as a result of the conflicting orders given by Johnston and Davis, Bragg was relieved of command, promoted to military chief of staff, and replaced with Johnston in December 1863. There Johnston reversed a number of Bragg's draconian rules and regulations, such as having men who stayed too long on leave shot for desertion, refusing to issue many leaves in the first place, issuing reduced rations when plenty were available, and requiring two and even three roll calls a day to catch anyone who might dare try to sneak away. Command of the Army of Tennessee was both Johnston's finest hour and where his natural abilities flourished. He honestly loved and cared for his men, and they returned his love with a devotion that lasted to their own deathbeds. One of the privates in the ranks of his army, Sam Watkins of Columbia, Tennessee, had this to say about the day Johnston assumed command:

> A new era had dawned; a new epoch had been dated. He passed through the ranks of the common soldier's pride; he brought the manhood back to the private's bosom; he changed the order of the roll-call, standing guard, drill, and such nonsense as that. The revolution was complete. He was loved, respected, admired; yea, almost worshipped by his troops. I do not believe there was a soldier in his army but would have gladly died for him. With him everything was his soldiers, and the newspapers, criticizing him at the time, said, "He would feed his soldiers if the country starved."
>
> We soon got proud; the blood of the old Cavaliers tingled in our veins. We did not feel that we were serfs and vagabonds. We felt that we had a home and a country worth fighting for, and, if need be, worth dying for. One regiment could whip an army, and did it, in every instance, before the command was taken from him in Atlanta.

General Joseph Eggleston Johnston of the Confederate Army. COURTESY OF THE LIBRARY OF CONGRESS

Johnston rebuilt his army just in the nick of time to face an army twice his size under Sherman, invading northern Georgia in May of 1864. Johnston was a past master at the running defense, as Sherman was a master at maneuver warfare, and his first priority was maintaining his force. Starting with the battles around Dalton, Johnston slowly gave ground before Sherman's juggernaut, making sure the Union armies bled heavily for every inch they gained. Whenever possible and prudent, the Confederate commander launched counterattacks, thinning the Union ranks at New Hope

Church and Pickett's Mill. In other places, he set up defenses so strong that the Union ranks bled nearly dry trying to take them, at Rocky Face Ridge, Resaca, and Kennesaw Mountain.

Although Johnston managed to keep his army intact and in fighting trim and lost not a single artillery piece in the long retreat from Dalton, criticism of him and his tactics reached a fever pitch after he pulled south of the Chattahoochee River, just outside Atlanta. Johnston's plan all along had been to force a costly campaign on Sherman, then pull into the nearly impenetrable defenses of Atlanta and allow the Union force to batter itself to pieces there. However, President Davis's enmity of Johnston reached a breaking point as he pulled back to Atlanta, and Davis fired the beloved commander on July 17, replacing him with one of his own corps commanders, the fiery and ill-tempered Lieutenant General John Bell Hood. To paraphrase what Sam Watkins said so well, let us close the book on that sad chapter after Hood's promotion, agonizing as it is to consider, suffice to say only that the once proud and able Army of Tennessee suffered the torture of misuse after misuse, before at last expiring on the ramparts around Nashville six months later. Sherman, incidentally, was delighted with the replacement, remarking that while Johnston was a dangerous foe, Hood was fairly predictable, and "I was never so nervous with him at my front."

Johnston was reappointed command of the pitiful remnants of the Army of Tennessee on February 23, 1865, and ordered to resist Sherman's march once again, this time in the Carolinas. Still more concerned about the lives of his men than the fate of the obviously doomed Confederacy, Johnston led them into only one more major battle, at Bentonville, North Carolina, on March 19. Reasonably successful in their first assault into the flanks of one of Sherman's four columns, Johnston wisely retreated before his Union nemesis could gather his own forces and crush him. Johnston opened surrender talks with Sherman shortly thereafter, the talks becoming more urgent after word reached them of Lincoln's assassination. Although Jefferson Davis, passing through the area on his flight from Richmond, rudely ordered Johnston to break contact with Sherman's force and retreat south with him, the courtly general instead signed the surrender documents on April 26.

After the war, Johnston worked in the insurance business in Savannah and Richmond and then served two terms in Congress as a representative from Virginia. He and Sherman became close friends after the war, and Johnston served as one of his old Union nemesis's pallbearers at his funeral. Going bareheaded during the ceremony, on a cold, misty day in 1891, Johnston developed pneumonia and died just weeks later. His aide had tried to get the aged general to at least wear a hat, but Johnston's only reply was, "He [Sherman] would not wear one if he was in my place."

third, the capture and control of the major river systems in the heartland of the Confederacy, the Mississippi, Cumberland, and Tennessee Rivers.

The naval blockade was effectively put into place on more than 3,500 miles of Southern coastline by July 1861, but Major General George Brinton McClellan's feeble attempts to take Richmond proved much less successful. To carry out the third portion of the grand plan, Brigadier General Ulysses S. Grant and Flag Officer Andrew Hull Foote (various sources list him as a captain, commodore, or admiral at this point in time) were given the mission of opening up the great Southern rivers to Union control. Together they decided to concentrate initially on taking control of the Tennessee and Cumberland Rivers in northern Tennessee.

The Union Army-Navy Plan

Grant and Foote agreed to start their campaign on the Cumberland River at Fort Donelson, near the Tennessee-Kentucky border, which would open up a river corridor to Nashville. Foote had overseen the construction of a new class of navy craft specifically designed for such interservice operations, the ironclad riverboat. These boats were relatively small, 75 feet long and 50 feet wide on average, shallow-draft craft with protected midship paddlewheels for propulsion, ironclad either entirely or at least protecting the gun decks, with rectangular casements covered by sloping iron armor with a small opening for cannon.

Early on, most of these gunboats were simply modified civilian riverboats, with widely varying sizes and gun capacities. One carried only four 8-pounder guns, while others carried guns as heavy as 42 pounds and mounted as many as 12 guns. Foote commanded three unarmed boats and four ironclads in the opening battles, manned by a rather motley assortment of 500 sailors who were formerly riverboat crewmen, Maine lumberboat sailors, New England whalers, New York ferrymen, and some only described as "Philadelphia sealawyers."

On the army side, Grant had about 15,000 soldiers organized into two divisions with five brigades. Brigadier General Charles Ferguson Smith took charge of three brigades, while Brigadier General John Alexander McClernand had two brigades under his command.

The Confederate Plan

In overall charge of the South's defense of the Mississippi River and its approaches was Major General Leonidas Polk, an Episcopalian bishop who was quite frankly more at home in the ministry than the military. He was convinced that the main Union attack would move down the Mississippi and accordingly placed most of his men and material in the buildup of fortifications at Columbus, Kentucky, for the defense of Memphis. He refused several requests for manpower and supplies to build up defenses on the Tennessee and Cumberland Rivers, believing that these were "backwater accesses with no real strategic value."

Governor Isham G. Harris of Tennessee, more concerned about the loss of the middle of his state than Polk was, personally ordered General Daniel S. Donelson of the Confederate Army to construct fortifications on these two rivers at the Kentucky border, where they are only 12 miles apart. Donelson chose a very poor site for the post guarding the Tennessee River; later named Fort Henry, it was placed on a floodplain that frequently flooded and was commanded by high ground across the river. The Cumberland River post was much better; later named Fort Donelson in his honor, the earthwork fort consisted of 2½ miles of fortifications surrounding two heavily entrenched artillery emplacements atop a 70-foot bluff overlooking the river.

The Tennessee River was so badly flooded during the battle for Fort Henry that the Union Navy was able to sail gunboats right inside the (formerly) riverside fort.

The right of revolution is an inherent one. When people are oppressed by their government, it is a natural right they enjoy to relieve themselves of this oppression, if they are strong enough, whether by withdrawal from it, or by overthrowing it and substituting a government more acceptable.

Lieutenant General Ulysses S. Grant, Union Army, from his *Memoirs*

The Battle of Fort Henry

Grant and Foote agreed to start their campaign by capturing Fort Henry. Foote started up the Tennessee River with his seven gunboats closely followed by Grant's force loaded on transport barges. Grant's plan was to land his force on either side of the fort, to prevent escape of the garrison, and march overland toward an assault while Foote's gunboats weakened the Confederate defenses by continuous bombardment.

Inside Fort Henry, things were getting soggy. The river was flooding again, and water was standing 2 feet deep in parts of the fort. Brigadier General Lloyd Tilghman, post commander, was disgusted; calling the fort's condition "wretched," he sent most of the 2,500-man garrison to nearby Fort Donelson and kept only a single 60-man artillery company to man the 17 guns.

On February 6, 1862, with Grant's troops landed and on their way over muddy, flooded roads, Foote sailed his gunboats nearly to the ramparts of the fort and opened fire. With the fort continuing to flood, Tilghman's gunners returned a telling fire, disabling two gunboats and killing or wounding nearly two score of their crew. The fort's crew fared little better, with four guns flooded out or disabled by enemy fire and 20 men killed or wounded. After less than two hours of bombardment, Tilghman

surrendered his post before Grant had a chance to close in. The fort was so flooded by that point that the Union officers accepting the surrender floated in the main gate by boat. Lost in the brief confrontation were 11 killed, 31 wounded, and 5 missing for the Union force; Tilghman reported his losses at 20 killed or wounded and the rest made prisoner.

The Battle for Fort Donelson

The day after the fall of Fort Henry, the commander of the Western Theater, General Albert Sydney Johnston, ordered the abandonment of Columbus and Bowling Green, Kentucky, and the movement of most of his armies south of the Cumberland River. To facilitate this movement and make safe his new positions, he ordered that Fort Donelson be reinforced and held.

Fort Donelson originally held a garrison of 5,000 troops, soon reinforced to a total of 18,000 (as few as 12,000 by some accounts) but burdened with a weird command structure where three generals shared the responsibility: Brigadier General John Buchanan Floyd, Brigadier General Gideon Pillow, and Brigadier General Simon Bolivar Buckner. To add to the unworkable situation of having three commanders, Buckner and Pillow were bitter political enemies back home in Kentucky; Pillow was a lawyer with no formal military training and a bad case of arrogance; Buckner was the only professional soldier of the three; and Floyd was a weak-willed politician who had been Buchanan's secretary of war. Floyd took over as senior commander strictly by virtue of his earlier date of commission.

While you were eating your good dinner we soldiers would have been glad to have the crumbs that fell from your table. I will tell you what our meals were this day:

Breakfast, rice and beef. Dinner, rice. Supper, beef and rice. Rice is our favorite dish now.

William Henry, 101st Illinois Infantry Regiment of the Union Army

The Advance to Fort Donelson

Grant waited several days before marching on Fort Donelson, building up his forces to as many as 27,000, with about 15,000 ready for an immediate investment of the Confederate stronghold. On the afternoon of February 13, the Union troops were in position to the south and west of the fort, with Foote on the way upriver with his gunboats and more troops to land on the north side of the fort. The day was clear and sunny, with quite a warm temperature for a winter's day, leading many of the Union soldiers to ditch their heavy overcoats by the side of the road as they marched in.

The night of February 13 a winter storm blew in, dropping the temperature down to 10 degrees and setting off a raging blizzard on the unprotected troops. Campfires had been forbidden, as any light brought a barrage from Fort Donelson's guns. A brief skirmish earlier in the day had resulted in numerous Union wounded, many of whom froze to death during the long night.

The Gunboats Enter the Action

Late in the afternoon of February 14, Foote arrived and swung into action. His four heavily armored gunboats closed to within 400 yards of the fort, exchanging heavy fire with the Confederate artillery crews until darkness set in. Foote was decisively defeated, his gunboats raked with heavy cannon fire until rendered useless, and most of his sailors aboard killed

or wounded. Foote himself was seriously injured aboard his flagship, the St. Louis, ultimately dying 16 months later of complications caused by the wound.

Although the Confederate force had been quite successful resisting the waterborne assault, it was obvious that they would not be able to make much of a stand against Grant's land-based assault, sure to come in the following days. The three generals agreed to break out toward the east and rejoin the rest of Johnston's force in Nashville. Launching a strong attack on the Union lines across the Nashville Road at daybreak, Pillow and Buckner managed to force the road open by noon. Unbelievably, though, Pillow ordered a retreat back into the fort on hearing a report that the Union troops in the area might be receiving reinforcements. Floyd, still in the fort, supported Pillow, and all the Southern soldiers who had forced the breakout were smartly marched back into the besieged garrison.

Pillow later claimed that he ordered the return to the fort because of a "confusion over orders," stating that he thought the men were to go back, pack their belongings, and presumably tidy up the place before leaving. Once back in the fort, he insisted that his men needed food and rest before embarking on such a long march, and Floyd timidly backed him up against the violently agitated Buckner, who rightfully insisted they had to leave immediately for any hope of escaping the Union envelopment. As they stood arguing, Grant launched his own attack.

Correctly assessing that as the attack had come from the Confederate left, their right must be weaker, he ordered an assault on that part of their line. General Charles Ferguson Smith led his division in a strong assault against the Confederate trenchlines, now held only by a single regiment of infantry. Buckner immediately moved his men back to counterattack, but Smith was able to capture and hold the outer line of defenses on that side of the fort before darkness brought an end to the day's fighting.

The Surrender of the Fort

The three Confederate generals again conferred, Pillow and Floyd in a sheer panic at their own capture and Buckner disgusted with their amateurish attempts at command. Floyd passed command of the post to Pillow, who immediately passed it to Buckner, who had made it clear that the only choice available was surrender. As Buckner made ready to end his resistance, Floyd and Pillow commandeered a steamboat and got themselves to safety across the river, along with a few hundred soldiers of Floyd's command. Newly appointed cavalry officer Lieutenant Colonel Nathan Bedford Forrest, disgusted with Buckner's intention to surrender, received his permission to escape through the surrounding swamps with as many men as possible.

On the morning of February 16, Buckner sent a message across to Grant asking for his surrender terms. Grant replied in a famous message, "No terms except unconditional and immediate surrender" (from which his nickname Unconditional Surrender came). Meeting at the Dover Inn later that afternoon, Buckner surrendered his command and the post. Casually discussing the action later with his prewar friend Grant, Buckner mentioned that he must have been disappointed not to have captured Pillow and Floyd as well. Well aware of Pillow's alleged "abilities" as a battlefield commander, Grant remarked that had he captured Pillow, he would have immediately released him, as Pillow

was more a danger to the Confederacy than an asset!

Numbers of those engaged, casualties, and prisoners made vary wildly from source to source, but somewhere in the neighborhood of 27,000 Union and 21,000 Confederate troops were involved in the action, with Grant losing about 2,800 dead, wounded, or missing. The Confederate force lost about 2,000 dead or wounded and had about 14,500 made prisoner, the rest escaping with Forrest or bugging out on their own.

THE TOUR

Getting There: Knoxville

Knoxville is in the eastern reaches of Tennessee, accessed by Interstate 75 from the north and south and Interstate 40 from the east and west. Nashville is 175 miles west on I-40, Chattanooga is 112 miles south on I-75, Asheville is 107 miles east on I-40, and Lexington, Kentucky, is 173 miles north on I-75. U.S. Highway 441 goes southeast about 30 miles to Pigeon Forge and Gatlinburg, directly adjacent to the Great Smoky Mountains National Park, a nice addition to tours in the area.

MODERN TIMES

All the defense works around Knoxville, including Fort Sanders, long ago disappeared. Most of the city then is on what is today the University of Tennessee at Knoxville campus, near the intersection of U.S. Highways 41/70 and U.S. Highway 129. A few of the older buildings on campus were used as barracks for both armies during their occupations.

The university has a marker commemorating Fort Sanders in front of Sophronia Strong Hall, unfortunately located 2 blocks south of the actual location. The United Daughters of the Confederacy have placed a monument at the actual location, the hill nearest the corner of 17th Street and Laurel Avenue.

ℹ️ *Both the Springfield and Enfield rifled muskets were capable of hitting an aimed target up to 1,000 yards away, but few soldiers could see well out to that range. Most opening shots occurred when the opposing lines were 150 to 300 yards apart.*

Also on the university campus is the location of Fort Byington, a smaller infantry and artillery fortification not engaged during the siege. As in all the other wartime forts, the ramparts have been leveled and the trenches filled in, but the hill it was located on may easily be seen from the university's main entrance on Cumberland Avenue.

POINTS OF INTEREST

Confederate Memorial Hall
3148 Kingston Pike, Knoxville
(865) 522–2371

Formerly known as Bleak House, for the Charles Dickens novel, this slave-built brick house was constructed in 1858 and was used as Longstreet's and McLaw's headquarters during the brief siege operation. The tower was used as a sniper post during the Confederate operations; Brigadier General William Price Sanders of the Union's Army, the fort's namesake, was killed by a shot from this tower while standing on the lawn of the still-existent Second Presbyterian Church on November 16, 1862. The house was damaged by Union artillery fire and reportedly still has bullets embedded in the walls.

The house is now owned by the United Daughters of the Confederacy and is preserved and open to the public as a museum with many period furnishings and decorations. It is open Tuesday, Wednesday, and Friday 1:00 to 4:00 P.M. Admission is $5.00 for adults, $4.00 for seniors, $3.00 for students, and $1.50 for children ages 6 to 12. The house is closed the entire month of January.

The Museum of East Tennessee History
600 Market Street, Knoxville
(865) 215–8824

Nicely laid out museum in the 1870s-era U.S. Post Office building, with a collection concentrating on the general history of the Knoxville area; the Civil War section has a small, well-presented collection of uniforms and weapons. The best feature is the price—free. Open Tuesday through

Saturday 10:00 A.M. to 4:00 P.M., Sunday 1:00 to 5:00 P.M.

ACCOMMODATIONS

Knoxville has a good selection of both independent and chain hotels and motels, as well as a sprinkling of bed-and-breakfast inns. For a complete listing and current information on local festivals and events, contact the Knoxville Convention and Tourist Bureau, 810 Clinch Avenue, (865) 523–7263. The visitor center there is open 8:30 A.M. to 5:00 P.M. daily.

Maplehurst Inn
Bed and Breakfast $$–$$$
800 West Hill Avenue, Knoxville
(865) 523–7773

This small inn has one big advantage: It is very close to the Civil War sites at the University of Tennessee campus. Eleven rooms and two suites are available. They all feature cable TV with movies, some have whirlpools, and one has its own fireplace. The adjoining restaurant serves breakfast only.

RESTAURANTS

Patrick Sullivan's
Steakhouse & Saloon $$–$$$
100 North Central Avenue, Knoxville
(865) 637–4255

This well-appointed tavern, built in 1888, is an upscale eatery in the best sense of the word, serving chicken, pork, fish, and pasta dishes prepared in several unusual varieties. The mesquite-grilled chicken was one of our favorites, as was the prime rib plate. Thanks to the wooden floors and bare brick walls, the noise level can be quite high; there is a balcony level usually available where the seating is a bit quieter.

Copper Cellar $$–$$$
1807 Cumberland Avenue, Knoxville
(865) 673–3411

Close to the university campus, this high-end steak-and-martini establishment serves chicken and seafood dishes as well. Portions are huge, as are the desserts, and the best thing is that you most decidedly will not go away hungry. No dress code is posted or apparently enforced, but this is not a blue jeans sort of place. Lunch is crowded, with a lot of corporate suits present; supper seems a bit more relaxed.

Getting There: Hartsville

Today, there is no sign (or signage) of the brief fight at Hartsville, but the still-rural section of the state will give you a very good idea of the challenges of defending such an isolated post. Take I–40 east out of Nashville to U.S. Highway 231 (exit 238), and then go north into Lebanon. Turn right onto Tennessee Highway 141, which crosses the Cumberland River just outside Hartsville very close to the site of the battle.

In Hartsville are two small museums: the Trousdale County Living History Museum, which centers around the extensive tobacco farming history of the area, and the Trousdale County Museum, which contains a small number of letters and artifacts from the Civil War. The latter is housed in the old railroad depot, circa 1892, and is open irregularly. To arrange a visit, call the Hartsville Chamber of Commerce at (615) 374–9243.

Getting There: Stones River

Stones River battlefield is in Murfreesboro, about 30 miles south of Nashville on Interstate 24. Take exit 78B, which will connect you directly with U.S. Highway 96 East. Stay on this highway until the intersection with US 41/70, turn left (north) on US 41/70 to Thompson Lane (just a short distance north on the highway), and turn left (west) onto Thompson. Follow this road to the turnoff onto the Old Nashville Highway, and the plentiful signs in the area will take you into the battlefield proper.

MODERN TIMES

After the battle, the Union troops stayed busy constructing one of the largest forts of the war, a 200-acre post surrounded by 14,000 feet of earthworks, soon named Fortress Rosecrans. Grateful men of Hazen's brigade built a large memorial to him and their comrades lost in the vicious fight before leaving later in 1863; this is considered the oldest intact monument of the war.

Today most of the battlefield is taken up by the urban sprawl of rapidly growing Murfreesboro. A small portion of the original 4,000-acre battlefield is preserved and protected by the National Park Service, which also oversees the inclusive Stones River National Cemetery. Only Union soldiers (and veterans of subsequent wars) are buried here; more than 2,000 of the Confederate dead are buried in a mass grave at nearby Evergreen Cemetery. Only 159 of this number are known and so marked. The remainder of the Confederate dead were buried in unmarked, now-lost mass graves by Rosecrans's men, who stayed in and around the battlefield for another five months.

POINTS OF INTEREST

Stones River National Battlefield
3501 Old Nashville Highway
Murfreesboro
(615) 893–9501
The 450-acre park includes only the portion of the battlefield involved in the first Confederate assault on December 31 and a section to the east close to the Round Forest area. The visitor center has a small but nicely presented collection of battlefield artifacts and a slide presentation about the battle, as well as a very nicely stocked bookstore. A self-guided driving tour audiotape is available (and recommended), as well as limited information about portions of the battlefield not on the property. The park is open seven days a week, 8:00 A.M. to 5:00 P.M., and is closed only on Christmas Day. Admission is free, but please do leave a donation in

the box at the visitor center entrance. During summer, ranger-led tours are offered, as well as occasional living-history exhibitions.

Oaklands Historic House Museum
900 North Maney Avenue, Murfreesboro
(615) 893–0022
Once the center of a 1,500-acre plantation, Oaklands was built in 1815 and is the best preserved of several existing antebellum mansions in the area. The plantation was the site of both the surrender of Murfreesboro to Forrest on July 13, 1862, and where President Jefferson Davis stayed when he visited the troops in December of the same year.

The house has been restored to its early Civil War splendor, with a beautiful sweeping main staircase and intricate fleur-de-lis wallpaper. It is open for tours Tuesday through Saturday 10:00 A.M. to 4:00 P.M. and Sunday 1:00 to 4:00 P.M. Admission is $7.00 for adults and $5.00 for children under 18.

ACCOMMODATIONS

Murfreesboro is a fair-size city, with plenty of food and lodging choices. For a complete listing, as well as information on local events, contact the Rutherford County Chamber of Commerce at (615) 893–6565 or (800) 716–7560.

Doubletree Murfreesboro $$–$$$
1850 Old Fort Parkway, Murfreesboro
(615) 895–5555, (800) 222–8733
A beautiful, open, and spacious hotel, with a nicely laid out and decorated atrium lobby and 168 rooms and suites. A fitness center, restaurant, bar, and whirlpool are on the property.

RESTAURANTS

Demo's Steak and Spaghetti House $$
1115 Northwest Broad Street
Murfreesboro
(615) 895–3701
A local favorite, Demo's specializes in spaghetti dishes and offers several varieties of other pastas, steaks, and seafood and a few Mexican dishes. The dining room is nicely decorated in dark green, with period-style lighting fixtures.

Getting There: Forts Henry and Donelson

Forts Henry and Donelson were located quite close to each other in an area of Tennessee now known as the Land Between the Lakes (or simply LBL to the locals). To get there from Clarksville, which is located just off I-24 northwest of Nashville, take U.S. Highway 79 for about 40 miles. Fort Donelson National Military Park, directly on US 79, is 3 miles west of the small town of Dover. The site of Fort Henry is on, appropriately, Fort Henry Road, about 6 miles farther west on US 79.

MODERN TIMES

Time and river floods have rendered invisible the ramparts of Fort Henry, now indicated only by a single historic marker and a hiking trail around the riverbank area. There are no amenities, restaurants, motels, or basically anything else at this location. The nearest town of any size is Dover, roughly 10 miles east on US 79.

Some of Fort Donelson has been preserved and protected by the federal government, which also located a National Cemetery at the site. The Cumberland River is no longer recognizable from its Civil War days, having been dammed up to form Lake Barkley. Very little survives today from the Civil War period, the local attraction being the massive Land Between the Lakes recreation area, toward which most of the few local businesses are oriented.

POINTS OF INTEREST

Fort Donelson National Military Park
US 79 West, Dover
(931) 232–5706
This 90-acre park features a small museum with a small collection of artifacts, as well

The only Confederate general to regain his commission and rank in the postwar U.S. Army was Joseph Wheeler. His last service was commanding the cavalry forces during the Spanish-American War.

as a 15-minute film about Grant's river campaign. Occasional ranger-led demonstrations of rifle and cannon firing are presented, mainly in the summer months, and brochures for a self-guided driving tour are available at the information desk. Several emplacements and river batteries are well preserved and give a good feel for what it was like here during the siege.

Don't miss the Confederate monument, which is rumored to be placed over a mass grave of Southern dead. After the fight, hastily buried Union dead were reinterred in what became a National Cemetery on the property, while the mass graves of Confederates were left undisturbed. As they were never marked, these final resting places lie scattered about the property, forgotten and lost. The National Cemetery contains 655 Union dead, only 151 of which are known. Soldiers from later wars are laid here as well, swelling the population to about 1,500.

The park is open daily from 8:00 A.M. to 4:30 P.M., closed only on Christmas Day. Admission is free, but donations are accepted and strongly encouraged.

The tale is told. The world moves on, the sun shines as brightly as before, the flowers bloom as beautifully, the birds sing their carols as sweetly, the trees nod and bow their leafy tops as if slumbering in the breeze, the gentle winds fan our brow and kiss our cheek as they pass by, the pale moon sheds her silvery sheen, the blue dome of the sky sparkles with the trembling stars that twinkle and shine and make nights beautiful, and the scene melts and gradually disappears forever.

> Corporal Sam Watkins, Confederate Army, on finishing his memories of the war, in *Co. Aytch*

Dover Hotel
Petty Street, Dover
(931) 232–5706

Originally built in the early 1850s, this was the site of Buckner's surrender to Grant and was later nicknamed the "Surrender Hotel." One of the few buildings to survive the war intact in this area, it stayed open until 1925, serving the riverboat traffic on the Cumberland River. Now partly preserved and restored, it has the same exterior appearance and some of the interior furnishings it did in 1862. Two rooms are open for tours between Memorial and Labor Day, noon to 4:00 P.M. daily. Admission is free.

ACCOMMODATIONS AND RESTAURANTS

There are no facilities worthy of mention in the immediate vicinity of Fort Henry or Donelson, as this is a rather rural section of the state that attracts very few tourists. The nearest town with adequate facilities is Clarksville to the east. There you will find the usual array of chain fast-food and midrange restaurants, as well as a selection of chain motels, mostly clustered around US 41 on the north side of town. Nearby Fort Campbell drives the local economy here, which leans heavily toward the sort of businesses young soldiers support, especially north of town to the Kentucky border. (Fort Campbell is actually in both states, and the entrance gates sit on either side of the state line.)

CHICKAMAUGA: THE ROCK AND THE ANGEL OF DEATH

BACKGROUND TO THE BATTLE

Following an unsuccessful campaign in Kentucky and failure to push back Major General William Starke Rosecrans's Union Army of the Cumberland at Stones River, Tennessee, in January 1863, General Braxton Bragg withdrew his still intact Army of Tennessee back to Tullahoma to attempt a stand. Charged with protecting the vital transportation center of Chattanooga, Bragg intended to let Rosecrans bleed his army to death in frontal assaults on the Confederate position along the Duck River rather than trying another offensive himself.

Months went by without action. Rosecrans had nearly wrecked his own army at Stones River and needed time to refit. Finally, under pressure from President Abraham Lincoln, the Army of the Cumberland moved south, bursting through multiple gaps south of Tullahoma on June 24 and taking Bragg completely by surprise. His own line of retreat in danger of being cut off, Bragg hastily withdrew his entire force into Chattanooga with barely a shot being fired.

Bragg had no idea of the actual position of the advancing Union columns. Believing that they still intended to envelop Chattanooga somewhere to the east from Knoxville, he spent several days fretting and giving conflicting orders. The Confederates reestablished their lines in the small mountain town by the Tennessee River, but when Union forces crossed unopposed at three points below the city, the Confederates again were ordered to withdraw south without a fight—this time completely out of

Tennessee and on to the northwest Georgia town of La Fayette. Without a firm grasp of the situation and in a nervous frustration over what to do about it, Bragg missed several excellent opportunities to strike the separate Union columns as they exited the Lookout Mountain passes. On September 9, as the last of Bragg's army left, the vanguard of Rosecrans's entered the city from the north.

At about the same time, Major General Ambrose Burnside's Army of the Ohio divided into four columns with 24,000 men and forced the Confederate garrison at Knoxville to abandon the city, again without a major fight. These forces joined Bragg's column in the general retreat south into Georgia. The Confederate commander was determined to protect the vital industrial center of Atlanta and to regain control of Chattanooga if possible, so he tried an interesting tactic to draw Rosecrans's forces into battle on his own terms.

Paying too much attention to planted "deserters," who convinced Rosecrans that Bragg was in full, panicked retreat, the Union commander placed his 60,000-man force in three widely separated columns in order to cut him off and force the Confederate Army into battle, where it could be destroyed once and for all. One column led by Major General Thomas L. Crittenden passed through Chattanooga and went on to Ringgold, Georgia. Another, led by Major General George H. Thomas passed through Bridgeport, Alabama, and with some difficulty crossed Sand Mountain to approach La Fayette. The third column, led by Major General Alexander McDowell McCook, went another 40 miles to the

i

The best known "rebel flag" was never an official flag of the Confederacy. The bloodred field flag with the blue saltire cross embossed with 13 stars is known by historians as the "Southern Cross" and was used as a naval jack and as a battle flag for the Army of Tennessee.

southwest of Chattanooga through northern Alabama toward Summerville, Georgia.

As the Union forces moved to his north and west, Bragg sent urgent requests for reinforcements and gathered his forces for battle.

TWO ARMIES AT CHICKAMAUGA

Bragg knew that to protect Atlanta, retake Chattanooga, or even hold on for long in the north Georgia mountains, he would need reinforcements, plentiful and soon. In addition to the men from the Knoxville garrison, two divisions were sent from Major General Joseph Eggleston Johnston's army in Mississippi. General Robert E. Lee agreed, reluctantly, to allow Lieutenant General James Longstreet to go to Bragg's aid with two divisions of his corps (the third, Major General George E. Pickett's division, was still combat ineffective after Gettysburg). All these reinforcements would bring the Confederate force to a higher available manpower than the Union's, an exceedingly rare event at any point during the war.

With help on the way, Bragg became impatient to go into offensive action. Between September 10 and 13, with Rosecrans's forces widely separated and cut off from mutual support, Bragg grabbed the tactical advantage and ordered divisional-size attacks at several points. Mysteriously, not a single attack was carried out; each divisional commander found one reason or another not to assault. Rosecrans shortly received word from spies and scouts about both the fizzled attacks and

the incoming reinforcements and ordered his columns to pull together just west of Chickamauga Creek. By September 17 the columns were in close proximity, and Rosecrans ordered them forward to concentrate in the vicinity of Lee and Gordon's Mill on Chickamauga Creek.

Engagements at the Bridges

On that same day, Bragg's forces were in place from near Reed's Bridge over Chickamauga Creek in the north to opposite Lee and Gordon's Mill in the south. With the leading elements of Longstreet's corps just arriving by train and still a few hours' march away, the order for attack was given. Bragg's strategy was to sweep forward and take control of the La Fayette road, hitting the Union forces from the east, cutting them off from a line of retreat back into Chattanooga, and hopefully driving them back toward Alabama. Brigadier General Bushrod R. Johnson's brigade was ordered to start the offensive by seizing and crossing Reed's Bridge, followed by movement forward all along the nearly 5-mile line.

Johnson moved forward early on the morning of September 18, but his and the other brigades' advances were slowed by a combination of bad roads and miscommunication. Colonel Robert Minty's 1st Brigade (2nd Cavalry Division) made the first contact with the advancing Confederate force, skirmishing about a mile east of Reed's Bridge before being pushed back to the creek itself. Before withdrawing, Minty ordered the bridge burned, further delaying the Confederate assault. Johnson's men did not actually cross the creek until late in the afternoon. By that time the leading element of Longstreet's corps, Major General John Bell Hood's division, arrived and took command of the column.

Just to the south at Alexander's Bridge, another contact was made about 10:00 A.M. between Colonel John T. Wilder's

1st Brigade (Mounted Infantry, 4th Division, XIV Corps), supported by the 18th Indiana Artillery, and Brigadier General St. John R. Liddell's Confederate division. Holding the line for most of the day, Wilder was forced to withdraw at about 5:00 P.M. when his right flank was turned by newly arriving elements of Major General William H. T. Walker's corps, who had crossed the creek farther downstream. Pulling back toward Lee and Gordon's Mill, Wilder was soon reinforced and managed to halt the sputtering Confederate advance after a fierce night attack.

Day Two, September 19, 1863, Morning

On Saturday morning, after a long night of shifting his forces about to meet the developing Confederate threat, Thomas's XIV Corps arrived at Kelley's field on the La Fayette road, and he ordered Brigadier General John M. Brannon's 3rd Division eastward to make contact with the Confederate force. About 7:30 A.M. they suddenly encountered dismounted troops in the vicinity of Jay's Mill and both sides opened fire. There was no opportunity for either side to get organized, and the fight rapidly turned into a confused melee, with men firing every which way and seeking whatever cover they could in the surrounding forest. A few minutes into the fight, none other than Brigadier General Nathan Bedford Forrest himself came charging up, pistol in one hand, saber in the other, and began bellowing orders. The dismounted troops were part of his cavalry corps, detailed to protect the northern flank of the Confederate lines. Quickly, his men got into line, lying down in the damp grass side by side and returning a disciplined fire into the Union ranks. Casualties were high, nonetheless, for the legendary cavalry commander, who lost almost 25 percent of his men in the first hour alone.

Both Forrest and Brannon quickly called for reinforcements, and shortly

Colonel John M. Connell's 1st and Colonel Ferdinand Van Derveer's 3rd Brigades (of Brannon's 3rd Division) arrived to shore up the Union line, while Walker and Liddell brought their divisions to Forrest's aid. The fight grew almost by itself; very soon additional units began pouring into the rapidly growing battle, extending the lines a few hundred yards to each side, then a half mile, a mile, and then finally a nearly 4-mile-wide solid front of combat existed over the fields and forest from near Lee and Gordon's Mill all the way up to well north of Jay's Mill. Throughout the early afternoon, assault after assault pushed one side back a bit, then the other, neither side gaining any real ground or advantage. Both lines were in close contact the entire time, with appallingly high casualties piling up by the minute.

From that point on through the end of the day the battle was a "soldier's fight," as the thick woods and disordered array of combat units made it nearly impossible for commanders on either side to make informed tactical decisions. Both lines overlapped at several points, and hand-to-hand combat was commonplace across the fields.

Day Two, Midday

Starting a little after noon, Thomas began shifting his forces north to oppose Confederate forces coming on line against his left flank. This opened up a hole in the main Union line that was quickly exploited by three brigades of Major General Alexander Stewart's division. Attacking straight across the La Fayette road at the Brotherton farm, they succeeded in breaking the thin Union line. Following his lead, just to the left at the nearby Viniard field, Brigadier Generals Jerome B. Roberton's and Henry L. Benning's brigades (of Hood's division) stormed across the La Fayette road and pushed the Union forces out of their entrenchments and back about 200 yards.

Ghost Stories

It doesn't take much traveling about in Civil War history circles until you start encountering ghost stories. Nearly as ubiquitous as tinny renditions of "Dixie," rebel flags, and poorly made "authentic" kepis, ghost stories are sort of a peripheral industry in and of themselves, with pricey ghost tours, books, and hallowed traditions of sightings, usually in places that were peripheral to the war itself. The litany of the tour guide is often the giveaway that a "real" story from somewhere else has been borrowed to spice things up: ". . . and here in the window of this upstairs bedroom, the ghostly image of Sally Jane Beauregard is often seen at midnight on the third of the month during a full moon, staring out down the lane as if pining away for her lover who left, to never return . . ." We have often wondered what would happen if Sally Jane Beauregard really did show up one night.

Despite all the crass commercialization of the supernatural in certain areas, there seems to be a widespread and firmly held belief that something not of the flesh is present in any number of places—throughout our travels over the years, we have had all sorts of sober, serious historians, park rangers, and reenactors broach the subject with us without prompting, telling us of sights, sounds, and even smells they have experienced in the places blood was shed. The author of this book must admit to a rather eerie encounter while a young soldier at Fort Campbell, Kentucky, in the 1970s. He saw what appeared to be a group of horsemen carrying a battle flag and crossing the road about a quarter mile ahead of his jeep; they disappeared from sight in a large empty field on the other side.

A few places seem obvious to have encounters of this sort—the battlefield at Gettysburg, Pennsylvania, has produced enough sightings to fill two books on that subject alone, and nearly the entire ranger staff at Andersonville National Historic Site had at least one or two stories of encounters to relate. Rangers and even some visitors at Shiloh had some stories, most of which seemed to circulate around the Bloody Pond section of the battlefield. One volunteer at the Castillo de San Marcos National Monument in St. Augustine (known as Fort Marion during the war) told a hilarious tale about the *layers* of "haints" around the 17th-century castle, where one is not certain if the ghost one encounters is Spanish, English, Native American, Confederate, or Union!

One story that has circulated around the reenactment community for years (and has been told to us as happening to "a friend of a friend" by no less than two dozen people) involves an incident one night at the Pickett's Mill battlefield, just west of Kennesaw Mountain near Marietta, Georgia. The details in the various retellings vary somewhat, but the gist is that two reenactors showed up after dark one night before the annual living-history exhibition on the battlefield (this is not unusual, for reenactors sometime travel hundreds of miles to events, not leaving until the workweek is done). Rather than go crashing through the thick, dark woods to the encampment site, they decided to sleep in their car in the visitor center parking lot, which is only feet from the Confederate lines during the battle. During the night they were awakened by the sound of masses of people moving around on the other side of the center, followed by "rebel yells" and (in some retellings of the story) the sounds of muskets discharging. Deciding that some of the other reenactors supposedly on the site were just out having a little moonlit fun, they stayed in their car and went back to sleep. The next morning upon rising and looking around for their compatriots, they discovered that the encampment area had been changed to one off-site and that no one except themselves had been on the battlefield all night.

Another story was related to us about an adjoining battlefield, New Hope Church, where an eminent artifact collector and historian from Atlanta was out with a companion walking the old battleground on the afternoon of May 27, 1964. A sudden spring thunderstorm blew in over the field, causing the two men to seek shelter in a nearby toolshed. Our source did not know what they encountered next, but the historian and his friend soon departed the field quickly, through the midst of the driving rain. Coming up to a nearby farmhouse, they sought shelter with the old farmer, who berated them for being out on the battlefield that day. "Don't you know that nobody goes down in there on *this* day?" he asked. It was 100 years to the day after that terrible battle was fought, also during the midst of a driving thunderstorm.

These are the sort of stories that are delicious to read about, but the real rising-hair-on-the-neck feeling can only come from hearing them firsthand in the places they happened. Don't hesitate to ask your guide or available rangers about what they may have seen, heard, or felt—it does give an exquisite flavor to the experience.

In all seriousness, there is something very different about the places we write about in this book. We have found the battlefields, ironically, to be some of the most peaceful places we've ever visited, as if all the energy has been sucked out of the area by the enormity of what happened there so long ago. As we have stood by the Peach Orchard at Shiloh, atop Snodgrass Hill at Chickamauga, on the ramparts of Fort McAllister near Savannah, on the porch at the Carter House at Franklin, in front of the row upon row of stark white tombstones at Andersonville, and in the open fields of Bentonville, there is an almost perceptible hush, as if the wind itself is reluctant to disturb the rest of those who are buried there. As we clambered through the overgrown trenches at Nickajack Ridge outside Atlanta and the thick woods near Griswoldville, we had the feeling that those who fell there have waited patiently for someone to tell of their sacrifice. These may not be ghosts in the proper sense, but the spirits of those who fought in those places are there all the same, and in some very real ways their bones are as well, given the "plant-them-where-they-fall" burial practices of the day. Tread lightly and allow them their well-deserved peaceful slumber.

At that point the Confederates had nearly split the Union forces in half and controlled their main line of communication to Chattanooga. Worse for Rosecrans, the momentum of their attack was carrying them straight toward his headquarters, across Brotherton field at Widow Glenn's cabin.

With the breach made, reinforcements would be all that was needed to completely break the Union lines and carry the day. Resistance in the retreating Union units was stiffening, and the breakthrough was bogging down after a few hundred yards' advance. Benning requested not only infantry reinforcements but artillery as well, to counter the batteries directly in front that were shattering his ranks. Stewart's division fared a little better, with Union batteries exhausting their loads of canister before his own attack drew too close.

Rosecrans sent word to his units to hold "at all costs," and they responded well, putting up a solid wall of resistance even while their own ranks were blown apart. Several witnesses mentioned that whole companies simply ceased to exist in the rain of lead balls and iron shot. In typical Bragg fashion, however, no reserves were ordered in to exploit the situation. Without fresh men and ammunition, the breakthrough halted before any serious gain was made. As darkness fell, Hood's brigades held their line, to be relieved later in the night, while Stewart's men stayed put and hastily dug in just west of the La Fayette road.

Day Two, Evening

Just after sunset, Major General Patrick R. Cleburne's division (Lieutenant General Daniel H. Hill's corps) was sent in from its reserve position up to the right of the rebel line and immediately swung into battle with its three brigades. Hitting Thomas's units in the process of shifting positions, another fierce hand-to-hand

combat ensued across nearly a mile-wide front, pushing the Union line back nearly three-quarters of a mile. Within an hour, however, it was too dark to see anything except the brilliant muzzle flashes seemingly coming from all directions, and both sides broke contact and pulled back after again suffering high casualties. The long day of fighting finally drew to a close without either side having gained any significant advantage.

The Union lines were now compacted into a 3-mile-wide continuous front, and all night long the men dug in and waited for the coming onslaught. Thomas's men constructed a milelong series of heavily reinforced, aboveground log emplacements, rather than entrenchments, during the night, along and just to the west of Alexander's Bridge Road. Longstreet himself finally arrived at Bragg's headquarters with the rest of his men about 11:00 P.M. Bragg divided his forces into two corps, giving Longstreet command of the left and Lieutenant General Leonidas Polk (an Episcopalian bishop in civilian life) command of the right.

All through the night both sides shifted their positions in preparation for the next day's action. The Union right moved back away from the Viniard field to the Glenn field at Crawfish Springs Road, "refusing" the Confederate line, which stayed near the La Fayette road all night. On the north end of the line, Cleburne's division was reorganized and reinforced by Breckinridge's division to the right, extending the line to Reed's Bridge Road and facing due west. Forrest's cavalry had confirmed that the line outflanked the Union defenses and stayed to the right to guard their own flank.

Bragg gave orders that night for Polk's corps to attack at daybreak in force on the extreme right, to be followed by attacks all down his line, and then followed in the same manner by Longstreet's on the left. Both corps were to hit the Union line with every man they had, no reserves were to be kept back, and the attack was to be maintained until the Union line broke.

A reckless and unprincipled tyrant has invaded your soil. Abraham Lincoln, regardless of all moral, legal and constitutional restraints, has thrown his abolition hosts among you, who are murdering and imprisoning your citizens, confiscating and destroying your property, and committing other acts of violence and outrage too shocking and revolting to humanity to be enumerated.

General Pierre Gustave Toutant Beauregard of the Confederacy, in a proclamation to the people of Virginia

Day Three, September 20, 1863, Morning

Sunday morning dawned with a bloodred sun through the fog and battle haze, but no sounds of gunfire reached Bragg's headquarters. Riding forward to reconnoiter the ground personally, the only sounds he heard were axes chopping and trees falling within the Union lines a few hundred yards away as they continued to strengthen their positions. Continuing on, he found the troops on the right flank drawing their rations and not even close to being ready for battle. No doubt throwing one of his famous temper tantrums, Bragg sent for Polk and his corps and divisional commanders.

Reading the naturally self-serving after-action reports of "who said what" and "when I received my orders," it was nearly impossible to ascertain with any degree of accuracy exactly what had caused the delay. The divisional commanders all stated that they had received their final orders at 7:25 A.M., but Hill claimed this was the first he had heard of any attack order. It is known that there was some serious infighting among the Confederate high command and that a rift over who was senior to whom had developed between Polk and Hill. Bragg himself was one of the most widely despised officers in the entire Confederate Army, hated and distrusted by officer and enlisted man alike, which only increased the communication problems. The only certainty was that no attack went off at dawn, and the Union line gained in strength by the hour.

About 9:30 A.M. the attack finally got under way (this time and subsequent ones are also disputed in different reports). Breckinridge's division led off with a three-brigade front. Moving forward about 700 yards, Brigadier General Benjamin H. Helm's rebel brigade was the first to make contact, with the 2nd and 9th Kentucky and 41st Alabama Infantry Regiments storming the barricades held by Brigadier General John H. King's 3rd Brigade (Brigadier General Absalom Baird's 1st Division, Thomas's XIV Corps). As each brigade advanced, the next in the line should have moved into position for support, but for some unknown reason, no brigade came up on Helm's left to support him, allowing enfilade fire to hit him from the Union forces now to his left.

The assaulting regiments were nearly torn to pieces, and the Union lines held fast. Helm, Mary Todd Lincoln's brother-in-law, was mortally wounded and died later that day. What was left of his brigade, along with Brigadier Generals Daniel W. Adams's and Marcellus A. Stovall's brigades, moved farther to the right and around the long line of fortifications, where they ran headlong into and captured a two-gun artillery battery and pushed back the extreme left of Baird's division. Stovall's brigade finally halted just to the Union left and rear at the La Fayette road (near the present-day visitor center), and Adams's moved up to his right in the Kelly field.

Day Three, Midday

Acting against specific orders, Polk had sent in his units one at a time rather than as a united front and had held back Walker's corps in reserve. To try to shore up this failed attack, Walker was sent in about 11:00 A.M. with orders to attack the same set of fortifications. Once again each brigade was thrown into the battle as it came into line, rather than as divisional- or corps-size assaults, and once again the attack was halted and repulsed. Another brigade commander was killed during the action, Colonel Peyton H. Colquitt.

A little to the south and the left, at about 10:00 A.M., Cleburne's division was ordered into the fight. Ordered to "dress" on Breckinridge, who was already heavily engaged, he instead moved too far to the left, and his units milled about getting organized for some time before committing to battle. Rather than pushing back Breckinridge's command, his three divisions stormed the heavily defended ramparts held by Major General John M. Palmer's 2nd Division (Major General Thomas L. Crittenden's XXI Corps), but they were thrown back with very heavy losses.

This piecemeal advance of regiments and brigades continued on down to the left of Polk's command, but while inflicting heavy casualties on the Union defenders, it proved unable to bring enough force at any one point to break the strong line of emplacements. Throughout the morning, Thomas shifted his units around to meet each newly developing threat, and so far Polk's tactics had not been able to counter this.

At about 10:00 A.M. Captain Kellogg of Thomas's staff was riding from his location to Rosecrans's headquarters. As he passed by Brannon's assigned position just north of the Brotherton farm, for some reason he failed to see the men in their entrenched position. Kellogg reported this to Rosecrans a few minutes later, who believed without confirmation that this meant that a hole existed in his lines and promptly issued orders for

Brigadier General Thomas J. Wood to move his 1st Division from in front of the Brotherton cabin north to link up with Major General Joseph J. Reynold's 4th Division and close this supposed gap.

Rosecrans had been having just as many infighting problems with his top commanders as Bragg, and Wood happened to have been personally and profanely berated by Rosecrans for failure to promptly obey orders only an hour previous. Wood knew full well that Brannon was exactly where he was supposed to be, and despite the warnings of his own staff officer that such a move would be disastrous, he decided to follow his orders to the letter. Wood's division moved out at 11:15 A.M., opening up a nearly 1,500-foot-wide undefended gap in the lines in the process.

Just on the other side of the La Fayette road at the Brotherton cabin, the spot Wood's men had just left, stood 16,000 men of Longstreet's corps drawn up in line of battle.

Longstreet's Breakthrough

Longstreet's men had moved up into position during the night, and it took several hours to get them fed and resupplied for the coming assault. It was not until just before 11:00 A.M. that he was able to advise Bragg that he was fully in position and ready to step off. Bragg then gave the go-ahead, and Longstreet moved forward into one of the luckiest accidents in military history.

Fully expecting to run headlong into the same strongly defended line of emplacements that had tied up Polk all morning, Longstreet had arrayed his main assault force into a powerful, compact formation. Surviving elements of three divisions had been rearranged into three divisions of eight brigades total, commanded as a corps by Hood. Directly adjacent to the south stood another division commanded by Major General Thomas C. Hindman, with three brigades arrayed two forward, one in reserve. Another division (Brigadier General William Preston's) stood in reserve to Hindman's left and rear.

No more than five minutes after Wood's division moved out of its position, four brigades assaulted side by side in a 3,500-foot-wide front (from left to right, those of Brigadier Generals Arthur M. Manigault, Zach C. Deas, John S. Fulton [Johnson], and Evander McNair) across the La Fayette road, the right two brigades smashing immediately through the just-abandoned breastworks. Raising their rebel yells, the leading regiments brushed aside what little resistance was left in the Union trenches and plunged ahead, passing on either side of the Brotherton cabin and heading for the tree line several hundred yards ahead at the double-quick.

The left two front brigades (Hindman's division) moved forward at the same time but ran into well-defended log breastworks after about 300 yards. Moving at the double-quick, Deas's and Manigault's brigades assaulted the works without faltering, driving Brigadier General William P. Carlin's 2nd Brigade (Davis's 1st Division, XX Corps) out of their trenches and back in wild disorder. For the Union, Major General Philip H. Sheridan's 3rd Division had also been shifting north just behind Carlin's position, but it was also driven off the field by the fury of Hindman's attack.

Brannon's men soon found themselves under attack from three sides and pulled back to the north. Wood's division, turning to go back to its original position, was pushed back also from the brunt of McNair's men advancing up the Dyer Road. One after another, Union regiments on line abandoned their positions under pressure from the massive Confederate attack until the right side of the line completely collapsed.

The rout of most units in this part of the field became complete. With his headquarters under threat of capture and a wild confusion of men and horses swirling around him running to the rear, Rosecrans himself joined the flight of roughly half his army (his headquarters was only about a half mile directly behind the Brotherton cabin). Abandoning the field with him was his aid, Brigadier General, and later President, James A. Garfield. Rosecrans headed dejectedly back to Chattanooga, believing that Thomas's men had been routed as well and the field already lost. Garfield accompanied his commander north to the outskirts of Chattanooga and then he turned back to try to help save the rest of his army.

STAND AT SNODGRASS HILL

Thomas realized that with Rosecrans abandoning the field, all hope for victory was gone and the best he could do was fight a rear-guard action to save as much of the army as possible. Leaving his men still successfully holding off Polk in the entrenchments along the La Fayette road, he moved his headquarters and what was left of units from the right flank back to Snodgrass Hill. With the broken and shattered remains of 19 regiments and 2 artillery batteries, he set up a line of defense around the top of Snodgrass Hill and the adjoining Horseshoe Ridge under the direct command of Wood and Brannon. All were terribly low on ammunition, and no resupply or reinforcement was thought possible.

Fast on Thomas's heels, Longstreet knew if he could throw him off the small hill then he could cut up the Army of the Cumberland piecemeal as it fled back to Chattanooga. He sent Bragg an urgent request for all available reserves, so to finish the battle as quickly as possible. Bragg replied that there were no available reserves, as everyone on the field was now committed with either his corps or Polk's, and Polk's men were "too badly beaten" to be shifted to Longstreet.

About 1:30 P.M., Longstreet's attack opened up again with Brigadier General Joseph B. Kershaw's division (McLaw's) attacking up the slope of Snodgrass Hill from the southeast. His force nearly gained the crest of the hill before being violently thrown back. Kershaw was followed in rapid succession by a continuous series of assaults all along Snodgrass Hill and Horseshoe Ridge, each one being beaten back with increasingly heavy casualties on both sides.

About 3:30 P.M., with Longstreet's assaults nearly piercing his lines at several points and his line of men becoming dangerously low, Thomas turned to look to the north and his line of retreat, wondering if the time had come to leave. Just then he spotted a column of infantry heading his way. Knowing that there were no reserves that could be sent his way, he prepared what defense against them that he could hastily muster, when their colors finally caught the breeze. It was Major General Gordon Granger with two brigades of his reserve corps, coming up from their position at Rossville, Georgia. Granger had observed Longstreet's men piling into Thomas, and in a great fury he violated his specific orders from Rosecrans and moved some of his reserves up to relieve Thomas's beleaguered post.

Going immediately into action, they shared the ammunition they had brought with Wood's and Brannon's men and jumped into the line of entrenchments just in time to meet another Confederate assault. It, too, was beaten back, along with the next, and the next. As sunset approached, almost everyone along the Union line had completely run out of ammunition, and the Confederates were massing for another assault. Granger gave the order to fix bayonets.

Three more assaults were thrown back at the very crest of the hill in fierce hand-to-hand combat. At 5:15 P.M., in the midst of yet another Confederate attack, Thomas received word from his absent commander Rosecrans, now safely in Chattanooga, for him to take charge of remaining forces and move them in a "threatening" manner to Rossville. He immediately passed the word along to the other commanders and made preparations to pull out at sunset.

Just as the sun was setting and Thomas's men started to pull out of their positions, another strong Confederate charge sent Longstreet's men up over the crest of both Snodgrass Hill and Horseshoe Ridge, into the midst of the retreating regiments. Massive confusion erupted, with many whole Union companies and regiments being made prisoner and others managing to slip away without harm. Their men exhausted but with "their dander up," Longstreet and Polk both begged permission to chase after the retreating Union army, but Bragg refused.

Terribly shaken by his own severe casualties and typically fretting over what he should do next, Bragg instead did nothing. Thomas slipped away unmolested back to Rossville with the remnants of his command, and Rosecrans began organizing his shattered army within the strong fortifications of Chattanooga. Not until September 22 did Bragg finally move the Army of Tennessee up to Missionary Ridge overlooking Chattanooga, only to find it was far too late to finish what had started off so well.

THE COST OF THE BATTLE

The Angel of Death was ever present during the two days of vicious fighting. Chickamauga was one of the bloodiest battles of the entire war, with more than 16,000 casualties among the 58,000 Union soldiers and 18,000 casualties among the 66,000 Confederate troops. Only the three days at Gettysburg produced a higher casualty figure. Dozens of officers on both sides were killed in the close fighting, including one Union and three Confederate generals.

Most of the dead were buried in unmarked trenches dotted around the battle areas, but one private lies today in the only marked grave on the battlefield. John Ingram, who had lived with his family in this area before the war, was a close friend of the Reed family, whose house stood in the area. Finding his body among his fellow slain of the 1st Georgia Infantry Battalion, they buried him near where he fell and maintained his grave for many years.

The Union Army was terribly affected by their defeat here, but in their despair they found a true hero. Thomas's efforts were widely publicized by Northern newspapers desperate for some good news from Chickamauga; they dubbed him the "Rock of Chickamauga" for his stand at Snodgrass Hill. Rosecrans fared less well, relieved of his command soon after for his continued displays of sheer incompetence in favor of Thomas.

THE TOUR

Getting There: Chickamauga

Chickamauga lies a little off the beaten path but still close enough to Chattanooga to nearly represent a suburb. Heavily traveled U.S. Highway 27 adjoins the Chickamauga and Chattanooga National Military Park, running from La Fayette in the south north to Fort Oglethorpe, right outside the main gate. For the easiest route, take the Battlefield Parkway exit off Interstate 75 (Georgia Highway 2, exit 350) and travel west about 5 miles, then south on US 27 about 1 mile to the park. This route takes you past a heavily built-up and quite congested shopping area.

Although it is several miles out of the way and takes you into the park "backwards," we prefer the much less traveled and more scenic southern route up from La Fayette; as a bonus, you will pass several other sites of the Chattanooga and Atlanta campaigns. From I-75, take exit 320 (Georgia Highway 136, also called the La Fayette–Resaca Road), turn left, and follow GA 136 about 25 miles to La Fayette. Turn right onto US 27; the park is about 15 miles north.

From either direction, make sure to go to the visitor center first. It is just inside the north entrance (nearest Fort Oglethorpe), and the entrance is very well marked.

POINT OF INTEREST

The Chickamauga and Chattanooga National Military Park
Fort Oglethorpe
(706) 866–9241

Today the Chickamauga portion of the Chickamauga and Chattanooga National Military Park is one of the best-preserved and marked battlefields of the war. Operated by the National Park Service, this was the first and largest of four parks established between 1890 and 1899 by Congress (the others being Shiloh, Gettysburg, and Vicksburg), largely as a result of efforts by Brigadier Generals Henry Van Ness Boynton and Ferdinand Van Derveer, veterans of the Union Army of the Cumberland. This park was officially dedicated in a three-day ceremony starting on September 18, 1895, the 32nd anniversary of the battle. Nearly all the 1,400-plus signs and monuments on the 5,000-acre park were personally located by Boynton and other veterans of the battle.

At the time of the dedication, very little had changed in these fields since the great battle, so little restoration work was required outside of clearing undergrowth and new forests. The National Park Service has done a superb job in maintaining the area, with improvements added to accommodate increasing numbers of tourists and to better interpret the action, while not detracting from the original look and feel of the grounds.

Just inside the north main gate is a large and well-appointed visitor center that houses a small collection of paintings and general artifacts, an excellent bookstore, and very informative displays on the battle. A special feature is one wing devoted to the Fuller Collection of American Military Shoulder Arms, a donated 335-piece collection of infantry small arms centering on Civil War pieces. A 150-seat multimedia theater presents one of the more unusual introductory presentations that we have seen, a 26-minute show that makes use of 43 slide projectors, 1,300 slides, 5 video projectors, dramatic lighting effects, and a surround-sound system to discuss both the battle and the subsequent establishment of the military park. Outside the newer portion of the restored and renovated 1935 building is a well-presented collection of the major types of artillery used during the battle.

The park is quite large, and it will take several visits to study the battle in real detail, but a well-marked, eight-stop, 7-mile auto tour will take you to most of the significant areas in two to three hours, depending of course on how often you pop out to read markers and view the monuments! A two-hour audiotape-guided tour is also available from the bookstore. Be sure to stop by the information desk and ask for a map of the tour.

For the serious student of military history, this place is absolute nirvana. There are about 700 cast-iron markers dotting the fields and woods detailing exactly who fought at that point and what they did. Blue-lettered signs detail Union movements; the red-lettered ones detail Confederate movements. Small cast-iron signs mark houses that stood during the battle, small piles of cannonballs mark army and corps headquarters sites, and eight large pyramids of cannonballs mark the deaths of brigade commanders. In addition, more than 600 monuments and 250 cannon mark other significant sites. Quite a few sites throughout the battlefield feature modern maps, photos, and even audio descriptions of the events that transpired. Miles of hiking trails wind all through the woods; maps and guides are available from the information desk in the visitor center.

An interesting note is the number of monuments with acorns as part of their design. These indicate units and positions of Thomas's XIV Corps, which "stood like an oak tree" atop Snodgrass Hill.

Be aware that a great deal of action occurred on either side of the La Fayette road, which is the old US 27 today. A modern "bypass" highway has reduced traffic levels inside the park. Please also be aware that the entire battlefield is for all practical purposes a graveyard. The standard practice throughout the Civil War was to bury the dead either where they fell or very close by, and here they were buried in shallow mass trenches that were never marked. No one knows where these graves are located, so please tread lightly.

Admission to the park and visitor center displays are free; the multimedia show is $3.00 for adults, $1.50 for children ages 6 through 16 and seniors over 62, and free for children under 6. The 26-minute show is repeated every half hour during peak visitor season (usually June through August), and you need to purchase tickets for it in the bookstore. The visitor center is open from 8:00 A.M. to 4:45 P.M.

ACCOMMODATIONS

Hotels and motels are available in limited quantity in Fort Oglethorpe, in Chattanooga to the north, and scattered all along I-75. For a central spot to tour both the Chattanooga and Atlanta campaigns, we suggest you stay in or near Dalton, east off I-75 at exits 333 and 336.

There is one very interesting hostelry we can highly recommend here—a former headquarters and hospital now open as a bed-and-breakfast.

Gordon-Lee House B&B $$-$$$
217 Cove Road, Chickamauga
(706) 375-4728, (800) 487-4728
One of the very few period structures on the battlefield itself that survived the war is in the adjacent Chickamauga Village. Used as Rosecrans's headquarters just before the battle, it became the center of seven large Union hospitals on its grounds during the battle. Some of the downstairs rooms were used for surgery, with wagons placed just under the windows for amputated limbs to be thrown onto. Originally built in 1847 by James Gordon, it is open now as a bed-and-breakfast.

RESTAURANTS

Both US 27 and GA 2 immediately outside the north gate of the park have just about any type of fast food you may care for; for finer dining, travel US 27 to Chattanooga 20 miles north. Check at the Chattanooga Visitor Center at 2 Broad Street (follow the signs to the Tennessee Aquarium; it is directly adjacent) for suggestions and directions.

Sonic Drive-In $
1783 Battlefield Parkway
Fort Oglethorpe
(706) 861-6705

As we mentioned in the Shiloh chapter, we don't usually recommend fast-food chains—but we must admit that we have a serious weakness for these '50s-style drive-ins where you give your order into individual parking-place menu speakers. Carhops still occasionally wear roller skates to deliver your food, which hangs in those silvery trays that clip onto the driver's window. The food can best be described as unabashedly un-PC: chiliburgers and foot-long hot dogs; high-cholesterol, greasy onion rings and french fries; some of the world's best milk shakes; and even, be still my (still) beating heart, cherry Cokes.

Day Trips

We strongly recommend that you follow your visit to Chickamauga with one to Chattanooga to see where these actions finally ended. See the chapter on Chattanooga for a full description of sites and directions.

Close by to the east is where the Atlanta campaign of 1864 started, and we recommend a visit to Dalton, Rocky Face Ridge, and Resaca, all well within an hour's drive. Please see the next chapter for details and directions.

DALTON TO JONESBORO: THE ATLANTA CAMPAIGN

BACKGROUND TO THE BATTLE

In the early spring of 1864, after three years of increasingly bitter fighting throughout the Southern states, Major General William Tecumseh Sherman saw that Georgia, and Atlanta specifically, held the key for the Union to bring the war to an end. There is a military axiom that states that while amateurs study strategy, generals study logistics as the crucial element of battle. General Robert E. Lee's forces in Virginia, the main focus of the war to that point, were able to hold the Union forces away from Richmond largely as a result of the supplies that flowed steadily up from the transportation and logistical center of Atlanta.

To complicate the picture, President Abraham Lincoln was facing a fierce election campaign against the former commander of the Union Army of the Potomac, Lieutenant General George B. McClellan, a War Democrat who nonetheless agreed with the Copperheads and Peace Democrats who saw the war as unwinnable and endless. There was a real possibility that if Sherman became bogged down in the same sort of stalemated combat that Lieutenant General Ulysses S. Grant faced in Virginia, the Northern Democrats who had pledged to end the war by peaceful means could very well take the White House that fall. "Peaceful means" meant armistice and, in reality, a Confederate victory.

The Union Commander

Sherman was a very modern general, not given to paroling prisoners or other gentlemanly considerations. He held a burning, very personal antipathy toward Georgia, which meshed well with his ideas about "total war." Literally years of seeing the words ATLANTA DEPOT stenciled on the sides of captured supply wagons and containers convinced him that the small city represented just as much a threat to his army as any military force. In his mind, the road to and from Atlanta needed not only to be taken but also laid to waste so that it could never again be used against the Union. An added benefit was that this "scorched earth" policy would horrify and subdue the populace, who might otherwise engage his forces in guerrilla warfare or other harassing actions.

With General Ulysses S. Grant's blessings, Sherman set about building an overwhelming force from his headquarters in Chattanooga. Other Union commands were asked to supply what men they could spare, and by late April 1864, three grand armies with more than 98,000 men stood ready to invade Georgia. A steady stream of reinforcements brought this force to more than 112,000 by June.

The Confederate Commander

To oppose Sherman stood General Joseph Eggleston Johnston with but a single grand army of just two corps strength, numbering just under 50,000 men. Reinforcements from Alabama, including Major General Leonidas K. Polk's entire corps and other commands not then under direct siege, bolstered his total strength to three corps with just under 65,000 men by late June.

Johnston faced a very serious situation. His own combatant forces would be required to protect the railroads leading to and from Atlanta and keep their own supply lines intact, while being both undermanned and underequipped. One key factor lay in their favor: Johnston was a master of defensive strategy, rarely overwhelmingly successful in the advance but almost supernatural in his ability to know the exact moment to withdraw—just at the point where fierce resistance to the usually superior numbers had delayed or disrupted his enemy's plans the most, while keeping his own forces as intact as possible. Very unusual for a combat commander, he was also a humanist who deeply cared about his men and sought to minimize casualties even at the advantage of the enemy.

Johnston had one other serious disadvantage—the enmity of President Jefferson Davis, who blamed him for the loss of Vicksburg the previous summer and all too readily listened to whomever had a complaint about his tactics.

Both commanders were highly experienced, experts in their own ultimate strategies, well versed in the latest military tactics developed over the previous three years, and very highly motivated to accomplish the goals that had been handed them. This was the campaign of the grand masters, unfolding almost like a dance, with each grand army moving in both opposition and concordance, swirling together in battle, only to separate intact and move with both purpose and grace to the next stage. Ironically, or perhaps not, after the war Sherman and Johnston became the best of friends.

THE OPENING BATTLES

A casual examination of a map makes it appear that Dalton, Georgia, was very nearly a natural fortress, but Sherman was no casual observer. He had explored most of this area while on detached duty in Marietta in 1844 (and not coincidentally unsuccessfully courting a certain Miss Cecilia Stovall of Etowah Heights near Allatoona at the time), and he had the

Less than 5 percent of the population in the Confederacy owned any slaves, although this accounted for about 26 percent of all the households.

remarkable ability to recall the lay of the land in great detail. He saw that Johnston's army could be trapped before the rocky ridge that was then their refuge if his own forces could get into the level, open ground between them and Atlanta. To this end, he sent two of his armies to distract Johnston by a strong direct assault at the northernmost gap, Mill Creek, while his third army slipped through the southernmost gap, Snake Creek, and cut off Johnston's retreat route at Resaca.

Johnston similarly was not a casual observer; anticipating that Sherman would merely feint toward Dalton and then break south to try to cut his army off from the rail line to Atlanta, he ordered preparation of defensive works on "good ground" 17 miles south, just north and west of Resaca. In addition, he ordered preparation of a series of "military roads" between the two positions so that he could rapidly shuttle his troops into the prepared positions when Sherman made his move.

On May 8, 1864, having received notice from his cavalry scouts that Sherman's forces were on the march toward him, Johnston set Lieutenant General John Bell Hood's army corps in position to the north of Dalton, with his men arranged on top of the ridgeline and across Crow Valley to Pickett Top and "refused" southward over Hamilton Mountain to the direct north of Dalton. Hardee's army corps took up position to his left, just to the west of the city and directly on top of the impressive ridgeline. The Confederate line snaked along roughly 5 miles of hill and valley, forming an almost fishhook shape, with Rock Face Ridge as the shank and Dalton just below the point. A detached division guarded the railway just to the northeast of Dalton, and a smaller detachment took up post above Dug Gap, 2 miles below the city.

Sherman Moves Out

Major General George H. Thomas's Union Army of the Cumberland moved down the railway from Ringgold on May 8 and took up position just to the west of Mill Creek Gap, while Major General John M. Schofield's Army of the Ohio moved in from the north and took up position across Crow Valley. Aided by these highly visible movements and the screening ridgeline between them and the Confederate positions, Major General James Birdseye McPherson's Union Army of the Tennessee quickly marched south through Snake Creek Gap.

Later that same day, two relatively small initial diversionary attacks were mounted by the Union troops against the very strong Confederate position just south of Mill Creek Gap and against the weaker position at Dug Gap. The attack at Mill Creek nearly turned into a full force battle, with part of Howard's IV Army Corps actually making it to the top of the northern end of the ridgeline before being violently repulsed. Both attacks were ultimately unsuccessful, though the attack at Dug Gap degenerated at one point into literal hand-to-hand combat—a comparatively rare event during the war—and featured the Confederates rolling large boulders down the steep mountainside toward the onrushing Union force.

Early in the morning of May 9, McPherson's men emerged from the gap and marched quickly toward Resaca, but the sight of Confederate cavalry and infantry troops along with the well-prepared roads gave him pause. Afraid that he would be caught on the open ground and unsure just how strong a force he was facing (actually less than one division of infantry and a few cavalry), McPherson became unusually cautious and elected to withdraw and entrench at the mouth of Snake Creek Gap. Sherman considered this act to be one of the major mistakes of the campaign; if McPherson had gone ahead and moved into Resaca at that time, Johnston would have been caught off guard and surrounded, and the campaign might well have been over for all practical purposes.

As McPherson made his move toward Snake Creek Gap, Thomas and Schofield both launched strong attacks on the Confederate line, reinforcing the previous day's assault directly against Mill Creek Gap and down the eastern slope of Rocky Face Ridge in Crow Valley. Multiple assaults over the next three days were successfully repulsed, leading Sherman to order a gradual withdrawal of forces from the fight, planning to follow McPherson's route down to Resaca. Johnston fully expected the move; by the afternoon of May 11, with the battle still fully under way, he began ordering his units to also gradually break off and march to their prepared positions outside Resaca. By midnight on the 12th, nearly all his army had broken off contact and moved south, staying intact as fighting units and taking all of their supplies with them. It was this sort of "fighting retreat" that Johnston specialized in, utilizing what resources he had to their maximum.

The Battlefield

Examination of this terrain shows the two weaknesses in Johnston's defensive position; first, his lines were stretched between the Union lines and the Oostanaula River, making a hasty withdrawal nearly impossible. Second, the rail line he had to defend lay nearly underfoot and all along the Confederate line, again limiting his chances for tactical maneuver. To his advantage was a "tight" line of battle, with his forces in proximity and the two flanks well placed directly on the banks of the river.

Sherman placed his forces in a semicircle anchored by the river on the right and curving around to face the northernmost Confederates directly. His position had little direct advantage over the Confederate line but was built up quickly by units traveling through Snake Creek Gap from the Dalton area.

Johnston's plan to defend the river and rail line from heavily fortified positions was clear, but Sherman's intent was less so. Starting early on the afternoon of May 13, uncoordinated and seemingly random attacks were made against the Confederate left, right, center, and the right again on the morning of the 15th. Most of these assaults were slowed and their lines broken up by the incredibly rough terrain immediately before the Confederate lines. Two divisions, Brigadier General Henry M. Judah's 2nd (Major General John M. Schofield's XXIII Army Corps) and Brigadier General Absalom Baird's 3rd (Palmer's XIV Army Corps) were involved in a three-corps-strength attack on the afternoon of May 14 on the "bend" of the Confederate line. The two divisions were nearly annihilated by coordinated artillery and long-range rifle fire before they could even get their men together through the muck, losing more than 600 in a few minutes' time. Judah was kicked out of the army four days later for his alleged incompetence during the battle.

The Union assaults were ultimately unsuccessful in much more than getting quite a few of their own men killed and failing to push back the Confederate line at all. Several divisions of Hood's army corps stepped out in the late afternoon of May 15 to counterattack the Union left but were withdrawn after Johnston learned of the only real Union success of the battle. Brigadier General Thomas W. Sweeney's 2nd Division (of Major General Grenville M. Dodge's XVI Army Corps) had crossed the Oostanaula River a few miles south at Lay's Ferry and threatened to cut the rail line and the Confederate line of retreat. Within hours Johnston evacuated his forces intact across the river and marched south toward Cassville, destroying all the bridges as soon as his forces made it across. The last, the railroad bridge just below Resaca, was set afire at 3:30 A.M.

THE RETREAT TO THE ETOWAH

Johnston, ever the wily strategist, came up with a unique plan while pulling back from Resaca on the night of May 15: to send Hardee's army corps with most of the supply wagons and ambulances straight through Adairsville to Kingston, 15 miles down the main road, while sending Hood's and Polk's army corps down a little-used route to the small town of Cassville, just 10 miles away. To give Hardee a little more time to ensure the safety of the supply train, Major General Ben F. Cheatham's division was placed across the road about 3 miles north of Adairsville. Hood and Polk were ordered to march rapidly and "tightly," to give the appearance that only a small force had passed down their path, and to be ready to launch a sudden counterattack when the unsuspecting Union forces appeared.

Cassville

Sherman followed Johnston south, delayed by the long river crossings necessary for his large force and by an almost comical spat between Major Generals Joseph Hooker and Schofield over which one had the right of way on the narrow roads. The Union forces had not paused to regroup after taking the Resaca battleground and headed south with McPherson's Army of the Tennessee wide to the Union right, Thomas's Army of the Cumberland marching straight down the railway, and Schofield's Army of the Ohio (also known as and consisting only of the XXIII Army Corps) wide to the left. Expecting Johnston to make a stand at Adairsville, he ordered his widely separated columns to close together just north of the small crossroads town. The large Union force arrived in Adairsville after a brief but spirited skirmish with Cheatham's division on the morning of May 18.

Sherman was apparently deceived by the Confederate diversionary tactic. Eager to engage Johnston before the Confederate force reached a good defensive ground south of the Etowah River, he hastily pushed all his units except Hooker's XX and Schofield's XXIII Army Corps down the single road to Kingston. These two corps were ordered down the road to Cassville to protect the flank of the main Union column.

Just to the west of the main Union line of advance, a single infantry division commanded by Brigadier General Jefferson C. Davis (the 2nd Division, Union XIV Army Corps) and supported by Brigadier General Kenner Garrard's 2nd Cavalry Division marched in and captured the important industrial center of Rome on May 18 after a one-day battle with Major General Samuel G. French's Confederate division. Johnston's willingness to give up Rome without much of a fight, and in effect most of northwest Georgia and northeastern Alabama, in order to preserve his fighting force would later be used as "evidence" of his alleged incompetence.

At Cassville, Johnston ordered Polk to set his corps across the road about one-half mile northeast of the town square, with Hood's corps positioned about 1 mile east and parallel to the road, so as to hit the Union flank as they approached. On the morning of May 19, just as Schofield's corps was walking into the trap, a small unit of Union cavalry led by Brigadier General Edward M. McCook stumbled into Hood's troops from the east, and a brief skirmish erupted. Fearful that McCook was supported by infantry columns, Hood suddenly, and against orders, pulled back from his ambush position to reposition facing east, to gain support from Polk's right. Johnston soon felt that the chance for surprise was lost and ordered both corps to a low range of hills southeast of the town before a full-force battle could develop.

Hood defended his overreaction to the end of his life, insisting that he had infantry to his rear and that he would have been unable to launch his attack on the main column of Union troops on the Cassville road. Surprisingly enough, he was partly correct; close behind McCook were two brigades of Union infantry supported by a single battery of horse artillery wandering around lost, looking for a road leading into the east side of Cassville when they ran into the rear column of Hood's corps.

On the Confederate left, Hardee put up stiff resistance against the massed Union forces near Kingston, but shortly after the Cassville disaster, and at the urging of Hood and Polk, Johnston ordered all forces to disengage and withdraw south of the Etowah River into the Allatoona Mountains. He finally halted about 11 miles southeast of Cassville and set up a strong defensive position around the railroad gap at Allatoona Pass, just northwest of the small town of Acworth. As usual, Johnston ordered the railroad bridge across the Etowah burned as they retreated. Sherman moved in and occupied Cassville and Kingston, giving his men a few days to rest while he studied the ground ahead.

THE APPROACH TO DALLAS

Sherman had ridden the area around Allatoona extensively as a young officer assigned to Marietta, and he knew the potential for making the gap into a natural fortress. Changing his usual frontal assault tactics, he abandoned his line of march straight down the railroad and moved westward toward the small town of Dallas. It is not clear whether he was trying to pull Johnston behind him into more open terrain (doubtful) or whether he was trying to take a more western approach into Atlanta. The real danger for Sherman was that by abandoning the railroad he was lengthening his own supply column, making it more vulnerable to a rear attack by Johnston's troops and cavalry.

Ordered up and out by buglers on the morning of May 22, the three grand Union armies moved out of camp at Cassville and Kingston in their usual three columns. Thomas and Schofield headed nearly due south while McPherson swung far to the right in order to eventually turn and approach Dallas from due west. The huge columns of massed Union infantry in a front nearly 20 miles wide were hard to conceal, and the move west was soon discovered by scouts from Major General Joseph Wheelers's cavalry corps. By the afternoon of May 23, Johnston ordered Hardee to a good defensive ground just east of Dallas and Polk to a tiny crossroads nearby called New Hope (some maps label it New Hope Church). Hood remained entrenched at Allatoona Gap overnight and was then ordered to New Hope when Johnston realized that all the Union forces were headed toward Dallas. On his arrival, Polk shifted his men slightly to the west, tying in with Hardee and forming a strong defensive line nearly 4 miles long from directly south of Dallas to 1 mile east of New Hope in the vicinity of a small community called Pickett's Mill.

THE BATTLE OF NEW HOPE CHURCH

Hood settled into line just before the forward Union skirmishers and scouts came into view. For the South, Major General Carter L. Stevenson's division set up on the right, Major General Thomas C. Hindman's division in the slightly higher ground on the left, and Major General Alexander P. Stewart's division deployed directly in front of the small log New Hope Church in the center. Just before 10:00 A.M. on May 25, Confederate skirmishers about a mile in front of their own lines encountered the forward elements of Hooker's XX Army Corps rapidly marching toward New Hope. They attempted to burn a bridge over Pumpkinvine Creek to set up a delaying action, but they were quickly overrun by Brigadier General John W. Geary's 2nd (Union) Division.

Warned that action was imminent, Stewart deployed his men in line astride

the crossroads, ordering them to dig in as rapidly as possible. Stovall's Georgia Brigade was positioned on an open hilltop in the midst of the church's graveyard and was unable or unwilling to dig in at all, but Brigadier General Henry D. Clayton's and Brigadier General Alpheus Baker's Alabama Brigades in the center and right of the line threw up hasty but strong works of felled trees and earthen embankments. Sixteen guns from Captain McDonald Oliver's Eufaula Alabama Battery and Captain Charles E. Fenner's Louisiana Battery were massed within Stewart's roughly one-half-mile front.

Sherman ordered Hooker to push through what he believed was a small force and march directly to Dallas, remarking, "There haven't been twenty rebels there today." Just before 4:00 P.M. a severe thunderstorm blew in over the battleground. Marching steadily on through the mounting wind and pounding thunder came Geary's 2nd Division, with Major General Daniel Butterfield's 3rd Division to his left and Brigadier General Alpheus S. William's 1st Division on his right, all spread across a one-half-mile front in column formation and bearing down directly on the massed Confederate front of Stewart's division. The natural earth and timber works, combined with the very thick underbrush, served to conceal the strength of the Confederate line from the Union attackers.

Just after 5:00 P.M., as Geary's skirmishers drove back Hood's, Union buglers sounded out the call to go forward double-quick. Stumbling and falling through the thick brush and unable to see what lay ahead, the men from Ohio, Pennsylvania, and New York hoped to brush straight through what they believed was a weak line of Confederate militiamen and detached infantry brigades. Just as the monsoon-force rains began, William's men broke out of the thickest part of the woods and rushed straight for the Confederate line.

Stewart had wisely ordered the artillery to load with double canister and positioned his 4,000 men nearly shoulder to shoulder on a very tight front, antici-

The last reported words of Robert E. Lee and James Longstreet were nearly the same: "Tell A. P. Hill to bring up his corps."

pating quite accurately that Hooker would be packed in heavy infantry formations on his approach. As lightning crackled all around and sheets of rain poured down, the shouting mass of more than 16,000 blue-coated infantry burst into sight less than 100 feet in front of his lines. Immediately the Confederate line opened up and disappeared again in a thick cloud of bluish-gray rifle and cannon smoke. William's men took the brunt of the concentrated fire, losing most of his more than 800 casualties in the first 10 minutes of battle.

For more than three hours this one-sided slaughter went on into the dark and stormy evening. Geary, Butterfield, and William all ordered assault after assault, trying to break through what was more and more obviously the main Confederate Army line, only to be thrown back each time by murderous artillery and rifle fire. Stewart's Confederate forces started running out of ammunition, the 60-round-per-man standard issue being depleted in as little as 30 minutes in some cases. Stewart brought his reserve forces in line primarily for their ammunition supply, and runners searched the wounded and dead for any extra cartridges. The Union's Hooker finally admitted defeat at about 7:30 P.M., pulling his men back a short distance to dig in for the night, while rebel yells and catcalls greeted their retreat.

Throughout the long night, as Union men dug in with shovels, bayonets, tin cups, or bare hands, sporadic rifle and artillery fire broke out, but no further assaults by either side were mounted. Hooker's command had lost more than 1,600 men in the short fight (most references back up this figure, but one source claims fewer than 700), while Confederate

losses amounted to "between 300 and 400" as reported by Stewart. One bitter Union infantryman remarked that Hooker had sent them into a "hell hole"; the name sticks as a common reference to the brutal fight there and at Pickett's Mill.

PICKETT'S MILL

After the pasting he received at New Hope Church, Sherman returned to his standard tactic of rapid flanking maneuvers, and ordered three divisions under the direct command of Howard to the far left in an attempt to turn the Confederate right. Johnston soon learned of the flanking attempt and ordered two divisions to shift to the right of Hood's line, covering the probable Union line of attack. To the far right of the newly extended Confederate line was one of Johnston's best, Major General Patrick R. Cleburne's division, which took up position on a hilltop overlooking Pickett's Mill.

Although his scouts reported fresh earthworks and Howard himself rode forward and observed gray-uniformed troops reinforcing them on the hill before them, the Union commander was somehow convinced that he had reached the flank, or rear, of the Confederate line of battle and possibly believed that only a small picket outpost was entrenching. His uncertainty was obvious in a message sent at about 3:30 P.M.: "I am now turning the enemy's right flank, I think." Just after noon on May 27, Howard brought his three divisions in line of attack on a hilltop just north of the small mill community, again forming the men into the same narrow, deep, heavy infantry formations that had failed so miserably two days earlier at New Hope Church.

At this point, the Confederate line curved to the east following the ridgeline atop a low rounded hill overlooking a steep, densely overgrown ravine. As the battle unfolded, two brigades of Cleburne's force were shifted to the far right of the line, refusing at right angles to the line so as to prevent any possibility of being flanked.

At 4:30 P.M. the Union line, or at least most of them, stepped off into the thick, entangling underbrush. There were very serious communication and land navigation problems, and one brigade ended up marching completely away from the growing sounds of battle "to get rations." That particular brigade's commander, Brigadier General Nathaniel McLean of Kentucky, was a political enemy of Howard and on that day chose a particularly poor way of demonstrating his contempt.

Howard's leading brigade, commanded by Brigadier General William B. Hazen's 2nd Brigade (of Brigadier General Thomas J. Wood's 3rd Division, Howard's IV Army Corps), easily drove away the Confederate pickets and moved into the ravine. The growth was so thick that the colors had to be encased to prevent them from being torn to pieces, and Hazen was forced to resort to his compass to keep moving in the right direction. Emerging suddenly in an open field, his troops first encountered a weak skirmish line of about a thousand dismounted cavalrymen from Brigadier General John Kelly's and Brigadier General William Hume's Confederate cavalry divisions, whom they mistook for unentrenched infantry. Steadily overpowering the cavalrymen, Hazen's men rushed cheering across the open ground upward to what they thought was an undefended rocky ridgeline. Just before gaining the heights, Brigadier General Hiram M. Granbury's Texas Brigade suddenly appeared in view and began pouring a galling fire into the face of the onrushing Union line.

Hazen's men kept up the pressure, although suffering appalling casualties from a two-gun battery to their right at the point of the ravine (part of Captain Thomas J. Key's Arkansas Battery) and from two more regiments rushing in to support Granbury, Colonel George Baucum's 8th/19th Arkansas Consolidated

Regiment to his left and Brigadier General Mark P. Lowrey's Alabama-Mississippi Brigade to his right. Hazen managed to stay in the fight for about 50 minutes before being forced to withdraw, leaving his more than 500 wounded and dead in place in the open ravine.

As Hazen withdrew, Colonel William H. Gibson's 1st Brigade advanced over nearly the same ground and met the same fate. Far from hitting a weakened Confederate line, as Brigadier General Thomas J. Wood (3rd Division commander) had hoped, Gibson's men advanced as far as the Confederate line itself before being thrown violently back. Roughly an hour of combat resulted in nothing more than an additional 687 Union casualties. Another brigade, Colonel Frederick Knefler's 3rd, was sent in about 6:30 P.M. in order to cover Gibson's retreat and to recover as many wounded as possible. They too were subjected to intense, nearly point-blank fire from the Confederate positions as soon as they entered the entangled ravine and withdrew in short order.

The major assaults ended by 7:00 P.M., but occasional firefights erupted until 10:00 P.M., when Granbury was ordered to "clear his front." The Texans fixed bayonets and, with wild rebel yells, charged forward into the darkened ravine, killing or capturing many of the remaining Union troops. The remaining Union troops either "skedaddled" or "retreated in good order, with no pursuit [by the Texans] even being attempted," depending on whose account you read. Both sides encamped in place for the night after the firing died down at about 11:00 P.M., their attention still fixed on the body-strewn battleground eerily lit by dead pine trees set afire during the hot exchange.

Union losses for the day's action totaled 1,689 killed, wounded, captured, or missing, while Cleburne reported only 398 killed or wounded. This failed action so upset Sherman that he apparently completely "forgot" it in both his official report and his postwar memoirs.

The following day, May 28, 1864, Sherman finally decided that this westward flanking movement was getting him nowhere quick. Short on rations, his lines stretched nearly to the breaking point trying to hold the entire 5-mile line of battle from south of Dallas to northeast of Pickett's Mill, as well as the lines of communication necessary to protect their supply line back to the railroad north of Allatoona. He ordered a gradual shifting motion of the line east toward Kennesaw and Marietta and sent his cavalry to capture Allatoona Gap itself. Johnston soon learned of this movement and ordered an attack on the Union right, straight toward Dallas itself, but was repulsed with no positive effects on the Union movement and at the cost of more than 600 casualties.

THE KENNESAW LINE

By the first of June Sherman had begun massing his armies at Big Shanty (now called Kennesaw) and made preparations to strike straight for the Chattahoochee River. In between stood the twin peaks of Kennesaw Mountain and Johnston's entire combat force. Johnston initially arranged his 65,000 troops in a thin, 10-mile-long line of battle that stretched from Brushy Mountain on the east to Lost Mountain on the west, about 3 miles northwest of Kennesaw Mountain itself. This line was known as both the Lost Mountain and First Kennesaw line.

In the late morning of June 14, 1864, Johnston, accompanied by Hardee, Polk, and several other general officers, climbed to the crest of Pine Mountain, in the rough center of the line. While observing the Union positions as related to their own lines, they were spotted by a Union artillery battery posted less than a half mile away, which immediately opened fire. The first round scattered the distinguished crowd; poor old, fat, and slow General Leonidas K. Polk, the Louisiana Episcopalian bishop, was struck directly in the chest by the second Parrott shot and died instantly.

After heavy attacks on June 14, 15, and 17, Johnston realized his men were spread much too thinly and withdrew 2 miles to the southeast quietly during the pitch-black night and heavy rains of June 18. There he heavily entrenched from the railroad to the right, up across Kennesaw Mountain, Little Kennesaw Mountain, and Pigeon Hill, and left over a low ridge later known as Cheatham Hill. This strong, compact 6-mile-long Kennesaw or Second Kennesaw line was reinforced by artillery batteries placed on the heights, and cavalry placed on both flanks. One Union officer noted that the natural barricade of the mountain seemed purposefully made to stop any attacking army. The sides facing the Union troops were steep and boulder-strewn, and most of the rest was covered with thick scrub brush. Confederate engineers cleared the peaks of trees and brush to serve as signal and artillery stations. The main entrenchments were dug at the proper military crests, with a series of screening entrenchments and rifle pits before them at the mountain base.

Cannon were hauled by hand up the steep slopes, 100 men per gun pulling, tugging, and cursing all the way. Eventually, two four-gun batteries were established on Pigeon Hill, one four-gun battery on the north end of Big Kennesaw (nearest present-day U.S. Highway 41), another nearly on the peak, and nine guns atop Little Kennesaw. Before they were even completely emplaced, firing erupted between them and newly arriving Union batteries.

As soon as each of his Union forces moved up into position, Sherman ordered constant probing and skirmish actions, trying to keep the pressure on until a weakness was revealed. One spot in the Kennesaw line, a small hilltop called Bald Knob, lay just outside the main Confederate defensive position between Pigeon and Cheatham Hills, held by a Kentucky unit of the Orphan Brigade, famous for its ferocity in battle, perhaps because their home state was held by the Union and they were unable to return there on leave throughout the war. After repeated assaults throughout much of the morning and early afternoon of June 20, two brigades of Major General David S. Stanley's 1st Division (Howard's IV Army Corps, Union Army) managed to wrest control of the small outpost. In a rather bizarre move, later that evening, one brigade was withdrawn when its commander thought that a relieving force had arrived. The Kentuckians quickly realized what had happened and moved back into their old positions, just as the Union troops realized their mistake and hastened back to the same spot. Just as the Union men jumped down into the trenches, the Kentuckians popped up and began shooting at point-blank range. A few minutes of swirling, confused carnage, which resulted in possibly more than one instance of "friendly fire" casualties, and the hill was left in Confederate control once again.

THE FIGHT AT KOLB'S FARM

Impatient as ever, Sherman saw that his probing actions were gaining nothing, so once again he returned to his classic flanking moves. Hooker's XX and Schofield's XXIII Army Corps were both sent on a sweeping movement to the south of the Kennesaw line to attempt to gain Marietta and cut off the Confederate line of retreat. Johnston's near-supernatural ability to "read" Sherman's intentions came to his aid once again; through a pounding thunderstorm on the night of June 21, Hood's entire corps marched from the far right of the line to the far left, consolidating and entrenching across the path of the approaching Union troops on Powder Springs Road.

As the Union troops prodded and advanced down that road on the afternoon of June 22, the South's Hood suddenly decided to abandon his fairly strong

defensive position to risk it all on a full-force assault. Hindman's division into the north and Stevenson's division on the left suddenly burst out of the thick woods into an open plain near the Kolb farm, heading straight into the massed fire of more than 40 Union artillery pieces. The attack gained nothing, falling apart before coming within rifle range of the hastily dug Union lines. The shattered remnants of Stevenson's division attempted to take refuge in a shallow creekbed, where they were continuously raked by artillery fire until able to pull back after dark.

This attack further strained relations between Hood and Johnston, which had not been very healthy to begin with. Johnston issued a sharp reprimand for attacking without orders, which Hood responded to with yet another letter to Jefferson Davis complaining about the strategy being used. Strangely, reprimands were issued on the Union side as well, for Hooker reported that during the short battle "three entire corps are in front of us," Johnston's entire force strength at that time. Sherman was not amused by this report, and it didn't help that Hooker and Sherman got along no better than their Confederate counterparts.

ACTION ON THE MOUNTAIN

With his probing actions indecisive and his flanking maneuver halted at Kolb's Farm, Sherman chose yet another tactic. Tiring of the way Johnston constantly slipped out of his flanking attacks, and possibly hoping to destroy the Confederate Army of Tennessee in one huge battle, he issued the order for a direct assault on the entrenchments of the Kennesaw line itself, to begin at 8:00 A.M. on June 27. McPherson was ordered to attack the southern side of the mountain, Thomas was ordered to attack south of the Dallas road in support of McPherson, and Schofield was directed to feint south of the Kolb's Farm area as a diversion.

At 9:00 A.M. on the hot morning of the 27th, three brigades of McPherson's corps stepped up onto the steep slopes of Pigeon Hill, straight into the rocky fortifications. Surprisingly, some made it far enough up the hill through increasingly heavy fire to engage in hand-to-hand combat atop the entrenchments before being forced back under heavy artillery fire. Union losses in this futile attack were more than 850, with Confederate losses described as "about 250."

Thomas chose to concentrate his attack against a salient in the Confederate line nearly 3 miles south of Pigeon Hill, later famous as the "Dead Angle." Believing that one mighty push would drive out the heavily entrenched Confederates of Cheatham's and Cleburne's divisions, he decided on the little-used heavy infantry formations. The five attacking brigades (from the Union right to left) were: Colonel John G. Mitchell's 2nd and Colonel Daniel McCook's 3rd—both of Davis's 2nd Division, XIV Corps; and Brigadier General Charles G. Harker's 3rd, Brigadier General George D. Wagner's 2nd, and Brigadier General Nathan Kimball's 1st—all of Brigadier General John Newton's 2nd Division, IV Corps). They spread out across a 200-yard front (1,500 to 2,000 yards was more normal) with about 10 yards between each brigade. The overwhelming fire from the Confederate line proved so intense that the 10-yard interval gradually closed until all five brigades ended up attacking as a single mass 12 ranks deep. An absolute slaughter ensued as every artillery piece and rifle within range concentrated on the 1,000-yard front line. One Confederate observer atop Kennesaw Mountain mentioned that as the massed Union troops approached the entrenchments, "they seemed to melt away or sink into the earth, to rise not more."

With so much fire coming within such a confined area, soon the dead leaves and underbrush were set afire, threatening to burn alive the wounded. Just to the right of the salient, Colonel William H. Martin of the South's 1st/15th Arkansas Regiments ran to the top of a breastwork and, waving a white flag, shouted that he was proposing a cease-fire while the fire was put out and the wounded moved. In what was surely a bizarre scene, Union and Confederates laid down their arms and worked side by side for a few minutes. Several reports mention that the Confederates "moved" whatever Union guns and ammunition they could get ahold of as well. With the fire out and the wounded safely moved, both sides returned to their weapons, and the slaughter renewed.

By nightfall, most Union units had been completely thrown back, those few left under some protection of the hilly terrain would stay within rock-throwing distance for the next six days and keep up a constant sniping harassment. Private Sam Watkins, a self-described "high-private" with the 1st/27th Tennessee Infantry Regiment (the Maury Grays) at the Dead Angle, described his feelings when the last Union attack of the day was finally repulsed:

I never saw so many broken-down and exhausted men in my life. I was as sick as a horse, and as wet with blood and sweat as I could be, and many of our men were vomiting with excessive fatigue, over-exhaustion and sunstroke; our tongues were parched and cracked for water, and our faces blackened with powder and smoke, and our dead and wounded were piled indiscriminately in the trenches. There was not a single man in the company who was not wounded or had holes shot through his hat and clothing.

The only gain of the entire day's action, ironically, was Schofield's diversionary attack to the south, which managed to get between Johnston's line and the Chattahoochee River while the Confederate forces were distracted by the main attack. Sherman was enraged over the failure to break the Confederate lines, however, and seriously contemplated ordering further attacks the next day. Thomas brought him back to reality by informing him that "one or two more such assaults would use up this army." Sherman finally relented and reported in a cable to Washington that night that his attack had failed and that he had suffered "about 3,000 casualties." Several reports dispute this figure, placing it closer to 7,000 or even 7,500. Included in this number were Brigadier General Harker and Colonel McCook, both killed in the assault on the Dead Angle, along with the death or wounding of nine other Union brigade and regimental commanders at this small place. Confederate losses for the day were placed at just under 1,000.

THE CHATTAHOOCHEE RIVER LINE

After his stunning defeat at Kennesaw Mountain, Sherman required more than a week just to regroup and resupply his demoralized soldiers. On July 1 he abandoned for good his frontal assault tactics on entrenchments and planned another flanking maneuver to the south and east to try once again to bypass Johnston and gain Marietta. Once again, Johnston's scouts observed the huge army getting under way before any real progress could be made. With no real natural defensive barrier to help stop the numerically superior Union Army, Johnston decided to abandon Marietta and fall back across the wide, shallow Chattahoochee River, burning or destroying whatever supplies and equipment Sherman might find useful along the way.

THE GEORGIA MILITIA ENTERS THE FIGHTING

By the afternoon of July 2, Johnston set up a new line of defense at the small town of Smyrna, just northwest of the Chattahoochee, while his main body crossed to the south bank. This line collapsed in less than a day of heavy skirmishing with forward elements of the Union line, and by the next afternoon Johnston pulled back to his last line of entrenchments north of the river.

Governor Joseph E. Brown of Georgia had repeatedly offered both his militia and his own "private army," the Georgia State Line, to Johnston for front-line service. Accepting them in May, just after the New Hope Church battle, both units had proven capable fighters in the line, although very unpolished. Private Sam Watkins gave a vivid description of their arrival:

By way of grim jest, and a fitting burlesque to tragic scenes, or, rather, to the thing called "glorious war," old Joe Brown, then Governor of Georgia, sent in his militia. It was the richest picture of an army I ever saw . . . Every one was dressed in citizen's clothes, and the very best they had at that time. A few had double-barreled shotguns, but the majority had umbrellas and walking sticks, and nearly every one had on a duster, a flat-bosomed "biled" shirt, and a plug hat; and to make the thing more ridiculous, the dwarf and the giant were marching side by side; the knock-kneed by the side of the bow-legged; the driven-in by the side of the drawn-out; the pale and sallow dyspeptic, who looked like Alex. Stephens, and who seemed to have just been taken out of a chimney that smoked very badly, and whose diet was goobers and sweet potatoes, was placed beside the three hundred-pounder, who was dressed up to kill . . .

After failing to hold the line at nearby Smyrna, Johnston was desperate to get his forces intact across the Chattahoochee, into the northern fringes of Atlanta, and to escape the overpowering Union frontal

CLOSE-UP

The Andrews Raid

Also (and probably better) known as the Great Locomotive Chase, the Andrews Raid was a daring attempt to cut the rail supply lines feeding the Confederate garrison in Chattanooga and allow an easy Union takeover of the strategic supply and transportation routes in and around the city. In command of the operation was James Andrews. The plan ultimately failed, but most decidedly not through lack of effort.

In early 1862 General Ormsby Mitchel had approved Andrews's plan, which involved stealing a locomotive somewhere north of Atlanta and running north on the Western & Atlantic Railroad tracks to Chattanooga, tearing up track, burning bridges, and blowing up tunnels along the way. The plan was to then move west to Huntsville, Alabama. Andrews handpicked a group of 22 railroad engineers and workers from the Union Army ranks and slipped into northern Georgia with his band of saboteurs in early April. Mitchel moved in and captured Huntsville on April 11 and waited there for Andrews to pull off his raid and come safely into the northern Alabama city. Notified of Mitchel's action, Andrews made a hasty reconnaissance of the train stations and stops along the W & A Railroad. Just

north of Atlanta, in the small town of Marietta, they found the opportunity they had been looking for.

On April 12 at 4:00 A.M. a Western & Atlantic railway engine—called the *General*—pulling a passenger car and two boxcars left Atlanta heading north and arrived in Marietta about an hour later, where Andrews and his men boarded unobserved. A few miles farther north the small train stopped at Big Shanty (now called Kennesaw), where the crew and other passengers disembarked and went into the Lacey Hotel for breakfast. Andrews had selected this site to commandeer the train knowing that everyone else would be at breakfast and that the small whistle-stop did not have a telegraph office. As the train crew sipped their coffee, the Union raiders jumped up into the *General's* cab and raced northward.

The two crewmen of the *General* raced out of the hotel as soon as they heard the engine start up, only to see it disappearing down the tracks. Engineer Jeff Cain, foreman Anthony Murphy, and conductor William Fuller ran down the tracks nearly 2 miles before finding a handcart and another work crew, who gave them the cart and helped move it north after the fleeing Union raiders.

assault. He ordered the few thousand men of the Georgia Militia under General Gustavus Smith to dig in on his left at hastily constructed trench lines on a steep hillside just below Smyrna, on the north bank of the Chattahoochee, near the small

Nickajack Creek. This near-suicidal and expendable position directly confronted the full-corps–strength vanguard of Sherman's army. With the Union forces bearing down rapidly, the 1st Regiment of the Georgia State Line under Colonel Edward

Andrews had no idea he was being pursued, even at a very low rate of speed, and his men busied themselves cutting telegraph lines, pulling rails out of the roadbed, and placing assorted obstacles across the tracks. As the Union raiders came to each station and stop along the way, they answered questions about their unscheduled train by stating that they were taking ammunition and supplies to the Confederate Army in Corinth, Mississippi, which seemed to satisfy the curious onlookers.

Fuller found a small "switch" engine at the Etowah station and headed north at maximum speed after his stolen train. Leaving the small engine in the massive rail yard at Kingston, the *General*'s own crew raced across the tracks on foot and then found another engine to carry them farther north. After only a few more miles of high-speed pursuit, they were forced to abandon this engine as well when tracks torn up by Andrews's men proved too tough an obstacle. Running north along the tracks once again, Murphy and Fuller finally found another suitable pursuit vehicle, the *Texas*, waiting on the southbound tracks at Adairsville.

The *Texas* was soon in full-speed pursuit running backward (north) on the rail line; Murphy and Fuller spotted their former engine and its Union captors just north of the Calhoun station. Andrews,

only now aware that he was being chased, initially ordered his men to hastily block and tear up the tracks to try to slow the onrushing Texas but soon abandoned his efforts and made full speed north on the tracks toward Chattanooga. The *General* managed to race north through Dalton and Ringgold but, running out of water for the boilers and unable to resupply because of the *Texas*'s close pursuit, was brought to a halt just south of the peak of Ringgold Gap. Andrews and his men hastily bailed out of the train and ran off into the surrounding mountains, even as Murphy pulled up in the *Texas*.

Confederate troops already en route down the tracks from Chattanooga immediately set out, scouring the mountains for Andrew's men, but it took nearly two weeks to round up the 22 raiders from points as far away as northern Alabama. Fourteen of the raiders were sent to prison camps. Eight of that number managed to escape in a mass breakout in October 1862, and the other six were paroled in March 1863. Andrews and seven other raiders were quickly tried in an Atlanta military court and just as quickly hung and dumped in unmarked graves. They were later interred in the Chattanooga National Cemetery, their final resting places marked by a stone model of the *General*.

M. Galt was sent in to reinforce the line on July 4. Relieving the militia at the forward primary fighting positions, the State Line troopers barely got into place before forward elements of Palmer's XIV Army Corps began their assault.

Palmer soon reported fierce resistance in this line, but Sherman was convinced that it represented a token rear-guard action while Johnston retreated across the river. Believing the line could be easily brushed aside, he ordered Palmer to "fiercely assault" the line with everything he had, nearly 20,000 men at that point. The total combat-effective manpower available to the State Line by this time was about 300, with the 2,000- to 4,000-strong Georgia Militia acting as reserves (most were not quite fit for even that duty) and one four-gun battery of artillery for support. Palmer's men assaulted and skirmished with the troopers all through the day of July 5 without result, until Sherman personally came up to reconnoiter.

Upon seeing the strength of the State Line's redoubts, he called off the attack, stating later that it represented "the best line of field entrenchments I have ever seen." Impressed with the fighting resistance of Joe Brown's Pets and worried that to continue the frontal attack would result in another disaster like Kennesaw Mountain, Sherman instead sent part of his army far to the left to cross the river at an unguarded site.

ROSWELL

Finding nearly all the ferries and pontoon bridges out due to the high water caused by weeks of heavy rains and what bridges remaining either heavily defended or burned, Sherman was hard pressed to find a crossing that wouldn't result in losing most of his army in the muddy water.

Garrard's 2nd Division Cavalry (of Brigadier General Washington Elliott's Cavalry Corps, Schofield's XXIII Army Corps) rode about 15 miles to the north and quickly captured the small town of Roswell, overlooking the Chattahoochee River. He found the bridge there burned but identified several spots nearby where the river could be safely forded. He was ordered to keep watch for Confederate movements and to stay concealed until the main force arrived. With Major General George Stoneman's cavalry division ranging as far south as Sandtown, McPherson's corps feinting to the right, and Thomas's corps keeping the pressure on the river

line, Schofield's corps quickly moved upriver on July 8 to find the best crossing site.

Roswell was a small but productive mill town, making uniforms, blankets, and other textile goods for the Confederacy. Even as word of approaching Union troops caused townspeople to leave in a panic, work continued in the mill. The wealthy and prominent Barrington King family, now headed at high speed away from the town, conferred the "ownership" of the property on the shoulders of one Theophilus Roche, a French citizen and relatively new employee of the mill. One story holds that Roche was in fact the mill's janitor. As the lead scouts of Garrard's cavalry approached, Roche ordered the Confederate national flag hauled down and replaced with the French tricolor.

Details on what happened next are poorly documented, but it is very clear that this attempt to claim foreign ownership of what was clearly a Confederate-supporting mill failed to impress the Union officers on the scene. Claiming they were acting on direct orders from Sherman (a point somewhat in dispute), the mostly women and children employees of the mill were arrested as traitors and sent under guard of a cavalry attachment to Marietta, while the mill and associated buildings were burned to the ground. Underscoring what must have been a horribly frightening and humiliating action for the women, several sources quote the Union cavalrymen escorts commenting on the "fine good looks" of the Roswell women, as pointedly different from the "fearfully homely" women they had seen elsewhere in northern Georgia. Once at Marietta, these women and children were grouped with other evacuees from the destroyed mill town of New Manchester and placed on northbound trains, ending up in Ohio and Indiana. Some records claim these women were placed in Northern prison camps in those states, while other records claim that they were "dumped out by the side of the [railroad] tracks," while still other records indicate that Northern families ended up taking in most or all of them.

Sherman Crosses the Chattahoochee

By nightfall the entire division was across, and with the news of the Union Army on the south bank, Johnston decided his only recourse was to once again retreat. Abandoning the river line to Sherman, Johnston pulled his forces back south of Peachtree Creek, on the very doorstep of Atlanta itself. In a little more than 60 days, the hardened rebel force had been forced back from no less than eight strongly prepared defensive lines by Sherman's flanking movements and had been forced to surrender all of northern Georgia.

Without further resistance to his river crossing, Sherman paused only long enough to rebuild pontoon and railroad bridges before striking south again. On July 11 McPherson was sent eastward toward Decatur and Stone Mountain with orders to cut the railway between Atlanta and Augusta. Sherman's greatest fear at this point was that Johnston would receive reinforcements by rail from Lee's Army of Northern Virginia. Thomas was sent south toward Peachtree Creek with Schofield marching just to his right, headed toward Buckhead.

Johnston carefully noted the Union approach and planned to wait until close contact was established and then to attack the gap between Thomas and Schofield before they were deployed for the fight. Before he could carry out this attack, Jefferson Davis fired Johnston in one of the worst decisions of the war. Late in the afternoon of July 17, Hood was promoted to general and given command of the entire Army of Tennessee. Just 33 years old and considered a hotheaded division-level commander who was

already out of his league as high as the corps level, the move delighted no one more than Sherman. In his postwar memoirs he mentioned, "I was always anxious with Johnston at my front." He knew Hood was rash and prone to ordering ill-timed and poorly planned movements and was anxious for him to do so before Atlanta. It would be much better to destroy the Confederate forces in the field and then easily take the vital transportation and supply center than to be forced to assault heavily fortified defenses.

Least happy of all were the Confederate soldiers, who had loved Johnston for his humane treatment of them and feared Hood would kill them all off in ill-considered battles. Private Sam Watkins said Johnston's removal was "like the successful gambler, flushed with continual winnings, who staked his all and lost. It was like the end of the Southern Confederacy."

ADVANCE TO PEACHTREE CREEK

The day after Hood took command, Union infantrymen of Palmer's XIV Army Corps advanced through heavy resistance by Wheeler's cavalry to the northern banks of Peachtree Creek, near Howell Mill Road. At just about the same time, Garrad's cavalry supported by McPherson's infantry reached the Georgia Railroad and captured the railroad depot at Stone Mountain, 15 miles east of Atlanta. On July 19 three brigades of Palmer's XIV Army Corps forced a crossing of Peachtree Creek toward Moore's Mill, followed by other crossings under fire by elements of Howard's IV Army Corps near Peachtree Road and Hooker's XX Army Corps near Collier Road. By nightfall the Union forces formed a solid line of blue-coated infantry on the south banks of Peachtree Creek itself, facing due south toward the Confederate line arranged atop low hills about one-half mile away.

The Battle

Pleased with the progress of his subordinates, Sherman ordered Thomas to cross Peachtree Creek and engage Hood, Schofield to capture Decatur, and McPherson to advance toward Atlanta, tearing up the railroad tracks along the way. Obsessed with detail, Sherman sent word on exactly how he wanted the tracks torn up, "Pile the ties into shape for a bonfire, put the rails across and when red hot in the middle, let a man at each end twist the bar so that its surface becomes spiral." Hood had a reputation as a battlefield brawler, and he wasted little time going on the offensive. A general attack was ordered at about 1:00 P.M. on July 20, intended to drive the dug-in Union infantry back across the creek and as far as the banks of the Chattahoochee River. Before the attack could commence, Hood ordered the entire line to shift a little less than 1 mile to the east, to protect his right flank from counterattack. Despite the fact that this movement threw the whole line into disarray and caused a general confusion as to exactly where they were to advance, he ordered the attack to begin at 4:00 P.M.

At about 2:45 P.M., Major General William W. Loring's division (Stewart's corps) stepped off, almost immediately encountering Union infantry and mistakenly initiating battle action in the center of the line. Major General William B. Bate's division of Hardee's corps, ordered to begin the general assault from the extreme right of the Confederate lines, didn't actually move out until nearly a half hour later. The rest of the 2-mile-long line followed in piecemeal, advancing more in small groups and masses than in well-formed lines, a result of the uneven terrain and thick underbrush.

The only real success of the entire assault was made by Brigadier General Thomas M. Scott's brigade (Stewart's corps) of mostly Alabama troops, who advanced through the Tanyard Branch and Collier Road vicinity, attacked, drove off, and captured the Union flag of Colonel Patrick H. Jones's 33rd New Jersey Infantry Regiment (Geary's 2nd Division, Hooker's XX Army Corps) as well as a four-gun artillery battery. Scott's men were soon forced to withdraw, as no other unit was able to break through to support them on either flank.

No other unit achieved even that modest of a success, and the entire attack was over with and all units back in their original positions by 6:00 that evening. The well-positioned Union forces had handed the advancing Confederates quite a mauling. Although the numbers engaged were fairly even, 21,450 Union to 18,450 Confederate, casualties were much more one-sided: 1,780 Union to 4,800 Confederate. Hood's first outing as an army commander was an unqualified disaster.

To add insult to injury, shortly before noon on July 20, Union soldiers led by Captain Francis DeGress set up four 20-pounder Parrott rifles and soon began firing the first of thousands of artillery shells into the Gate City itself. The first shell exploded at the intersection of Ivy and East Ellis Streets, killing a young girl who had been walking with her parents past Frank P. Rice's lumber dealership on the northwest corner. Shelling continued for several weeks at the rate of one round every 15 minutes, more as a harassment and reminder of the siege conditions than as a real destruction attempt. The DeGress battery would soon be the very object and center of fighting for the city.

THE BATTLE OF ATLANTA

Before the fighting died down at Peachtree Creek, Sherman was massing his forces for the next assault. McPherson's three corps were set in motion down the Georgia Railroad to attack Atlanta from the east, while Thomas and Schofield were ordered to close up and keep as much pressure on the Confederates as possible. By late in the day on July 20, forward elements of Major General Frank P. Blair's XVII Army Corps had engaged Wheeler's dismounted cavalry on a small hilltop 2 miles to the east of Atlanta. Heavy combat erupted as the two lines collided, until the overwhelmed Southern cavalrymen withdrew about midnight.

Leggett's Hill

Realizing the tactical importance of a ridge known as Bald Hill, in the early morning of July 21, Blair sent in Brigadier General Mortimer D. Leggett's 3rd Division and Brigadier General Giles A. Smith's 4th Division against Cleburne's division, which had replaced the decimated cavalrymen. Cleburne's men had spent the night reinforcing the hilltop position but were unable to stop the Union assault. The Confederates withdrew slightly and then spent most of the rest of the day attempting to retake the hill. While the battle raged on, Blair ordered up his artillery and set his guns into newly reversed entrenchments, bringing Atlanta itself within good artillery range for the first time. In honor of his heroics, the hilltop was renamed Leggett's Hill, a moniker that some maps still bear today.

The Night March through Atlanta

Hood had no intention of pursuing the same sort of well-planned-out, plodding, and slow retreat defense that Johnston utilized, and he saw an opportunity for offensive action against McPherson. Withdrawing Stewart's corps and the Georgia Militia to the strongly fortified positions in the outer ring of defenses around Atlanta, he ordered Hardee's corps on an all-night forced march. Moving due south down Peachtree Street through the middle of town (and panicking the civilians, who believed their entire army was deserting them), they swung eastward toward Decatur, attempting to get behind Blair's corps lines before moving north into the line of battle. Cleburne's division withdrew

with some difficulty from the Leggett's Hill action and joined Hardee's march. At the same time, two divisions of Wheeler's cavalry were sent around the Union left flank to attempt a strike at their supply wagons in Decatur.

To the lowly infantryman, this brilliant plan must have lost some of its luster. Having been in action off and on for more than two months, they had pulled back time after time only to spend hours in back-breaking labor—digging in and reinforcing when they arrived at new positions, for "spades is trumps," as the men said. Then, after doing this again and again with inadequate rest and dwindling supplies, they were ordered up on the line of battle only to be violently thrown back with heavy losses. Within hours of battle once more the order was given to withdraw and now to go immediately into an all-night march. Without a doubt this was nearly more than the poorly supplied, hungry, and thirsty men could endure.

Brigadier General Daniel C. Govan of Cleburne's division, Confederate Army, was equally unimpressed, deathly worried that "the loss of another night's rest was a heavy tax upon their powers of endurance." Hundreds of soldiers simply plopped down on the side of the road, unable to go any farther, until at last a two-hour rest was called. Hood intended for the attack to begin at daylight, but it became apparent that any possible attack could be launched no earlier than noon.

Unknown to the Confederates, McPherson was worried that they would attempt this exact movement and ordered his lines extended and turned to the south. Dodge's XVI Army Corps was ordered in to Blair's left, facing southeast and entrenching as had become the norm. At McPherson's urging, Blair's men heavily entrenched and blocked lanes of approach before them.

By the morning of July 22, Hardee's men had trudged down the McDonough Road south of Atlanta and then turned to the northeast on the Fayetteville Road toward Decatur. Still trying to make up time lost on the rest stops, Hardee ordered

Cleburne's and Brigadier General George E. Maney's divisions to begin deploying to the left when they reached Bouldercrest Road (now Drive), while Bate's and Major General William H. T. Walker's divisions continued on up the road before turning left on what is today called Wilkinson Drive. Both of these moves into line were short of their original goals.

Presently running into a large mill pond their guides had repeatedly warned them about, Walker's and Bate's divisions wandered around through the thick forest for nearly an hour trying to sort themselves out and get into the line of battle. As Walker roundly cursed their guides, grumbling that they must be "traitors" to allow him to get himself in such a fix, he raised his field glasses to try to figure out his next move. A nearby Union picket spotted Walker and killed him with a single, well-aimed shot.

Fighting in East Atlanta

Walker's place was taken over by Brigadier General Hugh W. Mercer, and the planned dawn attack commenced after more confusion and shifting troops at about 12:15 P.M. On advancing to the planned line of departure near the present-day intersection of Memorial Drive and Clay Street, the Confederates discovered to their horror that, far from being in the Union rear, they were advancing straight into a heavily invested front-line position. Pressing forward under intense fire from Sweeney's 2nd Division (Dodge's XVI Army Corps), they were immediately raked by fire from two well-sited artillery positions: one six-gun, 12-pounder Napoleon battery (Lieutenant Andrew T. Blodgett's 1st Missouri Light Battery) and one six-gun, 3-inch ordnance rifle battery (Captain Jerome M. Burrows's 14th Ohio Light Battery, noted as being replaced in command by Lieutenant Seith M. Laird in a few accounts).

About 30 minutes later, Cleburne's and Maney's divisions launched their attack to the left of the ongoing fight, straight into the "bend" of the Union line held by Giles Smith's 4th Division (Blair's XVII Army Corps). This attack was much more successful, driving the Union line all the way north to Leggett's Hill and capturing an entire infantry regiment (Lieutenant Colonel Addison H. Sander's 16th Iowa) and eight artillery pieces.

McPherson had been eating lunch with his staff and corps commanders less than a mile away when he heard the sudden crash of artillery fire. He hastily mounted his horse and rode south with a small group of officers to check on the situation, pausing atop a nearby hill. From there he could see that Sweeney's division was holding up well, but he couldn't see the situation on the other end of the line. Striking out immediately for the spot between the two Confederate assaults, he realized that his line was not continuous in that area and quickly ordered up more troops to fill the gap. Riding through the unmanned gap toward Giles Smith's position, his party suddenly burst out of the heavy forest into a clearing, coming face to face with the advancing 5th Confederate Regiment (Captain Richard Beard's Tennessee). The Confederates called on him to surrender, but in an attempt to escape, he wheeled his horse around, raised his hat in salute, and galloped off toward the tree line. A single shot fired by Corporal Robert F. Coleman tore through McPherson's lungs, killing him instantly.

Hood finally realized that the Union left flank was engaged, not the rear as planned, and ordered Cheatham's corps out of the east Atlanta defense line and in to assault the entrenched Union main line. At the same time, Maney's division was ordered to break off and move to Cleburne's left, where they could support Cheatham's attack. Maney's division started their assault at about 3:30 P.M. Cheatham's corps moved out a half hour later, possibly due to a confusion over orders. Once again Leggett's Hill was in the center of much of the action, but the repeated Confederate assaults failed to regain control of it.

The general assault found a weak spot at the Union position held by Brigadier General Joseph Lightburn's 2nd Brigade (Brigadier General Morgan L. Smith's 2nd Division, Logan's XV Army Corps). Brigadier General Arthur M. Manigault's brigade (of Cheatham's corps) led the rebel assault, pushing through the railroad cut (near the present day Inman Park MARTA Station) and capturing the infamous DeGress's 1st Illinois Light Battery H, consisting of four 20-pounder Parrott rifles that had been cutting them to pieces for hours. They then turned left and scattered four Ohio regiments (the 47th, 54th, 37th, and 53rd, in turn). More Confederate units poured through the opening, capturing another two-gun artillery battery and forcing a total of four Union brigades to retreat from a now nearly half-mile-wide breakthrough.

Sherman, observing from his head-quarters in the Augustus Hurt House a little less than a mile to the northwest, ordered Schofield to mass all his artillery (20 guns) at the Confederate breach and Logan to collect eight brigades to fill in the breach. Between the massed artillery and Logan's strong counterattack, the Confederates were soon forced back into their original positions at a heavy loss.

Wheeler's cavalry strike at Decatur met with more success, driving back two regiments of infantry and capturing 225 men and an artillery piece, but the troop was ordered back to the west to support Hardee in his attempt to capture or destroy the Union supply train, his main goal.

The day was another unqualified disaster for the Confederate Army of Tennessee. Total casualties ran more than 5,000 (Sherman claimed more than 8,000, but this was no doubt exaggerated) for no gain other than 12 briefly captured artillery pieces that could not even be withdrawn in the retreat, as all the caisson horses had been killed in the action.

The Union Army of the Tennessee fared little better, giving up no territory but losing 3,722 killed, wounded, or missing.

THE BATTLE OF EZRA CHURCH

Four days after the indecisive Battle of Atlanta, on July 26, Major General Oliver O. Howard of the North took over McPherson's Army of the Tennessee and immediately began moving out to the west along the northern arc of Atlanta's defenses. His targets were the last two open railroads leading into the besieged city, the Macon & Western and the Atlanta & West Point.

Hood soon learned of the Union movement and decided, once again, that it would be a good opportunity to launch an offensive action. He sent his old corps, now under command of Lieutenant General Stephen D. Lee, along with Stewart's corps, west down Lick Skillet Road (now Gordon Road) to confront Howard at the small crossroads where Ezra Methodist Church stood, before the Union troops could reach the vital railway.

In itself not a bad plan, the only problem was that Howard's corps had already reached the crossroads, was aware of Hood's intent, and was entrenching before Lee's corps ever left the city. As his corps marched out of the Atlanta defenses at about 10:00 A.M. on July 28, Lee was unaware of the new developments. Brigadier General John C. Brown's and Major General Henry D. Clayton's divisions led the Confederate column line. Within a mile or so, Brown encountered elements of Brigadier William H. Jackson's Cavalry Division, who informed him of the entrenched Yankee lines ahead. Lee made a very poor decision and ordered Brown's and Clayton's men to move straight ahead and to assault without wasting time waiting for additional support to come up.

Brown's division hastily formed in line of battle directly opposite more than three Union brigades of Morgan Smith's

2nd Division (Logan's XV Army Corps) and moved forward about 12:30 P.M. Clayton's division lagged a bit behind, moving through thick forest over to Brown's right flank, and formed up and moved forward about 10 minutes later, also into about four Union brigades. Both Confederate divisions were assaulting uphill into a barricaded, entrenched line of heavily supplied infantry (the Union troops had been issued 100 rounds per man before the battle, about 40 percent more than usual), and were being thrown into the headlong fight piecemeal as they arrived on scene. To top off the list of problems, the forest in this area was so thick that the assaulting Confederates couldn't see the Union entrenchment until they were nearly on top of them.

Only one unit managed to break through the Union barricade, Colonel William F. Brantley's Mississippi brigade over on the extreme left of the Confederate line of assault, but it was soon pushed back by a strong counterattack. The rest of the Confederate line melted away under rifle fire so intense that "no mortal could stand," as put by Colonel Hugo Wangelin (3rd Brigade Commander, Smith's 1st Division, Logan's Corps, Union Army).

Stewart's corps fared no better on their attempt. Leading the way was Major General Edward C. Walthall's division moving at the quickstep over the same ground Brown had charged through. Stumbling over the dead and wounded Confederates in the thick forest, his line was repulsed in quick order, and his dead and wounded now laid side by side with his predecessors'. Sporadic skirmishing and sniper fire continued until dark, when the Confederates withdrew into the Atlanta defenses, carrying as many wounded as the exhausted men were able to drag behind them.

For the third straight time in less than 10 days, Hood had wrecked a significant part of his once hardened and capable army by sending them against superior forces who were well-entrenched and better supplied. Total casualty figures for the brief attack are very difficult to accurately

assess, as few Confederate records exist, but the Confederates ended with somewhere between 2,500 and 5,000 killed, wounded, or missing, compared to the Union loss of about 600.

Both sides gained and lost something as a result of the 10-day, three-battle campaign around the Atlanta defenses. Sherman failed to take the city proper but did inflict serious damage on the Confederate Army of Tennessee. Hood failed to cripple or even drive back any of the three Union grand armies before him, but he did manage to hold both the city and two of the four railroads supplying it.

THE "GREAT RAID"

Following the battle at Ezra Church, Sherman turned to his cavalry corps to try to cut Hood's supply line. On July 27 McCook's 1st Division Cavalry with about 3,500 horsemen moved around the western flank of Atlanta's defenses, bound for Lovejoy Station about 25 miles south of the city. Later that same day, Garrard's 2nd Division Cavalry and Stoneman's cavalry division moved around the eastern line of defense toward the same destination with about 5,000 horsemen. The plan was to tear up the last remaining railroads supplying Atlanta along with their accompanying telegraph lines, then proceed to the Macon and Andersonville prisoner-of-war camps to release the more than 30,000 Union prisoners.

Sherman didn't have to wait long for word of his "great cavalry raid." On July 30 McCook's division was thoroughly routed near Newnan by two cavalry brigades under Wheeler's personal command, assisted by several infantry units. McCook's retreat north has been aptly described as "pathetic," poorly planned, and poorly executed. He managed to both lose most of the prisoners they had captured and be led by other prisoners into ambush after ambush. The fact that the Union cavalrymen would actually ask their Confederate prisoners to act as guides seems almost beyond comprehension, but it did indeed happen to McCook's sorrow. The Union commander was finally reduced to calling his commanders together and ordering them to scatter in an "every man for himself" headlong flight back toward the Union lines. McCook and about 1,200 men, the remnants of 10 cavalry regiments and artillery batteries, finally made it back to Marietta six days later.

The next day, Stoneman's entire force was captured, killed, or scattered at Sunshine Church just north of Macon. Stoneman not only failed to liberate the Union prisoners at Macon and Andersonville, he suffered the ignobility of joining their ranks at Macon's camp Oglethorpe. Garrard never even left the Atlanta area, where he skirmished with a detachment of Wheeler's around Flat Rock, 15 miles southeast of Decatur, until pulling back to the main Union line on July 29.

The "great raid" was not only a spectacular Confederate victory, so many cavalry horses were captured that an entire infantry brigade (Brigadier General Joseph H. Lewis's Kentucky Orphan) was able to be mounted later in the fall by the Confederacy. Sherman, noted for his extravagant prose in victory, was somewhat more terse in defeat, saying, "On the whole the cavalry raid is not deemed a success."

UTOY CREEK

Sherman grew more and more frustrated with his inability to pound or starve Hood's troops out of the city and ordered yet another attack on the remaining railroad tracks to try to force the Confederates out in the open where they could be destroyed once and for all. On August 4 Schofield's XXIII and Palmer's XIV Army Corps were ordered to swing around to the southwest and strike toward the two remaining railroad tracks near East Point. Another squabble between officers—this time between Palmer and Schofield over who was the senior officer—delayed the movement for nearly two full days.

Hood got word of the Union movement on August 5 and ordered a new line of emplacements built along the Sandtown Road (now called Cascade Road) and manned by Bate's division of Hardee's corps reinforced by a two-gun artillery battery, a brigade of the Georgia Militia, and Brigadier General Lawrence S. Ross's Texas Cavalry Brigade.

At dawn on August 6, after Sherman harshly reprimanded Palmer for his attitude and the delay it caused (he later stated, "I regard the loss of time this afternoon as equal to the loss of 2,000 men"), Brigadier General Jacob D. Cox's 3rd Division (Schofield's XXIII Army Corps) advanced with a 2,500-man front against the now heavily entrenched Confederate left. This attack got within 30 yards of the Confederate line before being broken up by severe losses and thrown back. Several other multibrigade assaults were attempted with the same result and nearly 400 casualties.

In the midst of all this action, still upset over his argument with Schofield and stinging from Sherman's rebuke, Major General John M. Palmer tendered his resignation and quit his command. Brigadier General Richard W. Johnson hastily took over command and ordered an immediate assault on the right of the Confederate line. They were no more successful, suffering 200 more casualties for no gain. Total Confederate losses for the day were about 200 and included those captured in their forward skirmish positions in the early part of the battle. Sherman tersely described the action as "a noisy but not bloody battle."

Frustrated with his inability to cut the rail lines, Sherman pondered his next move. A direct assault on the Atlanta fortifications was completely out of the question. Two, and in some places three, interlocking rings of artillery batteries and infantry parapets surrounded the city a little over a mile out from its center, reinforced by as many as four rows of abatis and long lines of chevaux-de-frise. These were manned with the tired, hungry, and undersupplied but highly experi-enced Confederate Army of Tennessee. Planned by Georgia's chief military engi-neer, Captain Lemuel P. Grant, and con-structed using slave labor from nearby plantations, the fortress city was "too strong to assault and too extensive to invest," according to Sherman's own chief of engineers, Captain Orlando M. Poe. Sherman decided to bombard the city into submission.

On August 1 Sherman had ordered Schofield's artillery to increase their rate of fire, and after the disaster at Utoy Creek, he sent for large artillery guns and plenty of ammunition. Two 30-pounder Parrott rifles were brought in from Chat-tanooga, specifically for building destruc-tion, and eight huge 4.5-inch siege guns were brought in and mounted by August 8. On August 9 Sherman ordered every battery within range to open fire "and make the inside of Atlanta too hot to be endured." That day alone more than 5,000 shells slammed into the city's heart.

JONESBORO

Sherman kept up the intense bombard-ment for more than two weeks, gradually wearing away the strength and endurance of the hollow-eyed soldiers within the city fortifications. Then, suddenly, on August 25 all the guns fell silent. Hood hoped for a moment that Sherman had given up and was withdrawing, but his hopes were dashed when word came of yet another Union flanking attempt. Thomas's entire Army of the Cumberland and Howard's Army of the Tennessee moved around the right of Atlanta and swept down on the Atlanta & West Point Railroad 9 miles southwest of East Point. Hood could not hope to muster any sort of force to stop them but pulled nearly his entire army out of Atlanta to try to protect the last remaining railway, leaving Stewart's corps and Smith's Georgia Militia to hold the city lines.

THE FINAL BATTLE FOR ATLANTA

Realizing that Sherman intended to strike at Jonesboro and cut the railway, after dark on August 30 Hood ordered Hardee's and Lee's corps to move hastily to defend the small town. Encountering Union pick-ets at about 3:00 A.M. and not wanting to risk a night battle, the two Confederate corps moved slightly to the east, not arriv-ing in line at Jonesboro until just after noon on the 31st. Hood was almost frantic to defend his railroad, sending Hardee message after message to attack "as soon as you can get your troops up."

At 3:00 that afternoon, the order came: fix bayonets, up and at 'em, and drive the Yankees from their trenches. The two-corps-wide Confederate assault advancing through open fields and con-centrated artillery canister fire into the Union-fortified positions never made it closer than 60 yards at any point before withdrawing. Losses were staggeringly one-sided, at least 1,700 Confederates ver-sus a mere 179 Union killed or wounded.

At the same time, Schofield's Army of the Ohio, reinforced by Major General David S. Stanley's IV Army Corps, moved around the southern Atlanta defenses and struck the Macon & Western Railroad near Rough & Ready (now called Mountain View). Quickly overwhelming the small dis-mounted cavalry unit stationed there, the Union troops quickly ripped up the tracks and moved north toward East Point.

At 6:00 that evening, Hood ordered Lee's corps back north to help defend Atlanta against the new attack, leaving Hardee alone in Jonesboro facing three full Union corps. At midnight Hardee sent a message by courier to Hood (the tele-graph wire having been cut about 2:00 P.M.) advising that the attack had failed and Atlanta should be abandoned. Through the rest of the long, hot night his forces shifted around to cover the gaps left by Lee's departure and to dig in as best they could. All knew their real job was to hold the main Union armies long enough for Hood to get the rest of their forces out of Atlanta.

The last Union attack began at 4:00 P.M. on September 1, led by two brigades of Brigadier General William P. Carlin's 1st Division (Brevet Major General Jefferson C. Davis's XIV Army Corps) and quickly followed by brigade after brigade, division after division, until all three corps were engaged in the assault. Amazingly, although one side of his line caved in and 865 prisoners and two full batteries of artillery were captured, Hardee managed to hold until the attack ended after nightfall. About midnight he withdrew his three remaining divisions south to Lovejoy Station, leaving behind about 1,400 dead and wounded. The Union force fared little better, losing a total of 1,272, but finally taking and cutting the last railway they had sought for so long.

On the morning of September 1, having received Hardee's dreadful message, Hood at long last ordered the evacuation of the doomed city. With the railway cut, it would be impossible to take much in the way of supplies with them, so warehouses were ordered opened up for the civilians. Stewart's corps and Smith's militia began marching out around 5:00 P.M., with the rear guard, French's divisional pickets, withdrawing about 11:00 P.M. Sappers and engineers hastily prepared the abandoned military supplies for destruction. Around midnight a thunderous roar announced the end of a large ammunition train that Hood was unable to withdraw. Sherman heard the blast 15 miles away in his headquarters at Jonesboro and knew he now had the city.

THE END OF THE ATLANTA CAMPAIGN

On September 3, 1864, Sherman telegraphed Major General Henry W. Halleck in Washington, "So Atlanta is ours, and fairly won."

Hood managed to slip away with his forces more or less intact, what remained of them, after blowing up his large ammunition train and abandoning warehouses full of supplies. No complete records exist, but somewhere close to 30,000 tired, starving, and ill-equipped troops were left to carry out Hood's desperate plan to strike at the Union rear. Well over 81,000 troops were still available to Sherman, who decided not to follow and finish off the badly mauled Confederate force but to simply rest and resupply within the fortifications of Atlanta.

The President [Jefferson Davis] never visited the army without doing it injury; never yet that it was not followed by disaster. He was instrumental in the Gettysburg affair. He instructed Bragg at Murfreesboro. He has opened Georgia to one hundred thousand of the enemy's troops and laid South Carolina liable to destruction. I charge him with having almost ruined the country, and will meet his champion anywhere to discuss it.

Congressman H. S. Foote of Tennessee, Confederate States of America, December 1863

Between Dalton and the gates of Atlanta lie the graves of 4,423 Union and 3,044 Confederate soldiers. The Union had 22,822 wounded and the Confederates 18,952 during the four-month campaign, and a total of 17,335 from both sides were captured or simply disappeared.

Sherman rested until mid-November, and then, leaving one corps behind to garrison the city and guard against the still-roaming Confederate Army of Tennessee, he divided his forces into two great columns and began his advance to Savannah and the sea. Almost as a parting gift to the vanquished rebels, he ordered every building "of military value"

"So Atlanta Is Ours . . ."

The fall of Atlanta was a huge relief, not only to the Union soldiers and their higher command but also very personally to Lincoln himself, who had been in grave danger of losing that year's presidential election to an advocate for immediate peace with the South. The messages that flew back and forth between Sherman in Atlanta and Washington give a good insight into the emotion that this victory brought.

ATLANTA, GA.,
September 2, 1864.
(Received 10:05 P.M.)

Hon. E. M. STANTON, Secretary of War: General Sherman has taken Atlanta. The Twentieth Corps occupies the city. The main army is on the Macon road near East Point. A battle was fought near that point, in which General Sherman was successful.

Particulars not known.

H. W. SLOCUM,
Major-General.

NEAR LOVEJOY'S STATION,
26 miles south of Atlanta, Ga.,
September 3, 1864—6:00 A.M.
(Received 5:30 P.M. 4th.)

Maj. Gen. H. W. HALLECK, Washington, D.C.: As already reported, the army drew from about Atlanta, and on the 30th had made a good break of the West Point road and reached a good position from which to strike the Macon railroad, the right (General Howard's) near Jonesborough, the left (General Schofield's) near Rough and Ready, and the center (General Thomas's) at Couch's. General Howard found the enemy in force at Jonesborough, and intrenched his troops, the salient within half a mile of the railroad. The enemy attacked him at 3 P.M., and was easily repulsed, leaving his dead and wounded. Finding strong opposition on the right, I advanced the left and center rapidly to the railroad, made a good lodgment, and broke it all the way from Rough and Ready down to Howard's left, near Jonesborough, and by the same movement I interposed my whole army between Atlanta and the part of the enemy intrenched in and around Jonesborough. We made a general attack on the enemy at Jonesborough on September 1, the Fourteenth Corps, General Jeff. C. Davis, carrying the works handsomely, with 10 guns and about 1,000 prisoners. In the night the enemy retreated south, and we have followed him to another of his well-chosen and hastily constructed lines, near Lovejoy's. Hood, at Atlanta, finding me on his road, the only one that could supply him, and between him and a considerable part of his army, blew up his magazines in Atlanta and left in the night-time, when the Twentieth Corps, General Slocum, took possession of the place. So Atlanta is ours, and fairly won. I shall not push much farther on this raid, but in a day or so will move to Atlanta and give my men some rest. Since May 5 we have been in one constant battle or skirmish, and need rest. Our losses will not exceed 1,200, and we have possession of over 300 rebel dead, 250 wounded, and over 1,500 well prisoners.

W. T. SHERMAN,
Major-General.

WAR DEPARTMENT,
September 3, 1864.

Major-General SLOCUM, Atlanta:
Accept my thanks for your telegram communicating the welcome news from Atlanta. Please keep me advised of events.

EDWIN M. STANTON,
Secretary of War.

ATLANTA, GA.,
September 3, 1864—9:30 P.M.
(Received 4:30 P.M. 4th.)

Major-General HALLECK, Chief of Staff:
Sherman, with his entire army, except this corps, is near Jonesborough, on the Macon road. Hood's army is south of him, except the troops left in Atlanta, consisting of militia and about one division of old troops. These troops, when they evacuated this place, took the McDonough road, and will probably effect a junction with their main army. Sherman has captured 2 batteries and 2,000 prisoners. The enemy, on evacuating, destroyed 7 locomotives and 81 cars, loaded with ammunition, small-arms, and stores, and left here 14 pieces of artillery, most of them uninjured, and a large num-

ber of small-arms. We have taken 200 prisoners, and deserters are constantly coming into our lines. We have on hand a good supply of ammunition, subsistence stores, and clothing. I earnestly hope that paymasters may be sent here as soon as possible, as some of my command have not been paid for eight months.

H. W. SLOCUM,
Major-General.

Order for Celebration of Victories at Atlanta, Georgia, and Mobile, Alabama

Executive Mansion,
Washington City,
Ordered, September 3d, 1864.

First.—That on Monday, the 5th. day of September, commencing at the hour of twelve o'clock noon, there shall be given a salute of one hundred guns at the Arsenal and Navy Yard at Washington, and on Tuesday September 6th., or on the day after the receipt of this order, at each Arsenal and Navy Yard in the United States, for the recent brilliant achievements of the fleet and land forces of the United States in the harbor of Mobile and in the reduction of Fort Powell, Fort Gaines, and Fort Morgan. The Secretary of War and Secretary of the Navy will issue the necessary directions in their respective Departments for the execution of this order.

Second.—That on Wednesday, the 7th. day of September, commencing at the hour of twelve o'clock noon, there shall be fired a salute of one hundred guns at the Arsenal at Washington, and at New York, Boston, Philadelphia, Baltimore, Pittsburg, Newport, Ky. and St. Louis, and at New Orleans, Mobile, Pensacola, Hilton Head & Newberne, the day after the receipt of this order, for the brilliant achievements of the army under command of Major General Sherman, in the State of Georgia, and the capture of Atlanta. The Secretary of War will issue directions for the execution of this order.

ABRAHAM LINCOLN

Order of Thanks to William T. Sherman and Others

Executive Mansion,
Washington City,
September 3d, 1864.

The national thanks are herewith tendered by the President to Major General William T. Sherman, and the gallant officers and soldiers of his command before Atlanta, for the distinguished ability, courage, and perseverance displayed in the campaign in Georgia, which, under Divine favor, has resulted in the capture of the City of Atlanta. The marches, battles, sieges, and other military operations that have signalized this campaign must render it famous in the annals of war, and have entitled those who have participated therein to the applause and thanks of the nation.

ABRAHAM LINCOLN

Proclamation of Thanksgiving and Prayer

Executive Mansion,
Washington City,
September 3d. 1864.

The signal success that Divine Providence has recently vouchsafed to the operations of the United States fleet and army in the harbor of Mobile and the reduction of Fort-Powell, Fort-Gaines, and Fort-Morgan, and the glorious achievements of the Army under Major General Sherman in the State of Georgia, resulting in the capture of the City of Atlanta, call for devout acknowledgement to the Supreme Being in whose hands are the destinies of nations. It is therefore requested that on next Sunday, in all places of public worship in the United-States, thanksgiving be offered to Him for His mercy in preserving our national existence against the insurgent rebels who so long have been waging a cruel war against the Government of the United-States, for its overthrow; and also that prayer be made for the Divine protection to our brave soldiers and their leaders in the field, who have so often and so gallantly perilled their lives in battling with the enemy; and for blessing and comfort from the Father of Mercies to the sick, wounded, and prisoners, and to the orphans and widows of those who have fallen in the service of their country, and that he will continue to uphold the Government of the United-States against all the efforts of public enemies and secret foes.

ABRAHAM LINCOLN

to be put to the torch; his troops broadly interpreted this order, burning all but about 500 of the 5,000 or so buildings left standing after the long campaign.

Both sides knew that with the fall of Atlanta and its surrounding factories and railroads, the war was, for all practical purposes, over.

THE TOUR

The main part of Sherman's march went from the Dalton area southeast to Atlanta in a path that almost exactly parallels today's Interstate 75, except for his movement west to Dallas. The adjacent US 41 goes down the same path but offers a slower-paced way of seeing the terrain and scenery. Be aware, also, that elements of his columns went quite a few miles east and west of this path, with battles, skirmishes, and other encounters encompassing an area from very close to the Alabama border to the west all the way east to the Athens area. There are literally dozens of historic markers and monuments in roadsides and town squares all over northern Georgia, commemorating each site's sideshow in the Atlanta campaign.

Getting There: Dalton

Dalton lies about 30 miles southeast of downtown Chattanooga, shielded from a direct advance by a long, sheer cliff face locally known as Rocky Face Ridge and called the "Georgian Gibraltar" by Union troops. Three gaps in the otherwise foreboding mountain ridge were large enough to allow an army to pass through in a reasonable amount of time but could be easily blockaded with a relatively small force of infantry and artillery.

Today, I-75 runs through the main line of battle just west of the town. Take the US 41 exit (number 336) and go west, away from Dalton. The fairly large level pass through the mountain range about 1 mile from the highway is Mill Creek Gap, where Lieutenant General William J. Hardee's army corps was arranged north-south facing the opening to the west. In this gap is a Georgia State Patrol post, with a very nice set of markers about the battle. This is known as the "Atlanta Campaign Pavilion Number 2," built by the WPA (Works Progress Administration) during the 1930s, one of five in the stretch from Ringgold to New Hope Church. Continuing west roughly 1 mile on US 41 is the intersection with Old Chattanooga Road (not well marked). This spot marks the connection between Major General Oliver O. Howard's IV Army Corps and Major General John M. Palmer's XIV Army Corps, both running northeast to southwest. Sherman's headquarters was on the hill directly in front of you, Blue Mountain. Most of the rest of both armies' lines are difficult to precisely locate today.

The Union forces marched out of Chattanooga and the Ringgold area toward the southeast, through Tunnel Hill and just to the west of Dalton, and down the long valley to the small settlements in the northwest section of Georgia, where this military campaign really started in earnest. Dalton lies about 20 miles below the Tennessee border, easily accessible from I-75 exits 333 and 336. From there through the action at Jonesboro, most of the major battlefields lie within a few miles east or west of I-75. US 41 parallels I-75 for most of this section and passes almost directly over the actual march route and through or very near many of the lesser-known sites. It is almost as if the highway planners laid out these roads just for the battlefield tourist! A warning: I-75 both north and south of Atlanta, and in particular this stretch, is noted for its very high-speed traffic and frequent serious accidents. US 41 is very congested in the suburban areas, and gridlock can develop in the Kennesaw-to-Atlanta stretch during rush hours.

To find the other significant landmark of the area, get back on I-75 southbound, and get off at exit 333 (Walnut Avenue). Turn right (west) and go up the large hill

The only state capital in the Confederacy not taken by Union troops during the war was Tallahassee, Florida.

for about 2 miles. On your right near the top of the rise is Dug Gap Battlefield Park. The park features a well-preserved section of Confederate emplacements. Make sure to walk to the top of the rocky defenses and see just what kind of terrain the Union assault was forced to deal with. A warning: There are no signs to guide you from I-75; make sure you are going west on Walnut Avenue away from the business district. Just about any sort of fast food is available on the other side of I-75 here, as well as a large outlet mall and other shopping centers.

POINT OF INTEREST

General Joseph Eggleston Johnston Statue
Intersection of Crawford and Hamilton
Downtown Dalton

Usually we would not recommend a special trip just to view a statue, but this is a must-see exception. A rather large, impressive bronze representation of Johnston in a pensive stance, the statue was commissioned in 1912 by the United Daughters of the Confederacy from Nashville artist Belle Kinney. Although we consider Johnston to be perhaps the finest battlefield commander in the western theater, his reputation suffered from both Davis's enmity and his own rather abrasive personality. As far as we have been able to establish, this is the one and only statue of the Virginia native.

ACCOMMODATIONS

Dalton is today a major shopping mecca for both the Atlanta and Chattanooga metropolitan areas, due to its reputation as a major manufacturing center of carpets and as the host to a number of outlet shopping centers, most of which are tied to the local carpet industry. However,

the majority of motels and restaurants are of the lower-middle range of chains, and there is little of note in the city itself related to the war. The best selection of the usual chain restaurants and motels can be found at exits 333 and 336 off I-75; exit 333 also features a large outlet mall.

RESTAURANTS

The Dalton Depot $$
110 Depot Street, Dalton
(706) 226-3160

One exception to the rule about Dalton eateries is this wartime railroad depot, in its original use until 1978 and now a mid-scale restaurant. This is the place where Johnston arrived to take over command of the Army of Tennessee, as well as the site of the celebrated arrival of Lieutenant General James Longstreet's corps, en route to the battle at Chickamauga. During the Andrews Raid, better known as the Great Locomotive Chase, the pursued and the pursuers raced by the station, the following train slowing down long enough to drop off a messenger boy to give an update to the depot's telegraph office.

The Depot specializes in steaks, pasta dishes, and premium hamburgers and has a full bar. The menu, outside of a handful of specials, is very similar to what one would find in the Applebee's and Chili's chains, but the atmosphere is much more pleasant here. The impressively sturdy, redbrick Depot is open 11:00 A.M. to 11:00 P.M. Monday through Saturday.

Getting There: Resaca

Resaca is now just a sleepy crossroads town just off a fairly unremarkable exit on I-75 (exit 320), but this was the site of the only known full-force battle of the Atlanta campaign, where the entire theater armies of both sides met at a single battleground. The small hamlet straddles a single rail line that runs nearly due north-south, following the same roadbed that the 1864 rail line utilized. A rail bridge on the south side of town contains some of the original abutments of the structure burned by Johnston's troops on their retreat southward. This bridge is off-limits to walk across, but you may easily see it from the adjacent US 41. Be very careful of the high-speed traffic in this area.

MODERN TIMES

What is remarkable about the modern-day vicinity of this battlefield is how much is visible from a car going 70 miles per hour! The Confederate line of battle lies almost exactly under the roadbed of I-75, stretching northward about 2 miles from exit 320 (the Resaca–La Fayette Road, Georgia Highway 143). The Union line of departure on May 13 and 14 was about one-half mile to the west, in the small hills you can see across the cleared fields. Battle on the 15th shifted to the northern part of town, where the Confederate line ran east-west about 4 miles outside town across US 41, roughly 1 mile each way. The Union line of departure on the 15th also ran east-west, about 1 mile north, filling the area from about one-half mile west of US 41 eastward across a 1-mile front. One note about these positions: The exact position of the Confederate and Union lines is currently undergoing some revision, helped in no small part by the excellent research of historian Dr. Philip L. Secrist of Kennesaw State University.

The terrain here today is quite as it was in 1864—primarily farm fields and other open areas, surrounded with thick woods featuring plenty of entangling underbrush. Numerous historical markers indicate exact placements of troops and their movements; all but one are located on or just off either Georgia Highway 136 west of town or US 41 north of town. The remaining sign is in the I-75 southbound rest area nearby. Aside from a single truck stop at exit 320 and two gas/convenience stations in the small town, there are no amenities at this location.

POINT OF INTEREST

The Confederate Cemetery at Resaca

One of the very few high-profile remnants of the battle is the small Confederate cemetery just north of the small crossroads town. Leave I-75 at exit 320, go east about one-half mile to the intersection with US 41, and turn left. Go north on US 41 about 2 miles, and then slow and look for a small sign pointing out the cemetery to your right down Confederate Cemetery Road.

This small cemetery houses the remains of about 420 soldiers, the vast majority of whom are unknown. Local Sons of Confederate Veterans and United Daughters of the Confederacy camps frequently maintain the cemetery, giving it a very parklike appearance. Ironically, these graves may prove to be the pickets that guard the only remaining preserved part of this battlefield; as of this writing, portions of the main battlefield have been sold to the state of Georgia, but free access to the area is still denied by a local landowner. This may result in action up to and including government seizure of the land; as of this writing, no firm plans are in place. This cemetery rests on what was part of Major General Alexander P. Stewart's division (Hood's corps), and a look around at the terrain makes it apparent that a good position would have been on the low hills just above the cemetery. Like so much else around this battlefield, unfortunately, these hills are on private property and not open to the public.

Getting There: Cassville

The area of these actions today is a rapidly growing suburb of Marietta and Atlanta, and landmarks are getting harder to find. Most of both Kingston and Adairsville were burned during the war, and just about all that remains are scattered markers and monuments. One of the five Atlanta Campaign Pavilions (small memorials to the campaign) is supposed to be at Cassville, but we were unable to find it. At last report most of its markers had been stolen and the stone wall was in bad repair.

Cassville itself is a little hard to find, but worth the effort to see graphic evidence of the destruction to civilians and their property this campaign caused. Look for the Cassville Road, a small two-lane road going to the east off US 41 about 9 miles south of Adairsville and 2 miles north of the U.S. Highway 411 intersection. The square burned by Sherman as retaliation for guerrilla operations after the battle was never rebuilt, and a large stone marker commemorates the empty lot. About one-half mile south of the square location is the St. James A.M.E. Church, known at the time as the Cassville Presbyterian Church, which was one of only three buildings in the town spared Sherman's wrath.

Getting There: Allatoona Pass

Today one of the best-preserved period locations of this area is Allatoona Pass, scene of a relatively small but very intense battle on October 5, 1864, between Hood's army advancing north from Atlanta and a heavily entrenched Union garrison (see the chapter Atlanta to Savannah for a complete description of this battle). It's a little difficult to find; no signs show the way, and you may think at first that you are on a dead-end street ending in Lake Allatoona. Take exit 283 off I-75, the Allatoona-Emerson Road, and go about 2 miles east, toward the lake. Except for the large earthen dam, this area is very similar to its appearance during the battle. A marker nearby shows a picture taken at the time; one building (the Clayton-Mooney House) still exists in just about the same condition. This house was used as a Union command post and hospital, and there is a marked mass grave where the driveway meets the street. Be

aware that this house and most of the surrounding area are private and not open to the public.

Getting There: New Hope Church

The New Hope battlefield area is a rapidly growing suburb today, and very few of the original landmarks remain. On the north side of the church, next to the road, are the original small WPA and new standard Georgia Historical Commission markers. On the south side of the church, in a small grove of trees, is the larger Atlanta Campaign Pavilion. Across Bobo Road stands the "old" New Hope Baptist Church, built after the war.

Across the Dallas-Acworth Highway is a large graveyard with a small part-stone building directly adjacent. This building is on the site of the wartime New Hope Church, and this graveyard is where Brigadier General Marcellus A. Stovall's Georgia Brigade was located during the fight. The men refused to dig in, taking heavy casualties as a result. Several individual and mass graves of unknown Confederate dead appear among the period and modern markers. Rumor has it that some of the period markers in this graveyard still bear scars from the battle, but we were not able to locate any damaged in such a way. There are no amenities of any sort at this location; the nearest gas and food are in Dallas just to the southwest.

From US 41 south of Emerson, take the Dallas-Acworth Road heading west (some maps mark this as Georgia Highway 381, but we did not find any such street markers on the route). About 7 miles down this road (and 2 miles past the small brown sign pointing to Pickett's Mill Battlefield Historic Site) you will suddenly come across the large brick New Hope Baptist Church on your left; turn into the parking lot, where you will find two sets of markers.

Getting There: Pickett's Mill

Pickett's Mill today is roundly celebrated as one of the best-preserved battlefields of any size in the nation. This area was not changed in any significant way after the war, and the state of Georgia has done a remarkable job of preserving without obscuring what remains. A state historic site, the battlefield is open Tuesday through Saturday 9:00 A.M. to 5:00 P.M. and Sunday noon to 5:00 P.M. It features guided and self-guided tours and several reenactment and nighttime events throughout the year. Three trails go over mostly wartime roads in the area, and points on the battlefield are marked by numbered and colored small wooden stakes. Maps available in the visitor center are used to describe the action; this is a very good system for getting a large amount of information across to the visitor without obscuring the view. For more information contact Pickett's Mill Battlefield State Historic Site, 4432 Mount Tabor Road, Dallas, GA 30157; (770) 443-7850.

Georgia has done a good job placing guidance signs to this out-of-the-way site; watch for roughly 1-foot-square brown signs with white lettering on the sides of the roads, with arrows pointing to turns. There are several ways to get to this site. From the New Hope battlefield, head north on the Dallas-Acworth road about one-half mile, and turn right on Due West Road. Drive about 1 mile to a four-way stop, and turn left on Mount Tabor Road. The entrance to the site is in the midst of a subdivision about one-half mile on your right. To go straight to Pickett's Mill from the Marietta-Kennesaw area, take Georgia Highway 120 about 12 miles west of the Marietta Square. This highway goes through the Kennesaw Mountain Battlefield Park between Cheatham Hill and Pigeon Hill. Turn right on Georgia Highway 92 (also called the Acworth-Hiram Road), and go about 3 miles to Due West Road. Turn left and go about 2 miles to Mount

Tabor Road; turn right and the site is one-half mile on your right. There are no amenities other than the visitor center in or near this site.

Getting There: Kennesaw

Kennesaw is just north of Marietta, Georgia, which in itself is just north of Interstate 285, the perimeter highway of Atlanta. US 41 goes directly through town, but the old section of the city is a short way east of this highway—look for the huge sign advertising the *General* and the Southern Museum of Civil War and Locomotive History just north of a small airport, about 1 mile north of the Kennesaw Mountain National Battlefield Park. From I-75 take the Barrett Parkway exit and go west about 2 miles to US 41; turn north and go about 2 miles. The way in to the old part of town is well marked, but the BIG SHANTY sign should catch your eye first.

MODERN TIMES

Kennesaw is an interesting small town, with many markers detailing its Civil War history. One note: Most period maps refer to this town as "Big Shanty"; the town was officially renamed much later. A local historian stated that this original name of the town came from the trainmen who were not impressed with the rather ramshackle look of the place and referred to the slight rise in town as the spot where the "big shanty" stood.

POINTS OF INTEREST

Kennesaw Mountain National Battlefield Park
900 Kennesaw Mountain Drive
Kennesaw
(770) 427-4686
Kennesaw Mountain today is a National Battlefield Park, stretching from just north of Big Kennesaw Mountain about 5 miles south to Kolb's Farm, 3 miles north and

west of Marietta. There are a multitude of hiking and equestrian trails throughout the large complex, which has become more or less a playground for the surrounding affluent community, as well as the third most visited battlefield park in the nation. The major combat areas are well marked with maps, photos, and explanatory markers, and Union and Confederate state memorials dot the open fields. The 11,900-square-foot visitor center houses an excellent relevant book selection and a film about the battle, as well as a very helpful and knowledgeable staff.

Southern Museum of Civil War and Locomotive History
2829 Cherokee Street, Kennesaw
(770) 427–2117

Housed in an old cotton gin, and home of the famed locomotive of the Andrews Raid, the *General*, this museum run by the city of Kennesaw does a very credible job of using its small collection of artifacts to best advantage. A short film about the Andrews Raid relates the story of the botched Union guerrilla attempt that started less than 100 yards away, and the museum has a good book collection for sale.

The museum, a member of the Smithsonian Affiliations program, is open Monday through Saturday 9:30 A.M. to 5:00 P.M. and Sunday noon to 5:00 P.M. Admission is $7.50 for adults; $6.50 for active military, AAA members, and seniors; and $5.50 for children ages 6 through 12. Children 5 and under are admitted free. Trains still rumble by regularly just outside the museum, giving it an authentic feel.

Wildman's Civil War & Relic Shop
2879 North Main Street, Kennesaw
(770) 422–1785

Across the street from the tracks and museum is another local institution, Wildman's Civil War & Relic Shop, which is a dusty and rambling building housing equal parts assorted books and artifacts for sale and museum (25 cents admission). Be

forewarned: This store has a very strong racial and "unreconstructed" feel, and there are many modern books, posters, and stickers exalting the Ku Klux Klan and the local gun laws. Kennesaw gained fame in 1982 by passing the first city ordinance in the nation requiring local residents to own firearms and ammunition, largely as a result of Dent "Wildman" Myers's efforts (this gun ordinance was in response to another town's antigun ownership ordinance). This said, we consider Mr. Myers to be one of the better sources of information on the Kennesaw campaign, and his contributions over the years to writing the local history have been invaluable.

ACCOMMODATIONS AND SUTLERS

This area is a heavily built-up suburb of the Atlanta metropolitan area and has nearly any amenity you could think of within a short drive. Just to the north of the battlefield park is Barrett Parkway; turn right and a major shopping and entertainment district is a very short drive to the east. In the vicinity of where Barrett Parkway intersects I-75 is a major regional mall (Town Center), several large strip shopping centers, an unusual bowling alley/microbrewery combination (U.S. Play), a good dozen chain hotels and motels, and every low- to midrange chain restaurant present in the Atlanta market.

RESTAURANTS

Shillings on the Square $$
19 North Park Square, Marietta
(770) 428–9520

This casual restaurant and bar has anchored a corner of the Marietta square for 20 years, hard by the Civil War–era Kennesaw House. Its neighborhood pub style is a favorite of locals looking for oversize sandwiches and finger foods late into the night or during a short lunch break. The kitchen opens at 10:30 A.M. and serves until midnight during the week, 2:00 A.M. on weekends.

For those with more elegant tastes, Upstairs at Shillings is an 80-seat fine dining room, with white tablecloths, candles, and soft piano tunes putting diners in a relaxed mood. Entrees include steaks, seafood, veal, lamb, and chicken. Dinner is served from 5:30 to 10:00 P.M. on weekdays, midnight on weekends. Sunday brunch is served downstairs from 10:30 A.M. to 2:00 P.M.

Pappadeaux Seafood Kitchen $$$
2830 Windy Hill Road, Marietta
(770) 984-8899

5635 Jimmy Carter Boulevard, Norcross
(770) 849-0600

10795 Davis Drive, Alpharetta
(770) 992-5566

This Cajun seafood house always draws a crowd; even at lunch, the wait can be more than 45 minutes! But it's worth it: The portions are large, the selection vast, and the tastes delectable. The wait passes quickly at the enormous bar. In addition to Cajun favorites, there are grilled, broiled, and baked items; soups; and salads. The setting is casual and noisy (no one will notice the kids' chatter in the large dining room). Lunch is served Monday through Friday; dinner begins at 3:00 P.M. on weekends. Pappadeaux does not take reservations.

Canoe $$$
4199 Paces Ferry Road SE, Atlanta
(770) 432-2663

On the banks of the Chattahoochee River in northwest Atlanta, Canoe is housed in a barrel-vaulted brick building once known as Robinson's Tropical Gardens. It's said that many a young romance bloomed at this riverfront restaurant and nightspot in the golden post–WWII years. Today wedding parties have been known to arrive in canoes for a luscious reception.

In accordance with its goal of offering delicious, healthful food for today's diner, Canoe's fare includes grilled farm-raised chicken with wild mushroom potato puree with port wine and cranberries; goat cheese and potato tortellini with arti-

chokes, autumn greens, pine nuts, and white truffle oil; and a wild mushroom soup with polenta croutons. There's also an assortment of beef and seafood. You can call ahead for reservations or take advantage of any waiting time to stroll riverside. Valet parking is available. Dinner is served nightly.

Getting There: Chattahoochee River Line

The entire Chattahoochee River Line area is now built-up suburbia and paved over by malls and large highways. Many parts of the main avenue of approach, from the northwest, are now industrial or in urban decay. To put it delicately, this is not the sort of area you would like to spend a lot of time in after dark. There have been some efforts to set up a River Line Park and preserve some of the works near Nickajack Creek, but as of this writing there are no publicized plans in place. Oakdale Road between Bankhead Highway and South Cobb Drive, just outside the Perimeter (I-285), runs roughly alongside Johnston's positions.

Getting There: Roswell

Roswell is easily accessible from the Marietta area by going east on Georgia Highway 120, also known as Roswell Road. GA 120 is not directly accessible from I-75; instead you will have to take one of the two (north and south) GA 120 Loop exits. This road bisects GA 120 and starts and ends at US 41. From the northern parts of Atlanta itself, the easiest route is Georgia Highway 400, which is a toll road inside I-285; go north about 12 miles from I-285, and exit at Holcomb Bridge Road. Be sure to take the second, most northerly exit for Holcomb Bridge, which will put you going westbound at the top of the ramp. Follow the signs in to the old part of the city. The signs are visible with a bit of difficulty through all the other signage; this is the "strip" where most chain establishments in the area reside.

MODERN TIMES

Around the Roswell area today, there is a popular local story that the women captured at Roswell "disappeared," presumably never to be heard from again. The truth is that some died of typhus and other infectious diseases during or shortly after the evacuation (not an unusual event at all during the war), some found other work and even families in the North and had no good reason to return, while King himself reported in an 1865 letter that some of his mill hands had already returned. The fact that Sherman was seen as nothing more and nothing less than a demon no doubt led to the rise of the "missing women of Roswell" myth.

ACCOMMODATIONS AND SUTLERS

Roswell is an upscale suburb of Atlanta and in fact sits in the midst of the "richest zip codes" in the Southeast (based on per-capita income of the area). The Roswell square has gentrified into a boutique and antiques-store zone, as have so many other small Southern towns, but has an unusually high percentage of decent restaurants and other amenities nearby. The northbound road through the square, Alpharetta Highway (U.S. Highway 19), leads to both fast-food heaven and very upscale shopping zones. Both Holcomb Bridge and Mansell Road running to the east of Alpharetta Highway just north of the square will take you to just about any chain restaurant you could imagine as well as the usual array of chain hotels and motels near the intersections with GA 400 (about 1 to 2 miles east). Just east of GA 400 on Mansell Road is the major regional North Point Mall, as well as associated strip malls and "big box" stores.

RESTAURANTS

While this area does feature a huge number of restaurants, it is a relatively new-growth area, and the playing field is still shaking itself out. Restaurants open and close at an astonishing rate; three separate establishments that we had attended on a more or less regular basis over the past few years (and had planned on highly recommending!) all closed during the course of researching this book.

Mittie's Tea Room Cafe   **$$**
952 Canton Street, Roswell
(770) 594-8822
This old store in Roswell's historic district has been a tearoom since 1987. A mix of antique tables and buffets are decorated with teapots, cups, and an assortment of tea paraphernalia. Lunch is light, with a variety of salads, quiches, soups, and a selection of wines and beers. And yes, tea-lovers, tea is served daily—and correctly, in a china pot. Mittie's is open Monday through Friday 10:00 A.M. to 4:00 P.M., Saturday and Sunday 8:00 A.M. to 4:00 P.M.

The Roasted Garlic   **$$**
281 South Main Street, Alpharetta
(770) 777-9855
Although it is somewhat north of the main Atlanta campaign lines of battle, it is well worth the time to take the short drive to this unheralded, out-of-the-way place that hits every note to near perfection. This small European-influenced restaurant combines well-prepared and presented food; a small but decent wine and beer selection; a warm, homey feeling; and some of the best service we have ever experienced in any restaurant, anywhere. One of the first in the Atlanta area to offer Spanish-style appetizers, the tapas are becoming one of its major draws—light appetizers that, in combination, can easily make a meal: ciabato bread with roasted garlic tappenade, spinach pies, eggplant capri, and marinated sirloin medallions over mixed field greens are a few examples.

Main entrees lean heavily toward variations of traditional Italian dishes—chicken parmigiana, euromixed grill, and lasagna, for example—but all have a care and love in preparation that would shame your grandmother. Salads and traditional American fare are served, but if it is available, Nicole's Pillows is an absolute must: asparagus and smoke mozzerella cheese–stuffed pasta in a walnut pesto cream sauce. Another very popular dish is the Masseria's chicken: baked chicken breasts with crushed roasted garlic, sundried tomatoes, and several imported cheeses topped with a paper-thin slice of prosciutto with a walnut fig pesto and aged provolone cheese. A nice selection of desserts is available, including a "to die for" Frutta Di Bosco (beg for the imported Italian mixed berry sorbeto on the side!).

Be aware that "foodies" in the northern suburbs have started to discover this place, and prime supper time tends to be rather crowded, even on the traditionally dead nights of Tuesday and Wednesday; reservations for such times are nearly mandatory. The Roasted Garlic is open for lunch Monday through Friday and for supper (dinner, outside the South!) from 5:00 to 9:00 P.M. Monday through Thursday, 5:00 to 10:00 P.M. Friday and Saturday, and 4:00 to 9:00 P.M. Sunday.

Krispy Kreme Doughnuts   **$**
791 North Atlanta Street (US 19)
Roswell
(770) 998-0779
This local branch of a well-known chain is just north of the Roswell square and formerly the northernmost outpost of a local institution. Krispy Kreme doughnuts are not the stomach-bombing variety of pastry commonly found in grocery stores and other similar chains. These are literally melt-in-your-mouth sugary delights that inspire intense loyalty among their devotees. It is by no means unusual to find all manner of society crowded into the small, warm, and delicious-smelling shops at 2:00 A.M., from the ubiquitous cops to punk rockers and business executives—all

drawn like moths to the bright red neon signs indicating that HOT DOUGHNUTS! are now coming out of the oven.

While the chain originates from North Carolina, it has the feel and following of a hometown original, much like the beloved Varsity (listed in the Atlanta to Savannah chapter). While Krispy Kreme has started offering other items in recent years, stick to the basics: coffee and sugar-glazed. You can't go wrong.

Getting There: Sope Creek

In the early afternoon of July 9, finding a 300-yard-wide, relatively shallow spot over a submerged fish dam near Sope Creek (Soap Creek on some maps), Colonel Daniel Cameron's 103rd Ohio Infantry (Union Army) swam across to establish a beachhead. Encountering no opposition, Schofield then ordered a crossing in force at 3:30 that afternoon. Led by a combat amphibious assault by the 12th Kentucky Regiment under Lieutenant Colonel Laurence H. Rousseau, part of Colonel Robert K. Boyd's 3rd (Kentucky) Brigade (the same brigade that had "withdrawn for rations" at Pickett's Mill), the crossing was an outstanding success. The only Confederates in the area were part of a small picket outpost, who only got off a single volley before running away.

The single spot remaining in more or less original condition is Sope Creek, part of the Chattahoochee River National Recreation Area. Ruins of a paper mill burned by Union cavalry scouting for crossing sites are still visible, as well as the nearby shallow ford across the river. Take I-75 to exit 261 (Delk Road), and travel east to Powers Ferry Road. Turn right, go about one-half mile, and turn left onto Terrell Mill Road. About 1½ miles down Terrell Mill is Paper Mill Road; follow the signs to the park from there. The park is in a residential area with no amenities of any kind.

Getting There: Atlanta

Atlanta has always been more of a transportation hub than a destination, as the excellent routes in and through the city show (there is a joke that you can't go straight to heaven after death—you have to change planes in Atlanta). I–75 goes northwest to southeast through the city, Interstate 85 goes northeast to southwest, Interstate 20 goes east to west, and all meet at one spot just south of the main downtown area. The gold-domed building at this spot is the Georgia State Capitol, site of the wartime city hall. I–285 circles the city (and is usually just called the Perimeter) about 6 to 10 miles out from the city center. On the north side (where the largest growth and most expensive property is), GA 400 connects I–75, I–85, and I–285 with the northern suburbs and goes all the way up to the foothills of the north Georgia mountains, about 65 miles away. On the east side, U.S. Highway 78, also known as the Stone Mountain Expressway, connects I–285 with Stone Mountain Park and Athens, about 45 miles away.

Hartsfield International Airport, one of the world's busiest (but surprisingly easy to navigate, just don't try parking there!), is on the south side, bordered by I–75 to the east, I–85 to the west, and I–285 to the south. The easiest way to get around the city, although it does not access every part of the city, is by using the MARTA train system. From a central station at 5 Points (where the first artillery rounds from Sherman's cannons killed a freed black man in 1864—a gas lightpost still standing there bears scars from the blast), lines run north and south from the Dunwoody and Doraville areas to the airport and east and west from Decatur to near the Cobb County line. If you plan on parking in Atlanta and flying out from Hartsfield, save yourself some grief and don't try finding a parking space at the airport itself. Even though there are more than 33,000 parking spaces there, a chronic shortage of all but the most expensive (up to $75 a day) makes this an exercise in futility. Park at one of the outlying MARTA train stations and take the train to Hartsfield. The station there is literally within the terminal itself, right next to the baggage pickup.

MODERN TIMES

The capital city of not only Georgia but of all the New South, Atlanta has been the center of commercial growth and development for the entire southeastern United States ever since the end of the war. Often called "The City Too Busy to Hate," in reference to the relatively few problems experienced here during the 20th-century civil rights struggles, it has also been called "The City Too Busy to Remember," in a bitter reference to the little concern there is for its rich history. Although there are some world-class museums and exhibits concerning the war here, the Atlanta History Center and the Cyclorama being two stellar examples, it is sometimes very hard to tell that anything existed here much before 1960. Atlanta has never paid very much attention to historic preservation, modeling itself more on the "let's get along with the carpetbaggers" mentality that Scarlett O'Hara used, and the explosive growth in business and immigration has left the city looking newly minted and rather sterile. This very un-Southern set of attitudes has led to jokes that there are really two states here, Atlanta and everything else outside I–285, and never the twain shall meet. This author has often joked that he did not really grow up in the South, he grew up in Atlanta.

In 1862 Robert E. Lee freed all the slaves his family owned. He had owned only one himself, an elderly servant he inherited from his mother, whom he kept as a means of ensuring that the old man got the care he needed.

All of this said, it is possible to find bits and pieces of Atlanta's role in the war, scattered like diamonds amid all the crass commercialism. Stone Mountain Park, on the east side of the city, rises up like a sentry to greet the dawn each day and was originally meant to serve as a permanent and vast Confederate memorial. The new private management that has taken over operation of the park from the state government has set about changing that aspect as rapidly as possible, so as not to offend the hordes of newly immigrated Yankees with dollars to spend, but if you hurry, you can still see the plantations, parks, museums, and the vast carving on the mountain itself. Peachtree Creek battlefield, or a small park containing about 5 percent of the original battleground, does still preserve a bit of original space in the midst of bustling Buckhead.

Underground Atlanta is an unevenly attended nightlife area in the very heart of downtown, which is actually the site of the original city. When Atlanta started growing after the war, the train tracks that had led to its rise started becoming a hindrance to its growth, so the city fathers decided to simply build over them. This led to a series of viaducts that still house the major part of that area of downtown. In the early 1970s this area was rediscovered by developers, who partly rebuilt part of the under-viaduct area to return it to its postbellum appearance. This commercial venture died in the early 1980s but was rebuilt again in the late 1980s, this time to a more contemporary appearance. It is still open, albeit stories of its imminent demise in the local newspaper, and it has become something of a "town square" for the city.

Other than these three sites and the ones we note below, it can be very difficult to find original, undisturbed areas in the city itself. However, even that can be a sort of testament to the spirit that got the city through the war—after surviving Sherman's wrath, the city rebuilt and in many ways eclipsed the cities that sent troops to destroy her.

POINTS OF INTEREST

Peachtree Creek Battlefield

Today this entire battlefield is in the middle of heavily urbanized Buckhead. The only remaining portion in more or less original condition is Tanyard Branch Park on Collier Road, scene of the most intense fighting. Several markers give a good idea of the layout of battle in this area, and a few cannon and embankments add to the flavor. Collier Road runs between Peachtree Road, about 2 miles north of I-85, and Howell Mill Road (which intersects I-75 1 mile to the west). At the corner of Collier and Peachtree is Piedmont Hospital, which has a large stone marker commemorating the battle. Another marker nearby indicates the spot where the Confederate assault began.

On the eastern flank of the battlefield is Peachtree Road, and the main entertainment district of Atlanta (Buckhead) is a short drive north. Be aware that the area around Peachtree, Pharr, and Paces Ferry Roads is simply crawling with bars (literally stacked on top of one another in some places!), which attracts large and nearly equal numbers of obnoxious young drunks and irritable police officers on weekend nights. "DUI check" roadblocks are common after dark, as are run-over pedestrians. Some upscale chain restaurants (Cheesecake Factory, Bones) are in the area, along with midscale retro (Johnny Rockets) and low-rent cheap fare (Waffle House, IHOP). For the non-ACW-fan spouse, a good distraction is the twin upscale shopping malls another mile north on Peachtree: Lenox Square and Phipps Plaza. A good scale to judge the quality of shops here (and matching prices) is the fact that the Ritz-Carlton Buckhead hotel sits between the two malls.

The Atlanta Battlefield

The area of battle on July 22 ranged around the area of Moreland Avenue and I-20, just east of the immediate downtown area. Literally nothing remains of the Atlanta battleground in the way of entrenchments or preserved area, however. Leggett's Hill itself was bulldozed down to make way for I-20 and Moreland Avenue expansions in the 1980s. A memorial marks the site where Walker died; it is an upturned cannon on the corner of Wilkinson Drive and Glenwood Avenue, directly adjacent to the north side of I-20. Close by is another upturned cannon marking the site of McPherson's death; it is at the corner of McPherson and Monument Avenues just off Maynard Terrace. A stone church building on DeGress Avenue off DeKalb Avenue (1 block north of I-20) stands where the center of battle swirled that day; a marker on the property notes that this was where the famed Troup Hurt House stood. Sherman's headquarters was in the Augustus Hurt House; the marked site is now on the grounds of the Carter Presidential Center on Copenhill Avenue off Moreland Avenue.

Atlanta History Center
130 West Paces Ferry Road, Atlanta
(404) 814-4000

Located just off the northeastern fringes of the Peachtree Creek battlefield, the Atlanta History Center is the crown jewel of Civil War museums in the South, and perhaps the nation. We were awestruck by the new buildings and displays on the many aspects of Atlanta history, but the Civil War display was simply beyond compare. Built around the large Beverly M. DuBose general artifact collection and the huge Thomas Swift Dickey ordnance collection (we bet you didn't know anyone actually collected old shells!), both donated permanently to the center,

The last surviving widow of a Union Civil War veteran, still drawing her late husband's pension, died in January 2003. It was customary in the early part of the century for aged veterans to marry young girls, specifically so that they would be eligible for these pensions.

changing exhibits keep the displays fresh and invite even the casually interested visitor back time and again.

The Civil War display, *Turning Point,* leads you through the stages of the war, with artifacts carefully chosen and displayed as appropriate and accurate for each year. Multimedia use is extensive, with four films, several sound displays, and many small scenes and dioramas. A unique display is the sole remaining Union supply wagon. As one curator mentioned, everyone wanted to save the unusual items, but they have a hard time finding the mundane.

The center hosts annual Civil War encampments, which provide a better-than-average display of the camp and battle life of the common soldier, around the circa-1845 Tullie Smith Farm. Recent encampments have featured rifle and artillery demonstrations, cavalry and infantry maneuvers, and even mail call and food ration distributions. A special treat at the fall 2001 encampment was an appearance by the 8th Regimental Band, a high-quality gathering of musicians playing period music on period instruments.

This is our absolute favorite museum, and we have returned quite a few times simply to enjoy the high quality of both artifacts and displays. A side benefit for the long-suffering Civil War buff's "widow" is the extensive collections present in other exhibits of everything from folk art to the 1996 Olympics.

The center is open Monday through Saturday, 10:00 A.M. to 5:30 P.M. and Sunday noon to 5:30 P.M. Admission is $12.00 for adults, $10.00 for students and seniors, $7.00 for children ages 4 through 12, and free for children 3 and under. These fees include the historic gardens and tours of two historic houses. If you live anywhere in the area, we strongly suggest considering a membership in the center. The annual cost is $50 for individuals and $75 for families, but there are good discounts for teachers, students, and certain other groups, and the membership gives free admission to all the center's facilities. In addition, a membership comes with sub-scriptions to the center's newsletter and *Atlanta History* magazine. Be aware that the AHC is in the midst of a multiyear rebuilding program and certain venues may not be open at all times.

The Atlanta Cyclorama
800 Cherokee Avenue, Atlanta
(404) 624-1071
The Cyclorama is an old favorite and comes close to tying with the Atlanta History Center as our favorite place to visit. The displays center around what they call "the world's largest painting," 42 feet tall and 385 feet around, weighing more than nine tons and with sculptures in front that give a very real three-dimensional feeling to the work. This painting is of a two-hour span of time, focusing just after 3:00 P.M. on July 22, 1864, as seen from a vantage point near the Troup Hurt House during the Battle of Atlanta.

The level of detail is amazing; we were astonished to discover recently that a detail portrays the charge of the obscure 1st Georgia State Line near the railway cut. A very well-produced short film narrated by James Earl Jones introduces the set-ting in a small, separate theater before you enter the main display theater. A 185-seat theater arranged in bleacher fashion slowly revolves in front of the painting and a taped historian narrates the action, com-plete with related spotlighting of the painting. A special treat is when one of the museum guides takes you on another spin around, highlighting some of the more obscure elements of the work; this happens more often during the winter off-season than during the peak visiting time.

Downstairs in the main entrance is the famed locomotive *Texas,* one of the heroes of the Andrews Raid (see the first Close-up in this chapter), along with a few other displays and an excellent bookstore. Upstairs is a good collection of artifacts, along with an excellent collection of con-temporary Civil War artwork.

The Cyclorama is open from 9:30 A.M. to 4:30 P.M. daily. Admission is $6.00 for ages 13 to 59, $5.00 for ages 60 and up, $4.00 for ages 6 through 12, and free for children under 6.

The Ezra Church Battlefield
As in most of the rest of the battlegrounds in Atlanta itself, nothing remains of the vast majority of the original emplacements but historical markers. Mozley Park, on Martin Luther King Jr. Drive just north of the I-20 intersection, was in the center of the fighting but is poorly marked and a bit difficult to find. Nearby Westview Ceme-tery (1680 Ralph David Abernathy) does contain a short section of preserved Con-federate trenches.

In the cemetery, atop a low hill close by the trench line, is one of the very few monuments erected by the Confederate veterans themselves (most were funded by either the states or the United Daughters of the Confederacy). Standing guard over the now nearly forgotten graves of his com-rades stands a lone concrete picket, with an inscription that talks mostly of peace: "Nation shall not rise up against Nation . . . Neither shall they learn war anymore."

Utoy Creek Battlefield
The Utoy Creek battlefield is centered in what is today the Cascade Springs Nature Preserve, off-limits to the public. The only extant structure in this area is the small Utoy Church, used as a hospital during the battle (now known as the Temple of Christ Pentecostal Church). Take I-20 west out of downtown Atlanta, exiting onto Martin Luther King Jr. Drive (exit 17). To the right (northeast) is the Ezra Church battle area. Turn to the left (southwest) and immedi-ately left again on Ralph David Abernathy Drive. On your right is Westview Ceme-tery, a major burial site for Confederates killed in the battles around Atlanta. Con-tinuing on Abernathy Drive, turn right onto Cascade Avenue. Travel 1½ miles, and then turn left onto Centra Villa; travel another half mile and turn left onto Venet-ian Drive. Drive less than one-half mile, and turn left onto Cahaba Drive; Utoy Church is on the corner.

Georgia's Stone Mountain Park
US Highway 78, Stone Mountain
(770) 498-5690

This 3,200-acre park, originally intended as a permanent Confederate memorial, is built around the world's largest outcropping of granite and features the world's largest carving on the mountainside. Larger than Mount Rushmore, the 90-foot by 190-foot figures of Jefferson Davis, Robert E. Lee, and Stonewall Jackson took nearly 60 years to carve. Two large museums in the park are a bit dated but do contain impressive displays of artifacts, paintings, and dioramas.

The park has become "the official playground of Atlanta," according to one source. On sunny weekends it can become hard to get around past all the hikers, bikers, picnickers, and sun worshipers, but it does have a large number of restaurants and attractions for the non–Civil War buff.

The park is open year-round 6:00 A.M. to midnight, and attractions are open 10:00 A.M. to 5:30 P.M., 8:00 P.M. during the summer months. The entrance fee is $7.00 per car, and a $30.00 annual pass is available; individual attractions within the park have various additional fees.

Georgia Department of
Archives and History
5800 Jonesboro Road, Morrow
(678) 364-3700

Not a museum, but a true gold mine of information for the hard-core buff or serious researcher, the Georgia Archives house a huge number of records ranging from muster and pension files to original letters and diaries. A large, comfortable "search room" houses an extensive number of reference works and is manned by staff members who will retrieve any other documents you may need.

The now-retired curator of Georgia's Civil War document collection, Charlotte Ray, was an invaluable source of information and inspiration in our research into other ACW projects, and her influence is still felt at every level. The staff is polite, polished, and highly professional, and they have proven over and over that they can work miracles in finding just the obscure document you might need!

The archives are open Tuesday through Saturday 8:30 A.M. to 5:00 P.M. There is no charge for admission.

ACCOMMODATIONS

Atlanta is a major tourist and convention destination, and the hospitality industry in Fulton County alone employs more than 115,000 workers and pays more than $215 million in taxes to the local governments. Needless to say, just about any chain hotel or motel in every price range is readily available; the Downtown Connector, the merging of I-75 and I-85 through downtown Atlanta, is the major corridor to all the listed amenities, and a short drive in (literally) any direction on the three highways (including I-20) is the best bet for lower-priced chain establishments at nearly any exit. The following recommendations are a tiny sampling of what is available in the downtown area itself. For a fuller listing, we suggest *Insiders' Guide to Atlanta.* Tax runs in the 13 percent range.

Atlanta Marriott Marquis $$$$
265 Peachtree Center Avenue NE
Atlanta
(404) 521-0000, (800) 228-9290

The 1,675-room Marquis is Atlanta's largest hotel and has received AAA's Four-Diamond Award. It has 150,000 square feet of function space, four restaurants, and 10 bars. There is also a health club (complimentary for guests) with an indoor/outdoor heated swimming pool.

Four Seasons $$$$
75 14th Street NE, Atlanta
(404) 881-9898

Formerly the Continental Grand, this Four Seasons hotel has retained all that was grand. In the three-story lobby, light from the 10-foot-high Baccarat chandelier plays across the rose-colored Spanish marble walls around the broad grand staircase. A lounge on the mezzanine serves cocktails and afternoon high tea. Park 75 is a sit-down, white tablecloth restaurant that serves breakfast, lunch and supper from early morning till 11:00 P.M. every day. The menu is "international with a Southern flair." The Ballroom showcases a skyline view from its 6,000-square-foot open terrace. The health club boasts the latest exercise equipment, and its gorgeous indoor lap pool suggests a Roman bath.

Westin Buckhead Atlanta $$$–$$$$
3391 Peachtree Road, NE, Atlanta
(404) 365-0065, (800) 253-1397
The Westin is patterned after the elegant fashions of modern Europe: sleek and smooth with curving lines and sweeping expanses of glass. The interior art is spectacular and belies the rather uninteresting exterior. Each of the 365 guest rooms in the 22-floor property features three phones and a modem hookup, voice mail, cable TV with HBO, bathrobes, and a hair dryer. The hotel's health club has an indoor pool.

RESTAURANTS

The Cyclorama (earlier in the Atlanta section) is painted from the vantage point of a person standing at a spot on Moreland Avenue about a mile north of I-20, just where the railroad tracks cross over the road. Do not be alarmed if you see a lot of strangely dressed people walking around here; this is the area known as Little 5 Points (locals call it L5P) and is the so-called "hippie" district. One block north of the railroad tracks on Moreland is the center of commerce for the area, where you can find any manner of macrobiotic food, incense, leather clothing, or artwork, and where you can get tattooed and pierced to your heart's content. We recommend Urban Tribe (1131 Euclid Avenue) or Sacred Heart Tattoo (483 Moreland Avenue) for the latter.

There is a distinct lack of the usual fast-food places in this area, which is actually a blessing. This area and the nearby Virginia-Highlands district (2 miles north on Moreland Avenue, west on Ponce de Leon Avenue, then immediately right onto Highland Avenue) are blessed with a large number of truly fabulous restaurants. Unfortunately, both districts suffer the Atlanta disease of quick open-and-shut doors; we recommend that you look for the bright green newspaper boxes and pick up a copy of *Creative Loafing* (free). Its main restaurant reviewer is Cliff Bostick, and we have never gone wrong with one of his recommendations. Be aware that he leans very heavily toward Vietnamese and other Asian cuisine.

La Grotta Ristorante $$$$
2637 Peachtree Road NE, Atlanta
(404) 231-1368
Ravina Center, 4355 Ashford
Dunwoody Road, Atlanta
(770) 395-9925
Fine Italian cuisine here includes pasta dishes and favorites such as roasted quail stuffed with Italian sausage, grilled polenta and balsamic vinegar sauce, and fillet of swordfish on a bed of spinach and Roma tomato with red pepper and fresh thyme coulis. Dinner is served Monday through Saturday at the Peachtree Road location, very close by the Peachtree Creek battlefield site, and reservations are recommended. The Ravina location, open for lunch and dinner, is more airy and modern than the Buckhead restaurant, with a wonderful view of the hotel's gardens from huge glass windows. Favorite menu items include grilled veal chop with herbs, shallots, and finocchio sautéed in butter and beef tenderloin grilled with Barolo mustard with mushrooms, spinach, and roasted-garlic mashed potatoes.

Manuel's Tavern $
602 North Highland Avenue NE, Atlanta
(404) 525-3447
Manuel's Tavern has been an in-town gathering place since 1956 when Manuel Maloof founded it. Maloof was politically active his entire life (at one time he was

CEO of DeKalb County), and today the walls of his tavern are covered with beer signs and pictures of sports heroes, Democratic Party leaders, and icons who frequent the place. Through the years, the Atlanta Press Club has held meetings and debates here, and the New York Times has described it as "Atlanta's quintessential neighborhood bar." Regulars roam from the main room to the "ballroom" (really the dining room), from bar to booth to table, catching up on all the latest while enjoying Manuel's wings, sandwiches, burgers, and salads. Most Atlanta cops, firefighters, and paramedics consider this "the" place to unwind after their shift, so expect to see quite a few uniforms at any given time. It can get hectic on a busy night, but the atmosphere is friendly and inviting. Manuel's is open daily for lunch and dinner.

Bacchanalia   **$$$$**
1198 Howell Mill Road, Atlanta
(404) 365–0410
This is, without a doubt, our favorite serious foodie Atlanta restaurant; in fact, it would fit very nicely alongside the finest that New Orleans or San Francisco can offer. This former Buckhead restaurant took a bold step and relocated to a renovated factory closer to downtown, in a neighborhood that is in transition, but most delicately can be described as

"interesting." However, the crowds who love the eatery's delectable fixed-price four-course dinners of California nouvelle cuisine ($65 each) are still putting their names on the reservation list. Along with an extensive wine list, you'll find plenty of seafood selections and updated American classics. Lunch is served Wednesday through Saturday, and dinner is served Monday through Saturday 6:00 to 9:30 P.M.; there's plenty of on-site parking.

Getting There: Jonesboro Battlefield

Jonesboro battlefield lies entirely within the present-day city limits of Jonesboro and almost entirely within the central business district. The town was almost completely destroyed during the battle, but a handful of period structures still exist. The center of action is well marked and can be found in Jonesboro's historic district, on US 41/19 (also called Tara Boulevard. Yes, that Tara). The heavy commercial buildup in this area can make finding the individual sites and structures difficult. We strongly encourage you to check with the Clayton County Visitors Center at 104 North Main Street for some excellent maps and directions.

ATLANTA TO SAVANNAH:
THE MARCH TO THE SEA

Sherman's Georgia campaign, another name given for his famed March to the Sea, can be viewed as simply an extension of his Atlanta campaign, which began in the northwestern mountains in May 1864. His original goal—cutting the critical transportation and manufacturing center of Atlanta off from the rest of the Confederacy—having been met by early September 1864, Sherman pondered what to do next. One of his earliest thoughts was to strike southwest toward LaGrange and West Point while Union forces stationed in Mobile and Pensacola marched north to meet him, opening the Chattahoochee and Appalachicola Rivers to Union control.

Another considered, then rejected, plan was to strike toward the state capital at Milledgeville, and then turn on Macon, Augusta, and "sweep the whole State of Georgia," but concern over the still undefeated Confederate Army of Tennessee just outside Atlanta gave him serious pause. His primary concern was that his supply line snaked through a relatively narrow corridor from Atlanta more than 100 miles to the north in Chattanooga and from there another 130 miles north to the main Union base at Nashville. Both the Confederate Army of Tennessee under Major General John Bell Hood and Major General Joseph Wheeler's cavalry corps up in Tennessee threatened to cut off this supply route at any given time.

Researching population and agricultural records for every county in Georgia, Sherman finally concluded that his 60,000-plus men could live off the land for a short time if they set off cross-country to join a Union army somewhere along the Atlantic Coast. Under great pressure to send his army south to rescue Union prisoners at the notorious Camp Sumter prisoner of war camp near Andersonville, Georgia, Sherman admitted that going down the Flint River to accomplish this would probably be the safest course of action. However, he had objectives other than simple, safe military maneuvers.

OCCUPIED ATLANTA

Sherman's grand army had simply walked into the contested city of Atlanta after Hood had abandoned it during the night of September 1, 1864. Hood, in one of his many rash decisions, had sent his entire cavalry force north to strike at the Union supply lines in Tennessee, leaving him without scouts to report on what his Union opposite was up to. Sherman, learning of the poor tactical decision, took advantage of the situation by shifting part of his forces to the south of Atlanta, near Jonesboro, and cut the single remaining railroad supply line into the city. Hood, left without means of supply or reinforcement and faced with the prospect of a protracted siege, took what opportunity was left and snuck his remaining combat forces out of the city under cover of dark.

Rather than face the small but combat-hardened group of veterans from Hood's army at their new defense lines near Lovejoy Station, Sherman elected to march his army into the city and take over the strong belt of fortifications himself. Hood, faced with the prospect of bleeding his army dry against the very fortifications they had built, decided instead to take his army north, cut the Union supply line, and try to starve Sherman out.

The Civilian "Problem"

Sherman had some interesting problems to deal with in Atlanta in addition to the roaming Confederate army at his gate. The extensive line of fortifications built by Confederate engineers and slaves around Atlanta was simply too large for even his huge army to fully man, so he ordered his own engineers to tighten it down to a smaller ring of artillery emplacements defended by trenches for infantry. The nearly 30,000 civilians still within the city troubled him, for he did not wish to "waste" any of the mountains of supplies flowing down from Chattanooga on the noncombatants.

On September 8, Sherman gave one of his most controversial orders of the war: "The city of Atlanta, being exclusively required for wartime purposes, will at once be evacuated by all except the armies of the United States." All civilians would be transported under flag of truce 10 miles south to Rough and Ready and then unceremoniously dumped in the unprepared area without provision for shelter or food.

Needless to say, this act provoked a howl of protest from Confederate civilian and military authorities. Hood stated in a letter to Sherman, "Permit me to say that the unprecedented measure you propose transcends, in studied and ingenious cruelty, all acts ever brought to my attention in the dark history of war." Mayor James M. Calhoun of Atlanta protested that the majority of citizens left (mostly women and children) could not stand up to the coming winter without shelter or food. In a letter to Sherman, he wrote that the act was "appalling and heartrending."

Sherman was not impressed. In a lengthy reply to Hood's letter, he reiterated his intentions and blasted Hood for suggesting it was anything truly unusual:

In the name of common sense, I ask you not to appeal to a just God in such a sacrilegious manner. You, who in the midst of peace and prosperity have plunged a nation into war, dark and cruel war, who dared and badgered us into battle, insulted our flag, seized our arsenals and forts that were left in the honorable custody of a peaceful ordnance sergeant, and seized and made prisoners of war the very garrisons sent to protect your people against negroes and Indians . . . Talk thus to the Marines, but not to me . . . if we must be enemies, let us be men, and fight it out as we propose to do, and not indulge in such hypocritical appeals to God and humanity.

Sherman had no intention of changing his orders, and on September 10 the first wagonloads of civilians left Atlanta. Hood was beside himself with the barbarity of Sherman's actions and just couldn't leave it be without a parting shot. "We will fight you to the death," he wrote back to Sherman, "better die a thousand deaths than submit to live under you."

SHERMAN MAKES HIS DECISION

By October 1, Sherman finally made up his mind where to go next. Ordering Major General George H. Thomas back to Chattanooga with two corps to defend Tennessee, he stripped down his remaining army to a handpicked fighting force of 55,255 infantry, 4,588 cavalry, and 1,759 artillerymen with 68 guns organized into four army corps. Writing a series of letters to his friend and commander, Lieutenant General Ulysses S. Grant, back in Washington, he outlined his planned offensive. "Until we can repopulate Georgia (with Unionists), it is useless for us to occupy it; but the utter destruction of its roads, houses, and people will cripple their military resources . . . can make this march and make Georgia howl." He further advised that he was sending his wounded and unfit soldiers back up to Tennessee, "and with my effective army, move through Georgia, smashing things to the sea."

Sherman's only real worry was that the few good roads and frequent stream and river crossings in southern Georgia could allow the remains of Hood's army and small bands of Georgia militia and home guards to delay his advance to an unhealthy degree. Unwittingly, Hood himself helped relieve some of this concern, with a renewed offensive against Sherman's rear.

THE BATTLE OF ALLATOONA PASS

Realizing that there was no way his battered army could ever hope to take Atlanta back by force, Hood, with President Jefferson Davis's blessings, marched his troops out of camp near Palmetto northward, hoping to cut Sherman's supply lines north of Atlanta and force him to turn and fight him there. Crossing the Chattahoochee River near Campbellton on October 1, he continued north for two days, finally encamping near Hiram. Major General Alexander P. Stewart was ordered to move east to attack and cut the Western & Atlantic Railroad line at Big Shanty (now Kennesaw), Acworth, and Allatoona.

Stewart's men surprised and captured about 170 Union troops at Big Shanty on October 4 and then quickly moved north and captured a larger garrison at Acworth. Flushed with these easy successes, Hood personally ordered Major General Samuel G. French to take his division on up the tracks to capture and destroy the bridge and railroad cut at Allatoona Pass. Hood was under the impression that the pass was only lightly held, as the two previous rail stops had been. However, Sherman had made the tiny settlement on the south side of the deep railway cut into a central base of logistical operations, had it heavily fortified, and had ordered another division under Brigadier General John M. Corse forward to garrison it. On both peaks over the 90-foot-deep railroad cut, heavily rein-

forced emplacements had been built. The westernmost set of peak defenses was dubbed the Star Fort, because of the arrangement of railroad ties surrounding it.

French divided his force and approached Allatoona from the north, west, and south. Once all were in position, he rather arrogantly sent Corse a terse message:

Sir: I have the forces under my command in such positions that you are now surrounded, and, to avoid a needless effusion of blood, I call upon you to surrender your forces at once, and unconditionally. Five minutes will be allowed for you to decide. Should you accede to this, you will be treated in the most honorable manner as prisoners of war.

Corse was somewhat less than impressed, and 15 minutes later he replied, "Your communication demanding surrender of my command, I acknowledge receipt of, and respectfully reply, that we are prepared for the 'needless effusion of blood' whenever it is agreeable with you."

French wasted no time, sending Brigadier Generals Francis M. Cockrell's Missouri Brigade and William H. Young's (Ector's) Brigade to assault from the west. Both pushed through the first line of defenses, then the second, and then through a third line of defense, all the while fighting hand-to-hand with clubbed rifles and bayonets. Advancing to within a few feet of the Star Fort, the fighting rapidly intensified, with the Confederate advance finally being stopped before it could overrun the fort. After receiving warnings that a Union force had been spotted moving rapidly toward the battle area, French disengaged and marched his depleted force west to rejoin Hood.

All through the daylong battle, a Union signal post at Kennesaw Mountain sent a message to Corse: "General Sherman says hold fast; we are coming." This message, which popularized the expression "Hold the fort, I'm coming," was nothing more than a morale booster, for Sherman did not order any additional infantry to the area until the next day, and none arrived until two days later. The forces spotted by the Confederate side were apparently just cavalry on a scouting mission.

Casualties in the brief, little-remembered battle were exceptionally high (one admittedly biased local historian said it was the "bloodiest battle of the war"), with Corse reporting 706 dead and wounded, and French also reporting 706 (including 70 officers), about 30 percent of each side's total force. Young himself was wounded just outside the fort and captured shortly afterward. Corse reported in a message to Sherman that he, too, had been wounded: "I am short a cheek bone and an ear but am able to lick all hell yet!" When Sherman came up later, he was unimpressed with the severity of his wounds and said, "Corse, they came damn near missing you, didn't they?"

This morning the enemy attacked our pickets. They planted their artilry so they had good range of us. They drove us out of our rifel pits about 11:00 A.M. and we fell back in the fort and then we held them and fought them until nearly 4:00 P.M. The timber is laying full of dead and some wounded. The wounded in our company Henry Hockman in left leg, J Garman fnger shot off, E Kahley shot in back, J Humpfrey in the side, (unidentified words), H C Carl through the breast, J Stewart slight in leg, Danil Dauber slightly in arm. Killed Simon (last name unidentified).

Private Thomas Jefferson Moses, 93rd Regiment, Illinois Volunteers, Union Army, description of battle of Allatoona Pass, October 5, 1864 (all spelling original, from his diary entry)

THE ARMIES ADVANCE IN OPPOSITE DIRECTIONS

Following the decisive loss at Allatoona Pass, Hood elected to continue north, hitting the Union garrisons at Rome, Resaca, Dalton, and Tunnel Hill before turning west into Alabama. Sherman initially sent a force of some 40,000 men chasing after him but soon wearied of the endless pursuit. Hood's strategy here is uncertain, but if it was to keep Sherman bottled up in northern Georgia, it both succeeded and failed. When Hood slipped away after the Union troops deployed for battle at La Fayette (just south of the Chickamauga battlefield) on October 17, Sherman remarked that Hood's tactics were "inexplicable by any common-sense theory . . . I could not guess his movements as I could those of Johnston." After a total of three weeks of chasing the fast-moving Army of Tennessee, Sherman ordered his forces to return to Atlanta and prepare for a march to the south.

Warned by Grant that Hood was taking his army north into Tennessee to threaten his supply lines, Sherman remarked, "No single force can catch Hood, and I am convinced that the best results will follow from our defeating Jeff Davis's cherished plan of making me leave Georgia by maneuvering."

At the same time, Davis was begging Hood "not to abandon Georgia to Sherman but defeat him in detail before marching into Tennessee." Hood replied that it was his intent to "draw out Sherman where he can be dealt with north of Atlanta." In his postwar memoirs, Hood clung to this unrealistic stance and his hopes of defeating both Sherman and Thomas's powerful force in Tennessee:

I conceived the plan of marching into Tennessee . . . to move upon Thomas and Schofield and capture their army before it could reach Nashville and afterward march northeast, past the Cumberland

*River in that position I could
threaten Cincinnati from Kentucky
and Tennessee . . . if blessed with a
victory (over Sherman coming
north after him), to send reinforcements to Lee, in Virginia, or to
march through gaps in the Cumberland Mountains and attack
Grant in the rear.*

It was whispered by not a few members of the Army of Tennessee that Hood
was half-mad from his injuries, shot in the
arm at Gettysburg and having a leg shot
off at Chickamauga shortly thereafter.
Widely viewed as a gallant fighter, his
leadership did not impress those under
him in the sense that his tactics killed a lot
of his men. Private Sam Watkins said, "As
a soldier, he was brave, good, noble and
gallant, and fought with the ferociousness
of the wounded tiger, and with the everlasting grit of the bull-dog; but as a general he was a failure in every particular."

Hood continued his march north, and
Sherman, upon hearing the news, couldn't
have been happier. "If he will go to the
Ohio River, I will give him rations." Just
before Hood's eastward-ranging cavalry
cut the telegraph lines, Sherman sent one
last message to Grant:

*If I start before I hear from you, or
before further developments turn
my course, you may take it for
granted that I have moved by way
of Griffin to Barnesville; that I
break up the road between Columbus and Macon good and if I feign
on Columbus, I will move by way of
Macon and Millen on Savannah; or
if I feign on Macon, you may take it
for granted I have shot toward
Opelika, Montgomery and Mobile
Bay, I will not attempt to send
couriers back, but trust to the
Richmond papers to keep you well
advised, I will see that the road is
completely broken between the
Etowah and the Chattahoochee,*

*and that Atlanta itself is utterly
destroyed.*

Content with his plans, happy about
Hood being more than 100 miles to his
rear, and with his army primed and ready
for action, Sherman had but one task left
before turning his attention on gaining the
sea before winter set in.

THE BURNING OF ATLANTA

Planning to begin his march out of Atlanta
southward on November 16, Sherman
issued orders that anything of military
value in the city be destroyed before they
departed. Giving the task over to his chief
of engineers, Captain Orlando M. Poe,
Sherman intended to render useless anything even remotely related to manufacturing, transportation, or communications.
Poe took this order and applied it quite
liberally, without any objection from Sherman. Starting on the afternoon of November 11, block after block was set afire,
the contents being pillaged and looted
beforehand by large gangs of drunken
Union soldiers and sober Southern citizens alike.

North of Atlanta, Sherman gave orders
that anything of "military value" be
destroyed by his troops gathering for the
march south. Rome, Acworth, and Marietta were all consigned to the torch, and
soon little was visible of the once pretty
small towns but heaps of smoldering ruins
and lonely chimneys standing like pickets.

*An authentic (hardtack) cracker
could not be soaked soft, but after
a time took on the elasticity of
gutta-percha.*

John D. Billings, in his book
Hardtack and Coffee

To conduct his destruction more efficiently, Poe had devised a new machine
consisting of a 21-foot-long iron bar
swinging on chains from a 10-foot-high

wooden scaffold. With a gang of soldiers to move and swing it, it was a devilishly clever way to knock down whatever struck his fancy. The railroad roundhouse, factories, warehouses, residences, and masonry buildings of all description were soon reduced to piles of rubble. Under other buildings Union soldiers piled stacks of mattresses, oil-soaked wagon parts, broken fence rails, and just about anything else that would burn. Atop everything they piled artillery shot and shells abandoned by Hood's retreating army. In a touch of irony, sentries were then posted to prevent "unauthorized" acts of arson.

Finally ready to move out of Atlanta, Sherman ordered Poe to start the fires late on the afternoon of November 15. Within a few minutes the "authorized" fires had been set, at first confined to factories and warehouses containing Hood's abandoned supplies. An early evening wind soon built up the fires, and spraying sparks and burning cinders in every direction, the fires spread like, well, wildfire. Pleased by the sight of the soon out-of-control fires raging through the city, Sherman was moved to remark only that he supposed the flames could be visible from Griffin, about 45 miles to the south.

As a sort of explanation to his staff, who were starting to view the wanton destruction with unease, Sherman remarked,

> This city has done more and contributed more to carry on and sustain the war than any other, save perhaps Richmond. We have been fighting Atlanta all the time, in the past; have been capturing guns wagons, etc. etc., marked Atlanta and made here, all the time; and now since they have been doing so much to destroy us and our Government we have to destroy them, at least enough to prevent any more of that.

As the huge fire built and built, block after block literally exploded into flame,

the thick smoke choking the Union soldiers who clapped and danced with glee among the ruins, barely waiting until the flames died down to start their looting and drunken revelry once again. What initially escaped the "authorized" fires did not escape these undisciplined wretches, who helped spread the flames by burning homes and businesses to cover up their crimes. In the midst of the chaotic riot, the 33rd Massachusetts Regimental Band stood, calmly and righteously playing "John Brown's Soul Goes Marching On." Major George Ward Nichols, Sherman's aide-de-camp, remarked without a hint of sarcasm that he had "never heard that noble anthem when it was so grand, so solemn, so inspiring."

Other Union soldiers and officers viewed the destruction differently, remarking that the burning and looting of private property was not necessary and a "disgraceful piece of business." Another summed up the view more widely held by their Confederate opponents: "We hardly deserve success."

As the flames died down overnight, dawn on November 16 revealed that more than 4,100 of the 4,500 buildings in town, including every single business, had been leveled by the flames and rioting Union troops. Sherman mounted his horse, Sam, and slowly led his men out of the ruined city, bound for Savannah and the Atlantic Ocean.

"THE WILD ADVENTURE OF A CRAZY FOOL"

With the "business" in Atlanta taken care of, his men up and ready, and prospects of an easy adventure before them, Sherman ordered the march out of the city to begin. The 60,598 Union soldiers were deployed in two huge columns, sometimes called "wings." On the morning of November 15, Brigadier General Alpheus William's XX Corps headed off due east through Decatur toward Augusta. General Peter Osterhaus's XV Corps and General

Frank Blair's XVII Corps formed the right column under overall command of Major General Oliver O. Howard and moved southward toward Macon. Early on the morning of November 16, Major General Jefferson C. Davis's XIV Corps moved out behind William's corps. The two-pronged attack was designed to fool Confederate defenders into thinking that Augusta and Macon were the targets of the separate wings, forcing them to divide their already inadequate forces while the two columns swung south and east and converged on the Georgia capital of Milledgeville.

To oppose the Union juggernaut was a pitiful handful of mostly irregular troops: Major General Gustavus W. Smith's (combined) Georgia Militia, the battered remnants of the Georgia State Line—freshly arrived after leaving the march north with Hood's army; a few home guard and hastily organized local militia groups; and the remnants of Major General Joseph Wheeler's cavalry corps. All told, fewer than 8,000 men were available to try to stop Sherman, most of whom had never fired a rifle in combat before.

About 7:00 A.M. on the morning of November 16, Sherman rode his horse slowly out of the bombarded, burned-out hulk of a once-thriving city along with the vanguard of his XIV Corps, down the dirt road leading toward Decatur and Stone Mountain. Stopping briefly, he turned to take another look at the scene of his greatest triumph and some of his greatest sorrows. From his vantagepoint he could barely make out the copse of trees where his beloved friend, Major General James Birdseye McPherson, had been shot and killed on July 22. Setting his battered hat back on his head and unwrapping another cigar to chew on along the way, he set his horse to a walk and left the city without uttering a word to anyone. In his memoirs, he remarked,

Then we turned our horses' heads to the east; Atlanta was soon lost behind the screen of trees, and became a thing of the past.

Around it clings many a thought of desperate battle of hope and fear, that now seem like the memory of a dream . . . There was a "devil-may-care" feeling pervading officers and men, that made me feel the full load of responsibility, for success would be expected as a matter of course, whereas, should we fail, this march would be adjudged the wild adventure of a crazy fool.

MARCHING THROUGH GEORGIA

Both columns moved out of Atlanta, one proceeding initially almost due east and the other south, with almost no opposition. Following Sherman's orders to the letter and spirit, nearly everything of any value that they encountered was confiscated or burned, and assigned work gangs destroyed most of the railroad tracks. The rails were lifted and the crossties pulled out from under them and piled high and set afire, then the rails were held over the burning ties until they glowed red hot and twisted and bent into unusable pretzel shapes called "Sherman's bow-ties."

The only Confederate opposition to the first part of the march was a series of small to moderate-size skirmishes between Rough and Ready (10 miles north of Jonesboro; now called Mountain View) and East Macon, with elements of Wheeler's cavalry.

Milledgeville

The skirmishers and foraging parties created a nearly 60-mile-wide path of destruction as they went across Georgia. Slocum's left wing moved like a blue buzzsaw through Stone Mountain, Lithonia, Conyers, Social Circle, and Madison before encountering any resistance to speak of. At Buckhead (a small town, not the

Atlanta suburb), Confederate sharpshooters caused a handful of casualties before being driven off; Sherman ordered the town totally burned to the ground in reprisal.

Howard's right wing had moved in a southeasterly direction, hoping to give the impression that Macon was their destination. Moving through McDonough and Locust Grove, Howard ordered a turn more to the east at Indian Springs, to close in tighter with the left wing and head more directly to Milledgeville. By November 20, the closest flanks of both wings were within 10 miles of each other and just a day's march from the Georgia capital.

EAST OF MACON

From the start of the march, Brigadier General Judson Kilpatrick's 3rd Cavalry Division had ridden to the far right of Howard's massed columns. He had been ordered to travel south—as close to Macon as he dared—and to tear up the railroad tracks as he went. He was then to close up again near Milledgeville. On November 20, he had a brief skirmish with Wheeler's cavalry just east of Macon, quickly driving the Confederates back into the line of entrenchments surrounding the city.

The next day, a single regiment, Captain Frederick S. Ladd's 9th Michigan, was sent to assault the small industrial town of Griswoldville, 10 miles east of Macon. Moving in without resistance, the cavalrymen soon destroyed most of the buildings in town, including the railroad station, a pistol factory, and a candle and soap factory. As they mopped up, Colonel Eli H. Murray's 1st Brigade settled in for the night about 2 miles to the east.

The Capital City

As the right wing set up just to their south, Slocum's left wing made ready to enter the Georgia capital. By November 19, it became obvious that the capital was Sherman's real target, and pandemonium erupted. The Georgia legislature was then in session, and upon hearing of the danger promptly sprang into action. A law was quickly passed requiring every physically able male citizen to join in the armed resistance to the Union invasion, exempting only themselves and sitting judges from the noble sacrifice. Turning to issues of a more immediate nature, they then authorized expenditure of $3,000 in public funds to hire a train to carry themselves, their families, their furniture, and their baggage to safety.

Georgia's governor, Joseph Emerson Brown, acted in an equally heroic manner. Stripping the governor's mansion of everything that wasn't nailed down (and a few things that were), he fled Milledgeville at a high rate of speed. Not far behind was the trainload of politicians from the legislature, who left with scarcely more dignity, actually pausing long enough to announce they were heading "for the front" before setting off in the opposite direction.

Civilians were equally panicked, but most lacked access to tax money to use to flee the city. A. C. Cooper, a local resident who had left Atlanta on Sherman's approach in July, later wrote about the effect of Sherman on the horizon:

> Reports varied; one would be that the enemy would be upon us ere long, as a few bluecoats had been seen in the distance, and we women were advised to pack up and flee, but there was blank silence when we asked, "Where shall we flee?" . . . Hurry, scurry, run here, run there, run everywhere. Women cried and prayed, babies yelled . . . dogs howled and yelped, mules brayed.

Late in the night of November 21, the first Union cavalry scouts entered the city, followed the next afternoon by the vanguard of the Union left wing, both without encountering the slightest act of resistance. Moving down Greene Street, officers of the XX Corps ordered the men into parade march, and with the bands playing selections of Northern patriotic tunes, made their way to the steps of the capitol building. With the bands sarcastically playing "Dixie," a large U.S. flag was raised on the building's tall flagpole.

As their men fanned out to see what they could steal in the city, officers amused themselves by occupying the recently deserted seats in the state legislature. In a high-spirited debate, the issue of secession was once again bandied about and promptly voted down. Sherman, who rode into town the next day, said that he "enjoyed the joke."

Griswoldville

As Sherman's officers were amusing themselves playing politician in the legislative chambers, things were a bit more subdued just to the south. At dawn on November 22, Wheeler's cavalry suddenly struck Murray's encampment. A short but furious fight ensued, ending when reinforcements from Colonel Charles C. Walcutt's 2nd Brigade (Union) rushed to Murray's aid. Together they pushed the Confederate cavalrymen back through the burned-out town of Griswoldville before breaking contact and returning to their original positions, where they heavily entrenched atop a small, wooded ridge.

The previous day Lieutenant General William J. Hardee, commander of the Confederate forces facing Sherman, had become aware that the Union forces were bypassing his location at Macon and made the assumption that they were heading toward the critical supply and manufacturing depot at Augusta. A hastily assembled force was pieced together around Major General Gustavus Woodson Smith's four regiments of the Georgia Militia and ordered to move out posthaste to protect the river city.

Besides the four brigades of Georgia Militia, the small task force contained Major Ferdinand W. C. Cook's Athens and

Augusta Local Defense Battalions; Captain Ruel W. Anderson's four-gun Light Artillery Battery; and the decimated ranks of the combined two regiments of the Georgia State Line under Lieutenant Colonel Beverly D. Evans. With the exception of the State Line, which had been in nearly continuous combat since May 29, the overwhelming majority of the command were the archetypal "old men and boys," this force representing the bottom of the barrel for reinforcements.

By Hardee's direction, Colonel James N. Willis's 1st Brigade, Georgia Militia, left early on the morning of November 22 along with Cook's command, bound for Augusta via the road to Griswoldville, to be followed later that same day by the remaining commands. Hardee left at the same time for Savannah to help prepare its defenses, and Smith elected to remain in Macon to do administrative chores, leaving command of the task force to the senior officer present, Brigadier General Pleasant J. Philips. As the Confederates left Macon, quite a few in the ranks remarked about how much Philips had been seen drinking that morning.

As Philips's command moved out, Howard's entire right wing was also on the move, swinging a little more to the south and heading straight toward Griswoldville.

THE BATTLE

Philips left Macon with the main part of his command and marched steadily on, arriving at the outskirts of Griswoldville just after noon. There he found Cook's defense battalions drawn up into a defensive perimeter, having spotted the well-entrenched Union lines just up the road.

Despite his explicit orders from both Hardee and Smith not to do so, Philips ordered preparations for an attack. Arranging his men perpendicular to the railroad tracks on the east side of town, Brigadier General Charles D. Anderson's 3rd Brigade, Georgia Militia, was placed on the left, just north of the tracks. Brigadier General Henry K. McKay's 4th Brigade was placed on Anderson's right, just south of the tracks, and Philips's own 2nd Brigade (now commanded by Colonel James N. Mann) moved in reserve to the rear of McKay. Evans's State Line troopers moved forward in the very center as skirmishers, and Cook's small battalions took the extreme right of the line. Anderson's battery set up just north of the tracks near the center of the line.

Facing Philips's small command was Walcutt's strong 2nd Brigade, 1st Division, XV Corps, consisting of no fewer than seven reduced-strength infantry regiments (the 12th, 97th, and 100th Indiana; 40th and 103rd Illinois; 6th Iowa; and 46th Ohio), two cavalry regiments (5th Kentucky and 9th Pennsylvania), and Captain Albert Arndt's Battery B, 1st Michigan Artillery. In all, about 4,000 mostly ill-trained and poorly equipped Georgia troops faced about 3,000 well-armed, well-entrenched, and combat-hardened veteran Union troops.

About 2:30 P.M. Philips ordered an all-out assault, and the ragged force began moving smartly across the open field toward the Union entrenchments. Major Asias Willison of the 103rd Illinois wrote in his after-action report what happened next:

> As soon as they came within range of our muskets, a most terrific fire was poured into their ranks, doing fearful execution . . . still they moved forward, and came within 45 yards of our works. Here they attempted to reform their line, but so destructive was the fire that they were compelled to retire.

While most of Philips's militiamen were being blown apart behind them, the State Line charged up the slope toward the Union position, only to be thrown back to the wooded base. The State Line charged several more times, meeting the same result, until Evans was seriously wounded and all retired from the field.

Most of the militiamen never got closer than 50 yards to the Union position but bravely held their ground and returned fire until dusk. Philips then ordered a retreat off the field, and the shattered ranks limped slowly back into Macon. Left behind were 51 killed, 422 wounded, and 9 missing. The Union lines were never in any real danger of being breached, but losses amounted to 13 killed, 79 wounded, and 2 missing in the brief fight. Walcutt himself was among the wounded and had to be carried off the field during the engagement, to be replaced by Colonel Robert F. Catterson.

SHERMAN DRIVES ON

With the pitiful remnants of Philips's command safely back inside Macon's defense by 2:00 A.M. on November 23, there was literally nothing standing between Sherman and any path he might choose to take next. That morning he issued new orders for all four corps to march east, the southern wing to head straight down the Georgia Central Railroad tracks toward Millen (near Buckhead Creek), while the northern wing and attached cavalry were to follow roads on the north side of the tracks. Their target was Camp Lawton, sometimes called Magnolia Springs, to rescue the estimated 11,000 Union prisoners recently brought there from Andersonville.

Early on the morning of November 24 the grand march resumed. Strangely, Milledgeville was left relatively intact, although all the government buildings, libraries, and some churches were ransacked and desecrated, and, once again, anything of value went along with the blue-suits.

Confederate resistance to this part of the march was nearly nonexistent, and those who did show up were grossly outnumbered. A good example is the defense of the Oconee River bridge near Oconee, where a force of exactly 186 men, the remnants of three separate commands, stood ready to keep Sherman from crossing. Even with nearly 1,000 cavalrymen from Wheeler's command backing them up, more than 30,000 Union soldiers moved like a blue tidal wave down the road to crush them. Fortunately, cooler heads prevailed, and the tiny command was withdrawn before it made contact.

Sherman still today has a reputation as a thief and firebug in certain parts of Georgia, and this section of the grand march is where it was earned. All along, "authorized" foraging parties had scoured the countryside, collecting food for both soldiers and animals, and "jes' a lil'" booty for themselves while they were at it. With military opposition nearly nonexistent, and no doubt with the blessings of many veteran officers, roving gangs of "bummers" roamed the countryside, casually stealing or destroying whatever caught their fancy. A 40-mile-wide path between Milledgeville and Millen was stripped down nearly to the roots; one traveler who crossed this area shortly after Sherman's passing remarked that everything down to and including fence posts had either been taken or burned.

The destruction the Union troops were creating started to disturb many Union officers, although Sherman himself wasn't among them. His attitude was that the Georgians had "forced" him to sponsor such actions by virtue of their secession and that he only regretted that he "had" to do such acts. The situation deteriorated so much at one point that even Sherman's blindly admiring aide, Major Henry Hitchcock, noted in his memoirs that "I am bound to say I think Sherman lacking in enforcing discipline."

Millen

Major General Blair's XVII Corps arrived in Millen completely without resistance on December 1. Brigadier General Judson Kilpatrick's 3rd Cavalry Division, moving rapidly to the north on Sherman's personal order, arrived at the site of Camp Lawton on November 27, after a fierce resistance

by Wheeler's cavalry, only to discover that the Union prisoners had been moved again, this time to a rude camp near Blackshear, 10 miles northeast of Waycross and the Okefenokee Swamp in deep southeastern Georgia.

Sherman entered Millen on December 3 with the rest of his army. Deeply angered that he had been unable to rescue the POWs, he issued orders to march directly on Savannah beginning the next morning and took out his wrath on the small town as they left. In a classic understatement, he mentioned in his memoirs, "I caused the fine depot of Millen to be destroyed, and other damage done . . . "

THE LAST OF THE MARCH

Leaving Millen on the morning of December 4, all four corps marched directly toward Savannah and arrived nearly unmolested on the outskirts of the city between December 10 and 12. Along the way, two separate Confederate defenses were mounted with what remained of the Georgia Militia and the Georgia State Line supplemented by Wheeler's cavalry and some local defense forces. On both occasions their commanders elected to withdraw in the face of such overwhelming Union opposition.

Savannah's defenses were formidable, stretching more than 13 miles from the Savannah River to the Little Ogeechee River and manned by just under 10,000 men—the bare remnants of every militia and state defense force that could be scraped together. In addition, more than 50 artillery pieces with a fair supply of ammunition sat in the ring of strong earthwork fortifications.

Sherman had a serious problem by this time; his supplies of food and clothing were running critically low, and there was nothing much in the surrounding salt marshes and swamps that he could send foraging parties out for. He desperately needed to make contact with the Union Navy, lying just off the coast, but the two possible river approaches were both guarded by powerful Confederate fortifications. Needing the supply line open and open fast, he personally ordered Brigadier General William Babcock Hazen to take his 2nd Division (XV Corps) down to the Ogeechee River 14 miles below Savannah, assault and take the Confederate fort there, and open the river to the Union Navy.

Fort McAllister

Fort McAllister, on Genesis Point guarding the entrance to the Ogeechee River, had been designed by Major John McCrady, chief engineer for the state of Georgia, in the late spring of 1861. Ordinarily, a massive masonry fort like Fort Pulaski or Jackson east of Savannah would be desirable, but these were time-, money-, and manpower-intensive projects, and McCrady had none of those resources.

Instead he settled on a star-shaped, four-gun emplacement earthwork fort with walls 20 feet tall and 17 feet thick, originally intended to be equipped with four 32-pounder smoothbore cannons. The walls originally only faced the river, and a large earthen bomb-proof stood behind the gun emplacements to serve as a hospital. On June 7, 1861, the DeKalb Rifles, Company A, 1st Georgia Infantry Regiment under Lieutenant Alfred L. Hartridge was sent in to build and man the structure.

Having an infantry company build and man an artillery post strikes one as an odd move, but the relatively few trained cannoneers were needed at posts where actual combat was expected. At backwa-

ter posts like Fort McAllister, infantry companies were customarily sent in to while away the war years.

Hartridge's men did a very good job, clearing away the thick forest for a mile behind the fort site to provide clear lanes of fire and almost immediately setting about building up and improving the design.

FORT MCALLISTER IN COMBAT

By the time of Sherman's arrival, the earthwork fort had been tripled in size and assaulted without success some seven separate times by Union gunboats. The DeKalb Rifles had long since departed for hotter action to the north, and a new commander had taken over, Major George W. Anderson. The garrison now consisted of about 230 men of the Emmet Rifles and the Georgia Reserves, along with real artillerymen of Captain Nicholas B. Clinch's Georgia Light Artillery Battery.

The post by this time looked quite different, having been expanded into a five-sided fort 650 feet long and 750 feet wide, with a dry ditch studded with sharpened stake abatis surrounding it. More and heavier artillery had been brought in; two 32-pounder rifled guns, three 10-inch Columbiads, and three 8-inch Columbiads guarded the river approaches. To guard against expected infantry attacks, a rear wall slightly smaller than the front wall had been built and 12 field artillery pieces mounted atop it. To complete the armament, a 10-inch Tredegar Seacoast Mortar was mounted just outside the main defense walls.

The reluctant decision to make the post an earthwork arrangement proved most fortuitous. Fort Pulaski, a few miles to the north and long regarded as an impregnable guardian of the northern approaches to Savannah, had been breached by heavy rifled cannon fire on April 11, 1862, and surrendered after a mere 30 hours of shelling. The earth walls of Fort McAllister were nearly impervious to incoming fire, the walls either deflecting or swallowing up the Union artillery fire. Even if a shell buried deep in the earth before exploding, repairing the crater was a simple matter of shoveling a few wheelbarrow loads of dirt back in it. The thousand-year era of the heavy masonry fort had come to an end.

HAZEN'S APPROACH

Sherman's choice of the West Point graduate's division to assault the Confederate fort was not a random one; not only had Hazen proven to be a capable and brave battlefield commander, but the 2nd Division was the same that Sherman had commanded at Vicksburg and Shiloh, one in which he "felt a special pride and confidence." Hazen was ordered to take the fort as soon as possible, and he left the morning of December 13, marching rapidly down the old Hardwicke Road (now Georgia Highway 144).

Shortly after noon, Hazen reached the causeway leading out to the fort and promptly captured the lone Confederate sentry posted there, Private Thomas Mills. After his capture, Mills revealed that his unit had placed "torpedoes," or buried shells that exploded when stepped on, all along the soft sand causeway. Hazen ordered his men to immediately search for and dig up the land mines, delaying his approach to the fort.

By the time the road was made safe and the rest of his command came into line, it was after 4:30 P.M. Leaving nine regiments behind as reserves, Hazen moved the other nine regiments forward until they were arrayed in a semicircle around the isolated post, but no closer than 600 yards out. Confederate guns opened up, but with little effect. Union skirmishers ran forward, closing to within 200 yards of the fort and began a damaging fire on the gunners. One of the fort's major weaknesses was the fact that all the guns were mounted en barbette, or up on top of the ramparts, leaving the gunners exposed to rifle fire.

THE BATTLE FOR FORT MCALLISTER

Sherman, watching the action from atop a rice mill across the river, was nearly beside himself with impatience. As the afternoon wore on and dusk approached, he had a signal sent over to Hazen: "You must carry the fort by assault tonight, if possible." A few minutes later a reply came back: "I am ready and will assault at once!" At 4:45 P.M. Hazen ordered a general assault to begin.

As the Union infantry sprang to their feet and began moving toward the fort at the double-quick, a furious rain of fire came from both sides. Moving up close to the ramparts, the Union men had almost entered the outer defense bands when huge explosions rocked the earth; more torpedoes had been buried all around the fort in the soft sand, making them nearly impossible to spot. Forcing their way forward despite the deadly mines and deafening cannon fire to their front, the 47th Ohio quickly gained the west wall and began running down it, looking for an opening to enter the fort. At the far northwestern corner, they discovered that the line of abatis stopped above the high-tide mark (it was then low tide), and they quickly ran through the opening and up onto the ramparts.

Almost at the same moment, the 70th Ohio and 111th Illinois Regiments pushed through the tangle of fixed defenses and appeared atop the ramparts nearby, and the fight quickly escalated into a vicious hand-to-hand brawl. The Confederate garrison refused to surrender, even in the face of such overwhelming odds. As each artillery position was overrun, the cannoneers continued to resist with ramrods swung as clubs and even just their fists, until bayoneted or beaten to the ground by the swarming blue masses. Each bombproof emplacement had to be taken individually, and the fight ended only when every last Confederate was killed, wounded, or beaten into submission. Hazen stated in his after-action report that "...the line moved on without checking, over, under and through abatis, ditches, palisading and parapet, fighting the garrison through the fort to their bombproofs, from which they still fought and only succumbed as each man was individually overpowered."

Although the whole action took only 15 minutes to complete, the fight was somewhat more than the Union soldiers had expected. The resistance of Captain Nickolas B. Clinch, commanding Clinch's Light Battery, which was stationed on the landward side of the fort, was typical:

When [Clinch was] summoned to surrender by a Federal captain [Captain Stephen F. Grimes of the 48th Illinois], [he] responded by dealing a severe blow to the head with his sabre. (Captain Clinch had previously received two gunshot wounds in the arm.) Immediately a hand to hand fight ensued. Federal privates came to the assistance of their fellow officer, but the fearless Clinch continued the unequal contest until he fell bleeding from eleven wounds (three sabre wounds, six bayonet wounds, and two gun shot wounds), from which, after severe and protracted suffering, he has barely recovered. His conduct was so conspicuous, and his cool bravery so much admired, as to elicit the praise of the enemy and even of General Sherman himself.

Anderson had to know that his position had no hope of reinforcement from Hardee's troops inside Savannah, nor did he have any real chance of stopping Hazen's men from taking his post. However, in the archaic Southern fashion, he stood his ground and resisted until there was no one left standing. In his afteraction report he noted, "The fort was never surrendered. It was captured by overwhelming numbers."

With the fall of Fort McAllister, the March to the Sea for all practical purposes ended. By 5:00 P.M. Sherman was able to signal the route was clear to a navy steamer already coming up the river with badly needed supplies. Losses were high for such a short fight, with Hazen losing 24 killed and 110 wounded and Anderson losing 17 killed, 31 wounded, and all the rest made prisoner.

SAVANNAH

As soon as news reached Hardee of the fall of Fort McAllister, he knew that holding onto Savannah would be futile and began making preparations to evacuate his army into South Carolina. His engineers immediately set about making a series of pontoon bridges from the foot of West Broad Street, across the network of tidal rivers, to Hardeville on the South Carolina border. This escape route ran along the narrow top of Huger's Causeway (roughly the route that U.S. Highway 17 follows today). A thick layer of rice straw was put over the wooden planks of the bridges to deaden the sound of wagon and gun carriage wheels. All was ready by December 19, and everyone impatiently awaited Hardee's order to leave.

Meanwhile, back on the siege line, Union gunners had kept up a steady drumbeat of fire on the city since setting up on December 10. Sherman's engineers built a series of large, well-fortified gun emplacements for the large siege cannon they expected to receive via the navy in short order, and most began settling in for what was expected to be another long stand.

On December 17 Sherman sent a rather harsh note to Hardee demanding his immediate surrender, warning that he had plenty of large guns and ammunition and that unless quarter was given he would "make little effort to restrain my army burning to avenge the great national wrong they attach to Savannah and other large cities which have been so prominent in dragging our country into civil war."

Hardee, obviously bidding for a little more time, replied the next morning that he refused to surrender and indicated that if Sherman carried out his threats to ignore the conventions of war and carry out unrestrained rape and pillage, then Hardee would "deeply regret the adoption of any course by you that may force me to deviate from them in the future." For the time, this was a rather crude and uncivilized exchange of threats. Both men knew it—and neither was fully prepared to back them up.

To cover up his planned movement, Hardee requested what help was available from the Confederate Navy and sent three regiments of infantry to reinforce Wheeler's cavalry up on the line. Late on the afternoon of December 20, the Confederate ironclad *Savannah* steamed upriver a bit and began lobbing shells at the Union positions. As darkness fell, every heavy artillery position began shooting up what was left of their ammunition supply, heavy shells raining down with some accuracy on the Union positions for more than two hours.

While the shot, shell, and canister rounds kept the Union troops' heads down, Hardee began his retreat out of the city. All the field guns that could be moved left first, while work gangs set the remaining boats afire at their moorings. When the big guns' ammunition ran out, their crews spiked the barrels and watered down the remaining gunpowder in the magazines. Major General Ambrose R. Wright's division was the first to leave at about 8:00 P.M., followed by Major General Lafayette McLaw's division two hours later and Smith's Georgia Militia at 11:00 P.M.

Acting as the rear guard, the Georgia State Line, now under command of Colonel James D. Wilson, stayed in their skirmish line and, along with Wheeler's cavalry, kept up a steady fire toward the Union lines. When a signal rocket flared up about 1:00 A.M., both commands gradually ceased fire, and one company at a time left the trenches and quickly moved across the bridges into South Carolina. The bridges were then sunk in place or cut loose from their moorings by engi-

neers, the last link setting adrift at 5:40 A.M. on December 21.

Union Troops Enter the City

When all firing ceased about 3:00 A.M., forward skirmishers of a dozen different Union regiments cautiously moved forward and dropped into the newly abandoned Confederate positions. Sending word back of their discovery, a general advance was soon ordered, and Sherman's "bummers" began moving east into the city itself. The advance was led by Brigadier General John W. Geary's 2nd Division (XX Corps). About 4:30 A.M., as the last of Hardee's men were filtering across the river to the north, Colonel Henry A. Barnum of the 3rd Brigade, Geary's division, encountered Mayor Richard D. Arnold of Savannah near the intersection of Louisville and Augusta Roads. There the mayor handed the Union colonel a formal letter of surrender of the city, addressed to Sherman:

Savannah, Dec. 21, 1864

Maj. Gen. W. T. Sherman, Commanding U.S. Forces near Savannah:

Sir: The city of Savannah was last night evacuated by Confederate military and is now defenseless. As chief magistrate of the city I respectfully request your protection of the lives and private property of the citizens and of our women and children. Trusting that this appeal to your generosity and humanity may favorably influence your action, I have the honor to be, your obedient servant,

R. D. Arnold
Mayor of Savannah

Barnum's men continued into the city, where as the rosy light of dawn appeared

i

The last state to be rid of its military occupation by the Union army was Georgia, in February 1870.

over the horizon, the Stars and Stripes were once again raised over the U.S. Customs house. Two brigades moved on east to take the newly abandoned post at old Fort Jackson. As they entered and raised the national banner on the ramparts, the *Savannah*, retreating downriver, lobbed a few shells their way. Union batteries returned fire, but these last shots of the campaign had no real effect on either side.

Sherman had been at nearby Hilton Head Island conferring with navy officers on the next plan of action and did not return to the city until late on the night of December 21. Making his headquarters in the large, comfortable Green-Meldrin House at Madison Square (still existent), he sent a telegram from the parlor to President Lincoln the next day:

Savannah, Ga., Dec. 22, 1864

His Excellency President Lincoln,

I beg to present to you, as a Christmas gift, the city of Savannah, with 150 heavy guns and plenty of ammunition, and also about 25,000 bales of cotton.

W. T. Sherman
Major General

THE TOUR

It is difficult today to travel directly down all of Sherman's path between Atlanta and Savannah, bearing in mind that it was a 40- to 60-mile-wide route filled with wandering, looting bummers. Most of his route went through what is today very lightly traveled east central Georgia south of I-20 and north of Interstate 16. To get a flavor of the terrain, we suggest you travel Georgia Highway 24 east out of Milledgeville,

which lies over many of the original roadbeds that Davis's XIV Corps traveled. This route passes through Sandersonville, Louisville, Waynesboro, and close to Sylvania; to complete that corps' march route, take Georgia Highway 21 south from the intersection at Newington to Interstate 95 just outside Savannah.

The southern part of the right wing, Blair's XVII Corps, marched a route that is closely paralleled in places by Georgia Highway 57 east from the Griswoldville area. This route passes through Gordon, Irwinton, and Wrightsville before entering Swainsboro; there take U.S. Highway 80 east to Savannah to complete the march route.

If you would rather skip the scenery and travel on to Savannah, the best and quickest route is I-16 east from Macon. The trip should take between two and three hours, depending on what warp factor you are traveling. I-16 between Macon and Savannah is without a doubt one of the lightest-traveled interstates in the eastern United States and has few, widely spaced amenities. Although a few other exits have one or two gas stations or perhaps a small restaurant, most food, gas, and lodging facilities can be found at the exits for Dublin and Metter (exits 51 and 104, respectively). Be very aware that Georgia state troopers are quite active along I-16, as this highway gained a reputation in the past as a speeder's dream because it is a mostly level straightaway. We have noticed quite a number of troopers recently around the Dublin and Metter vicinities and around the I-95 intersection just west of Savannah.

The "scenic" route passes through a very lightly populated part of the state, and food and gas are even more of an iffy proposition outside the few small towns. Make sure to fill up before you go! It is a good idea to stop along Riverside Drive in Macon, which parallels I-75 south of Interstate 575 and north of I-16, because once you exit onto I-16 you will rapidly leave the commercial center of Macon.

Getting There: Allatoona Pass

The battlefield is accessible from I-75 north from Atlanta. You will take exit 283 (Emerson-Allatoona Road), turn right (east), and go about 2 miles to the pass area. On the way you will cross over a set of railway tracks—the modern relocation of the tracks the soldiers were fighting over.

MODERN TIMES

Nearly all the area covered by the battle of Allatoona Pass is today heavily overgrown or equally heavily developed, and the east side of the battlefield is under the murky waters of Lake Allatoona. The dug railroad gap is also heavily overgrown, and it is difficult to get a clear picture of the tactical situation, but at least one period structure remains. The Mooney House, the yellow-and-white, tin-roofed structure in the sharp curve in the road at the pass entrance, was used as a field hospital during the battle and can be seen in a well-known photograph of the area taken just after the battle by George M. Barnard. A small marker next to the house's mailbox indicates the location of a mass grave of soldiers who died in the hospital following the brief battle; it is now partially covered by the road and driveway.

There is a small parking area with two historic markers across the street from the Mooney House, which indicate quite well the 1864 layout and tactical situation. One contains a fair reproduction of the Barnard photo, which gives landmarks still visible today. The Star Fort still exists, although overgrown and in deteriorating condition on top of the left peak of the railway cut. A warning: Both the fort and the Mooney House are private property and not open to the public; please be respectful and observe them from the parking lot. The eastern redoubt, on top of the right peak, is on U.S. Army Corps of Engineers property and can be accessed by a steep, partially overgrown path just inside the entrance to the pass walking north.

Satan is a pretty bad fellow, but he can't give us worse than we got at Chickamauga.

Wounded Union soldier, to a "fire and brimstone" preacher who was visiting his hospital bed

POINTS OF INTEREST

For suggested places to visit in and around Atlanta, please see the recommendations in our chapter on Dalton to Jonesboro. We emphasize the near necessity for anyone even remotely interested in the war to visit the Atlanta History Center in Buckhead and the Atlanta Cyclorama at Grant Park.

ACCOMMODATIONS

Atlanta is a major tourist and convention destination, and the hospitality industry in Fulton County alone employs more than 115,000 workers and pays more than $215 million in taxes to local governments. Needless to say, just about any chain hotel or motel in every price range is readily available. The Downtown Connector, the merging of I-75 and I-85 through downtown Atlanta, is the major corridor to all the listed amenities, and a short drive out in (literally) any direction on the three highways (including I-20) is the best bet for lower priced chain establishments at nearly any exit. The following recommendations are a tiny sampling of what is available south of the downtown area itself; for a fuller listing, may we suggest *Insiders' Guide to Atlanta*. Tax runs in the 13 percent range.

Country Inn and Suites $-$$
759 Pollard Boulevard, Atlanta
(404) 658-1961,
You can't get much closer to big-league action than this 87-room hotel just up the street from Turner Field, the home of the Atlanta Braves. The hotel has an outdoor pool and a weight room and is convenient to downtown, the Georgia capitol, city hall, and the Atlanta Cyclorama. It is just off I-75/85 and I-20 where they meet just

Sherman's General Orders from Atlanta

Sherman wrote in his memoirs regarding the two general orders he gave for the conduct of his March to the Sea that "no account of that historic event is perfect without them," so here they are in their entirety.

Special Field Orders, No. 119
Headquarters Military Division of the Mississippi, in the Field, Kingston, Georgia, November 8, 1864

The general commanding deems it proper at this time to inform the officers and men of the Fourteenth, Fifteenth, Seventeenth, and Twentieth Corps, that he has organized them into an army for a special purpose, well known to the War Department from our present base, and a long and difficult march to a new one. All the chances of war have been considered and provided for, as far as human sagacity can. All he asks of you is to maintain that discipline, patience, and courage, which have characterized you in the past; and he hopes, through you, to strike a blow at our enemy that will have a material effect in producing what we all so much desire, his complete overthrow. Of all things, the most important is, that the men, during marches and in camp, keep their places and do not scatter about as stragglers or foragers, to be picked up by a hostile people in detail. It is also of the utmost importance that our wagons should not be loaded with any thing but provisions and ammunition. All surplus servants, non-combatants, and refugees, should now go to the rear, and none should be encouraged to encumber us on the march. At some future time we will be able to provide for the poor whites and blacks who seek to escape the bondage under which they are now suffering. With these few simple cautions, he hopes to lead you to achievements equal in importance to those of the past.

> By order of Major-General W. T. Sherman,
> L. M. Dayton, Aide-de-Camp.

Special Field Orders, No. 120
Headquarters Military Division of the Mississippi, in the Field, Kingston, Georgia, November 9, 1864

1. For the purpose of military operations, this army is divided into two wings, viz.: The right wing, Major-General O. O. Howard, commanding, composed of the Fifteenth and Seventeenth Corps; the left wing, Major-General H. W. Slocum commanding, composed of the Fourteenth and Twentieth Corps.

2. The habitual order of march will be, wherever practicable, by four roads, as nearly parallel as possible, and converging at points hereafter to be indicated in orders. The cavalry, Brigadier-General Kilpatrick commanding, will receive special orders from the commander-in-chief.

3. There will be no general train of supplies, but each corps will have its

ammunition-train and provision-train, distributed habitually as follows: Behind each regiment should follow one wagon and one ambulance; behind each brigade should follow a due proportion of ammunition-wagons, provision-wagons, and ambulances. In case of danger, each corps commander should change this order of march, by having his advance and rear brigades unencumbered by wheels. The separate columns will start habitually at 7:00 A.M., and make about fifteen miles per day, unless otherwise fixed in orders.

4. The army will forage liberally on the country during the march. To this end, each brigade commander will organize a good and sufficient foraging party, under the command of one or more discreet officers, who will gather, near the route traveled, corn or forage of any kind, meat of any kind, vegetables, corn-meal, or whatever is needed by the command, aiming at all times to keep in the wagons at least ten days' provisions for his command, and three days' forage. Soldiers must not enter the dwellings of the inhabitants, or commit any trespass; but, during a halt or camp, they may be permitted to gather turnips, potatoes, and other vegetables, and to drive in stock in sight of their camp. To regular foraging-parties must be intrusted the gathering of provisions and forage, at any distance from the road traveled.

5. To corps commanders alone is intrusted the power to destroy mills, houses, cotton-gins, etc.; and for them this general principle is laid down: In districts and neighborhoods where the army is unmolested, no destruction of such property should be permitted; but should guerrillas or bushwhackers molest our march, or should the inhabitants burn bridges, obstruct roads, or otherwise manifest local hostility, then army commanders should order and enforce a devastation more or less relentless, according to the measure of such hostility.

6. As for horses, mules, wagons, etc., belonging to the inhabitants, the cavalry and artillery may appropriate freely and without limit; discriminating, however, between the rich, who are usually hostile, and the poor and industrious, usually neutral or friendly. Foraging-parties may also take mules or horses, to replace the jaded animals of their trains, or to serve as pack-mules for the regiments of brigades. In all foraging, of whatever kind, the parties engaged will refrain from abusive or threatening language, and may, where the officer in command thinks proper, give written certificates of the facts, but no receipts; and they will endeavor to leave with each family a reasonable portion for their maintenance.

7. Negroes who are able-bodied and can be of service to the several columns may be taken along; but each army commander will bear in mind that the question of supplies is a very important one, and that his first duty is to see to those who bear arms.

8. The organization, at once, of a good pioneer battalion for each army corps,

composed if possible of Negroes, should be attended to. This battalion should follow the advance-guard, repair roads and double them if possible, so that the columns will not be delayed after reaching bad places. Also, army commanders should practice the habit of giving the artillery and wagons the road, marching their troops on one side, and instruct their troops to assist wagons at steep hills or bad crossings of streams.

9. Captain O. M. Poe, chief-engineer, will assign to each wing of the army a pontoon-train, fully equipped and organized; and the commanders thereof will see to their being properly protected at all times.

> By order of Major-General W. T. Sherman,
> L. M. Dayton, Aide-de-Camp.

south of downtown. Guests enjoy complimentary continental breakfasts and free local phone calls.

Renaissance Concourse Hotel $$$–$$$$
One Hartsfield Centre Parkway, Atlanta
(404) 209-9999, (800) 228-9290

Just seven minutes from the airport, this hotel has 380 rooms and 7 suites. Call from the airport to receive direct pickup services when you arrive. When departing, the free shuttle takes you to MARTA (the Atlanta–metro area public transportation service) from the hotel so that you may catch the train directly to the airport. Each room has a coffeemaker, cable TV, and a minibar. The hotel's health club has a swimming pool, sauna, and whirlpool open to all guests. There's a restaurant serving breakfast, lunch, and supper; a bar; and a lobby gift shop.

RESTAURANTS

As a primary travel destination and a large, well-populated urban center all in one, Atlanta has more than its fair share of eating establishments. More than 7,500 exist in the 10-county metro area; with so many newly built restaurants opening nearly daily, the five major newspaper

reviewers admit regularly that they can't keep up. A fair warning, though: Nearly as many close just as quickly, which makes the eating-out scene here quite dynamic. Again, the following is a bare sample. For the best and most recently updated listings, look for a copy of the Friday or Saturday edition of the *Atlanta Journal-Constitution* or (preferably) a copy of *Creative Loafing* (free), which shows up in green-colored newspaper racks on Wednesday. The price range in each restaurant listing gives the cost of dinner for two, excluding cocktails, beer or wine, appetizer, dessert, tax, and tip.

The Varsity $
61 North Avenue NW, Atlanta
(404) 881-1706

The one and only, the Varsity is a long-beloved Atlanta institution. At the corner of Spring Street and North Avenue, the original Varsity (there are Junior Varsitys in the Cheshire Bridge Road area of Atlanta, in Norcross, and in Athens) is just across the North Avenue bridge from Georgia Tech. It opened in 1928 and claims the distinction of being the world's largest drive-in. Every day, this single restaurant serves up to 2 miles of hot dogs, a ton of onion rings, and 5,000 fried pies. Friendly, sometimes eccentric carhops will bring your food out to your car, or you can eat inside in one of several "TV rooms." The serving counters here are a beehive of activity; the slogan is "Have your money in your hand and your order in your mind." The onion rings may just be the best on the planet. The Varsity does not serve alcohol.

As native Atlantans, we consider the Varsity to be an essential part of our lives and experience digestive problems without regular applications of its food. Credit cards not accepted.

Atkins Park   **$-$$**
794 North Highland Avenue NE, Atlanta
(404) 876-7249
With a liquor license first issued in 1927, Atkins Park has the distinction of being the oldest bar in Atlanta. It hearkens back to the age of dark, wood-paneled, beery neighborhood bars. A perennial favorite of the Virginia-Highlands neighborhood, Atkins Park offers a changing menu, including herbed grouper, rosemary ocean scallops, pasta, and burgers. Atkins Park is open nightly until 3:30 A.M. and serves brunch on Saturday and Sunday until 3:00 P.M.; when available, there is free parking in the rear.

Son's Place   **$**
100 Hurt Street, Atlanta
(404) 581-0530
Son's Place traces its lineage back to the defunct Burton's Grill, a soul food landmark in Atlanta, where the late Deacon Burton, regal in his tall chef's hat, presided over a small army of women (all of whom he called "mama") who cooked up the best skillet-fried chicken in town. The vegetables, such as mashed potatoes, collard greens, and creamed corn, are deliciously flavored and thoroughly cooked in traditional Southern style. Son's is a favorite with everyone from media people to civil rights leaders. It's right beside the Inman Park/Reynoldstown MARTA station; breakfast and lunch are served Monday through Friday, and no alcohol is offered. Credit cards not accepted.

Getting There: Milledgeville

Milledgeville lies about 70 miles southeast of Atlanta, as the crow flies, and nearly equidistant between I–20 and I–16. The easiest route that stays fairly close to Sherman's march route is to take I–75 south from Atlanta to exit 205, turn left onto Georgia Highway 16, go east 22 miles to Monticello, staying on GA 16 another 18 miles to Eatonton, then right onto U.S. Highway 441 for 20 miles to Milledgeville. Be aware that while GA 16 is a relatively sedate route, both I–75 and US 441 feature very heavy, high-speed traffic.

POINTS OF INTEREST

Old Governor's Mansion
120 South Clark Street, Milledgeville
(478) 445-4545
Built in the Greek Revival style in 1838, this was the home of 10 Georgia governors, including Joseph Emerson Brown, who was arrested here by Union authorities in May 1865. Sherman rolled out his bedroll on the bare wooden floor downstairs to spend the night on November 23, remarking good naturedly how rude it was of Brown to have left before such a distinguished visitor had arrived!

At press time the mansion was closed for a $10.5-million renovation but scheduled to reopen in February 2005. Call to confirm hours and admission fees.

State Capitol Building
Statehouse Square, on campus
of Georgia Military College
210 East Greene Street, Milledgeville
(478) 445-2035
This imposing Gothic-style building is considered to be the oldest public building in the nation built in such a style. Begun and first used in 1803, the building served as the state capitol until 1863. The original structure was severely damaged in several post–Civil War fires and was restored to nearly original condition in

The last surviving Confederate general was Brigadier General John McCausland, who died in 1927 at the age of 91.

1943. Another restoration was completed in the fall of 2001.

Today this building is the main administration office for the Georgia Military Academy and has no original interior furnishings, decorations, or even period arrangement of rooms. Tours are available by special arrangement, but quite frankly the exterior is the only really interesting thing here.

The Gothic-style gates at the north and south entrances to the campus were constructed just after the war from bricks salvaged from the arsenal and powder magazine blown up by Sherman's troops.

Milledgeville Visitor Center
200 West Hancock Street, Milledgeville
(478) 452–4687, (800) 653–1804
We suggest a visit here for a copy of the excellent map and guide for a walking tour of the old part of town. Trolley tours are available here as well as information on the series of festivals held throughout the year.

Getting There: Griswoldville

Griswoldville is not only off the beaten path, it is downright difficult to find! The town was completely destroyed during Sherman's march, not resettled after the war, and does not appear on any present-day maps. The easiest route—easy being relative here—is to take I-16 east out of Macon and get off at exit 6, U.S. Highway 129 Alternate. Turn left (north) and go 3 miles to the intersection with US 80. A warning: Be careful not to turn at the rather confusing intersection just before this one—it will take you on US 80 west to Macon instead.

Turn right (east) on US 80, travel 2½ miles to the US 80/GA 57 split, and take the left fork onto GA 57. Continuing east, in about 3½ miles you will come across a Primitive Baptist Church on your left, with a historical marker in front with some details about the battle. This is not the site of the original town, although the sign seems to imply so. Travel farther east on GA 57 about another mile to an intersection with an unnamed, well-traveled paved road on the left (exactly 4⁴⁄₁₀ miles from the US 80/GA 57 split). Turn left onto Ridge Road and travel 1½ miles to the railroad tracks. Just before the tracks, you will see a small sign pointing to the new battlefield park, down a series of unnamed roads. The route is well signed, however, and easy to follow.

MODERN TIMES

On the right of the road at Griswoldville is a series of historical markers about the town and the battle and the site of a wartime church. The present-day Henderson Road Baptist Church across the road is on the site of the wartime pistol factory that produced about 3,500 Colt's Navy Repeaters and Brass-Framed Confederate Colts. The thickly wooded area on the south side of the tracks on both sides of the road was the main residential area of town.

The open fields to the east, about a half mile from town, is where the battle actually took place. They were taken over by a preservation group, and a new battlefield park was dedicated in 2000.

Getting There: Fort McAllister

Fort McAllister State Historic Park is relatively easy to find, especially considering the intricately undulating coastline and rivers in the area. Take I-95 south from Savannah to exit 40, and turn left onto GA 144. Travel east about 10 miles to Spur GA 144, turn left and go about 2 miles to the park. The route is well marked all the way from the interstate. There is a small gas station/convenience store at the latter intersection; otherwise, there are no amenities in the area.

Fort McAllister State Historic Park
3894 Fort McAllister Road
Richmond Hill
(912) 727–2339

This 1,700-acre park between the Ogeechee River and Red Bird Creek has two alluring identities: It's the site of the earthen fort that guarded the southern approach to the Savannah area, and it's a recreational area with amenities for campers and picnickers. These two attractions once existed as Fort McAllister State Historic Park and Richmond Hill State Park; in 1980 they were combined, and today the Georgia Department of Natural Resources operates the site. There is a $2.00 fee to enter the park, which is open 8:00 A.M. to 5:00 P.M. daily.

Fort McAllister is one of the best-preserved earthwork fortifications built by the Confederacy during the Civil War. The site was once owned by Henry Ford, who began an extensive restoration in the late 1930s; the fort eventually fell into the hands of the state of Georgia, which restored it to near its 1863–64 appearance.

You can wander around the walls and through the interior of the fort and look inside its central bombproof, but be careful not to climb on these earthen structures, which are extremely susceptible to erosion from foot traffic. Take the self-guided tour of the fort and check out a 32-pounder smoothbore gun that fired red-hot cannonballs and the furnace where these projectiles were heated; the reconstructed service magazine, which held shells, powder, and fuses for the rebels' 32-pounder rifled gun; and the fort's northwest angle, where the 47th Ohio Infantry Regiment placed the first U.S. flag planted on the parapets.

The fort site also has a museum containing Civil War shells and weapons; implements such as those used in the construction of the fort; artifacts from the Confederate blockade runner *Nashville*,

which was sunk in the Ogeechee by the Union ironclad *Montauk;* a diorama of the assault on the fort; and a display depicting life at the fort as experienced by its 230 defenders. Museum admission is $2.50 for adults, $2.00 for seniors, and $1.50 for children ages 6 to 18; children younger than 6 are admitted free. The park admission fee is counted as a credit toward these rates.

For day-trippers, the main attraction of the recreational area is the tree-filled picnic ground running along a high bluff overlooking the Ogeechee River. Tall pines and hardwoods make this a shady, serene spot for walking or sitting in a glider-type swing and watching the river flow by. You'll find 50 sites with picnic tables and grills, a fishing pier that extends out over the river, and plenty of rustic-looking playground equipment for the kids in this area, which borders the main road leading to the fort.

If you plan on making your visit to Richmond Hill–Liberty County last longer than a day and you like roughing it, consider staying at the park's Savage Island Campground, which has 65 campsites—50 for recreational vehicles and 15 with tent pads—all with water and electrical hookups, grills, and tables. Two comfort stations provide campers with toilets, heated showers, and washer/dryers, and the campground also has a playground, nature trail, and dock and boat ramp on Red Bird Creek. The RV sites rent for $19.00 a night, and the tent pads are $17.00 a night, with rates for senior citizens about $3.00 less.

Getting There: Savannah

Savannah is easily accessible from the interior of Georgia via I-16, which runs straight into the heart of the city. From the north or south, I-95 intersects I-16 about 8 miles west of town.

To get to the old section of town, simply stay on I-16 until it ends on Liberty Street, and turn left. This will take you straight to the Savannah Visitors Center and River Street. Most of the major attractions and historic sites are well marked and signed from this point.

POINTS OF INTEREST

Savannah Visitors Center & History Museum
301 and 303 Martin Luther King Jr. Boulevard, Savannah
(912) 944-0460, (912) 238-1779
Housed in the old Central Georgia Railroad Station, the visitor center is large and rather imposing, with a very helpful staff and a moderate selection of maps and brochures of local attractions. A large museum houses a nicely presented, small selection of artifacts from every phase of this city's long history, including uniforms and equipment belonging to Savannah's own regiments, as well as Forrest Gump's park bench. A short film gives a breathless overview of the area history but hardly touches on the Civil War period. A small bookstore and no fewer than three gift shops round out the offerings, and several tour companies load up just outside the side entrance. Admission to the visitor center is free; the museum and film are $4.00 for adults and teens, $3.00 for seniors and children 6 through 12. The center is open 9:00 A.M. to 5:00 P.M. daily.

Confederate Memorial
Located in Forsyth Park (on Bull Street between Gaston Street and Park Avenue) is the large, rather imposing monument honoring the area's Civil War dead. This is claimed to be the largest such memorial in the South and was the most expensive by a long shot. When unveiled in 1875, the original monument showcased two statues: *Judgement* and *Silence*. The public reaction to the gaudy original was harshly negative, and the monument quickly

underwent a multi-thousand-dollar renovation, unveiled again in 1879 with only a simple sculpture of a soldier on top. Used as a Union encampment during the occupation, today the park is the setting for quite a number of festivals and events.

Green-Meldrim House
St. Johns Church
14 West Macon Street, Savannah
(912) 233-3845
Built in Gothic Revival style in 1853 for wealthy cotton grower Charles Green, the house was offered to Sherman for his headquarters by the owner. Green was concerned that if Sherman did not use the structure, another Union general would, and he would "suffer the indignity of such a situation." The famous "Christmas gift" telegram was sent to Lincoln from the front parlor, where Sherman also learned of the death of his infant son Charles, born during the long Georgia campaign. Sherman never saw his son alive.

Today the home is owned by its neighbor, St. Johns Church, and serves as the parish house. The home is open for tours from 10:00 A.M. to 4:00 P.M. on Tuesday, Thursday, Friday, and Saturday; admission is $5.00 for adults and $2.00 for students.

Fort Jackson
1 Fort Jackson Road, Savannah
(912) 232-3945
Located 2½ miles from the center of town on the (only) road out to Tybee Island, this is the oldest standing brick fortress in the United States, built in 1808. The 20-foot-high walls contained five 32-pounder smoothbore cannon, one 32-pounder rifled gun, two 8-inch Columbiads, and one 12-pounder mountain howitzer, all manned during the war by the 22nd Battalion of Heavy Artillery commanded by Major Edward Clifford Anderson (later the Mayor of Savannah). A small museum inside houses displays centering on the Confederate naval history of the area, including several about the CSS *Georgia*, whose watery grave is marked by a red buoy about 300 yards away in the Savannah River.

---

i

The last words of Stonewall Jackson were "Let us cross the river and rest in the shade of those trees."

The only action here during the war came in a brief 1862 skirmish with two Union gunboats and when it was fired upon by the CSS *Savannah* as Union troops raised their flag atop it in December 1864. The fort is open 9:00 A.M. to 5:00 P.M. daily except Thanksgiving, Christmas, and New Year's Day; admission is $2.50 for adults and $2.00 for seniors, active military, and children 6 through 18.

ACCOMMODATIONS

Savannah is a city of great diversity, and that characteristic holds true when it comes to the accommodations it offers its visitors. Savannah has several hotels that are large and contemporary and others that are medium-size and quaint. It has motels that are moderately priced but comfortable and others where, for a few dollars more, you'll be awash in amenities. Many of the hotels and motels offer suites in addition to rooms with the standard two double beds or one king-size bed, and a couple of establishments have nothing but suites.

Each of the hotels and motels listed here accepts major credit cards and is wheelchair-accessible. Almost all have nonsmoking rooms, and most do not allow pets. All establishments have color cable TV; if you're looking for premium channels, a phone call might be in order.

The in-season generally runs from mid-March through October. Some establishments decrease their rates during the hot summer months, and others jack them up on weekends, so call in advance to ascertain how much you'll have to spend. If you're planning to stay here on St. Patrick's Day weekend, expect to fork out considerably more than you would at any other time of year and make reservations months in advance.

Best Western Historic District $–$$
412 West Bay Street, Savannah
(912) 233-1011
Once you arrive at the Best Western Historic District, you can park your car and leave it for the rest of your stay, according to the folks who run the 143-room motel. The Best Western fronts Bay Street, and the motel's rear building is on the western end of River Street, placing the three-story establishment about a block from the shops and restaurants along the river and in City Market. It's within walking distance of much of the Historic District. If you want to do your sightseeing while riding, hop on a tour bus or trolley at the motel's front door. There is a complimentary continental breakfast and a fenced-in pool for swimming and sunning on the River Street side of the property. Eighty-seven of the rooms have two full-size beds, and the rest have kings. Parking is free at this motel, which has been accommodating visitors to Savannah since the early 1970s.

DeSoto Hilton Hotel $$$$
15 East Liberty Street, Savannah
(912) 232-9000, (800) HILTONS
A $6 million renovation completed in the summer of 1997 left the 246-room DeSoto Hilton looking like . . . well, 6 million bucks. The extensive makeover gave the hotel an aura that's both classical and rich: The lobby, hallways, and rooms are adorned with white columns, dark wood paneling, and burgundy and forest-green furnishings. The 15-story hotel stands in the midst of the Historic District, and the views from rooms on the upper floors, particularly those with balconies, are spectacular. The concierge floor—the 13th, numbered as such by hotel officials apparently unconcerned with superstition—offers what staff members call the "skyline view." You'll pay $30 extra to stay there, but you'll get the view, a room featuring deluxe amenities such as the Hilton's trademark terry-cloth bathrobes, and the use of a private lounge serving continental breakfast in the morning and drinks and hors d'oeuvres in the evening. Step out on the balcony of the lounge and enjoy a panoramic look at the graceful Eugene Talmadge Memorial Bridge and Savannah's riverfront. If you really want to

CLOSE-UP

Fort Pulaski National Monument

Construction of this massive fortress began in 1829, partially under the direction of a new graduate from West Point, 2nd Lieutenant Robert E. Lee. The 25-foot-high, 7½-foot-thick walls required 18 years, 25 million bricks, and the then-princely sum of $1 million to complete. The "Third System" fort was armed with 48 heavy guns manned by 385 officers and men of the 1st Regiment of Georgia Volunteers and the 25th Regiment of Georgia Regulars. Five 8-inch and four 10-inch Columbiads, one 24-pounder Blakely rifle, and two 10-inch seacoast mortars stood on the ramparts facing Tybee Island; in the casements below, one 8-inch Columbiad and four 32-pounder guns faced the seaward island. In batter-ies outside the wall stood two 12-inch and one 10-inch seacoast mortars to add to the fire that could be directed against any seaward Union attack.

The massive walls were thought to be impregnable to artillery fire, the only danger of capture coming from a protracted siege. Post Commander Colonel Charles H. Olmstead carefully laid in over six months' worth of rations to forestall this possibility.

Union troops landed and took over the abandoned emplacements on Tybee Island on November 24, 1861, and soon began bringing in heavy guns to deal with Fort Pulaski. Secretly constructing 11 batteries on and around the island, by April 1862, Major General Quincy A. Gill-

stay in style, request a "corner king"—a room with a king-size bed, balcony, two large corner windows, and a bathroom equipped with a double vanity. You can dine on the premises at Magnolia Restaurant, which serves breakfast, lunch, and dinner Southern-style, and you can unwind at the Lion's Den lounge, where the bar brings back memories of TV's *Cheers* and the library is stocked with real books.

The hotel pool is on a second-floor deck that can accommodate outdoor gatherings of as many as 150 people. The Hilton has 19,000 square feet of meeting space indoors in the form of executive board suites with seating for 5 to 30 people; the Harborview Room, whose 15th-floor location makes it the highest meeting room in the city; and a 5,408-square-foot ballroom with 18-foot ceilings and elaborate crystal chandeliers. Also available for get-togethers is a recently refurbished atrium on the hotel's ground floor. The Hilton was built in 1968 on the site of the DeSoto Hotel, which was constructed in 1890 and was a Savannah landmark for decades. A sitting room off the lobby of the Hilton affords guests a glimpse of the old hotel—the walls are covered with memorabilia, including framed banquet programs from visits by several U.S. presidents. Covered, secured parking is available for $7.00 a day, and valet service is $10.00. There is also a limousine shuttle service.

Courtyard Savannah Midtown   **$$$$**
6703 Abercorn Street, Savannah
(912) 354-7878, (800) 321-2211
The Marriott's Courtyard Savannah Midtown stands between two of the city's

more, now in command on Tybee Island, was ready to begin his assault on the massive fortress. In battery were 36 heavy guns, including a new weapon, the James rifled cannon.

With all in place, Gillmore called for the fort's surrender. Olmstead merely replied, "I am here to defend the fort, not surrender it." Within minutes of the reply, at 8:10 P.M. on April 10, 1862, Gillmore ordered his batteries to open fire. Five James rifles (two 84-pounders, two 64-pounders, and one 48-pounder) along with 15 slightly smaller cannon and 14 heavy mortars fired a total of 5,275 shots and shells at the fort in the next 31 hours.

With the massive walls actually breached by the new rifled cannon in several places, his rampart guns knocked off their mounts, and useless and solid

shot threatening to penetrate to the powder magazines, at 2:00 P.M. on April 11, Olmstead raised the white flag of surrender. The thousand-year era of masonry fortresses as main defenses came to a sudden end.

The old, still-battered fort is now restored and operated by the National Park Service and open for tours. A small museum with a good bookstore contains a bare handful of artifacts and some reasonably well-preserved regimental battle flags, and there are several rather nice mini-museums within casements of the fort itself. The fort is open during spring, summer, and fall from 9:00 A.M. to 7:00 P.M. daily. Winter hours are 9:00 A.M. to 5:00 P.M. daily. Admission is $3.00 for adults.

busiest thoroughfares, Abercorn Street and White Bluff Road, but the three-story motel's beautifully landscaped grounds will give you a feeling of being away from the madding crowd. The centerpiece of the motel is the tree-filled courtyard with its quaint gazebo and swimming pool. Just off the pool is an enclosed whirlpool surrounded by lots of space for lounging, and a recently renovated fitness room near the lobby sports all-new exercise equipment. The Courtyard's large dining area is open for breakfast, with a full meal and continental servings available. There are 144 interior rooms including 12 suites, and all have sleeper sofas. Rooms on the upper floors open onto balconies. There are two meeting rooms, each of which can accommodate 24 persons seated at tables.

La Quinta Inn $–$$
6805 Abercorn Street, Savannah
(912) 355–3004

La Quinta opened in the late 1970s and is one of the older motels on Savannah's main drag, Abercorn Street (although the rooms were remodeled in 1996). With its red-tile roofs and stucco exterior, the motel has the distinctive Southwestern appearance of all La Quinta Inns and espouses the chain's credo of providing spacious, comfortable rooms and "100 percent guest satisfaction." The two-story motel has 154 rooms with kings and doubles housed in two buildings that ramble over nicely landscaped grounds between Abercorn and White Bluff Road. The outdoor pool is tucked in a secluded nook set way back off the street, and there is HBO on the tube. A complimentary continental

Fleshing Out the Family Tree

To find the military records of an ancestor, you need his name, state, regiment, and company, if possible. Then contact the following office and request NATF Form 80: General Reference Branch (NNRG-P), National Archives and Records Administration, Seventh and Pennsylvania Avenue, Washington, DC 20408; e-mail: inquire@arch2.nara.gov

Be sure to give your name, snail-mail address, and phone number if ordering by e-mail. Always ask for at least three copies of the form.

breakfast is available from 6:00 until 10:00 A.M. each morning in an area off the lobby. La Quinta accepts pets weighing 20 pounds and less.

RESTAURANTS

Your taste buds will be glad they came to Savannah—but your waistline might not be. The city offers a quantity and variety of restaurants completely out of proportion to its size. The local specialties lean heavily toward seafood, naturally, with shrimp fresh off the boats a particular favorite.

Williams Seafood Restaurant $$–$$$
8010 Tybee Road, Savannah
(912) 897–2219

Members of the Williams family have been providing Savannahians with seafood since 1936, when Tom Williams began selling the fish and crabs he caught while tending the bridge over the Bull River on the road to Tybee Island. Tom's wife, Leila, developed a special recipe for deviled crab, and sales to motorists headed to and from the beach boomed; the Williamses opened a roadside stand and eventually a restaurant near the bridge. On the site of that original spot is the existing Williams Seafood Restaurant, operated by a third generation of the Williams family.

The deviled crab is still on the menu. Other favorites of the families who have made Williams a regular part of their lives through the years are the shrimp and flounder. This large, unpretentious-looking restaurant seats upwards of 500 people and also serves steak, hamburger, and chicken. Beer and wine are available, as are catering and banquet facilities. The restaurant is open for lunch and dinner.

Williams is just off US 80 at the western end of the newest bridge over the Bull River. Remnants of the bridge Tom Williams once tended can be seen nearby.

I worked night and day for twelve years to prevent the war, but I could not. The North was mad and blind, would not let us govern ouselves, and so the war came. Now it must go on until the last man of this generation falls in his tracks and his children seize his musket and fight our battles.

President Jefferson Davis, Confederate States of America, in a private letter, July 17, 1864

Crystal Beer Parlor $
301 West Jones Street, Savannah
(912) 443–9200

We go to the Crystal for the onion rings and the burgers, which are made from fresh sirloin ground in the beer parlor's kitchen, but there are many other selections on the menu—crab stew, shrimp-salad sandwiches, chili-dog platters, hot roast beef sandwiches, and baked stuffed flounder.

The Crystal is a local landmark, having been a favorite of Savannahians since it opened in 1933. With its high-back, padded booths and dark-wood paneling, the restaurant retains the feel of the 1930s. If you want to get an idea of what Savannah and its people were like 40 or 50 years ago, take a look at the Crystal's walls, which bear enlarged photographs depicting those times.

The restaurant serves lunch and dinner Monday through Saturday. Reservations aren't required, but they're taken and are recommended for groups of 10 or more.

Spanky's Pizza Gallery & Saloon $
317 East River Street, Savannah
(912) 236-3009

308 Mall Way, Savannah
(912) 355-3383

200 Governor Treutlen Road, Pooler
(912) 748-8188

404 Butler Avenue, Tybee Island
(912) 786-5520
Ansley Williams, Alben Yarbrough, and Dusty Yarbrough opened the first Spanky's on River Street in 1976, intending to bring pizza to the area. They also served burgers and chicken sandwiches at the restaurant, which is housed in what had been a cotton warehouse. According to Williams, the chicken breasts used for the sandwiches were too large for the buns on which they were served, so the restaurants sliced off the excess chicken and not wanting to be wasteful, battered and fried the strips of meat and sold them as "chicken fingers." Their concoction was a hit with locals and has become a mainstay of eateries throughout southeast Georgia and the rest of the country.

The success of the River Street location led to the opening of Spanky's restaurants in other parts of the state and locally on the Southside near Oglethorpe Mall, in Pooler, and on Tybee Island (that one's called Spanky's Beachside). Williams and the Yarbroughs eventually went their

separate ways, with Williams retaining ownership of the Spanky's on River Street and the Yarbroughs remaining involved with the others.

Although the Spanky's restaurants have different owners, the menus are basically the same, with the chicken fingers, pizza, and burgers still featured. Another favorite of veteran customers are Spanky's Spuds, which are circular-sliced potatoes that are battered and fried. The restaurants are open daily for lunch and dinner.

Carey Hilliard's Restaurant $
3316 Skidaway Road, Savannah
(912) 354-7240

8410 Waters Avenue, Savannah
(912) 355-2468

11111 Abercorn Street, Savannah
(912) 925-3225

514 US 80, Garden City
(912) 964-5671

5350 GA 21, Garden City
(912) 963-0060
That there are five Carey Hilliard's in the Savannah area should tell you something about the popularity of these restaurants, which provide casual dining in an atmosphere geared toward families. Founder Carey Hilliard opened his first establishment in 1960 on Skidaway Road in what had been an A&W Root Beer stand. The drive-in, curb-service feature was retained, and all five restaurants offer it today. Order from your car, and you receive many of the amenities you would by dining inside, including china plates and silverware.

Barbecue has always been and still is a big seller at Carey Hilliard's, which serves lunch and dinner, but seafood dishes account for about half the orders these days. Among the favorites of customers are the fried shrimp, oysters, and deviled crabs. Seating at the restaurants averages 250. Beer and wine are available.

ANDERSONVILLE: THE WORST PLACE ON EARTH

Confederate officials searching for a place to hold thousands of Union prisoners as the war intensified in late 1863 found what they thought was a perfect place, on the Georgia Southwestern Railroad track at what they called Station Number 8, and the tiny adjacent village inhabitants called Andersonville. Captain William Sidney Winder, the officer in charge of the search, apparently had no intention of creating a hellhole when he chose this location. On the contrary, in his official report he mentions the "plentiful food" and water available, easily accessible transportation, and location far from the battle lines as the makings for a fine location.

THE PRISONER-OF-WAR SYSTEM

Until well into the second year of the war, the old European tradition of exchanging and "paroling" prisoners prevailed. After a given battle, equal numbers of prisoners from both sides were released, and those left were allowed to sign an oath that they should not take up arms again and were sent home. In theory this system worked rather well for the holding side; by allowing the prisoner to go home, you no longer had to feed, house, or guard him, and by virtue of his oath he had become a noncombatant.

This system required the mutual cooperation and honesty of each side, which did exist in the early part of the war. What makes the study of the Civil War so fascinating to many researchers is this very period, when war was conducted almost on a medieval model. Officers exchanged salutes before battle, quarter was given when requested, and opponents were addressed with the same honor and courtesy as fellow officers and men. General Robert E. Lee took this concept to a high level; throughout the war he was noted for his refusal to refer to the Union Army or any member of it as the "enemy," preferring the terms "those people over there" or "our friends opposite us."

Prisoners, and in particular officers, were usually quite well treated during the brief period they spent in captivity. It was routine for relations on opposite sides to "look each other up" if in the same area; tobacco, whiskey, and rations were often exchanged between inmates and guards; and even newspapers, debating societies, dances, and other parties were organized at some prisons. No one expected to have to house and feed prisoners for any serious length of time.

Both sides were so unprepared to deal with any real number of prisoners in the beginning, in fact, that some were held in local jails along with murderers, thieves, and other riff-raff. The North began using old coastal fortifications and the South old factory buildings to hold the rapidly increasing numbers. Even with exchanges and paroles, the administrative bottlenecks soon caused overcrowding in each side's prisons.

The situation finally became critical after July 1863, when the exchange system collapsed because it became increasingly obvious that while Northern POWs honored their parole and went home to stay, the Confederates either went back to their units or joined another one. Numbers of POWs on both sides rapidly climbed, helped in no small part by the increasing number and severity of battles then taking place. The North attempted to control the problem by appointing a central authority over all the prison camps. Colonel William H. Hoffman (who had been a POW himself at the beginning of the war) set up a vast bureaucratic network of regulations, inspections, and standards for his camps. The South followed suit by appointing Brigadier General John H. Winder to a similar position, putting him in charge of all the Richmond POW camps, where nearly all the Union prisoners were being held at first.

Life in the Prison Camps

Again in theory, the system should have worked to encourage both sides to treat prisoners in a relatively humane manner, but unfortunately neither side lived up to its charge. Both in the North and in the South, camps became crowded very rapidly, and space to house prisoners and build more camps became harder to find. By early 1864 both sides resorted to building simple wooden enclosures with no interior housing to "corral" the prisoners—in short, building nothing more than concentration camps.

At that time the South was barely able to feed its own army and citizens, and despite the efforts of camp commandants, most Union prisoners barely subsisted on diets of rough corn bread occasionally supplemented by half-rotted and spoiled meat. This was frequently what the camp guards and staff were eating as well. Rail routes were being decimated by Union attacks, and what little food was being produced often rotted in warehouses for lack of transportation.

News leaking out of the South about these conditions was seized on and amplified by the Northern press. Indignant articles about the Southern "abuses" of POWs enraged the public, which demanded that "justice be done" and that the Confederate prisoners be treated the same. Some Union officers were more than happy to satisfy this misplaced lust for vengeance; at war's end, Hoffman returned $1.8 million to the Federal treasury (roughly

equivalent to $38 million in today's dollars), bragging that this was money he had saved by cutting prisoner rations.

More than 150 prison camps were built on both sides during the war. Almost all were filthy, disease-ridden hellholes fit for no man. Many prisoners vomited uncontrollably on entering the gates of Andersonville or its Northern counterpart, Elmira; the overpowering stench of open sewers, dead bodies, and rotting flesh hung like a cloud over the open field. At most prisons, "fresh fish" (new prisoners) had to be shoved through the doorway, where they would stand for hours at first trying not to touch or sit on anything. The walls and floors of prison buildings were normally covered with thick layers of greasy slime, dirt, mold, dead lice, and other vermin.

The prisoners themselves were nearly universally filthy, lice and flea infested, and covered with open sores and rashes. Many became despondent, not caring what happened to themselves or others, and quit bothering to use the slit latrines to relieve themselves or even to cover up the mess afterwards. Diarrhea, dysentery, and typhoid fever ran rampant, killing many more prisoners than starvation or failed escape attempts.

Boredom was an equally lethal killer; by the height of the war many camps were so crowded that it could take literally hours to walk from one side to another, and most activities were forbidden for security reasons. Sitting in the same spot day after day, too hungry to sleep and too tired to talk, with the noise from dying and delirious fellow prisoners ringing in their ears day and night, wearing encrusted and filthy clothes, and with all hope for release or exchange gone, some prisoners finally chose suicide as a means of escape. Andersonville became notorious during the war for its "deadline," a small wooden fence 20 feet inside the main stockade wall, where guards could and usually did shoot anyone who ventured inside it (actually, most open prisons on both sides had this feature). Some

i *At the battle of Franklin, Tennessee, in December 1864, 9,239 of Hood's 34,732 men were killed or wounded—27 percent of the force, and some weren't even present on the battlefield.*

prisoners "went over" just to end their suffering.

The filth that these prisoners existed in on both sides cannot possibly be overstated. Several prisoners wrote in their journals that their skin actually changed color from the layers of grime; and a Northern surgeon testified that it took months of bathing to completely remove the encrusted dirt. Most prisoners were not allowed to bathe for most or all of their incarceration; many reported that if they were allowed a bath, it would be six months or longer before another.

Comparative Ratios of Prisoner Deaths

By the third year of the war, vast numbers of prisoners were falling into Southern hands, times were tough for everyone as a result of the Union naval blockade and the cutting of railroads throughout the Confederacy, and few were in the mood to deal kindly with the "Northern invaders." However, although this chapter deals specifically with the most notorious prison of all, it is important to note that the North did not treat their prisoners much better.

Roughly 29 percent of Andersonville's 45,000 prisoners died in captivity, where conditions were wretched for all concerned, but 24 percent of the 12,123 Confederates held at Elmira, New York, died in captivity as well. Elmira suffered from many of the same supply and environmental problems Andersonville faced, but there is a great deal of evidence that at least part of their prisoners' suffering was deliberately induced. The evidence is much stronger for this deliberate retaliation at

other notorious Union prisons—Camp Douglas (Chicago) and Rock Island, Illinois; and Camp Morton, Indiana—all of which had relatively high prisoner mortality rates.

CAMP SUMTER

Construction of the new camp near Andersonville was delayed for a few months after the initial scouting report, both by local opposition to the project (fear of vindictive escaped prisoners) and a general shortage of labor. By the time work crews started on the new facility, in early January 1864, shortages of money and rapidly increasing numbers of Union prisoners caused the Confederate government to order a strong fence built, without any interior buildings to house the POWs. Under pressure to have the facility ready at the earliest opportunity, the workmen simply stripped the entire area of all but two trees, using the tall pines to build a 15-foot-high double wall of roughly shaved logs butted closely together. Guard towers, known as "pigeon roosts," were built against the outside of the interior wall and spaced every 30 feet.

A "star fort" (a simple fort built with protruding artillery redoubts, which from above looks like a four-, five-, or six-pointed star) on the southwest corner and six other earthwork emplacements guarded against any Union cavalry attempt to free the prisoners, and inward-facing cannon guarded against prisoner uprisings. A smaller enclosure called Castle Reed located one-half mile west housed the officer prisoners sent to this area until they were transferred to Macon's Camp Oglethorpe in May 1864. Afterwards, only enlisted prisoners languished in Camp Sumter.

The first prisoners moved in on February 25, 1864, even before the stockade walls were completed. Within a week the first escape attempt was mounted, when prisoners climbed the stockade wall using a rope handmade of torn shirts and blankets. All were caught within a day or two, but their attempt inspired construction of the ill-famed deadline.

Lacking even the crudest sort of structure to protect themselves from the elements, the first arrivals were able to use leftover scraps of wood to built rude huts. Later prisoners built "shebangs" by digging shallow pits in the red clay ground and covering them with some sort of tarp. Others simply sat out in the open—totally exposed to the sun, wind, and rain.

The Camp's Unbeloved Commander

The commandant of the camp in early 1864 and through most of the early buildup was Colonel Alexander W. Persons, replaced by General Winder (Captain Winder's father) on June 17. By that date the prison already held more than twice the number it was designed for. Many of the arriving prisoners had been held at other Confederate POW camps and arrived already filthy, weak, sick, and diseased. The stage was set for a real disaster to take place, the responsibility for which would be placed on the next arrival, Winder's subordinate, Captain Henry Wirz.

Wirz was not only not a Southerner, he was not even American. A native of Switzerland, he had immigrated to the United States and was living in Louisiana when the war broke out. Wounded during the Battle of Seven Pines in the spring of 1862, he was promoted and assigned as adjunct general to General Winder in Richmond. Given various tasks after that, including a strange "secret mission" to carry documents to Confederate agents in Europe, he was eventually assigned as keeper of the inner stockade of Camp Sumter in March 1864.

Wirz had a disagreeable personality and no real flair for command. Some of his more outrageous orders and comments were later used as "evidence"

against him in his war crimes trial. Many prisoners attempted to escape by tunneling under the walls, digging in the open under the pretense of digging wells for water (there also were some legitimate wells dug by the prisoners). Wirz decided at one point that the Union prisoners were "covering up" this digging with their shebangs, so he ordered that no prisoner build or inhabit any sort of overhead shelter. This insane command was soon overturned.

There were also quite a few reports that Wirz habitually walked around the stockade with pistol in hand and that he personally shot several prisoners (although this last point is the object of heated debate). Camp Sumter's best-known inmate, Private John Ransom (author of *Andersonville Diary*), certainly was no great fan of Wirz:

> *May 10.—Capt. Wirtz [sic] very domineering and abusive. Is afraid to come into camp anymore. There are a thousand men in here who would willingly die if they could kill him first. Certainly the worst man I ever saw.*

The Decline and Fall of Andersonville

By the end of the summer of 1864, Camp Sumter's population reached 33,000, making it the fifth largest city in the entire Confederacy. One thousand three hundred prisoners occupied each acre of land within the compound, and things went from bad to worst. Atlanta was under siege, and Sherman's cavalry was ranging all through the northern half of Georgia and Alabama laying waste to railroads and warehouses. Rations started to get short and then nearly disappeared. Salt was the first to go, then what few fresh vegetables that had been available and then meat totally disappeared. Most prisoners started to subsist on rough cornmeal

Fort Jefferson

Besides the filth and hunger, there were other terrors for the prisoners in the Civil War camps. Weather was a serious factor, with Confederate prisoners suffering from the northern cold, and Union suffering from the intense heat and humidity of the South. One of the most wretched prisons, ironically holding both Union and Confederate prisoners at different times, was Fort Jefferson in the Dry Tortugas Islands, 68 miles west of Key West, Florida. A massive structure with walls 8 feet thick and 50 feet tall, Fort Jefferson had been planned as the most outlying coastal fortification in the Keys, originally intended to house 1,500 men and 450 artillery pieces.

Never completed as planned, the massive fort was occupied by Union troops from the start of the war and originally used to house Union mutineers and other such military prisoners. Most civilians, even those living in Florida, had no idea this place even existed, but it rapidly gained a foul reputation among Union troops, who called it "America's Devil's Island" and believed being sent there was little more than a death sentence.

Unspeakably hot in summer and plagued with mosquitoes and scorpions, it wasn't long before Union prison authorities decided to use it to hold POWs. Prisoners were kept in the dank, dark, and hot casements, with walls liberally coated with slime and mildew. Guards were housed in proper barracks, but conditions on the island were so terrible that there was at least one riot among the guard companies, and afterward they were shuttled in and out fairly rapidly.

To add to the strain, escape was unlikely through the shark-infested waters, although there were several unfortunate attempts, and scurvy was common among the prisoners who couldn't afford to pay the high prices demanded by Union sutlers for fruits and vegetables.

The total number of prisoners, deaths, or escapes from Fort Jefferson will never be known; the camp commandant, Colonel Charles Hamilton, never kept or turned in any records.

delivered only four days a week and turned to eating rats and even birds that the stronger men were able to catch.

Some of the less-enlightened guards started amusing themselves by dropping bits of food over the wall into the mass of prisoners, just to laugh at the riot that would ensue. A few of the nastier ones would drop food within the deadline, just to get the opportunity to kill a prisoner.

A very small stream runs through the stockade site; when the camp opened, it was the only source of drinking, bathing, and toilet water in the entire facility. Needless to say, it became overwhelmed and contaminated in short order, and no other source of decent water was to be had. When a violent thunderstorm in August 1864 reopened an old spring that had been covered up by construction debris, the prisoners insisted that God himself had opened the spring with a lightning bolt and named the spot Providence Spring.

The number of prisoners dying from diarrhea and dysentery skyrocketed soon after the camp opened, claiming more than 4,500 in just a five-month period. Deaths were so common that some prisoners managed to escape by pretending they were dead, waiting until after they were carried outside the walls to the rude "death house" to make their escape. By the end of the war, exactly 12,914 had died and another 329 had escaped. Largely through the work of a single prisoner, Private Dorence Atwater of the 2nd New York Cavalry, only 460 of the graves are marked as "unknown." Atwater was assigned the responsibility of recording the names of all those who died at the camp, and fearing the loss of this record in the Confederate archives, he painstakingly handwrote another, which he kept in hopes of notifying the families of the deceased.

Prisoners were also stalked by some of their own number. A group of thugs known as the "Mosby Raiders" beat, robbed, terrorized, and even murdered their fellow prisoners quite openly for many months. Led by a particularly unpleasant character, Private William "Mosby" Collins of Company D, 88th Pennsylvania Infantry, they were finally brought down by another group of prisoners. With Wirz's cooperation, the Raiders were subjected to a trial by the prisoners themselves, and six were hanged. Three others were later beaten to death by their former victims. The six hung are buried in a special part of the cemetery, away from any other prisoner by the prisoners' request.

After the fall of Atlanta in September 1864, many prisoners were quickly relocated to other camps, farther away from the action. Only the sickest 8,000 remained by the end of September; all but about 1,300 of that number died by the end of November. The camp stayed open with a much-reduced number of prisoners, operating mainly for the sick and dying until war's end.

THE TOUR

Getting There: Andersonville

Andersonville National Historic Site is in southwest Georgia, about 120 miles south of downtown Atlanta, 30 miles west of Interstate 75, and 10 miles northeast of Americus. There is not a really direct route to the site; a recommended route from the Atlanta area is to take I-75 south from Macon and exit onto Georgia Highway 49 (exit 149), the Andersonville POW Memorial Trail. This will take you more or less straight to the site over about 40 miles of two-lane highways and is preferable to fighting the high-speed truck traffic on I-75 just to get 5 or 10 miles closer. To avoid the interstate crush altogether, take U.S. Highway 19 about 100 miles south of downtown Atlanta to the small town of Ellaville and then turn left onto Georgia Highway 228, which ends about 10 miles east directly across from the site on GA 49.

Coming from south of the site, take I-75 north to Cordele (exit 101). Turn left onto U.S. Highway 280 and go about 18 miles to a right turn onto Georgia Highway 195, which ends on GA 49 just below the site.

Andersonville National Historic Site
GA 49, Andersonville
(229) 924-0343
Camp Sumter today would be unrecognizable to the more than 45,000 Union prisoners who passed through its gates. The original burial site of prisoners who died in camp was established as Andersonville National Cemetery on July 26, 1865, just after the end of the war, primarily to preserve and honor the graves of 12,914 who died in the adjacent POW camp over a 14-month span. Initially there was no attempt

to preserve or mark the site of the notorious camp and stockade site, but the land was finally purchased in December 1890 by the Georgia Department of the Grand Army of the Republic, a Union Army veterans group. This group was unable to properly care for or maintain the property and shortly after sold it for $1.00 to the Women's Relief Corp (WRC), the national ladies' auxiliary of the Grand Army of the Republic (GAR).

The WRC proved good caretakers, making many improvements and keeping the grounds in good shape until donating the entire site to the U.S. government in 1910. The War Department and subsequent Department of the Army took care of the site until 1970, when the National Park Service was given the responsibility. Both the GAR and the army were primarily concerned with the national cemetery, and it wasn't until the Park Service took over that real efforts were made to preserve the stockade site and initiate education programs about it.

Today the site has a triple charge; in addition to protecting the National Cemetery and stockade site of Camp Sumter, construction began in 1996 on a new National Prisoner of War Museum, which is charged with preserving the memory and telling the story of all American prisoners of war throughout our many conflicts. This museum, opened in an emotional ceremony on April 9, 1998, is designed from the ground up as a powerful reminder to each visitor of the intensity of the stories it holds.

Walking toward the building from the parking lot, you are forced to walk in single file through a narrow passage between two brick buildings reminiscent of guardrooms. This, plus the black entry gates, gives the proper sense of foreboding and tension that a real prisoner would have faced. Once inside, the atmosphere is lightened by the high ceiling and skylights (make sure to notice the painted murals above), but the stark hallways of the exhibit corridors seem far too peaceful to hold the pictures and stories that

seem almost to explode off the wall. A quiet place for reflection is provided under two small sunlit towers.

In back of the museum, on the side facing the stockade site, is the Commemorative Courtyard with a small brick-lined stream flowing past brick and bronze statuary. A short pathway takes you from the courtyard to the partially reconstructed northeast corner stockade wall of Camp Sumter.

The entire site is haunting and disturbing, as it should be. On entering the grounds you drive through a quiet woods and then turn right into the National Cemetery. The closely packed, militarily straight, and in proper file and rank tombstones seem almost like formations of ghostly infantry drawn up in some vast line of battle. It seems impossible to comprehend that so many thousands of dead actually lie in such a small space; men were buried shoulder to shoulder without a coffin in long trenchlike graves and covered with about 3 feet of earth. These are not true mass graves, as each man was buried more or less independently and properly interred by the Confederate work details, not just hastily dumped in a hole.

Driving the short distance over to the stockade site, we were struck by how peaceful and quiet the vast open space is; similar to the site of many violent battlefields, it is as if all the energy was sapped from the very ground by the overwhelming suffering and carnage that took place here. A few state memorials dot the northwest corner, and white stakes placed every 50 feet or so show where the stockade wall and deadline were. Except for these and two short sections of reconstructed walls, the place is utterly empty.

A narrow paved road allows one to do a driving tour of the 26-acre site. A small memorial building built after the war by grateful ex-POWs houses Providence Spring, and the star fort and most of the earthworks are still intact. Several markers on the roadway contain photos of what the scene looked like during the war, and in most places the contrast between that period and the modern one is startling.

The National Cemetery is still active, with veterans of all the American wars (including the American Revolution) interred here, and about 150 burials take place each year. Please be respectful if you visit during a ceremony.

The visitor center and museum has a 20-minute orientation film, narrated by Colin Powell, introducing both Andersonville and the general topic of POWs. It also contains an excellent small bookstore and research library as well as the before-mentioned exhibits. Admission is by donation, and the grounds are open year-round 8:00 A.M. to 5:00 P.M. Water and restrooms are available, and picnicking is permitted in a designated area, but no food is sold on the grounds.

ACCOMMODATIONS

There is a single small bed-and-breakfast in Andersonville village, A Place Away Cottage (110 Oglethorpe Street; 229–924–1044; $). The village also features one restaurant with an adjacent RV park, Andersonville Restaurant; call the visitor center to check on hours and availability (229–924–2558). The nearest hotels and motels are in Americus, 10 miles to the southwest on Georgia Highway 49. We have heard many compliments on the Windsor Hotel (125 West Lamar Street, Americus; 229–924–1555; $$$–$$$$). Several chain motels and the usual fast-food restaurants are on GA 49 as you enter town and US 19 as you leave to the west. Going back to I–75, you have a wide range of chain hotel, motel, and restaurant choices clustered around Cordele (exits 101/102), Vienna (exit 109), Perry (exits 135/136), Fort Valley (exit 142), and Byron (exit 149).

Andersonville village is worth visiting after leaving the historic site. The hamlet contains a seven-acre pioneer farm, several antiques and craft shops, and the Drummer Boy Civil War Museum, which has garnered praise for its high-quality private collection. Across the street is

Brigade Sutler, which sells reproductions of uniforms, weapons, and equipment aimed at the reenactor crowd. This shop is usually closed during weekends when major reenactment events are going on, as John and Patricia usually work out of a field tent on "sutlers row." Call (706) 648–4268 first to see if they will be in. Right smack in the middle of town is a 45-foot-tall obelisk memorial to Captain Henry R. Wirz, the last commandant of Camp Sumter. We believe that this is the only monument to a convicted war criminal in this country and has inscribed upon it the "unreconstructed" view of Wirz and the POW situation. After the war there were quite a number of people who refused to accept that the Confederacy had been finally and decisively defeated. There are still folks around who believe that the Lost Cause was a spiritual one as well as a political and military one and that at some point in the future, "The South will rise again," to quote frequently seen bumper stickers.

Day Trips

We highly recommend a trip to Columbus, about 60 miles west of Andersonville, while you are in this part of the state. Take GA 49 through Americus and turn right on US 280. This will take you straight into Columbus, with the side benefit of going through Plains, the birthplace, residence, and historic site of President Jimmy Carter. Just before you enter Columbus you will drive through Fort Benning Military Reservation, which contains an exquisite collection of Civil War artifacts in its excellent National Infantry Museum (Building 396, Baltzell Avenue, Fort Benning; 706–545–2958).

US 280 is called Victory Drive within Columbus, and 2 miles before it goes over the Chattahoochee River into Alabama is the National Civil War Naval Museum, which houses the remains of the never finished 224-foot ironclad ram CSS *Jack-*

son and the 130-foot wooden gunboat CSS *Chattahoochee,* as well as a nice collection of models, weapons, and artifacts of the Confederate Navy. A warning: Although there are a few signs pointing the way, it is easy to get confused about where to enter the parking lot for this museum due to the very heavy traffic and urban blight of Victory Drive. Turn left off Victory Drive at the large sign marking SOUTH COMMONS, the Columbus Civic Center, and then go through the large parking lot to the right until you see the museum building. The museum, located at 1002 Victory Drive, Columbus (706–327–9798) is open Monday through Sunday 9:00 A.M. to 5:00 P.M. Admission is $4.50 for adults, $3.00 for students, $3.50 for active military and seniors, and free for children under 6.

Another interesting day trip is to Jefferson Davis Historic Site near Irwinville, the site of the Confederate president's capture by Union troops at the end of the war. Take I–75 south to Georgia Highway 32 (exit 78), and travel east approximately 15 miles into town. Turn left onto Jeff Davis Park Road; the site is about 1 mile on the left. Run by the state of Georgia, the 13-acre park contains a small museum and a few markers commemorating the event. The major attraction here is an impressive 12-foot-tall granite monument with a bronze bust of Davis on top, depicting his capture.

Unfortunately, the carved scene hints at one of the sillier myths of the war, that Davis was captured wearing women's clothing. Davis had been traveling west through southern Georgia to Texas or possibly Mexico, to try to continue the war from the Trans-Mississippi Theater. A unit of Union cavalry was in hot pursuit, and just before dawn on May 10, 1865, they suddenly raided his camp. In the confused skirmish, two columns of Union cavalry started firing on each other, killing two troopers before realizing their mistake.

Hearing the gunfire, Davis jumped up and threw on his wife's cloak by mistake in the darkened tent, ran outside, and tried to mount his horse to escape. A Union officer drew down on him, as his wife, Varina, ran up and threw her arms around him to shield him from being shot. Union soldiers in a very high spirit after his capture exaggerated the event, claiming that Davis had on bloomers and even a hoop skirt!

The site is open Tuesday through Saturday 9:00 A.M. to 5:00 P.M. and Sunday 2:00 to 5:30 P.M. You can find it at 338 Jeff Davis Park Road, Fitzerald (912–831–2335). Admission to the park is free; the museum admission is $2.50 for adults, $1.50 for youths ages 6 through 18, and free for those 5 and under.

MOBILE BAY: DAMN THE TORPEDOES

M obile, Alabama, lies at the south-ernmost point in the state, at the northwestern tip of a 36-mile-long and 18-mile-wide bay that allows the state its only sea access. With a population of just over 29,000 when the war started, it was one of the largest cities in the state and second only to New Orleans as a port for international trade. Although never a city noted for strong secessionist feelings, no doubt due to the strong ties with Northern traders, Mobile was proposed by local boosters as the first capital of the Confederacy. Some radical secessionists felt that the Confederacy was bound to eventually include Mexico and some or all of the Caribbean islands, so it would be in a favorable central location.

After Lincoln's election in 1860, seces-sion fever swept the state, and Governor Andrew B. Moore soon moved to provide for military defense. On January 3, 1861, several days before a state convention met to formally declare Alabama free from the Union, he ordered local companies of the 1st Alabama State Troops to seize and man forts and arsenals around Mobile Bay. The next day, two companies moved to take Forts Morgan and Gaines, while several other companies went 30 miles north to seize the Mount Vernon Arsenal. Seven days later, on January 11, 1861, Alabama for-mally declared secession.

FORTRESS MOBILE

Mobile not only had a valuable and large deepwater port to help supply the newly formed Confederacy, it also had a series of fortifications to protect it, thanks to the U.S. Army Corps of Engineers. At the east side of the entrance to the bay stood mas-sive Fort Morgan, supported by Fort Gaines and Fort Grant across the ship channel on Dauphin Island. Mobile itself was protected by a series of small forts and artillery batteries on both shores of the northern end of the bay, as well as a series of trench lines surrounding the city on the west (landward) side.

Within days of Alabama's secession, a massive project was under way to clean up and improve the still-unfinished forts. With volunteer citizens and slaves provided by local planters, all available guns were mounted, living quarters for the garrisons built up outside the walls, wells cleaned out, and sloping glacis constructed. In March, when the Confederate government took over responsibility for area defense from the state, Colonel (later Lieutenant General) William Joseph Hardee was named commander of Fort Morgan.

Hardee, the author of the then stan-dard text on infantry tactics, was only in command at Mobile for three months, but he managed a near whirlwind of action. The untrained militia and local guard infantrymen were properly trained, artillerymen were trained and readied to repel the inevitable naval attack, and Hardee's own command was soon expanded to the entire Mobile Bay area. In addition, he was placed in command of the "Mobile Navy," the revenue cutter *Lewis Cass,* soon augmented by a grossly inadequate ironclad, the CSS *Baltic.* Later, after Hardee had departed, this "navy" was expanded to include two ironclad rams, the CSS *Tennessee* and CSS *Nashville;* two ironclad "floating batteries" (gunboats sim-ilar to the rams), the CSS *Huntsville* and CSS *Tuscaloosa;* and three side-wheeler gunboats, the CSS *Morgan,* CSS *Gaines,* and CSS *Selma*—all at the time of the major last battles under the command of Admiral Franklin Buchanan. The CSS *Tennessee,* Buchanan's flagship, was typical of the large, powerful Confederate-designed ironclads—209 feet long with a 48-foot beam, covered with 4 to 6 inches of armor plating and mounting two 7-inch and four 6.4-inch Brooke rifled guns.

FORT MORGAN

The centerpiece of Mobile's defense against naval attack was a massive, five-sided masonry post at the very tip of Mobile Point, Fort Morgan, supplemented by two other smaller forts across the ship channel on Dauphin Island. The three-story-high brick fort still under construction when hostilities broke out in 1861 had replaced earlier defense posts dating back to a French outpost in 1699 at the site. However, it was only after the Spanish concession of Florida to the fledgling United States in 1813 that any attempts were mounted for strong, permanent fortifications on the two narrow barrier islands guarding Mobile Bay.

Fort Gaines on Dauphin Island, named for General Edmund Pendleton Gaines (best known for commanding Fort Erie with great skill during the War of 1812), and Fort Morgan on Mobile Point (named for General Daniel Morgan, Revolutionary War) are of the Third System of Fortification planning period of the 1830s and 1840s. A continuous series of strong masonry forts was planned to guard ports, towns, and strategic locations along the entire eastern seaboard and Gulf Coast. First proposed in 1821, Fort Gaines was still unfinished when the war began, described as a "shell of masonry" by one visitor. Although mounting few guns and for all practical purposes nearly unmanned early in the war, it still posed an impressive defensive obstacle, with a five-sided outer wall 22½ feet tall and 4½ feet thick. Unlike so many other Gulf Coast fortifications, Fort Gaines possessed gun emplacements well situated to defend against attacks from either land or water. By 1864 the garrison under Colonel Charles D. Anderson consisted of about 800 infantry and artillerymen, about half poorly trained local militia, and 26 heavy guns. Some of the garrison were of the Pelham Cadets, boys as young as 14 who ended up fighting about as well as any other irregular unit there.

> [The Civil War] *was a fearful lesson, and should teach us the necessity of avoiding wars in the future.*
>
> Lieutenant General Ulysses S. Grant, Union Army, from his *Memoirs*

Fort Morgan was a star-shaped pentagon of similar construction begun in 1819 and completed in 1834, although with a particular design feature that proved seriously hazardous during the battle. A three-story-tall, 10-sided barracks building in the center of the fort known as the "citadel" stuck up well above the surrounding parapet, lending both a perfect aiming point for Union gunners and providing a shrapnel hazard if hit during battle. To help protect the fort's gunners, wooden traverses across the side and rear of the casements as well as sandwork glacis all around the exterior masonry walls were planned, although little work was completed before the Union attacks commenced. At the time of the last battle for control of the bay, Brigadier General Richard L. Page commanded a garrison of 400 regular army and artillery troops, and the fort mounted 45 guns of various sizes and calibers.

A third major defensive point centered around Fort Powell, a smaller earthwork redoubt named for the former commander of Fort Morgan, Colonel William Llewellyn Powell, who had died on duty in September of 1863. Guarding (and formally named for) the westernmost approach to Mobile Bay, Grant's Pass, the post only mounted eight heavy guns and contained at its peak only 140 troops under Lieutenant Colonel James M.

Williams, but it was able to stand up against repeated Union attacks with little damage.

Perhaps the most famous, and certainly one of the most effective, defense arrangements was the stringing of a series of "torpedoes" across the bay from Fort Morgan to Fort Gaines. The floating mines were built to explode when touched by a ship or gunboat and had enough power to shatter an armored ironclad's hull. By the third year of the war, every water approach to Mobile Bay had at least one line of torpedoes across most of the passage, and the main ship channel was guarded by no less than 180 in three rows that covered the entire channel up to within 700 feet of Fort Morgan.

BACKGROUND TO THE BATTLE OF MOBILE BAY

Following the Union Navy's largely successful tight blockade of eastern Confederate-held ports, the Union Army campaigns in the Carolinas and Florida, and the utter failure of the weak Confederate Navy to do much more than snipe at the Union blockade, only the ports of Wilmington, North Carolina, and Mobile, Alabama, were left open to receive the critical supplies brought in by blockade runners by the third year of the war. Wilmington was able to supply, barely, General Robert E. Lee's Army of Northern Virginia, with a trickle of supplies sent westward to Lieutenant General Braxton Bragg's Army of Tennessee. Mobile was the only remaining open port by 1864 still able to bring the majority of supplies in to the Western and Trans-Mississippi Theater armies.

Even more important than Mobile's port to the supply and reinforcement of the Army of Tennessee was the city's railroad network. After the loss of the rail center at Corinth, Mississippi, following the Shiloh-Corinth campaign in the summer of 1862, Mobile became the only rail link between Confederate forces in the East-ern and Western Theaters. Its importance was underscored in early July 1862, when Major General John Porter McCown's division moved through the city from Tupelo, Mississippi, en route to Chattanooga, Tennessee, to reinforce the garrison there. By later July, the rest of General Bragg's 25,000-strong Army of Mississippi followed McCown's route, abandoning northern Mississippi in order to try to save Chattanooga.

Despite the extreme value Mobile posed to the Confederacy as both a rail center and port, neither side made any serious early moves to take or protect it. The series of Confederate Western Theater commanders in the first years of the war consistently looked to Forts Morgan and Gaines to provide the majority of protection for the city, supplemented by small infantry and artillery redoubts and emplacements in and around the city to guard against the "unlikely" event of a land-based attack. Major General Benjamin Franklin Butler and Flag Officer (later Rear Admiral) David Glasgow Farragut determined to concentrate their Northern forces initially on New Orleans and the Mississippi River, leaving Mobile (and Pensacola) for a later attack.

A few months after Confederate troops had abandoned Fort Massachusetts on nearby Ship Island, Butler and Farragut moved to seize the strategically positioned island. On December 3, 1861, 1,900 Union soldiers stepped ashore to take back possession of the post 12 miles off the shore of Gulfport, Mississippi, providing the Union Army and Navy an ideal base from which to threaten the entire Gulf coastal region of eastern Florida, Alabama, Mississippi, and Louisiana. However, Mobile remained securely in Confederate hands for nearly three more years, with Farragut busy along the Mississippi River and the land forces concentrating on Vicksburg and the Mississippi interior. Prior to the 1864 battle, the only serious attack was a weak attempt by Commander David D. Porter to force a passage into Mobile Bay in the summer of 1862, easily repulsed by the rebels without any immediate Union follow-up.

Naval Attacks on Mobile Bay

Due primarily to its isolated location, well south of any other major city or supply depot, any military action at Mobile was probably going to be either purely naval or an amphibious landing heavily supported by naval gunfire. This was confirmed by the first action, in December 1861, when the part-ironclad (armor only protected the boilers, leaving the gundeck open and exposed to enemy fire) CSS *Florida* sailed out from Fort Morgan's pier to engage the blockade steamer USS *Huntsville* near Sand Point. Typical for early-war encounters, naval or otherwise, both sides withdrew after firing a relatively few ill-aimed shots that did little or no damage, and subsequently both sides claimed victory.

In April 1862 the Mobile Bay naval commander, Captain Randolph, ordered the newly readied wooden gunboats CSS *Morgan* and CSS *Gaines* to sail out and try to break through the Union blockade "fleet," which consisted of only two ships at the time. Even with this weak enemy force to attack, the two Confederate gunboats only fired a total of about a dozen shots before retreating at high speed back to the safety of their harbor. In the next two years, five other such small naval actions against the blockade fleet or the Confederate forts were mounted; all had the same negative results.

The most serious attack during this period, although actually only a feint to draw attention away from a Union Army attack toward Meridian, Mississippi, had Farragut sailing four gunboats and six "mortar schooners" (wooden small ships mounting heavy mortars that could stand off from the main action a bit and lob shells inside a fort's walls) into Grant's

Pass. Over the course of five days of bombardment in February 1864, his ships fired about 2,000 shots and shells into the earthwork fort, killing one man and wounding five, including post commander James Williams. In exchange, the fort stood nearly intact with the little damage done being repaired in one day, and one of Farragut's own mortar schooners was hit by Confederate gunners and nearly sunk. Although the channel had been seeded with torpedoes, and Union gunboats struck several, none exploded as expected. An after-action inspection revealed that marine worms had infested the wooden casks and rendered the triggers inoperative.

THE BATTLE OF MOBILE BAY

With most of the Gulf Coast and Mississippi River now under Union control, Farragut's next objective was to shut down the port of Mobile once and for all. Using his assembled naval force, his primary objective was to neutralize the three main Confederate forts and completely cut off the blockade runners from a safe port. A separate army force under Major General Gordon Granger would land on Dauphin Island with about 1,500 men and attack the two forts there. To oppose the assault, Commander Page (3rd Brigade, District of the Gulf) could muster about 1,040 men in the three forts and their surrounding batteries.

At dawn on August 5, 1864, Farragut began his attack. Fourteen wooden, lightly armored gunboats and four ironclad monitors sailed toward the main ship channel in a tight formation, the gunboats lashed together in pairs with the better protected monitors alongside starboard (eastward) to protect them from Fort Morgan's artillery fire. Well aware of the torpedoes strung across the channel, Farragut deliberately ran his small fleet close to Fort Morgan, attempting to sail through the narrow space between the fort and the first line of torpedoes, although at a terrible risk from near point-blank Confederate fire. At about 7:00 A.M. Farragut ordered his point vessel, the USS *Tecumseh,* to open fire, which was followed in short order by a concentrated fire from Page's guns. For the next 45 minutes both sides kept up a blistering fire, but amazingly, although they were literally only a few yards apart, very little damage was done to either side.

One of Farragut's major objectives was the sinking or disabling of the CSS *Tennessee.* As his fleet sailed past Fort Morgan, the USS *Tecumseh* swung slightly west to engage the Confederate ironclad awaiting her near the middle of the ship channel but almost immediately struck a torpedo, shattering her hull and sending her quickly to the bottom. Only 21 of her 114-man crew managed to escape. The wooden gunboat USS *Brooklyn,* next in line to the USS *Tecumseh,* slowed and started turning away from the lethal minefield back toward Fort Morgan. Confederate gunners cheered then quickly loaded their guns with grapeshot and canister, preparing to rake the enemy decks as soon as they moved within range.

Farragut, lashed by his crew into the rigging of his flagship, USS *Hartford* (to keep him from being killed from falling to the deck if wounded while in his high observation post), allegedly screamed out to his helmsman, "Damn the torpedoes! Drayton! Ahead, Full Speed! Hard astarboard; ring four bells! Eight bells! Sixteen bells!" (there is much debate over whether he really said this famous quote) and thus ordered his own ship to take the lead. Moving at near maximum speed, the small Union fleet pushed through the torpedo belts without setting off any more, although several officers reported hearing fuses firing as their ships hit the floating mines.

For the South, Buchanan's own fleet opened fire as soon as their guns were unmasked to the onrushing Union gunboats. While their shots raked the Union ships for several minutes before they were able to return fire, the Confederates definitely got the worst of the exchange. Within a few minutes the CSS *Gaines* was sinking from multiple shots below the waterline, the CSS *Selma* was run down by the USS *Metacomet* and forced to surrender, and the CSS *Morgan* soon broke contact and fled east to the safety of her namesake. Only the CSS *Tennessee* remained by 8:00 A.M. to threaten Farragut's assault, and the Union fleet now safely past the forts quickly turned on the powerful but slow and ungainly ironclad.

The CSS *Tennessee* moved in for her own attack, but Farragut's ships surrounded her and began maneuvering for ram attacks. At 9:25 A.M. the USS *Monongahela,* the USS *Lackawanna,* and Farragut's own ship rammed the Confederate ship in turn, inflicting little damage but disrupting the gun crew's ability to fire. Buchanan suffered a broken leg when an 11-inch solid shot struck the after port cover he was standing next to. In the meantime, the three surviving Union ironclad monitors had moved up alongside the CSS *Tennessee* and had begun hammering fire on her armored decks. At 10:00 A.M., with his steering gear shot away and his gun crews no longer able to return fire, Captain James D. Johnston surrendered his ship.

The short naval action resulted in 12 Confederates killed, 20 wounded, and 280 captured. Farragut reported a loss of 145 killed, 170 wounded, and 4 captured.

Forts Powell and Gaines

At the same time Farragut was racing through the main ship channel, Lieutenant Commander George H. Perkins aboard the USS *Chickasaw,* along with three other gunboats, moved up Mississippi Sound toward Grant's Pass and opened fire on Fort Powell. Williams's gunners returned fire, but once again, neither side suffered in the short exchange. The USS *Chickasaw* withdrew, along with the other gunboats, but returned alone just before noon and again late in the afternoon. This time her gunners were more effective, raking the fort's exposed parapets with a hot fire and penetrating the bomb-proof. Convinced that a renewed bombardment the next day would result in his magazine being penetrated and exploded, Williams ordered his men to evacuate to nearby Fort Gaines during the night, setting fire to and destroying his post as he left.

Granger landed his troops on Dauphin Island late in the afternoon of August 3, and Page immediately requested reinforcements from the Mobile garrison. About 200 local militia and Confederate marines managed to slip past the Union fleet lying close by and get into the fort before Granger's attack commenced. By midnight on August 4, the Union landing force had closed in enough to set up their artillery batteries and opened fire on Fort Gaines's water battery as Farragut's fleet sailed through the channel. Anderson ordered his own guns to open up on the Union battery, but with no apparent success.

Just after noon on August 6, the USS *Chickasaw* moved within range and began pounding the fort's masonry walls. Little damage was suffered, but several patients in the post hospital were killed by flying debris. Before the infantry or even other Union gunboats could get involved in the fight, Anderson decided he had had enough. Showing a sad lack of leadership, Anderson first signaled Page over in Fort Morgan for instructions, consulted with two of Page's staff officers, and was then presented with a petition signed by most of his own officers imploring him to surrender rather than fight on. With Page frantically signaling him to hold his post, Anderson raised a white flag and requested terms from Granger and Farragut. Into Union captivity went 864 officers and men, as well as 26 artillery pieces, a large amount of ammunition, and a year's supply of food.

The early surrender of both forts caused a storm of protest in both Mobile and the Confederate high command. Area commander Page said publicly that the surrenders were a "deed of dishonor and disgrace to its commander and garrison," and both Williams and Anderson were crucified in the Mobile press. Williams was quickly removed from command, although some responsibilities were gradually restored later. In all fairness, these officers faced a near impossible defensive position, bombarded from the sea, threatened by infantry by land, and cut off from any hope of continued resupply or reinforcement. When the CSS Tennessee surrendered, the last best chance for a naval victory was surrendered with her.

Infantry Attacks

With the western approaches to Mobile Bay now secured, Granger and Farragut turned their attention on Fort Morgan. Granger's heavily reinforced command, now numbering some 5,500 infantry and artillerymen, landed just east of the isolated Confederate fort uncontested on August 9. Page pulled his infantry inside the fort, obviously outmatched in an open land battle, and prepared for a long siege. Just before noon the Union fleet moved in and began shelling the fort; a few hours later a note was delivered demanding the unconditional surrender of the last Confederate outpost. Page adamantly refused, and Granger ordered his troops to close in on the fort.

Rather than a headlong assault, Granger decided to slowly move his troops forward, building heavy artillery emplacements and siege entrenchments as they went. Farragut's sailors had repaired the CSS *Tennessee*'s steering gear and, along with the three surviving ironclad monitors, began a heavy bombardment of the fort on August 13. Two days later the now close-in Union infantry and their heavy siege artillery joined in on the bombardment and sniping. For some unknown reason, Page refused his gunners permission to return fire, except for occasional, short barrages toward the Union infantry encampment.

Granger continued to bring in more heavy artillery, and by the morning of August 21 he was able to report 25 heavy artillery pieces and 16 siege mortars mounted and ready for action. That afternoon his gunners, joined by every Union monitor and gunboat, opened up a massive, pounding barrage on Fort Morgan. Page reported later that the barrage soon "disabled all the heavy guns save two . . . partially breached the wall in several places, and cut up the fort to such an extent as to make the whole work a mere mass of debris." Although the heavy barrage lifted somewhat during the night, it resumed in full force at dawn the next day. Page was forced to admit that his command could not hold out much longer. He ordered what ammunition remained destroyed and his guns spiked, and he sent a message offering unconditional surrender to Granger. The formal surrender was signed on the afternoon of August 23.

Despite the rather heavy fighting that took place at Fort Morgan, Page reported only very light casualties: 3 killed and 16 wounded, with more than 600 marching into captivity.

The Defense of Mobile

While Page had fought off both Farragut and Granger for a few weeks, Major General Danny Herndon Maury, District of the Gulf commander headquartered in Mobile, hastily prepared the city for the coming invasion. He urgently requested reinforcements from Bragg and conscripted every available male in the city. Even with his officers rounding up anyone who could tote a rifle, by August 9 Maury still only had about 4,000 troops in entrenchments and batteries all around the city, a pitifully small force to resist the attack that all were sure was coming in days, if not hours.

However, neither Farragut nor Granger was in any particular hurry to attack

Mobile. A waterborne reconnaissance on August 15 revealed to the Union admiral that the harbor defenses were far too strong for him to bring up his fleet within gun range and that an attack on the city would have to be primarily a land-based one. The Union commanders returned to Fort Morgan and sent word to Washington that they would need a serious number of reinforcements to overcome the Confederate defenses and take Mobile.

It is well that war is so terrible, lest we grow too fond of it.

> General Robert E. Lee to Lieutenant General James Longstreet, both of the Confederate Army, December 13, 1862

Maury sent word that he, too, badly needed large numbers of reinforcements, but he knew that his prospects for getting them were slim. He spent the next few months fortifying the city as well as possible, centering the defenses around a series of fixed and floating batteries, rebuilt or reinforced entrenchments and redoubts, and even building up and improving an old Spanish fort on the eastern shore of the bay, known, appropriately, as Spanish Fort. Outside of ordering out a handful of naval and land-based raids and skirmishes on the Mobile defenses, both Farragut and Granger seemed perfectly content to wait in Fort Morgan until reinforcements or other orders arrived.

THE RENEWED MOBILE CAMPAIGN

Late in 1864, the commander in chief of all Union armies, Lieutenant General Ulysses S. Grant, was not at all convinced that Mobile was worth the intense manpower needed to take it, but he wanted Granger to move his force north and take Selma and Montgomery. These two cities brought under Union control would help a planned cavalry raid through Alabama and

CLOSE-UP

The Confederate Flag

The first Confederate flag, or Stars and Bars, incorporated two horizontal red stripes separated by a white stripe. It included seven white stars in a blue field. This flag was adopted in March 1861 and raised over the Confederate capitol, then in Montgomery, Alabama, by the granddaughter of former U.S. president John Tyler. But this flag caused confusion at the Battle of First Bull Run in Virginia because it looked very much like the union's Stars and Stripes. Following the battle, General Pierre Gustave Toutant Beauregard designed a battle flag for the Confederate Army of Northern Virginia. This flag, erroneously referred to today as the Confederate Stars and Bars, was a red square with a blue St. Andrew's cross and 13 superimposed white stars (representing the 11 seceded states, plus the "enemy held" states of Kentucky and Maryland).

A variation of this flag was used by armies in the Western Theater, being the same basic design but rectangular rather than square. This same flag was used by the Confederate Navy and called the "Naval Jack." This is what many still call the Confederate flag, and most historians refer to as the "Southern Cross." In May 1863 the Confederacy adopted a new national flag to replace the first Stars and Bars. It was white with the more familiar battle flag in the upper left corner.

This flag is sometimes referred to as the "Stonewall Flag," as one of its first uses was to drape Lieutenant General Thomas Jonathan "Stonewall" Jackson's casket after he was mortally wounded following the Battle of Chancellorsville. Also known as the "Stainless Banner," this flag showed mostly white unless flying in a stiff breeze and was frequently mistaken for a flag of truce or surrender, so a new design in 1865 added a red bar on the flag's white edge. This last flag design came about too late in the war to see much actual service. Today, however, the Army of Northern Virginia's battle flag (or the western variation) is the one most people identify as the "Confederate flag."

Georgia by Major General James Harrison Wilson, even then on his way south through Tennessee. Granger was promised more troops and ordered to bypass Mobile if a short campaign was insufficient to take it.

After many delays, Granger's reinforcements finally arrived in mid-March 1865, and shortly after that the Union columns moved out. Major General Edward Richard Sprigg Canby moved north with about 32,000 troops from the base at Fort Morgan on March 25. A second column led by Major General Frederick Steele marched out of Fort Barrancas at Pensacola, Florida, on March 20 with about 13,000 troops. At this time on the Confederate side, Maury could muster a total of about 9,000 soldiers, militia, conscripts, and sailors to man the 209 artillery pieces and miles of trenches and redoubts around the city and upper bay.

As soon as he was notified of the Union columns' route of approach, Maury moved all his infantry to the eastern shore, into Spanish Fort and nearby Fort Blakely. Brigadier General Randall Lee Gibson took over command of Spanish Fort, with a garrison consisting of his own Louisiana Brigade, with about 500 men, another 950 infantrymen from the Alabama reserves, and about 360 artillerymen to man the 6 heavy guns, 14 field guns, and 12 Coehorn mortars. Brigadier General St. John Richardson Liddell at Fort Blakely was in a slightly better position, with a peak force of about 2,700 troops manning a 3,000-yard-long line of entrenchments and redoubts.

Spanish Fort

Canby came on fast, approaching Spanish Fort early on the morning of March 27. To give his engineers a little more time to improve their emplacements, Gibson ordered Lieutenant Colonel Robert H. Lindsay to take about 500 men and hit the Union column before they could deploy for battle. Lindsay assaulted through the Union vanguard, but he withdrew when the column's forward regiments began deploying in line of battle. His delaying tactic worked, however, forcing Canby to delay several hours getting his forces reorganized and moving again. By nightfall Canby's men were starting to establish siege lines only 1,000 yards from the fort, with some forward skirmishers less than 300 yards from Gibson's line.

Most siege operations during the war tended to be all-artillery affairs, with infantry on both sides primarily just trying to dig in deep enough not to be hit. However, from the morning of March 28 on through the end of the siege, Union sharpshooters kept up a steady and accurate fire inside the fort's walls, small infantry attacks were launched by both sides on the other's trench lines, and Canby's men steadily extended their line of entrenchments until they were nearly to the walls of the Confederate fort itself.

The artillery kept up a steady barrage through it all, with one massive two-hour barrage on April 4 coming from no less than 40 heavy siege guns and about 12 siege mortars.

The worst bombardment of all came on April 8 at sundown, when 53 Union heavy siege guns, joined by 37 field guns and mortars and Union gunboats just off-shore, started a concentrated fire directly on the fort. Ironically, Gibson had planned his own barrage for that same date and time, but his gunners were only able to crank off a few rounds before the Union barrage drove them to their shelters. During the heavy barrage, troops from Colonel James L. Geddes's 3rd Brigade leading Brigadier General Eugene Asa Carr's 3rd Division (of Major General Andrew Jackson Smith's XVI Corps) assaulted the left of the Confederate line. Overrunning the first line of entrenchments, they were nearly to the fort itself when a rebel counterattack led by Lieutenant Alfred G. Clark with about 100 men stopped the assault before it could overrun the parapet walls.

Clark was killed in the counterattack, but his small command managed to stop the Union assault. Aware that he was not going to be able to hold against a renewed attack, Gibson ordered his gunners to spike their guns and gradually withdrew his command out of the fortification walls. During the night the remnants of his force worked their way across the marshes to Fort Blakely then were transferred by steamboat across the bay into Mobile. While he was able to take most of his 395 wounded out with him, he left behind 93 dead and about 750 missing or captured.

Fort Blakely

While Canby advanced on and laid siege to Spanish Fort, Steele moved north in a feint on Montgomery then west to attack Fort Blakely. Early on April 1 his vanguard,

Lieutenant Colonel Andrew B. Spurling's 2nd Cavalry Brigade, encountered Captain J. B. Hart's 46th Mississippi Infantry Regiment, deployed about 5 miles east of Fort Blakely as skirmishers. Spurling's cavalry immediately charged, driving the small Confederate command nearly the whole way to the fort, and captured 74 of the 100 men as well as the regimental colors. Their charge was only halted by concentrated fire from another regiment posted outside the fort, fewer than 100 Missourians from Colonel James McCown's (Cockrell's) brigade.

Throughout April 1 and 2 Steele's advancing command came into line and launched into a running fight with Liddell's advance guard, gradually pushing them to within a half mile of the fort, where both sides dug in for another protracted siege. The next week was spent beefing up the lines and launching isolated attacks, none of which gained any territory from the other. When Spanish Fort fell on the night of April 8, Canby moved his infantry north and ordered Steele to join in a general attack the next day. At 5:30 P.M. on April 9, four Union divisions jumped out of their trench line, leading a mass assault of more than 16,000 infantrymen on the small Confederate fort. Within a few minutes they completely overran Fort Blakely, capturing 3,423 Confederate soldiers in the process.

The siege at Fort Blakely broke the back of the entire Confederate command at Mobile. Casualty reports are apparently missing, but fewer than 200 Confederate soldiers escaped into the bay and the relative safety of the remnants of the Mobile fleet. All three generals present were captured, while Canby and Steele's command lost a combined total of 113 killed and 516 wounded.

The last two batteries remaining under Confederate command, Battery Huger and Battery Tracy, remained, blocking any Union advance toward Mobile until nightfall on April 11. Their ammunition exhausted, Maury's last artillerymen spiked their guns then escaped by steamboat back to Mobile, where they joined the retreat north toward Montgomery. These were the last shots fired in the last battle of the Western Theater; final commander of the Department of East Louisiana, Mississippi, and Alabama, Lieutenant General Richard "Dick" Taylor, met with Canby at Citronelle, Alabama, on May 2 to discuss surrender terms. The last 4,500 Confederate soldiers under his command formally surrendered on May 4, 1865 (some sources state May 8), nearly a month after Lee had surrendered in Virginia and more than a week after Johnston had surrendered in North Carolina. Only General Edmund Kirby Smith held out longer, surrendering his Trans-Mississippi Department on May 26, ending all formal military action in the war.

THE TOUR

Getting There: Mobile

Mobile is at the extreme southwestern corner of Alabama, just a few miles from the Mississippi state border. Interstate 10 connects Mobile with Biloxi and New Orleans to the west and Pensacola and Tallahassee to the east. Interstate 65 runs northeast out of the city to Montgomery. Battle areas of the Mobile campaigns (naval- and land-based) are nearly all outside the city proper; Spanish Fort and Fort Blakely are across Mobile Bay just off I-10 East, and Forts Morgan and Gaines are south of the city on the Gulf of Mexico coastline.

The two existing coastal forts offer an interesting journey in turn. We suggest you follow Alabama Highway 193 south out of the city (intersection with I-10 West at exit 17) about 20 miles to Dauphin Island. Turn left at the stop sign (end of AL 193) onto Bienville Road and travel about a mile to Fort Gaines. After your visit there, backtrack about one-quarter mile to the car ferry landing, near the fishing boat ramps. A privately run car ferry runs about every 90 minutes across the bay to Pleasure Island and Fort Morgan State Park. The ferry has a range of prices from $3.00 to $25.00, depending on your mode of transportation, and some discounts are offered for round-trip passages. Both forts are (barely) within walking distance of the ferry landing, providing the weather cooperates and you are in reasonable shape.

Traveling east out of Fort Morgan State Park, the small town of Gulf Shores is 22 miles away on Alabama Highway 180. Turn left onto Baldwin County Route 59 in the main business district, which intersects I-10 about 25 miles north at exit 44. Fort Blakely and Spanish Fort are about 8 miles west and Mobile is 15 miles west on the interstate from this intersection, allowing an interesting, if lengthy, roundabout tour of the battle areas.

Originally located roughly near where AL 193 crosses Grant's Pass before it enters Dauphin Island, Fort Powell no longer exists, but the tour brochure at Fort Gaines points out its location, barely visible from one bastion.

POINTS OF INTEREST

Fort Gaines Historic Site
51 Bienville Boulevard, Dauphin Island
(251) 861-6992

This well-preserved and lovingly cared for fort was used as a coastal defense outpost during the Spanish-American War and both World Wars and later as a Coast Guard base, modified to suit each new role. Now owned and operated by the Dauphin Island Park and Beach Board, it is very well preserved and managed and an absolute delight to visit. An excellent brochure outlines the self-guided tour, and one of the "disappearing" gun mount magazines has been converted into an unusual but well-presented museum of uniforms, weapons, maps, photos, and documents spanning the 140-year history of the fort.

The old guardhouse next to the main sally port (entrance) contains a rather extensive collection of souvenirs as well as

When visiting Fort Morgan and Fort Gaines at the sea entrance to Mobile Bay, make plans to use the cross-bay ferry between the two. It will save a significant amount of driving, the ride is usually pleasant, and it gives you a Union Navy view of the two Confederate forts.

a nice collection of books, and some of the former garrison would no doubt be amused to note that their former commandant's office on the other side of the sally port now houses the restrooms. The tour brochure notes the location of Fort Powell, which no longer exists.

Fort Gaines is open daily from 9:00 A.M. to 6:00 p.m., closed only on Christmas and New Year's Day. The entrance fee is $5.00 for those 13 and over, $2.50 for children ages 5 through 12, and free for children under 4. The fort is located near the end of Bienville Road, about 1 mile east of the intersection with AL 193 and about one-quarter mile east of the car ferry port.

Fort Morgan State Park
51 AL Highway 180 West, Gulf Shores
(251) 540-7125

The basic shape and masonry walls of Fort Morgan still exist more or less intact, but the post was heavily modified for service in the Spanish-American War and both World Wars. Now operated by the Alabama Historical Commission, the site includes several postwar buildings used as part of a radically expanded post at the turn of the 20th century, several artillery pieces from various periods of the post's history, and a self-guided tour of the partially restored fort.

As a general rule (with several significant exceptions), we have found that the lower the level of ownership and management of a historic site (i.e., federal is high, local historical commission is low), the more informed, helpful, and friendly the staff is, and accordingly the more pleasant the visit is. Unfortunately, Fort Morgan is not a good example of this rule. On our visits over the past five years, we have encountered staff ranging from ill-informed to downright rude, incorrectly labeled or attributed signs and markers, a very confusing arrangement for paying entrance fees, poorly maintained and dangerous stairwells, and a distinct shortage of basic amenities. Reluctantly, we must recommend that perhaps the best visit of the fort and battle area can be taken in while just offshore aboard the Mobile Bay Ferry.

The fee for visiting the fort is $5.00 for those 13 and over, $3.00 for students and children ages 6 through 12. "Group rates are available," although we were not able to find out any specifics. You are supposed to pay your entrance fee about one-half mile east of the site at the same gate where you pay your fee for the Mobile Bay Ferry (which is only collected on the Fort Morgan side for trips either way), although there are no signs to indicate this, and you must inform the fee collector of your intentions. There is a single set of restrooms on-site next to the main parking lot and a single soft drink machine in a tiny, unmarked brick building next to the fort's sally port (under the flagpoles). A small museum with maps, photos, and artifacts shares space with a large gift shop near the main entrance. The fort is open daily from 8:00 A.M. to 5:00 P.M. and the museum/gift shop from 9:00 A.M. to 5:00 P.M.; closed only on Thanksgiving, Christmas, and New Year's Day.

Historic Blakely State Park/Spanish Fort
33745 State Route 225, Spanish Fort
(251) 626-0798
This 3,800-acre park is the site of the last major battle of the war, in April 1865. Although none of the earthworks or entrenchments still exists, there are several paths through the woods that run through the battle area, and two observation platforms overlooking the Tensaw River, where Battery Huger and Battery Tracy were located. A battle reenactment is held here the first weekend in April each year.

Nearby Spanish Fort is now a heavily built-up suburb of Mobile; no trace of the old fort remains. The park is open daily 9:00 A.M. to 5:00 P.M., closed only December 24 and 25. Admission is $3.00 for adults, $1.50 for children ages 6 through 12.

Fort Conde Welcome Center
150 South Royal, Mobile
(251) 208-7304
While all of the Civil War actions took place outside the city of Mobile proper, there are still some worthwhile sights there for the dedicated buff. For a complete listing of this historic city's sights and attractions, most of which lean toward the antebellum, contact the welcome center, which can also supply maps (which are absolutely necessary here).

Admiral Raphael Semmes Statue
Government Street at
Water Street, Mobile
The admiral was the famed commander of the CSS *Alabama,* the most successful Confederate commerce raider, which sank 57 Union ships before being shot to pieces and sunk by the USS *Kearsarge* off the coast of France.

The Museum of the City of Mobile
111 South Royal, Mobile
(251) 208-7569
This museum houses a truly massive collection of artifacts detailing the long history of Mobile. A nice Civil War–era exhibit contains a small but well-presented weapons display. The museum is open 9:00 A.M. to 5:00 P.M. Monday through Saturday and 1:00 to 5:00 P.M. on Sunday; it is closed on city holidays. Admission is $5.00 for adults, $4.00 for seniors, and $3.00 for students and children.

USS *Alabama* Battleship Memorial Park
2703 Battleship Parkway, Mobile
(251) 433-2703
No, this isn't Semmes's famed warship, which lies in the murky depths 3 miles off the coast of Cherbourg, France. This is the equally famous WW II battleship, now

nicely preserved as a floating museum. The decks, massive maingun turrets, mess rooms, berthing compartments, bridge, and officers' quarters are open for tours. Also in the encompassing 100-acre park is the USS *Drum,* a WW II fleet submarine also open for tours, as well as a rather eclectic selection of combat aircraft, including a B-52D, B-25 Mitchell, P-51D Mustang, F4U Corsair, and even an A-12 (the interceptor version of the super-secret SR-71 Blackbird).

This attraction has absolutely nothing to do with the Civil War history of Mobile, but it is nearly irresistible to the historical traveler and an absolute must for any military buff. Open 8:00 A.M. to 6:00 P.M. daily, the park is closed only on December 25. Admission is $10.00 for adults, $5.00 for children ages 6 through 11. If you park in the adjoining lot, the fee is another $2.00. The park is across the Mobile River from the downtown area; take I-10 east to exit 27 and follow the signs.

ACCOMMODATIONS

There are very few lodgings available near either fort, and those on the two islands tend to be the very high-priced resort variety with lengthy minimum stays required. We recommend you look for more reasonably priced establishments a few miles north in the metro Mobile area, particularly near the I-10 intersections, and we have noted a few of the better choices.

Gulf Breeze Motel $-$$
**1512 Cadillac Avenue, Dauphin Island
(251) 861-7344, (800) 286-0296**
While most facilities on the Gulf Coast area of Mobile are expensive resorts, this small motel is a significant exception. The two-story, blue-and-white facility houses 31 fairly good-size units, each of which contains a refrigerator as well as the usual amenities. Less than 2 miles from Fort Gaines (turn right instead of left at the water tower, where AL 193 ends on the island), Gulf Breeze is just up the street

from the beaches and an 18-hole golf course; a boat launch and slips are on the grounds. A bit unusual is the 48-hour cancellation notice needed for reservations (so your credit card is not charged for a night's stay), and the check-in time is quite early, at 1:00 P.M. The island is very pleasant, so if you wish to stay for a week, one night of your stay is free.

> *SOLDIERS—The Commanding General takes pleasure in announcing to his troops that victory and success is now within their grasp; and that the Commanding General feels proud and gratified that in every attack and assault the enemy have been repulsed; and that the Commanding General will further say to his noble and gallant troops, "Be of good cheer—all is well."*
>
> Order read to the Army of Tennessee just before the December 1864 battle of Nashville, from Lieutenant General John Bell Hood of the Confederate Army (as quoted by Sam Watkins in *Co. Aytch*)

The Gulf Shores Plantation $$-$$$$
**AL 180 West, Gulf Shores
(251) 540-5000, (800) 554-0344**
If you want to go whole hog in an upscale resort, this is the place to do it. Located very conveniently between Fort Morgan and Gulf Shores along a rather long and mostly deserted island road, this full-service resort has 325 rooms arranged as one- to three-bedroom condos and is rated three-diamond by AAA. All the rooms feature kitchens. There are six swimming pools on the property, as well as a golf course, lighted tennis courts, a sauna and Jacuzzis, and a game room for the kiddies. Most restaurants on this stretch of Gulf Shores are few and far between, but there is a Pizza Hut on the property as well as a beachside cafe. Isolation has its advantages, as the beach is practically a private one.

RESTAURANTS

As for the lodgings, we recommend look-ing for dining establishments off the two islands, as the ones nearest the two forts tend to be overpriced and not really supe-rior to those closer to the city, with one significant exception.

Lighthouse Bakery $
919 Chaumont Avenue, Dauphin Island
(251) 861–BAKE (2253)
This small bakery and sandwich shop is fairly well hidden away on a side street across from the Ship and Shore Store and facing the Baptist church. It appears sparkling new and caters to both the resort and fishing crowds. The best time to visit is at breakfast, when the pleasant staff has fresh, large cinnamon rolls, dan-ishes, and muffins ready (well before most historians of our acquaintance have their eyes cranked open!), as well as a variety of ever-changing daily specials.

Cajun roast beef, smoked turkey, and turkey pastrami sandwiches are available for dinner or early suppers, as well as a variety of other meat, cheese, and salad sandwiches. This is a "for-real" bakery, and fresh breads and rolls are available daily. Try to visit on a Thursday, when the to-die-for pepperjack cheese rolls are offered. The popularity this bakery has already engendered is reflected in the notice that you must call ahead to reserve one of the French bread loaves, available on Saturday.

Another highlight is the freshly ground and properly prepared coffees—a hearty espresso or "real" cappuccino is highly rec-ommended. The Lighthouse is open Tues-day through Friday 6:00 A.M. to 4:00 P.M., Saturday 6:00 A.M. to 6:00 P.M., and Sunday 9:00 A.M. to 3:30 P.M.; closed on Monday.

OTHER ALABAMA AND MISSISSIPPI BATTLEFIELDS

With the exceptions of the Vicksburg-Jackson, Mobile, and Shiloh-Corinth campaigns, the Civil War actions in Alabama and Mississippi largely consisted of smash-and-grab cavalry raids and small militia engagements. These two states, the very heartland of the Southern Confederacy, ironically came through the war nearly unscathed, as the major battles raged in their neighboring states to the east. Even where major battles did occur within their borders, as at Vicksburg and Mobile, the combat action stayed relatively close geographically to those cities, leaving the surrounding countryside mostly unmolested.

In this chapter we will concentrate on one relatively small but very significant battle in Mississippi and try to point out some of the other significant landmarks in both states. For a more in-depth discussion of the major campaigns fought in these states, please turn to the specific chapters on Mobile, Vicksburg, and Shiloh.

ALABAMA

Alabama was perhaps the Confederate state least directly affected militarily by the war. The fourth state to secede from the Union, the "Cradle of the Confederacy" served as the first national capital, was the home and first office for President Jefferson Davis, and remained throughout the war an important munitions and iron manufacturer and supplier to the Southern

armies, but no grand campaigns marched through her until the very end, when nearly all resistance had faded away. Accurate records are very difficult to obtain or evaluate, but somewhere in the neighborhood of one-fifth of the entire population of the state enlisted in the military forces (about 100,000 men out of 500,000). About half of these men were killed or wounded during the war.

The population of Alabama was by no means unanimous in their support for the war, as in most other states both North and South. The mountainous northern sections were particularly noted for their strong pro-Union stance; in one there was a very serious attempt to "secede" from the state of Alabama and form an independent, county-size, and pro-Union sovereign nation. The Free State of Winston died in its planning stages, but both sides took note of the seeming anti-Confederate fever there and tried in their own ways to exploit it. Their efforts failed, for just as in mountainous regions all over the world, the local population wanted to be left to their own devices and not to be involved in "flatlander" squabbles.

Even this independent train of thought had its limitations. Part of a Union cavalry—the 1st Alabama Cavalry—was raised in Randolph County (on the southeastern edge of the independence-minded area), but the same county sent men to fill out in whole or in part some 30 artillery, cavalry, and infantry regiments for the Confederacy, not to mention a whole host of local militia and home guard units.

Union Raid into Central Alabama

Although the Union controlled most of northern Alabama by the second year of the war, it was not able to mount an offensive deep into the state until the strong Confederate garrisons in Mobile were eliminated. It was not until the last two months of the war, with Mobile safely under Union control and most of the other Alabama garrisons killed, captured, or scattered, that a raid deep into the state aimed at eliminating the strong arsenal at Selma and as many other manufacturing facilities and supply warehouses as could be safely captured or reduced. To this end, Major General James Harrison Wilson gathered more than 14,000 cavalrymen in extreme northwestern Alabama, just east of Corinth, Mississippi, in the early spring of 1865, preparing to mount a massive raid through the industrial heartland of Alabama and Georgia.

Wilson's Raid to Selma, as it was originally known, was the largest single operation of its kind during the war, and one of the most successful, but to be perfectly blunt, it could not have succeeded at any objective if Confederate resistance was not collapsing everywhere just as it kicked off. The only combat forces available to resist during this 28-day raid were three seriously decimated brigades of Brigadier General Nathan Bedford Forrest's cavalry command, along with small remnants from Brigadier General James Ronald Chalmer's Mississippi and Brigadier General William Hicks "Red" Jackson's Tennessee Cavalry Divisions, and a small detachment from Brigadier General Philip Dale Roddy's Alabama Cavalry Brigade. In a few places this pitiful force was joined by local militia, but at no point did Wilson face a force stronger than 5,000 Confederates. Forrest claimed that he had a total force available of some 12,000 men in early March, but it is much more likely that he had somewhere around half that number actually still sticking around.

Wilson's Raid Sets Off

Wilson's force concentrated at Eastport, Alabama, just across the border from northeastern Mississippi and left on its great raid on March 22. With only scattered resistance from bands of Forrest's cavalry and small groups of infantry, they moved quickly in three columns southeast through the state, aiming straight for Selma. Forrest attempted to make a stand just north of Plantersville, 18 miles north of Selma, with a hastily assembled force of about 2,000 cavalrymen and militia. On the morning of April 2, Wilson's vanguard on the Randolph-Plantersville Road (now Alabama Highways 139 and 22), the 72nd Indiana Mounted Infantry, encountered rail barricades set up by Roddey's cavalry across the road. The Union force immediately attacked, forcing most of the Confederate cavalrymen to abandon their positions and fall back, while the rest covered their retreat. Wilson ordered his men to keep the pressure on, and a sort of "leapfrog" running battle soon ensued. The Confederates continued to fall back but kept a hot fire as they did (this is a tactic known as a "fighting retreat").

Forrest had deployed the rest of his small force about a mile behind Roddey's position, and the Union force finally ran into his main line about 4:00 P.M. Believing they could just blow through Forrest's thin line, the men of the 17th Indiana Mounted Infantry charged, led by Captain Frank White. Wilson had described White as a "berserker of the Norseman breed," and the captain did his best to live up to that description. Charging into the line, into the very teeth of Forrest's only battery of artillery, a vicious hand-to-hand combat broke out with the for-once superior numbers of Confederate infantry. Forrest himself joined in the fray, soon wounded by a saber blow from Captain James D. Taylor, but he killed his assailant moments later with his pistol. White and his men were soon hurled back with significant losses.

Wilson ordered another attack to begin at once, this time with a brigade-wide front of dismounted cavalry and infantry, well supported by a heavy attack on the right of the Confederate line. That part of Forrest's line was held by the untrained and untried Alabama State Troops under Brigadier General Daniel Weisiger Adams. The militiamen soon caved in under the brutal attack, exposing Forrest's whole line and within a few minutes forcing him to pull his command south into Selma. Although a relatively short affair, one Union soldier called the fight, "a right smart little skirmish."

There is many a boy here today who looks on war as all glory, but, boys it is all hell. You can bear this warning to generations yet to come. I look upon war with horror.

Major General William T. Sherman, Union Army, in an address to a Grand Army of the Republic convention, 1880

The Battle of Selma

A 5-mile-long series of earthworks and redoubts had been established in a semi-circle around Selma, anchored on both ends to the Alabama River that flows across the south side of town. The most likely avenue of attack was from the north, the very direction Wilson was coming from, and the strongest parts of the line were here. In front of the trench line ran a parapet 6 to 8 feet tall, 8 feet thick at the base, and with a 5-foot-deep, 5-foot-wide ditch in front. While the fortifications were formidable, the garrison manning them was not. By the time Wilson closed in, Forrest's command was so small that he had to space them nearly 10 feet apart to cover the entire line (the standard was something more like elbow distance apart, ideally). Again, an exact figure as to the strength of this force is impossible to ascertain, but somewhere between 4,000 and 8,000 men manned the line, a bad mixture of hardened veterans of the Army

of Tennessee alongside civilian preachers hastily "recruited" from the city churches.

The battle at Selma was almost anticlimactic from the start. Wilson's men moved south quickly on the morning of April 2, and by 3:00 P.M. they were just outside the city defenses and moving in line ready to assault. A little after 4:00 P.M. one of Wilson's divisions (Brigadier General Eli Long's 2nd Cavalry) stormed the northwestern ramparts astride the Summerfield Road, clearing the formidable obstacle in one great charge. The Confederate defenders put up a mighty defense during the assault—as Long and his staff rode forward, one was killed by a sharpshooter and four were wounded, including Long himself, who was shot in the head. Major General Emory Upton's 4th Cavalry Division had launched into the northeastern ramparts at nearly the same time, easily pushing over the parapet and encountering less resistance than Long suffered. As darkness fell, all Confederate resistance in the city broke, leaving Wilson his prize.

Wilson rested briefly in the small Alabama town and then gathered his force and headed east, toward his fateful rendezvous with the Confederate president himself.

MISSISSIPPI

The second state to declare secession (January 9, 1861), Mississippi was so enthusiastic as a whole to the new Confederacy that it somehow managed to contribute more fighting men to the Southern cause than the total number of white males it had in its 1860 census. More than 80,000 men served, mostly outside the state's borders, although Mississippi was a heavily fought-over battleground most of the war. Less than one-fourth of that number were still present in their regiments at war's end. While cavalry raids and operations ranged over most of the state repeatedly between 1862 and 1865, most large combat operations were concentrated in two areas: northeastern portions of the state around Corinth and Tupelo and the triangle between Vicksburg, Natchez, and Jackson (see the chapter on Vicksburg for a more thorough study of that campaign).

Corinth

This small town in extreme northeastern Mississippi came into prominence far out of proportion to its size during the war for two reasons—the Memphis & Charleston and Mobile & Ohio Railroads, which crossed in town. It was critical for the Confederacy to maintain control of these rail lines in order to maintain a cohesive and easily reinforceable front across the Western Theater, and it was equally critical for the Union to control them to prevent that very same thing.

After the disastrous fall of Forts Henry and Donelson in northern Tennessee in early 1862 (see the chapter on Other Tennessee Battlefields for a discussion of these battles), Western Department commander General Albert Sidney Johnston moved his headquarters to Corinth and tightened his lines of defense. As his western armies were badly outnumbered by the Union armies still assembling, Johnston decided to make the roads linking Memphis to Charleston his main line of resistance; pulled troops away from Arkansas, Charleston, Savannah, Mobile, and most of Florida; and initially abandoned plans to retake Kentucky. His strategy was to gather his forces in northern Mississippi, wait until the Union armies collected in Tennessee, and then strike hard and try to destroy their fighting capability before they could recover. While an excellent (and classic) strategy, it relied heavily on surprise and massive force, both of which were difficult to manage given the battlefield tactics and transportation methods of the day.

Johnston gave General Pierre Gustave Toutant Beauregard overall responsibility for assembling the scattered forces at Corinth and making them ready for battle.

As Beauregard set about his task, Major General Henry Wager Halleck (commander, Department of the Mississippi) was sending his combined armies south to attack and take Corinth and Jackson, thus (hopefully) splitting the Confederate Western Theater neatly in half. Starting in early March 1862, Union forces started arriving in Savannah, Tennessee, to establish their forward base of operations for the move to Corinth, 30 miles to the south. Learning of the Union presence, Johnston decided to move out and strike the enemy force before it could fully deploy, even though a major portion of his own army had not yet arrived.

Johnston led about 40,000 men of his newly minted Army of the Mississippi north to the place where Union forces were landing for their own invasion—a small riverboat landing called Pittsburg Landing and better known for the local small country church, Shiloh (see the chapter on Shiloh for a discussion of this battle). After a two-day fiercely contested fight on April 6 and 7, which included the death of Johnston himself, Beauregard withdrew the battered army back to Corinth and dug in, while the Union Army was too exhausted and battered itself to pursue immediately.

Background to the Battle

Even before Johnston ordered the army out to Shiloh, work was under way to fortify Corinth. First begun as a series of simple breastworks on the north and east sides of town, after Beauregard brought the army back to town on April 8, 1862, work began in earnest to expand and improve the line. Work was complicated by the fact that hospitals, churches, and ordinary homes were filled to overflowing with Confederate wounded, as many as 8,000 by several accounts. Major General Earl Van Dorn's Army of the West had finally arrived from Arkansas, along with a division under Brigadier (later Major) General Sterling "Pap" Price, joining General Braxton Bragg's Army of the Mississippi, fresh back from Shiloh, to give Beauregard nearly 66,000 combat troops in the small city.

Halleck moved his great Northern army very slowly south, starting out on April 29 and taking nearly a month to move the 20 miles to the outskirts of Corinth. His nearly 130,000-man army was composed of Brigadier (later Lieutenant) General Ulysses S. Grant's Army of the Tennessee, Major General Don Carlos Buell's Army of the Ohio, and Major General John Pope's Army of the Mississippi, the very combined Union force that had so worried Johnston.

Johnston had only had to worry about Grant's army the first day at Shiloh, and his successor Beauregard had been pushed off the field of battle when Buell's army showed up the next day. As the three great Union armies slowly moved into an encompassing siege position around the city, it was obvious that there was no way the smaller Confederate force could win in open battle and to stay would be a slow starvation after the supply lines were cut. Beauregard decided to evacuate his forces while he still had the chance and hopefully work his armies into a position where they could take out the superior Union forces piecemeal.

On May 29 most of the sick and wounded, along with most of the available supplies, were moved down the Mobile & Ohio Railroad line south to Tupelo, while regimental and brigade commanders shuffled their commands around the city to give the Union force the idea that they were about to try a breakout attack. "Quaker guns" (logs painted black) replaced the artillery in their redoubts, and buglers blew their calls in deserted camps while the infantry quietly slipped out the unguarded back door, following the trains to Tupelo. During the night what was left of the cavalry slipped out just as quietly, leaving startled Union pickets to see only a deserted line of earthworks and redoubts guarding an equally deserted town when the dawn broke. Some historians state that this withdrawal was the beginning of the end for the western Confederacy, as it left the Union Army in a strong position with a large force deep in the Southern lines of communication.

The Battle of Corinth: Act 1

With Beauregard's army safely out of the city, Halleck's men cautiously entered Corinth, fully expecting some sort of trap or ambush. When a thorough search of the area turned up no sign of gray-clad infantry, Halleck undoubtedly breathed a sigh of relief—and then set about strengthening the city's fortifications for an expected attack. Over the next few months, a series of artillery batteries ringed by infantry emplacements were built on the south side of town (called Batteries A through F), soon joined by an inner ring of five more such batteries, called the College Hill line.

By late summer 1862, the main focus of activity started moving away from Mississippi into Tennessee and northern Georgia. Bragg had replaced Beauregard as overall commander, but he soon moved with his Army of Tennessee to Chattanooga to counter an expected Union move against that transportation and manufacturing center. Van Dorn was given command of the District of Mississippi and moved his headquarters and most of his command southwestward to Vicksburg, while Price shifted his reduced Army of the West into Iuka, Mississippi, to keep an eye on the Union movements east.

There had been several command changes in the Union army at Corinth as well. Halleck had been recalled to Washington to serve as the latest in a continuing series of unsuccessful commanding generals of all the Union armies, the very position his lieutenant Grant would successfully fill some time later. Grant set about preparing his army to move east into central Tennessee, while the beloved but inept Major General William Starke "Old Rosy" Rosecrans, a divisional commander during the brief siege, took over command of both the Army of the Mississippi and the Department of Corinth.

Iuka

Ordered to prevent any of the three Union armies in Corinth from traveling east to attack Bragg in Tennessee, Price was in a bad position. He had 14,000 men strung across a wide line in northeastern Mississippi, really more of a guard and early-warning force than any significant combat threat; his only reinforcements lay on the other side of the Union positions, several hundred miles away in Vicksburg; and Grant appeared determined to move his armies through his position. Grant was also worried that Price might move his force north to join Bragg and resolved to attack the Confederate force before he could do so. As one might imagine, Civil War–era generals spent a lot of time in their tents worrying, usually about the most unlikely of things. On September 16, 1862, Grant ordered Major General Edward Otho Cresap Ord to take his 2nd Division (Army of the Tennessee) and Rosecrans to take his Army of the Mississippi and assault Price's force in a coordinated attack on the morning of September 19.

The attack at Iuka did not come off as planned, to say the least. Ord's order to attack at a given time was changed to an order to move in when he heard Rosecrans's attack start, the intention being to better coordinate the two-pronged assault. Price had learned of Ord's movement against him from the northwest around dusk on September 18, although not of Rosecrans's from the southwest, and telegraphed Van Dorn with the news. The Confederate commander ordered Price to pull his troops out of Iuka, join his force now moving out of Vicksburg, and threaten Grant's armies from Tennessee.

As Price's men moved out of town on the afternoon of September 19, they ran straight into Rosecrans's force, the Union movement to attack having been delayed by poor navigation skills.

While Rosecrans's and Price's troops rapidly deployed and launched into a vicious fight, Ord's force stayed unmoving on the north side of town. He later claimed that he heard no gunfire all the rest of the day, a claim supported by his command staff, but Grant remained suspicious ever after that he had simply decided to let Rosecrans do all the fighting. This is perhaps one of the better known examples of a phenomenon known as "acoustic shadow," where someone many miles away may hear the noise of battle, but someone close in might hear nothing.

Price's northernmost battlefield commanders had warned him about Ord's presence, but when he did not join in Rosecrans's attack, the Confederate commander decided his force was just a ruse to try to get him to split his small command. However, when the Union attack was unsuccessful in breaking his own lines by nightfall, Price decided that, ruse or not, Ord was bound to join in the continued assault the next morning. Just before dawn on September 20 Price led his men safely south out of the besieged town, heading to join Van Dorn's force bearing north out of Vicksburg. Rosecrans initially ordered his men to pursue, but fearful of getting lost again and facing a strong rearguard action from Price's men, he soon called off the chase.

The Battle of Corinth: Act 2

With Price and Van Dorn both now safely out of his immediate area of concern, Grant moved north to Jackson, Tennessee, with most of his army, leaving Rosecrans with only four divisions to garrison the town and protect the northern Mississippi supply lines. Van Dorn knew that Corinth was a key town for either side to control and, with most of the Union armies now gone, determined to attack it. On the first of October, the 22,000 men of the combined Confederate armies in Mississippi moved north from their base near Ripley, 22 miles southwest of Corinth, in an attempt to take the fortified town from the northwest and by surprise.

By the very next day, the element of surprise was lost when the Confederate infantry skirmished with Union cavalry scouts at the Hatchie River Bridge on the outskirts of Corinth. Alarmed, Rosecrans concentrated his forces in the strong north and west fortification positions and waited for Chewalla, Tennessee, less than 8 miles from Corinth.

On the early morning of October 3, Major General Mansfield Lovell's, Brigadier General Dabney H. Maury's, and Brigadier General Louis Hebert's divisions burst out of the woods and stormed the northwest-ernmost line of outer defenses, easily driving in the Union pickets and advancing through the line of works with few casualties. As they dressed ranks again in preparation for assaulting the city's inner defenses, three small earthquakes shook the ground under them, frightening the men and shattering their confidence. Van Dorn ordered an hour's halt to give the men time to eat, drink, and rest before what he assumed would be a final assault. This delay only granted Rosecrans the time he needed to strengthen his line of inner defenses.

RENEWED ATTACKS

About noon Van Dorn ordered the men up and in line of battle again, but repeated assaults the rest of the afternoon failed to crack the Union line. At dusk Van Dorn ordered a halt to the battle, and plans were made with his division commanders for the next morning's assault. Hebert was to lead the attack by a strong assault on the Union right, followed in close order by Maury in the center and Lovell hitting the Union left flank. A predawn heavy artillery barrage was planned to help screen the

infantry movements into line and reduce the Union defenses.

At 4:00 A.M. the Confederate artillery batteries opened up to "soften" the Union fortifications for the assaulting infantry, but they were soon silenced by very effective Union counter-battery fire. Just before he was to move out on assault, Hebert suddenly fell ill and was replaced by Brigadier General Martin E. Green, who wasted a precious hour trying to get reorganized. Maury had started his assault in the meantime, allowing Rosecrans to concentrate his artillery fire and troop strength on his small part of the assault line. For some unknown reason, Lovell never ordered his men to attack.

When Green's men finally came into line, the two Confederate divisions succeeded in blowing through the Union defenses and into the city itself. At the height of the battle, several brigades managed to fight their way to the rail crossroads in the center of town, while Colonel William P. Rogers led his 2nd Texas Infantry Regiments up and over the ramparts of Battery Robinett, the last line of Rosecrans's defenses. However, since Lovell had failed to support the attack, Union troops from the south side of the city were able to move forward and hit the Confederates on their flank, violently breaking up the attack. Rogers was killed and his force shattered before they could consolidate their gain. Within two hours the Confederates were forced to withdraw from the city, and Rosecrans once again had full control of his lines. Van Dorn once again was forced to order a general retreat, which, once again, Rosecrans was unable to pursue, possibly out of fear of becoming lost once more.

For a relatively short fight, casualties were staggeringly high on both sides. Rosecrans reported that he had lost 315 killed and 1,812 wounded, with another 232 missing or captured (out of 21,147 engaged) during the two-day battle, while Van Dorn reported a loss of 1,423 killed, 5,692 wounded, and another 2,268 missing and presumed captured (out of his approximately 22,000-strong command). Corinth remained either occupied or under Union control for the rest of the war, and no Confederate army tried again to retake it.

THE TOUR

Alabama Sites

We suggest a visit to significant Alabama sites as part of a larger tour of the battle areas in Georgia, Tennessee, and Mississippi; accordingly, we list these areas from east to west, and from the northern part of the state to the southern half.

JACKSONVILLE

Scene of a small cavalry raid in 1862, this small town north of Anniston is best known today as the home of Jacksonville State University. Just off the main square next to city hall is the First Presbyterian Church, one of a handful of antebellum structures still in existence in the city. This church, built in 1861, was used as a hospital during and after the short battle here; it is still in use and does not offer formal tours.

In the city cemetery 2 blocks south, at the corner of South Church and Mays Streets, is the resting place of General Robert E. Lee's "boy artillerist," Major John Pelham. A tall, well-sculpted statue of the young officer looks west out of the Confederate section of the cemetery (at the very edge of the cemetery, at the cross streets given above). Pelham had resigned from West Point after his home state of Alabama seceded, just a few weeks before he was due to graduate. Assigned to Lee's Army of Northern Virginia, Pelham displayed an amazing skill at gunnery, particularly with his fast-moving "horse artillery" battery.

Pelham was a good-looking and rather dashing sort and a favorite of the equally dashing cavalry officer Brigadier General James Ewell Brown ("Jeb") Stuart, who took Pelham along on his many cavalry raids. Officially just a casual observer, Pelham joined in on a mass charge of the 3rd Virginia Cavalry at Kelley's Ford on March 17, 1863. Struck on the neck by a bursting artillery shell, he was quickly taken to the nearby home of his fiancée, Bessie Shackelford, where he died that same night. He was just 24 years old.

Jacksonville is just off the (very) well-beaten path between Anniston and the shopping mecca of Boaz, about 15 miles north of Interstate 20 (exit 185) on Alabama Highway 21. Both Anniston and Gadsden, a few miles to the northwest on U.S. Highway 431, have plentiful food and lodging establishments.

ADDISON

The center of the onetime Free State of Winston, this tiny northwest Alabama community was ground zero for the antisecessionist movement. The center of all this activity was in a roadside stopover, Looney's Tavern, which stood just outside town. The original building is long gone, but the site has a historic marker and can be found on Winston County Highway 41 about 2 miles north of its intersection with U.S. Highway 278, on the eastern edge of town. This road is very poorly marked; watch for the road sign pointing toward Decatur just before you start into the business district of the small settlement.

This area was seriously pro-Union during the war, as a few known statistics bear out. Not only was the little-known 1st Alabama Cavalry raised in this area (and went on to march with Sherman through Georgia), but an estimated 2,000 local citizens joined this and other Union regiments during the war. Another estimated 10,000 "Tories" lived in northern Alabama, actively assisting Confederate deserters and helping Union raiders. Three thousand of these Unionist citizens met at Looney's Tavern on July 4, 1861, to draft documents formally protesting Alabama's secession and to explore ways their county could secede from the state. In the end nothing ever came of the attempt.

Just to the west of Addison is the private Looney's Amphitheater & Park, which presents a highly colored version of the events leading up to the meeting at Looney's Tavern, advertised as "Alabama's official outdoor musical drama." Shows are presented yearly in July and August, but ironically not on July 4! A whole range of other activities are offered at the same time—a riverboat cruise with "master storytellers [who] spin yarns of yesteryear," a gift shop with "Civil War memorabilia," a home-style restaurant, and the "Looney Putt Miniature Golf" course. Every ACW site should be so blessed! For ticket prices and dates and times of the production, call (205) 489–5000. The amphitheater is just west of Addison on US 278.

DECATUR

Located at an extremely strategic point on the Tennessee River served by the newly built Tuscumbia Railroad (known during the war as the Memphis & Charleston), this small town became an important transportation and supply center during the war. Although the target of both sides as "ownership" changed hands relatively early in the war, no pitched battles were fought in or around the town.

Immediately after the Union victory at Shiloh (April 7, 1862), Brigadier (soon Major) General Ormsby McKnight Mitchel was directed to take a reinforced division of about 8,000 men and take Huntsville and Decatur for the North at his earliest opportunity. This would cut the Confederate supply lines through north Alabama and south-central Tennessee, while providing a good base to use for a planned invasion of Montgomery and Mobile, as well as a nod of protection for the Unionist Tories who populated the surrounding area. On April 12 the lead brigades of Mitchel's force entered Decatur unopposed and immediately set out reconnaissance parties farther west toward Florence and Tuscumbia.

The Union kept control of Decatur the remainder of the war, suffering only iso-lated and brief cavalry attacks on its garrison for the next two and a half years. In late October 1864, General John Bell Hood's decimated Army of Tennessee camped just outside the city for three days, "making demonstrations" against the Union garrison to keep them bottled up inside the city until the rest of his force had safely passed to the west. It is highly unlikely that he actually sought any battle, which did not come in any stead, as his target was badly needed supplies he expected to find at Tuscumbia.

Decatur is located west of Huntsville, just off Interstate 65. U.S. Highway 72 Alternate connects the town with I-65 at exit 340, about 5 miles east of downtown. Although little military action occurred here, there are three interesting stops in the town.

The Old State Bank
925 Bank Street, Decatur
(256) 350–5060
Built in 1833, this large, impressive Greek Revival building originally housed one of the three first branches of the Bank of the State of Alabama. Legend has it that then President Martin Van Buren attended the dedication ceremony. During the war it served as a hospital and supply depot (which Hood would no doubt have loved to get his hands on) and is reportedly one of only five structures left standing in town after the war. The huge columns gracing the front porch have damage that is claimed to be from some of the Confederate cavalry raids.

Now restored to its bank-era appearance (the state bank system in Alabama died in 1846), the Old State Bank stands on a beautifully landscaped downtown park and is open as a city museum. The bank is open Monday through Friday 9:30 A.M. to 4:30 P.M. and closed noon to 1:00 P.M. daily for lunch. Weekend hours vary; the staff advises that you call ahead to check. The bank is closed Thanksgiving, December 24 and 25, and New Year's Day. Admission is free.

Hines-McEntire Home
120 Sycamore Street, Decatur

This two-story brick mansion on the Tennessee River bank was a headquarters for both sides during the war. Local legend holds that General Albert Sydney Johnston of the Confederacy planned his Shiloh campaign here and that, for the Union, General Ulysses S. Grant and Major General William Sherman met here for strategic discussions after the Vicksburg campaign.

The home is empty and up for sale at this writing; no tours are currently offered, and the grounds are fenced off, but a good view of the house can be obtained from the street. Sycamore Street runs north off Wilson Street/US 72 west of the Keller Memorial Bridge over the Tennessee River and just past a small bridge over the railroad tracks.

Parham's Civil War Relics
and Memorabilia
721–723 Bank Street, Decatur
(256) 350–4018

This small shop upstairs over an antiques store is a short walk from the Old Bank and offers an interesting variety of small artifacts for sale, as well as books and modern memorabilia concerning the war. Owner Robert Parham is a local authority on the Civil War era and a good conversationalist; be prepared to stay awhile if you really want to know what happened here!

Some of the larger, better known "relic" shops we have visited could take some lessons from Parham; he runs a tidy shop with artifacts priced for the average collector, concentrates on his immediate area, and has a refreshing lack of "the very bullet that killed A. S. Johnston" style of labels and identifications.

WHEELER

General Joe Wheeler Plantation
12280 Alabama Highway 20, Wheeler
(256) 637–8513

Although most maps point to this location 15 miles west of Decatur as a "town," it really consists of one thing alone: the plantation and last home of Major General Joseph "Fighting Joe" Wheeler of the Confederate Army. Perhaps one of the best combat cavalry officers produced during the war, Wheeler fought primarily with the Army of Tennessee under Bragg, Johnston, and Hood and commanded what was for all practical purposes the only unit resisting Sherman's Georgia campaign of fall 1864. He led his cavalry in more than 500 skirmishes and 127 pitched battles, lost 16 horses shot out from under him, had 36 of his staff officers wounded, and was himself wounded three times. Although he and the equally famous Major General Nathan Bedford Forrest of the South loathed each other, they were both past masters at the art of employing cavalry to disrupt enemy lines of communication. Wheeler went on to a successful postwar career as a cotton planter and U.S. congressman, and during the Spanish-American War, he became the only Confederate general officer to regain his U.S. commission as a general officer.

During the Santiago campaign (Spanish-American War), U.S. Major General Wheeler commanded the cavalry division that included Teddy Roosevelt's Rough Riders. Perhaps showing his advancing age (he was 62 at the time) or just hearkening back to a happier time, upon seeing the Rough Riders storming up Kettle Hill (not San Juan Hill, as is so often erroneously attributed), he allegedly turned to his aide and remarked, "Just look at them! They got the Yankee sons-of-bitches on the run!"

The Wheeler Plantation is a work still in progress, being restored as a living-history park, but it's a very interesting and highly recommended stop. The main house has been restored to its original condition, most furnishings are period and original to the house, and another 13 buildings round out what is shaping into a close approximation of a postbellum working plantation. The main house contains a selection of personal and professional artifacts from Wheeler's long and fascinating life.

The main house and museum will undergo continued reconstruction into 2005, so call to confirm hours and admission fees. The plantation is most decidedly not the easiest place to find; take the four-lane AL 20/US 72 Alternate 15 miles west from the Decatur square, and watch carefully for a historic marker to your left (south) in a small parking lot—it is directly in front of the plantation entrance. There is no sign on the westbound route that we could see (there is one showing the evacuation route for the nearby Brown's Ferry Nuclear Power Plant!), but there is one on the eastbound side to direct you in.

FLORENCE

This city dates its founding from a year before Alabama even became a state (1818) and was an important trade and commerce center when this was the "western frontier." Although right smack in the middle of Union offenses aimed at Corinth to the west and Decatur to the east and violently taken over by both sides several times during the war, it came through the war relatively unscathed. Today it is the home of the University of North Alabama and has retained its status as a trade and commerce center for industrial traffic on the adjacent Tennessee River.

Civil War sites are hard to find in this heavily urbanized city, but it can boast at least one gem of the era.

Pope's Tavern Museum
203 Hermitage Drive, Florence
(256) 760-6439
Originally a stagecoach stop built in 1811 in the middle of a dense wilderness, this small building in the midst of an equally dense urban neighborhood now houses a museum of Civil War–era and early pioneer artifacts. The tavern was used as a hospital for both Confederate and Union troops during and after the local skirmishes and the nearby Battle of Elk River and as a supplemental hospital for the wounded from the Battle of Franklin (Tennessee).

The museum is open Tuesday through Saturday 10:00 A.M. to 4:00 P.M. and closed all major holidays. Admission is $2.00 for adults and 50 cents for those under age 18 and students with identification.

SELMA

Better known in modern times for its pivotal role in the civil rights movement, Selma was a very important manufacturing and supply center during the war, with several gun factories, foundries, warehouses, and a large armory. The Selma Naval Works produced rams, including the CSS *Tennessee,* and during the last two years of the war, nearly half the barrels and nearly two-thirds of the cartridge ammunition used by the armies in the Western Theater were produced here. The small town survived most of the war untouched, due in no small part to its isolated location deep in west-central Alabama.

Selma is about 40 miles west of both Montgomery and I-65, on U.S. Highway 80. Take exit 167 off I-65 on the south side of town, and go west on US 80 for a straight shot to the city.

While almost all of the town was destroyed either during the battle or burned by Wilson's men as they left a week later, there are a handful of extant structures. Just off US 80 on the north part of town, on Broad Street at the Trinity Lutheran Church, is a marker about the battle and a small section of breastworks, the only remaining part of the line.

Old Dallas County Courthouse
(Smitherman Historic Building)
109 Union Street, Selma
(334) 874-2174
The courthouse is a large, impressive Greek Revival building well restored and kept up, which was used as a hospital and military school during the war. Now used as a museum, it houses a small but rather impressive collection of Civil War artifacts and antiques, as well as a sample of the goods that Selma's factories produced for

John Bell Hood

Of all the hard-luck cases who were living examples of the Peter Principle (that everyone eventually rises to his or her level of incompetence), John Bell Hood tops the list. Hood was born in Owingsville, Kentucky, in 1831 and secured a berth at West Point by virtue of his uncle, Congressman Richard French. He graduated after an undistinguished career at the military academy in 1853, ranked 44th out of 52. The custom at that time was to "brevet" newly minted officers (i.e., to give them the rank but not the pay, position, or real responsibility of a certain rank), and Hood was brevetted a 2nd lieutenant and sent to California soon after his graduation. In 1855 he was commissioned in the same rank and reassigned to the 2nd Cavalry in Texas, joining future Confederate and Union generals Robert E. Lee, William J. Hardee, Albert Sydney Johnston, and George H. Thomas. While there, he suffered the first of his many combat injuries in skirmishes with hostile Indians.

With the outbreak of war in 1861, Hood resigned his U.S. commission and was almost immediately granted a Confederate one to the rank of 1st lieutenant. By March of 1862 he had been promoted to brigadier general and placed in charge of the Texas Brigade (soon afterward named Hood's Texas Brigade, in the fashion of the day), under the overall command of Colonel John B. Magruder at Yorktown, Virginia. Five months later he was promoted to major general and given command of a division in Lieutenant General James Longstreet's corps, Lee's Army of Northern Virginia. He developed a reputation there as a gallant and brave fighter, inspiring deep love and devotion among his own men. At Gettysburg, however, an ill-conceived plan forced Hood under protest to charge his division uphill into a well-positioned Union force. His division was decimated, and Hood suffered a crippling injury to his left arm.

After a brief recovery period, Hood traveled with Longstreet west to reinforce General Braxton Bragg's army, about to engage at Chickamauga, Georgia. In a nearly unbelievable stroke of luck, Longstreet's corps arrived on the field at the exact place and time a Union brigade had been mistakenly moved out of the way. Longstreet was able to exploit the breach most successfully, but Hood suffered another gunfire wound, this time resulting in the amputation of his right leg. While recuperating, Hood developed an addiction to the painkiller laudanum, which many historians believe led directly to the poor battlefield decisions he subsequently made.

Upon returning to the field, Hood was promoted to lieutenant general and given command of a corps in General Joseph E. Johnston's Army of Tennessee, just in time for their rolling defense against Major General William T. Sherman's 1864 invasion of Georgia. Hood ranted against Johnston's careful hoarding of his strength while slowly giving way before Sherman, preferring the charging attack over the static defense, and said as much in a series of letter to Bragg, then President Jefferson Davis's military chief of staff, as well as to Davis himself. Davis was equally unhappy with the strategy Johnston had adopted and on June 17, 1864, replaced him with Hood, with orders to attack Sherman. Three days later her ordered an all-out attack on the Union positions at Peachtree Creek, which failed at the cost of nearly one-fourth of his command. Two days later, after a forced, nightlong march through the city of Atlanta, he attacked Sherman's positions again, this time on the eastern outskirts of the city. This attack failed as well, and follow-up attempts at Ezra Church on the western outskirts and at Jonesboro to the south accomplished nothing but reducing his available force to less than half its original strength. Forced to abandon the city on September 1, Hood soon led what was left of his army on a hare-brained campaign, designed, he said, to lure Sherman out of the strongly fortified city and north into open ground, where the vastly larger Union army could be destroyed. More than one grizzled veteran of the Army of Tennessee started saying openly that Hood had gone mad but, as good soldiers, they followed his commands.

This plan resulted in nothing more than making a portion of Sherman's available force chase Hood all up through northern Georgia before they were recalled to prepare for Sherman's march to Savannah. Hood concocted another hare-brained plan, this time to storm north through Tennessee, seizing the Union supply headquarters at Nashville, and then continue north through Kentucky, threatening Cincinnati, Ohio, and eventually moving east to join Lee's army

Lieutenant General John Bell Hood of the Confederate Army, in a postwar photo. COURTESY OF THE NATIONAL ARCHIVES

at Petersburg, where they would join forces and crush the huge Union Army commanded by Lieutenant General Ulysses S. Grant. Davis, very reluctantly this time, agreed to Hood's idea and allowed him to proceed. Moving through very scattered and light resistance at first, Hood soon ran into a rapidly retreating force at Franklin, Tennessee, on November 30 and ordered the attack with only two of his three divisions in position and only two hours of daylight left. The attack was an unmitigated disaster, with Hood being only one of 2 alive and uninjured generals (out of 12) at the end of the fight. Still he pressed on, finally washing the remnants of his army up on the shores of Union ramparts at Nashville in December 1864.

With his army nearly completely destroyed, Hood tendered his resignation quietly, which was wisely accepted. Hood spent his postwar years in New Orleans as a modestly successful businessman and vehemently defended his war record to anyone who would listen—including readers of his own book of experiences, the aptly named *Advance and Retreat,* and his writings in the monumental *Battles and Leaders of the Civil War.* His bad luck plaguing him to the end, Hood, his wife, and his eldest daughter died in a yellow fever epidemic in 1879, leaving behind 10 orphaned children.

the war effort. The museum is open Tuesday through Friday 9:00 A.M. to 4:00 P.M. and is closed all major holidays. Admission is $3.00 for persons ages 14 and over.

Old Depot Museum
4 Martin Luther King Jr. Street, Selma
(334) 874-2197
The former Tennessee & Alabama River Railroad depot, nearly destroyed during the battle, has been restored and serves as the Selma–Dallas County Museum of History and Archives. Emphasis is equally divided between Civil War, railroading, and civil rights–era exhibits, and a very nice archival room is available. Additional displays cover the Native American history of the area, WPA murals, and a selection of very rare photos showing African Americans at work on a postbellum local plantation. The depot is open Monday through Saturday 10:00 A.M. to 4:00 P.M. and on Sunday by appointment.

Live Oak Cemetery
West Dallas Avenue, Selma
A great number of Confederates who died in the battle are buried here in the cemetery's Confederate section, graced by a large monument. Lieutenant General William Joseph Hardee is also buried here, as is Navy captain Catesby ap Roger Jones, executive officer of the CSS *Virginia* (usually and erroneously identified as the *Merrimac*) and commander of the

ironclad during the fight with the USS *Monitor,* later commander of the Selma Iron Works.

MONTGOMERY

Montgomery saw no combat during the war, thanks to her position deep in the state well away from the major battle areas, but her position in Confederate lore was established even before the first shots were fired. This was the home of the first Confederate capital, before it was moved to Richmond, Virginia, and the place where President Jefferson Davis took his oath of office. Wilson's Raid came through and took the city, a transportation and supply hub, without resistance a little more than a week after Selma fell. While this capital city is a large and bustling metropolis, there are a few reminders about the war to be found.

Alabama State Capitol
Capital Hill on Dexter Avenue
Montgomery
(334) 242-3935, (800) 252-2262
The State Capitol was built in 1851 in a style very similar to the U.S. Capitol. A bronze star mounted on the west portico marks the very spot where Jefferson Davis took his oath of office. Forty-five-minute guided tours are given of the building. Make sure to see the impressive three-story, self-supporting double-spiral staircase built by former slave Horace

King, a postbellum legislator. The capitol is open for tours Monday through Saturday 9:00 A.M. to 4:00 P.M.; admission and tours are free.

First White House of the Confederacy
664 Washington Avenue, Montgomery
(334) 242–1861

The home of Jefferson Davis and his family during the first months of the Confederacy is right across the street from the capitol building and is now restored and open as a museum. The house is furnished with Davis's own furniture from his home in Mississippi, and the second floor is kept just the way it was when he was in residence. A small collection of Confederate relics and artifacts as well as some of Davis's personal belongings are on display. The museum is open Monday through Friday 8:00 A.M. to 4:30 P.M. and closed on Thanksgiving, Christmas, and New Year's Day. Admission is free, but donations are accepted and appreciated.

Mississippi Sites

CORINTH

Corinth is a bit off the beaten path, which in this case is a very good thing—there simply hasn't been enough "progress" there to erase much of its past. The town is 89 miles east of Memphis, 226 miles southwest of Nashville, 168 miles west of Birmingham, and 218 miles north of Jackson; it helps the traveler to remember that getting there is half the fun! Corinth lies in extreme northeastern Mississippi very close to the Alabama border, at the crossroads of US 72 between I-65 (exit 340) and Memphis, and U.S. Highway 45 between Interstate 40 at Jackson, Tennessee (exit 82), and Tupelo. If you are approaching from the east, we heartily recommend US 72, as it goes through Florence, Wheeler, and Decatur, Alabama—all interesting Civil War–related stops.

Corinth is without a doubt the most Civil War–oriented town we have visited, at least in the Western Theater. Information on its preserved houses, buildings, entrenchments, and museums could literally fill a good-size book. We strongly advise that you contact the Corinth Area Tourism Promotion Council and ask for its excellent package of information before starting your trip.

Corinth Area Tourism Promotion Council
602 East Waldron Street
P.O. Box 1089, Corinth, MS 38835
(662) 287-8300, (800) 748–9048

While these folks do have a visitor center in downtown Corinth, most of the information they provide can be obtained at some of the venues and attractions as well as a new satellite visitor center on the west side of town at US 45. However, we strongly suggest you call or write them to get their free mail-out package, as this is one of the best presentations we have seen from any city of any size. The devotion this town has to the Civil War historian or traveler is truly astonishing and makes the visit here an absolute must. The council also has an excellent Web site for the wired: www.corinth.net.

Northeast Mississippi Museum
Off US 45 Business north
on Fourth Street
P.O. Box 993, Corinth, MS 38835
(662) 287-3120

This small museum should be your very first stop in town. Although it is quite small physically, this is one of the finest museums of its type that you will ever step into. Largely the result of efforts by Margaret Greene Rogers, this museum relies on its highly knowledgeable and informative staff to supplement the well-laid-out displays of letters, paintings, models, and relics.

The displays themselves are rather eccentric, with a mixture of fossils from the Paleozoic and Cretaceous periods next to Chickasaw Indian relics, which are next to turn-of-the-20th-century photos of Corinth alongside battlefield-dug Civil War relics. A separate room contains a selection of largely 19th-century household items, and a small research room contains a rather impressive amount of local history books and publications, with a heavy emphasis on the Civil War era.

Do not let this eccentricity and the relatively small size of the museum fool you; we fully expected to make this a "10-minute in and out" when we first visited and ended up spending well over an hour just talking with the staff about some of the more unusual items on display. This is most decidedly not the sort of place where you see the same "bullets-n-belt buckles" that so many small town museums seem to have in common (to the point that most are hard to distinguish from one another), and we not only highly recommend a visit here but insist that this is a crucial stop for any visit to the town. The museum is open daily except for holidays, and there is no admission fee. Please help this small gem stay open, however, by giving a donation or making a purchase from the unusually small selection of "stuff for sale."

Curlee House
301 Childs Street
P.O. Box 1089, Corinth, MS 38835
(662) 287–9501

This 1857 home just off US 45 Business was the headquarters for both Bragg and Halleck and is one of the 16 National Historic Landmarks in Corinth. Central to the campaigns that were waged here, the home also houses the Corinth Civil War Interpretive Center on its grounds (see below) and offers tours of its well-restored and elegant interior. The house is open Monday through Saturday 9:00 A.M. to 5:00 P.M. and Sunday 1:00 to 4:00 P.M.; admission is $2.50.

Corinth Civil War Interpretive Center
501 West Linden, Corinth
(662) 287–9273

The Civil War Interpretive Center once was a small building behind the Curlee House. In July 2004 a $9.5-million, 12,000-square-foot replacement opened its doors, ready to educate visitors about

Corinth's importance during the war. The multiacre site highlights the 1862 Siege and Battle of Corinth as well as 16 historic landmarks in and around town. Open every day except Christmas (call to confirm hours); there is no admission fee.

Corinth National Cemetery
Horton Street, Corinth
(901) 386–8311

This cemetery was established in 1866 as the 16th National Cemetery, just three-quarters of a mile from the railroad intersection that was the focus of so much of the fighting here. Union dead were gathered here from the battlefields of Corinth, Iuka, Parker's Crossroads, and some 17 other battle and skirmish areas, as well as hospitals and camps across Mississippi and Tennessee. There are 1,793 known and 3,895 unknown Union soldiers buried in this still-active cemetery, where more than 7,000 veterans of subsequent wars also have been laid to rest. National cemeteries are usually shrines to the Union cause, but this one is unusual: Three Confederate soldiers were buried here, too, just under the flagpole. Open daily 8:00 A.M. to 4:30 P.M.; there is no admission fee.

A number of men were before [Union major general Benjamin Butler] to take the oath of allegiance. One of them, a wag in his way, looked at the General, and with a peculiar Southern drawl, said: "We gave you hell at Chickamauga, General!"

The General was furious at the man's familiar impudence and threatened him with all sorts of punishment, but again came that drawling voice, repeating the first part of the statement, but he was stopped by the General, who ordered him to take the oath of allegiance to the United States at once or he would have him shot. After some hesitation, looking into General Butler's fierce eye, he reluctantly consented to take the oath. After taking the oath, he looked calmly into General Butler's face, and drew himself up as if proud to become a citizen of the United States and a member of the Yankee Army, and said: "General, I suppose I am a good Yankee and citizen of the United States now?"

The General replied in a very fatherly tone, "I hope so." "Well, General, the rebels did give us hell at Chickamauga, didn't they?"

From *Civil War Treasury of Tales, Legends & Folklore*, edited by B. A. Botkin

Battery Robinett
Linden Street, Corinth
(662) 287-5269

The center of Corinth's inner defenses and then scene of some of the heaviest fighting, the earthworks here were rebuilt to the original specifications in 1976. A small park surrounding the earthworks, display cannons, and monuments is always open. There is no admission fee.

Battery F
Davis Street, Corinth

One of several original and well-preserved earthworks in and around town, this was the one through which Confederate forces successfully assaulted on October 3, 1862. It is a redoubt of the type called a "lunette," with mountings for four guns and several surrounding infantry rifle pits. Well outside the main part of town, take Smith Bridge Road west across US 45, turn right onto Kimberly Road and then left onto Davis Street.

Accommodations

There are surprisingly few places to stay here, other than the ubiquitous B&Bs, and most of the available motels tend to be a little road-weary from the very heavy fishing and hunting crowds that come here. The most convenient facilities are three relatively new chain motels on the west side of town near the intersection of US 72 and US 45; our other recommendation is to travel to the larger town of Tupelo, 55 miles south on US 45, which has a much larger selection of mid- and low-priced chain lodging. Be aware that these facilities fill up very fast during special events and on most summer weekends; we recommend you make prior reservations or plan on staying somewhere well outside of town.

Restaurants

As with the lodging availability, there seems to be a distinct shortage of good restaurants in Corinth and only a few that we felt we could wholeheartedly recommend. We were quite surprised when even the locals were recommending the usual chain fast-food places (grouped together on US 72), and we actually left two local establishments because of the lack of cleanliness and service. This is a serious hunting and fishing area, and the restaurants show it. For other choices, we recommend you make the drive to Tupelo.

Gloster 205 Restaurant $
205 North Gloster Street, Tupelo
(662) 842-7205

This restaurant in a spiffed-up old house serves steaks, fresh seafood, prime rib, pasta dishes, and salads. The atmosphere here is more formal than in most other Tupelo establishments, but this is a very casual town. Expect good food in an upscale and trendy atmosphere. The ambience is complete with lots of green plants, nice woodwork, and white tablecloths and napkins.

Jefferson Place $
823 Jefferson Street, Tupelo
(662) 844-8696

In a residential neighborhood, this regional-favorite restaurant is known to serve hand-trimmed beef, seafood, and great sandwiches. Jefferson Place has a bar and a sometimes-enthusiastic crowd. The old house it calls home has dark wood paneling, which is brightened up by open windows and light tablecloths. It is casual and open for lunch and dinner six days a week; it's open for lunch only on Sunday.

Day Trips

Brices Cross Roads
Highway 370, Baldwyn

In late spring 1864, with Sherman raging through northern Georgia and the entire Confederacy threatened with being cut in half, Major General Nathan Bedford Forrest received orders to hit Sherman's supply and communications lines in Tennessee and try to make him slow down or even withdraw from the Deep South. Moving out of his base at Tupelo with 3,500 cavalrymen, Forrest soon learned that a column of more than 8,500 Union cavalry and infantry under Brigadier General Samuel D. Sturgis was en route from Memphis with orders to stop him. As usual for the fiery cavalry commander, he turned his columns west and made all speed to Sturgis's force to surprise and destroy him before he was ready for battle.

On June 10, 1864, the rapidly advancing Confederate cavalry encountered the first Union patrols along the Baldwyn Road, about 1 mile east of the small settlement of Brices Cross Roads. Immediately launching into a strong attack, Forrest's men were upon the Union patrols almost before they had made it back to their main column. Union reinforcements were hastily brought up, but by midafternoon the Confederate force had completely smashed the Union lines and sent Sturgis's command in a panicked rout back to Memphis. The small Confederate command not only took the field and scattered their aggressor, but also managed to capture more than 1,500 Union soldiers!

The Brices Cross Roads site today is a very small park with a single monument and some good interpretive signs, but the drive to the site off US 45 features several roadside historic markers that give a good

visualization of the action here. Adjacent to the small historic park is a cemetery containing the remains of 99 Confederate soldiers; all but one are unidentified. Aside from the usual collection of scattered mobile homes, the surrounding area seems little changed from the war, which adds to the historic flavor. We highly recommend a visit here, which does not add very much to the travel time from Corinth to Tupelo.

Recently, the nearby town of Baldwyn has opened the Brices Cross Roads National Battlefield and Visitor Center, on Mississippi Highway 370 and across US 45 from the actual battlefield. Hours of operation are Tuesday through Saturday 9:00 A.M. to 5:00 P.M. and Sunday 12:30 to 5:00 P.M. There is a small entrance fee, and the site has a small collection of artifacts, some good displays about the battle, and a very friendly staff.

Tupelo National Battlefield Site
Mississippi Highway 6, Tupelo

This small park within the city limits of Tupelo commemorates a rare unsuccessful attack by Forrest against a superior Union force here on July 13, 1864. Although the Union column did withdraw from the area after the three-hour battle and Forrest's cavalry followed in a sort of low-intensity running battle, the Union force managed to get its column through the area more or less intact (which was their original intention).

Florewood River Plantation
U.S. Highway 82 West, Greenwood
(601) 455-3821

Florewood is a living-history re-creation of 1850s plantation life in the Mississippi Delta. At the "big house," also known as the planter's mansion, guests are greeted by costumed docents who conduct tours of the furnished house. On the grounds, visitors view and visit the adjunct buildings or those outbuildings necessary to plantation life: the schoolroom, the blacksmith shop, the smokehouse, the overseer's house, the carriage house/tutor's home, and even a sorghum mill. A cotton museum and gift shop are at the entrance to the park property; both are open year-round.

Florewood is open Tuesday through Saturday 9:00 A.M. to 5:00 P.M. and Sunday 1:00 to 5:00 P.M. (March through November); short tours are given December through February; closed major holidays. Admission is $3.50 for adults, $3.00 for senior citizens and groups, and $2.50 for youths ages 5 through 18; children younger than 5 are free.

Beauvoir
2244 Beach Boulevard, Biloxi
(800) 570–3818

The restored last home of the only president of the Confederacy, Beauvoir was the seaside estate of Jefferson Davis. A National Historic Landmark, Beauvoir was built in the mid-1800s, and its 74-acre landscaped grounds and handsome buildings are open to visitors. In addition to the furnished presidential residence, there is a Confederate museum and cemetery where the Tomb of the Unknown Confederate is located. The beautiful grounds contain large oaks, magnolias, pines, gardens, and a lagoon.

It was at this spacious house facing the Gulf of Mexico that President Davis, after his release from a federal prison, wrote *The Rise and Fall of the Confederate Government.* Here's an interesting anecdote about Jefferson Davis: According to local legend, Davis was visited at Beauvoir by the Union soldier who had captured him. The man had no money, so Davis loaned him enough to get back home and gave him this suggestion: "If you ever meet any of our boys in want, relieve them if possible." The Davis family showed their appreciation for Confederate veterans even after Davis died in 1889. His widow refused to sell Beauvoir and the surrounding property to a hotel developer for $100,000; instead she sold it to the Sons of Confederate Veterans for $10,000.

Open daily March 1 to Labor Day, 9:00 A.M. to 5:00 P.M.; open 9:00 A.M. to 4:00 P.M. the rest of the year; closed Christmas. Admission is $7.50 for adults, $6.75 for persons over age 64 and military, and $4.50 for youths ages 6 through 15.

VICKSBURG: SEALING THE CONFEDERACY'S FATE

Nearly before the first shots on Fort Sumter ended, visionary general officers of the Union Army foresaw that this would not be any "90-day struggle," as the Washington bureaucrats and woefully inadequate top army brass claimed. Not only were the very cream of the prewar U.S. Army officer corps resigning their commissions in order to serve their Southern home states, but the level of rhetoric coming from the near-fanatical secessionist politicians ensured that once separate, it would be a long, hard climb to reconstruct the whole nation.

The de facto leader of this visionary group was none other than General Winfield Scott, the aged veteran of the War of 1812 and the Mexican-American War (not to mention his less heroic involvement in the southeastern Native American removals of the 1820s and 1830s). Despite his ill health and dated military strategies, he insisted that not only was the nation headed for a long war, but that the South could only be defeated by a long, grinding campaign aimed at cutting its lines of supply and communication. His grand scheme, dubbed the Anaconda Plan, called for an absolute blockade of the entire Southern coastline by the U.S. Navy to prevent resupply from friendly foreign countries and stop waterborne reinforcement of the Confederate armies, followed by the capture and use of the Mississippi River from Illinois to the Gulf of Mexico to cut the Southern Confederacy in half and allow it to die from lack of supplies.

"Old Fuss and Feathers" Scott's plan was seriously derided at first, as few Union politicians or generals saw the need to do anything so drastic. The widely held belief on both sides was that one big battle would be all that was needed to send the opposing army fleeing from the field and resolve the conflict instantly. The laughter stopped, however, after the shocking Union defeat at the First Manassas (First Bull Run) battle in Virginia; and even as Scott was being replaced as general in chief by Major General George Brinton "Little Mac" McClellan, essential elements of the Anaconda Plan were being expanded into the overall Union strategy for the war.

SPLITTING THE SOUTH

The Union strategy during the war had three parts: first, the total naval blockade of the Southern coastline, envisioned by Scott; second, an overland campaign to capture the Confederate capital of Richmond, Virginia; and third, control of the Mississippi River and all the port towns along it. Brigadier General (later General in Chief) Ulysses S. Grant opened the third part of this grand strategy in early February 1862 with the assault on and capture of Forts Henry and Donelson on the Tennessee and Cumberland Rivers in northern Tennessee. With the way cleared toward Nashville and other points south in Tennessee, Grant then turned west along the Ohio River toward the Mississippi, swung around and isolated a strong Confederate garrison at Columbus, Kentucky, and then turned inland to move toward Corinth, Mississippi. Memphis fell soon afterward, after another short, fierce naval battle, completely opening the northern stretches of the Mississippi to Union control.

Major General John Pope successfully moved his Union Army of the Mississippi against fortified Confederate positions at Island Number 10 and New Madrid on the Mississippi, well supported by Union gunboats, and opened the northern stretches of the great river to Union control by early April 1862. Later that same month Flag Officer (later Admiral) David Glasgow Farragut and Major General Benjamin Franklin Butler captured New Orleans after a short naval battle, opening up the southern stretches of the river. By early spring 1862, only Port Hudson, Louisiana, and Vicksburg, Mississippi, remained in Confederate hands and prevented a complete Union domination of the river.

BACKGROUND TO THE BATTLE

The Vicksburg campaign was an unusually long and costly operation for both sides. From the earliest assault attempts in December 1862 to the final surrender on July 4, 1863, only the horrible siege at Petersburg, Virginia, from June 1864 to May 1865 was longer or more destructive in lives to both soldiers and civilians. As the best defensive ground of any port between Memphis and the Gulf Coast, Vicksburg was an obvious target that the Union commanders wasted little time in attacking.

Most histories of the Vicksburg campaign concentrate on the famous siege of the small town, which lasted from April 29 to July 4, 1863, but in fact the battle for this critical river port started many months earlier.

Grant had been given the task of completely clearing the Mississippi of any Confederate threat when he assumed command of the newly formed Department of Tennessee on October 16, 1862. Under his command were some 43,000 men, reinforced to about 75,000 as the campaign wore on. Two days earlier Lieu-

tenant General John Clifford Pemberton had assumed command of the Confederate Department of Mississippi and East Louisiana, which for all practical purposes simply meant the area immediately surrounding Vicksburg. The number of men he commanded has been the subject of countless debates since the war: While the force probably numbered in the 40,000 range, Grant claimed he faced well over 60,000, while Pemberton himself stated he had only 28,000.

Chickasaw Bluff

With his victory at the Battle of Shiloh and the fall of Corinth, Mississippi, assuring his dominance over western Confederate armies, Grant immediately set about moving against Vicksburg, which he considered one of the most vital targets in the entire Western Theater. He split his command into two great columns; led by Major General William Tecumseh Sherman, the westernmost column was to move south with 32,000 men on transport barges down the Mississippi River from Memphis to directly attack Vicksburg. To keep Confederate forces divided and unable to concentrate on the city's defense, Grant personally led 40,000 men overland south along the Mississippi Central Railroad tracks from Grand Junction, Tennessee, 35 miles west of Corinth.

Grant moved south on November 26, 1862, slowly moving his large force through northern Mississippi. Passing through Holly Springs and Oxford, he established forward supply bases in both towns and left small garrisons to guard against expected Confederate raids. His major problem during the march south was that his supply lines back to Columbus, Kentucky, were growing longer and more vulnerable. On December 20, just as the vanguard of Grant's column was approaching the small town of Granada, a 3,500-man Confederate cavalry force under Major General Earl Van Dorn captured and destroyed his supply base at Holly Springs. At about the same time, another cavalry force under Brigadier General Nathan Bedford Forrest stormed through western Tennessee and southern Kentucky, destroying more than 60 miles of the critical railroad lines supplying the Union overland campaign. Grant was forced to call off his part of the attack and move northwest into Memphis.

The same day Grant lost his base at Holly Springs, Sherman and his men boarded a naval flotilla in Memphis and cast off toward Vicksburg. The infantry-men were loaded onto 59 transport ships and barges, escorted by seven gunboats. A message about Grant's defeat reached Sherman the next day, but he decided to continue on, risking that his strong surprise assault might be enough to carry the com-ing battle. On Christmas Eve the Union flotilla arrived at Milliken's Bend, Louisiana, just north of Vicksburg, and prepared to start disembarking the troops.

DECEMBER 24, 1862, VICKSBURG

Vicksburg had been an island of relative calm at this point, a safe harbor from the vicious naval battles that ranged north and south along the Mississippi. Social life went on, little changed from antebellum times, with frequent parties, cotillions, and afternoon barbecues—the major differ-ence being that the men wore Confeder-ate gray dress uniforms instead of their civilian garb. Dr. William Balfour and his wife, Emma, had prepared a grand Christ-mas Eve ball in their house on Crawford Street, inviting the local garrison's officers to join the society elite in an elaborate party. As the band played and couples danced, mud-splattered Private Philip Fall burst through the door searching for the ranking officer present, Major General Martin Luther Smith, carrying the startling news that Sherman and his force were nearly upon them at that very moment. Signaling for the band to stop playing,

Smith addressed the crowd, "This ball is at an end—the enemy are coming down the river, all noncombatants must leave the city." With that, Smith and his officers immediately departed, calling out the gar-rison to man the defenses while still in their dress uniforms.

Aware that Sherman was coming from the north, area commander Pemberton (who arrived on December 26 from his position at Grenada) placed the majority of his men in a northeast-to-southwest line at the foot of the Walnut Hills on the north side of town (nearly directly atop present-day U.S. Business Highway 61 on the north side of the military park), facing northwest toward where Sherman's troops were expected to approach. Pemberton had about 25,000 men total (including reinforcements brought in during the bat-tle) divided into two divisions to stand against Sherman's four divisions with 30,000 men (some sources state 33,000). The Confederate lines were formidable, with several lines of entrenchments well supported by artillery emplacements and fronted by a thick tangle of abatis made of felled trees that also gave the infantry a well-cleared field of fire.

The Assault on Chickasaw Bluff

The Union troops disembarked starting in late afternoon on December 26 and by the next day were pushing inland toward Vicksburg, led by Colonel John F. DeCourcy's 3rd Brigade (3rd Division). As the infantry advanced slowly on the road past Mrs. Anne E. Lake's house, they came under heavy fire from advance Confeder-ate pickets in the nearby woods. This advance to contact ended after a brief but heavy firefight; DeCourcy pulled his men back to camp and the pickets retired within the Confederate line. Other actions took place over the next two days, while Sherman tried to figure out where Pem-berton's weakest spot was.

Finding no part of the Confederate line notably weaker than any other, Sherman decided to try a massive head-on assault. At 7:30 A.M. on December 29, his artillery opened a heavy fire on Pemberton's line, answered quickly by counter-battery fire from massed Confederate guns on the bluff above them. About 11:00 A.M., Union infantry officers ordered their men into line of battle—Brigadier General Frank Blair's brigade on the left, DeCourcy's and Brigadier General John M. Thayer's brigades in the center, and Brigadier General Andrew Jackson Smith leading both the 1st and 2nd Divisions on the right, all arrayed to strike the Confederate line at about the same time.

Under heavy and accurate rifle fire as soon as they exited the woods, DeCourcy's and Blair's brigades stormed across the bayou and managed to push through the entangling defenses and take the first line of rifle pits. Soon joined by the 4th Iowa Regiment of Thayer's brigade (the only one to make it across the open fields), the Union infantrymen attempted to keep their assault moving and push back through the layers of defensive entrenchments, but they were soon stopped by murderous rifle and artillery fire. As they started to pull back and retreat to their encampment, General Stephen Dill Lee ordered his rebels forward in a counterattack. The 17th and 26th Louisiana Infantry Regiments surged forward, overrunning the hapless Union infantry, and soon returned with their prize: 21 officers, 311 enlisted men, and four regimental battle flags.

This scene was repeated all down the line. Although Smith's two divisions managed to make it literally within spitting distance of the Confederate lines on the right, they were not able to carry the works even after five assault attempts. As darkness fell, the Union troops abandoned what little gains they had made and returned to their encampments. That night, during a drenching and chilling rainstorm, Sherman made plans to assault again the next day, this time aimed at taking the artillery emplacements atop the

bluff, but finally he canceled the attack after deciding that it would be too costly an attempt. Another planned attack, this time against Confederate fortifications on nearby Snyder's Bluff on New Year's Day, was canceled when a thick fog prevented easy movement.

> *For twenty months now I have been a sojourner in camps, a dweller in tents, going hither and yon, at all hours of the day and night, in all sorts of weather, sleeping for weeks at a stretch without shelter, and yet I have been strong and healthy. How very thankful I should feel on this Christmas night! There goes the boom from a cannon at the front.*
>
> John Beatty, 3rd Ohio Infantry Regiment, Union Army

Late on the afternoon of January 1, 1863, Sherman ordered his men back aboard the transport ships and barges and set sail down the Yazoo River to its mouth on the Mississippi. The next day he was placed under the command of Major General John A. McClernand, who decided to carry the battle away from Vicksburg for the time being. Sherman's report of the battle, and his failure, is a model of terseness: "I reached Vicksburg at the time appointed, landed, assaulted and failed." His failure cost 208 dead, 1,005 wounded, and 563 captured or missing. Despite the personal responsibility he seemed to take in his report for the failed assault, in letters and his postwar memoirs he blamed a lack of fighting spirit in his own infantry for the failure, most notably DeCourcy's brigade, which had ironically advanced the farthest into the Confederate entrenchments. Pemberton reported a loss of 63 killed, 134 wounded, and 10 missing after the battle.

ATTEMPTS TO BYPASS VICKSBURG

Grant waited a few weeks, building up his army before attempting to reduce Vicksburg again. His major tactical problem, underscored by Sherman's failure, was that the town was built on a steep bluff footed by swamps and the Yazoo and Mississippi Rivers, making any assault from the east, north, or south a near suicidal venture. The only approach that might have worked was from the east, along the spine of ridges that arced nearly 200 miles above and below the town. This favorable approach had its own set of problems, most notably, how to get his troops in position atop the eastern bluffs. To add to all these problems, the winter rains that year had been unusually heavy, increasing the flooding problems and widening the rivers.

Grant's problems can be illustrated by the near-desperate attempt he had his engineers make, digging a 1½-mile-long canal across one of the peninsulas below Vicksburg, known locally as De Soto Point, which would hopefully allow his troop and supply ships to bypass the powerful artillery batteries and land unmolested south of the city. Now known as Grant's Canal, work continued through March of 1863, when early spring flooding destroyed some of the works and covered the peninsula and the Confederate defenders moved some of their artillery batteries to cover both ends of the canal.

Meanwhile, Major General James Birdseye McPherson was attempting to bring his XVII Corps in to reinforce Grant and hit the city from the south by cutting and blasting a passage through the labyrinth of swamps and small rivers from Lake Providence, 75 miles north of Vicksburg, to a point in the Mississippi River some 200 miles south of the city. A 400-mile-long route was mapped and partially pre-pared before the entire project was scrapped as unworkable.

A third attempt to gain the eastern bluffs was mounted by blasting through a natural levee at Yazoo Pass, 320 miles north of Vicksburg, and plotting a water-borne route south to the city. Before they could make much progress, Major General William W. Loring's division rushed north to stop the Union raid. About 90 miles north of Vicksburg, the Confederate troops hastily built an earthwork and cotton bale post (dubbed "Fort Pemberton") and engaged the onrushing Union gunboats on March 11. The Union infantry could find no way to assault the fort in the swampy terrain, and this expedition soon turned away in defeat. Less than a week later a fourth and last attempt to sail through the bayous north of the city, known as Steele's Bayou Expedition, ended in both defeat and the near capture of all the Union gunboats.

THE BATTLE OF GRAND GULF

With every attempt to bypass the Vicksburg defenses proving unsuccessful, Grant decided to take the head-on approach. McClernand had just been placed under Grant's overall command, and he was ordered to have his command build a road to move down the western bank of the Mississippi River to a forward base directly across from the Confederate outpost at Grand Gulf, 60 miles south of Vicksburg. Planning to try an amphibious assault under fire against the Confederate fortifications, Grant also directed McClernand to have his gunboats and troop transports run past the Vicksburg Mississippi River batteries and meet up with his Army of the Tennessee at a point ironically named Hard Times. On the night of April 16, 1863, eight gunboats and three transports set sail downriver under the direct command of Commodore William David Porter, each specially prepared to meet the expected hot Confederate fire. The port (left) side of each ship, which would face the Confederate batteries, was piled high with cotton and hay bales, and small coal scows and supply barges were lashed to each side of the ships.

Just before midnight the small flotilla approached Confederate outposts just north of Vicksburg, which promptly raised the alarm. Artillery crews raced in to man their guns, and within minutes a furious firefight broke out along the river. Porter reported later that every one of his ships was hit in the exchange, some multiple times, but he also stated that his own broadsides into the town could not help but do great damage to the city, as they were firing at near point-blank range. One sailor reported that they were so close that falling bricks from buildings struck by the Union cannon could clearly be heard.

Despite the heavy and accurate Confederate fire, only one transport was sunk, and the other ships limped down to join the infantry at Hard Times. Another flotilla ran the same gauntlet on the night of April 22—six transports towing 12 supply barges—but this time Confederate gunners managed to sink one transport and six of the barges.

Grant had planned to use the transports and barges to bring 10,000 infantrymen across the Mississippi to a landing point at Grand Gulf, at the mouth of the Big Black River. Porter's gunboats opened fire on the Confederate fortifications at Grand Gulf on April 29 but failed to inflict any serious damage or silence their guns after nearly six hours of continuous bombardment. To add to Grant's problems, return fire from Confederate gunners inflicted serious damage to the Union gunboat fleet. Grant reconsidered his plan and decided to move his men downriver to a "cooler" landing zone. The next day, in the largest amphibious operation mounted by an American army until World War II, Grant crossed the river and landed at Bruinsburg with 24,000 troops and 60 cannon. After months of campaigning, Grant at last had a toehold on the east side of the river close to Vicksburg.

THE BATTLE OF PORT GIBSON

While Grant was crossing the river downstream, Sherman had mounted a strong demonstration against Haine's Bluff, while Colonel Benjamin Henry Grierson moved his Union cavalry south out of Tennessee and mounted another demonstration against the railroad lines between Meridian and Jackson before turning south toward Baton Rouge. Grant's men began moving north almost as soon as they reached dry land, aiming for the town of Port Gibson. By late in the afternoon of April 30, more than 17,000 Union troops were ashore and moving out rapidly, with several thousand more still en route across the river.

Two Confederate brigades had already marched south from Grand Gulf to oppose the Union assault: Brigadier General Edward D. Tracy's and Brigadier General Martin E. Green's, which by nightfall were astride the Bruinsburg and Rodney Roads directly in the path of the Union advance. Starting about midnight the advance skirmishers of the Union column met up with the Confederate pickets, and a lively firefight broke out. The firing died down about 3:00 A.M. but picked up again with vigor about the first light of dawn (about 5:30 A.M.).

The Confederate lines held well until about 10:00 A.M., when Green's brigade was pushed back up the road about 1½ miles by a heavy Union assault. There they were reinforced by two other brigades hastily dispatched from Grand Gulf: Brigadier General William E. Baldwin's and Brigadier General Francis M. Cockrell's, which helped shore up a strong line along the Rodney Road. Tracy's men managed to hold up well in their position on the right, despite losing Tracy himself, who was killed early in the fighting. Although several vicious counterattacks were mounted that managed some limited success, the Union assault was simply overwhelming, and all the Confederate commanders began retiring from the field about 5:30 P.M.

Three states were admitted to the Union during the war: Kansas (1861, the 34th), West Virginia (1863, the 35th), and Nevada (1864, the 36th).

The daylong battle cost Grant 131 killed, 719 wounded, and 25 missing or captured, while the Confederate commanders reported a loss of 60 killed, 340 wounded, and 387 missing or captured. Accounts vary, but the total Confederate force in the field amounted to about 8,000, while Grant had an estimated 23,000 engaged in the fight by late afternoon. Confused by the Union attacks toward Vicksburg seemingly coming from all directions, Pemberton ordered Grand Gulf evacuated and all the troops to move within the defenses of Vicksburg, instead of confronting and attacking Grant's bridgehead.

THE BATTLE OF RAYMOND

Rather than directly move in and seize Grand Gulf, Grant decided to move northeast and cut the Southern Railroad lines between Jackson and Vicksburg, Pemberton's only remaining line of communications, supply, and retreat. Similar to Sherman's later march through Georgia, Grant set his forces in a three-corps-abreast formation, with McClernand's XIII Corps on the left, Sherman's XV Corps in the middle, and McPherson's XVII Corps on the right. Grant planned to move nearly directly northeast toward Jackson, then turn right and cut the rail line somewhere east of the small settlement of Edwards. On May 7 the three corps moved out, a total of 45,000 Union soldiers moving deep into the very heart of the Confederacy and dangerously far from their own base of supplies.

Pemberton guessed correctly what Grant was up to and sent word to his garrison in Jackson to move out and confront the Union advance, while he moved part of his own force in Vicksburg out to strike the Union line from the west. Brigadier General John Gregg moved his 3,000-man brigade out of Jackson promptly, arriving in Raymond on May 11 and setting up pickets along the west and south roads into the town. For artillery support Gregg could boast a single battery, the three guns of Captain Hiram Bledsoe's Missouri Battery.

At dawn on May 12, Gregg's pickets sent word that the Union vanguard was approaching their position along the Utica Road (today known as Mississippi Highway 18). The Confederate commander hastily deployed his men to strike what he thought would be the right flank of a small Union force, along both the Utica and Gallatin Roads, and placed the Missouri Battery atop a small hill commanding the bridge crossing Fourteenmile Creek. As the first regiments of McPherson's column moved into the small valley of Fourteenmile Creek, Gregg ordered volley fire into their flank.

The sudden burst of fire shattered the front Union ranks, and Gregg ordered his men to keep up a hot fire. After about two hours of volleys, Gregg ordered up his Tennesseeans and Texans in line of assault, planning to roll up the Union line and finish up the day. As the Confederates advanced into the dry creekbed and through the easternmost Union formations, they ran smack into the newly reorganized division led by Major General John A. Logan, who was leading his men into battle with "the shriek of an eagle." By 1:30 P.M., with Union regiments and brigades piling onto the field, Gregg finally realized that he was facing a full Union corps and started ordering his units to pull back. The battle had become a confused swirling of Union and Confederate units nearly invisible to their commanders in the thick, choking dust, and it took most of the rest of the afternoon for both commanders to get a complete grasp of their own positions and issue appropriate orders.

Gregg attempted to break contact and retreat, but McPherson's troops kept a running battle going until they reached Raymond itself. The Confederates hurried past townspeople who were preparing a "victory" picnic for them, before stopping for the night at Snake Creek. McPherson's men broke off the pursuit in Raymond, where the Union troops helped themselves to the picnic dinner. The next morning Gregg moved his brigade back into Jackson, reporting a loss of 73 killed, 252 wounded, and 190 missing or captured. McPherson reported to Grant that he had faced a force "about 6,000 strong" but emerged victorious, at the cost of 68 killed, 341 wounded, and 37 missing or captured.

THE BATTLE OF JACKSON

Surprised at the strong show of force so far east of Vicksburg, Grant decided that he would have to take Jackson before he could safely turn back west toward "Fortress Vicksburg." On May 13 he ordered his army forward once again— McPherson north from Raymond along the Clinton Road, Sherman northeast through Raymond toward Mississippi Springs, and McClernand's corps arrayed in a defensive line from Raymond to Clinton to guard against any more unpleasant surprises. The same day, General Joseph Eggleston Johnston (commander, Department of Tennessee and Mississippi) arrived in Jackson by train to assume overall command of Vicksburg's defense. With Grant's army nearly knocking on Jackson's door, Johnston ordered an immediate evacuation of the city toward the north, with Gregg's brigade and parts of two other brigades remaining as long as possible to mount a rear-guard action. After a heavy rainfall in the morning of May 14 briefly delayed their attack, Sherman's and McPherson's corps charged the weak Confederate defenses with bayonets fixed starting about 11:00 A.M., driving the Confederate defenders back after a bitter hand-to-hand struggle and capturing the outer defenses of the city without much loss.

Although strong Confederate artillery emplacements delayed the Union advance in the center, Sherman sent part of his command around the right flank and north along the railroad line into the heart of the city. With his left flank breached, Gregg ordered his brigades to move out of the city along the Canton Road to the north, while Union troops invested the city right behind them. By 3:00 P.M. the Stars and Stripes was being hoisted again over the state capitol building. The few hours of combat resulted in about 300 Union soldiers killed, wounded, and missing and an estimated 850 Confederate casualties.

With Grant's army between him and Vicksburg, Johnston believed that he had arrived too late to do any real good, but he sent a series of messages to Pemberton urging him to march out of Vicksburg and join the 6,000 troops he had moved north out of Jackson in a battle to destroy Grant's force. Pemberton, a great believer in the use of fixed fortifications, was extremely reluctant to enter a campaign of movement and maneuver. He made it very clear that he wished to remain in his line along the Big Black River, but finally he agreed to move out. In a clear act of disobedience of orders, instead of moving to join Johnston, Pemberton decided on his own to strike against Grant's line of communication back to Grand Gulf, now occupied and a major supply center for the Union army.

On May 15 Pemberton initially moved his 23,000 men *southeast* to near Edward's Station, effectively moving farther away from Johnston and placing Grant's army between the two commands. Unknown to either Confederate commander, Grant's men had intercepted the series of orders and communications between them, and the Union commander was maneuvering his own forces to exploit the confusion. Johnston issued another order on May 16 to Pemberton to move northeast and join him, which for some reason he decided to obey, but by this time Grant was ready to strike.

THE BATTLE OF CHAMPION HILL

As Pemberton moved northeast early on the morning of May 16 along the Ratliff road just south of Champion Hill, his three divisions strung out along the road for nearly 3 miles, a courier brought word that a large Union contingent was bearing down upon him from the Jackson road to the northeast. Pemberton immediately halted his march and arrayed in line of battle to protect the high ground of Champion Hill itself, as well as the cross-roads leading to Edwards and Vicksburg. Major General William Wing Loring's division covered the Raymond road to the south, the right flank of Pemberton's line; Brigadier (soon after Major) General John S. Bowen's division deployed along the Ratliff road to Loring's left; and Major General Carter Littlepage Stevenson's division covered the left flank and the crest of the small knob of Champion Hill.

Just before noon Brigadier General Alvin P. Hovey's and Logan's divisions of McPherson's corps attacked along the Jackson road against Stevenson's positions atop Champion Hill. Stevenson's men were soon forced off the crest under heavy fire, but Bowen's division shifted north and succeeded in regaining the hill. Grant ordered his artillery massed and directed all fire on the hilltop Confederate positions, quickly followed by renewed infantry assaults. About 1:00 P.M. Stevenson's and Bowen's men were forced to retreat under the crushing Union assault, escaping south along Baker's Creek to the Raymond road before turning west toward Vicksburg.

Brigadier General Lloyd Tilghman's brigade was ordered to act as a rear guard, to cover the escape "at all costs." Joined by Loring's men, they put up a fierce resistance but were cut off by massive artillery fire and forced to move farther south and east, eventually circling around north and meeting up with Johnston near Jackson. Tilghman himself was killed during the rear-guard action.

Pemberton led his army's retreat west through Edwards before taking up a defensive position at the Big Black River for the night, while McClernand's corps moving in from the south entered and occupied Edwards about 8:00 P.M. Grant reported losses of 410 killed, 1,844 wounded, and 187 missing or captured, while Pemberton suffered 381 killed, 1,018 wounded, and 2,441 missing or captured, but the real damage was the decisive defeat of the Confederate forces. Pemberton would eventually limp back into Vicksburg minus Loring's division, which never returned to his command, but Grant had succeeded in isolating Vicksburg to an island outpost completely cut off from any hope of resupply or reinforcement.

BIG BLACK RIVER BRIDGES

Pemberton was unaware that Loring, who had circled around to the south and east to join up with Johnston at Jackson, was not following him back into Vicksburg. Instead of immediately moving all his forces back within Vicksburg's formidable defense, Pemberton ordered Bowen's division reinforced by Brigadier General John Vaughn's brigade to hold a defensive perimeter around the bridges over the Big Black River, in the hopes that Loring would soon show up and have a safe passage over the river. On the morning of May 17, with the rest of Pemberton's troops marching the 12 miles west to Vicksburg, McClernand's XIII Corps rapidly swept forward and engaged Bowen's small command.

Bowen had established a seemingly tight line of battle, well anchored on the river on the left and a waist-deep swampy area on the right, with 18 artillery pieces arrayed along the line to sweep a wide area of fire that any Union assault would have to march through. Even before McClernand's corps was fully arrayed for battle, Brigadier General Michael Lawler saw an opportunity to gain a quick Union victory and ordered his brigade to fix bayonets and hit the center of the Confederate line. In a hand-to-hand combat that lasted less than three minutes, Vaughn's brigade broke under the fierce assault and ran for the bridges, followed quickly by the rest of Bowen's command, as more and more Union infantry brigades fixed bayonets and followed Lawler's lead.

Many of the retreating Confederates drowned while attempting to cross the river, forced into the water by Pemberton's chief engineer, Major Sam Lockett, who had set fire to the bridges to keep them out of Grant's hands. There is no known surviving record of Confederate dead and wounded in the brief battle, but Grant reported capturing more than 1,700 prisoners and all 18 artillery pieces, while suffering a total of 279 dead, wounded, and missing out of his own commands.

Burning the bridges slowed Grant's advance less than a single day. His engineer threw up three bridges across the river by the morning of May 18, and the great Union army quickly crossed and moved out toward Vicksburg.

FORTRESS VICKSBURG

Shortly after the fall of New Orleans in the spring of 1862, Flag Officer (soon afterward Rear Admiral) David Glasgow Farragut sailed his West Gulf Blockading Squadron north along the Mississippi River and captured Baton Rouge and Natchez without resistance. Joined just outside Vicksburg on July 1, 1862, by Flag Officer Charles Henry Davis's Western Flotilla, sailing south along the Mississippi after capturing Memphis and reducing the Confederate river fleet to a shattered remnant, the two powerful gunboat fleets had managed to take control of nearly the entire river for the Union after only a few months of campaigning. Now the only thing that stood in the way of complete and free Union transit of the river, other than the weaker Confederate bastion at Port Hudson across the river in Louisiana, was a few artillery batteries stationed high

on a bluff next to the river in the small but very important port town of Vicksburg.

Farragut's fleet had passed Vicksburg several times, starting in late May, and had exchanged fire with the rapidly growing city defenses to no real effect. Before Davis's arrival, his own mortarboats and sloops had kept a steady bombardment of the town, irregularly at first, but growing in intensity as both sides brought more guns into action. After three weeks of numbing and near continuous fire, and after the intense heat and disease had rendered all but 800 of his 3,000 sailors unfit for duty, Farragut called off the operation and sailed south, while Davis returned his fleet to Memphis. Farragut reported that Vicksburg could only be successfully reduced by a combined army and naval force attacking from land and water simultaneously.

Confederate independence with centralized power without State sovereignty . . . would be very little better than subjugation, as it matters little who our master is, if we are to have one.

> Governor Joseph Brown of Georgia, in a November 1864 speech to the Georgia General Assembly

Even before the first Union assaults on the town, General Pierre Gustave Toutant Beauregard (commander, Department of the West) had prepared a plan of defense for the town after the defeat at Shiloh and sent engineer Captain D. B. Harris south from Fort Pillow to oversee the initial construction of a series of fortifications. Major (later Major General) Martin Luther Smith soon arrived from constructing the defenses of New Orleans to take over building the Vicksburg defenses and ended up commanding troops during the siege from behind his own line of fortifications.

In September 1862, following Farragut's failed attempts, this line of fortifications was extended to the inland side of Vicksburg, neatly surrounding the town with a powerful, near unassailable, and continuous line of forts, infantry positions, and artillery emplacements. Within a few months the defense line ran from Fort Hill on the north side of town along the curving ridges some 9 miles south to South Fort then back north along the river for some 4½ additional miles. The defensive line mounted about 115 heavy guns, with another 31 mounted in batteries alongside the river.

The only approaches into the city through the surrounding ridges were six roads and one railroad track that ran across natural bridges over rather steep ravines. To guard these natural avenues of attack, Harris's engineers had built nine well-constructed and powerful forts, some with walls nearly 20 feet thick. Each one of these forts was surrounded by a maze of interconnected and interlocking rifle pits, artillery batteries, and communications trenches. In front of this line was a deep and wide ditch, and all the trees were cut down for quite some distance in front of the line to provide a clear field of fire, making any direct assault a suicidal venture at best. The town was now a massive fortified redoubt, nearly impregnable to reduction by weapons of the day, that could either prove a safe haven for its Confederate defenders or a deadly trap, depending entirely on what Grant chose to do.

First Assaults on Vicksburg

Grant believed he had Pemberton's 31,000 men demoralized and not fully prepared to make much of a fight after his two-week-long running battle from Port Gibson to the Big Black River, and he wanted to storm the Vicksburg defenses before they could recover. On May 19, with 50,000 men under his command but only 20,000 in position to strike, he ordered an immediate assault on the town.

Sherman's XV Corps was the only command in position to strike, and about 2:00 P.M. he ordered a general attack. Mov-

ing against the northeastern corner of the Vicksburg line, his men attempted to storm and reduce the powerful fort called Stockade Redan. Advancing under heavy and accurate Confederate fire, part of one regiment (the 13th U.S. Infantry) got close in enough to place their colors on the exterior sloping wall before being thrown back with heavy losses. This was the only "gain" Sherman managed before withdrawing; McPherson's XVII and McClernand's XIII Corps made some demonstrations against other parts of the line, but neither did any better than Sherman, who lost nearly 1,000 casualties to no gain.

Three days later Grant ordered another assault attempt, this time preceded by a four-hour-long artillery barrage against the Confederate line followed by a 45,000-man attack against a 3-mile front. Portions of all three corps managed to make it to the base of the Confederate defenses, but only one regiment penetrated the line. An Iowa regiment of McClernand's corps led by two sergeants shot their way into the Railroad Redoubt through a hole made by their artillery and in a fierce firefight managed to kill or drive out the Confederate defenders. Before this regiment could be reinforced and the breach in the wall exploited, men of Colonel Thomas N. Waul's Texas Legion counterattacked and regained the fort. No other Union gain was made before the entire assault line was once against thrown back with heavy losses.

Pemberton had managed to rest many of his combat troops even during these assaults, using only about 18,000 of his men in the defense while inflicting a total of 3,200 Union casualties. Pemberton's casualties in these assaults are not recorded but were undoubtedly much less severe than Grant's. With his powerful assault forces turned aside without much difficulty, Grant changed his plans and settled in for a long siege of the fortified town, something Johnston had already warned Pemberton would be inevitable and disastrous if he pulled his forces back into the city as planned.

THE SIEGE

Grant officially began his siege operation on May 25 and, with the exception of two isolated events, made no further attempts to take Vicksburg by force. With all lines of supply, communications, or reinforcement successfully cut, Grant directed his engineers and infantry to begin construction of a series of siege trenches, designed to gradually grow nearer and nearer the Confederate positions. He had no intention of simply allowing Vicksburg to starve itself out, at least initially, but planned to try digging a series of mines (or tunnels) under the massive fortifications, pack them full of explosives, and literally blast his way through the walls into the city.

While the infantry was busy digging their way through Mississippi, Grant's artillery and Porter's naval flotilla set about making life miserable within the town. While the city had suffered sporadic shelling from Union gunboats on the river ever since the first days of the campaign, nearly constant incoming fire began soon after Pemberton brought his army inside the defenses and did not cease until the final surrender some 47 days later. It did not take long for Vicksburg's citizens to move out of their homes and into caves dug deep into the sides of the hills. It also did not take long to figure out when they could safely venture out to try to find food and water: 8:00 A.M., noon, and 8:00 P.M., when the artillerymen would cease firing to eat their meals. Grant continuously built up his siege artillery force, and by the end of June he had 220 guns of various sizes engaged around the city.

Within a relatively short time, the siege made life nearly untenable for civilians and soldiers alike within the city. Food supplies had not been abundant when the campaign began, and when all supply routes were cut, what few items were still available commanded premium prices. Flour sold for as high as $1,000.00 per barrel, molasses for $10.00 per gallon, spoiled bacon for $5.00 a pound, and what little cornmeal remained went for $140.00 per bushel. Beef, coffee, sugar, bread, and even horse or mule meat was nearly nonexistent. For a while a bread made of ground peas was available, for a price, but soon even this disgusting fare was gone. Some accounts even claim that the rat population of the city nearly disappeared by the middle of June, but this is undoubtedly an apocryphal tale. The truth, however, is just as stark: By late June the average soldier ration consisted of one biscuit, four ounces of usually rotted bacon, peas, and sometimes a little rice each day—less than half the normal combat ration.

One odd shortage that reared its head in June was that of cartridge bags for Pemberton's remaining heavy guns. These bags were made of flannel and held a measured charge of gunpowder, and not a single bolt of the cloth could be found anywhere in town. The soldiers were being asked to give up their outer shirts for the cause, and when the ladies of the town found out, they immediately volunteered their petticoats. A newspaperman in town later remarked that every outgoing shell from the city's 10-inch Columbiads was powered by these women's underwear.

Sherman Gets Impatient

Only two days after the siege operation began, Sherman displayed his usual impatience and requested help from Porter's naval flotilla to reduce the fortifications before him. The gunboat *Cincinnati* was reinforced with heavy logs and bales of cotton along her ironclad sides and then moved downriver to directly confront the river batteries below Fort Hill, clearing the way for the infantry to move in.

The *Cincinnati*'s captain, Lieutenant George M. Bache, brought her downriver on May 27 and turned close to shore on the north end of town to prepare to open a broadside fire on the Confederate batteries. However, before his guns could open fire, the swift river current caught his boat and spun it around, forcing Bache to unmask his stern batteries in order to maintain control. This was the weakest and least-armored section of the ironclad, and the Confederate gunners took full advantage. From atop Fort Hill and from the multiple batteries along the river, rains of 8- and 10-inch fire raked the Union gunboat, soon smashing through her stern and shooting away her steering gear. Within minutes the huge gunboat was an uncontrollable mess of smashed gundecks and wounded and dying men.

Bache attempted to run his boat aground on the far side of the river to allow his crew to escape safely, but the boat was too badly damaged to stay afloat that long. The *Cincinnati* went down in 3 fathoms of water, taking 40 of her men with her, her colors still flying from the blasted stump of a flagpole where they had been nailed during the brief but vicious battle.

The Mines

From the very start of the siege, Grant had planned to try to blast his way through the Confederate defenses by using mines, and by late June the first were ready to go. A tunnel had been dug under the 3rd Louisiana Redoubt, near the center of the arcing Confederate line, and filled with more than a ton of gunpowder. On June 25 the mine was ready, and Grant ordered every gun he had to open fire all along the Vicksburg line to prevent Pemberton from shifting his forces around. At 3:00 P.M. the powder was fired, and with a deafening roar the entire top of the hill was blown off, opening a crater 50 feet in diameter and 12 feet deep. With nearly 150 heavy guns and every infantry unit along the line supporting, two regiments led by Brigadier General Mortimer D. Leggett charged into the breach, only to discover that the Confederates had discovered their mining attempt and moved back to a second fortified position.

From there, the Louisiana troops directed near point-blank volleys of shot and canister into the Union infantry ranks, whose survivors were then soon joined in hand-to-hand combat by the 6th Missouri Infantry Regiment. The Illinois infantrymen attempted to stay in the crater, throwing up a hasty wall in front of them and forming in a double line of battle to keep up a continuous volley fire of their own. The Louisiana defenders responded by throwing hand grenades down into the crater, which Leggett later said did fearful damage to his surviving infantry. The firing died down after the Union infantry managed to pull back slightly and build a parapet across the crater for their own protection. Grant reported a loss of 30 men, but this is not thought to be accurate; his true loss in the short action was most likely between 300 and 400 killed or wounded. Pemberton reported a loss of 90 dead and wounded.

The next morning Pemberton's men exploded two mines of their own on the north side of the line, near where Sherman's troops were working on a mine near the Stockade Redoubt. No one was killed, but the Union mining operation there was destroyed. Another mine was started that day under the new position of the 3rd Louisiana Redan and fired off on July 1. This time a large number of Confederate defenders were killed or wounded in the explosion, which completely destroyed the large redoubt and blasted a hole 50 feet wide and 20 feet deep in the parapet walls. Colonel Francis Marion Cockrell led his Missouri regiment immediately forward to seal the breach, although himself wounded by the explosion. Under extremely heavy artillery and rifle fire, the breach was gradually filled in and reinforced, although at a cost of more than 100 infantrymen during the six-hour-long operation. Grant never ordered an infantry attack forward to exploit this breach.

With mining operations continuing all along the Vicksburg line, Grant decided to hold his forces in place until all was ready then fire all at once and assault in one huge wave over the line. By July 2 the siege trenches were so close to the Confederate positions that the defenders would only have time for one volley before the Union infantry would be on top of them. The only crimp in this plan was a possible attempt to relieve Vicksburg from Grant's rear.

Johnston had returned to Jackson after Grant's departure and had spent the intervening weeks building up his forces. In addition to the men he had pulled out of the capital in the face of the Union assault, he now commanded Loring's division, joining him after being cut off from Pemberton after the Battle of Champion Hill, as well as every militia unit, local defense command, home guard, or individual able man that could be scraped together from all around Mississippi. Johnston had appealed to both Bragg in Georgia and Davis in Richmond for more troops and supplies, but the building Chickamauga campaign in north Georgia had taken up every spare man and all the available supplies. In Jackson he had nearly 30,000 troops, but the vast majority were green troops totally untrained and ignorant of battle, with a curious collection of shotguns, muskets, and old rifles.

Despite the odds, Johnston was determined to do what he could and sent a message to Pemberton that he was on the way and would attempt to break through Grant's siege line, probably on July 7. Grant had intercepted this message and promptly shifted his forces around to face Johnston, who he feared far more than Pemberton, and requested immediate reinforcements from any command in the west. Several thousand men arrived from the Trans-Mississippi Theater and from Union armies in Tennessee later in June, and Grant sent Sherman to take control of the growing threat from the east.

In the end Johnston never did anything with the army he had raised, remaining in Jackson until June 28 and then hesitantly moving west. On July 4, still not in contact with Sherman's line at the Big Black River, he learned of Pemberton's

surrender and immediately returned his army to Jackson.

July 4, 1863: The End

By early July nearly half of Pemberton's men were unfit to fight, suffering from malaria, dysentery, gangrene, and a host of other illnesses, and the rest capable of holding on but weakened by the severe food shortage. Nearly every building in the city had been hit by the ceaseless artillery fire, and most were reduced to blasted hulks. Snipers fired at any man who dared poke his head out of his trench or above the parapet of his redoubt; civilians were now living full time in dug-out caves, many with ventilation so poor that candles wouldn't stay lit. The stench from blasted-apart horses and mules filled the air, and everyone was approaching complete exhaustion from the strain of the prolonged siege.

Pemberton knew that Grant was about to make a move against him and that his men probably wouldn't be able to stop it. Multiple communications begging Johnston to attack went unanswered or came back with replies saying the Jackson garrison needed more time to organize. In answer to Pemberton's predicament, a letter appeared in his headquarters on June 28, signed "Many Soldiers," praising his own inspired leadership but asking that he surrender. The letter went on to threaten a general mutiny if he did not. On July 1 Pemberton circulated a letter among his top commanders asking if their troops would be able to fight their way out of the siege, which came back with a decidedly negative answer. On July 2 he called a conference of all his officers and point-blank asked if they thought he should surrender the city. Only two disagreed but could offer no other feasible plan.

At 10:00 A.M. on July 3, 1863, white flags of truce were raised all along the Vicksburg line, and for the first time in weeks the guns fell silent. After some difficulty in discussing the terms of surren-

Ulysses Simpson Grant

Usually called "Sam" by his friends, Grant was born on April 27, 1822, in Point Pleasant, Ohio. His name is a bit confusing, as he was christened Hiram Ulysses, but the name was changed in error by the congressman who appointed him to West Point—Simpson is actually his mother's maiden name. Grant had a difficult childhood, constantly under pressure from his Puritan-stock parents to improve his rather abysmal school performance, and he had quite a reputation for laziness. Today he would no doubt be diagnosed with a learning disability of some sort, but his parents obtained an appointment to West Point for him, as they did not believe he would be able to make it in the civilian world—then, as now, the military was seen in some circles as a haven for the incompetent and unaccomplished. Grant showed very little promise at West Point, being considered a poor student by professors and classmates alike, although showing great abilities as a horseman and some aptitude for mathematics. Preferring popular novels to the study of tactics, Grant somehow muddled through his years at the military academy, graduating in 1843 ranked 21st out of a class of 39. Several sources claim that Grant intensely hated both West Point and the military itself and closely followed rumors that Congress was considering closing the academy.

Although Grant was seduced by the romantic glamour of the cavalry, the army saw fit to assign him to the infantry instead, with a berth in the 4th Infantry as his first post. Along with a score of other future Confederate and Union officers, Grant saw his first combat action during the Mexican War. He performed well enough under fire to win two citations for gallantry and a promotion to captain. Just after the war he married Julia Dent, the sister of one of his classmates at West Point, in a ceremony in which his future opponent, James Longstreet, served as his best man. He was subsequently assigned to a series of remote stations in California, where, desperately missing the company of his beloved Julia, he turned to the bottle for company. Although his alleged alcoholism was grossly overstated, it was clearly more than an officer of the U.S. Army was expected to indulge in, and after a rather harsh reprimand from his commanding officer, Grant resigned his commission in 1854 and returned to his family, then living in St. Louis, Missouri.

Grant was a walking disaster area as a private citizen, forced to peddle firewood at one point to earn enough for food and reduced to asking his parents for money to pay the rent. He soon moved his family into his parents' home in Galena, Illinois, where he proved no more successful at civilian occupations. His rescue, and resurrection, occurred with the opening shots of the Civil War, where, after being rebuffed in his efforts to rejoin the regular army, he was offered the colonelcy of the 21st Illinois Infantry. After a few false starts, he finally achieved a great victory on the battlefield at the fights over Forts Henry and Donelson in Kentucky. Leading a corps in General Henry W. Halleck's

Department of Missouri, he was caught by surprise in the vicious Confederate attack at Pittsburg Landing (Shiloh Church) in April 1862, but he managed to hang on just long enough for reinforcements to be rushed to his aid. Although this was technically a victory for him, rumors that he had been drinking during the movement south, causing his army to be caught by surprise, started spreading through the army, and his early failed attempts at capturing Vicksburg nearly completely derailed his career once again. However, a subsequent brilliant campaign of maneuver brought the Mississippi River outpost back under Union control, and a follow-up campaign broke the long Confederate siege at Chattanooga and swept them out of Tennessee altogether. Impressed, Lincoln recalled Grant to Washington, promoted him to lieutenant general (the first to hold this rank in a U.S. army since George Washington), and placed him in overall command of all Union armies.

Major (later Lieutenant) General Ulysses S. Grant of the Union Army. COURTESY OF THE LIBRARY OF CONGRESS

Grant earned a reputation in Virginia after assuming overall command as a "butcher" who used brute force and the lives of too many of his own men to break the Confederate Army of Northern Virginia's defense of Richmond. However, his major gains came not from costly frontal assaults but from the very tactics of speed and maneuver his critics claimed he failed to use. One significant exception was at the battle of Cold Harbor, where an ordered frontal assault took the lives of 6,000 Union soldiers in the first 20 minutes of battle.

After the war, Grant served two terms as president of the United States, both of which were wrecked by scandal after scandal. Grant's ignorance of the very intricate game of 19th-century politics, coupled with his blind devotion to the friends he appointed to office, who were as inept in their positions as he had been as a businessman, made his administration one of the worst in the history of the presidency. Returning to private life, his subsequent forays into business were no more successful than his prewar ones. His family fortune depleted and near destitute, one last blow for the aging general came with his diagnosis of a fast-spreading and lethal throat cancer, no doubt a result of his well-known and lifelong fondness for cigars. To try to provide for his family, he bowed to pressure from friends and began writing his memoirs. Wreaked by pain and unable to sleep throughout the last weeks of his life, he finished the two-volume work just days before his death on July 23, 1885. Mark Twain published the memoirs personally and gave all the proceeds to Julia, nearly bankrupting himself in the process. This magnificent work, the *Personal Memoirs of U. S. Grant,* has been called one of the finest autobiographies ever published in the English language and is a remarkable portrait of a man who was clearly modest about himself and his accomplishments but was able to forthrightly write about what he had done.

der, with Pemberton showing some late-stage theatrics and Grant calmly insisting upon unconditional surrender, a deal was finally struck late in the day. Confederate soldiers would surrender their weapons but would not enter prison camps, instead being paroled as soon as rolls could be made out. Grant wanted to avoid the expense and logistical nightmare of feeding and transporting 30,000 prisoners, and Pemberton found the offer quite acceptable, undoubtedly knowing that most of the men would soon return to the army anyway.

At 10:00 A.M. on July 4, 1863, the day after the great Union victory at Gettysburg, Pemberton ordered each of his divisions in turn to get out of their trenches, form up, and march under their own colors to the surrender point. Union regiments stood alongside the road watching silently as their beaten opponents passed, offering in a soldier's way a salute to the gallant defenders of Vicksburg.

With the Confederates stacking arms and tenderly laying down their colors, Major General John Alexander Logan led his 3rd Division into the town to occupy it, and soon one of his regimental flags and the Stars and Stripes were raised over the courthouse. The long campaign was at last over, and the end of the Confederacy in the West had begun.

Soldiering is a rough coarse life, calculated to corrupt good morals and harden a man's heart.

Private Henry W. Prince, 127th New York Infantry, Union Army

THE COST

Both sides suffered terribly in the long campaign to capture Vicksburg and ultimately the Mississippi River. There are fairly complete records for Grant's losses: 1,514 killed, 7,395 wounded, and 453 captured or missing. Confederate records are very spotty on this period, but during the siege operation alone Pemberton lost a reported 1,260 killed, 3,572 wounded, and 4,227 missing or captured. Union records indicate that a total of 29,491 surrendered on July 4, but this figure includes all the civilians left in town as well as the remnants of the Confederate defenders.

THE TOUR

Getting There: Vicksburg

Vicksburg lies 45 miles due west of Jackson, Mississippi, easily accessible on Interstate 20. The battlefield park lies just off I-20 exit 4; turn right at the bottom of the exit ramp (approaching from Jackson) onto Clay Street, and the well-marked entrance to the park is just ahead on your right. The main business district of Vicksburg is farther west along Clay Street, which is dotted with directional signs to guide you to all the prominent and most of the obscure sites and attractions. The Vicksburg Convention & Visitors Bureau Welcome Center is across the street on the left from the battlefield park entrance and is a must-stop for detailed directions, as well as the vast selection of brochures, discount coupons, maps, and other information on the local establishments and attractions. The staff is quite friendly and has demonstrated an outstanding willingness to go far out of their way to help meet visitors' needs.

MODERN TIMES AT CHICKASAW BAYOU

Almost all of the Chickasaw Bayou battlefield is now private property and not open to touring, but you can get a good view of the area from a highway that runs through the area and from certain points in the battlefield park. US 61 Business, also known in town as Washington Street, runs northeast out of town, and just past the boundaries of the battlefield park it passes over the remains of the Confederate line of defense. About 1½ miles north on US 61 Business is a turnoff to the left leading to an old Indian mound; this was the position held by the 31st Louisiana and 52nd Georgia Infantry Regiments, supported by a battery from the 1st Mississippi Light Artillery, which successfully held off five strong assaults by Union troops.

One of the best views of the general area can be had from Fort Hill, within the battlefield park (Stop 9 on the tour map). From the north ramparts, look straight ahead and a bit to your right: The bluffs you can see about 2 miles away are the positions of Confederate artillery during the battle, the Confederate infantry was in

---

Six future U.S. presidents served in uniform during the war: Grant, Hayes, Garfield, Arthur, Harrison, and McKinley.

i

---

emplacements at the base of the bluffs, and the swampy area you can see a little to your left is where the Union troops assaulted through.

MODERN TIMES IN VICKSBURG

Today Vicksburg is a bustling small town, driven in about equal parts by Civil War–related tourism and the new boom in riverboat gambling. As you drive down the "main drag," Clay Street, you can't help but notice the extreme frequency of markers and monuments scattered among the fast-food restaurants and small businesses. Even many of the completely non-ACW–related businesses make some reference to the long siege and battle in their names: the Battlefield Inn, Vicksburg Battle Campground, the Pemberton Square Mall, and so on. Although obviously the destination at the end of a well-worn path leading hoards of tourists from Jackson and other points east (and west and north and south), it is a surprisingly pleasant place to visit. Unlike our stops at a great number of other tourist and Civil War–related destinations, we did not have a single unpleasant encounter during our visits, and aside from a few government employees in the national park, we experienced nothing but the warmest and most gracious of welcomes wherever we went.

> *Well, I would be very happy to oblige you, if my passes were respected, but the fact is, sir, I have, within the last two years, given passes to 250,000 men and not one has got there yet.*
>
> Abraham Lincoln, to a visitor who requested a pass through the lines to the Confederate capital of Richmond

This no doubt was the result of Vicksburg's "other" and perhaps least obvious face: that it is ground zero for that most revered of all surviving Southern traditions, the Southern belle. Scarlett O'Hara of *Gone With the Wind* fame is the idea that most people not of the South have of belles, and in some ways it is an accurate portrayal. Belles are known here (and across the Old South) as an effective combination of sugar-sweet politeness covering the tenacity and effectiveness of a tank, women who would never think of being rude to a stranger any more than they would wear white shoes before Easter (or after Labor Day, for that matter). While some of their traditions seem a bit dated, such as never putting dark meat in a chicken salad or avoiding Miracle Whip like the plague ("real" Southern belles make their own, or at least buy Hellman's and add a little lemon), it is an absolute delight to be in the presence of people who would never dream of making you feel uncomfortable or unwelcome. As opposed to the standards set by certain television talk shows and the average rush-hour commute, these ladies can think of no word stronger than "tacky" to describe the worst possible aspect of someone's behavior. And they would never, ever say that to their faces.

Old times are indeed not forgotten here, as the annual Spring and Fall Pilgrimages open the many antebellum homes for tours, the fees from which help keep many of them open and in the same family. Many of these homes claim rightfully to have survived the vicious fighting here, and several have visible damage to the structure as proof. While the main visitor center on Clay Street can give you maps and brochures of the even-dozen homes open year-round for tours, some of which are listed below, a casual drive around the small city takes you past many others that wear their scars from the war as badges of honor.

One last word about touring Vicksburg before we recommend some specific sites and attractions: When you go (and you must!), prepare to stay awhile and let the charm of this Confederate mecca embrace you. This is not the sort of historic site that treats its history as a sideshow to help get you to empty out your wallet; these folks rightfully treat their town as hallowed ground, where the sacrifices of both sides are respectfully preserved and, for the most part, tastefully presented.

POINTS OF INTEREST

Vicksburg National Military Park and Cemetery
3201 Clay Street, Vicksburg
(601) 636-0583

This 1,858-acre park is called the best-preserved Civil War battlefield in the nation. A trail more than 16 miles long carries one through the major sites of the long campaign here. We suggest you start out in the visitor center in order to view the 18-minute film *Vanishing Glory* and see the life-size exhibits and artifacts telling the story of the campaign. This will give you a much better bearing over the complex actions than if you simply try to drive through the park and get a feel for it yourself. After your visit to the visitor center (and be sure to walk over and see the replica artillery emplacements next to the parking lot), drive through the park's rolling hills, past markers and monuments recounting the military campaign. The driving tour goes through the Vicksburg National Cemetery, where nearly 17,000 Union soldiers are buried. Also in the north section of the park are the remains of the Union gunboat USS *Cairo* and its adjacent museum.

USS *Cairo* is open daily from 8:30 A.M. to 5:00 P.M.; the museum is open daily from 8:30 A.M. to 5:00 P.M. November through March, 9:30 A.M. to 6:00 P.M. April through October.

Admission: $5.00 per car. For a guide in your vehicle, it's $30.00 per car, $40.00 per van, and $60.00 per bus. Cassette tapes can be bought for about $6.00. No credit cards are accepted.

The Duff Green Mansion
1114 First East Street, Vicksburg
(601) 636-6968, (800) 992-0037

A former hospital for Confederate and Union soldiers, this three-story mansion, built circa 1856, offers 30-minute tours daily on the hour. Visitors will see what is considered to be one of the finest examples of Palladian architecture in the state. The mansion was built by Duff Green, a wealthy merchant, for his bride, Mary Lake, whose parents donated the property as a wedding gift. In a cave near the mansion, she gave birth to a son during the siege of the city and named him, appropriately, Siege Green. Before the war, the 12,000-square-foot home was the site of many lavish parties. Now it offers bed-and-breakfast accommodations. Open daily for tours, noon to 5:00 P.M. Admission is $6.00 for adults and $4.00 for children 6 through 12.

Anchuca
1010 First East Street, Vicksburg
(601) 661-0111, (888) 686-0111

Take a 25-minute tour through this grand mansion filled with magnificent period antiques and gas-burning chandeliers. Built in 1830, Anchuca was one of the city's first mansion-type homes. Additions were made from 1840 to 1845. After his release from serving 2½ years in prison, President Jefferson Davis went to Anchuca to visit his oldest brother, Joe, who was living in the mansion, and made a speech from Anchuca's balcony. In addition to the two-story main house, Anchuca visitors can see the original slave quarters, also built in 1830, and the turn-of-the-20th-century guest house. Open daily 9:30 A.M. to 3:00 P.M.; admission is $6.00 for adults and $3.00 for children ages 6 through 12.

McRaven
1445 Harrison Street, Vicksburg
(601) 636-1663

No less an authority than *National Geographic* described this home as the South's time capsule. Spend an hour and a half touring this home that was built from 1836 to the 1850s in Frontier, Empire, and Greek Revival styles. Watch for the damage done by wartime cannons, and enjoy the antiques and three-acre garden. Open Monday through Saturday 9:00 A.M. to 5:00 P.M. and Sunday 10:00 A.M. to 5:00 P.M.; the house is closed December through February. Admission is $5.00 for adults, $3.00 for children 12 through 18, and $2.50 for children ages 6 through 11.

Balfour House
Crawford Street, Vicksburg

Built in 1835, Balfour House hosted many prominent military figures during the Civil War and eventually became the headquarters for Union soldiers after the city's fall. A key feature of the Greek Revival house is its elliptical staircase that spirals for three floors. It's named for owner Emma Harrison Balfour, a diarist who recorded events during the city's war years. Open Monday through Saturday 9:00 A.M. to 4:30 P.M. and Sunday 1:00 to 5:00 P.M. Admission is $5.00 for adults.

ACCOMMODATIONS

The main road through town and its intersection with I-20 has just about every major national low- and midlevel chain establishment, but for a real Vicksburg experience, we recommend you try one of the numerous bed-and-breakfast establishments dotted around town; check at the city visitor center for an up-to-date listing. Other than these, we can recommend two interesting places to stay, one on the Mississippi River and the other in Jackson.

Horizon Casino Hotel $$-$$$
1310 Mulberry Street, Vicksburg
(800) 843-2343

This seven-story hotel, adjacent to the casino with its shops and restaurants, offers free continental breakfast to its guests. There are 117 rooms with 16 suites plus covered parking and child-care facilities. Due to Mississippi's rather eccentric gambling laws, which require that all casinos must be aboard boats, this rather massive complex is on the river.

Edison Walthall $-$$
225 East Capitol Street, Jackson
(601) 948-6161, (800) 932-6161

This hotel, one of Mississippi's finest, is right downtown, near the governor's mansion, state capitol, and museums. It's a AAA four-diamond hotel with a Mobile three-star restaurant. It offers an outdoor heated pool with a hot tub and a fitness center plus meeting rooms, airport transportation, and true Old World charm. It has 208 rooms and 3 suites. Edison Walthall was originally built in 1928 but recently refurbished to modern standards. Also expect room service, a gift shop, fax, copier, and a courtesy van for trips within 3 miles of the hotel.

RESTAURANTS

Mayflower Restaurant $
123 West Capitol Street, Jackson
(601) 355-4122

The Mayflower has been feeding Jacksonians since 1935. Owner Mike Kontouris has a philosophy: Treat the customers well, serve them good food at a good price, and they'll come back. He does, and they do. The Mayflower has been featured in American Airlines' inflight magazine and other publications, but the important thing at the Mayflower is the food, which they serve 18 hours every day. A favorite is the Greek salad with lump crabmeat. They also serve up seafood specials, including speckled trout and redfish, and lots of pastas, too.

Beechwood Restaurant & Lounge $-$$
4451 East Clay Street, Vicksburg
(601) 636-3761

Beechwood's menu features delicious steaks, seafood, and po'boys. There's a lunch special Sunday through Friday. Try the popular Beechwood Classic, a filet with shrimp. The restaurant is open daily from 11:00 A.M. to 10:30 P.M. (to 12:30 A.M. on Friday and Saturday).

Walnut Hills $-$$
1214 Adams Street, Vicksburg
(601) 638-4910

Walnut Hills's round tables filled with down-home cooking are well known and for good reason. A typical menu features some of the best fried chicken found anywhere, plus country-fried steak, fried corn, snap beans, okra and tomatoes, corn bread, and blackberry cobbler. The restaurant is open Monday through Friday starting at 11:00 A.M. Service from the round tables is available until 2:00 A.M.; a la carte is available until 9:00 P.M.

Mary Mahoney's Old French
House and Cafe $-$$
138 Rue Magnolia, Biloxi
(228) 374-0163

This is a Coast landmark and longtime favorite. In one of the oldest houses in Mississippi, built in 1737, the restaurant has served presidents, entertainers, and dignitaries with such dishes as lobster, fresh fish, shrimp, and lump crabmeat. The cafe offers po'boys and sandwiches 24 hours a day, seven days a week. The restaurant hours are Monday through Saturday from 11:00 A.M. to 10:00 P.M. Reservations are recommended.

Day Trips

Mississippi State Historical Museum
100 South State Street, Jackson
(601) 576-6920

This museum is something of which Mississippians are most proud. Called the Old Capitol Museum, it was built in the late 1830s and restored in 1961, and what a grand Greek Revival structure it is. It houses award-winning exhibits spanning the early days of the state's colorful history through the civil rights movement and beyond. Plan to spend awhile here for there's much to see and do, and there's also a bookstore and gift shop. Admission is free.

The Manship House
420 East Fortification Street, Jackson
(601) 961-4724

The Gothic Revival house built in 1857 and called a "cottage villa" will be forever known as the home of the Jackson mayor who surrendered the town to Union Army general W. T. Sherman during the Civil War in 1863. Not that the mayor had much choice, since Sherman was wont to ride his fiery trail through the South, wreaking havoc in his wake. Mayor Manship's house-museum uses photos, diaries, and letters to interpret family activities and events of the 1800s. The Manship House is administered by the Mississippi Department of Archives and History. Open 9:00 A.M. to 4:00 P.M. Tuesday through Friday, 1:00 to 4:00 P.M. Saturday; admission is free.

Grand Gulf Military Monument
Route 2, Box 389, Port Gibson
(601) 437-5911

Grand Gulf Military Park is dedicated to the former town of Grand Gulf and to the Civil War battle that took place there. The park is 8 miles northwest of Port Gibson, off US 61 and consists of approximately 400 acres that incorporate Fort Cobun, Fort Wade, a cemetery, a museum, campgrounds, picnic sites, hiking trails, an observation tower, and a number of restored buildings. The museum contains Civil War memorabilia plus antique machinery and an assortment of horse-drawn vehicles. Open Monday through Saturday 8:00 A.M. to noon and 1:00 to 5:00 P.M.; Sunday 10:00 A.M. to 6:00 P.M. Admission is $2.00 for adults and $1.00 for children.

Ruins of Windsor
Mississippi Highway 552, Port Gibson

All that remains today of a gracious mansion 10 miles southwest of Port Gibson is 23 columns. The mansion, completed in 1861, was a Confederate observation post. After the Battle of Port Gibson, it was turned into a hospital to treat Union soldiers. The grounds are generally open year-round during daylight hours. If the gate is locked, you can walk the 150 yards from the road to the ruins, but keep an eye out for hunters during deer-hunting season (late November through late January). There have been a few isolated instances of illegal hunting near the ruins, and illegal hunters aren't mindful of tourists. Admission is free.

Beauvoir
2244 Beach Boulevard, Biloxi
(800) 570-3818

The restored last home of the only president of the Confederacy, Beauvoir was the seaside estate of Jefferson Davis. A National Historic Landmark, Beauvoir was built in the mid-1800s, and its 74-acre landscaped grounds and handsome buildings are open to visitors. In addition to the furnished presidential residence, there is a Confederate museum and cemetery where the Tomb of the Unknown Confederate Soldier is located. The beautiful grounds contain large oaks, magnolias, pines, gardens, and a lagoon. Open daily 9:00 A.M. to 5:00 P.M. from March 1 to Labor Day; closes at 4:00 P.M. the rest of the year. Closed Christmas. Admission is $7.50 for adults, $6.75 for persons over age 64 and military, and $4.50 for youths ages 6 through 15.

NEW ORLEANS AND PORT HUDSON: THE RIVER WAR

Soon after the first shots of the war had been fired, an overall Union strategy based on a gradual strangulation of the South was adopted. Based on the previously derided Anaconda Plan first proposed by General in Chief Winfield Scott of the U.S. Army, the multiphased strategic plan relied on one basic and yet crucial component for success: the control and free transit of the Mississippi River by the Union Army and Navy, splitting the Confederacy in half and denying an important route of supplies to the blockaded states from ports in Texas and Mexico.

As this was in many ways still a frontier area with few roads (and even fewer that could be used to support an army), the task of wresting control of the great river was given in equal parts to army and navy commands. One combined command was established in Cairo, Illinois, and given the task of clearing out Confederate outposts along the river moving to the south, and another was formed at Ship Island, Mississippi, and given the task of fighting their way upriver to join the Cairo-based squadron in taking complete control of the river. Given command of the assembling fleet at Ship Island was a highly experienced naval captain, Tennessee born but Union loyalist David Glasgow Farragut.

BACKGROUND TO THE BATTLE

The fact that military operations would have to be conducted on relatively shallow inland rivers that were choked with debris and had poorly charted and ever-shifting ship channels, and with enemy artillery and infantry emplacements literally only feet away from the ship channel, meant that some serious rethinking in ship design and naval tactics would have to be done. The U.S. Navy possessed 90 ships of all types when the war began, but only 42 were listed "in service" at spots all around the globe, and not a single warship would suffice for river warfare. Although other navies had experimented with metal-clad armored warships, and the French had used several to good success in the Crimean War, almost every U.S. ship was both wooden and sail-powered.

On the other hand, the fledgling Confederate Navy had not a single ship at the outbreak of hostilities and a host of problems to overcome. Another part of the Union strategic plan called for a tight blockade of the Southern coastline and ports, which the Confederate Navy would be charged with either breaking or at least preventing from totally closing down the most critical ports. It was obvious that the Mississippi River was going to be a major area of conflict, and suitable ships for port defense there were needed as well. The final and greatest problem was where these ships would come from, as nearly every major shipyard and heavy industrial facility was located in the North.

THE TARGETS

Aside from a series of strong Confederate river forts and outposts from Memphis northward along the Mississippi, the major points of concern for the Union Navy were New Orleans, Port Hudson, and Vicksburg. New Orleans would be the immediate problem; the largest city in the Confederacy, it had the greatest number of shipbuilding and other industrial facilities of any other single area of the South, and to leave it untouched was to guarantee a strengthened Confederate military. However, it was located on a curve of the Mississippi surrounded by swamps and marshy lowlands that precluded an overland campaign and was well protected from attack by sea by two powerful forts 70 miles downstream just above the Head of the Passes, Forts Jackson and St. Philip.

The two masonry forts were originally ordered constructed by Andrew Jackson in 1822 following his victory over the British force in the area in 1814. Fort Jackson was the larger of the two, roughly star-shaped and positioned on the western bank of the river, manned by about 700 troops and mounting 74 guns, including several 10-inch Columbiads, the largest gun in the Confederate inventory at the time. A smoothbore cannon, the Columbiad was capable of throwing a 128-pound shell over 1,800 yards with deadly accuracy. It was more than capable of destroying any of the U.S. Navy's wooden ships of the day. Fort St. Philip was across the river on the opposite bank, about one-half mile farther upstream, and was an unusual construction of thick brick walls covered by dirt ramparts in a sort of "squished" star arrangement, also manned by about 700 troops and mounting 52 guns. Both forts were well located in a bend in the river that any ship would have to slow down to navigate, making any attempt to "blow by" the posts unlikely.

To add to the riverborne defenses, a third ancient fort, Fort Chalmette, just upstream, was also garrisoned and armed. This was the site where Andrew Jackson fought the British during the War of 1812 (a battle that was fought more than two weeks after the war was officially over). No one thought it really necessary to man this old post, but it provided some insurance in case an enemy fleet managed to get past the two forts downstream. Between Forts Jackson and St. Philip, heavy chains holding several old ship hulks were placed across the river and strongly anchored, blocking the river passage.

THE NAVIES

The defense at Forts Jackson and St. Philip was further backed up by the fledgling Confederate Navy's western gulf fleet, consisting of four ships of the line: the *McRae,* the ironclad-ram *Manassas,* and the ironclads *Louisiana* and *Mississippi.* These were backed up by two ships of the Louisiana Navy, the *Governor Quitman* and the *Governor Moore,* and a group of converted riverboats mounting a single gun each and rather grandiosely called the River Defense Fleet: the *Breckenridge, Defiance, Stonewall Jackson, General Lovell, Warrior,* and *Resolute.* Records are incomplete, but the ships probably mounted a total of about 100 guns.

> *A Baptist. And always have been.*
>> Old civilian woman in north Georgia, when asked by Union troops if she was "secesh" or a Union supporter

By the end of March 1862, Farragut had assembled two small fleets to take on the enormous task of opening up the lower Mississippi: an 18-ship gunboat fleet led by his own flagship, the *Hartford*—a 2,900-ton screw sloop 225 feet long and 44 feet wide that had a top speed of just under 14 knots. The 2 frigates, 5 sloops, and 11 ironclad gunboats mounted a total of 243 guns. A second fleet known as the Mortar Flotilla, commanded by Commander David Dixon Porter, Farragut's own foster brother, consisted of 22 two-masted sail-powered schooners roughly 100 feet long each, mounting a single 13-inch mortar that fired a 200-pound shell up to 4,000 yards, landing nearly vertical and easily lobbed over fortification walls. These mortar schooners sailed under their own power while at sea but were towed upriver by their own assigned support fleet of 8 gunboats and unarmed towboats.

On April 8, 1862, Farragut moved all but one of his ships across the shallow passes and sandbars that marked the entrance to the Mississippi River at the Head of the Passes. A few days later he was followed by a large troopship fleet bearing Major General Benjamin Franklin Butler and his 18,000-man army command, and both began moving upriver on their campaign to take New Orleans.

THE BATTLE OF FORT JACKSON AND FORT ST. PHILIP

Farragut decided to let Porter's mortar flotilla handle the problem of the powerful Confederate forts before he brought his own fleet into firing range. On April 18, the 22 mortar schooners were towed into position just south of a bend in the river below Fort Jackson and commenced a heavy bombardment of the two posts. Over the next five days, about 17,000 rounds of ammunition were fired, which slightly damaged the forts but failed to kill many men of the garrisons or destroy any of their gun emplacements.

Farragut, displaying his usual impatience, decided to cancel the bombardment (which was not doing much good anyhow), send his fleet in to directly attack the Confederate stronghold, and as quickly as possible get past it upriver—his main goal being to capture New Orleans as soon as possible. The first of several obstacles in his way was the chained-together old ships across the river below the two forts, and he assigned Lieutenant Charles H. S. Caldwell, captain of the *Itaska,* to find a passage through.

After several failed attempts to blast through the line of obstacles by cannon fire and explosives, Caldwell decided to simply ram his way through. Bringing his gunboat up to full speed, he hit the chains

about midchannel and swiftly parted them, leaving a clear passage for the rest of the fleet. Farragut arranged his gunboats into three divisions and then signaled for them to move out at 2:00 A.M. on April 24.

The first division was led by the large gunboat *Cayuga,* in front of two screw sloops, two corvettes, and three more gunboats strung out in a single column. The small task force was not seen until nearly upon Fort Jackson, but then the Confederate gunners opened up with every available cannon. The *Cayuga* was raked by fire not only from the forts but also from three of the Confederate gunboats lying anchored nearby. All three gunboats were quickly sunk by the lead Union ship and two others that rapidly closed in.

The second division, led by Farragut's own flagship *Hartford,* soon entered the growing fight and was nearly immediately attacked by a Confederate ship pushing a fire raft, which struck and nearly threatened to set ablaze the Union ship. Farragut calmly ordered the fire to be doused and the enemy ship sunk, both of which occurred in rapid secession, and then he just as calmly turned his attention to the rest of the battle.

A wild naval melee had broken out by now, with the Confederate ram *Manassas* attacking the Union ships *Mississippi* and *Brooklin,* both of which escaped with little damage, before moving downstream toward the rest of the Union fleet. Before the *Manassas* could mount another attack, the *Mississippi* turned on her and forced the Confederate ship aground under a near blizzard of shot and shell. The crew barely escaped with their lives while the boat was shot to pieces on the bank. While this drama was unfolding downstream, the Louisiana Navy steamer *Governor Moore* attacked the onrushing Union fleet led now by the corvette *Varuna.* Each ship raked the other with concentrated fire, inflicting heavy casualties on both, while the *Governor Moore* actually shot its own bow away in order to place point-blank fire into the Union gunboat. After a follow-up ramming attack, the Union corvette sank near the far bank, taking most of her crew with her. The *Governor Moore* did not have much time to celebrate; moments later, as she turned away from the sinking Union ship, exposing her sides to the rest of the Union fleet, a heavy blast of fire from several ships exploded her magazine and sent her burning to the bottom with almost all her crew.

Seeing the burning and wrecked Confederate ships drifting past his schooners just downstream, Porter ordered his mortars to renew their fire on the forts. The fort's gunners were forced to stop their own fire on the Union fleet, but once again, little physical damage was done to the two Confederate outposts. However, the real damage was already done, as Farragut's fleet was now safely past the two forts, having wrecked the Confederate naval fleet at the cost of 37 dead, 149 wounded, one ship sunk, and two ships damaged. Farragut signaled Butler to bring his troopships upriver and bypass the forts, which would be allowed to simply starve themselves out when New Orleans was taken and their supplies cut off.

THE END OF THE BATTLE FOR NEW ORLEANS

As soon as Butler had moved his troopships above the two Confederate forts, Farragut ordered his fleet to set sail once again toward New Orleans. Nearing old Fort Chalmette, he noticed that the Confederate defenders had installed river batteries on both banks, threatening his passage. The *Brooklin* opened fire on both sides with her swivel-mount 80-pounder Dahlgren gun, sending only about 20 shots into the batteries before their gunners broke and ran, leaving the river passage open. This action was probably the best showing of the entire war for that particular model of Dahlgren gun, as most

80-pounders had a tendency to burst after a few rounds.

Watching Farragut's actions from a levee nearby, New Orleans garrison commander Major General Mansfield Lovell at once ordered his 4,000-man command to destroy what supplies they could, along with the tons of cotton bales sitting on the docks ready for shipment, and then pulled out of the city before Farragut's ships approached.

On the morning of April 25, Farragut's fleet sailed into the New Orleans port and docked without a single shot being fired, although his gun crews were standing by at the ready. The civil authorities of the city reacted with ill-thought-out impudence at first, actually daring Farragut to "try and take the city," but they finally bowed to the obvious and formally surrendered the city on April 29. The commanders of Forts Jackson and St. Philip originally intended to hold fast to their posts, but the men mutinied and demanded the forts be abandoned. On April 28 the forts' guns were spiked, and the officers formally surrendered their posts to Butler's men. The short action had cost the Confederates only 12 dead and 40 wounded, but they lost one of the most critical ports in the entire Western Theater.

NEW ORLEANS AFTER THE BATTLE

With the Big Easy rather easily taken, Butler was placed in charge of the occupation force, and Farragut soon moved out to points upriver. Butler, an unpleasant and rather corrupt administrator, managed to outrage the local populace to the point that even his own commanders in Washington were soon debating his judgment. He soon earned the nickname Spoons for his habit of raiding local plantations and wealthy estates, where he "confiscated" the silverware and other valuables. Several sources claimed he had a habit of doing this at dinner parties. Only a day after assuming his post, he began issuing a series of imperial-sounding edicts, including harsh pronouncements demanding the civilian population treat his men and the national flag with the utmost reverence at the threat (and delivery) of harsh punishments.

A local gambler, William Mumford, was arrested for pulling down a Union flag that one of Farragut's men had placed over the Old Mint Building before Butler even arrived. Mumford was tried for treason, quickly convicted, and just as quickly hanged on June 7. On May 15 Butler issued his General Order Number 28, which became better known as his "Woman Order." In short, this order stated that any lady of the town that dared treat any Union soldier with contempt in any way would be immediately assumed to be a prostitute and arrested as such. Newspapers as far away as London condemned this act, which ultimately helped lead to Butler's removal from his command in December, but curiously, the order was never revoked or changed.

LAST GUARDIAN OF THE RIVER: PORT HUDSON

With New Orleans and Memphis successfully taken, only two last Confederate outposts remained in the way of complete control of the river by the Union Navy— the heavy batteries controlling access between Port Hudson, Louisiana, and Vicksburg, Mississippi. Worse for the success of the grand Union strategy, this stretch of Confederate-controlled river included the mouth of the Red River, giving a clear waterborne supply and communications route to the Trans-Mississippi Theater.

Port Hudson is about 120 miles by air south of Vicksburg but more than 200 miles by the meandering Mississippi River; it served primarily as a tiny cotton port before the war. Settled by small farmers early in the 19th century, the small town never "caught on" with the large landown-

ers and was in danger of disappearing when the war began. What the town lacked in amenities it more than made up for in abundance of good terrain for defense of the river passage. Eighty-foot-high bluffs lined the river to the west of the small settlement, where the river curves around nearly upon itself, making a high-speed passage impractical. Swamps, ravines, and nearly impenetrable woods surrounded Port Hudson on three sides, making the only practical land approach one from due east.

Despite this very favorable position and the urging of then Western Theater commander General Pierre Gustave Toutant Beauregard, the town remained without a significant garrison or serious fortifications until after nearby Baton Rouge was occupied in May 1862. Major General Earl Van Dorn, Vicksburg area commander, realized nearly too late the vital nature of this position and sent a 5,000-man force under Major General John C. Breckinridge to attack and try to retake the state capital in order to gain time to reinforce and build up Port Hudson.

BATON ROUGE

Now a forward base for Farragut's fleet attacking Vicksburg, Baton Rouge was garrisoned by a 2,500-man force under Brigadier General Thomas Williams, supported by a varying number of naval gunboats. Breckinridge's command moved south in late July 1862, preparing to assault and retake the capital, but ran into several delays caused primarily by some unspecified disease sweeping through the camps. Although the Confederate commander received some reinforcements from a small outpost 60 miles north of Baton Rouge, by early August he was in position to attack with only about 2,600 effective combat troops. To reinforce his attack, Van Dorn had ordered a small naval task force south, led by the ironclad *Arkansas*.

Breckinridge arrived just outside town on the afternoon of August 4 and divided his decimated command into two weak divisions led by Brigadier Generals Daniel Ruggles and Charles Clark. Lieutenant Henry K. Stevens was having serious engine trouble with his *Arkansas*, adding to the growing problems with the Confederate attack, but Breckinridge gave the order to attack at 4:30 A.M. on August 5.

The plan was to attack with the two divisions nearly line-abreast against the Union line running parallel to the river, while the gunboats moved in and neutralized the Union gunboat threat. As was almost the usual during this war, nothing went off as planned. A thick fog prevented a coordinated movement of the two divisions; heavy skirmishing on the Union right confused the two division commanders, who moved their units in such a manner that several actually ended up firing on one another; and Stevens's problems with his gunboat delayed his entry into the battle until nearly the end. Despite this, the Union line caved in rather quickly, sending the blue-clad troops scurrying to the relative safety of their own gunboats' covering fire, while Ruggles and Clark moved forward into the town, fighting house to house and street to street with the scattered Union commands.

As the town was being overrun, Stevens moved into position and prepared to attack the three Union gunboats at the dock, when his engines suddenly seized up again, and the naval battle ended before it had even really begun. Reorganizing a hasty defense under the covering fire of the gunboats, Williams personally led a failed counterattack, dying in the attempt, and his scratch force once again fled to the cover of the gunboats. With no naval support coming, Breckinridge held the town until about 10:00 A.M. and then pulled out and marched north to Port Hudson. As the Confederate troops pulled out, Colonel Thomas W. Cahill assumed overall command for the North and moved his remaining force back into their original positions. Union losses in the brief fight were 84 dead and 299 wounded or missing, while Breckinridge reported a loss of 84 dead

and 372 wounded, missing, or captured, including a seriously wounded Clark, left on the battlefield and later captured. Two weeks later, Butler ordered the city evacuated, looted, and razed to the ground and the garrison returned to New Orleans. His officers made sure the finest furniture, art, silver, and anything else of value went south safely in their own possession. As a final act, Spoons Butler ordered the inmates at the Louisiana State Prison at Baton Rouge released but involuntarily enlisted into Union service.

THE DEFENSE OF PORT HUDSON

Nearly the moment his rebel troops entered Port Hudson, Ruggles put them to work building defensive works and gun emplacements for the coming assault. The lines soon extended nearly 8 miles in a wide semicircle around the small settlement and mounted 10 heavy guns by the end of August. Two attempts by Farragut's fleet to bypass the fortifications afterward met with a hot and accurate fire, leading the newly promoted admiral to set aside his plans to attack Mobile and concentrate on building up a land and naval force to attack the remaining Confederate river strongholds.

By early March 1863 both sides had built up impressive forces in the area. Major General Franklin Gardner had assumed command of the Confederate garrison, now reinforced to four brigades with nearly 16,000 men manning 11 pentagonal gun emplacements mounting 21 heavy guns along 3 miles of the river, as well as another 5 miles of infantry entrenchments and gun emplacements guarding the inland approaches. In total, 107 heavy guns, field pieces, and mortars guarded the lines from 25 separate batteries, ranging from relatively small field howitzers up to three 9-inch naval Dahlgren guns and seven 30-pounder Parrott rifles.

Farragut had prepared a squadron to run the Port Hudson batteries and join the

---

CLOSE-UP

The Song of the South

"Dixie" was a song written in 1859 by an Ohio musician, Daniel Decatur Emmett, while he was living in New York City. Emmett had never traveled through the South at the time and had only third-hand or worse knowledge of what the area was actually like. However, he was under pressure to compose a new song for a failing minstrel show. The show folded shortly thereafter, but his song became a surprising hit. Originally entitled "I Wish I Were in Dixie's Land," it became the unofficial song of the Confederacy after being played at President Jefferson Davis's inauguration. Many Southerners objected to a proposal to make it the official anthem, as it was not considered "dignified" enough. In April 1865, just after receiving the news that General Robert E. Lee had surrendered his troops in Virginia, Lincoln stepped out of the White House and walked up to an army band that was playing nearby. He asked them to play "Dixie" for him, and when his shocked aides commented on the seemingly strange request, he remarked that it was the "finest tune I ever heard."

---

gathering force assaulting Vicksburg, consisting of his flagship *Hartford,* three other heavy seagoing ironclads, three smaller "river" ironclads, and the side-paddle ironclad *Mississippi,* along with six mortar boats. After dark on March 14, 1863, he ordered the squadron forward, trying to slip past the Confederate batteries under cover of darkness. *Hartford* and the smaller ironclad *Albatross* managed to get past the first set of batteries before the Union ruse was discovered and Confederate gunners opened a near point-blank fire.

A thunderous fire from the Confederate batteries raked the Union ships, pounding through the thick iron plating and destroying engines and steering gear. Two hours later, only Farragut's two lead ships had managed to pass the batteries more or less unscathed, while the rest of his fleet was nearly wrecked. All managed to limp back south, except for the *Mississippi,* which fought alone while grounded on a mudbank for nearly an hour until an

onboard fire grew out of control. Her crew abandoned ship about 1:00 A.M.; an hour later she slipped free and drifted south, finally ending her life in a massive explosion about 5:30 A.M., when the fire finally reached her powder magazine. Farragut had managed to get two ironclads past the defenses and on to Vicksburg at the cost of 26 killed, 38 wounded, and 64 missing, as well as one ship destroyed and the rest seriously damaged. Confederate losses amounted to 3 killed and 22 wounded.

Assault on Port Hudson

With Farragut's failure to blast through the Confederate river defenses, it became obvious that a land attack to neutralize the position would be necessary. Major General Nathaniel P. Banks's Army of the Gulf, with nearly 35,000 men, was assigned the task of storming and taking the strong Southern position. Most decidedly a "political" general (he had been the Speaker of the U.S. House before the war and won his commission by pulling strings), Banks was not viewed as exactly the Confederacy's worst enemy; in the Shenandoah campaign against Major General Thomas Jonathan "Stonewall" Jackson during late 1861, his command suffered so many defeats and huge amounts of captured supplies that the delighted Confederate troops nicknamed him "Commissary" Banks.

Despite the expressed feeling that his 35,000-man force was "inadequate" to take the Confederate stronghold, Banks moved out in mid-May 1863 with only a portion of his men to take it. The rest were left to garrison Baton Rouge, New Orleans, and several other smaller posts. Encircling the Confederate position by May 23 with roughly 15,000 (some accounts say 20,000) men and a handful of Union gunboats, Banks made his first attempt to assault on May 27. An ill-coordinated attack limped off at dawn on the Union right, followed hours later by attacks along the rest of the line.

This battle featured the first use of large numbers of African-American troops, including two regiments of Louisiana Native Guards—almost all former slaves. Although Banks outnumbered his Confederate opponents nearly four to one at nearly every place along the line, the attack was a dismal failure. The greatest Union advance was the advancement into the outer trench lines at a few points, all of which were quickly retaken and the attacks blunted. Total casualties for the failed attack were about 2,000 Union soldiers and about 250 Confederates.

A little over two weeks later, Banks attempted another assault. As in the May 27 attack, a nearly hourlong heavy bombardment preceded the attack, followed by a formal call for the Confederate garrison to surrender. When they refused, the

bombardment was resumed and a general assault against the center of the Confederate line was prepared. At 4:00 A.M. on June 14, with only three hours to organize and prepare their men for the attack, a three-division front assaulted three points on the Confederate line, centered on a large fort known as the Priest Cap. The uncoordinated attack fared no better than the earlier attempt and gradually petered out before noon. The two attacks had cost Banks a total of 708 killed, 3,336 wounded, and 319 captured or missing, to gain nothing. Confederate losses amounted to 176 killed and 447 wounded, with none reported missing or captured.

Banks settled down into a tight siege of the Confederate garrison, which was running low on supplies even as the campaign began. As at Vicksburg, Union engineers and infantry cut a series of siege trenches growing ever closer to the Confederate line, while sappers attempted to mine under the line and blow it up. This last attempt was foiled by the Confederates' own countermining efforts, while sharpshooters kept everyone's head down in the trenches and occasional firefights lit up the line. This siege, the longest in American history, lasted 48 days. Many accounts confirm that after the regular rations, horses, and mules were all gone, the men turned to eating dogs and rats until they, too, were all gone.

Banks had planned another general assault for July 7, which was postponed due to poor weather. Before it could be rescheduled, news arrived about the fall of Vicksburg; when informed, Gardner decided he could not hold out alone against additional Union forces surely heading his way. Formal surrender of the garrison took place on July 9, with 5,500 prisoners walking into captivity. With this act, the Mississippi River was at long last once again under full Union control, and the Confederacy had suffered a devastating breach from which it would never recover.

THE TOUR

Getting There: New Orleans

New Orleans is in extreme southeastern Louisiana, not far from the Mississippi state line and easily accessible via Interstate 10 from the east or west, Interstate 55 south from Jackson, Mississippi, or Interstate 59 south from Hattiesburg, Mississippi. Fort Jackson still exists, although most of the other forts and locations mentioned either disappeared under the meandering flow of the great river or long ago fell into disrepair and neglect. Fort Jackson is near the small town of Buras; south of New Orleans, take Louisiana Highway 23 south from U.S. Highway 90 on the south side of town, and follow it about 53 miles south to the marked historic site. It is very hard to get lost here, as it is the only major hardtop road in the vicinity! Still, you need to watch carefully for the turnoff (on the left going south), as the fort itself is on the other side of both a rather high levee and a sports complex.

MODERN TIMES

Very little remains in the Big Easy from Civil War times, including any of the few fortifications constructed for its defense. A few houses noted for being Butler's headquarters or various Union officers' residences dot the city, but the dearth of really historic sites can be illustrated by the Cable House, whose claim to fame is that it was the residence of a California poet, Joaquin Miller, who was denied the use of the mail in the 1880s for his pro-

---

A great source for personnel and unit information on the Internet is the CWU-NITS site, updated about every three months, with contacts for just about every unit that fought in the war. The address is http://sunsite.utk.edu/civil-war/warweb.html#rosters.

Southern views. The most significant sites in the area are Fort Jackson and the Chalmette National Historic Park.

POINTS OF INTEREST

**Louisiana Historical Association Civil War Museum
929 Camp Street, New Orleans
(504) 523-4522**
A very nice collection of Civil War relics, concentrating on those from Louisiana regiments. The flag collection is unusual and well presented, as are a nice weapons collection, some period currency and documents, and displays of personal effects of Jefferson Davis and Robert E. Lee. Open Monday through Saturday 10:00 A.M. to 4:00 P.M.; closed all major holidays. Admission is $5.00 for teens and adults; for those under 12 it's $2.00. Across the street is the National D-Day Museum, also highly recommended.

**Jackson Barracks Military Museum
6400 St. Claude Avenue, New Orleans
(504) 278-8242**
Originally built in 1833, this was the main defense barracks for the New Orleans area until the end of World War I, and a host of high Confederate officers called this place home during their service as young U.S. Army officers before the war. Originally the barracks consisted of four two-story brick buildings with walls 20 inches thick, surrounded by a brick wall with four towers mounting cannon at each corner. Partially restored, this museum now houses weapons and artifacts from every American war through the 1991 Persian Gulf War and has a nice collection of flags, personal equipment, cavalry and artillery artifacts, and ammunition from the Civil War era. Open Monday through Friday 8:00 A.M. to 4:00 P.M.; admission is free. Please be aware that post–September 11 security concerns may affect the hours or even accessibility, as this museum is on an active military post.

Fort Jackson
LA 23, Buras
(985) 657-7083

Sixty miles southeast of New Orleans, this fort survived both the encounters with Farragut's fleet and the Union occupation and was used as a training base during World War I, only to almost disappear due to flooding and the incredibly humid environment. The fort has been restored but is still in very poor condition, despite constant efforts by the staff and a protective surrounding levee. A self-guided tour goes through several powder magazines, guardrooms, barracks, and casemates, as well as around several surviving earthworks that protected the fort from infantry attack. A small museum, not always open, has artifacts from here and nearby Fort St. Philip (now in ruins, on private property and inaccessible), as well as a small gift shop with the usual souvenirs.

In the center of the parade ground is one of the original 6-inch Rodman Columbiads, which was mounted on the parapet during the war, as well as the remnants of several hot shot ovens. The fort is open 7:00 A.M. to 5:00 P.M. daily; admission is free, but donations are accepted (and encouraged—let's keep this place open).

Chalmette Battlefield and National Cemetery
(part of Jean Lafitte National Historic Park and Preserve)
Louisiana Highway 46, Chalmette
(504) 281-0510

Six miles southeast of the French Quarter, still within the metropolitan New Orleans area and surrounded by the gigantic Shell Oil Arabi facility, this area gained its highest fame as the site of General Andrew Jackson's victory over the British during (or more accurately, several days after) the War of 1812. During the New Orleans campaign, earthwork batteries mounting ten 32-pounder guns provided the last-ditch defense of the city. The 141-acre park is now a memorial to the 1812 battle and Jackson, with very little information presented about the Civil War use of the site, although the remaining earthworks are the original Confederate gun emplacements. The park is open 9:00 A.M. to 5:00 P.M. daily, closed on December 25 and Mardi Gras; admission is free.

ACCOMMODATIONS

New Orleans is a major convention and tourism destination, so reserving a room at pretty much any given price is not terribly difficult. However, *finding* that room might be. We heartily suggest that you contact the New Orleans Metropolitan Convention & Visitors Bureau before your trip, for both a map of this sometimes confusing city and an updated list of available hotels. The staff is exceptionally helpful and pleasant and can be called at (800) 672-6124; information is also available on the Web at www.nawlins.com.

There are literally dozens of hotels in the metro area, an unusually high percentage of which are the usual and expected chains. However, there are two fine establishments that we feel are worthy of special mention.

Avenue Plaza Hotel $$$-$$$$
2111 St. Charles Avenue, New Orleans
(504) 566-1212

One of the nicest hotels in the Garden District, the Avenue Plaza offers 256 suites on its 12 floors, all with a king- or queen-size bed; half have kitchens and radios, and all rooms feature microwave ovens and small refrigerators. A rooftop sundeck with adjacent Jacuzzi is available, as are a sauna and steamroom, valet laundry, and massages.

Soniat House $$$$
1133 Chartres Street, New Orleans
(504) 522-0570, (800) 544-8808

A relatively small, 33-room hotel in a restored 1830s-era mansion at the edge of the French Quarter, the Soniat is one of the most elegant and beautiful hotels in the city. The sort of place where locals send someone they wish to impress, the exquisitely restored mansion is filled to the brim with fine antiques, the staff is exceptionally pleasant and attentive, and a high degree of attention to detail is obvious in everything we observed. The only drawbacks are the three-night minimum stay required during parts of the year and the outrageous prices for parking. If money is not a concern, head straight for the Soniat.

RESTAURANTS

New Orleans is a town devoted to the finer things in life, most notably, food. A comprehensive list of the good, nonchain restaurants here would fill a good-size book; we refer you to *Insiders' Guide to New Orleans* for a more complete listing. Here are a few of our favorites, where we can honestly say we have never had a bad meal (possibly because we have never had a bad meal *anywhere* in New Orleans, excepting the fast-food places!).

Antoine's $$$-$$$$
713 St. Louis Street
French Quarter, New Orleans
(504) 581-4422
This institution is as inseparable from New Orleans as the Mississippi River and nearly as ancient. First opened in 1840, it is the oldest continuously operating restaurant in the United States and has one of the largest wine cellars with well over 30,000 bottles on hand at any given time. This is a place where tradition lives on both in the quality of its food and the experience and longevity of its staff. A regular haunt of the New Orleans society class, during Mardi Gras the Carnival Kings take over their own private dining rooms, and reservations are almost exclusively the domain of the "permanent table" variety.

More than 130 dishes adorn the Edwardian French menu; specialties include *huitres a la Foch* (fried oysters served on toast, covered with pâté de foie gras), Oysters Rockefeller (invented here), *Oeufs Sardou* (poached eggs covered with artichoke hearts and hollandaise sauce), and broiled Gulf shrimp rémoulade. When you make reservations, make sure to request the Omelette Alaska Antoine for dessert, which must be ordered in advance. Antoine's is open Monday through Saturday for lunch and supper. Reservations are for all practical purposes mandatory and should be made well in advance.

Bayona $$$$
430 Dauphine Street
French Quarter, New Orleans
(504) 525-4455
The finest jewel in this most elegant and traditionally refined restaurant town and a personal favorite of this author. Bayona is housed in an unexpectedly romantic, more than 200-year-old cottage nestled along a lesser traveled avenue in the northern part of the French Quarter. Chef Susan Spicer tends toward well-considered game dishes, such as pecan-crusted rabbit with a Creole mustard-tasso cream sauce, and is noted for her signature cream of garlic soup. The service is understated but perfect in execution, and the wine list is extensive, very well selected, and unusually inclusive of both moderate and higher-range European and California vintages. The dessert list is equally extensive and inclusive, ranging from fine cheese plates to cakes, tarts, sweet roulades, ice creams, pies, and the best sorbets we have experienced on this side of the Atlantic.

In short, Bayona is the sort of place that justifies a short vacation trip in and of itself and is absolutely not to be missed when you find yourself anywhere in the region. Open for lunch Monday through Friday 11:30 A.M. to 2:00 P.M. and supper Monday through Thursday 6:00 to 10:00 P.M. and Friday and Saturday 6:00 to 11:00 P.M.

Getting There: Baton Rouge/Port Hudson

Baton Rouge is about 80 miles northwest of New Orleans on I-10, which also connects the state capital with Lafayette to the west. Interstate 12 runs east out of Baton Rouge to connect with I-55 at Hammond and Interstates 10 and 59 near Sidell, close to the Mississippi state line. Port Hudson is about 12 miles north of Baton Rouge, just off U.S. Highway 61.

Port Hudson State Commemorative Area
236 US 61, Zachary
(225) 654-3775, (888) 677-3400
This 650-acre park encompasses the northern portion of the Confederate lines and represents one of the better-preserved battlefields of the war. The town was basically destroyed during the battles and siege and abandoned by its civilian population after the war, so little has changed in either the remaining fortifications or earthworks. An unusual feature of the park is the three 40-foot observation towers that give an excellent view of the rugged terrain of the battlefield. An interpretive center on-site has displays about the battle as well as a few artifacts and an excellent display featuring a 20-pounder Parrott rifle and limber. Several other outdoor displays illustrate the artillery positions, including one original gun used during the battle, an 8-inch siege howitzer originally manufactured at West Point in 1841. An extensive trail system winds through the park, passing both original and reconstructed earthworks.

Getting to the park is a bit tricky: Take Interstate 110 north out of Baton Rouge until it ends at US 61. Turn right and go about 12 miles north until you see the rather small sign for the Port Hudson State Commemorative Area. The park is open daily from 9:00 A.M. to 5:00 P.M. Admission is $2.00 for adults; children under 16 and seniors are free.

FLORIDA: MORE TROOPS THAN VOTERS

In 1860 Florida boasted a population of 78,686 free citizens and 61,753 slaves, the smallest population by far of any of the soon-to-be Confederate states. In terms of simple statistics, Florida fought and bled more than any other Confederate state in relation to its small population. By 1865 more than 15,000 troops would come out of this meager populace, most of which left the state by mid-1862, contrasted with about 14,000 registered voters in the entire state. One in 11 served; one-third of those did not return. About 5,000 of these soldiers died in action or as a result of disease during the war. Compared with today's population, it is the equivalent of Florida providing 1.4 million soldiers and losing 465,000!

Florida had only been in the Union for 16 years, after 300 years of being passed back and forth from Spanish to English to American control, when it voted for secession on January 10, 1861. Different sources claim either widespread opposition to or equally widespread enthusiasm for secession, but the simple fact was that Florida was more a liability than an asset to the Confederacy. The relatively few troops it provided did help the critical manpower shortage, but the state legislature could earmark only $100,000 for arms and equipment, soon exhausted in the inflated wartime market and leaving most of the men still unarmed.

Appeals to the Confederate government in Richmond for funds to equip the troops only revealed that there was no money to be had and that Florida would have to somehow equip the soldiers it was requested to provide. Additionally, the very troops requested by the national government would not be accepted for service until somehow properly equipped at the state's own expense. As late as mid-1862, official calls were asking civilians to provide what "shot guns, double and single barrel rifles, and muskets" that they had available.

As additional liabilities, Florida had more than 6,000 miles of difficult-to-defend shoreline, a scarce and widespread population at least partly sympathetic to the Union, and an interior easily penetrated by the multiple large river outlets. Despite all this, the state could not be ignored by the newly formed rebel government, as it was a valuable source of cotton, turpentine, and beef as well as a port and haven for blockade-runners.

BACKGROUND TO THE BATTLE

The populated areas of 1861 Florida were concentrated in the northern reaches, as were nearly all the ports and railroads. Ironically, the second largest city was Key West, with a population of 2,832 (including 591 slaves), but it was isolated from the mainland by the lack of connecting roads or railroads.

The railroad network was still in the process of building up across the state when war broke out; as a result, no line connected Pensacola (the largest city) with the eastern portions, nor did any line connect eastern Florida with Georgia or Alabama. Forts originally built by the Spanish or by the U.S. government starting in the 1840s guarded the most critical approaches to Pensacola, Fernandina, St. Augustine, and the Keys. Both sides recognized that besides these major approaches, the capital at Tallahassee, the railroad crossroad town of Baldwin, and the river towns of Jacksonville, New Smyrna, St. Marks, Appalachicola, Cedar Key, and Tampa all were strategic locations to the control of the state.

There never seems to have been a grand strategy for control of Florida by the Union Army, nor was there a concerted effort by the Confederate government to provide for its defense. After Florida seceded, the Union all but surrendered all but three of the coastal forts with little or no resistance. Most of the troops called up in the state left for either the Army of Northern Virginia or Army of Tennessee, leaving a bare 2,000 for home defense throughout most of the war.

The Civil War in Florida can be divided into three phases: first, the seizure or defense of coastal fortifications early on; second, a withdrawal of Confederate forces from the eastern coast followed by a long period of uncontested garrison by Union forces in these abandoned positions; and finally, a short but intense period of combat for control of the northern reaches toward the end of the war, ironically all won by the Confederates.

FERNANDINA

Fernandina, on (and sometimes referred to as) Amelia Island, is at the very northeastern tip of Florida, just across Cumberland Sound and the St. Marys River from Georgia's Cumberland Island and adjacent town of St. Marys. Guarding the mouth of the river that separates the two states (for a few miles, at least), the island was a Spanish-held haven for pirates and smugglers before the United States took over in 1821. To guard the waterborne approach and the new port town, construction of a fort began on the northernmost tip in 1847.

Most local publications trumpet that this was the only U.S. location to have been under eight flags in its history: French, Spanish, British, "Patriots," Green Cross of Florida, Mexican Rebel, U.S., and Confederate. The Patriot flag flew for the shortest time, when the U.S.-backed Patri-ots of Amelia Island overthrew Spanish control and declared their own territory, only for the day of March 17, 1812. The next day they raised the U.S. flag, but soon afterward the island was returned to Spanish control.

A Real Pirate Story

The most unusual flag, almost certainly unique in American history, was the Mexican Rebel flown while the pirate Luis Aury controlled the island from September to December of 1817. The island, where pirates, smugglers, and assorted riffraff roamed freely, had been a black-market haven since the 1808 U.S. embargo on slave importing. Aury was a Frenchman who was allowed to fly the Mexican flag and roam under its protection so long as he sent Mexico a percentage of his plunder. Using a secret act passed by Congress in 1811 as an excuse, the United States sent military forces under Captain J. D. Henley and Major James Bankhead to seize the island with its valuable port from Aury on December 23, 1817. The island was "held in trust" for the Spanish until formally ceded in 1821.

FORT CLINCH

Fort Clinch was named for General Duncan Lamont Clinch of Second Seminole War fame. The land was purchased in 1842 on the north end of Amelia Island, and construction began about 1847 but progressed very slowly; by the onset of war only two of the five planned bastions, two walls, the guardhouse, and a prison building were complete. A few other smaller buildings were in various stages of construction, but no cannon of any caliber had been mounted, and the post was only a military stronghold in the most liberal sense of the word.

Florida militia took over the fort without a struggle in May 1861, as the Union garrison had either already withdrawn or was simply at another fort. Over the next six months, several sand dune batteries were constructed around the island to supplement the unfinished fort, and a total of 33 artillery pieces were brought in and mounted. No real effort was made by the Confederate garrison to continue any of the work on the fort itself.

General Robert E. Lee, newly appointed commander of the Department of South Carolina, Georgia, and East Florida, had by this time changed his coastal defensive strategy from one of static, fort-based defense to one of mobile infantry and artillery strike forces, preferably arranged near railroad lines so as to be able to move quickly against enemy threats. Lee made two brief inspections of the fortifications at Fernandina in November 1861 and January 1862 and found that despite the best efforts of the Florida troops, the defenses were inadequate at best. He ordered naval officers from Savannah to help mount the cannon and train the gunners and the 24th Mississippi Infantry Regiment to the fort as reinforcements.

Before the fort could be placed into full operation, Union seizure of barrier islands in Georgia and South Carolina showed just how vulnerable the isolated and lightly manned post was to an attack of any significant strength. Lee ordered evacuation of forces on both Cumberland and Amelia Islands in late February 1862. The Mississippi and Florida troops abandoned Fort Clinch by February 29, just as Union gunboats sailed up into Cumberland Sound and began shelling the fortifications. The Confederate troops were able to withdraw only 18 of the artillery pieces before the gunboats showed up; the other 15 were captured and left in place to serve their new masters.

Confederate sympathizers abandoned Fernandina along with the combat troops, leaving only a tiny, windswept, bug-infested island for the Union garrison to enjoy. No shots were fired in combat from the rude fort by either side during the entire war, the action soon shifting away from the coastline up to the north and west. Despite the decisive demonstration at Fort Pulaski a little over a month later that the era of masonry forts was over, the garrison spent the rest of the war and early postwar period working on the walls and emplacements. By 1867 the fort was nearly complete when abandoned once again, this time for more than 30 years.

ST. AUGUSTINE

The nation's oldest city remained a Confederate-held town for just a little over 1 year of its 430-year history and endured 3 years of sometimes hostile Union occupation but supplied both fighting men and a well-protected harbor to the fledgling nation. Originally founded in 1565 by the Spanish, the town has been continuously inhabited ever since by the ebb and flow of one empire after another.

Civil War Times in the Ancient City

After only 16 years as part of a full-fledged state and "24 years of territorial vassalage," as one secessionist agitator charged, St. Augustine embraced the idea of secession and the new nation with gusto. Following Lincoln's election in 1860, when not a single vote for him was recorded in the entire state of Florida, the only debate seemed to be whether to secede immediately or to wait a bit. With their representatives voting solidly along with the vast majority for the ordinance of secession in Tallahassee on January 10, 1861, the town held a mighty independence celebration. On the fall of Fort Sumter in Charleston Harbor, another joyous celebration was held under the new flag of rebellion in the town plaza.

With secession fever rising in 1860, the town raised a militia unit for defense known variously as the Florida Independent Blues or St. Augustine Blues. They were soon joined by another infantry unit, the Milton Guards, and by the Marion Artillery in January 1861. The only U.S. fortification in the area, Fort Marion (formerly and today known as the Castello de San Marcos), was manned by a "garrison" of a single U.S. Army ordnance sergeant, who gave up the post several days before the secession vote with only verbal resistance and a demand for a receipt.

Despite the seeming invincibility of the old Spanish-built fort, competent military engineers realized early in the war that the town was vulnerable and would be difficult to adequately defend. General Robert E. Lee, during one of his Fernandina inspection trips, commented that "the small force posted at Saint Augustine serves only as an invitation to attack" and ordered that only the essential harbors of Charleston, Savannah, and Brunswick were to be fortified and defended. By February 1862, with the situation deteriorating in Tennessee, most of the town's defenders marched off to duty with the Confederate Army of Tennessee.

For all intents and purposes, Florida was left to her own devices without regular army troops for defense through most of the rest of the war. Newly elected Florida governor John Milton lamented that he "almost despaired of protection from the Confederate Government." In St. Augustine, a Union naval blockade in place since December 1861 had reduced the town almost to the point of governmental collapse. The prewar tourist industry had come to a complete halt, business could only be conducted at the most elemental level, and very few citizens were able to pay their taxes.

The Occupation

Almost as a blessing, a Union assault force arrived off the coast of St. Augustine, and on March 12, 1862, Commander C. R. P. Rogers arrived at the seawall to request the town's surrender. He was greeted

there by friendly politicians and local Unionists; the offer was quickly accepted, and in short order the Stars and Stripes once again flew over Fort Marion.

With such an easy transition, the occupying Union garrison at first assumed the town was full of Northern sympathizers. Rogers received a rude awakening on his first walk around town, where he was greeted with loud comments of disapproval from some of the town's ladies. Another group of women chopped down the town plaza flagpole so that he would not be able to hoist the U.S. flag upon it.

Although there never was any concerted effort to regain the city, after the discovery of several Confederate Army deserters in town and the assassination of several Unionists nearby, all Southern sympathizers still living in St. Augustine were ordered expelled. Many had already left to live with friends or family in the Confederate-held interior, and most of the male population had entered military service.

Confederate Sympathizers Are Forced Out

The first forced expulsion began in September 1862, consisting of all those who had refused to take an oath of allegiance and agree to report on "subversive" activities. In typical military bureaucratic style, an order countermanding the removal arrived just as a shipload of women and children was on its way out of the harbor. Most of the women had been forced to give up their homes and possessions before boarding the ship and thus had no place left to stay. A few remained, but most went into the interior with the blessing of both townspeople and Union authorities, happy to reduce the number of mouths to feed.

A more orderly evacuation commenced in January 1863, apparently consisting primarily of those ladies who particularly irked the Union officials. The official decree was for those with "husbands and sons in the rebel army," but that could be applied to just about anyone left in town. Mrs. Victoria Williams was rather outspoken in her assessment of the situation and those in charge of it, to the extreme discomfort of their guards. By the time their ship reached Fernandina, she and her family were put off and given over with thanks to the Confederate authorities just outside the island town. Other families were put off in small groups at a number of other Southern ports.

Throughout the rest of the war, other individuals and small groups would be expulsed from town, mostly into the Confederate-held interior. Presumably many returned after hostilities ceased, but there is no consistent record of this.

Soldier Life in the Ancient City

The only real military opposition to the continued Union occupation was by a small Confederate cavalry force commanded by Captain J. J. Dickison. Mostly confining his activities to patrolling the west bank of the St. Johns River to warn of any Union offensive, Dickison occasionally raided the outskirts of town, inflicting a few casualties and capturing some unlucky Union soldiers. Even with this threat, the Union soldiers and authorities became complacent in their relatively comfortable post, to the point that Colonel William H. Noble (who had replaced Rogers) was himself captured in December 1864, while riding with his aide to Jacksonville. Even with this serious loss, Union authorities failed to change their security procedures, and two more groups of soldiers were taken prisoner within the next month.

Before the war, St. Augustine had been both a tourist destination (as it is very much today) and a wintertime health resort for sickly Yankees. In the fall of 1863,

it resumed one of these roles when the Union Army decided to make the town into a convalescent camp and hospital.

Slowly but steadily, the town's population grew with the arrival of more Unionists and soldiers and with growing numbers of disenchanted Confederate Army deserters. By the end of the war, the town was nearly back to its prewar norm, with the Federal courts reopened, the churches nearly filled to capacity, and trade with Northern cities restored. Even news of the Confederate Army commander in chief General Robert E. Lee's surrender in Virginia failed to change life to any great degree.

As in so many other Southern cities, the great emotion of the Confederate loss gradually changed into a wistful nostalgia for the Lost Cause. In 1872 the United Daughters of the Confederacy, locally headed by Anna Dummett, erected a tall stone obelisk in the central plaza as mute testimony to the 44 local men killed in the war. This monument still stands in the Plaza de la Constitution at the end of King Street, directly across from the Bridge of Lions downtown, guarded by 8-inch "Rodman" Columbiad artillery pieces and a nearby 10-inch seacoast mortar, part of the wartime Fort Marion defenses.

THE INVASION OF NORTHEAST FLORIDA

The largest battle in Florida began as nothing more than yet another occupation of Jacksonville, the fourth in half as many years. In overall command was Brigadier General Truman A. Seymour, charged with securing the small port town for the Union once again and then moving westward into the interior area between the St. Johns and Suwanee Rivers with four goals in mind. First, to cut the railroads and stop the northward flow of food and supplies to the Confederate Army of Tennessee, several hundred miles north in Georgia. Second, to capture the valuable store of cotton, turpentine, and lumber for the

Union Army's own use. Third, to "free" and recruit blacks for the increasing numbers of "colored" regiments. Lastly, and possibly least important, Seymour was to "inaugurate measures for the speedy restoration of Florida to her allegiance."

With some advance preparation by the Union garrison already at Fernandina, and with some difficulty passing through the sandbar-choked entrance to the St. Johns River, troop transports guarded by gunboats started upriver at daybreak on February 7, 1864. Seymour had under his command a force of about 7,000 men organized into 10 infantry regiments, 1 cavalry battalion, and 3 artillery batteries. One of the infantry regiments present was the all-black 54th Massachusetts (of Battery Wagner fame, as featured in the movie *Glory*).

The movement of Union troops toward the northeast Florida coast had not gone unnoticed by the Confederates, who quickly began scouting for a suitable place to mount a proper defense. In command of the Department of East Florida was Brigadier General Joseph Finegan, with a mere 1,200 men at his disposal, all widely scattered in small groups across the interior portions of the state from Fernandina to Tampa. Alerted to the danger, General P. G. T. Beauregard, Department of South Carolina, Georgia, and Florida (who had replaced Lee), immediately sent word to Finegan that help was on the way, to hold the Union forces at bay as best he could, and to "prevent capture of slaves."

Jacksonville

Meanwhile, the Union flotilla proceeded up the St. Johns River, pausing only long enough to engage and pursue a small number of Confederate pickets just below Commodore's Point, less than 2 miles from the wharves of Jacksonville itself. (Commodore's Point contains no marker or sign that we were able to locate but lies at the northern base of the Isaiah D.

Hart Bridge on U.S. Highway 1 Alternate, the Commodore Point Expressway. The area is now largely industrial.)

With little resistance, the flotilla of Union transports tied up to the Jacksonville docks about 3:40 P.M. on February 7, and the troops began off-loading immediately. There was very little to secure in town, as three previous Union invasions and departures over the past two years had reduced most of the houses and shops to unreconstructed rubble. Nearly 3,000 people had lived in town in 1860; when Seymour arrived on the *Maple Leaf,* there were fewer than 200 remaining, almost all women and children who assured the invaders that they were "Union."

By nightfall Seymour's troops had full command of Jacksonville, digging in for the night in an existing defensive position on the west side of the city, and he passed on orders for them to prepare to move rapidly toward the inland rail junction at Baldwin at dawn. For some unknown reason, this dawn assault did not take place; instead, after an uneventful night the men moved out in three columns about 3:00 P.M. on February 8, their objective being the South Prong of the St. Marys River about 35 miles due west.

The Move West

The deliberate movement was the result of changed orders. Instead of a quick attempt to seize and cut the railroads, Seymour apparently desired a somewhat deeper and more thorough disruption of the Confederate-held territory, tearing up what rails they could, destroying stockpiles of supplies, and reconnoitering the Confederate positions and emplacements. The troops were still only supposed to march about 35 miles inland, but there was no order or suggestion to avoid contact with any Confederate forces.

The three Union columns consisted of Colonel W. B. Barton's brigade (47th, 48th, and 115th New York Infantry Regiments) marching straight up the Lake City–Jacksonville road (roughly following the route of present-day U.S. Highway 90, paralleling Interstate 10); Colonel Guy V. Henry's Mounted Brigade (40th Massachusetts Mounted Infantry, the Independent Battalion of Massachusetts Cavalry, Langdon's Light Artillery Battery, Elder's Horse Artillery Battery, and Batteries B and C of the Third Rhode Island Artillery) on a parallel road to the left; and Colonel J. R. Hawley's Brigade (7th Connecticut and 7th New Hampshire Infantry Regiments, and the 8th U.S. Colored Troops) on another road to the right. These three roads converged about 3 miles from Jacksonville, and Seymour expected Confederate opposition before that point.

Camp Finegan

Instead of making contact, the men marched on through the growing darkness before stopping for the night at the road junction. Henry's mounted troops continued before finally encountering an abandoned picket outpost about 5 miles down the road. Easing through the woods, the Union men quietly came upon a small manned outpost and seized it with a rapid assault. Quickly remounting and riding on for another 10 minutes, they soon came upon a major Confederate outpost known as Camp Finegan. (The exact location of Camp Finegan cannot be definitely placed, but it should be approximately in the area known as West Jacksonville, near the intersection of Lane Avenue and Beaver Street [US 90], about 1 mile east of the I-10 and Interstate 295 intersection. The CSX Railroad track through this area runs over the roadbed of the Civil War–era tracks.)

Observing about 200 heavily armed Confederate defenders waiting in the camp (Lieutenant Colonel Abner McCormick's 2nd Florida Cavalry), Henry elected to bypass the camp and travel another 4 miles west to attack a reported artillery camp at Twelve Mile Station. Finding the camp manned but unguarded and

the Confederates in the process of cooking and eating, Henry ordered a sudden, loud assault. Most of the artillerymen took off for the surrounding woods at the first notes of the Union bugles. The Confederates lost 18 men and 45 horses and mules, but the hardest blow was the loss of five critically needed artillery pieces.

Meanwhile, the Union infantry columns abandoned their plans for encamping at the road junction and began moving west through the thick, dark woods. Encountering Camp Finegan, they began to surround the camp before assaulting. Although they quietly captured all the Confederate pickets, something warned the men inside, and the Confederates deserted the camp before the Union attack could be mounted. After briefly searching the surrounding woods the next morning for deserters, the Union infantrymen moved out toward Baldwin, 15 miles to the west.

Baldwin

Henry's men left Twelve Mile Station at 4:00 A.M. on February 9, riding the 10 miles in to Baldwin and tearing up the rail tracks as they went. Baldwin itself was taken without resistance by 7:00 A.M., and in just this short time most of Seymour's objectives had been met. Major General Quincy Adams Gillmore, in overall command of the Union operation and now in Jacksonville, ordered more regiments forward for support and directed Seymour to continue inland. Henry ordered his men to move out once again on the morning of February 10.

Barber's Ford

Riding west of Baldwin and capturing occasional stocks of food and supplies along the way, no resistance was met until the bridge over the South Prong of the St. Marys River at a place known as Barber's Ford. There, the bridge had been burned and the 2nd Florida Cavalry waited in ambush. The lead Union pickets were gunned down as they approached the burned-out bridge, but the Confederates melted away with the loss of only 4 men as the Union Independent Battalion charged their position. Union losses were set at 17 dead and wounded. (The bridge over the South Prong of the St. Marys River was destroyed before the skirmish, and no period structure remains there today. No sign of Barber's Ford could be located, but the skirmish took place between Macclenny and Glen St. Mary on US 90; the CSX Railroad bridge just south of the road over the river is the historic site.)

LAKE CITY

Seymour received additional orders from Gillmore that same day directing him to push his forces as far west as the Suwanee River and advising that additional infantry support was headed his way. At the same time, Finegan, in Lake City, was hurriedly concentrating all his forces to meet the Union invasion force.

Moving out from Barber's Ford about 1:00 P.M. on February 11, Henry's mounted force soon entered Sanderson, only to find three large warehouses full of supplies set afire only 15 minutes beforehand by the last departing Confederate train. After a short rest, the mounted troops continued westward through the night, arriving 3 miles east of Lake City by midmorning.

Slowly advancing through a thick morning fog, Henry's troops suddenly encountered Confederate infantry already drawn up in line of battle. Due to the thickness of the fog and the noise discipline exercised by both sides, neither saw each other until they were fewer than 100 yards apart, and both sides then immediately opened fire. The 1st Georgia Regulars, under the command of Lieutenant John Porter Fort, withstood the initial Union assault led by the 40th Massachusetts and the Independent Battalion and soon forced the Union line into retreat.

With food and ammunition running short, and the main body of infantry support more than 30 miles to their rear, Henry decided to retreat all the way back to Sanderson before halting.

The sometimes dubbed "Battle of Lake City" took place just east of the main commercial district of Lake City, approximately where Price Creek Road intersects US 90, just to the west of the airport. The Confederate line was reported to be a mile in length, running north and south across US 90 and the adjacent CSX Railroad track.

Olustee

For 10 days after ordering his forces to retreat back to the relative safety of Sanderson and Barber's Ford, Seymour marked time by slowly reinforcing his garrison and limiting his offensive actions to a single raid on Gainesville and another to the Georgia-Florida border area. Finegan wasted no time building up his small force, sending every available unit from western and southern Florida into his line east of Lake City, and appealing to Confederate authorities for more infantry and artillery.

By the afternoon of February 19, Seymour had consolidated a force of eight infantry regiments, one mounted infantry regiment, three batteries of artillery, and a cavalry battalion, numbering just over 5,400 men and 16 artillery pieces. Swinging once again into the offensive, he ordered his men west along the Jacksonville–Lake City road, with the intention of confronting the Confederate forces at Lake City, driving through them, and destroying the railroad bridge over the Suwanee River.

Finegan remained at his headquarters in Lake City, placing command of the Confederate force on Colonel Alfred H. Colquitt. He had moved his main body of troops a few miles east of Lake City to a tiny settlement named Olustee Station. By nightfall on the 19th, Finegan had collected some eight full infantry regiments, parts of two other infantry battalions, four artillery batteries, and two cavalry regiments, numbering about 5,200 men. Committed to holding a line of defense at Olustee Station, he ordered his men to construct a line of hasty emplacements and prepared to meet the expected Union assault.

Colquitt soon chose a good ground to make a stand; with a large lake to his left and a dense swamp just to the right, the railroad tracks and adjoining road ran through a narrow patch of high ground that would be much easier to defend than the usual flat, wide-open terrain of northern Florida. Ironically, although both sides were nearly evenly matched, both commanders believed they were facing a superior force, and neither ordered their cavalry force forward to scout the opposing army.

Learning about the Confederate position at Olustee during the night of February 19, Seymour hastily gave orders for his force to march out and confront it in the morning. Leaving Sanderson and Barber's Ford about 7:00 A.M. in road march formation, once again the mounted forces under Henry rapidly pulled ahead of the main body of infantry. There was apparently little or no concern about encountering a major Confederate force anytime soon, as neither flankers nor skirmishers had been deployed, no order to load and prepare the artillery for action had been given, and most of the infantrymen had not yet loaded their guns or otherwise prepared for imminent action. The Union cavalry casually rode down the road at a trot, expecting to simply scatter whatever enemy force they chanced upon, as they had been doing for weeks.

Encountering a small group of Confederate pickets, Henry's men returned their fire until they broke for the rear. Feeling a bit more prudent, Henry decided to wait a bit until the infantry could catch up with him. About 2:00 P.M. the vanguard of the Union infantry arrived, led by the 7th Connecticut Infantry, and were immediately ordered up front to probe for the

main Confederate line. With the Confederate force still coming into line and Union infantry rapidly marching up the road, contact was not long in coming.

As the 7th Connecticut advanced slowly forward deployed as skirmishers, they came under increasingly heavy but still sporadic fire from Confederate skirmishers falling back. Seymour ordered a "reconnaissance by fire" from one of the cannon just arriving on the field, and the response was swift. As the line of Union infantry broke out of the pine woods into the railroad track clearing, they discovered a line of heavy entrenchments manned by no fewer than four full infantry regiments (the 6th, 8th, 19th, and 64th Georgia Infantry). Soon under fire from three directions, Seymour ordered the Connecticut men to fall back a few yards to a cleared area next to a small pond.

Within a few minutes, five other Union infantry regiments rushed up into line of battle (the 7th New Hampshire; 8th U.S. Colored Troops; and the 47th, 48th, and 115th New York), while the four Georgia regiments moved out of their entrenchments and deployed into a three-quarter-mile line of battle directly facing the field.

Under intense fire from the Confederate line, one by one the Union infantry retreated farther to the rear, with one notable exception. Well-drilled for dress parade but totally untrained for combat, the 8th Colored Troops were rushed into line of battle with still-unloaded rifles and then deployed and attempted to load and make ready while under intense and accurate fire from the Georgia line. At first the troops wavered and hesitated, threatening to break and run, but soon they loaded up and began to return a steady, if inaccurate, fire. Refusing to be pushed back, the troops ended up losing more than 300 of the 550-man command in the withering Confederate fire.

As the fighting intensified, more units rushed in on both sides. Three more Georgia regiments (the 1st, 23rd, and 32nd Georgia Infantry) deepened and extended the Confederate line while the 6th Florida

Infantry Battalion dressed the right of the line, slightly overlapping the Union line and enabling them to pour a galling fire on the now-exposed flank of the Florida men. As the men came into line, Colquitt ordered a general advance on the weakened Union position. As the attack mounted, two more Union infantry regiments (the 54th Massachusetts and the 1st North Carolina Colored) rushed into the growing battle at the double-quick.

As the two lines of battle slammed together, a near impenetrable volume of fire erupted from the Georgians. Between bullets and mixed grape and canister shot from the handful of Confederate cannon newly arriving on the field, the 115th New York lost 296 officers and men dead, wounded, or missing in action. To their far left, the newly baptized-by-fire 8th Colored Troops had three successive regimental flag bearers shot down, while the fourth lost an arm in the intense fire but held on to the flagstaff and carried it off the field.

Despite the arrival of the two fresh black regiments, the Union line could hold only a few more minutes. By 2:30 P.M. their line was in full retreat, with the 54th Massachusetts and 1st North Carolina Colored Troops slowly pulling back, still dressed in ranks, and keeping up a steady fire to protect their fleeing comrades. The Confederate line surged ahead, fully intending to stay close on the heels of Seymour's broken command. By 3:00 P.M. their own charge ended, not by Union resistance but by lack of ammunition for rifles and cannon.

Resupplying from the filled ammunition pouches of the Union dead and some supplies newly moved up by rail, the Confederate line managed to shortly resume pursuit, completely chasing the Union units off the field by dusk. By Sunday night the shattered remnants of all the Union regiments were in or near Jacksonville, having burned both supplies and bridges behind them, while the Confederates seemed contented just to ransack the abandoned Union equipment rather than engage in any serious pursuit.

PENSACOLA

One of the first permanent settlements in America, preceded only by St. Augustine a mere three years before the town was established in 1568, Pensacola contained both an excellent harbor and nearby entrances to river access into the interior. Both made it a ripe target for the newly established Confederate government and a vital post to hold for the U.S. Army.

Forts of Pensacola Bay

Surprisingly, or not so according to your own disposition, nearly all the history books are wrong about one significant fact. The first shots of the Civil War were not fired at Charleston's Fort Sumter, as widely assumed, but actually at Pensacola's Fort Barrancas several hours earlier. Along with its sister outpost to the southeast, Fort Pickens, Fort Barrancas was a bayside post held by a small, isolated Union garrison heavily outnumbered, outflanked, and outgunned by a growing number of Alabama and Florida militias and state troops on the mainland.

THE FIRST SHOTS

Lieutenant Adam J. Slemmer was in charge of a small garrison of Union troops in Fort Barrancas when news of Florida's secession came in. Quickly consolidating weapons and ammunition in Fort Barrancas, Slemmer ordered his men into the fort, gun batteries to be prepared for action, and drawbridges to be raised. The young Union officer had foreseen that combat was imminent, and he was not going to surrender without a good fight. Just before midnight on January 8, 1861, Union sentries spotted movement outside the fort. Issuing a challenge that went unanswered, the guard force opened fire without drawing blood. These were the first real shots fired in anger of the Civil War; about five hours later the bombardment of Fort Sumter in Charleston Harbor began.

Two men were widely reported to be the last surviving veterans of the war, both dying in 1959. However, research of census records revealed that they had been five and two years old when the war began.

Realizing that his small force had no real chance of withstanding a strong land-based attack from the rapidly growing Confederate forces in the area, Slemmer spiked his guns, destroyed powder stores in another nearby small fort, and evacuated his force to Fort Pickens. The next day, seven companies of infantry from Florida and Alabama took over the newly abandoned posts and immediately demanded Slemmer's surrender.

FORT PICKENS

The southernmost and largest of the Pensacola Bay fortifications, Fort Pickens was named for American Revolution brigadier general Andrew Pickens of South Carolina. The large masonry fort was originally designed in 1829 as part of an interlocking band of forts around Pensacola Bay. Fort Pickens sat within 200 yards of the ship channel as it existed then and was intended to serve as defense against attacks coming only from seaward.

Completed late in 1834, the fort was a massively complex project, requiring 21.5 million locally made bricks, 26,000 barrels of lime from Maine, large quantities of granite from New York, lead for water-proofing from Illinois, and copper drains from Switzerland. Most of the construction was done by slaves sent from New Orleans, all under the direction of William Henry Chase, area supervisor for the U.S. Army Corps of Engineers.

The five-sided fort was designed to resist attack from any angle, including close-in infantry attack. Each corner had a bastion with cannon positions arrayed to enable fire right alongside the walls, the walls themselves rose some 40 feet above the surrounding dry moat, and positions were originally included for two hundred 24- to 32-pound cannon, 20 mortars, and 28 carronade on two levels. This number changed through the years, peaking at a recommendation for 221 guns in 1855, including forty-two 8-inch and four 10-inch Columbiads. As a sort of "last-ditch" defense, each bastion had three "mine" chambers filled with explosives, which could be selectively set off to wipe out an occupying force if one should gain control of the structure.

Chase took a liking to the pleasant climate of Pensacola and moved back there after retiring from the army, shortly before the outbreak of hostilities. Following Florida's secession, Chase was given a commission as a colonel in the Florida army, and his first mission, ironically, was the capture or destruction of the fort he had built.

The Union Defenses Build Up

Having moved his men safely from Fort Barrancas and spiking the guns he could not remove, Slemmer refused a total of three demands for his surrender, believing that the massive fort could safely harbor his small command until reinforcements could be landed. Although reinforcements soon arrived in Pensacola Bay via the U.S. steam sloop of war *Brooklyn,* high-level politics between outgoing U.S. president James Buchanan and Florida senator Stephen R. Mallory forged an agreement that as long as Fort Pickens was not reinforced, it would not be attacked.

Slemmer had reason to be concerned about the delay in reinforcements. Although the fort had been designed for up to 1,200 soldiers manning well over 200 cannon, he had only 88 soldiers and sailors and 40 cannon in place. While the truce was under way, his men managed to mount another 14 cannon, but the majority of casements remained empty. To add to his headaches, although the fort did have defensive positions all around its perimeter, it had originally been designed to resist a naval push into the bay from the southwest, while simultaneously defending against a land-based push from the east. With the Confederates holding Fort Barrancas to the north and the small Fort McRee to the west, the lighter-built north and west walls, containing two of the three powder magazines, would be most vulnerable.

Confederates Attack

Eight days after newly elected U.S. president Abraham Lincoln took office, he ordered the *Brooklyn* to go ahead and land her troops to reinforce Fort Pickens. During the night of April 11, these troops entered the fort without opposition or answer from the surrounding Confederate positions. More troops arrived on April 16 and again landed without opposition on the seaward side of the fort.

After the formal organization of the Confederacy in February 1861, tensions ran very high in Pensacola, although, astonishingly, Slemmer was still permitted to buy food in town and use the local post office without fear of arrest or harassment. A handful of relatively minor raids and skirmishes prevented the Confederates from fully utilizing the deepwater harbor and eventually led to a determination to violently take over Fort Pickens.

On the morning of October 9, 1861, a landing force of just over 1,000 men under command of General Dick Anderson arrived on Santa Rosa Island about 4 miles east of the fort (roughly where the main commercial area today begins) and split into three groups to strike the fort from three sides. Within two hours, the assault force had overrun a small Union picket post but was soon forced to retreat under heavy fire from infantry and artillery. Without getting any closer than a

mile from the fort itself, the Confederates sailed back off the island leaving behind 87 dead, wounded, or captured.

This was the only serious attempt to capture Fort Pickens during the war, but it did not go completely unanswered. A few weeks later, on November 22 and 23, 1861, joined by the Union gunboats *Niagara* and *Richmond* with their 24- and 32-pound guns, Slemmer ordered a massive bombardment of the Confederate positions. Five thousand outgoing shells badly damaged and silenced Fort McRee, destroyed most of the small village of Warrington and the Pensacola Navy Yard, and did some relatively minor damage to Fort Barrancas. The Confederates managed to return fire, lobbing some 1,000 shells at Fort Pickens and the gunboats, without serious effect on either.

A second bombardment on January 1 and 2, 1862, succeeded in exploding Fort McRee's powder magazine, rendering the post useless, and raked what was left of the Navy Yard with shot and shell. Fort Barrancas's defenders managed to return an intermittent fire toward Fort Pickens, again without effect.

While Slemmer and his command had absolute control over the entrance to the harbor and the immediate shoreline, their now-reinforced garrison was far too weak to assault the Confederate positions overland. A Union invasion of west and central Tennessee a few weeks later proved the deciding factor, however, with the subsequent withdrawal of more than 8,000 Confederate troops from Pensacola to fight with the Army of Tennessee. A small garrison remained behind, but when U.S. Navy commander David Farragut's fleet anchored just outside Mobile Bay on May 7, 1862, about 40 miles to the west, the remaining Confederates pulled out to help Mobile's defense, burning most of the military installations and supplies left behind.

Pensacola was formally surrendered by Mayor Dr. John Brosnaham to Lieutenant Richard Jackson on the morning of May 10, 1862. For the remainder of the war the port city remained in Union control and was used primarily as a staging base for small raids into southern Alabama and western Florida.

THE TOUR

Reasoning with Hurricane Season

Weather experts say that hurricane seasons peak and ebb in relative strengths and numbers of major hurricanes and that the East and Gulf Coasts can expect high levels of both for the next eight years or so. It is strongly suggested that you call just before your trip to make sure that the roads are passable and that your hotel is open, and it pays to monitor weather conditions during the hurricane season (roughly June through November, peaking in late August and September).

Getting There: Amelia Island/Fernandina Beach

Fernandina is an easy drive from Interstate 95—get off on exit 373 (Florida Highway A1A) just south of the Georgia state line and travel east about 10 miles. Both the historic district and Fort Clinch are just off FL A1A a few miles farther. Turn left on Centre Street to go to the district and left into the fort; park just before FL A1A reaches the beaches. Be sure to watch carefully for the turn, as the signs are parallel to the road and nearly hidden in the thick vegetation.

MODERN TIMES AT FORT CLINCH

After the Civil War, this forlorn outpost was relegated to "caretaker" status, meaning that while no troops garrisoned it, and no upkeep or maintenance was done, the army intended to still claim it as insurance against a future crisis. That emergency did

not come until the early spring of 1898, when the post was activated for service in the Spanish-American War. Abandoned again in September of that same year, the still-unfinished fort lay dormant for another 43 years until activated one last time for use as a watch station in World War II. Today Fort Clinch still stands as the centerpiece of 1,121-acre Fort Clinch State Park, a narrow peninsula with more than 2 miles of shoreline on the Atlantic Ocean and Cumberland Sound.

Fort Clinch State Park
**2601 Atlantic Avenue, Fernandina Beach
(904) 277-7274**

The still-unfinished fort is in a remarkable state of preservation, considering that wind, tide, and storms have been battering its earthen walls more than 150 years. A small, tidy museum with a small number of well-presented artifacts begins your tour, and be sure to purchase your admission tickets in the gift shop before heading outside; rangers do occasionally check for receipts, as it is relatively easy to just walk in from the beach side. Make sure to ask for the pamphlet *History of Fort Clinch,* which gives a good capsule history and a good map of the fortifications.

A short path leads from the museum to the main gate of the fort, just through a tall earthwork glacis and across a narrow drawbridge. Inside are several brick buildings containing replica period furnishings, and occasional outlines of foundation stones reveal what portions were never completed. Atop the earthwork rampart are several large replica artillery pieces, 10-inch Rodman Columbiads, which were capable of firing a 128-pound shot well over 5,500 yards at full charge.

These replicas cannot be fired, as the gun tubes are actually made of concrete, not iron. Also on top are mounts for several 15-inch Rodmans, for which there is no record of ever actually being mounted before the post was abandoned. Just outside the glacis next to the entrance path is an actual 15-inch Rodman, the only period piece at the fort.

Forts of this type had a multilayered array of artillery, with the large Columbiads upstairs typical of those used for long-range defense. Smaller pieces would have been mounted in the downstairs curtain wall for close-in defense, and different shot charges would be on hand to handle tasks from setting ships afire to wrecking sails and rigging to stopping close-in charging infantry.

The first weekend of every month features an extensive living-history program of a typical day in the lives of a Union garrison. Don't talk to these folks about anything post–Civil War, as they are quite realistically "in character" and will simply stare at you. A full-garrison encampment of Union troops is held one weekend in May, and a full-Confederate encampment is held the last full weekend in October.

All of these encampments show quite effectively how the typical soldier lived and worked. Artillery crews are usually on hand at these times and demonstrate the firing of a replica 3-inch ordnance rifle. Candlelight tours of the post are scheduled periodically; check with the visitor center for dates and details.

Departing the fort, the path takes you back through the museum and gift shop, which contains the usual assortment of souvenirs as well as a small but good book collection, an unusual selection of videotapes, and a large assortment of patterns for historic dress.

The surrounding state park is very interesting and enjoyable in its own right, featuring shelling, hiking trails, beaches, very nice bicycle paths, and picnicking and camping sites. Nature trails wind through a coastal hammock, where a wide variety of wildlife from egrets to alligators thrives.

The park entrance fee is $5.00 per vehicle (up to eight people included), and admission to the fort is an additional $2.00. The park is open 8:00 A.M. to sundown every day, and the fort and visitor center are open 9:00 A.M. to 5:00 P.M. daily.

OTHER POINTS OF INTEREST

Amelia Island/Fernandina Beach Chamber of Commerce
102 Centre Street, Amelia Island
(904) 261-3248, (866) 813-2937

For a complete list of local businesses, contact the friendly people at the Amelia Island/Fernandina Beach Chamber of Commerce, housed in the old railroad station at the end of the "main drag" near the shrimp-boat docks.

Two Web sites give a good overview of businesses and attractions: Amelia Now at www.amelianow.com and Amelia Island Destinations at www.ameliaisland.com.

Amelia Island Museum of History
233 South Third Street, Amelia Island
(904) 261-7378

"Florida's Only Oral History Museum" is an exceptional experience, centered around the twice-daily interpreter-led tours of the former Nassau County Jailhouse. The museum covers the history of the local area from the time of Timucuan Indians through the French, Spanish, English, and American periods, climaxing with Amelia Island's "golden age" in the late 19th century. These tours are at 11:00 A.M. and 2:00 P.M. Monday through Saturday; no reservation is required. Special tours for groups of 10 or more cover the age of Spanish galleons and island archaeology.

The museum itself is open 10:00 A.M. to 4:00 P.M. Monday through Saturday and offers a well-stocked research facility containing local publications and documents on the second floor, as well as arranged, special out-of-museum guided walking tours for groups of four or more. Admission is $5.00 for adults and $3.00 for children.

Kingsley Plantation
FL A1A, Fort King George Island
(904) 251-3537

Just south of Amelia Island, on Fort King George Island north of the Mayport ferry dock, stands one of the oldest antebellum structures in the state. Zephaniah Kingsley purchased and began construction of the large plantation in 1814, which still exists today in nearly unchanged form. While not specifically related to the war, the exhibits and ranger-guided tours give an unblinking view of what life was really like on Southern plantations; it rarely resembled Tara of *Gone with the Wind* fame.

Slave quarters are tiny and resemble jail cells more than residences—mute testimony to the plantation owner's treatment of those who toiled in his cotton, sugar cane, and corn fields. Twenty-three of these cabins remain, as well as the main ("big") house, kitchen house, barn, and part of one of the original gardens.

Kingsley Plantation is owned and operated by the state of Florida and is open Monday through Friday 9:00 A.M. to 5:00 P.M. and Saturday and Sunday 1:00 to 3:00 P.M. Ranger-led tours are given at 1:00 P.M. Admission is free, but donations are accepted.

Fort Caroline National Monument
12713 Fort Caroline Road, Jacksonville
(904) 641-7155

The largest city in the United States (in area if not in population) has its own Civil War history, unfortunately nearly completely obscured by urban sprawl. Taken and occupied a total of four times during the war by Union troops, both sides recognized that Jacksonville represented both a valuable protected port and a gateway into the northeastern interior of the state.

Fort Caroline is a rare reminder of the past here, consisting of a two-thirds-scale reconstruction of a fort built by French Huguenots in 1562, approximately at this site. Somewhere along the river bluffs nearby stood a reinforced Confederate artillery battery under the command of Lieutenant Colonel Charles F. Hopkins; the exact location could not be precisely located by any source we consulted.

On September 30, 1862, 1,500 troops under the command of Brigadier General John M. Brannon departed Hilton Head Island, South Carolina, with orders to challenge this battery and other Confederate defenses and to free the approach to Jacksonville on the St. Johns River. On October 1, now joined by six naval gunboats led by Commander Charles Steedman, Brannon's men began disembarking at Mayport Mills, about 5 miles to the rear of the Confederate emplacement. As the Union infantry approached overland and the gunboats sailed downriver to catch him in a two-pronged assault, Hopkins abandoned his position as untenable. This battery never came under fire or fired its guns in combat.

Fort Caroline itself is an interesting park, with a large area of pristine wilderness along the river, shell mounds left by the original inhabitants, a small but nice visitor center with videos and publications on area wildlife, and guided tours of the fort and nature preserve on Saturday. Admission is free.

ACCOMMODATIONS

Amelia Island/Fernandina Beach is a decidedly unusual mixture of upscale vacation destinations with overtones of shrimping, timber, and paper-mill industries. Two very high-end resorts grace the south end of the island: the Ritz-Carlton Resort and the Amelia Island Plantation. Several very nice bed-and-breakfast inns dot the old town, and there is ample boutique shopping available for long-suffering "Civil War widows."

Unfortunately, lodging and dining for those on a tighter budget are harder to come by. There are exactly two chain motels on the island, but their prices are markedly higher than in "nonresort" areas. Dining establishments are equally upscale, but we find it easier to justify premium prices for food of this quality.

Ritz-Carlton Resort $$$
4750 Amelia Island Parkway
Amelia Island
(904) 277-1100, (800) 241-3333

This Ritz-Carlton has everything you could possibly want in a resort and then

Olustee Remembered

While Florida, along with other southern states were [sic] gravely concerned over the prospects of war and the contention for the freedom of our slaves, our real trouble began again when Florida along with other states, drew out of the Union and the Federal armies sought to seize all our coastwise towns, tear up our few railroads and take our State Capitol at Tallahassee, and this trouble came as near our home as Lake City, which is only four miles distant, at the time of the battle of Olustee, when the Federal army was defeated and driven back to Jacksonville. My first actual knowledge of this battle was the sound of guns which I heard very clearly in the late morning of the day of the battle.

I was at my home where my father and our faithful slaves were gathered with me and my children to protect us if needed. My husband at that time was a soldier with the Confederate forces in Virginia.

We heard the report of the guns from the battle of Olustee for several hours and of course every one for many miles around was in a state of great fear and anxiety, though before the next day we had learned that our men had won the battle and had driven the Union forces away after killing and wounding many of them. The Union men carried their dead and wounded to Jacksonville. The dead and wounded of our army were brought to Lake City. The wounded were cared for in a hospital set up for that purpose, in the Cathey building, then located on what is now North Marion Street in Lake City. The dead were buried in Lake City cemetery, and once each year on a day set apart in May, the graves of these soldiers are decorated and appropriate ceremonies held in their honor.

Lake City, Florida, resident
Sarah Rebecca Rivers Moore
to her granddaughter, Orrie Moore
Kendrick, in about 1937

some. Each of the 444 rooms and suites has its own private balcony; twice each day the rooms are cleaned and primped; there is 24-hour room service, 1½ miles of exclusive beachfront, and the overall quality of impeccable service that is a Ritz-Carlton trait.

For those who desire even more exclusive treatment, there is a special Club Level floor with its own private lounge, concierge, and five complimentary food and drink presentations each day. We must state that we were quite taken aback by the very friendly and accommodating nature of everyone we spoke to here, and

they really do pull out all the plugs to do whatever they can for guests' comfort.

Four restaurants on the premises serve nearly anything you desire from afternoon tea to cocktails and cigars to macrobiotic cuisine to multicourse gourmet meals. To work off all this, there are nine tennis courts, an 18-hole golf course, a well-appointed fitness center with steam and sauna, an indoor lap pool and whirlpool, an outdoor pool and whirlpool, and our personal favorites, plush terry robes and really comfortable chairs. More details are at the Ritz-Carlton Web site: www.ritzcarlton.com.

Beachside Motel Inn $-$$
3172 South Fletcher Avenue
Amelia Island
(904) 261-4236

On the other end of the accommodations spectrum from the Ritz-Carlton is this small, neat, unpretentious beach motel with an exceedingly polite staff. As proof positive that this is most decidedly not a spring break kind of place, this represents the only motel actually on the beach. Rates fluxuate with the "seasons." Call ahead.

RESTAURANTS

Brett's Waterway Cafe $$-$$$
Fernandina Harbour Marina
Amelia Island
(904) 261-2660

This dockside restaurant is surprisingly upscale, given the sometimes grubby shrimp-boat dock alongside. Just across the railroad tracks from the visitor center at the very end of Centre Street, Brett's offers a good selection of fresh Florida seafood, steaks, chicken, and an interesting assortment of specials.

The food here is very good, the prices (for this area) are quite reasonable, and the waitstaff is attentive and friendly, but the overall atmosphere is dampened a bit by some frosty greetings we witnessed and received. Be forewarned: They are quite serious about "casual resort wear" being expected of patrons.

Getting There:
St. Augustine

St. Augustine is in northeastern Florida, about 35 miles south of Jacksonville and 10 miles east of Interstate 95. The easiest route into the historic part of town is via Florida Highway 16 off I-95 (exit 318); go east about 11 miles to where FL 16 ends at San Marco Avenue (*not* US 1), turn right, and the old city gate is about a mile down the road. For a more scenic route, take FL A1A down from Amelia Island; it is a long

trip but well worth it for the view and salt air. Be careful not to miss the sharp turn into the parking lot at the Mayport Ferry, where FL A1A goes over the water, or you'll end up in one of the most confusing urban interstate highway tangles we have ever seen.

MODERN TIMES

St. Augustine has regained its prewar reputation as a premier tourist attraction with a vengeance; on warm summer afternoons it can be hard to get through the throngs on St. George Street and San Marco Avenue. This is an incredibly pleasant place and one of our favorite destinations, even if its very real and important Civil War history is downplayed in favor of the rather longer Spanish era. Most sights and attractions are within walking distance of one another in the downtown area, which is bisected by the pedestrian-only St. George Street.

The historic zone roughly outlines the Civil War–era city limits, running from the old city gate on Orange Street, across from the old Spanish fort, east to the Matanzas Bay seawall, south to St. Francis Street, and west to the San Sebastian River. Most modern shops and conveniences are just to the west of this area, running north and south along US 1. Just south and east on FL A1A over the Bridge of Lions (named for the two white marble lion statues guarding the prominent 1926 Mediterranean Revival–style drawbridge over Matanzas Bay) are Anastasia Island and St. Augustine Beach, one of the cleanest, nicest, and least crowded beach towns in all Florida.

We strongly suggest that you contact the chamber of commerce's visitor information center before you travel and ask them to send you their large packet of information on local attractions, restaurants, motels, shops, and events (904-825-1000). As soon as you arrive in town, go by the center at 10 Castillo Drive, across the street from the Ripley's Believe It or Not! Museum and just up the street from the

Castillo de San Marcos. This is one of the best put-together visitor centers we've seen, with a nicely designed building, small museum, film on the history of the city, gift shop, and literally thousands of booklets, brochures, and maps free for the asking. Behind the center is a large parking lot that we suggest you use while visiting the old town area; it is only $3.00 for all day and relatively easy to get into and out of.

POINTS OF INTEREST

Castillo de San Marcos National Monument
1 South Castillo Drive, St. Augustine
(904) 829-6506

Old Fort Marion, relabeled with its Spanish-era name in 1942, is the oldest masonry fort in the United States and the only 17th-century fort still standing in the United States. Replacing nine previous wooden forts dating back to 1565, construction of the large structure began in 1672 and took 27 years to complete. The Castillo is primarily made of an unusual material called coquina, a type of masonry block consisting of a compressed mixture of oyster shells and lime.

There are remnants of nearly every era of the fort's history still visible, and a large number of actual Spanish-era cannon are mounted on the upstairs gundeck. In front of the seawall, next to the ravelin (main entrance) are a number of Florida Territory–era (circa 1842) cannon laid on the ground. Original powder magazines and storerooms under the gundeck have been converted to small museums detailing nearly every aspect of the more than 300-year-old fort.

Operated by the National Park Service, the fort is open for "wandering," four ranger presentations per day, frequent cannon-firing demonstrations, and occasional guided tours from 8:45 A.M. to 4:45 P.M. weekdays; closed on Christmas Day. The fort is undergoing renovation, so these hours may vary. Admission is $5.00 for adults, $2.00 for children 6 to 16, and free for children under 6 (accompanied by an adult) and Golden Age Passport holders. This last category is a real deal—anyone over age 65 (with proof of age) may purchase a lifetime pass for a one-time fee of $10.00, which gives free admission to most federal-level parks and monuments.

Museum of Weapons and Early American History
81-C King Street, St. Augustine
(904) 829-3727

This one-large-room museum has a hands-down fantastic collection of small Civil War–era artifacts (dug and collected), as well as a complete representation of every major firearm used during the war. Swords, cutlasses, unusual and unique firearms, flags, documents, photos, and a small but nice selection of artifacts from other early eras in American history round out the somewhat eclectic collection. Our personal favorites were the unusually complete display of both small arms ammunition and artillery fuses and the very nicely presented collection of waist and cartridge belt buckles.

A similar-size room adjacent holds a good-size gift shop, containing a nice selection from the standard faux belt buckles and kepi caps up to decent books, prints, and actual artifacts for sale. We highly recommend a stop here and that you allow at least an hour to really peruse the large collection. The museum is nearly hidden away just off King Street 2 blocks west of the Plaza de la Constitution, in the rear of a parking lot between the Zorayda Castle (which is hard to miss) and Flagler Auditorium; look for the row of flags hanging from the roof. Open daily 9:30 A.M. to 5:00 P.M. Admission is $4.00 for adults and $1.00 for children ages 6 through 12; 6 and under are free.

This town is literally full of authentic and fascinating historic sites and attractions—to give even a short description of each would require a book in itself! Two we can recommend as having a documented connection with the Civil War; the other Spanish- and British-era buildings most likely were used for one purpose or another by the occupying Union forces.

Government House Museum
48 King Street, St. Augustine
(904) 825-5033

A museum covering almost exclusively the early Spanish and British history of the area, this house was used as the U.S. Provost Guard House during the Union occupation, and the exterior is nearly unchanged in appearance from that time. Open 10:00 A.M. to 4:00 P.M. daily except Christmas Day. Admission is $2.50 for adults, $1.00 for students and children 6 through 18; children ages 6 and under are free.

Gonzales-Alvarez House
(also called the Oldest House)
14 St. Francis Street, St. Augustine
(904) 824-2872

This structure claims, with some justification, to be the oldest house in America, dating from the early 17th century and continuously occupied ever since. The house was a noted tourist attraction even in Civil War times, and there are several documents from the era that complain of Union soldiers damaging the house by picking off pieces of wood and coquina—a masonry block made of oyster shells and lime—as souvenirs. The house is open daily for tours from 9:00 A.M. to 5:00 P.M.; admission is $6.00 for adults, $5.50 for seniors, and $4.00 for students and children 6 through 18.

Fort Matanzas National Monument
FL A1A South, St. Augustine
(904) 471-0116

Although this 250-year-old structure lacks any Civil War connection, it is still well worth a visit. Fourteen miles south of St. Augustine on FL A1A, the small coquina structure was built to protect the southern approaches of the city at Matanzas Inlet. An unusual feature of the small park is that you must ride across the Matanzas River on a (free) ferry to tour the fort itself. Never used in full-scale combat, the

fort is tower-shaped, with a second-floor gundeck containing two original artillery pieces, restored barracks room, and a third-story officers quarters.

A small visitor center contains a handful of artifacts, some good maps and brochures, a short film on the fort's history, and exceptionally friendly rangers. The park is administered by the National Park Service and is open from 9:00 A.M. to 5:30 P.M. daily except Christmas Day. Admission is free for both the park and ferry, which runs roughly every half hour except in bad weather or turbulent water.

ACCOMMODATIONS

St. Augustine is also well blessed with an abundance of decent chain and privately owned motels and bed-and-breakfast establishments. Most of the chain motels are clustered around the Old Town section on both San Marcos Avenue and US 1 just west of the main part of town; a few others are located on St. Augustine Beach. Please note that nearly every establishment charges extremely high rates during "special events," which are not confined to those taking place in St. Augustine itself. Daytona Beach, 60 miles to the south, hosts a series of racing and motorcycle events for several weeks in February and early March each year; unless you are attending these events, we strongly suggest you pick another time to visit this area. We can recommend the following independent establishment.

Beacher's Lodge $$-$$$$
6970 FL A1A South, Crescent Beach
(904) 471-8849, (800) 527-8849

Actually in Crescent Beach about 8 miles south of St. Augustine Beach, this beachfront lodge has 143 suites with small but very functional kitchens, separate bedrooms, nice sitting areas, and a fantastic view from every room. Rates and occasional minimum-stay lengths vary significantly based on the season, the time of week, the size of beds, the floor desired, and with local and nearby special events.

Tribute to a Major General

Tis old Stonewall the Rebel that leans on his sword,
And while we are mounting prays low to the Lord:
"Now each cavalier that loves honor and right,
Let him follow the feather of Stuart tonight."

CHORUS: Come tighten your girth and slacken your rein;
Come buckle your blanket and holster again;
Try the click of your trigger and balance your blade,
For he must ride sure that goes riding a raid.

Now gallop, now gallop to swim or to ford!
Old Stonewall, still watching, prays low to the Lord:
"Goodbye, dear old Rebel! The river's not wide,
And Maryland's lights in her window to guide." (CHORUS)

There's a man in the White House with blood on his mouth!
If there's knaves in the North, there are braves in the South.
We are three thousand horses, and not one afraid;
We are three thousand sabres and not a dull blade. (CHORUS)

Then gallop, then gallop by ravines and rock!
Who would bar us the way take his toll in hard knocks;
For with these point of steel, on the line of the Penn
We have made some fine strokes—and we'll make 'em again. (CHORUS)

A tribute song to Major General James Ewell Brown Stuart of the Confederate Army, sung to the tune of the old Scottish air *Bonnie Dundee*.

The staff is extremely friendly, and there is direct, gated beach access for guests as well as a nice pool.

RESTAURANTS

St. Augustine became one of our favorite destinations not only because of the history and pleasant surroundings but also because of the surplus of great restaurants. While we honestly never had what we would consider a bad meal at any of the non-chain establishments, the following are our favorites.

Beachcomber Restaurant   **$-$$**
2 "A" Street, St. Augustine Beach
(904) 471-3744
This is hands-down our favorite place for breakfast. Perched on a small dune literally on the beach, Beachcomber features a large open deck that hangs out over the sand, where you have salt water, sun, and surfers along with your bacon and eggs. There is a rather small indoor seating section with a large U-shaped bar for those who don't care for alfresco dining. Open now for more than 50 years, Beachcomber

offers the standard American breakfast menu and features fresh seafood, fried shrimp, oysters, burgers, and bar-type finger food the rest of the day. A nice selection of domestic and imported beers and wines helps make their deck a popular "locals" attraction in the evenings.

Open from 7:00 A.M. to 9:00 P.M. Sunday through Thursday and 7:00 A.M. to 10:00 P.M. Friday and Saturday, Beachcomber is hidden away in a largely residential beachfront neighborhood and a bit difficult to find. Travel down FL A1A and carefully watch the cross-street signs, which go down in number from north to south. "A" Street is just past First Street, behind the A Street Surf Shop and Sharkey's Shrimp Shack.

The Oasis Deck & Restaurant $-$$
4000 FL A1A South, St. Augustine Beach
(904) 471-2451

The Oasis is a close second choice of ours for breakfast. The only drawback is that it is very well known among both locals and regular tourists, and getting a table at peak hours is difficult at best. The Chef's Special at breakfast is for the hearty appetite: three eggs scrambled with ham, cheese, tomatoes, bell peppers, and onions, with potato and onion home fries and biscuits; the whole thing slops over the edges of a rather large platter. Other meals feature equally huge portions of delicious food: grilled and fried seafoods, sandwiches, burgers, salads, a raw bar, and bar-food munchies. Be sure to ask about the daily special. There is an upstairs deck and bar that caters heavily to the singles beach crowd. Open from 6:30 A.M. to 1:00 A.M. daily, the Oasis is at the corner of FL A1A and Ocean Trace Road, just south of the main beach area (where the main drag is known as A1A Beach Boulevard).

A1A Ale Works $$-$$$
1 King Street, St. Augustine
(904) 829-2977

Directly across the street from the Bridge of Lions and the Municipal Marina, A1A Ale Works is upstairs in the large two-story white building with intricately delicate iron gingerbread on the corner. The food is described as "New World cuisine," which means heavily Cuban- and Caribbean-influenced sandwiches and seafood. Grilled portobello mushroom sandwiches served on yucca rolls are one of our favorites, along with New World Flatbread du jour (toppings vary daily), Cuban-style smoked chicken pressed sandwiches, rag-time shrimp, and conch bollos. The in-house microbrewery produces a nice selection of very good beers and one really great root beer. If the weather is nice, ask to be seated on the open-air patio; the view is fantastic and it is usually cooler outside than you might think. A1A is open daily from 11:00 A.M. to 10:30 P.M., open weekends until 11:00 P.M.

Getting There: Olustee

Olustee Battlefield State Historic Site is about 45 miles west of Jacksonville and 15 miles east of Lake City in a partially cleared area just north of the railroad tracks surrounding a small, swampy pond. Easy access is via US 90 that runs between Lake City and I-10 just east (and north) of the battlefield. The tiny village of Olustee is about 2 miles west of the battlefield. The occasionally used alternative name for this conflict, Ocean Pond, refers to a fair-size round pond just west of the battlefield.

MODERN TIMES

Olustee has returned today to its prewar status as a sleepy roadside settlement, though the local major industry is staffing two large nearby state prisons instead of farming cotton. The battlefield itself is in a state of remarkably good preservation, although kept up primarily for the annual reenactment (the weekend closest to February 20). The only markers on the field itself pertain to the reenactment weekend. There is a small and unstaffed but nicely laid-out visitor center, set up to automatically turn on whenever someone enters the building, along with a short "self-serve" film on the battle. To the rear of the center is a large, striking monument to the Confederate victory, flanked by two cannon and two historic markers.

POINT OF INTEREST

Natural Bridge Battlefield
State Historic Site
7502 Natural Bridge Road, Tallahassee
(850) 922-6007

Both the place of the second largest battle in Florida and the site of the "last gasp" of the Confederacy, Natural Bridge today is a tiny park 15 miles southeast of Tallahassee, about 120 miles west of Olustee.

In early 1865 Tallahassee was the last unoccupied state capital in the Western Theater and a tempting target for overly confident Major General John Newton of the Union Army. From his poorly made topographic maps of the area, Newton convinced himself that it would be a relatively easy task to sail from his base at Key West to the mouth of the St. Marks River, march quickly overland, and take the capital by surprise.

Joined in his quest by Navy commander William Gibson, their flotilla sailed up from the Keys, landing in Apalachee Bay on March 3, 1865. That same day 300 sailors and marines stormed ashore and captured the East River Bridge 4 miles up the St. Marks River and prepared to advance their gunboats upriver toward the Confederate-held capital. Meanwhile, Newton's infantry had landed and was rapidly advancing overland toward Tallahassee.

As Newton attempted to sail upriver the next morning, all his boats ran aground in the shallow, sand-choked water. He was observed by townspeople nearby, and a message was sent to the capital warning of the assault force. A hastily assembled force under Lieutenant Colonel George Scott headed toward the only place to cross the St. Marks River without getting wet, at Natural Bridge, a natural phenomenon where the river runs underground for a short distance.

By the holy Saint Patrick, Colonel, there's so much good shooting here, I haven't a minute's time to waste fooling with that thing.

Irish private of the 10th Tennessee Infantry, when ordered to pick up the battle flag dropped by the wounded color sergeant

Scott's force could most charitably be called eccentric. The fewer than 700 men represented recuperating wounded veterans, local militia, home guards, and civilian volunteers from the surrounding counties. From Quincy came a group of some elderly men called the Gadsden Grays, mostly made up of veterans of the Seminole Wars. Rounding out the command were 24 teenagers from West Florida Seminary, aged from 14 to 18, each going off to battle with a note of permission from his mother.

Unaware of Gibson's problems downstream and still expecting his gunboats for support, Newton moved rapidly overland toward the river crossing. The 700 men of the 2nd and 99th U.S. Colored Infantry Regiments closed in on the area just before dawn, apparently unaware of any hostile force ahead. Scott's force had arrived just a few hours before, hastily throwing up earth and log breastworks in a crescent shape on the west bank of the natural bridge.

As dawn peeked through the piney woods on March 6, the Union advance guard made contact. A well-aimed volley of fire from the Confederate works both opened the battle and threw the Union infantry back temporarily. All through the rest of the day, the Union tried to crack the Confederate line with a series of both major assaults across the narrow bridge and flanking movements through the surrounding swamplands. All attempts to dislodge the irregular defenders failed, and by nightfall Newton ordered a hurried retreat back to the still-grounded gunboats several miles to the south.

Today, there is only a tiny park with a single set of three memorials and two sets of reproduced log breastworks to mark the site of the small but significant battle. One very general interpretive marker explains the general setting of the battle, and a set of restrooms and a few picnic tables stand across the road.

To access the site, take I-10 west from Olustee/Lake City to exit 203, turn right on Florida Highway 61 and then almost immediately right again onto U.S. Highway 319/Capital Circle Road, and go south about 10 miles to Florida Highway 363/Woodville Highway. Travel south about 15 miles to Woodville, and turn left just past the elementary school onto Natural Bridge Road (also called County Road 2192). The park is about 6 miles down this very lightly traveled country road.

ACCOMMODATIONS AND SUTLERS

There are no amenities at Olustee itself, but just about anything you need can be obtained 15 miles west in Lake City. This is a major stopping-off point for the large numbers of tourists headed for Disney World (150 miles to the southeast), so nearly every chain restaurant and motel has a presence here. However, the sheer numbers of tourists passing through tend to fill up the available rooms and seats rapidly, so we would advise you to plan your travel through here during nonpeak seasons (January through April, except during spring break season, or the fall until just before Christmas). The majority of motels and restaurants can be found on the western side of town, straddling the intersection with Interstate 75.

Getting There: Pensacola

Pensacola lies at the extreme western end of the Florida panhandle, accessible by I-10 from either Tallahassee or Mobile, Alabama. Most of the sites of interest are situated directly adjacent to Pensacola

Bay, which lies at the south and east side of town. The easiest, if not the most direct route, is via I-10 South at exit 12. The major attractions are fairly well marked; to go to Fort Pickens, stay on I-10 until the end (where it becomes U.S. Highway 98 and later Florida Highway 399), and follow the signs to Pensacola Beach, finally turning right on Fort Pickens Road. Although there is really only one east-west road on the narrow beach area, the turn is in the middle of a built-up beach town area and is easily missed (it is just beyond the Tourist Information office).

The other significant sites are within Pensacola Naval Air Station. Take State Route 295 West off Interstate 110, and travel about 7 miles until you reach the main gate. This route is called Fairfield Drive, Warrington Road, and Navy Boulevard at various times along its length.

MODERN TIMES

Fort Barrancas and Fort Pickens were used for a variety of purposes until the end of World War II. But their only real claim to fame in these later years was that Geronimo and 14 other Apaches were confined at Fort Pickens from October 1886 to May 1888, when they were moved to another post in Alabama. These Native Americans sparked the first tourist boom in the area. Hundreds of sightseers crossed the bay by boat to see the famous Apache chief, and the garrison was briefly reinforced to protect the public from these "dangerous" prisoners.

At the end of the 19th century, during the Spanish-American War era, Fort Pickens was reinforced with modern gun emplacements both inside and alongside the old brick walls. Abandoned again just after the turn of the 20th century, these emplacements saw their last military service as observation and coastal defense stations during WWII.

Fort McRee guarded the western end of the entrance to Pensacola Bay, on the eastern tip of Perdido Key. It was of a very unusual design, resembling a long, slightly bent aircraft wing with rounded ends, possibly the only one of this design ever built. Walls 35 feet high, 150 feet wide, and 450 feet long faced the ship channel, with mounts for 128 cannon in two tiers. The entire fort was surrounded by a dry moat 60 feet wide with a 3-foot glacis just outside it. The fort was originally planned to hold up to 500 soldiers. Construction began in 1840 and took three years to complete, using some 15 million bricks in the process. Unfortunately, no trace of this post remains. Having been battered by wind and wave for many years, the old walls finally crumbled away in the hurricane of 1906.

Today Fort McRee is completely gone, lacking even a historic marker to indicate where it stood, but Forts Pickens and Barrancas have been restored and opened for touring by the National Park Service. Fort Pickens is open from 9:30 A.M. to 5:30 P.M. daily April through October and 8:30 A.M. to 4:00 P.M. November through March. Guided tours are given daily at 2:00 P.M., with an additional tour at 11:00 A.M. on weekends. Just inside the main fort entrance is the visitor center. In the clump of green-and-white buildings near the fishing pier, you'll find the Fort Pickens Museum (same hours as the fort) and the Fort Pickens Auditorium, which shows a movie or provides some kind of program on the fort, island, weather, local history, marine life, or the like at scheduled times during the year. Admission is free, and the old fort is easy to locate: Go west on the only east-west road on Pensacola Beach, Fort Pickens Road, about 8 miles west of its intersection with FL 399/Pensacola Beach Road.

Fort Pickens, part of the Gulf Islands National Seashore, lies at the far end of a rather sizable National Park Service natural preservation area, about a 4-mile drive from the commercial zone of Pensacola Beach. This area was used for defensive fortifications from 1829 until the mid-1940s and still houses a number of fortification emplacements, batteries, and command

and control bunkers dating from different war eras during these years. Fort Pickens itself is a low-ranging, two-story masonry fort oriented northeast-southwest; a number of WWII–era buildings used by the Park Service are arrayed on the Pensacola Bay side. Fort Barrancas is open from 9:30 A.M. to 5:00 P.M. daily April to September. From here on, hours get fairly complicated; call (850) 934-2600 for hours during the remainder of the year (guided tour times tend to vary as well). Outside the visitor center, a ranger does a program on artillery at 9:30 A.M.

The 65 acres surrounding the forts contain oak and pine forests, a picnic area, and a nature trail. Fort Barrancas is on the grounds of Pensacola Naval Air Station and is free to the public. The fort was constructed between 1829 and 1859, along with three other masonry forts surrounding Pensacola Bay. This large masonry and earthwork post stands on the site occupied by two previous forts, built by the English and Spanish beginning in 1763. The name is a reflection of this heritage, recalling the original post title of San Carlos de Barrancas. Six million bricks are in the surprisingly small structure, built primarily by slave labor contracted from New Orleans. The 300- by 330-foot structure contained mounts for 8 large howitzers and 33 smaller artillery pieces, but on the eve of hostilities in 1861 it actually contained thirteen 8-inch Columbiads, two 10-inch mortars, and 24 smaller cannon.

POINTS OF INTEREST

Pensacola Convention and Visitor Information Center
1401 East Gregory Street, Pensacola
(850) 434-1234, (800) 874-1234
This very nicely laid-out and managed visitor center at the base of Pensacola Bay Bridge (on the mainland side) should be your first stop. The staff is exceptionally friendly and helpful, and there are literally thousands of maps, fliers, newspapers, and brochures on area attractions, amenities, and services.

Civil War Soldiers Museum
108 South Palafox Place, Pensacola
(850) 469–1900
This gem of a museum is a perfect example of why you should not judge a museum by its entrance. What looks like a fairly unassuming storefront in the Pensacola historic district opens up to reveal a wonderfully presented, 4,200-square-foot facility with professional-quality displays and mountings. Based around the extensive collection of local gastroenterologist Dr. Norman W. Haines Jr., the collection (naturally) has a distinct leaning toward the rarely seen medical aspects of the war.

The museum chronicles every facet of the war to one degree or another, with a special emphasis on letters, diaries, quotes, and photographs to bring a human element to the four years of suffering. The whole period of struggle is documented by paintings, photos, and artifacts from John Brown and Frederick Douglass to the last Civil War veteran. The Pensacola Room records the significant people and events of the immediate area and includes a 23-minute video presentation, *Pensacola and the Civil War.*

One side of the two-room display is devoted entirely to medical equipment and procedures—primitive surgical equipment, early attempts at field anesthesia (including a minié ball with teeth marks!), amputations, and many photographs of the results.

Although relatively small, this fine museum is well worth a few hours' visit and includes a small bookstore, which (thankfully!) avoids the usual tacky "rebel" souvenirs in favor of quite a nice selection of more than 700 related titles. We admit we have a weakness for locally produced history books and pamphlets, and this bookstore had a very nice selection. We cannot emphasize enough how highly we recommend this small museum; it is in itself worth a trip to Pensacola.

The museum is open Tuesday through Saturday, 10:00 A.M. to 4:30 P.M.; admission is $6.00 for adults, $5.00 for active-duty military, $2.50 for children 6 through 12, and free for children under age 6. Annual memberships that offer free admission, a newsletter, notice of special events, and other benefits are available for $20.00 for individuals and $35.00 for families.

National Museum of Naval Aviation
Pensacola Naval Air Station, Pensacola
(850) 452–3604
Although this facility has absolutely nothing to do with any aspect of the Civil War (well, there were balloons used for reconnaissance back then . . .), its location less than a mile away from Fort Barrancas and the extremely high quality of the facility makes it a "must-see."

It's not only one of a kind, it's also one of the three largest air and space museums in the world. Pensacola became the country's first Naval Air Station back in 1914, and up through World War II, every naval aviator got his initial training here. The 250,000 square feet of museum space contain more than 100 navy, marine corps, and coast guard aircraft and trace the history of naval aviation from biplanes to the space shuttle. There's the single remaining gigantic NC-4 taking up most of the front space, the first aircraft to cross the Atlantic; the first F-14A Tomcat (flown in the movie *Top Gun*); and a navy F-18 Hornet in Blue Angels colors.

The seven-story Blue Angels Atrium, used for ceremonies and social events, features four A-4 Skyhawks in Blue Angels regalia suspended in their famous "diamond-four" formation from the ceiling. An IMAX theater with a 70-foot screen and surround sound presents several films throughout the day, and an upstairs flight simulator lets you "ride along" on a violently bumpy bombing mission. Several cockpits of transports, fighters, attack aircraft, and helicopters are on the second floor, where you can climb in to try one for yourself. Free ramp-tours are given on a bus that loads just outside the main entrance, which we recommend; when the Blue Angels aerobatics demonstration team isn't on tour, the adjacent airfield is their home base, and you might get a chance to see them.

This is a really wonderful museum, even if aviation isn't your main interest, and we highly recommend you stop by before or after visiting the forts in the area. The museum is open 9:00 A.M. to 5:00 P.M. daily except Thanksgiving, Christmas, and New Year's Day. Admission is free, with some films, rides, and events requiring a small fee. Every Tuesday during the off-season (roughly October to March), the Blue Angels rehearse their act over Pensacola Bay, so try to be in the area then!

ACCOMMODATIONS

Five Flags Inn $$-$$$
**299 Fort Pickens Road, Pensacola
(850) 932-3586**
This small mom-and-pop motel has the best rates on the beach, and all the rooms on both floors face the beach. Rooms with two doubles or one king bed are available; you need to specify your preference, if you have one, as they rarely ask first. The rooms are very small and have uncarpeted floors, but they are immaculately clean (especially for a beach motel), and a large Gulf-front cement porch is right outside your door. Local calls and good coffee are free, and the motel is less than 3 blocks from the main restaurant and nightclub district. Room rates vary depending on the season (there are eight seasons listed!). We very highly recommend this place, especially since it is one of the closest motels to Fort Pickens, just 7 miles west.

The Dunes $-$$$
**333 Fort Pickens Road, Pensacola
(850) 932-3536**
Located right next door to the Five Flags Inn but on the other end of the economic spectrum, the Dunes is the most luxurious high-rise hotel on the beach. Rooms are decked in beach peach and seafoam green with tropical wallpaper, bedspreads,

---

The official end of the war did not occur until President Andrew Johnson declared that the "insurrection" in Texas had ended on August 20, 1866.

---

and pictures. Double rooms offer a king-size or two queen-size beds. Penthouse suites are available with two rooms, a full kitchen (without a stove), a four-person Jacuzzi, and either a rooftop terrace or double balcony overlooking the Gulf.

RESTAURANTS

Flounder's Chowder
& Ale House $$-$$$
**Pensacola Beach Road at
Fort Pickens Road, Pensacola
(850) 932-2003**
Flounder's has fun with everything from the menu to the decor and only gets serious when it comes to making good food. "Eat, drink and Flounder" is the motto, and several other "famous" quotes appear on the menu, somewhat differently than we remember, such as "Better to have Floundered and Lost, Than Never to have Floundered at All"—Alfred, Lord Flounder.

Florida seafood is presented in almost three dozen ways; steaks start at 10 ounces if you're not very hungry and grow to 16 ounces if you are! Chowders, salads, light pasta dishes, poultry, burgers, and sandwiches offer all patrons something they like, including Julius Flounder, who said, "I came, I saw, I Floundered." Open every day for lunch and supper with live entertainment Friday and Saturday; a full bar is available both indoors and outside. There is a very nice, large deck overlooking Santa Rosa Sound, with what they call a "Key West–style Beach Bar featuring the world's finest beach bands." We heartily agree!

Peg Leg Pete's Oyster Bar $$-$$$
**1010 Fort Pickens Road, Pensacola
(850) 932-4139**
Don't let the rather ramshackle building and hordes of surfer-sorts in the bar fool

you—this is one of the best seafood restaurants in the area. An extensive raw bar features no fewer than eight variations on the naked oyster; local seafood is available fried (this is the South, after all!), grilled, stuffed, or steamed; and steaks, chicken, sandwiches, and burgers round out the rather extensive menu. Cajun food is a side specialty of the house, and we highly recommend the Shrimp Orleans. If the weather permits, try the Underwhere Bar directly underneath the restaurant; it's a Tiki bar–style deck with live entertainment.

A warning: This is a very popular restaurant with both locals and knowledgeable tourists, and it fills to capacity nearly every night. If you don't want to wait in line for a seat, try to go before or after peak meal times, which can run until after dark in warmer months. Open 11:00 A.M. to 11:00 P.M., but "sometimes we stay open longer if business warrants it."

THE WORLD OF CIVIL WAR REENACTMENT

At the end of the Civil War, the sound of shots fired had not even died away before the first reenactments of the war were attempted. For the vast majority of the veterans involved, the war had been the highlight and focus of their entire lives, and it proved very difficult to let go. Many were eager to tell their stories of campaigns and battles to their long-suffering wives and wide-eyed children, and more than one took to open fields to demonstrate their prowess with rifles. Union veterans had the chance to purchase their weapons when discharged, for the then astronomical sum of $5.00, and those that declined to do so soon had the chance again on the surplus market for a markedly lower sum (incidentally, today rifles in fair to good condition are available on the collector's market, for the somewhat higher sum of $1,500 to $2,500 for an "unidentified" example or $3,500 and up for one that can be linked to a specific veteran).

Veterans organizations such as the Union's Grand Army of the Republic and the United Confederate Veterans were established shortly after the end of the war and soon began organizing "camp life" displays for families of the veterans so that Dad could tell, once more, what it had been like to suffer under "Spoons" Butler or to march proudly barefoot for "Marsh" Robert. Large-scale reunions started occurring in the 1880s, and by the turn of the 20th century, the dwindling ranks of the veterans were being watched by increasing crowds of spectators as they marched in parades or reenacted parts of famous battles. The favorite during this period was the re-creation of the Battle of Gettysburg, with huge camps set up for reunions of the 35th (1898), 50th (1913), and 75th (1938) anniversaries of the battle. The later reunions were caught on film, and the sight of aged men staggering up Cemetery Ridge only to shake hands with their former foes across the stone wall at the top cannot help but bring a lump to the throat.

The United States Army had gotten in on the fun as early as 1904, with a large training maneuver on the old Manassas battleground. In May 1935, on the 72nd anniversary of the Battle of Chancellorsville, a huge training maneuver loosely attempting to re-create the battle involved cadets from the Virginia Military College (where "Stonewall" Jackson taught before the war), U.S. cavalry squadrons, and the U.S. Marine Corps. The U.S. Army maneuvered again at Manassas in 1961, this time dressing the troops in inauthentic blue and gray uniforms and having them carry modern weapons, and attempted to re-create the battle for a large group of spectators. One source claims this was "militarily speaking, perhaps the most authentic reenactment of Manassas that has ever been carried out," although the uniforms and equipment were not even close to authentic in appearance, and the whole affair, called a "sham battle" at the time, was simply done as part of the centennial celebration of the war.

During the lead-up to the national celebration of the centennial of the war in the early 1950s, an organization was formed that would transform the public's view of both the Civil War and of the re-creation of it—the North-South Skirmish Association, or simply N-SSA, as it is most widely known. This organization, which still exists and is highly active, promoted the research and construction of truly authentic dress and equipment and centered around target-shooting competitions using authentic and replica weapons up to and including artillery pieces. This organization takes the re-creation of the war very seriously, as evidenced by its own literature:

In the early morning sun you can see the dew on the grass. There is a chill in the air, but little breeze. The flags hang limp. You can hear the sounds of measured activity as men check their weapons and fill cap pouches and cartridge boxes. Anticipation hangs in the air. You take your place in the skirmish line that extends over a quarter of a mile. At last, the order is given, "Load and come to the ready." 400 ramrods glint in the sun as 400 Minié balls are rammed home. 400 hammers click back to full-cock. And then the silence. You can cut the tension with a knife . . .

When the firing starts, the ghosts return. Farmboys from Michigan, Indiana, Alabama, and Mississippi. Young men from the small towns of Ohio and Virginia, and the street-wise city kids from the big ports of New York, Philadelphia, and New Orleans. You can almost hear their voices: "There! On the left! On the left! Git it! Somebody take the one on the left!"

from the N-SSA Web site, www.n-ssa.org

Every year the N-SSA holds two national shooting competitions at its dedicated range at Fort Shenandoah, near Winchester, Virginia, in late May and early October. We highly recommend that you attend at least once—it is perhaps the most exciting single event in all of Civil War reenacting and living history—to watch gun crews firing live rounds under pressure at targets a half mile away (if only the pressure of competition and not counter-battery fire, although we have

heard rumors that it has been considered from time to time!).

By the late 1960s interest in re-creating the accurate history of the war increased and started moving away from the organized target-shooting emphasis of the N-SSA. With help from the hoopla surrounding the 1976 bicentennial celebrations, agencies such as the National Park Service and organizations supporting local museums and battlefields began promoting "living history." Amateur (and sometimes professional) historians donned accurate uniforms and equipment in order to put on displays to explain to the public how the men of that era had lived and fought. In the best spirit of capitalism, manufacturers and suppliers sprang forward to meet the needs of these historians, producing at first reasonably acceptable replica equipment and firearms. Throughout the 1970s and early 1980s, this display-oriented activity slowly grew into a full-fledged hobby, with increasing numbers joining the ranks of fledgling reenactment units that took on the names and colors of actual Civil War–era units. The available equipment, now obtained from the archaic-termed "sutlers," became much more accurate in appearance (and higher in price) to the point that many of the firearms and leather gear had to be marked REPRODUCTION so that they would not be sold to an unsuspecting collector by the unscrupulous as authentic.

By the early 1980s this growing camp of reenactors proved to be a third split in the overall Civil War re-creation community; the N-SSA was (and is) still around, the museum- and battlefield-based living historians were (and are) still around, but now the major focus of attention turned to the re-creation of actual battles and campaigns, not just camp life and occasional shooting competitions. A turning point in the hobby came with the 125th anniversary of First Manassas in 1986. An estimated 6,000 reenactors took to the field in front of a crowd conservatively estimated to be twice that, catching the attention of the mass media. An article in the August 11, 1986, issue of *Time* magazine brought national attention; and Hollywood, ever ready to catch the coattails of a trend, produced (frankly rather bad) miniseries and films that used some of the reenactment crowd as extras.

In the mid-1990s a series of events connected with the 135th anniversary of the war proved what an explosive growth had occurred in the hobby. Feature films such as *Glory* and *Gettysburg* used large numbers of reenactors, and events such as the 135th anniversary Battle of Gettysburg drew in an estimated 24,000 reenactors (this number, like all crowd estimates, is the midpoint of a rather extensive range of estimates). Mass media once again turned their attention to the strangely dressed hordes running across old battlefields, the *New York Times* proclaiming that this was the "fastest growing family hobby" in America. The "family" connection is interesting to note, as for the first time large numbers of women and children were participating, both in drag (as it were) as soldiers and perfectly in character as wives, families, and camp followers in the evermore authentic camps. For the first time, even male civilian reenactors started appearing in large numbers, as authentically dressed and mannered sutlers (who are not reluctant to take "farb" money, by the way), photographers (who use authentic, and very difficult, wet-plate methods), doctors (yes, re-creating amputations), musicians, carpetbaggers, and so on.

Today this hobby has morphed into a wide variety of activities—so wide, in fact, that it is rather difficult to keep track of it all. Old "real" veterans organizations have changed into organizations of the descendants of soldiers (Sons of Confederate Veterans, United Daughters of the Confederacy) who don authentic dress and study the mannerisms of the period to put on balls and cotillions and to serve as honor guards for remembrance ceremonies and Confederate Memorial Day parades. Newsstands are filled with periodicals dedicated to the history of the war (*Civil War Times*

Illustrated, America's Civil War, Blue & Gray, and *North & South* are a few examples). A vast and bewildering array of sutlers dedicated to the hobby have sprung up, many of which argue about how their particular product is so much more authentic than the dregs that preceded it (actually, this is very similar to advertising habits of merchants of the 19th century!). And nearly every weekend throughout the year, at least one reenactment, a "tactical" (a more authentic re-creation, usually open-ended, not scripted to a historic battle, and closed to public view), ball, "school of the soldier," or other living-history event is going on in some part of the country. The hobby has even spread internationally, with events in Canada, England, and Germany. The number of reenactment units is very difficult to ascertain, with new ones popping up every month and older ones fading away, but a conservative estimate is somewhere in the neighborhood of 1,500 distinct units.

In addition to the divisions between those considering themselves and their activities as living history, reenactment, or N-SSA related, a subsection of the reenactment community has more recently appeared that can most delicately be termed the "hardcore," although they refer to themselves as "authentics." These are people, almost exclusively male, who take the concept of "authenticity" to its maximum. Not only do they obsessively research every single piece of clothing and equipment they wear and use, they consider their overall physical appearance—deliberately starving themselves to get the typical look of the later-war Confederates, not bathing for protracted periods of time, and usually going around barefoot. All of their leather gear is worked over until it obtains a desired "worn-out" appearance, and anything made of brass is treated to give it a brownish patina. The author of this work ran into an encampment of these "hardcores" just south of the Shiloh battlefield one early spring day in 1998, and the whole camp appearance was so correct to the smallest detail that he had trouble

CLOSE-UP

How To Fire a 12-Pounder Field Gun, Model 1857

Actually, this process is essentially the same for all the muzzle-loading cannons, but the drill comes from a training manual of the era. This piece is more commonly know as the Napoleon cannon, one of the most frequently seen artillery pieces in the national parks. The smoothbore tube is made of bronze, the carriage is wood (although the ones you see in national parks are metal carriages painted to look like the wooden ones, to reduce mainte-nance costs), and this piece is known as a "light" gun, although it weighs about 1,200 pounds. It was designed to fire solid round shot weighing 12 pounds (hence the des-ignation), although during the war explo-sive shells and canister rounds were used more frequently. Artillerymen considered this piece to be without peer when it came to dealing with onrushing infantry-men; it could accurately fire canister shot out to 300 yards, and being a short-tubed smoothbore, it could be reloaded signifi-cantly faster than a rifled gun.

Once the battery comes into firing position, the caisson and gun are pulled into place by the caisson teams. The cais-son itself is then positioned directly behind the gun, separated by about 5 to 10 yards, so that a single hit would not destroy both elements of the piece. By the book, artillery pieces were positioned side by side 14 yards apart, but of course this was often ignored in combat. When the caisson and gun are in position, the caisson horses are led to the rear and cared for by the drivers and teamsters. The eight-man gun crew then take up their assigned positions, seven of which are referred to by numbers:

Numbers One and Two stand to the right and left (facing downrange), respec-tively, of the front of the tube's muzzle.

Numbers Three and Four stand to the right and left of the tube directly behind the wheels, on either side of the vent hole. The Gunner stands to the left rear of the trails.

Numbers Six and Seven stand behind the ammunition box on the caisson.

Number Five is the ammunition run-ner and positions himself at the left side of the caisson with his bag open, ready to take a round forward.

believing he was not looking at ghosts. *Confederates in the Attic: Dispatches from the Unfinished Civil War* by Tony Horwitz, published in 1998, talks about these "hard-cores" among other current Civil War top-ics. While it has gotten mixed reviews from the reenactment crowd, it is a highly entertaining, admittedly biased view of how all this activity looks to outsiders.

To keep track of all the goings-on, a subsection of media totally devoted to the hobby has appeared, with one monthly magazine, *Camp Chase Gazette,* and sev-eral newspaper-format monthly periodi-

When the battery commander gives the command "commence firing," the Gunner orders, "load!" and states what is to be fired (shot, shell, canister, etc.). Number Seven removes the designated round from the ammunition box, and hands it to Number Six, who prepares a fuse for it (if used on that round). Number Six hands the round to Number Five, who places the round in a special heavy leather or canvas bag hung off his shoulder and walks the round forward, always on the left side of the tube.

While this is going on, Number One has taken his sponge tool, dunked it in a barrel of water, and sponged out the barrel (to ensure there are no lingering sparks from any earlier shots fired, which would cause the next step to be brief and exciting). Number Two takes the round from Number Five (who immediately returns to the caisson) and places the round in the muzzle of the tube. Number Three places his gloved thumb over the vent hole, while Number One flips his sponge tool around to the rammer end and rams the round down the barrel. Both move aside while the Gunner takes his removable sight out of his pocket, places it in position over the vent

hole, and sights the gun. Number Three has moved back to the trail and moves the piece left or right as ordered by the Gunner.

When he is satisfied that the piece is aimed properly, the Gunner steps back to his left, and orders, "ready!" Numbers One and Two turn away from the muzzle and cover their ears. Number Three takes a vent prick (which looks much like a thin knitting needle), pushes it through the vent hole, and pricks the powder charge bag attached to the loaded round. Number Four inserts a friction primer into the vent hole and attaches his lanyard to it. While he steps back to his left rear, pulling the slack out of the lanyard, Number Three covers the primer assembly with his gloved left hand to prevent a premature firing. The Gunner then orders, "fire!" Number Three lets go and turns away to his right, and Number Four yanks the lanyard, firing the piece. The four front cannoneers then wheel the cannon back into position (it usually is pushed back about 2 or 3 feet by the recoil), Number One swabs out the tube, and this whole drill is repeated until the "cease fire" order is given by the battery commander.

cals: *Civil War News* (sounds like an oxymoron, but it is surprisingly chock-full of recent happenings), *Civil War Courier,* and *Smoke & Fire News.* There is even a magazine devoted to the growing civilian aspect of the hobby, *The Citizen's Companion,* and the whole aspect of the vast

array of offerings from sutlers, both good and bad, has led to the creation of a quarterly newsletter, *The Watchdog,* which provides insightful (and fair) reviews of both sutlers and their products.

While there is a natural problem with authentically re-creating the war—the

How to Fire an 1853 Model Enfield .577 Caliber Rifled Musket

The main infantry weapons of the Union Army and the Confederacy, the 1861 Springfield and the 1853 Enfield, respectively, used the same loading and firing drill. While different tactical and drill manuals of the day give various "step by step" methods of precision loading, the following is the usual battlefield drill:

Place the butt of the rifle between your feet, muzzle side toward your body.

Holding the rifle in your left hand, reach in your cartridge box and remove one paper-wrapped cartridge.

Tear open the "pigtail" of the cartridge with your teeth on the right side of your mouth.

Holding the cartridge between your thumb and index finger, pour the gunpowder down the barrel.

Push the remaining part of the cartridge, containing the minié ball, down into the barrel.

Grasp the ramrod between thumb and index finger and smoothly draw it out of its housing. It should clear the weapon when your arm is at full extension.

Turning the ramrod over, place the butt (wide portion) inside the barrel of the rifle as far as it will easily slide.

Grasping the other end of the ramrod only with the crook of the little finger of the right hand, briskly push the ramrod down until the charge is fully seated at the bottom of the barrel.

Grasping the ramrod between thumb and index finger, swiftly withdraw it from the barrel, turn it over, and reinsert it into its housing inside the rifle stock.

Grasping the rifle stock with the left hand at about the level of the rear sight, raise the rifle while at the same time, moving the barrel downwards, until the stock is roughly at waist level. With the right thumb, pull the hammer back to half-cock.

Reach into the cap box with your right hand and remove one cap.

With the thumb and index finger, place the cap on the nipple, and push it firmly down until it is seated.

Move the right hand back to grasp the stock just behind the trigger housing—this is the "charge" position.

If the rifle is not going to be fired immediately, do not place the cap on the nipple under the hammer, as this makes an accidental discharge all too easy. If firing is "at will," or as rapidly as you can reload, then bring the rifle up to your shoulder, pull the hammer back to full cock, and aim and fire the rifle. If a volley fire is ordered, the following three orders are given by whomever has command:

"Ready"—With the rifle at the "charge" position, pull back the hammer to full cock.

"Aim"—Place the butt of the rifle against your right shoulder, pick a target, and take careful aim. Place your right index finger through the trigger housing, and lightly place it on the trigger.

"Fire"—Squeeze the trigger, (do not pull it, as this affects the aim), fire the weapon, and immediately go through the loading process again.

reenactors are only shooting off gunpowder, no minié balls are loaded, the surgeons are only pretending to saw off limbs (we think), and relatively few people actually get shot—most of the participants in this hobby take their roles very seriously, and an event open to the public is well worth attending, if only to get a flavor of what the real thing was like. One of the more transcendent experiences we have had was watching a very small reenactment in Greensboro, Georgia, that was re-creating a Virginia battle called the "Mule Shoe." It was a cool morning and had rained hard all the previous night, leaving the ground unpleasantly muddy, and a heavy mist was hanging in the air. From a hillside viewing area, shivering in the damp air, we watched the approach of the Union regiments, bayonets affixed to their Springfields, battle flags hanging limply on their staffs. As they turned in to the field in front of us, a nearby Confederate artillery battery opened fire, its deep boom shaking the ground. At that moment a weak winter sun briefly peeked through the mist, highlighting the approaching gleaming bayonets and catching the brilliant colors of the battle flags, now flying out proudly as the men in lines of battle gave a deep "huzzah" and charged the entrenched Confederate line. It was the sort of moment where you get a lump in your throat, and just for that one moment, you were transported back into the midst of a desperate battle.

There are innumerable sources on how you can either watch or get involved in this hobby. The best we can recommend is the *Camp Chase Gazette*, $28 for a one-year subscription (P.O. Box 625, Morristown, TN 37814). However, if you have Web access, there are innumerable sites to look into, starting again with the *Camp Chase Gazette*, www.campchase .com. Another excellent source is the cyber version of *Civil War News*, www.civilwar news.com. The be-all, end-all of Web links can be found at the U.S. Civil War Center at Louisiana State University, www.cwc.lsu .edu. While it does not have every single

link concerning the Civil War, at least yet (their stated purpose is to index them all), there is enough there to provide several years' worth of hotlinking. Another very good source is the museums and visitor centers attached to battlefield and historic sites, which are more frequently hosting reenactments and living-history exhibits.

If you decide that this is the hobby for you, we suggest purchasing one (or both) of a pair of excellent books on the subject, *Springing to the Call!: How to Get Started in Civil War Reenacting*, published by the *Camp Chase Gazette*, or *Reliving the Civil War: A Reenactor's Handbook* by R. Lee Hadden. Both give good overviews of what the hobby entails, including warnings about how much it costs to get started. A decent outfit, including leather gear and weapons, will set you back between $1,500 and $2,000, although there are ways, that these books explain, to start participating for considerably less.

Like any other endeavor, the field of reenactment has a language of its own. Here are a few examples of what you may hear as you wander through the camps:

Bridge: sometimes simply called a "translator," the person you will see at events open to the public who speaks to the public in 21st-century language, explaining what is going on.

Bulletproof: reenactors who do not die on schedule or as appropriate given the tactical situation. Not a term of endearment.

Early war/late war: referring to the uniform chosen, especially on the Confederate side, whether you are going for the gaudier appearance of uniforms worn in 1861–62 or the more practical uniforms worn toward the end of the war, 1863 on.

Farb: completely unauthentic, fake, or fake-appearing; used as a noun or verb. Many new reenactors wear cowboy boots, for example, which is "farb," or talk about the latest political problems, which is "talking farbish." One prime example of a "farb" we saw at a living-history exhibit in Alabama had on a silvery-gray cowboy hat with a bright brass "officers" cord, a brown barn coat with bright blue sergeants' stripes sewn on, blue jeans, black cowboy boots, and a pair of Elvis-style mirrored sunglasses.

Galvanize: for very obvious reasons (better looking uniforms, better officers, prettier women, general gallantry, etc.), the vast majority of reenactors want to portray Confederates. This poses a problem when you have 2,000 Confederate re-enactors at an event with only 50 or so Union, so many events require participating units to take turns portraying Union, called being "galvanized." Many established reenactment units are so used to this that they portray specific Union as well as Confederate units.

"Peeing on his buttons": one method the hardcore crowd uses to get the proper brownish patina on their brass coat buttons. Used as a term to indicate someone may be getting into the hobby a bit too much.

Powder burner: usually refers to someone who loads and fires much too fast for authenticity (a soldier of the period could fire at a maximum rate of three shots a minute, but it is possible to load blank charges much faster). Also refers to events where there is an unusually high amount of shooting.

Road apples: presents left on the trail by passing cavalry horses.

Thread counters: reenactors who obsess about having the most authentic possible uniforms and equipment, to the point where they literally count the number of threads per inch of fabric to make sure it has been woven to the historically correct size.

INDEX

ABOUT THE AUTHOR

John McKay is very nearly a native of Atlanta; he was born in Carrolton, Georgia, but moved into the city before he was four. He entered the army immediately after graduating from high school and was eventually assigned to the famed "Currahees" (1st Battalion, 506th Infantry Regiment) of the 101st Airborne Division at Fort Campbell, Kentucky. He later served in West Germany and in the Georgia National Guard.

After his discharge from the service, John spent more than 15 years as a firefighter and paramedic in and around Atlanta and then turned his interests to teaching and writing history, especially that of the American Civil War. John taught high school American history, government, and military history for several years; he is currently the lead teacher for the Georgia National Guard's STARBASE program. Among his recently published works are the "Atlanta Campaign" section of the *Encyclopedia of the American Civil War* and the seventh edition of *Insiders' Guide to Atlanta,* coauthored by John's wife, Bonnie, and published by The Globe Pequot Press.

John resides in the north Fulton County town of Alpharetta, Georgia, with Bonnie, a recovering debutante who is a much-beloved but long-suffering "Civil War widow" as well as an invaluable source of information on the social mores of the Old South. The "Orphan Brigade"—a constantly changing assortment of critters who appear seemingly out of nowhere at regular intervals—does picket and skirmisher duty around their property.